VCP5: VMware Certified Professional on vSphere 5 Study Guide

Exam VCP-510 Objectives

Section 1: Plan, Install, Configure and Upgrade vCenter Server and VMware ESXi

OBJECTIVE	CHAPTER
Objective 1.1: Install and Configure vCenter Server	2
Objective 1.2: Install and Configure VMware ESXi	2
Objective 1.3: Plan and Perform Upgrades of vCenter Server and VMware ESXi	2
Objective 1.4: Secure vCenter Server and ESXi	3
Objective 1.5: Identify vSphere Architecture and Solutions	3

Section 2: Plan and Configure vSphere Networking

OBJECTIVE	CHAPTER
Objective 2.1: Configure vNetwork Standard Switches	4
Objective 2.2: Configure vNetwork Distributed Switches	4
Objective 2.3: Configure vSS and vDS Policies	4

Section 3: Plan and Configure vSphere Storage

OBJECTIVE	CHAPTER
Objective 3.1: Configure Shared Storage for vSphere	5
Objective 3.2: Configure the Storage Virtual Appliance for vSphere	5
Objective 3.3: Create and Configure VMFS and NFS Datastores	5

Section 4: Deploy and Administer Virtual Machines and vApps

OBJECTIVE	CHAPTER
Objective 4.1: Create and Deploy Virtual Machines	6
Objective 4.2: Create and Deploy vApps	6

Sybex®
An Imprint of
WILEY

Objective 4.3: Manage Virtual Machine Clones and Templates	7
Objective 4.4: Administer Virtual Machines and vApps	7

Section 5: Establish and Maintain Service Levels

OBJECTIVE	CHAPTER
Objective 5.1: Create and Configure VMware Clusters	8
Objective 5.2: Plan and Implement VMware Fault Tolerance	8
Objective 5.3: Create and Administer Resource Pools	8
Objective 5.4: Migrate Virtual Machines	9
Objective 5.5: Backup and Restore Virtual Machines	9
Objective 5.6: Patch and Update ESXi and Virtual Machines	9

Section 6: Perform Basic Troubleshooting

OBJECTIVE	CHAPTER
Objective 6.1: Perform Basic Troubleshooting for ESXi Hosts	10
Objective 6.2: Perform Basic vSphere Network Troubleshooting	10
Objective 6.3: Perform Basic vSphere Storage Troubleshooting	10
Objective 6.4: Perform Basic Troubleshooting for HA/DRS Clusters and vMotion/ Storage vMotion	10

Section 7: Monitor a vSphere Implementation and Manage vCenter Server Alarms

OBJECTIVE	CHAPTER
Objective 7.1: Monitor ESXi, vCenter Server and Virtual Machines	11
Objective 7.2: Create and Administer vCenter Server Alarms	11

Exam objects are subject to change at any time without prior notice and at VMware's sole discretion. Please visit the VMware certification website (http://mylearn.vmware.com/portals/certification/) for the latest information on the VCP5 requirements.

Sybex®
An Imprint of
WILEY

VCP5

VMware® Certified Professional on vSphere™ 5

Study Guide

VCP5

VMware® Certified Professional on vSphere™ 5

Study Guide

Brian Atkinson

WILEY

John Wiley & Sons, Inc.

Senior Acquisitions Editor: Jeff Kellum
Development Editor: Susan Herman
Technical Editors: Troy Clavell, André Pett
Production Editor: Liz Britten
Copy Editor: Kim Wimpsett
Editorial Manager: Pete Gaughan
Production Manager: Tim Tate
Vice President and Executive Group Publisher: Richard Swadley
Vice President and Publisher: Neil Edde
Media Project Manager: Laura Moss-Hollister
Media Associate Producer: Marilyn Hummel
Media Quality Assurance: Shawn Patrick
Book Designer: Judy Fung; Bill Gibson
Proofreader: Jen Larsen, Word One, New York
Indexer: Ted Laux
Project Coordinator, Cover: Katherine Crocker
Cover Designer: Ryan Sneed
Cover Image: ©Jeremy Woodhouse/Photodisc/Getty Images

Copyright © 2012 by John Wiley & Sons, Inc., Indianapolis, Indiana

Published simultaneously in Canada

ISBN: 978-1-118-18112-6

ISBN: 978-1-118-22731-2(ebk.)

ISBN: 978-1-118-23623-9(ebk.)

ISBN: 978-1-118-26499-7(ebk.)

For general information on our other products and services or to obtain technical support, please contact our Customer Care Department within the U.S. at (877) 762-2974, outside the U.S. at (317) 572-3993 or fax (317) 572-4002.

Wiley publishes in a variety of print and electronic formats and by print-on-demand. Some material included with standard print versions of this book may not be included in e-books or in print-on-demand. If this book refers to media such as a CD or DVD that is not included in the version you purchased, you may download this material at http://booksupport.wiley.com. For more information about Wiley products, visit www.wiley.com.

Library of Congress Control Number: 2012935797

10 9 8 7 6 5 4 3 2

Dear Reader,

Thank you for choosing *VCP5: VMware Certified Professional on vSphere 5 Study Guide*. This book is part of a family of premium-quality Sybex books, all of which are written by outstanding authors who combine practical experience with a gift for teaching.

Sybex was founded in 1976. More than 30 years later, we're still committed to producing consistently exceptional books. With each of our titles, we're working hard to set a new standard for the industry. From the paper we print on, to the authors we work with, our goal is to bring you the best books available.

I hope you see all that reflected in these pages. I'd be very interested to hear your comments and get your feedback on how we're doing. Feel free to let me know what you think about this or any other Sybex book by sending me an email at nedde@wiley.com. If you think you've found a technical error in this book, please visit http://sybex.custhelp.com. Customer feedback is critical to our efforts at Sybex.

Best regards,

Neil Edde
Vice President and Publisher
Sybex, an Imprint of Wiley

Acknowledgments

Writing this book has been a learning experience in so many ways. I learned that balancing writing with work, family, and friends is nearly impossible. I also learned that attention to detail can consume a rather large amount of time. Speaking with someone about a virtualization topic is one thing, but putting words on a page about the same topic is a very different experience. Most important, I learned a lot about vSphere 5 in writing this book that I did not previously know. I took and passed the VCP511 BETA exam in July 2011, shortly before work on this book began. In some ways, I wish I had waited and taken the VCP5 after I had finished writing this book! I also learned that writing a book requires a great deal of help, and there are many people who were instrumental in making this book happen.

I would like to thank Jeff Kellum for his patience and for helping me become the author of this book. Jeff and I had been discussing many different projects for a while, and I am thankful that we were able to decide on this book. Thank you, Jeff!

I would like to thank Susan Herman for her patience and her willingness to coach me in the writing and editing process. Susan was a great help and a constant source of information that helped make the writing process much easier.

I would like to thank my technical editor, Troy Clavell, for his attention to detail and for calling me out on my mistakes. I am constantly amazed at the amount of knowledge Troy has and the level of detail that he was able to help me bring to this book.

I would like to thank André Pett for his eagerness to help and for his role in technical proofreading this book.

I would like to thank Kim Wimpsett for her patience and willingness to listen to me about various VMware wording and phrasing issues. Kim did a great deal of work, and I appreciate it.

I would like to thank John Troyer and Alex Maier of VMware for their help and for routing my many questions the right way. I give many thanks to Marshall Rozario for introducing me to VMware GSX all those years ago and making all of this possible. I also want to thank Elias Khnaser for helping me get my foot in the door of the publishing industry.

Thanks to Laans Hokanson, Brad Johnson, Brandon Atkinson, and Kyle Hughes for the support, listening, and advice. I know I both isolated and drove some of you crazy along the way, and I appreciate your help and patience.

I also must thank my family for their support in this project. We knew that writing this book was going to be a significant undertaking, and I cannot thank my wife, Jennifer, enough for her help. She was a great listener, advisor, motivator, and so much more in this process. Thank you, Jenn, for everything! Thanks to my children, Cooper, Cohen, and Calden, for their understanding and patience with me in this process. I look forward to having so much more time to spend with you all!

About the Author

Brian Atkinson is a senior systems engineer with 15 years of experience in the IT field. For the past six years, he has been focused on virtualization and storage solutions. Brian holds the VCP3, VCP4, and VCP5 certifications and has been awarded the VMware vExpert designation from VMware for 2009, 2010, and 2011. He is a VMware Technology Network (VMTN) moderator and guru. He maintains his personal blog in the VMTN communities at `http://communities.vmware.com/blogs/vmroyale/` and can also be found @vmroyale.

Contents at a Glance

Introduction   *xxxiii*

Assessment Test   *liii*

Chapter   **1**   What's New in vSphere 5   1

Chapter   **2**   Plan, Install, Configure, and Upgrade
                        vCenter Server and VMware ESXi   27

Chapter   **3**   Secure vCenter Server and ESXi
                        and Identify vSphere Architecture and Solutions   95

Chapter   **4**   Plan and Configure vSphere Networking   143

Chapter   **5**   Plan and Configure vSphere Storage   219

Chapter   **6**   Create and Deploy Virtual Machines and vApps   299

Chapter   **7**   Manage and Administer Virtual Machines
                        and vApps   373

Chapter   **8**   Establish Service Levels with Cluster, Fault
                        Tolerance, and Resource Pools   421

Chapter   **9**   Maintain Service Levels   499

Chapter   **10**   Perform Basic Troubleshooting   593

Chapter   **11**   Monitor a vSphere Implementation and
                        Manage vCenter Server Alarms   641

Appendix   **A**   Answers to Review Questions   703

Appendix   **B**   About the Additional Study Tools   719

Index   *723*

Contents

Introduction   *xxxiii*

Assessment Test   *liii*

Chapter   1   What's New in vSphere 5   **1**

    ESX Retirement   3
    VCB Retirement   4
    VMI Paravirtualization Retirement   4
    VMware GUI Toolbox Retirement   4
    Windows 2000 Guest OS Customization Support   4
    Newly Created VMCI Sockets Unsupported   5
    Requirement of LAHF and SAHF CPU Instruction Sets   5
    Intel SMT–Related CPU Scheduler Enhancements   5
    Notable Configuration Maximums Changes   5
    ESXi Firewall and Management Networks   6
    Swap to SSD   7
    Support for Hardware and Software FCoE Adapters   7
    Host UEFI Boot Support   8
    Improved SNMP Support   8
    New Command-Line Interface   8
    vSphere High Availability Improvements   8
    Virtual Machine Enhancements   9
    Expanded Support for VMware Tools   9
    Mac OS X Server Support   11
    vCenter Server Enhanced Logging   11
    VMware vCenter Server Heartbeat Improvements   11
    Fault Tolerance Improvements   13
    iSCSI UI Support   13
    GUI to Configure Multi-core Virtual CPUs   14
    vNetwork Distributed Switch Improvements   14
    Network I/O Control Improvements   17
    Storage vMotion Improvements   17
    VAAI Thin Provisioning Improvements   17
    NFS Support Improvements   18
    Storage Accelerator   18
    VMFS-5   18
    vMotion and Metro vMotion   19
    vCenter Server Appliance   19
    vSphere Storage Appliance   19
    Storage DRS   20

Profile-Driven Storage   21
Image Builder   21
Auto Deploy   22
VMware Data Recovery 2.0 Improvements   23
Update Manager Improvements   24
Licensing   24
Summary   25

**Chapter   2   Plan, Install, Configure, and Upgrade
                    vCenter Server and VMware ESXi   27**

Introduction to vCenter Server   29
  Identifying Available vCenter Server Editions   29
  Deploying the vCenter Server Appliance   30
  Installing vCenter Server into a Virtual Machine   34
  Sizing the vCenter Server Database   39
  Installing Additional vCenter Server Components   41
  Installing and Removing vSphere Client Plug-ins   46
  Enabling and Disabling vSphere Client Plug-ins   50
  Licensing vCenter Server   51
  Determining Availability Requirements for a
     vCenter Server in a Given vSphere Implementation   55
  Determining Use Case for vSphere Client and Web Client   56
Introduction to VMware ESXi   57
  Performing an Interactive Installation of ESXi   58
  Deploying an ESXi Host Using Auto Deploy   60
  Configuring NTP on an ESXi Host   61
  Configuring DNS and Routing on an ESXi Host   64
  Enabling, Configuring, and Disabling Hyperthreading   69
  Enabling, Sizing, and Disabling Memory
     Compression Cache   70
  Licensing an ESXi Host   73
Planning and Performing Upgrades of vCenter
  Server and VMware ESXi   75
  Identifying Upgrade Requirements for ESXi Hosts   75
  Identifying Steps Required to Upgrade a vSphere
     Implementation   76
  Upgrading a vNetwork Distributed Switch   78
  Upgrading from VMFS-3 to VMFS-5   80
  Upgrading VMware Tools   81
  Upgrading Virtual Machine Hardware   82
  Upgrading an ESXi Host Using vSphere Update Manager   83
  Determining Whether an In-Place Upgrade Is
     Appropriate in a Given Upgrade Scenario   88

Summary	89
Exam Essentials	89
Review Questions	91

Chapter 3 Secure vCenter Server and ESXi and Identify vSphere Architecture and Solutions 95

Securing vCenter Server and ESXi	96
Identifying Common vCenter Server Privileges and Roles	96
Describing How Permissions Are Applied and Inherited in vCenter Server	98
Configuring and Administering the ESXi Firewall	100
Enabling, Configuring, and Disabling Services in the ESXi Firewall	105
Enabling Lockdown Mode	108
Configuring Network Security Policies	110
Viewing, Sorting, and Exporting User and Group Lists	112
Adding, Modifying, and Removing Permissions for Users and Groups on vCenter Server Inventory Objects	114
Creating, Cloning, and Editing vCenter Server Roles	118
Adding an ESXi Host to a Directory Service	121
Applying Permissions to ESXi Hosts Using Host Profiles	124
Determining the Appropriate Set Of Privileges for Common Tasks in vCenter Server	129
Identifying vSphere Architecture and Solutions	130
Identifying Available vSphere Editions and Features	130
Explaining ESXi and vCenter Server Architectures	130
Explaining Private, Public, and Hybrid Cloud Concepts	134
Determining Appropriate vSphere Edition Based on Customer Requirements	135
Summary	136
Exam Essentials	137
Review Questions	138

Chapter 4 Plan and Configure vSphere Networking 143

Configuring vNetwork Standard Switches	145
Identifying vNetwork Standard Switch Capabilities	145
Creating and Deleting a vNetwork Standard Switch	148
Adding, Configuring, and Removing vmnics on a vNetwork Standard Switch	151
Configuring VMkernel Ports for Network Services	155
Adding, Editing, and Removing Port Groups on a vNetwork Standard Switch	158
Determining Use Case for a vNetwork Standard Switch	162

Configuring vNetwork Distributed Switches   163
    Identifying vNetwork Distributed Switch Capabilities   163
    Creating and Deleting a vNetwork Distributed Switch   165
    Adding and Removing ESXi Hosts to/from a vNetwork
        Distributed Switch   169
    Adding, Configuring, and Removing dvPort Groups   173
    Adding and Removing Uplink Adapters to dvUplink
        Groups   179
    Creating, Configuring, and Removing Virtual Adapters   182
    Migrating Virtual Adapters to and from a vNetwork
        Standard Switch   187
    Migrating Virtual Machines to and from a vNetwork
        Distributed Switch   191
    Determining Use Case for a vNetwork Distributed Switch   195
Configuring vSS and vDS Policies   196
    Identifying Common vSwitch and dvSwitch Policies   196
    Configuring dvPort Group Blocking Policies   196
    Configuring Load Balancing and Failover Policies   198
    Configuring VLAN Settings   201
    Configuring Traffic Shaping Policies   202
    Enabling TCP Segmentation Offload Support for a
        Virtual Machine   207
    Enabling Jumbo Frames Support on Appropriate
        Components   209
    Determining Appropriate VLAN Configuration
        for a vSphere Implementation   212
Summary   213
Exam Essentials   214
Review Questions   215

Chapter   5   Plan and Configure vSphere Storage   219

Configure Shared Storage for vSphere   221
    Identifying Storage Adapters and Devices   222
    Identifying Storage Naming Conventions   223
    Scanning and Rescanning Storage   225
    Enabling, Configuring, and Disabling vCenter
        Server Storage Filters   227
    Describing Zoning and LUN Masking Practices   230
    Identifying Use Cases for FCoE   231
    Identifying Hardware/Dependent Hardware/Software
        iSCSI Initiator Requirements   231
    Determining Use Case for Hardware/Dependent
        Hardware/Software iSCSI Initiator   232

Configuring and Editing Hardware/Dependent
    Hardware Initiators   233
Enabling and Disabling Software iSCSI Initiator   236
Configuring and Editing Software iSCSI
    Initiator Settings   238
Configuring iSCSI Port Binding   239
Enabling, Configuring, and Disabling iSCSI CHAP   242
Comparing and Contrasting Array Thin Provisioning
    and Virtual Disk Thin Provisioning   245
Determining Use Case for and Configuring Array
    Thin Provisioning   246
Create and Configure VMFS and NFS Datastores   247
Identifying VMFS-5 Capabilities   247
Creating, Renaming, Unmounting, and Deleting a
    VMFS Datastore   248
Identifying VMFS Datastore Properties   255
Extending and Expanding VMFS Datastores   257
Upgrading a VMFS-3 Datastore to VMFS-5   262
Placing a VMFS Datastore in Maintenance Mode   264
Determining Appropriate Path Selection Policy for a
    Given VMFS Datastore   264
Selecting the Preferred Path for a VMFS Datastore   266
Disabling a Path to a VMFS Datastore   268
Creating an NFS Share for Use with vSphere   269
Connecting to a NAS Device   270
Identifying NFS Datastore Properties   272
Mounting and Unmounting an NFS Datastore   272
Determining the Use Case for Multiple VMFS/NFS
    Datastores   273
Configure the vSphere Storage Appliance   274
Determining the Use Case for Deploying the VSA   274
Defining vSphere Storage Appliance (VSA)
    Architecture   275
Determining Appropriate ESXi Host Resources
    for the VSA   277
Configuring ESXi Hosts as VSA Hosts   278
Configuring the Storage Network for the VSA   279
Deploying and Configuring
    the VSA Manager   280
Administering VSA Storage Resources   283
Summary   291
Exam Essentials   292
Review Questions   294

Chapter 6   Create and Deploy Virtual Machines and vApps   299

Creating and Deploying Virtual Machines   301
    Identifying Capabilities of Virtual Machine
       Hardware Versions   301
    Configuring and Deploying a Guest OS into a New
       Virtual Machine   303
    Placing Virtual Machines in Selected ESXi
       Hosts/Clusters/Resource Pools   313
    Identifying Methods to Access and Use a Virtual
       Machine Console   313
    Installing, Upgrading, and Updating VMware Tools   316
    Identifying VMware Tools Device Drivers   319
    Configuring Virtual Machine Time Synchronization   320
    Identifying Virtual Machine Storage Resources   323
    Configuring and Modifying Disk Controller for
       Virtual Disks   324
    Configuring Appropriate Virtual Disk Type for a
       Virtual Machine   329
    Creating and Converting Thin/Thick Provisioned
       Virtual Disks   332
    Configuring Disk Shares   334
    Determining Appropriate Datastore Locations for
       Virtual Machines Based on Application Workloads   335
    Configuring and Modifying Virtual CPU and Memory
       Resources According to OS and Application
       Requirements   336
    Configuring and Modifying Virtual NIC
       Adapter and Connecting Virtual Machines to
       Appropriate Network Resources   337
    Converting a Physical Machine Using
       VMware Converter   340
    Importing a Supported Virtual Machine Source
       Using VMware Converter   345
    Modifying Virtual Hardware Settings Using
       VMware Converter   349
Create and Deploy vApps   354
    Determining When a Tiered Application Should Be
       Deployed as a vApp   354
    Creating a vApp   355
    Adding Objects to an Existing vApp   356
    Identifying and Editing vApp Settings   357
    Configuring IP Pools   359
    Suspending and Resuming a vApp   363

	Cloning and Exporting a vApp	364
	Summary	366
	Exam Essentials	367
	Review Questions	368

Chapter   7   Manage and Administer Virtual Machines and vApps   373

Managing Virtual Machine Clones and Templates	375
Identifying Cloning and Template Options	375
Cloning an Existing Virtual Machine	376
Creating a Template from an Existing Virtual Machine	379
Deploying a Virtual Machine from a Template	381
Updating Existing Virtual Machine Templates	383
Deploying Virtual Appliances and vApps from an OVF Template	384
Importing and Exporting an OVF Template	385
Determining the Appropriate Deployment Methodology for a Given Virtual Machine Application	386
Identifying the vCenter Server–Managed ESXi Hosts and Virtual Machine Maximums	387
Administering Virtual Machines and vApps	389
Identifying Files Used by Virtual Machines	389
Identifying Locations for Virtual Machine Configuration Files and Virtual Disks	391
Configuring Virtual Machine Options	393
Configuring Virtual Machine Power Settings	395
Configuring Virtual Machine Boot Options	397
Configuring Virtual Machine Troubleshooting Options	399
Identifying Common Practices for Securing Virtual Machines	400
Determining When an Advanced Virtual Machine Parameter Is Required	402
Hot Extending a Virtual Disk	403
Adjusting Virtual Machine Resources (Shares, Limits, and Reservations) Based on Virtual Machine Workloads	406
Assigning a Storage Policy to a Virtual Machine	408
Verifying Storage Policy Compliance for Virtual Machines	413
Summary	414
Exam Essentials	414
Review Questions	416

**Chapter   8   Establish Service Levels with Cluster, Fault
                  Tolerance, and Resource Pools   421**

Creating and Configuring VMware Clusters   423
   Determining the Appropriate Failover Methodology and
      Required Resources for an HA Implementation   424
   Describing DRS Virtual Machine Entitlement   424
   Creating and Deleting a DRS/HA Cluster   425
   Adding and Removing ESXi Hosts from a
      DRS/HA Cluster   428
   Adding and Removing Virtual Machines to/from a
      DRS/HA Cluster   431
   Enabling and Disabling Host Monitoring   433
   Configuring Admission Control for HA and
      Virtual Machines   435
   Enabling, Configuring, and Disabling Virtual
      Machine and Application Monitoring   441
   Configuring Automation Levels for DRS and
      Virtual Machines   443
   Configuring Migration Thresholds for DRS and
      Virtual Machines   447
   Creating VM-Host and VM-VM Affinity Rules   448
   Configuring Enhanced vMotion Compatibility   456
   Monitoring a DRS/HA Cluster   458
   Configuring Storage DRS   462
Planning and Implementing VMware Fault Tolerance   466
   Determining Use Cases for Enabling VMware
      Fault Tolerance on a Virtual Machine   466
   Identifying VMware Fault Tolerance Requirements   467
   Configuring VMware Fault Tolerance Networking   469
   Enabling and Disabling VMware Fault
      Tolerance on a Virtual Machine   475
   Testing an FT Configuration   478
Creating and Administering Resource Pools   480
   Describing the Resource Pool Hierarchy   480
   Defining the Expandable Reservation Parameter   481
   Creating and Removing a Resource Pool   484
   Configuring Resource Pool Attributes   485
   Adding and Removing Virtual Machines to/from
      a Resource Pool   487
   Determining Resource Pool Requirements for a
      Given vSphere Implementation   488
   Evaluating Appropriate Shares, Reservations, and
      Limits for a Resource Pool Based on Virtual
      Machine Workloads   488

	Cloning a vApp	493	
	Summary	493	
	Exam Essentials	494	
	Review Questions	495	

Chapter   9   Maintain Service Levels   499

Migrating Virtual Machines	501
Migrating a Powered-Off or Suspended Virtual Machine	501
Identifying ESXi Host and Virtual Machine	
Requirements for vMotion and Storage vMotion	505
Identifying Enhanced vMotion Compatibility CPU	
Requirements	506
Identifying Snapshot Requirements for	
vMotion/Storage vMotion Migration	507
Configuring Virtual Machine Swap File Location	507
Migrating Virtual Machines Using	
vMotion/Storage vMotion	511
Utilizing Storage vMotion Techniques	514
Backing Up and Restoring Virtual Machines	518
Identifying Snapshot Requirements	518
Creating, Deleting, and Consolidating	
Virtual Machine Snapshots	521
Installing and Configuring VMware Data Recovery	528
Creating a Backup Job with VMware Data Recovery	541
Performing a Test and Live Full/File-Level Restore with	
VMware Data Recovery	544
Determining Appropriate Backup Solution for a	
Given vSphere Implementation	550
Patching and Updating ESXi and Virtual Machines	552
Identifying Patching Requirements for ESXi	
Hosts and Virtual Machine Hardware/Tools	553
Creating, Editing, and Removing a Host	
Profile from an ESXi Host	554
Attaching and Applying a Host Profile to an	
ESXi Host or Cluster	556
Performing Compliance Scanning and	
Remediating an ESXi Host Using Host Profiles	557
Installing and Configuring VMware vSphere	
Update Manager	559
Configuring Patch Download Options	567
Creating, Editing, and Deleting an Update	
Manager Baseline	570
Attaching an Update Manager Baseline to an	
ESXi Host or Cluster	577

Scanning and Remediating ESXi Hosts and
Virtual Machine Hardware/Tools Using
Update Manager   578
Staging ESXi Host Updates   586
Summary   587
Exam Essentials   .   588
Review Questions   589

Chapter   10   Perform Basic Troubleshooting   593

Perform Basic Troubleshooting for ESXi Hosts   595
Troubleshooting Common Installation Issues   595
Monitoring ESXi System Health   596
Identifying General ESXi Host
Troubleshooting Guidelines   598
Exporting Diagnostic Information   599
Perform Basic vSphere Network Troubleshooting   602
Verifying Network Configuration   603
Verifying a Given Virtual Machine Is Configured
with the Correct Network Resources   605
Troubleshooting Virtual Switch and Port
Group Configuration Issues   605
Troubleshooting Physical Network Adapter
Configuration Issues   607
Identifying the Root Cause of a Network Issue
Based on Troubleshooting Information   610
Perform Basic vSphere Storage Troubleshooting   611
Verifying Storage Configuration   611
Troubleshooting Storage Contention Issues   612
Troubleshooting Storage Overcommitment Issues   617
Troubleshooting iSCSI Software Initiator
Configuration Issues   617
Troubleshooting Storage Reports and Storage Maps   618
Identifying the Root Cause of a Storage Issue
Based on Troubleshooting Information   620
Perform Basic Troubleshooting for HA/DRS
Clusters and vMotion/Storage vMotion   620
Identifying HA/DRS and vMotion Requirements   620
Verifying vMotion/Storage vMotion Configuration   621
Verifying HA Network Configuration   622
Verifying HA/DRS Cluster Configuration   623
Troubleshooting HA Capacity Issues   625
Troubleshooting HA Redundancy Issues   626
Troubleshooting DRS Load Imbalance Issues   627
Interpreting the DRS Resource Distribution
Graph and Target/Current Host Load Deviation   630

Troubleshooting vMotion/Storage vMotion
Migration Issues 633
Interpret vMotion Resource Maps 633
Identifying the Root Cause of a DRS/HA Cluster or
Migration Issue Based on Troubleshooting
Information 635
Summary 635
Exam Essentials 636
Review Questions 637

**Chapter   11   Monitor a vSphere Implementation and Manage
vCenter Server Alarms   641**

Monitor ESXi, vCenter Server, and Virtual Machines 643
Describing How Tasks and Events Are Viewed in
vCenter Server 644
Creating, Editing, and Deleting Scheduled Tasks 646
Configuring SNMP for vCenter Server 650
Configuring Active Directory and SMTP Settings
for vCenter Server 651
Configuring vCenter Server Timeout Settings 653
Configuring vCenter Server Logging Options 654
Creating a Log Bundle 655
Starting, Stopping, and Verifying vCenter Server
Service Status 656
Starting, Stopping, and Verifying ESXi Host
Agent Status 659
Monitoring and Administering vCenter
Server Connections 661
Configuring, Viewing, Printing, and Exporting
Resource Maps 663
Explaining Common Memory Metrics 666
Explaining Common CPU Metrics 668
Explaining Common Network Metrics 669
Explaining Common Storage Metrics 670
Comparing and Contrasting Overview and
Advanced Charts 671
Creating an Advanced Chart 674
Identifying Critical Performance Metrics 677
Determining Host Performance Using resxtop and
Guest Perfmon 679
Given Performance Data, Identifying the
Affected vSphere Resource 683
Create and Administer vCenter Server Alarms 684
Listing vCenter Default Utilization Alarms 685
Listing vCenter Default Connectivity Alarms 685

Listing Possible Actions for Utilization and
Connectivity Alarms   685
Creating a vCenter Utilization Alarm   687
Creating a vCenter Connectivity Alarm   691
Configuring Alarm Triggers   694
Configuring Alarm Actions   695
For a Given Alarm, Identifying the Affected
Resource in a vSphere Implementation   696
Summary   697
Exam Essentials   698
Review Questions   699

Appendix   A   Answers to Review Questions   703

Chapter 2: Plan, Install, Configure, and Upgrade
vCenter Server and VMware ESXi   704
Chapter 3: Secure vCenter Server and ESXi
and Identify vSphere Architecture and Solutions   705
Chapter 4: Plan and Configure vSphere Networking   707
Chapter 5: Plan and Configure vSphere Storage   708
Chapter 6: Create and Deploy Virtual Machines and vApps 709
Chapter 7: Manage and Administer Virtual
Machines and vApps   710
Chapter 8: Establish Service Levels with Cluster,
Fault Tolerance, and Resource Pools   712
Chapter 9: Maintain Service Levels   713
Chapter 10: Perform Basic Troubleshooting   715
Chapter 11: Monitor a vSphere Implementation and
Manage vCenter Server Alarms   716

Appendix   B   About the Additional Study Tools   719

Additional Study Tools   720
Sybex Test Engine   720
Electronic Flashcards   720
PDF of Glossary of Terms   720
Adobe Reader   721
System Requirements   721
Using the Study Tools   721
Troubleshooting   721
Customer Care   722

Index   *723*

Table of Exercises

Exercise **2.1** Deploying the vCenter Server Appliance 31

Exercise **2.2** Installing vCenter Server into a Virtual Machine 35

Exercise **2.3** Installing the vSphere Client 41

Exercise **2.4** Installing the vSphere Web Client (Server) 43

Exercise **2.5** Installing the VMware Syslog Collector on vCenter Server 47

Exercise **2.6** Installing VMware Auto Deploy 49

Exercise **2.7** Adding License Keys to vCenter in Evaluation Mode. 53

Exercise **2.8** Performing an Interactive Installation of ESXi 5 58

Exercise **2.9** Deploying an ESXi Host Using Auto Deploy 61

Exercise **2.10** Configuring NTP on an ESXi Host 62

Exercise **2.11** Configuring DNS and Routing Using the vSphere Client 64

Exercise **2.12** Configuring DNS and Routing from the ESXi DCUI. 65

Exercise **2.13** Enabling/Configuring/Disabling Hyperthreading. 69

Exercise **2.14** Enabling and Disabling the Memory Compression Cache. 71

Exercise **2.15** Sizing the Memory Compression Cache. 72

Exercise **2.16** Adding License Keys to ESXi in Evaluation Mode 73

Exercise **2.17** Upgrading a vNetwork Distributed Switch 78

Exercise **2.18** Upgrading an ESXi Host Using vSphere Update Manager 84

Exercise **3.1** Disabling the NTP Client in the ESXi Firewall 101

Exercise **3.2** Configuring Allowed IP Address Settings for the NTP
Client in the ESXi Firewall. 103

Exercise **3.3** Configuring Startup Policies for ESXi Services 105

Exercise **3.4** Enabling Lockdown Mode Using the vSphere Client 109

Exercise **3.5** Viewing, Sorting, and Exporting User and Group
Lists from an ESXi Host. 113

Exercise **3.6** Adding Permissions for Users on vCenter Server
Inventory Objects 114

Exercise **3.7** Modifying Permissions for Users on vCenter Server
Inventory Objects 117

Exercise **3.8** Removing Permissions for Users on vCenter Server
Inventory Objects 117

Exercise **3.9** Creating a New Role in vCenter Server 119

Exercise **3.10** Cloning and Editing a Sample Role in vCenter Server. 120

Exercise   **3.11** Adding an ESXi Host to Active Directory 122

Exercise   **3.12** Applying Permissions to an ESXi Host Using Host Profiles 124

Exercise   **4.1** Creating a vSwitch 149

Exercise   **4.2** Adding a vmnic to a vSwitch and Configuring It 152

Exercise   **4.3** Removing a vmnic from a vSwitch .154

Exercise   **4.4** Configuring a vSwitch with a VMkernel Port Group for vMotion. . 155

Exercise   **4.5** Editing a Port Group in a vSwitch .159

Exercise   **4.6** Adding a Port Group in a vSwitch .160

Exercise   **4.7** Removing a Port Group in a vSwitch 162

Exercise   **4.8** Creating a dvSwitch 166

Exercise   **4.9** Adding an ESXi Host to a dvSwitch 169

Exercise   **4.10** Removing an ESXi host from a dvSwitch. 172

Exercise   **4.11** Adding a dvPort Group to a dvSwitch. 173

Exercise   **4.12** Configuring a dvPort Group 175

Exercise   **4.13** Removing a dvPort Group. 179

Exercise   **4.14** Adding and Removing Uplink Adapters to
                    dvUplink Groups. 179

Exercise   **4.15** Adding a Virtual Adapter to a dvSwitch. 183

Exercise   **4.16** Configuring a Virtual Adapter 186

Exercise   **4.17** Migrating a Virtual Adapter to a vSwitch 187

Exercise   **4.18** Migrating Virtual Machines to and from a dvSwitch 191

Exercise   **4.19** Configuring dvPort Group Blocking Policies 197

Exercise   **4.20** Configuring Traffic Shaping Policies on a vSwitch 203

Exercise   **4.21** Configuring Traffic Shaping Policies on a dvSwitch 205

Exercise   **4.22** Enabling TSO for a Virtual Machine 207

Exercise   **4.23** Enabling Jumbo Frames for a vSwitch 209

Exercise   **5.1** Identifying Storage Adapters and Devices in ESXi 222

Exercise   **5.2** Rescanning Storage in ESXi 225

Exercise   **5.3** Disabling, Configuring, and Enabling vCenter Server
                    Storage Filters 228

Exercise   **5.4** Configuring and Editing a Dependent Hardware iSCSI Adapter . . 233

Exercise   **5.5** Enabling the Software iSCSI Initiator. 236

Exercise   **5.6** Disabling the Software iSCSI Initiator 237

Exercise   **5.7** Configuring and Editing the Software iSCSI Initiator Settings . . . 238

Exercise   **5.8** Configuring iSCSI Port Binding on the Software iSCSI Initiator. . 240

Exercise   **5.9** Enabling, Configuring, and Disabling iSCSI CHAP on
the Software iSCSI Adapter. 243

Exercise   **5.10** Creating and Renaming a VMFS Datastore 249

Exercise   **5.11** Unmounting a VMFS Datastore 252

Exercise   **5.12** Deleting a VMFS Datastore. 254

Exercise   **5.13** Growing an Extent in a VMFS Datastore 257

Exercise   **5.14** Adding an Extent in a VMFS Datastore 260

Exercise   **5.15** Upgrading a VMFS-3 Datastore to VMFS-5 262

Exercise   **5.16** Selecting the Preferred Path for a VMFS Datastore 267

Exercise   **5.17** Disabling a Path to a VMFS Datastore. 268

Exercise   **5.18** Connecting to a NAS Device 270

Exercise   **5.19** Deploying and Configuring the VSA Manager 280

Exercise   **5.20** Installing a New VSA Cluster Using VSA Manager. 283

Exercise   **5.21** Entering VSA Cluster Maintenance Mode 288

Exercise   **5.22** Entering Appliance Maintenance Mode 290

Exercise   **6.1** Configuring and Deploying a New VM with the vSphere Client. . 303

Exercise   **6.2** Configuring and Deploying a New VM with the vSphere
Web Client. 308

Exercise   **6.3** Accessing a Virtual Machine Console with the vSphere
Web Client. 314

Exercise   **6.4** Installing VMware Tools Using the vSphere Client 316

Exercise   **6.5** Upgrading VMware Tools Using the vSphere Client 317

Exercise   **6.6** Updating VMware Tools Using the vSphere Client 318

Exercise   **6.7** Configuring Periodic Time Synchronization in a
Virtual Machine. 321

Exercise   **6.8** Configuring and Modifying a Disk Controller in the
vSphere Client 326

Exercise   **6.9** Adding an RDM to a Virtual Machine with the vSphere Client . . 330

Exercise   **6.10** Converting a Thin Disk to a Thick Disk 332

Exercise   **6.11** Configuring Disk Shares for a Virtual Machine
                Using the vSphere Web Client 334

Exercise   **6.12** Adding, Configuring, and Connecting a Virtual NIC
                Adapter Using the vSphere Client 338

Exercise   **6.13** Installing VMware Converter Standalone and
                Converting a Physical Server to a Virtual Machine 341

Exercise   **6.14** Importing a Hyper-V VM Using VMware Converter 346

Exercise   **6.15** Performing a V2V Conversion to Modify Virtual Hardware
                Settings Using VMware Converter 350

Exercise   **6.16** Creating a vApp Using the vSphere Web Client 355

Exercise   **6.17** Identifying vApp Settings 357

Exercise   **6.18** Configuring an IP Pool and vApp 360

Exercise   **6.19** Cloning a vApp Using the vSphere Client 364

Exercise   **6.20** Exporting a vApp Using the vSphere Client 365

Exercise   **7.1** Cloning an Existing Virtual Machine 376

Exercise   **7.2** Creating a Template from an Existing VM 380

Exercise   **7.3** Deploying a VM from a Template 381

Exercise   **7.4** Updating Virtual Machine Templates 384

Exercise   **7.5** Importing an OVF Template 386

Exercise   **7.6** Configuring Virtual Machine Options 393

Exercise   **7.7** Configuring Virtual Machine Power Management Settings 396

Exercise   **7.8** Configuring Virtual Machine Boot Options Using the vSphere
                Web Client 398

Exercise   **7.9** Hot Extending a Virtual Disk Using the vSphere Web Client . . . 403

Exercise   **7.10** Adjusting Virtual Machine Resources 407

Exercise   **7.11** Implementing Storage Profiles 409

Exercise   **7.12** Verifying VM Storage Policy Compliance 413

Exercise   **8.1** Creating a New Cluster with HA and DRS Enabled 425

Exercise   **8.2** Adding and Removing ESXi Hosts to and from a Cluster 428

Exercise   **8.3** Adding a VM from an Existing ESXi Host to a Cluster 432

Exercise   **8.4** Configuring Admission Control and Admission Control Policies . . 436

Exercise   **8.5** Configuring VM Options for vSphere HA 439

Exercise   **8.6** Enabling and Configuring VM Monitoring
                and Application Monitoring 442

Exercise   **8.7** Configuring Automation Level for Cluster and a VM 444

Exercise   **8.8** Configuring the Migration Threshold for DRS 447

Exercise   **8.9** Creating a VM-Host Affinity Rule 449

Exercise   **8.10** Creating a VM-VM Affinity Rule 454

Exercise   **8.11** Enabling EVC for a Cluster 456

Exercise   **8.12** Configuring Storage DRS 463

Exercise   **8.13** Configuring VMware FT Logging Traffic 469

Exercise   **8.14** Enabling FT for a Powered-Off Virtual Machine 475

Exercise   **8.15** Disabling FT for a Powered-Off Virtual Machine 477

Exercise   **8.16** Testing Failover of FT 478

Exercise   **8.17** Configuring and Testing Expandable Reservations 481

Exercise   **8.18** Creating a Resource Pool 484

Exercise   **8.19** Evaluating Memory Reservations for a FT VM 489

Exercise   **9.1** Migrating a Powered-Off Virtual Machine
                            Using the vSphere Client 502

Exercise   **9.2** Migrating a Suspended Virtual Machine Using the
                            vSphere Web Client 503

Exercise   **9.3** Configuring the Virtual Machine Swap File Location 508

Exercise   **9.4** Migrate a Virtual Machine with vMotion Using the
                            vSphere Web Client 512

Exercise   **9.5** Migrate a Virtual Machine With Storage vMotion
                            Using the vSphere Client 513

Exercise   **9.6** Performing a Storage vMotion with Advanced Techniques 515

Exercise   **9.7** Creating a Virtual Machine Snapshot and Then Revert To It 521

Exercise   **9.8** Deleting a Virtual Machine Snapshot 523

Exercise   **9.9** Consolidating Virtual Machine Snapshots 525

Exercise   **9.10** Installing the VMware Data Recovery Client Plug-in 529

Exercise   **9.11** Installing the VMware Data Recovery Backup Appliance 531

Exercise   **9.12** Adding a Virtual Disk to the VMware Data
                            Recovery Backup Appliance 533

Exercise   **9.13** Installing the FLR Client in Ubuntu 535

Exercise   **9.14** Configuring the VMware Data Recovery
                            Backup Appliance 536

Exercise   **9.15** Connecting the VMware Data Recovery
                            Backup Appliance to vCenter Server 538

Exercise   **9.16** Creating a Backup Job with VMware Data Recovery 541

Exercise   **9.17** Performing an Individual File-Level Restore
Using the FLR Client 544

Exercise   **9.18** Restoring a VM with VMware Data Recovery 547

Exercise   **9.19** Testing the Restore of a VM with VMware Data Recovery 549

Exercise   **9.20** Creating an ESXi Host Profile 554

Exercise   **9.21** Editing an ESXi Host Profile 555

Exercise   **9.22** Attaching a Host Profile to an ESXi Host. 556

Exercise   **9.23** Compliance Scanning and Remediating an ESXi Host. 557

Exercise   **9.24** Installing vSphere Update Manager 560

Exercise   **9.25** Configuring vSphere Update Manager Network Settings 563

Exercise   **9.26** Configuring vSphere Update Manager
Virtual Machine Settings. 564

Exercise   **9.27** Configuring vSphere Update Manager Cluster Settings 565

Exercise   **9.28** Configuring vSphere Update Manager Download Settings 568

Exercise   **9.29** Creating a Dynamic Patch Baseline for ESXi 5 571

Exercise   **9.30** Editing a Dynamic Patch Baseline for ESXi 5 574

Exercise   **9.31** Attaching a Baseline to an ESXi Host 577

Exercise   **9.32** Manually Scanning an ESXi Host for Compliance 579

Exercise   **9.33** Manually Remediating a Noncompliant ESXi Host 580

Exercise   **9.34** Creating a Group Baseline and Attaching It to
a Virtual Machine 581

Exercise   **9.35** Manually Scanning and Remediating a Virtual Machine. 584

Exercise   **9.36** Staging ESXI Host Updates. 586

Exercise   **10.1** Exporting System Logs from vCenter Server. 600

Exercise   **10.2** Using the vmkping Command from ESXi Shell 606

Exercise   **10.3** Troubleshooting Physical Network Adapter Configuration
Issues Using the vSphere Client. .608

Exercise   **10.4** Viewing Storage Contention with esxtop 614

Exercise   **10.5** Viewing Storage Contention Data 616

Exercise   **10.6** Creating and Correcting a DRS Load Imbalance. 627

Exercise   **11.1** Creating, Editing, and Deleting a Scheduled Task in vCenter
Server Using the vSphere Client. .647

Exercise   **11.2** Configuring SNMP for vCenter Server 651

Exercise   **11.3** Verifying, Stopping, and Starting the VMware VirtualCenter
Server Services Using the Windows Services Management
Console. 656

Exercise   **11.4** Verifying, Stopping, and Starting the ESXi Host Agent 659

Exercise   **11.5** Configuring, Viewing, Printing, and
                        Exporting a Resource Map 664

Exercise   **11.6** Creating an Advanced Performance Chart. 675

Exercise   **11.7** Using resxtop Data and Perfmon to Monitor ESXi Host
                        Performance. 679

Exercise   **11.8** Monitoring Virtual Machine CPU and Memory Usage with a
                        vCenter Server Utilization Alarm. 687

Exercise   **11.9** Monitoring Datastore Connectivity with a vCenter Server
                        Connectivity Alarm 691

Introduction

Obtaining the VCP5 certification is a key step for vSphere administrators. Having the VCP5 proves that you know how to install, configure, and administer a vSphere 5 environment. Gaining the VCP5 certification is challenging and rewarding, and the process will teach you many things about vSphere that you may not have previously known.

Regardless of the experience level you bring to this book, I aim to provide you with additional experience by including multiple exercises per chapter. Some of these exercises may seem easy if you have a considerable amount of vSphere experience, but I believe there is no better way to learn vSphere than to actually perform these exercises. The exercises line up directly with the VCP5 exam objectives, and knowing how to do the steps in these exercises will be very beneficial when you take the VCP5 exam.

Aside from Chapter 1, each chapter also includes 20 review questions. That means by the time you work your way through this book, you will have been presented with 200 questions. (There are also an additional 150 questions included in the Sybex test engine on the web site, along with 150 flashcards.) Chapters also include case studies, warnings, tips, and notes that encompass many of the issues I have encountered in my experiences with vSphere.

Choosing the VCP5 certification is a great decision, and with this book, you are that much closer to achieving this goal. Certification is extremely valuable for a variety of professional and personal reasons, and obtaining the VCP5 certification will reward you with a wealth of knowledge about vSphere 5. The VCP5 is just the first step of VMware's certification path, so becoming a VCP5 is the also the first step in obtaining additional VMware certifications in your future. Whichever path you choose, I wish you the best of luck!

What Is the VMware Certified Professional on vSphere 5 (VCP5) Certification?

The VCP5 is the first of three certifications offered in VMware's datacenter virtualization certification area. The VCP5 will test your ability to install, configure, and administer a vSphere 5 environment. VMware believes VCP5 candidates will have approximately six months of vSphere experience and a general IT experience level of two to five years. This general IT experience is likely because virtualization incorporates so many different aspects of IT. Experience with networking, storage, systems, security, programming, command-line interfaces, and more will all serve a vSphere administrator well.

While having general IT experience and familiarity with vSphere 5 is a step in the right direction, there is also the requirement of a VMware-authorized course to obtain VCP5 certification. This course requirement assures that anyone who passes the VCP5 exam actually has some hands-on experience with the products. The classes are comprehensive and very good at introducing students to subjects they might not otherwise have experience with. While the courses are a great learning experience, do not assume that these few days of coursework will be a suitable substitute for months or years of real-world experience. There is no substitute for actually knowing how and when to use the vSphere.

 While it would obviously be better to take the course prior to the VCP5 exam, the course requirement can be satisfied either before or after taking the VCP5 exam.

The VCP5 exam blueprint is the official guide to be used for the VCP5. Any objective listed in the VCP5 exam blueprint is fair game for the VCP5 exam, and you should expect to be tested on each objective. This book follows the VCP5 exam blueprint and covers each and every objective contained therein.

Why Become VCP5 Certified?

Become certified because you have a strong desire to be a VCP5! Becoming a VCP5 shows that you have the skills necessary to install, configure, and administer a vSphere 5 environment. These skills, along with the VCP5 certification, can lead to your ability to stand out among your peers, lead to career advancement opportunities, and ultimately increase your market value. Perhaps the most important reason is the simple fact that in this journey you will learn more about vSphere 5 than you ever thought possible.

How to Become a VMware Certified Professional on vSphere 5 (VCP5)

If you are new to VMware certifications or have a VCP certification older than VCP4, then the following requirements exist for the VCP5 certification:

- VMware vSphere: Install, Configure, Manage 5.0
- VMware vSphere: Fast Track 5.0
- VCP5 exam

If you have a previous VCP4 certification or if you have taken an authorized VMware VCP4 qualifying course, then the following requirements exist for the VCP5 certification:

- VMware vSphere: What's New 5.0
- VCP5 exam

This information was accurate at the time this book was written, but it is subject to change. Always consult the VMware certification website for the latest information on the VCP5 requirements: (`http://mylearn.vmware.com/portals/certification/`).

The actual VCP5 exam consists of 85 questions, and there is a time limit of 90 minutes. The exam is offered in English, but an additional 30 minutes is offered to candidates in a country where English is not a primary language. There is also a pre-exam survey that consists of 8 questions, and you will have 15 minutes to complete these questions and the pre-exam agreements. Note that this survey has no effect on the types of questions offered in your exam. The passing score for the VCP exam is 300, which uses a scaled scoring method that ranges from 100 to 500. There is a wait of seven calendar days before exam retakes are allowed. Once you have passed the VCP5 exam, you are not allowed to take the exam again.

The VCP5 exam is administered through Pearson VUE. For registration and more information about the exam, visit the VMware page at the Pearson VUE website (www.pearsonvue.com/vmware).

Tips for Taking the VCP5 Exam

In addition to experience, coursework, and studying, another part of ensuring success on the VCP5 exam is preparing to take the test. Here are a few helpful hints:

- Schedule the test on a date that offers you plenty of time to prepare and when you can be focused 100 percent on the exam.
- Be sure to get good consistent sleep in the days leading up to the exam.
- Eat breakfast, lunch, or a snack before going in. You want to be fresh, focused, and not distracted in any way.
- Know exactly where the testing center is and be sure to arrive there early.
- If possible, bring this book or your notes along with you to the testing center. This will allow you to review if you have time to spare.
- Relax and focus on what you know.
- Read each exam question carefully, and then read it again. I tried to provide some misleading questions in this book to prepare you for this possibility on the VCP5 exam.
- If you are unsure of a question or it is simply taking too much of your time, flag it for review and move on.
- If you don't know the answer to a question, make an educated guess. Never leave questions unanswered!

- For those difficult questions, make a mental note of them and then find the answer after you leave the testing center.

Who Should Read This Book?

Any experienced vSphere administrator who is ready to pass the VCP5 exam should read this book. This book covers each objective of the VCP5 exam as listed in the exam blueprint. Using this book as your study guide for the VCP5 exam will streamline your studying process and increase your odds of passing the VCP5 exam.

What Does This Book Cover?

This book covers every single objective of the VCP5 exam as outlined in the exam blueprint. Access to a test lab is an essential part of using this book, but a copy of VMware Workstation 8 or newer on a host system with plenty of memory can make an excellent physical lab substitute in most cases. Many of the exercises in this book actually utilized VMware Workstation 8; I had to do something on that long flight! In some ways, using VMware Workstation can even teach you more about virtualization, because it forces you to think about the additional layer of abstraction in use. There are eleven chapters in this book, and they are as follows:

Chapter 1: What's New in vSphere 5   This chapter offers a quick look at what is new and changed in vSphere 5. This chapter doesn't include assessment questions or chapter review questions and is simply intended to get you up to speed on what is new with vSphere 5.

Chapter 2: Plan, Install, Configure, and Upgrade vCenter Server and VMware ESXi   This chapter covers planning, installing, and configuring vCenter Server and ESXi 5. Upgrading vCenter Server and ESXi 5 are also included here.

Chapter 3: Secure vCenter Server and ESXi and Identify vSphere Architecture and Solutions   This chapter covers securing vCenter Server and ESXi and also discusses vSphere architecture and solutions.

Chapter 4: Plan and Configure vSphere Networking   This chapter is completely focused on vSphere networking and covers vSwitches, dvSwitches, and the various aspects of configuring each.

Chapter 5: Plan and Configure vSphere Storage   This chapter is completely focused on vSphere storage. VMFS, NFS, and the various connectivity options are discussed, along with how to use the different datastore options.

Chapter 6: Create and Deploy Virtual Machines and vApps   This chapter covers creating and deploying virtual machines and vApps in vSphere 5.

Chapter 7: Manage and Administer Virtual Machines and vApps   This chapter covers managing and administering virtual machines and vApps. Clones, templates, and more are covered in this chapter.

Chapter 8: Establish Service Levels with Clusters, Fault Tolerance, and Resource Pools   This chapter covers a lot of material and includes HA, DRS, FT, and resource pools.

Chapter 9: Maintain Service Levels   This chapter covers migrating virtual machines, backing up and restoring with VMware Data Recovery, and implementing patching solutions for vSphere 5. vSphere Update Manager is also covered in this chapter.

Chapter 10: Perform Basic Troubleshooting and Alarm Management   This chapter covers troubleshooting for ESXi hosts, storage, networking, HA, DRS, vMotion, and Storage vMotion.

Chapter 11: Monitor a vSphere Implementation   The final chapter in this book covers monitoring ESXi hosts and vCenter Server, in addition to using vCenter Server alarms.

Each chapter also includes tips, notes, warnings, case studies, and exercises. As mentioned, aside from Chapter 1, all chapters include 20 review questions.

What's Included in the Book?

There are many helpful items intended to prepare you for the VCP5 exam included in this book. These items include the following:

Assessment Test   There is a 40-question assessment test at the conclusion of this introduction that can be used to quickly evaluate where you are with vSphere 5. This test should be taken prior to beginning your work in this book and should help you identify areas that you are either strong or weak in. Note that these questions are purposely simpler than the types of questions you may see on the VCP5 exam.

Objective Map and Opening List of Objectives   The front-inside cover of this book contains a detailed exam objective map showing you where each of the exam objectives are covered, but know that this book also follows the exam blueprint in order! Each chapter, excluding Chapter 1, also includes a list of the exam objectives that are covered.

Exam Essentials   The end of each chapter includes a listing of exam essentials. These are essentially repeats of the objectives, but remember that any objective on the exam blueprint could show up on the exam.

Chapter Review Questions   Chapters 2 through 11 include 20 review questions each. These are used to assess your understanding of the chapter and are taken directly from the chapter content. These questions are based on the exam objectives and are similar in difficulty to items you might actually receive on the VCP5 exam.

You can obtain the Sybex test engine, flashcards, and glossary at www.sybex.com/go/vcp5.

Sybex Test Engine   There are 150 questions included as practice exams in the Sybex test engine. These questions are taken from Chapters 2 through 11 and cover the exam objectives. It may be helpful to wait and take these tests until after you have completed the book and are feeling ready for the VCP5. If you do well on these tests, then you should also be ready for the VCP5 exam.

Electronic Flashcards   The flashcards are included for quick reference and are great tools for learning quick facts. You can even consider these as 150 additional simple exam questions, which is essentially what they are.

PDF of Glossary of Terms   There is a glossary included that covers the key terms used in this book.

How to Use This Book

This book aims to provide the missing pieces required to pass the VCP5 exam. You bring the experience and the desire to learn, and I will cover the objectives in detail and get you ready to pass the exam! This book contains a wealth of resources, but knowing how to use them is also important. Here is my recommendation for how to use these resources:

1. Review the VCP5 exam blueprint that follows this section. Make notes of the objectives and rate where you think you are with each objective. Be honest in your assessment, since the ultimate goal here is to learn and improve.

2. Take the assessment test located at the end of this introduction. Be honest here, and when the assessment test is complete, adjust your ratings from the previous step. Remember that the goal is to identify where you are strong and weak. The assessment test should help with this.

3. Take your time and read each chapter attentively. Allocate extra time to objectives you don't understand as well. Rushing through the chapters for the sake of completing them does you no favor. If there are sections that you don't understand, read them again.

4. Take the time to actually complete the exercises in each chapter. Think about how features work and how you could modify the exercises for different results. Understand what the exercise is trying to teach you, and do not view the exercises as obstacles in the way of your completing the chapter. Be prepared to tear your lab down and rebuild it several times!

5. Take your time at the end of each chapter to answer the review questions. Think of them as mini-VCP5 exams. Take these tests only after reading the chapter and feeling confident that you understand the material presented in the chapter.

6. Use the flashcards included with this book. Think of them as easy questions you might receive on the exam or facts that you may need to be able to answer actual exam questions. The flashcards cover the objectives!

7. Review additional materials, specifically the tools listed in the VCP5 exam blueprint. These official VMware resources contain significant detail and can provide answers to just about any question you may have.

8. Use the VMTN communities and ask questions. I have learned as much, or possibly more, from the communities than all other resources I have used. It might even be me who answers your question, because I still spend a great deal of time in the VMTN communities!

9. Experiment with your lab. Break it! Never consider your lab a permanent setup. Learn how vSphere works, and understand its abilities and limitations. This is experience that can help pay dividends on exam day.

Obtaining your VCP5 certification will require experience, hard work, and time. There is no quick route to the VCP5, and any shortcut is simply shorting you of the benefits of this certification. Take your time and study the content of this book. Understand the content and ask questions if you have them. It is this process of learning and experimenting that will help you become VCP5 certified. Follow this advice, and you will do well!

Exam Objectives

The following list of exam objectives is taken directly from the VCP 5 exam blueprint. These objectives are based on exam blueprint version 1.4 and may have changed since this book was written.

> **NOTE** Always ensure that you are using the latest version of the VCP 5 exam blueprint. The exam blueprint is available at http://mylearn.vmware.com/ register.cfm?course=103110.

Section 1: Plan, Install, Configure and Upgrade vCenter Server and VMware ESXi

Objective 1.1: Install and Configure vCenter Server

Knowledge

- Identify available vCenter Server editions
- Deploy the vCenter Appliance
- Install vCenter Server into a virtual machine
- Size the vCenter Server database

- Install additional vCenter Server components
- Install/Remove vSphere Client plug-ins
- Enable/Disable vSphere Client plug-ins
- License vCenter Server
- Determine availability requirements for a vCenter Server in a given vSphere implementation
- Determine use case for vSphere Client and Web Client

Tools

- VMware vSphere Basics guide
- vSphere Installation and Setup guide
- vCenter Server and Host Management guide
- VMware Virtualization Toolkit
- vSphere Client

Objective 1.2: Install and Configure VMware ESXi

Knowledge

- Perform an interactive installation of ESXi
- Deploy an ESXi host using Auto Deploy
- Configure NTP on an ESXi Host
- Configure DNS and Routing on an ESXi Host
- Enable/Configure/Disable hyperthreading
- Enable/Size/Disable memory compression cache
- License an ESXi host

Tools

- VMware vSphere Basics guide
- vSphere Installation and Setup guide
- vCenter Server and Host Management guide
- vSphere PowerCLI
- vSphere Client

Objective 1.3: Plan and Perform Upgrades of vCenter Server and VMware ESXi

Knowledge

- Identify upgrade requirements for ESXi hosts
- Identify steps required to upgrade a vSphere implementation
- Upgrade a vNetwork Distributed Switch
- Upgrade from VMFS3 to VMFS5

- Upgrade VMware Tools
- Upgrade Virtual Machine hardware
- Upgrade an ESXi Host using vCenter Update Manager
- Determine whether an in-place upgrade is appropriate in a given upgrade scenario

Tools

- VMware vSphere Basics guide
- vSphere Installation and Setup guide
- vSphere Upgrade guide
- VMware vSphere Examples and Scenarios guide
- Installing and Administering VMware vSphere Update Manager

Objective 1.4: Secure vCenter Server and ESXi

Knowledge

- Identify common vCenter Server privileges and roles
- Describe how permissions are applied and inherited in vCenter Server
- Configure and administer the ESXi firewall
- Enable/Configure/Disable services in the ESXi firewall
- Enable Lockdown Mode
- Configure network security policies
- View/Sort/Export user and group lists
- Add/Modify/Remove permissions for users and groups on vCenter Server inventory objects
- Create/Clone/Edit vCenter Server Roles
- Add an ESXi Host to a directory service
- Apply permissions to ESXi Hosts using Host Profiles
- Determine the appropriate set of privileges for common tasks in vCenter Server

Tools

- vSphere Installation and Setup guide
- vCenter Server and Host Management guide
- VMware vSphere Examples and Scenarios guide
- vSphere Security guide

Objective 1.5: Identify vSphere Architecture and Solutions

Knowledge

- Identify available vSphere editions and features
- Explain ESXi and vCenter Server architectures

- Explain Private/Public/Hybrid cloud concepts
- Determine appropriate vSphere edition based on customer requirements

Tools

- VMware vSphere Basics guide
- VMware vCloud: Requirements for a Cloud
- VMware vCloud: Service Definition for a Public Cloud
- VMware vCloud: Service Definition for a Private Cloud
- vSphere 5.0 Licensing, Pricing and Packaging Whitepaper

Section 2: Plan and Configure vSphere Networking

Objective 2.1: Configure vNetwork Standard Switches

Knowledge

- Identify vNetwork Standard Switch (vSS) capabilities
- Create/Delete a vNetwork Standard Switch
- Add/Configure/Remove vmnics on a vNetwork Standard Switch
- Configure vmkernel ports for network services
- Add/Edit/Remove port groups on a vNetwork Standard Switch
- Determine use case for a vNetwork Standard Switch

Tools

- vSphere Installation and Setup guide
- vSphere Networking guide
- vSphere Client

Objective 2.2: Configure vNetwork Distributed Switches

Knowledge

- Identify vNetwork Distributed Switch (vDS) capabilities
- Create/Delete a vNetwork Distributed Switch
- Add/Remove ESXi hosts from a vNetwork Distributed Switch
- Add/Configure/Remove dvPort groups
- Add/Remove uplink adapters to dvUplink groups
- Create/Configure/Remove virtual adapters
- Migrate virtual adapters to/from a vNetwork Standard Switch
- Migrate virtual machines to/from a vNetwork Distributed Switch
- Determine use case for a vNetwork Distributed Switch

Tools
- vSphere Installation and Setup guide
- vSphere Networking guide
- vSphere Client

Objective 2.3: Configure vSS and vDS Policies

Knowledge
- Identify common vSS and vDS policies
- Configure dvPort group blocking policies
- Configure load balancing and failover policies
- Configure VLAN settings
- Configure traffic shaping policies
- Enable TCP Segmentation Offload support for a virtual machine
- Enable Jumbo Frames support on appropriate components
- Determine appropriate VLAN configuration for a vSphere implementation

Tools
- vSphere Installation and Setup guide
- vSphere Networking guide
- vSphere Client

Section 3: Plan and Configure vSphere Storage

Objective 3.1: Configure Shared Storage for vSphere

Knowledge
- Identify storage adapters and devices
- Identify storage naming conventions
- Identify hardware/dependent hardware/software iSCSI initiator requirements
- Compare and contrast array thin provisioning and virtual disk thin provisioning
- Describe zoning and LUN masking practices
- Scan/Rescan storage
- Identify use cases for FCoE
- Create an NFS share for use with vSphere
- Connect to a NAS device
- Enable/Configure/Disable vCenter Server storage filters
- Configure/Edit hardware/dependent hardware initiators

- Enable/Disable software iSCSI initiator
- Configure/Edit software iSCSI initiator settings
- Configure iSCSI port binding
- Enable/Configure/Disable iSCSI CHAP
- Determine use case for hardware/dependent hardware/software iSCSI initiator
- Determine use case for and configure array thin provisioning

Tools

- vSphere Installation and Setup guide
- vSphere Storage guide
- VMware vSphere Examples and Scenarios guide
- vSphere Client

Objective 3.2: Configure the Storage Virtual Appliance for vSphere

Knowledge

- Define Storage Virtual Appliance (SVA) architecture
- Configure ESXi hosts as SVA hosts
- Configure the storage network for the SVA
- Deploy/Configure the SVA Manager
- Administer SVA storage resources
- Determine use case for deploying the SVA
- Determine appropriate ESXi host resources for the SVA

Tools

- VMware vSphere Storage Appliance Installation and Configuration guide
- VMware vSphere Storage Appliance Administration guide
- VSA Manager

Objective 3.3: Create and Configure VMFS and NFS Datastores

Knowledge

- Identify VMFS and NFS Datastore properties
- Identify VMFS5 capabilities
- Create/Rename/Delete/Unmount a VMFS Datastore
- Mount/Unmount an NFS Datastore
- Extend/Expand VMFS Datastores
- Upgrade a VMFS3 Datastore to VMFS5
- Place a VMFS Datastore in Maintenance Mode
- Select the Preferred Path for a VMFS Datastore
- Disable a path to a VMFS Datastore

- Determine use case for multiple VMFS/NFS Datastores
- Determine appropriate Path Selection Policy for a given VMFS Datastore

Tools

- vSphere Installation and Setup guide
- vSphere Storage guide
- vSphere Client

Section 4: Deploy and Administer Virtual Machines and vApps

Objective 4.1: Create and Deploy Virtual Machines

Knowledge

- Identify capabilities of virtual machine hardware versions
- Identify VMware Tools device drivers
- Identify methods to access and use a virtual machine console
- Identify virtual machine storage resources
- Place virtual machines in selected ESXi hosts/Clusters/Resource Pools
- Configure and deploy a Guest OS into a new virtual machine
- Configure/Modify disk controller for virtual disks
- Configure appropriate virtual disk type for a virtual machine
- Create/Convert thin/thick provisioned virtual disks
- Configure disk shares
- Install/Upgrade/Update VMware Tools
- Configure virtual machine time synchronization
- Convert a physical machine using VMware Converter
- Import a supported virtual machine source using VMware Converter
- Modify virtual hardware settings using VMware Converter
- Configure/Modify virtual CPU and Memory resources according to OS and application requirements
- Configure/Modify virtual NIC adapter and connect virtual machines to appropriate network resources
- Determine appropriate datastore locations for virtual machines based on application workloads

Tools

- vSphere Virtual Machine Administration guide
- Installing and Configuring VMware Tools Guide
- vSphere Client / vSphere Web Client

Objective 4.2: Create and Deploy vApps

Knowledge

- Identify vApp settings
- Create/Clone/Export a vApp
- Add objects to an existing vApp
- Edit vApp settings
- Configure IP pools
- Suspend/Resume a vApp
- Determine when a tiered application should be deployed as a vApp

Tools

- vSphere Virtual Machine Administration guide
- vSphere Client / vSphere Web Client

Objective 4.3: Manage Virtual Machine Clones and Templates

Knowledge

- Identify the vCenter Server managed ESXi hosts and Virtual Machine maximums
- Identify Cloning and Template options
- Clone an existing virtual machine
- Create a template from an existing virtual machine
- Deploy a virtual machine from a template
- Update existing virtual machine templates
- Deploy virtual appliances and/or vApps from an OVF template
- Import and/or Export an OVF template
- Determine the appropriate deployment methodology for a given virtual machine application

Tools

- vSphere Virtual Machine Administration guide
- VMware vSphere Examples and Scenarios guide
- VMware Open Virtualization Format Tool
- OVF Tool User Guide
- vSphere Client / vSphere Web Client

Objective 4.4: Administer Virtual Machines and vApps

Knowledge

- Identify files used by virtual machines
- Identify locations for virtual machine configuration files and virtual disks
- Identify common practices for securing virtual machines

- Hot Extend a virtual disk
- Configure virtual machine options
- Configure virtual machine power settings
- Configure virtual machine boot options
- Configure virtual machine troubleshooting options
- Assign a Storage Policy to a virtual machine
- Verify Storage Policy compliance for virtual machines
- Determine when an advanced virtual machine parameter is required
- Adjust virtual machine resources (shares, limits and reservations) based on virtual machine workloads

Tools

- vSphere Virtual Machine Administration guide
- vSphere Client / vSphere Web Client

Section 5: Establish and Maintain Service Levels

Objective 5.1: Create and Configure VMware Clusters

Knowledge

- Describe DRS virtual machine entitlement
- Create/Delete a DRS/HA Cluster
- Add/Remove ESXi Hosts from a DRS/HA Cluster
- Add/Remove virtual machines from a DRS/HA Cluster
- Configure Storage DRS
- Configure Enhanced vMotion Compatibility
- Monitor a DRS/HA Cluster
- Configure migration thresholds for DRS and virtual machines
- Configure automation levels for DRS and virtual machines
- Create VM-Host and VM-VM affinity rules
- Enable/Disable Host Monitoring
- Enable/Configure/Disable virtual machine and application monitoring
- Configure admission control for HA and virtual machines
- Determine appropriate failover methodology and required resources for an HA implementation

Tools

- vCenter Server and Host Management guide
- vSphere Availability guide

- vSphere Resource Management guide
- vSphere Client

Objective 5.2: Plan and Implement VMware Fault Tolerance

Knowledge

- Identify VMware Fault Tolerance requirements
- Configure VMware Fault Tolerance networking
- Enable/Disable VMware Fault Tolerance on a virtual machine
- Test an FT configuration
- Determine use case for enabling VMware Fault Tolerance on a virtual machine

Tools

- vSphere Availability guide
- vSphere Client

Objective 5.3: Create and Administer Resource Pools

Knowledge

- Describe the Resource Pool hierarchy
- Define the Expandable Reservation parameter
- Create/Remove a Resource Pool
- Configure Resource Pool attributes
- Add/Remove virtual machines from a Resource Pool
- Determine Resource Pool requirements for a given vSphere implementation
- Evaluate appropriate shares, reservations and limits for a Resource Pool based on virtual machine workloads
- Clone a vApp

Tools

- vSphere Resource Management guide
- vSphere Virtual Machine Administration guide
- vSphere Client / vSphere Web Client

Objective 5.4: Migrate Virtual Machines

Knowledge

- Identify ESXi host and virtual machine requirements for vMotion and Storage vMotion
- Identify Enhanced vMotion Compatibility CPU requirements
- Identify snapshot requirements for vMotion/Storage vMotion migration
- Migrate virtual machines using vMotion/Storage vMotion
- Configure virtual machine swap file location
- Migrate a powered-off or suspended virtual machine

- Utilize Storage vMotion techniques (changing virtual disk type, renaming virtual machines, etc.)

Tools

- vSphere Resource Management guide
- vSphere Virtual Machine Administration guide
- VMware vSphere Examples and Scenarios guide
- vSphere Client/vSphere Web Client

Objective 5.5: Backup and Restore Virtual Machines

Knowledge

- Identify snapshot requirements
- Create/Delete/Consolidate virtual machine snapshots
- Install and Configure VMware Data Recovery
- Create a backup job with VMware Date Recovery
- Perform a test and live full/file-level restore with VMware Data Recovery
- Determine appropriate backup solution for a given vSphere implementation

Tools

- vSphere Virtual Machine Administration guide
- VMware Data Recovery Administration guide

Objective 5.6: Patch and Update ESXi and Virtual Machines

Knowledge

- Identify patching requirements for ESXi hosts and virtual machine hardware/tools
- Create/Edit/Remove a Host Profile from an ESXi host
- Attach/Apply a Host Profile to an ESXi host or cluster
- Perform compliance scanning and remediation of an ESXi host using Host Profiles
- Install and Configure vCenter Update Manager
- Configure patch download options
- Create/Edit/Delete an Update Manager baseline
- Attach an Update Manager baseline to an ESXi host or cluster
- Scan and remediate ESXi hosts and virtual machine hardware/tools using Update Manager
- Stage ESXi host updates

Tools

- vSphere Host Profiles guide
- Installing and Administering VMware vSphere Update Manager guide
- Reconfiguring VMware vSphere Update Manager

- VMware vSphere Examples and Scenarios guide
- vSphere Update Manager Utility
- vSphere Client

Section 6: Perform Basic Troubleshooting

Objective 6.1: Perform Basic Troubleshooting for ESXi Hosts

Knowledge

- Identify general ESXi host troubleshooting guidelines
- Troubleshoot common installation issues
- Monitor ESXi system health
- Export diagnostic information

Tools

- vCenter Server and Host Management guide
- vSphere Monitoring and Performance guide
- vSphere Troubleshooting guide
- vSphere Client

Objective 6.2: Perform Basic vSphere Network Troubleshooting

Knowledge

- Verify network configuration
- Verify a given virtual machine is configured with the correct network resources
- Troubleshoot virtual switch and port group configuration issues
- Troubleshoot physical network adapter configuration issues
- Identify the root cause of a network issue based on troubleshooting information

Tools

- vSphere Networking guide
- vSphere Troubleshooting guide
- vSphere Client

Objective 6.3: Perform Basic vSphere Storage Troubleshooting

Knowledge

- Verify storage configuration
- Troubleshoot storage contention issues
- Troubleshoot storage over-commitment issues
- Troubleshoot iSCSI software initiator configuration issues
- Troubleshoot Storage Reports and Storage Maps
- Identify the root cause of a storage issue based on troubleshooting information

Tools

- vSphere Storage guide
- vSphere Troubleshooting guide
- vSphere Client

Objective 6.4: Perform Basic Troubleshooting for HA/DRS Clusters and vMotion/Storage vMotion

Knowledge

- Identify HA/DRS and vMotion requirements
- Verify vMotion/Storage vMotion configuration
- Verify HA network configuration
- Verify HA/DRS cluster configuration
- Troubleshoot HA capacity issues
- Troubleshoot HA redundancy issues
- Interpret the DRS Resource Distribution Graph and Target/Current Host Load Deviation
- Troubleshoot DRS load imbalance issues
- Troubleshoot vMotion/Storage vMotion migration issues
- Interpret vMotion Resource Maps
- Identify the root cause of a DRS/HA cluster or migration issue based on troubleshooting information

Tools

- vSphere Availability guide
- vSphere Resource Management guide
- vSphere Monitoring and Performance guide
- vSphere Troubleshooting guide
- vSphere Client

Section 7: Monitor a vSphere Implementation and Manage vCenter Server Alarms

Objective 7.1: Monitor ESXi, vCenter Server and Virtual Machines

Knowledge

- Describe how Tasks and Events are viewed in vCenter Server
- Identify critical performance metrics
- Explain common memory metrics
- Explain common CPU metrics
- Explain common network metrics
- Explain common storage metrics

- Compare and contrast Overview and Advanced Charts
- Configure SNMP for vCenter Server
- Configure Active Directory and SMTP settings for vCenter Server
- Configure vCenter Server logging options
- Create a log bundle
- Create/Edit/Delete a Scheduled Task
- Configure/View/Print/Export resource maps
- Start/Stop/Verify vCenter Server service status
- Start/Stop/Verify ESXi host agent status
- Configure vCenter Server timeout settings
- Monitor/Administer vCenter Server connections
- Create an Advanced Chart
- Determine host performance using resxtop and guest Perfmon
- Given performance data, identify the affected vSphere resource

Tools

- vCenter Server and Host Management guide
- vSphere Resource Management guide
- vSphere Monitoring and Performance guide
- vSphere Client

Objective 7.2: Create and Administer vCenter Server Alarms

Knowledge

- List vCenter default utilization alarms
- List vCenter default connectivity alarms
- List possible actions for utilization and connectivity alarms
- Create a vCenter utilization alarm
- Create a vCenter connectivity alarm
- Configure alarm triggers
- Configure alarm actions
- For a given alarm, identify the affected resource in a vSphere implementation

Tools

- vCenter Server and Host Management guide
- vSphere Resource Management guide
- vSphere Monitoring and Performance guide
- VMware vSphere Examples and Scenarios guide
- vSphere Client

Assessment Test

1. Which of the following are supported methods for providing high availability for vCenter Server? (Choose all that apply.)

    A. vCenter in a VM protected with HA and DRS

    B. vCenter in a VM protected with HA and FT

    C. vCenter Server Heartbeat

    D. Microsoft Cluster Server (MSCS)

2. You need to uninstall a vSphere Client plug-in. Which of the following is the proper way to uninstall the plug-in?

    A. Use the vSphere Client Plug-in Manager to disable it.

    B. Use the add/remove or uninstall functionality included in Windows to uninstall the plug-in.

    C. Use the vSphere Web Client to remove the plug-in.

    D. None of these is correct.

3. What is the minimum system requirement for memory in an ESXi 5 host?

    A. 1GB

    B. 2GB

    C. 3GB

    D. 4GB

4. vCenter Server 5 requires which of the following?

    A. Compatible 32-bit Windows OS

    B. Compatible 32-bit Linux OS

    C. Compatible 64-bit Windows OS

    D. Compatible 64-bit Linux OS

5. What are the preferred methods for configuring and administering the ESXi firewall? (Choose two.)

    A. DCUI

    B. vSphere Client

    C. esxcli

    D. esxcfg-firewall

6. Which vCenter Server Edition is no longer available in vSphere 5.0?

    A. Essentials

    B. Essentials Plus

    C. Advanced

    D. Enterprise Plus

7. Amazon's Elastic Compute Cloud (Amazon EC2) is an example of which type of cloud computing model?

   A. Private

   B. Public

   C. Hybrid

   D. Community

8. Which of the following may be used to perform operations against an ESXi host that is in lockdown mode?

   A. vSphere CLI commands

   B. vSphere Management Assistant (vMA)

   C. vSphere Client connected directly to ESXi host

   D. vSphere Client connected to vCenter Server managing the ESXi host in lockdown mode

9. What is the maximum number of ports in a vSwitch?

   A. 4,084

   B. 4,088

   C. 4,095

   D. 4,096

10. You add a new NIC to a vSwitch used for virtual machine network traffic. What additional actions must be taken before virtual machines will begin to use this NIC?

    A. Refresh networking.

    B. Reboot ESXi host.

    C. Restart ESXi Management Network.

    D. None of the above.

11. Which of the following are port binding types used in a dvSwitch? (Choose all that apply.)

    A. Static binding

    B. Dynamic binding

    C. Persistent binding

    D. Ephemeral binding

12. Which load-balancing policy is available only in the dvSwitch?

    A. Route Based On IP Hash

    B. Route Based On Source MAC Hash

    C. Route Based On Physical NIC Load

    D. Use Explicit Failover Order

13. Supported storage adapters in ESXi include which of the following?

    A. iSCSI

    B. RAID

C. Fibre Channel

D. All of these

14. Storage array thin provisioning can be configured through which feature of the vSphere Client?

   A. VMFS datastore properties

   B. NFS datastore properties

   C. Storage adapter properties

   D. None of these

15. What is the minimum memory requirement for ESXi hosts that will host a vSphere Storage Appliance?

   A. 2GB

   B. 4GB

   C. 6GB

   D. 8GB

16. When creating VMFS datastores, what is the relationship that should be maintained between VMFS datastore and LUN?

   A. 1-1

   B. 1-2

   C. 2-1

   D. None of these

17. What is virtual machine hardware version introduced in vSphere 5?

   A. 3

   B. 4

   C. 7

   D. 8

18. Disk shares can have which of the following values? (Choose all that apply.)

   A. Custom

   B. Default

   C. High

   D. Low

19. You have a virtual machine that will be configured to use VMware FT. What is the appropriate virtual disk type to choose for this virtual machine?

   A. Flat

   B. Thick

   C. Thin

   D. None of these

20. To completely disable all time synchronization for a virtual machine, what must occur?

    A. Disable the sync device driver.

    B. Edit the VMX file.

    C. Use the vSphere Client to configure time properties.

    D. None of these.

21. Which of the following most accurately describes a virtual appliance?

    A. Preconfigured and ready-to-use virtual machines that include an operating system and applications

    B. Preconfigured and ready-to-use virtual machines that cannot be modified

    C. Preconfigured vApp

    D. None of these

22. What is the maximum number of vCPUs per VM in vSphere 5?

    A. 8

    B. 16

    C. 32

    D. 64

23. Which of the following is not a valid virtual machine file?

    A. `-flat.vmdk`

    B. `-psf.vmdk`

    C. `-ctk.vmdk`

    D. `-00000#.vmdk`

24. Which of the following terms is used to describe increasing the size of a VMDK while the virtual machine is powered on?

    A. Warm extend

    B. Hot extend

    C. Disk grow

    D. Disk extend

25. VMware FT supports which of the following virtual machines? (Choose two.)

    A. Windows Server 2008 with one vCPU

    B. Windows Sever 2008 with two vCPUs

    C. Windows Server 2000 with one vCPU

    D. Windows Server 2000 with two vCPUs

26. Which of the following statements is true about individual virtual machine automation levels?

    A. The automation level defined for the DRS cluster will override the individual virtual machine automation level.

B. The automation level defined for the individual virtual machine will override the automation level defined for the DRS cluster.

C. The automation level defined for the individual virtual machine must match that of the DRS cluster.

D. None of these.

27. Which of the following objects can be part of the resource pool hierarchy? (Choose all that apply.)

A. Virtual machines

B. vApps

C. Folders

D. Resource pools

28. Which of the following can be used to provide application-level fault tolerance for a virtual machine? (Choose all that apply.)

A. VMware FT

B. VMware HA

C. Microsoft Clustering Services

D. vCenter Server Linked Mode

29. You want to migrate a virtual machine to a new host and datastore in a single operation. This option is grayed out in the Migrate Virtual Machine Wizard. What is the most likely reason?

A. vCenter Server is not licensed for this operation.

B. The virtual machine is virtual hardware version 7.

C. The virtual machine is powered on.

D. The virtual machine is powered off.

30. VMware Data Recovery can back up to which of the following media types?

A. Tape only

B. Disk only

C. Tape and disk

D. Optical media

31. A virtual infrastructure administrator has been asked to restore a virtual machine to its previous configuration from a snapshot. Which of the following actions should she take?

A. Delete

B. Delete All

C. Revert

D. Consolidate

32. vSphere Update Manager can be used to update which of the following? (Choose all that apply.)

   A. The VMware Tools

   B. ESXi 5 hosts

   C. Virtual machine hardware

   D. ESX 3.5 hosts

33. Which of the following commands can be used to test connectivity of a vMotion interface?

   A. `ping`

   B. `vmkping`

   C. `esxcli network`

   D. All of these

34. Which of the following can be used to troubleshoot storage contention issues? (Choose all that apply.)

   A. `esxtop`

   B. `resxtop`

   C. The vSphere Client

   D. Tools from your storage vendor

35. Which of the following should be used for ESXi hosts that will participate in HA-enabled clusters?

   A. Static IP addresses

   B. DHCP-assigned IP addresses

   C. IPv6

   D. vMotion

36. Which of the following admission control policies in HA offers the most customization for capacity in the cluster?

   A. Host Failures The Cluster Tolerates.

   B. Percentage Of Cluster Resources Reserved As Failover Spare Capacity.

   C. Specify Failover Hosts.

   D. None of these is correct.

37. When the vSphere Client is used and directly connected to an ESXi host, which of the following tabs is used to view tasks and events?

   A. Events

   B. Tasks & Events

   C. Scheduled Tasks

   D. Logs

38. Which of the following is used to control the vCenter Server services on the Windows host that it is installed on?

    A. `services.exe`

    B. `services.msc`

    C. `services.cpl`

    D. `services.chm`

39. Overview charts are available for which of the following? (Choose all that apply.)

    A. vSphere Client connected to ESXi host

    B. vSphere Client connected to vCenter Server

    C. vSphere Web Client

    D. All of these

40. Which of the following are alarm-type monitors? (Choose all that apply.)

    A. Datastore cluster

    B. Datacenters

    C. Datastores

    D. Distributed port groups

Answers to Assessment Test

1. **A, C.** vCenter Server is supported in a VM protected with HA and DRS. VMware vCenter Server Heartbeat is a VMware product and will be fully supported by VMware. For more information, see Chapter 2.

2. **B.** vSphere Client plug-ins are Windows applications, so they are quite easily uninstalled by using the native application uninstall functions in the Windows OS. For more information, see Chapter 2.

3. **B.** ESXi 5 hosts require a minimum of 2GB of RAM. For more information, see Chapter 2.

4. **C.** vCenter Server 5 requires a compatible 64-bit Windows OS, such as Windows 2008 R2. For more information, see Chapter 2.

5. **B, C.** There vSphere Client and the `esxcli` command are the preferred methods for configuring the ESXi firewall. For more information, see Chapter 3.

6. **C.** The Advanced edition is no longer available. Customers who were previously licensed for the Advanced edition will be upgraded automatically to the Enterprise edition. For more information, see Chapter 3.

7. **B.** Amazon's Elastic Compute Cloud (Amazon EC2) is an example of a public cloud. In the public cloud, you would pay for the consumption of resources from the third party delivering those resources. For more information, see Chapter 3.

8. **D.** All operations performed against an ESXi host in lockdown mode must originate from the vCenter Server that is managing the ESXi host. For more information, see Chapter 3.

9. **B.** A vSwitch can have a maximum of 4,088 ports. For more information, see Chapter 4.

10. **D.** The addition of a vmnic to a vSwitch is a nondisruptive action, and virtual machine network traffic will begin to use this NIC immediately with no further action. For more information, see Chapter 4.

11. **A, B, D.** Static, dynamic, and ephemeral are the three types of port binding used in a dvSwitch. For more information, see Chapter 4.

12. **C.** The Route Based On Physical NIC Load policy is available only when using a dvSwitch. For more information, see Chapter 4.

13. **D.** iSCSI, RAID, and Fibre Channel are all supported adapter classes used to provide storage connectivity in ESXi. For more information, see Chapter 5.

14. **D.** The configuration of thin provisioning on storage devices is not supported in ESXi. You will have to use the vendor's management tools instead. For more information, see Chapter 5.

15. **C.** ESXi hosts that will host a VSA appliance must have a minimum of 6GB of RAM. For more information, see Chapter 5.

16. **A.** When creating VMFS datastores, it is important to maintain a one-to-one relationship between each VMFS datastore and LUN. For more information, see Chapter 5.

17. **D.** Virtual machine hardware version 8 is the latest version. For more information, see Chapter 6.

18. **A, C, D.** Shares may have the values of Low, Normal, High, and Custom. For more information, see Chapter 6.

19. **B.** A thick provisioned disk, which is also known as a Thick Provision Eager Zeroed disk, is a VMDK file that is created and all of the space is provisioned and zeroed immediately. This type of disk is required for VMware FT. For more information, see Chapter 6.

20. **B.** To completely disable all the VMware Tools initiated time synchronization functionality for a VM, the virtual machine's VMX file must be modified. For more information, see Chapter 6.

21. **A.** Virtual appliances are preconfigured and ready-to-use virtual machines that include an operating system and applications. For more information, see Chapter 7.

22. **C.** Thirty-two vCPUs is the maximum number of vCPUs supported in vSphere 5. For more information, see Chapter 7.

23. **B.** There is no `-psf.vmdk` file type. For more information, see Chapter 7.

24. **B.** The process of increasing the size of a VMDK while a VM is powered on is known as hot extend. For more information, see Chapter 7.

25. **A, C.** Windows Server 2000 and Windows Server 2008 are both supported guest operating systems for use with VMware FT, but only a single vCPU configuration is supported. For more information, see Chapter 8.

26. **B.** Individual virtual machine automation level settings override the settings defined in the DRS cluster. For more information, see Chapter 8.

27. **A, B, D.** Virtual machines, vApps, and other resource pools can all be members of the resource pool hierarchy. For more information, see Chapter 8.

28. **C.** Of the choices listed, only Microsoft Clustering Services can provide application-level fault tolerance. For more information, see Chapter 8.

29. **C.** To change a virtual machine's host and datastore in one operation, the virtual machine needs to be powered off. For more information, see Chapter 9.

30. **B.** VMware Data Recovery is a disk-based backup solution. For more information, see Chapter 9.

31. **C.** Revert will restore the virtual machine to its previous state. For more information, see Chapter 9.

32. **A, B, C, D.** vSphere Update Manager can update virtual machine hardware, the VMware Tools, and ESX/ESXi 3.5 and newer hosts. For more information, see Chapter 9.

33. **B.** The vMotion interface is a VMkernel connection type, and the `vmkping` command can be used to test its connectivity. For more information, see Chapter 10.

34. **A, B, C, D.** All of these tools can be used to troubleshoot storage contention issues. For more information, see Chapter 10.

35. **A.** It is always a good idea to use static IP addresses for any server. For more information, see Chapter 10.

36. **B.** Percentage Of Cluster Resources Reserved As Failover Spare Capacity allows the percentage of CPU and memory resources to be reserved, making it the most customizable option available. For more information, see Chapter 10.

37. **A.** When the vSphere Client is connected directly to an ESXi host, the Events tab is used to view recent events. Tasks are possible only with vCenter Server. For more information, see Chapter 11.

38. **B.** The Services MMC snap-in, or `services.msc`, is used to control services in Windows. For more information, see Chapter 11.

39. **B.** Overview charts are available only when the vSphere Client is connected to a vCenter Server. For more information, see Chapter 11.

40. **A, B, C, D.** All of these are alarm-type monitors. For more information, see Chapter 11.

Chapter

1

What's New in vSphere 5

THIS CHAPTER COVERS THE FOLLOWING TOPICS:

- ✓ ESX Retirement
- ✓ VCB Retirement
- ✓ VMI Paravirtualization Retirement
- ✓ VMware GUI Toolbox Retirement
- ✓ Windows 2000 Guest OS Customization Support
- ✓ Newly Created VMCI Sockets Unsupported
- ✓ Requirement of LAHF and SAHF CPU Instruction Sets
- ✓ Intel SMT–Related CPU Scheduler Enhancements
- ✓ Notable Configuration Maximums Changes
- ✓ ESXi Firewall and Management Networks
- ✓ Swap to SSD
- ✓ Support for Hardware and Software FCoE Adapters
- ✓ Host UEFI Boot Support
- ✓ Improved SNMP Support
- ✓ New Command-Line Interface
- ✓ vSphere High Availability Improvements
- ✓ Virtual Machine Enhancements
- ✓ Expanded Support for VMware Tools
- ✓ Mac OS X Server Support

- ✓ vCenter Enhanced Logging
- ✓ VMware vCenter Server Heartbeat Improvements
- ✓ Fault Tolerance (FT) Improvements
- ✓ iSCSI UI Support
- ✓ GUI to Configure Multi-core Virtual CPUs
- ✓ vNetwork Distributed Switch Improvements
- ✓ Network I/O Control Improvements
- ✓ Storage vMotion Improvements
- ✓ VAAI Thin Provisioning Improvements
- ✓ NFS Support Improvements
- ✓ Storage Accelerator
- ✓ VMFS-5
- ✓ vMotion and Metro vMotion
- ✓ vCenter Server Appliance
- ✓ vSphere Storage Appliance (VSA)
- ✓ Storage DRS
- ✓ Profile-Driven Storage
- ✓ Image Builder
- ✓ Auto Deploy
- ✓ VMware Data Recovery 2.0 Improvements
- ✓ Update Manager Improvements
- ✓ Licensing

vSphere 5 continues to build on the rich feature set of vSphere 4.1, which is the industry-leading virtualization platform for building cloud infrastructures. There are new capabilities at all levels of the product, and the introduction of these new features will in many ways be what will differentiate the VCP4 from the VCP5. In this chapter, I will review these new vSphere 5 features. The purpose here is simply to introduce what is new in vSphere 5. Many of these features will be covered in much greater detail in the following chapters.

ESX Retirement

As of vSphere 5, ESX is no longer available. ESXi is the hypervisor architecture that will be used in vSphere 5 and beyond. For those who have been using only ESX and not ESXi, one of the most notable changes is the absence of the Service Console. This represents new operational and administration challenges, but it also improves security, reliability, and management. There is a menu-driven Direct Console User Interface (DCUI) and an ESXi Shell that can each be used in ESXi 5. The ESXi Shell looks similar to the Service Console in ESX.

The ultimate idea with removing the Service Console is to move away from the concept of using the Service Console as a direct means to administer your hosts. As mentioned earlier, removing the Service Console improves security, reliability, and host management. The host should almost be thought of as a piece of hot-swappable hardware in your virtual infrastructure. The removal of the Service Console helps enable this way of thinking. If you haven't done so already, take a look at either the VMware vSphere PowerCLI, the vSphere Command-Line Interface (vCLI), or the vSphere Management Assistant (vMA). You will notice that these utilities offer equivalent functionality, but the syntax may be quite different. If you have come to rely on the Service Console for operational or administrative tasks and are not familiar with the vCLI, PowerCLI, or vMA, you will have a bit of a learning curve. Also, you'll need to consider items such as SAN agents, multipathing software, backup agents/software, hardware monitoring, UPS software, and any scripts that were being used in ESX and how these functionalities will work, or be replaced, in ESXi.

VCB Retirement

VMware Consolidated Backup (VCB) is no longer supported in vSphere 5. VMware Data Recovery will be covered in the exam. If you are interested in using third-party backup applications, you should look into whether these vendors support the VMware vStorage APIs for Data Protection.

VMI Paravirtualization Retirement

vSphere 5 does not support the Virtual Machine Interface (VMI) guest operating system paravirtualization interface. This is because innovations made in CPU hardware acceleration technologies from Intel and AMD have allowed these newer processors to outperform VMI. Virtual machines that use paravirtualization can be migrated to vSphere 5, and more information is available in VMware KB 1013842.

VMware GUI Toolbox Retirement

vSphere 5 will be the final vSphere release to support the VMware Tools graphical user interface, VMware Toolbox. The Toolbox command-line interface (CLI) will continue to be updated and supported. The Toolbox command-line interface provides the same functionality that was previously available in the VMware Tools control panel. The Toolbox command-line interface is named differently, depending on the guest operating system it is accessed from:

- In Windows, use `VMwareToolboxCmd.exe`.
- In Mac OS X, use `./vmware-tools-cli`.
- In Linux, FreeBSD, and Solaris, use `vmware-toolbox-cmd`.

For example, to list the available devices for a virtual machine running a Windows OS, you would run the following command from the Windows command line:

`VMwareToolboxCmd.exe device list`

Windows 2000 Guest OS Customization Support

vSphere 5 will be the last vSphere release to support guest customization of the Windows 2000 guest operating system. Newer versions of Windows guests will continue to be supported for guest customization.

Newly Created VMCI Sockets Unsupported

Virtual machine–to–virtual machine communications are no longer supported in vSphere 5. This functionality will be removed in the next major vSphere release, but VMware will continue to support host-to-guest communications.

Requirement of LAHF and SAHF CPU Instruction Sets

For ESXi 5 hosts, only CPUs that contain the Load Register AH From Flags (LAHF) and Store AH Register into Flags (SAHF) CPU instruction sets are supported. The ESXi installer will check the compatibility of the host CPU during an installation or upgrade. If your host hardware is not compatible, a purple screen will appear with an incompatibility information message. The install or upgrade cannot continue beyond this point. Always use the VMware HCL (www.vmware.com/go/hcl) to verify host compatibility with ESXi 5 before you begin the installation.

Intel SMT–Related CPU Scheduler Enhancements

The Intel simultaneous multithreading (SMT) architecture exposes two hardware contexts from a single processor core. Utilizing two hardware contexts yields a 10 percent to 30 percent improvement in application performance, depending on the workload. The ESXi 5 CPU scheduler's policy is tuned for this type of architecture and ensures high efficiency and performance for mission-critical applications.

Notable Configuration Maximums Changes

While the VCP5 exam is unlikely to quiz you on simple configuration maximum questions, this data is extremely important to know for the exam. It is much more likely that you will see a question where knowing a specific configuration maximum is a prerequisite for knowing the correct answer to the question. The following list is only a sampling of the configuration maximums and focuses only on those that have changed from vSphere 4.1.

- vCPUs per VM changes from 8 to 32
- RAM allocation per VM changes from 255GB to 1TB
- VM swap file size changes from 255GB to 1TB
- VMs per host changes from 320 to 512
- vCPUs per host changes from 512 to 2048
- RAM per host changes from 1TB to 2TB
- NFS mounts per host changes from 64 to 256
- LUN size changes from 2TB minus 512 bytes to 64TB
- Port groups per vSwitch changes from 512 to 256
- Maximum concurrent host HA failover changes from 4 to 32
- Resource pools per cluster changes from 512 to 1,600
- Resource pools per host changes from 4,096 to 1,600
- Number of hosts per datacenter changes from 400 to 500

ESXi Firewall and Management Networks

With the removal of the Service Console in vSphere 5, VMware now provides a new firewall to protect the ESXi host management interface(s). This firewall is provided through a VMkernel network adapter (vmknic)–level firewall module. The following are the key features of this firewall:

- Service-oriented and stateless
- Supports ability to restrict access to services based on IP address and subnet mask
- Can be managed through the vSphere Client or the new `esxcli` command-line interface
- Supports host profiles
- Eliminates the use of iptables

  To provide the ability to create new services and firewall rules, you can also define firewall services through XML description files. You create these XML files manually and activate them by running an `esxcli refresh` command.

Swap to SSD

In vSphere 5, the VMkernel automatically recognizes and tags solid-state drive (SSD) devices. These devices can be located on the local ESXi host or on the network, and the VMkernel scheduler allows ESXi swap to extend to these local or network SSD devices. Swapping to SSD is significantly faster than swapping to a traditional spinning disk, and this feature can help minimize the performance impact of swapping resulting from memory overcommitment.

Support for Hardware and Software FCoE Adapters

Support has been added for many software and hardware Fibre Channel over Ethernet (FCoE) adapters. The following are some of the supported software FCoE adapters:

- 10 Gigabit BR KX4 Dual Port Network Connection
- 10 Gigabit Dual Port Backplane Connection
- 10 Gigabit CX4 Dual Port Network Connection
- 10 Gigabit Network Connection
- 10 Gigabit Dual Port Network Connection
- 10 Gigabit Network Connection
- 10 Gigabit BX Network Connection
- 10 Gigabit AT2 Server Adapter
- 10 Gigabit KX4 Network Connection
- 10 Gigabit KR2 Network Connection
- 10 Gigabit TN Network Connection

These are some of the supported hardware FCoE adapters:

- Emulex OneConnect OCe10100 10GbE, FCoE UCNA
- Emulex OneConnect OCe11100 10GbE, FCoE UCNA

As with any storage or network adapter, always consult the VMware HCL (www .vmware.com/go/hcl) to check the compatibility or availability for specific FCoE adapters.

Host UEFI Boot Support

ESXi 5 hosts are supported for booting from the Unified Extensible Firmware Interface (UEFI). UEFI allows the host server to boot from hard disks, CD-ROM drives, or USB media.

Improved SNMP Support

The capability to convert Common Information Model (CIM) indications to Simple Network Management Protocol (SNMP) traps has been added to vSphere 5. vSphere 5 also supports the Host Resources MIB (RFC 2790) and allows for greater control over the types of traps sent from the SNMP agent.

New Command-Line Interface

vSphere 5 introduces a new command-line interface (CLI) called `esxcli`. The introduction of the `esxcli` command marks the beginning of efforts by VMware to standardize on a single command-line interface for both local and remote administration. The `esxcli` command is available on ESXi 5 hosts from the ESXi Shell. It is also available in the vSphere Command-Line Interface or through the vSphere Management Assistant.

vSphere High Availability Improvements

vSphere High Availability (HA) has been completely rewritten for the vSphere 5 release to increase scalability, reliability, and usability. HA now uses the concept of a master-slave relationship between the nodes in a cluster, where before it relied on the concept of primary and secondary nodes. The master host is responsible for the following:

- Monitoring the state of the slave hosts
- Monitoring the power states of all protected VMs
- Managing the lists of cluster hosts and protected VMs
- Serving as the vCenter Server management interface by reporting the cluster health state

The slave hosts run virtual machines locally, monitor their runtime states, and report their state updates to the master host. This new model simplifies planning and design considerations and allows for easier scalability. This is particularly true for vSphere environments running on blade servers and for stretched cluster environments.

HA also no longer has any dependency on DNS servers and can also communicate between the cluster nodes through the storage subsystem in a process called *datastore heartbeating.* Datastore heartbeating allows a master host that has lost communication with a slave host over the management network to communicate over the storage network to determine whether the slave host has failed, is in a network partition, or is network isolated. If a slave host cannot be reached via datastore heartbeating, it is considered failed. Using multiple paths of communication allows for a greater level of redundancy and better identification of the node's actual health.

The HA user interface has been improved to more easily show the role a node plays in the cluster and its current state. There is now a single log file for HA, which should allow for easier troubleshooting of HA events.

Virtual Machine Enhancements

With the release of vSphere 5, VMware introduces a new virtual hardware version for virtual machines. This newest release is virtual hardware version 8. Improvements in this latest version include the following:

- 32-way vCPUs
- Virtual NUMA (vNUMA) support
- 1TB RAM maximum
- Non-hardware-accelerated 3D graphics for Windows Aero support
- USB 3.0 device support
- UEFI virtual BIOS
- Client-connected USB devices
- Smart card reader support

Figure 1.1 shows the new capabilities of virtual hardware version 8.

The CPU and memory capabilities are provided to handle the virtualization of even more Tier 1 applications, while the enhanced graphics capabilities, USB 3.0 support, and smart card reader support are clearly targeted at providing more features to virtual desktop infrastructure (VDI) environments.

Expanded Support for VMware Tools

vSphere 5 supports hosting virtual machines running prior versions of VMware Tools and virtual hardware. This means virtual machines with the 4.*x* version of VMware Tools and older virtual machine hardware versions can run fully supported in a vSphere 5 environment. This compatibility will make the vSphere 5 upgrade process much easier to manage.

Table 1.1 shows the vSphere 4.*x* and vSphere 5 compatibility for VMware Tools and the virtual hardware versions.

FIGURE 1.1   Virtual Machine Properties editor

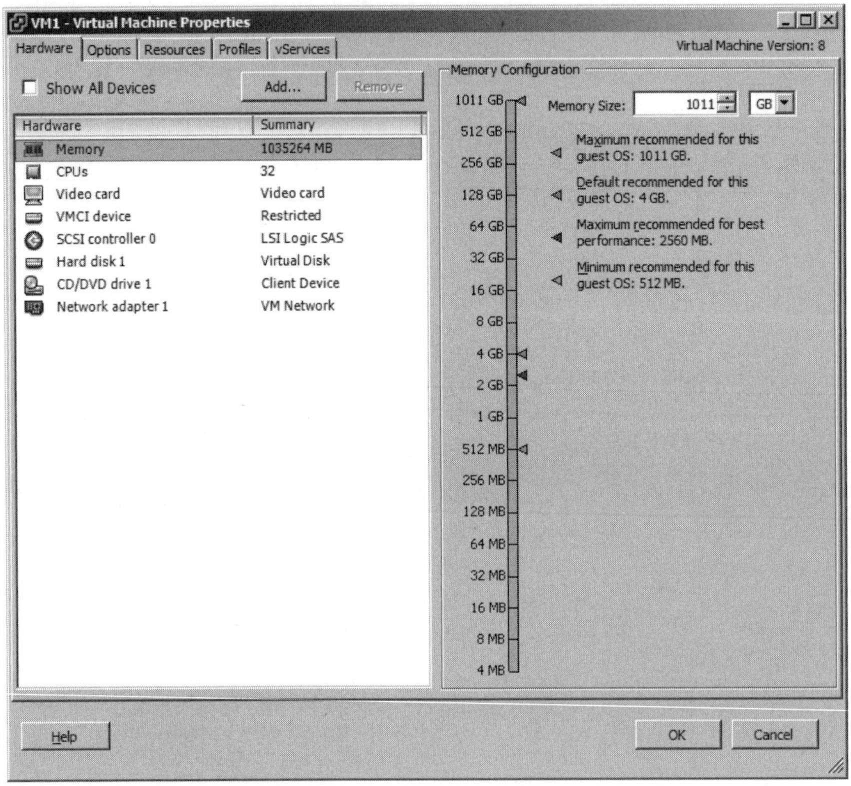

TABLE 1.1   vSphere 4.*x* and vSphere 5 VMware Tools compatibility

Version	vSphere 4.*x*	vSphere 5
VMware Tools 4.*x*	Yes	Yes
VMware Tools 5	Yes	Yes
Virtual hardware	3, 4, 7	4, 7, 8

Mac OS X Server Support

vSphere 5 supports OS X Server 10.6 (Snow Leopard) as a guest operating system when ESXi is installed on Apple Xserve servers. It is important to note that Apple hardware is an absolute requirement for this guest OS support, and the ESXi host will verify whether Apple hardware is being used when provisioning an OS X Server 10.6 guest.

The use of vMotion to migrate Mac OS X Server virtual machines requires both the source and destination ESXi 5 hosts to be on Apple Xserve hardware. Mac OS X 10.6 running in a virtual machine will also require the virtual hardware version 8 EFI BIOS option, which vSphere 4.*x* does not support. It is also important to note that VMware Fault Tolerance (FT) is not supported with Mac OS X Server virtual machines.

vCenter Server Enhanced Logging

vCenter Server system message logging has several enhancements. All log messages are now syslog-generated, and these messages can be logged locally or on one or more remote syslog servers. There is also a bundled VMware Syslog Collector on the vCenter Server installation media that can be used to collect these syslog messages. If you plan on using the vCenter Server Appliance, know that it can use the native Linux syslog-ng facility for syslog messages. You can configure this message logging with either the vSphere Client or the `esxcli` command.

VMware vCenter Server Heartbeat Improvements

When designing your virtual infrastructure, you must consider the availability of vCenter Server. This availability is covered in objective 1.1 of the VCP5 exam, so it is important to understand how to leverage VMware vCenter Server Heartbeat. vCenter Server Heartbeat is used to provide a highly available vCenter Server. The latest version of VMware vCenter Server Heartbeat, version 6.4, provides improvements in the areas of manageability, usability, and application support. Figure 1.2 shows the basic design of vCenter Server Heartbeat.

FIGURE 1.2   vCenter Server Heartbeat architecture

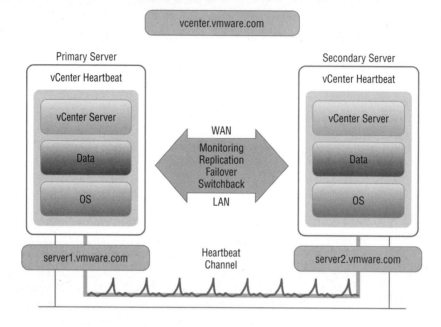

vCenter Server Heartbeat provides a high availability solution that is easy to manage. While other clustering solutions can be used to provide a highly available vCenter Server, the complexity can also be high with these solutions. If a solution becomes too complicated, errors could inadvertently be introduced and decrease the overall effectiveness of the solution.

Like other clustering solutions, VMware vCenter Server Heartbeat 6.4 works with two servers. vCenter Server Heartbeat allows both the active and passive servers to be represented as unique entities within Microsoft Active Directory. Each vCenter Server is assigned a unique IP address, and each vCenter Server is accessible on the network at all times.

Each vCenter Server instance can be associated with a virtual IP address. The virtual IP address follows the active VMware vCenter Server instance, if and when a failover is required. This means that users need to know only a single vCenter address to connect to and that administrators can perform maintenance actions in a transparent manner.

vCenter Server Heartbeat leverages vCenter Server and the vSphere Client to allow a single pane of glass for VMware vCenter Server Heartbeat operations. Administrators now have the ability to monitor and perform management functions from within the vSphere Client via a new vSphere Client plug-in. In addition, vCenter Server Heartbeat operational tasks and alarms are registered with the vCenter Server.

vCenter Server Heartbeat now also provides availability for VMware View Composer and Microsoft SQL Server 2008 R2. This support provides high availability for virtual desktops and protection for the vCenter Server database, even if it is installed on a separate server.

It is important to note that VMware vCenter Server Heartbeat is a separately licensed product available from VMware, and it is not included with any edition of vSphere 5. Although it is not an included component, a separate clustering solution used to provide high availability for vCenter Server would likely also include additional costs. There is more information on these scenarios in the next chapter, including supported configurations for achieving high availability for vCenter Server.

Fault Tolerance Improvements

With vSphere 5, VMware Fault Tolerance (FT) gains support for new CPU architectures and guest operating systems. Refer to VMware KB 1008027 for the most up-to-date information on supported CPUs and guest operating systems that can be used with VMware FT. Also, check out my regularly updated blog entry "VMware Fault Tolerance Requirements and Limitations" for much more information on VMware Fault Tolerance:

```
http://communities.vmware.com/people/vmroyale/blog/2009/05/18/vmware-fault-
tolerance-requirements-and-limitations
```

iSCSI UI Support

For anyone who has ever had to configure iSCSI in previous versions of vSphere, the iSCSI GUI will be a welcome addition in vSphere 5. The new iSCSI GUI allows you to configure dependent hardware iSCSI and software iSCSI adapters along with their network configurations and port bindings in a single dialog box from within the vSphere Client. Figure 1.3 shows the new Network Configuration tab.

FIGURE 1.3   iSCSI configuration GUI

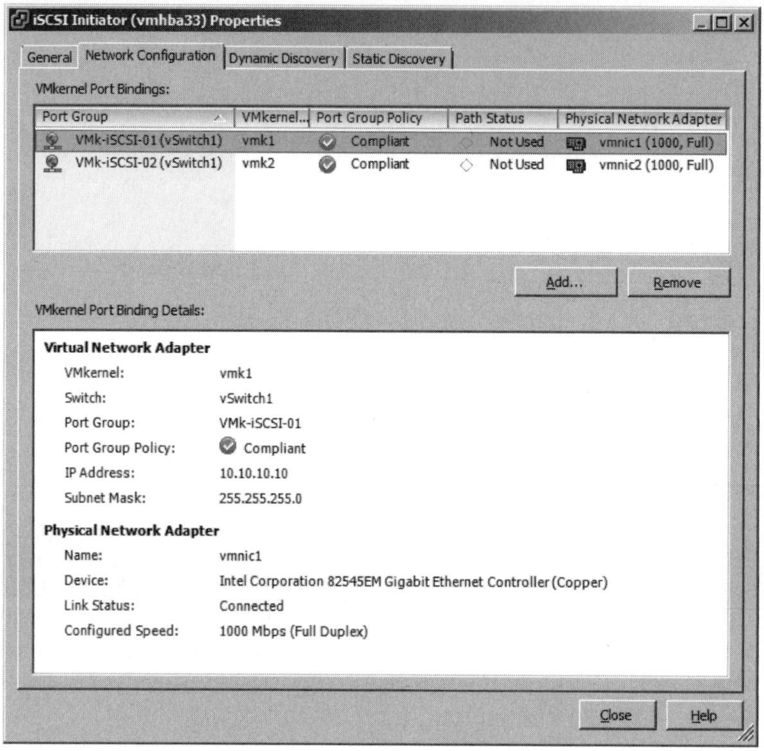

GUI to Configure Multi-core Virtual CPUs

The new GUI on the Virtual Machine Properties dialog box allows you to configure multi-core vCPUs. You can now modify the number of virtual CPU cores per socket without having to use the Advanced Settings options. Figure 1.4 shows the new CPU/multi-core configuration settings.

vNetwork Distributed Switch Improvements

vSphere 5 introduces two new features in the Distributed vSwitch that provide more visibility into traffic that is flowing in the virtual infrastructure. The first of these features is

NetFlow; vSphere 5 supports NetFlow 5. The NetFlow capability provided in vSphere 5 provides the following visibility:

- Intrahost virtual machine traffic (virtual machine–to–virtual machine traffic on the same host)

- Interhost virtual machine traffic (virtual machine–to–virtual machine traffic on different hosts)

- Virtual machine–to–physical infrastructure traffic

FIGURE 1.4 New CPU/multi-core configuration settings

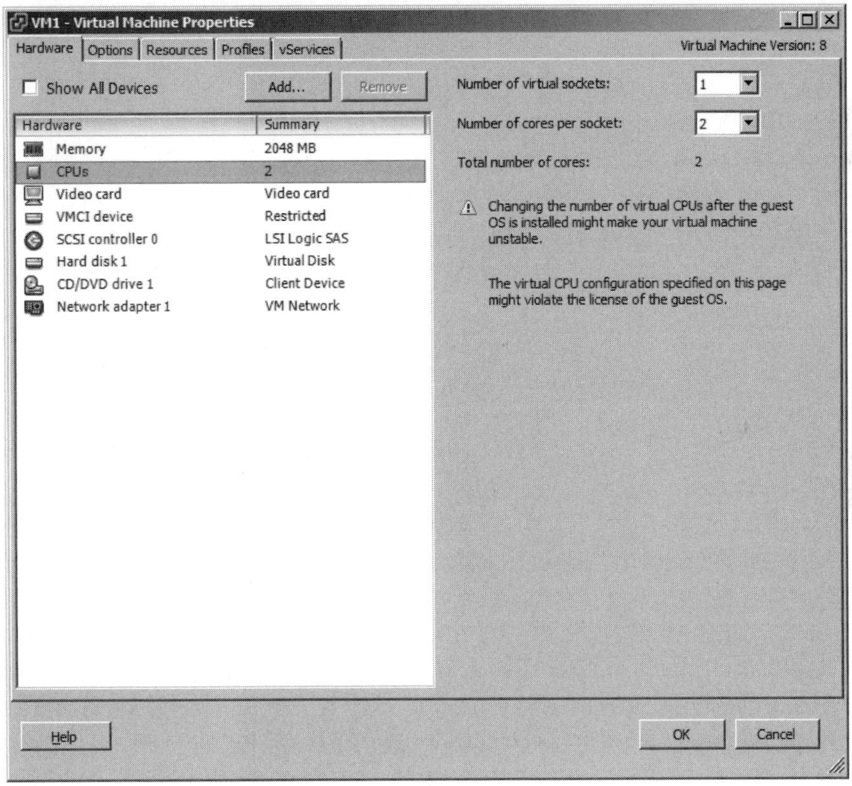

NetFlow can be enabled on Distributed vSwitches at the port group level, at the individual port level, or at the uplink level. Enabling flow monitoring on a Distributed vSwitch allows the monitoring of application flows. This NetFlow data helps in capacity planning and in ensuring that I/O resources are properly utilized.

The second new feature in the Distributed vSwitch is port mirroring. *Port mirroring* is when a network switch sends a copy of network packets seen on a switch port to a network monitoring device connected to another switch port. This is also known as Switch Port Analyzer (SPAN) on Cisco switches. Port mirror configuration can be done at the distributed switch level and is used for network monitoring or troubleshooting. The port mirroring capability in vSphere 5 provides the following visibility:

- Intrahost virtual machine traffic (virtual machine–to–virtual machine traffic on the same host)

- Interhost virtual machine traffic (virtual machine–to–virtual machine traffic on different hosts)

FIGURE 1.5   Configuring Discovery Protocol settings

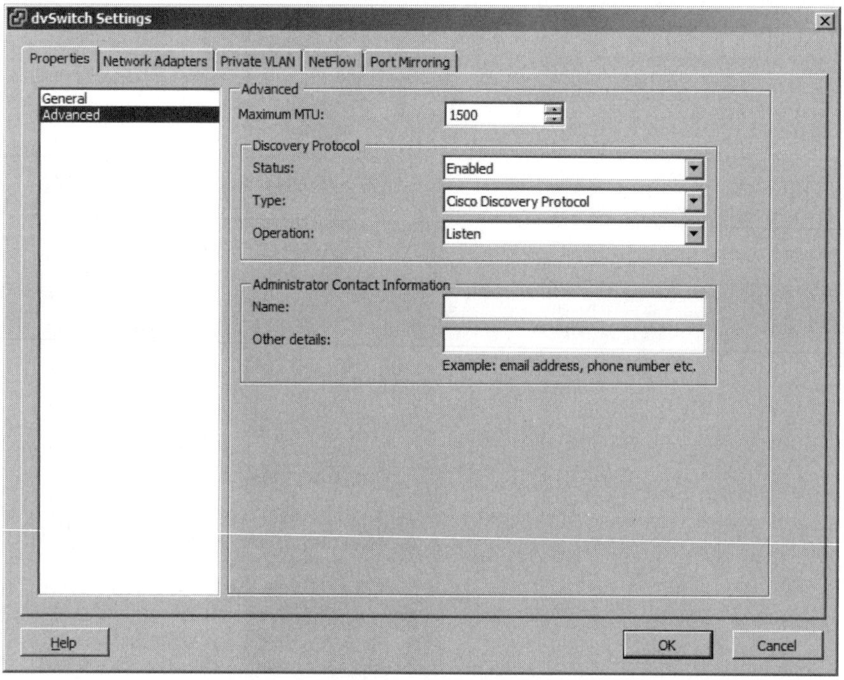

If you have been using vSphere 4.x, then you have likely used Cisco Discovery Protocol (CDP) data before and know the value it brings to identifying network devices and their associated configurations. vSphere 5 now also supports IEEE 802.1AB standards-based Link Layer Discovery Protocol (LLDP). Like CDP, LLDP is used to discover information about network devices, but it is a vendor-neutral discovery protocol. LLDP can be enabled at the distributed switch level by selecting either the CDP or LLDP discovery protocol type. You can also configure the operation mode for the discovery protocol from the distributed switch settings. The following are the three available options:

Listen   Only listen for upstream network information.

Advertise   Only advertise information about this distributed switch.

Both   Listen for upstream network information and advertise information about this distributed switch.

You can configure the Discovery Protocol settings in the distributed switch settings, under Advanced, as shown in Figure 1.5.

Network I/O Control Improvements

Network I/O Control (NIOC) allows the creation of resource pools containing network bandwidth. Users can create new resource pools to associate with port groups and specify 802.1p tags, allowing different virtual machines to be in different resource pools. This allows a subset of virtual machines to be given a higher or lower share of bandwidth than the others.

In vSphere 5, NIOC supports traffic management capabilities for the following traffic types:

- Virtual machine
- Management
- iSCSI
- NFS
- Fault Tolerance logging
- vMotion
- vSphere replication
- User-defined

Storage vMotion Improvements

Storage vMotion now supports virtual machines in snapshot mode and the migration of linked clones. In addition, there have been improvements made in the copying mechanisms used by Storage vMotion, which will result in greater efficiency and migration time predictability.

VAAI Thin Provisioning Improvements

VAAI enhancements have been introduced in vSphere 5 to optimize thin provisioning capabilities. The challenges around using thin provisioning have typically been the reclamation of dead space and monitoring the storage to ensure that an out-of-space condition never occurs. VAAI Thin Provisioning introduces Dead Space Reclamation and Out-of-Space Conditions to address these problems.

Dead Space Reclamation does exactly what its name implies. When a virtual disk is deleted or migrated off of the datastore, the storage device will be made aware that these blocks are no longer in use, and the blocks may then be reclaimed. Out-of-Space Conditions is a set of advanced warnings and errors that may be used to notify administrators when important thresholds are reached for thin-provisioned datastores. Also introduced are mechanisms that can temporarily pause a virtual machine, when disk space is depleted. This enables the issue to be addressed by a virtual infrastructure administrator, without resulting in the failure of a virtual machine.

NFS Support Improvements

vSphere 5 introduces NFS support for Storage I/O Control. Also introduced is hardware acceleration for NAS, which will allow faster provisioning and the use of thick virtual disks on NFS volumes. This is accomplished through two newly introduced VAAI primitives:

- Full File Clone: Enables virtual disks to be cloned
- Reserve Space: Enables creation of thick virtual disk files

It is important to point out that the NAS VAAI plug-ins do not come with vSphere 5. This means your NAS vendor will have to develop and distribute this technology.

Storage Accelerator

A storage accelerator has been added, to be specifically used with VMware View (VDI) workloads. When this setting is configured in ESXi, a read cache is constructed in memory. This read cache is optimized for recognizing, handling, and deduplicating VDI client images and can result in a significant reduction in IOPs from ESXi hosts to the storage.

VMFS-5

VMFS-5 is arguably one of the best new features in vSphere 5. VMFS-5 is the latest version of VMware's Virtual Machine File System (VMFS). VMFS volumes can now be up to 64TB in size using a single extent, but it should be noted that a single VMDK is still limited to 2TB minus 512 bytes. If this VMDK size limit is considered bad news, then the good news is that pass-through (physical) RDMs larger than 2TB are supported.

Also absent in VMFS-5 are the different VMFS block size options, because a unified block size of 1MB is now used for newly created VMFS-5 volumes. Upgraded

VMFS-3 volumes will retain their given block sizes, but these volumes may be upgraded while VMs are running on them. Coupling VMFS-5 capacity with 32-way vCPU and 1TB memory support could lead to some pretty massive workloads running in vSphere 5!

vMotion and Metro vMotion

vMotion is certainly not new, but there are some new capabilities of vMotion in vSphere 5 that are worth mentioning. Performance enhancements made to vMotion now allow it to effectively saturate a 10 GbE network adapter's bandwidth. vSphere 5 also introduces the ability for vMotion to use multiple network adapters. Even a single vMotion will see the VMkernel transparently load-balance the traffic over all vMotion-enabled vmknics. These enhancements speed up vMotion and are especially beneficial for VMs with large memory footprints. There seems to be a theme here of vSphere 5 having the ability to support large Tier 1 workloads.

vSphere 5 also introduces the Metro vMotion feature. Metro vMotion is a latency-aware feature that allows vMotion to work with higher network latencies than were supported in previous versions of vSphere.

vCenter Server Appliance

The vCenter Server Appliance (vCSA) is a preconfigured Linux-based VM that has been optimized to run only vCenter Server and its associated services. It is deployed as an Open Virtualization Format (OVF)–formatted VM and is supported only on ESX/ESXi 4.0/4.1 and ESXi 5.

Limitations of the vCenter Server Appliance include no IPv6 support, no Linked Mode capability, and no use of Microsoft's SQL Server. The vCenter Server Appliance can be an appealing option to non-Windows environments but can also be used for smaller deployments because it includes a bundled database.

vSphere Storage Appliance

The vSphere Storage Appliance (VSA) is aimed at small-to-medium business (SMB) customers and provides a shared storage solution, without requiring these customers to purchase a SAN or NAS. The VSA can be deployed in a two-node or three-node configuration and uses the local disks from the ESXi hosts to create a mirrored NFS share, as shown in Figure 1.6. The VSA allows features like High Availability (HA), Distributed Resource Scheduler (DRS), and vMotion to be used.

FIGURE 1.6 VSA cluster with two members

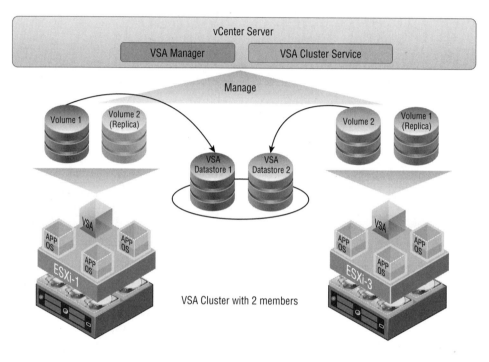

Storage DRS

This is essentially VMware's Distributed Resource Scheduler (DRS) for storage. Storage DRS, much like DRS, provides virtual machine placement and load-balancing mechanisms based on disk I/O and capacity. Storage DRS allows you to group similar datastores into a load-balanced storage cluster.

A new object called the *datastore cluster* is the basis of Storage DRS. A datastore cluster is simply an aggregated group of VMFS or NFS datastores (see Figure 1.7). A datastore cluster can contain either all VMFS or all NFS datastores. Mixing and matching VMFS and NFS is not allowed in the same datastore cluster.

FIGURE 1.7   Datastore cluster

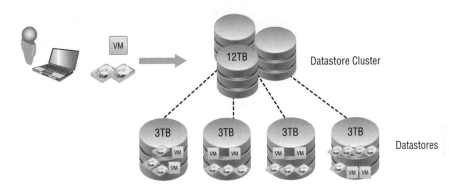

Profile-Driven Storage

Referred to as VM Storage Profiles in vCenter, profile-driven storage decreases the amount of administrator interaction required to deploy VMs. Instead of the VMware administrator having to know (or learn) a VM's particular disk requirements, a profile is created, and the VM is placed accordingly on the appropriate storage.

Image Builder

Image Builder is a new feature of vSphere 5; it is a PowerShell CLI command set that is used to manage software depots, image profiles, and VMware Installation Bundles (VIBs). These components, shown in Figure 1.8, are used to create and maintain ESXi images to be used during ESXi installations and upgrades.

FIGURE 1.8   Image Builder components

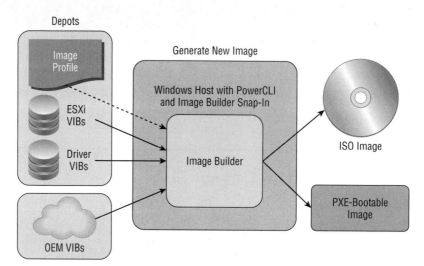

Auto Deploy

Auto Deploy is used to provision ESXi hosts, using a vCenter Server (see Figure 1.9). With Auto Deploy, the ESXi host will use the Preboot Execution Environment (PXE) at boot, and then vCenter Server will load the ESXi image directly into the host's memory. Auto Deploy stores no ESXi state on the host disk and allows diskless ESXi host configurations.

There are several benefits of using Auto Deploy, including the decoupling of the ESXi 5 host from the physical server. For example, if an ESXi 5 host fails and needs to be replaced, there is no manual ESXi 5 installation required when using Auto Deploy. Think about the manual steps required to install ESXi 5 and the configuration that has to happen. Using Auto Deploy, the ESXi host configurations will be consistent and significantly faster to provision. Another benefit of using Auto Deploy with diskless servers would be no RAID monitoring! Because Auto Deploy relies on vCenter Server, you should give serious consideration to providing high availability for vCenter Server when using Auto Deploy.

FIGURE 1.9   Auto Deploy architecture

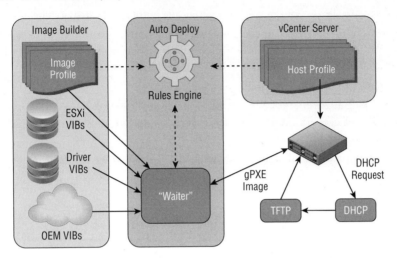

VMware Data Recovery 2.0 Improvements

VMware Data Recovery 2.0 has new capabilities that make it faster, more reliable, more easily managed, and better integrated with vCenter Server. These improvements include the following:

- You can generate and email scheduled reports to as many as 10 e-mail addresses. Reports include an application summary, job summary, destination summary, virtual machines that failed backup, virtual machines not backed up, virtual machines successfully backed up, and nonbackup warnings and errors.
- It includes user-specified Destination Maintenance Windows in which backups will not run.
- You can suspend individual jobs by right-clicking the backup job and selecting Suspend Future Tasks.

- You can change the number of days between automated integrity checks.

- You can specify the day of the week on which the automated integrity check is run.

- Deduplication improvements include a new compression algorithm to improve the commit speed of compressed data, utilization of the I/O path, and a more efficient layout of data on disk that reduces time to restore from backup.

- Improvements to the integrity check process include periodic checkpoints during integrity checking of the datastore and bulk processing of similar jobs.

- VMware Data Recovery 2.0 is built on CentOS 5.5 64-bit, allowing for better scalability and stability for the appliance.

- Linux swap partitions and Windows paging files are no longer included in backups.

- If an integrity check is stopped, the check can now be resumed without having to restart the entire process.

- Data Recovery is now more resilient against transient network failures.

Update Manager Improvements

vCenter Update Manager 5 has also been updated for vSphere 5. Improvements include the following:

- Support for ESX/ESXi 4.*x* to ESXi 5 upgrades

- Improved integration with vSphere clusters

- Improved VMware Tools upgrade

- Enhanced Update Manager download service

- Update Manager UI improvements

The Update Manager 5 release also includes the VMware vSphere Update Manager Utility. This utility helps users reconfigure the setup of Update Manager, change the database password and proxy authentication, re-register Update Manager with vCenter Server, and replace the SSL certificates used by Update Manager.

Licensing

There have been changes to the licensing in vSphere 5. Gone are the restrictions on physical core counts for processors and the amount of physical RAM installed in an ESXi 5 host. While the physical RAM limitations are gone, there is a new concept introduced called vRAM. vSphere 5 is still licensed per processor but will now include a vRAM entitlement for each processor license purchased. vRAM is the amount of memory configured to powered-on virtual machines, and it can be pooled across an environment.

Another change in vSphere 5 licensing is in the number of versions being offered. There are now five editions, or "kits," being offered:

- Essentials Kit
- Essentials Plus Kit
- Standard Acceleration Kit
- Enterprise Acceleration Kit
- Enterprise Plus Acceleration Kit

The Advanced Edition of vSphere 4 is gone, and customers who were licensed for this edition of vSphere 4 will be entitled to the vSphere 5 Enterprise Edition.

It is highly unlikely that the specifics of licensing will be covered in the VCP 5 exam, because the exam blueprint specifies only that users know how to license ESXi and vCenter Server. With that being said, understanding VMware licensing is a very beneficial thing for a VMware administrator to understand.

Summary

There have been many changes and new features introduced in vSphere 5. Some of these changes are around retired features like the ESX hypervisor architecture, VCB, and paravirtualization. These technologies served their purpose at one point in the VMware road map but have been replaced by improved technologies.

Many of the new features in vSphere 5 are targeted at being able to support large Tier 1 workloads in VMs. You can now have a 32-vCPU virtual machine with 1TB of RAM and a single disk of up to 64TB. That is a huge improvement over vSphere 4.1, where you could have an 8-vCPU virtual machine with 255GB of RAM and a single disk of up to 2TB minus 512 bytes. There also have been improvements to vMotion, Storage I/O Control, and Network I/O Control to accommodate these large workloads.

There are also many improvements in management included in vSphere 5. New features like Storage DRS, Profile-Driven Storage, and Auto Deploy will go a long way in making the VMware administrator's day-to-day tasks simpler. Improvements made to vSphere HA, Update Manager, and VMware Data Recovery will all help simplify the management of the virtual infrastructure.

There are also several exciting firsts for vSphere 5, like Mac OS X support, a vCenter Server Appliance that runs on Linux, and a cross-platform vSphere Web Client. Of course, with all these changes in feature sets, there also comes a new licensing model that you will need to get familiar with.

Although there are many changes to vSphere 5, many of which we will explore in the coming chapters of this book, there will be features that are not covered by the VCP5 exam blueprint. Thinking that these features omitted on the blueprint are not likely to show up on the exam would be a mistake. I encourage you to learn all of the vSphere 5 products and explore the feature sets as you move through this book. Learn how the products work and where they might effectively be used in your virtual infrastructure, but also be mindful of the "why" of these products and feature sets.

Chapter

2

Plan, Install, Configure, and Upgrade vCenter Server and VMware ESXi

---

VCP5 EXAM OBJECTIVES COVERED IN THIS CHAPTER:

✓ **Install and Configure vCenter Server**

- Identify available vCenter Server editions

- Deploy the vCenter Appliance

- Install vCenter Server into a virtual machine

- Size the vCenter Server database

- Install additional vCenter Server components

- Install/Remove vSphere Client plug-ins

- Enable/Disable vSphere Client plug-ins

- License vCenter Server

- Determine availability requirements for a vCenter Server in a given vSphere implementation

- Determine use case for vSphere Client and Web Client

✓ **Install and Configure VMware ESXi**

- Perform an interactive installation of ESXi

- Deploy an ESXi host using Auto Deploy

- Configure NTP on an ESXi Host

- Configure DNS and Routing on an ESXi Host

- Enable/Configure/Disable hyperthreading

- Enable/Size/Disable memory compression cache
- License an ESXi host

✓ **Plan and Perform Upgrades of vCenter Server and VMware ESXi**

- Identify upgrade requirements for ESXi hosts
- Identify steps required to upgrade a vSphere implementation
- Upgrade a vNetwork Distributed Switch
- Upgrade from VMFS-3 to VMFS-5
- Upgrade VMware Tools
- Upgrade Virtual Machine hardware
- Upgrade an ESXi Host using vSphere Update Manager
- Determine whether an in-place upgrade is appropriate in a given upgrade scenario

This chapter will cover part of Section 1 of the VCP5 exam blueprint. The first part of the chapter will cover planning, installing, configuring, and upgrading vCenter Server and VMware ESXi. These are the first tasks that all of the other objectives in the exam will build upon. Without ESXi and vCenter, we wouldn't get very far, would we?

This chapter will also cover identifying the available editions of vCenter Server and installing vCenter Server. It will cover installing the vCenter Server Appliance and sizing the vCenter Server database. In addition, it will cover installing, removing, and enabling and disabling vSphere Client plug-ins, as well as understanding vCenter licensing, determining vCenter Server availability, and determining specific use cases for the vSphere Client and the vSphere Web Client.

This chapter will cover installing and configuring ESXi, both using interactive installations and using the Auto Deploy feature. It will also cover configuring ESXi hosts for specific NTP, DNS, routing, and hyperthreading settings, along with memory compression cache settings and ESXi host licensing.

Finally, this chapter will cover upgrading vCenter Server and ESXi hosts. It will also cover how to identify requirements and steps for upgrades, along with how to upgrade a vNetwork Distributed Switch, VMFS-3 volumes, VMware Tools, and virtual machine hardware. Using vSphere Update Manager and determining whether an in-place upgrade is appropriate will round out the chapter.

Introduction to vCenter Server

vCenter Server is used to manage ESXi hosts and the resources they contain. This can include virtual machines, networks, storage systems, *resource pools*, and much more. vCenter Server comes in three editions, and these editions will be discussed first.

Identifying Available vCenter Server Editions

Part of planning your virtual infrastructure is being able to identify the available editions of vCenter Server in vSphere 5. VMware vCenter Server is available in the following editions:

- VMware vCenter Server for Essentials
- VMware vCenter Server Foundation
- VMware vCenter Server Standard

VMware vCenter Server for Essentials is integrated into two available vSphere Essentials *Kits*. Both vSphere Essentials Kits are all-in-one solutions targeted at small-to-medium businesses (SMBs). The differentiator with the vSphere Essentials Kits is that they are entirely self-contained and cannot be used with other editions. These kits are limited to three hosts (two CPUs each) and a maximum pooled *vRAM* capacity of 192GB, but they include everything you need to get started.

The two available options for the vSphere Essentials Kits, both of which come with VMware vCenter Server for Essentials, are the vSphere Essentials Kit and the vSphere Essentials Plus Kit. The vSphere Essentials Plus Kit adds the vMotion, High Availability (HA), and VMware Data Recovery features to the vSphere Essentials Kit.

VMware vCenter Server Foundation is used for centralized management of up to three ESXi hosts. This version is not sold as part of a kit but instead allows the purchase of the individual component of vCenter Server.

VMware vCenter Server Standard is used in all other vSphere 5 Kits, including Standard, Enterprise, and Enterprise Plus. There are no limits or restrictions on the number of hosts that it can manage except for the supported maximum of 1000 hosts. vCenter Server Standard includes vCenter Orchestrator and vCenter Server Linked Mode as additional features.

Three editions of vCenter Server are available, and for the exam it is important to know the differences between these editions. Now that I have covered the editions of vCenter Server, I will move on to deploying one of the exciting new features of vSphere 5: the vCenter Server Appliance.

Deploying the vCenter Server Appliance

The vCenter Server Appliance is a preconfigured Linux-based *virtual machine* (VM) that has been optimized to run only vCenter Server and its associated services. It is deployed as an *Open Virtualization Format* (OVF)–formatted VM and is supported only when deployed on ESX/ESXi 4.0/4.1 and ESXi 5 hosts. To deploy the vCenter Server Appliance, several prerequisites must first be met:

- The vSphere Client must be installed.

- A minimum of 7GB of disk space is required, and a maximum of 80GB of disk space is required.

- Both the VMDK and OVF files for the vCenter Server Appliance must have already been downloaded.

Once all of the prerequisites are met, you can follow the steps in Exercise 2.1 to deploy the vCenter Server Appliance.

EXERCISE 2.1

Deploying the vCenter Server Appliance

1. Open the vSphere Client and connect to a supported ESX/ESXi 4.0/4.1 or ESXi 5 host.

2. From the File menu, choose Deploy OVF Template. This will launch the Deploy OVF Template Wizard.

3. The first step in the wizard is to browse to the downloaded VMDK and OVF files for the vCenter Server Appliance and select the OVF file. Once the OVF file has been selected, it will appear in the Deploy From A File Or URL field, as shown here.

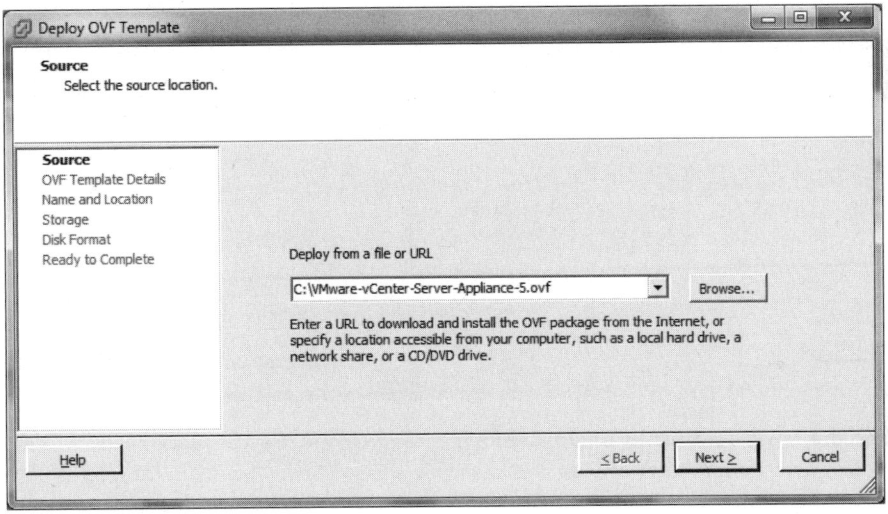

4. Click the Next button to continue. Verify the OVF template details for accuracy and then click the Next button to continue.

5. Specify a name and location for the deployed template. This name will be the name of the deployed VM. Click the Next button to continue.

6. Choose a datastore and/or disk format to house the vCenter Server Appliance. You can be presented with different options here depending on the type of storage your ESXi host has or the version of your ESXi host. Click the Next button to continue.

(continued)

7. Choose the appropriate network for the vCenter Server Appliance, and click the Next button to continue.

8. Finally, review the details of the task deployment, as shown here.

9. Click the Finish button to begin deploying the vCenter Server Appliance. A dialog box will appear that shows the task progress. Verify the task completes in the vSphere Client.

   The vCenter Server Appliance has now been deployed. The remainder of this exercise will cover the steps to configure it.

10. Power on the vCenter Server Appliance.

11. Right-click the vCenter Server Appliance in the left pane of the vSphere Client and choose the Open Console option from the context menu that appears.

12. After ensuring that the console window has focus, press the down-arrow key to select the Configure Network option.

13. Press the Enter key.

14. You will first be prompted to configure an additional IPv6 address. Press N and then press the Enter key.

15. You will next be prompted to choose between DHCP and static IP addressing. Press N and then press the Enter key.

16. Enter the IP address for the vCenter Server Appliance and press the Enter key.

17. Enter the appropriate subnet mask and press the Enter key.

18. Enter the gateway address and press the Enter key.

19. Enter the first DNS server address and press the Enter key.

20. Enter the second DNS server address and press the Enter key.

21. Provide a hostname and press the Enter key.

22. You will be prompted to specify whether an IPv4 proxy server is necessary to reach the Internet. Choose the appropriate response and press the Enter key on the keyboard to continue.

23. You will be prompted to review the information just entered and confirm whether it is correct. If the information is correct, press Y and then press the Enter key on keyboard. The final configuration should appear similar to what is shown here.

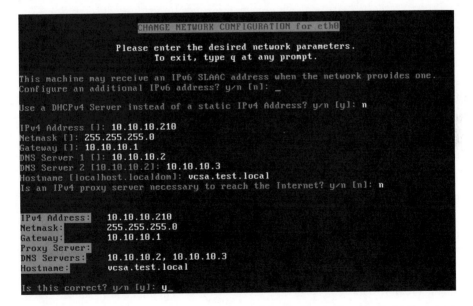

24. When the networking setup is complete, the window will refresh to the start-up screen.

25. Locate the second line in this window. It contains the URL to manage the vCenter Server Appliance.

NOTE The vCenter Server Appliance has the default username of *root* and the default password *vmware*.

The vCenter Server Appliance is a welcome addition to vSphere 5, but it may not be suitable for every environment. The lack of SQL Server support alone could keep this appliance from being deployed in many Windows-based environments. For environments that want to use SQL Server or the Windows operating system, there is still the option to install vCenter Server on a Windows server. I will cover installing vCenter Server in the following section.

Installing vCenter Server into a Virtual Machine

vCenter Server can be installed on a physical server or a virtual machine. Both are supported configurations, and the installation process is the same once the Windows server is deployed. There are obvious benefits to having vCenter run in a VM, including the ability to protect it with *vSphere High Availability* (HA), *VMware Distributed Resource Scheduler* (DRS), and vMotion, as well as the ability to *snapshot* the virtual machine. These reasons can make a strong case for running vCenter Server in a virtual machine. To install vCenter Server in a virtual machine, you must meet many prerequisites. Some of these include the following:

- The installation media should be downloaded and available.

- The Microsoft .NET 3.5 SP1 Framework is required to be installed on the Windows server. The vCenter Server Installer can install the .NET 3.5 SP1 Framework; however, the installation may require an Internet connection.

- Ensure that the vCenter Server system requirements are met, including two 64-bit CPUs or one 64-bit dual-core CPU, 4GB RAM, and 4GB free disk space.

- Ensure that all required network ports are open.

- Verify that your database is supported.

- Verify that DNS entries are resolving correctly for the server that vCenter Server will be installed on.

- Verify that there is no Network Address Translation between the vCenter Server system and the ESXi hosts that it will manage.

- If using a remote database, have the vCenter database created.

- If using a remote database, create and test a 64-bit system *data source name* (DSN). If using Microsoft SQL, create the DSN using the SQL Native Client driver.

- Preferably, vCenter Server should be installed on a Windows server that is a member of a domain.

- Verify that the computer name is no longer than the 15-character maximum.

- Verify that the Windows server that will house vCenter is not a domain controller. vCenter will not install on domain controllers, because Active Directory Application Mode (ADAM) is used.

- Ensure that a static IP address is used for the Windows OS hosting vCenter Server.

 If vCenter Server is installed on a system configured with IPv6, then vCenter Server will use IPv6.

Once you've met the vCenter Server prerequisites, you should give some thought to the account that will be used to run the vCenter Server services. Either the Windows built-in SYSTEM account or a user account can be used to run vCenter Server.

The Microsoft Windows built-in SYSTEM account has more permissions and rights on the server than the vCenter Server system needs, which can contribute to security problems.

The benefit of using a user account is that greater security is provided by using Windows authentication for SQL Server. This user account must be an administrator on the Windows server that vCenter Server will be installed on. If you plan on using SQL authentication for SQL Server or if you plan on using an Oracle or DB2 database, you will also set up a local user account for the vCenter Server system. This user account is required to be an administrator on the local machine.

It is also important that you log on to Windows with the correct user account, when you run the vCenter Server Installer. If you are going to use the bundled Microsoft SQL 2008 R2 Express database, then log in with any user account that has Administrator privileges. If you are using either a local or remote SQL database with Windows authentication, then log in to Windows with the account that has access to the database to run Setup.

Exercise 2.2 covers the process of installing vCenter Server on a virtual machine.

EXERCISE 2.2

Installing vCenter Server into a Virtual Machine

1. Open a console session on the Windows server using the vSphere Client.

2. Ensure that the media for vCenter Server is attached or available locally on the virtual machine.

3. Log on to the Windows server that vCenter Server will be installed on, and launch the VMware vCenter Installer application by running the autorun.exe file.

(continued)

EXERCISE 2.2 *(continued)*

4.   The VMware vCenter Installer will launch.

Take note of what is included on the vCenter Server Installer screen. There are new items now available in vSphere 5, and some familiar items from vSphere 4.x (such as *vCenter Guided Consolidation and vCenter Converter)* are no longer there.

5.   Select vCenter Server under the VMware Product Installers section and then click the Install button to begin.

6.   Select the language to be used for installation and click the OK button to continue.

7.   Accept the end-user patent agreement and the license agreement to continue.

8.   Enter a username and organization. You can enter a vCenter Server license key now or wait until after install.

9.   The next step is to choose the database to be used for vCenter Server. The options here are to use a Microsoft SQL Server 2008 Express instance or to

use an existing supported database. If you are using an existing supported database, select the appropriate 64-bit DSN. Click the Next button to continue.

10. Once you've selected the database, if you are using the bundled Microsoft SQL Server 2008 Express instance, you can select either the SYSTEM account or a user account. If you use either a local or remote SQL Server, with Windows authentication, the account that has access to the database will be used for the vCenter Server services to run under. The option to use the SYSTEM account is not available if you use a local or remote SQL Server with Windows authentication.

11. After the database has been selected, the destination directories for vCenter Server and the *Inventory Service* are chosen. These installation paths cannot contain commas or periods.

12. The next step is to decide whether this vCenter Server instance will be installed in stand-alone mode or *Linked Mode*.

    Linked Mode provides visibility across multiple vCenter Server instances, with roles, permissions, and licenses replicated across the infrastructure. This can allow a single login to manage the inventories of all vCenter Servers.

13. If this is the first vCenter Server deployed in the environment, simply choose the Create A Standalone VMware vCenter Server Instance option and click the Next button to continue.

(continued)

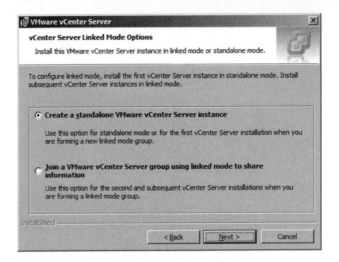

14. Next, you will configure the ports used for vCenter. These are the ports that vCenter Server will use for various communications. Change these ports only if you know exactly what you are doing or have a very good reason to do so. Changing ports here would typically be performed with the assistance of security or network personnel.

15. The next step is to configure the ports for the Inventory Service. Again, you should change the ports only if you know what you are doing or have a good reason to do so.

16. The vCenter Server Java Virtual Machine (JVM) memory is configured next. This setting simply adjusts the amount of memory allocated to the vCenter JVM. Choose the correct size for your environment, and know that this setting can be changed at any time after installation using the information contained in http://kb.vmware.com/kb/1039180.

17. The final, and also optional, step before installing vCenter Server is choosing whether to increase the ephemeral port value. This will increase the number of ephemeral ports available, which is important if your vCenter Server manages hosts on which there will be more than 2,000 virtual machines powered on. If this setting is appropriate for your environment, select it.

18. Finally, click the Install button to begin the vCenter Server installation.

 If you did not enter a license key during installation, vCenter Server will be in evaluation mode. Evaluation mode allows the use of the full vSphere 5 product feature set for 60 days. At any point within this 60 days after installation, you can enter a license key to convert vCenter Server to licensed mode.

vCenter Server 5 is now installed on a virtual machine and is ready to use, but before you install the vSphere 5 Client and start using vCenter Server, I will cover the very important topic of sizing the vCenter Server database.

Sizing the vCenter Server Database

An important part of configuring your vCenter environment is sizing the vCenter database. Improperly sized vCenter Server databases can lead to performance issues in vCenter or even unplanned system downtime. The vCenter Server database stores many items, including host and virtual machine configurations, resources and virtual machine inventory, user permissions, roles, alarms, events, tasks, and performance statistics. This performance statistic data can account for 90 percent of the information contained in the vCenter Server database, but the amount of resources your vCenter Server database consumes will ultimately depend on the number of managed VMs, the number of managed ESXi hosts, and the amount of performance statistics you plan to collect.

Fortunately, vCenter Server allows you to specify the interval duration, retention, and statistics level of the statistics counters. There is even a Database Size calculator included in the vCenter Server Settings Statistics window (see Figure 2.1). To access this tool, choose Administration ➢ vCenter Server Settings. Next, choose the Statistics option, and the Database Size calculator appears at the bottom of the screen.

FIGURE 2.1   vCenter Server Settings Statistics window

```
vCenter Server Settings                                                    [x]

Statistics
   Select settings for collecting vCenter statistics


  Licensing              ┌─Statistics Intervals──────────────────────────────┐
  Statistics             │  Interval Duration    Save For      Statistics Level│
  Runtime Settings       │  ☑ 5 Minutes          1 Days        1               │
  Active Directory       │  ☑ 30 Minutes         1 Week        1               │
  Mail                   │  ☑ 2 Hours            1 Month       1               │
  SNMP                   │  ☑ 1 Day              1 Years       1               │
  Ports                  │                                                     │
  Timeout Settings       │                                            Edit...  │
  Logging Options        └─────────────────────────────────────────────────────┘
  Database               ┌─Database Size─────────────────────────────────────┐
  Database Retention Policy│ Based on the current vCenter and inventory size, the vCenter database can be │
  SSL Settings           │ estimated. Enter the expected number of hosts and virtual machines in the │
  Advanced Settings      │ inventory to calculate an estimate.                 │
                         │                                                     │
                         │   50   Physical Hosts    Estimated space required:  14.32 GB │
                         │                                                     │
                         │  2000  Virtual Machines                             │
                         │                                                     │
                         │ Click Help for details on how the vCenter database size is calculated. │
                         └─────────────────────────────────────────────────────┘



   Help                                            OK          Cancel
```

If vCenter Server is not yet installed, VMware also provides calculators that can be used to estimate the size of the vCenter Server database. These sizing calculators are available here:

- VMware vCenter Database Sizing Calculator for Oracle:

  www.vmware.com/support/vsphere4/doc/vsp_4x_db_calculator_oracle.xls

- VMware vCenter Database Sizing Calculator for Microsoft SQL Server:

  www.vmware.com/support/vsphere4/doc/vsp_4x_db_calculator.xls

These URLs are specific for vCenter 4.1. At the time this book was written, there were no published URLs available for vSphere 5.

vCenter Server comes bundled with a Microsoft SQL Server 2008 R2 Express edition database. This bundled database can be used with up to 5 VMware ESX/ESXi hosts and 50 virtual machines in the inventory. It is important to note that the Microsoft SQL Server 2008 R2 Express database cannot be installed as part of a vCenter Server upgrade. Upgraded vCenter Server systems will require Microsoft SQL Server 2008 R2 Express to be manually installed prior to running the vCenter Server Installer.

> **WARNING**   The maximum database size in SQL Server 2008 R2 Express is 10GB.

Keep in mind the limitations of the bundled Microsoft SQL 2008 R2 Express database when planning for your vCenter Server. If you suspect that the environment will grow beyond the limits of Microsoft SQL 2008 R2 Express, your design should likely include a supported database.

Regardless of the database server used to house the vCenter Server database, once vCenter Server is installed and operational, you should perform standard database maintenance as suggested by the database vendor. This can include actions such as monitoring the growth of the log file, compacting the database log file as needed, and scheduling regular backups of the database.

Now that I have covered the importance of sizing the vCenter Server database and maintaining it, I will cover installing two additional vCenter Server components:

- vSphere Client
- vSphere Web Client (Server)

Installing Additional vCenter Server Components

The first additional component that you will learn how to install is the vSphere Client. The vSphere Client is a Windows application that can be used to manage and configure both ESXi hosts and vCenter Server instances.

Exercise 2.3 covers the steps to install the vSphere Client.

EXERCISE 2.3

Installing the vSphere Client

1. Connect to a console session on a supported Windows client or server and log on with an administrator account.

2. If the Windows client or server has Internet access, open a web browser and enter the following URL: http://vcenter.domain.com or http://ESXi.domain.com.

(continued)

EXERCISE 2.3 *(continued)*

3. When the page loads, click the Download vSphere Client link located under the Getting Started section.

 N⦸TE If you connected to the ESXi host's URL in step 2, the vSphere Client will be downloaded from the VMware web site!

4. Once the file has been downloaded, run it.

5. If the Windows client or server does not have Internet access, ensure that the media for vCenter Server is attached or available locally. Then use autorun.exe to launch the VMware vCenter Installer application.

6. Once the installation wizard starts, first select the language.

7. On the Welcome screen, click the Next button to begin.

8. Click the Next button on the End-User Patent Agreement screen to continue.

9. Agree to the terms of the license agreement, and click the Next button to continue.

10. Enter both your username and organization information, and click the Next button to continue.

11. Choose a destination directory for the vSphere Client, and click the Next button to continue.

12. Click the Install button to install the vSphere Client.

After the installation of the vSphere Client completes, you can use the vSphere Client to connect to either an ESXi host or a vCenter Server system. After starting the vSphere Client, log in to either an ESXi host or a vCenter Server system using the appropriate credentials. You can use the Use Windows Session Credentials option to pass through the credentials of the currently logged on Windows user.

 N⦸TE Security warnings about certificates will appear when logging in, because the vSphere Client detects certificates signed by an ESXi host or vCenter Server (default setting). This is the default behavior, and if you trust these certificates, you can safely ignore these warnings.

You can now turn your focus to installing the *vSphere Web Client* (Server).

The vSphere Web Client is a *cross-platform* web application that allows you to connect to a vCenter Server system to manage an ESXi host. It can be particularly useful to virtual infrastructure administrators, help-desk staff, operations, VM owners, and users who are not using the Windows OS. It is important to remember that the vSphere Web Client cannot be used to connect directly to an ESXi host.

> Determining use cases for the vSphere Web Client will be discussed in more detail later in this chapter, in the section "Determining Use Case for vSphere Client and Web Client."

There is also a licensing report included in the vSphere Web Client Server that allows customers to query vRAM utilization. This report is actually accessed through the standard vSphere Client, but the functionality is provided by the vSphere Web Client Server. This license reporting feature is why a note is included on the vCenter Server Installer screen about the vSphere Web Client being required.

The naming of the vSphere Web Client feature can also be a bit confusing. The vSphere Web Client installer actually installs the vSphere Web Client Server. It is this web server that will host the web application known as the vSphere Web Client. So, remember that there are two distinct pieces to this feature: a web server that gets installed and a client that is accessed from this web server via a web browser. Before installing the vSphere Web Client (Server), you must meet several prerequisites:

- The vCenter Server installation media should be downloaded and available.

- Verify membership in the Administrators group on the system.

- Verify that the system requirements are met; this includes a 64-bit operating system for installation.

- Microsoft Internet Explorer 7 and 8 and Mozilla Firefox 3.6 are the supported web browsers for use with the vSphere Web Client.

- Adobe Flash Player version 10.1.0 or newer needs to be installed for your supported web browser.

Once the prerequisites have been met for the vSphere Web Client (Server), installation can begin. Exercise 2.4 covers how to install the vSphere Web Client (Server).

EXERCISE 2.4

Installing the vSphere Web Client (Server)

1. Connect to a console session on any supported Windows client or server and log on with an Administrator account.

2. Launch the vCenter Server Installer, select vSphere Web Client (Server) from the list of VMware Product Installers, and then click the Install button to begin.

3. When the installation wizard starts, select the language.

4. On the Welcome screen, click the Next button to begin.

(continued)

EXERCISE 2.4 *(continued)*

5. Click the Next button on the End-User Patent Agreement screen to continue.

6. Agree to the terms of the license agreement, and click the Next button to continue.

7. Enter both your username and organization and click the Next button to continue.

8. Port configuration is next. These are the ports that the vSphere Web Client (Server) will use for various communications. Change these ports only if you know exactly what you are doing or have a very good reason to do so. Changing ports here would typically be performed with the assistance of security or network personnel.

9. Choose a destination directory for the vSphere Web Client (Server), and click the Next button to continue.

10. Click the Install button to install the vSphere Web Client (Server).

11. When the vSphere Web Client (Server) installation completes, a web browser opens and loads the *vSphere Web Client Administration application*. This interface is used to register vCenter Servers on the vSphere Web Client Administration Application page (as shown here).

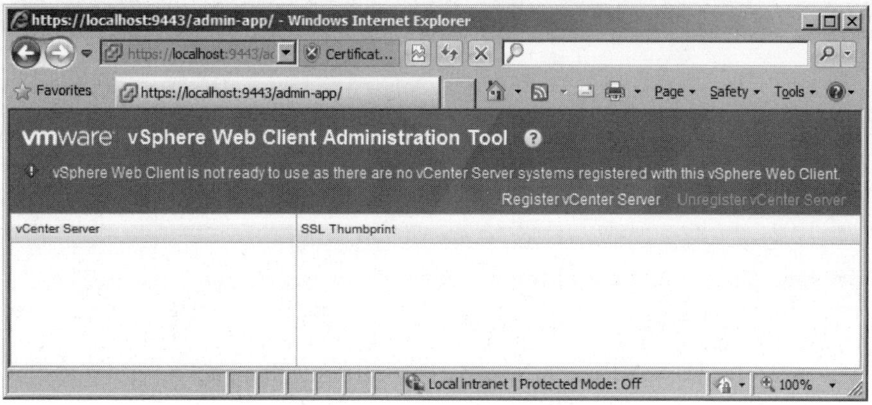

If the web browser fails to open or to display the registration tool page properly, you can later open the application from the Windows Start menu. Select Programs ➢ VMware ➢ VMware vSphere Web Client ➢ vSphere Administration Application.

12. Use the Register vCenter Server link at the top of the page to add a vCenter Server. Enter the URL of vCenter Server as https://vcenter.domain.com, and provide the appropriate credentials. Provide the vSphere Web Client server name or IP address, and then click the Register button to continue. The information entered should appear similar to what is shown here.

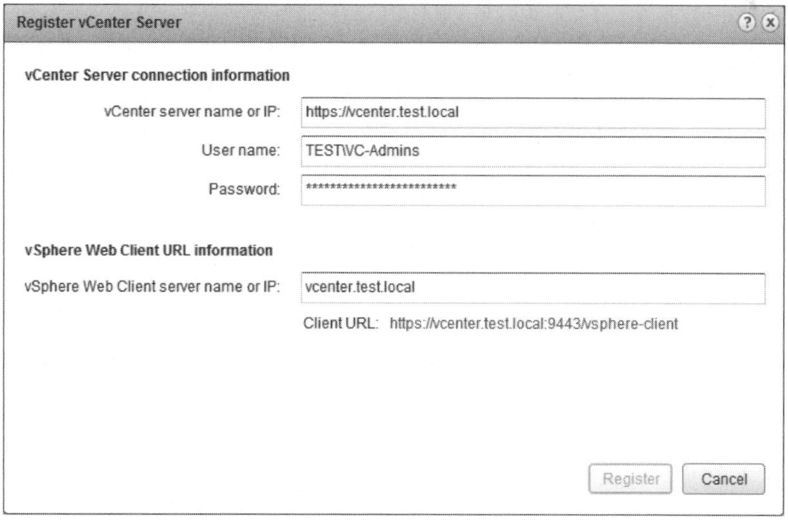

(continued)

13. A Certificate Warning screen will appear. Select the Install This Certificate check box and then click the Ignore button to continue.

14. Verify that at least one vCenter Server is now listed in the vSphere Web Client Administration application.

To access the vSphere Web Client from a web browser, open a supported web browser and enter the following URL: http://vcenter.domain.com. Use the Log In To vSphere Web Client link provided on the vSphere Welcome page to launch the vSphere Web Client. You will be prompted to log in to continue. After successfully logging in, you can use the vSphere Web Client for VM deployment and monitoring functions.

Next you will learn how to install two of the vCenter Support Tools from the vCenter Server Installer.

Installing and Removing vSphere Client Plug-ins

Plug-ins are applications that provide additional features or functionality to vCenter Server. Plug-ins are normally composed of both a server component and a client component. The plug-in server components are installed and registered with a vCenter Server, and the plug-in client component is available to vSphere Clients.

Installing plug-ins can modify the vCenter Server interface by adding such things as additional views, tabs, toolbar buttons, and menu options. These additions typically serve to add functionality and can be managed using the vSphere Client's *Plug-In Manager.*

Occasionally there may also be a need to remove a vSphere Client plug-in. Since vSphere Client plug-ins are just Windows applications, they are quite easily uninstalled by using the native application uninstall functions in the Windows OS.

Some vCenter Server features that are implemented as plug-ins include the following:

- vCenter Storage Monitoring
- vCenter Service Status
- vCenter Hardware Status

Two additional components that make use of the vSphere Client plug-ins are the VMware Syslog Collector and VMware Auto Deploy.

The VMware Syslog Collector is essentially a syslog server for Windows. The idea is that ESXi system logs can be directed to a *syslog server*, rather than to a local disk on the ESXi host. As you will learn later, a local disk may not be required for an ESXi 5 host. The possibility of a diskless ESXi host makes it essential to have the ability to collect logs. The VMware Syslog Collector provides this capability.

The VMware Syslog Collector can be installed on the same machine as the associated vCenter Server or on a different machine. If installed on a different machine, that machine must meet the system requirements and have a network connection to vCenter Server. The VMware Syslog Collector supports both IPv4 and IPv6. There are several prerequisites for installing the VMware Syslog Collector:

- Verify membership in the Administrators group on the system.
- Verify that the system requirements are met.
- Verify that the host machine has Windows Installer 3.0 or newer.

Once these prerequisites have been met, the installation of the Syslog Collector may begin. Exercise 2.5 covers the installation steps.

EXERCISE 2.5

Installing the VMware Syslog Collector on vCenter Server

1. Connect to a console session on the Windows server that houses vCenter Server. Be sure to log on with an Administrator account.

2. Launch the vCenter Server Installer and select VMware Syslog Collector from the list of vCenter Support Tools. Click the Install button to begin.

3. When the installation wizard starts, select the language.

4. On the Welcome screen, click the Next button to begin.

5. Click the Next button on the End-User Patent Agreement screen to continue.

6. Agree to the terms of the license agreement, and click the Next button to continue.

7. Choose a destination directory for the Syslog Collector. You will also need to choose a directory for the syslog repository and configure the repository settings.

   Depending on the number of hosts and a variety of other factors, the log file size and rotation settings may need to be tweaked over time. It is also important to keep in mind that the location for the repository could potentially require significant space. For this reason, a drive other than the system drive of the server should be used.

(continued)

EXERCISE 2.5 *(continued)*

vSphere Syslog Collector

Destination Folder
Click Next to install to this folder, or click Change to install to a
different folder.

Install vSphere Syslog Collector to:

C:\Program Files (x86)\VMware\VMware Syslog Collector\   Change...

vSphere Syslog Collector Configuration

Repository directory:

S:\logs\   Change...

Size of log file before rotation: 2   MB

Log rotations to keep: 8

InstallShield

   < Back   Next >   Cancel

8. For this exercise, choose the VMware vCenter Server Installation setup type and click the Next button to continue.

9. Enter the FQDN or IP address of vCenter Server, along with the appropriate vCenter Server Administrator credentials. Accept port 80, unless you have customized the vCenter ports. Click the Next button to continue.

10. Review the Syslog Collector port settings. The UDP protocol on port 514 is the combination that syslog servers typically use and is the default presented here. These settings can be modified as required. Once the port settings are selected, click the Next button to continue.

11. Use the pull-down menu to specify how the Syslog Collector should be identified (which IP address or hostname) on the network, and click the Next button to continue.

12. Finally, click the Install button to begin the installation.

You will verify the installation of the Syslog Collector after the next task of installing VMware Auto Deploy. This is because the tasks required to configure both the Syslog Collector and Auto Deploy are the same.

The Auto Deploy server is a component that simplifies the deployment and patching of VMware ESXi hosts. Auto Deploy server can be used to provision multiple physical hosts with VMware ESXi software, while specifying the exact image to deploy and the host to provision with the image. ESXi hosts that utilize Auto Deploy will PXE boot, and the Auto Deploy server will stream the ESXi image into the host's memory. No state is stored on the ESXi host. Instead, the Auto Deploy server will manage state information for each ESXi host configured to use Auto Deploy.

> The Auto Deploy feature must be installed separately for each instance of vCenter Server that Auto Deploy will be used with.

There are several prerequisites for installing Auto Deploy:

- Verify membership in the Administrators group on the system.
- Verify that the system requirements are met.
- Verify that the host machine has Windows Installer 3.0 or newer.

Once the prerequisites have been met for Auto Deploy, installation may begin. Exercise 2.6 covers the steps for installing Auto Deploy.

EXERCISE 2.6

Installing VMware Auto Deploy

1. Connect to a console session on the Windows server that houses vCenter Server. Be sure to log on with an Administrator account.

2. Launch the vCenter Server Installer, select VMware Auto Deploy from the list of vCenter Support Tools, and then click the Install button to begin.

3. When the installation wizard starts, select the language.

4. On the Welcome screen, click the Next button to begin.

5. Click the Next button on the End-User Patent Agreement screen to continue.

6. Agree to the terms of the license agreement, and click the Next button to continue.

7. Choose a destination directory for Auto Deploy. You will also need to choose a directory for the Auto Deploy repository and configure the maximum size of the repository. It is important to keep in mind that the location for the repository could eventually grow quite large, so the volume selected should have plenty of free space. The default value of 2GB is designed to hold four image profiles. Click the Next button to continue.

(continued)

8. Enter the FQDN or IP address of vCenter Server, along with the appropriate vCenter Administrator credentials. Accept port 80, unless you have customized the vCenter ports. Click the Next button to continue.

9. Review the Auto Deploy port settings, and click the Next button to continue.

10. Specify how vSphere Auto Deploy should be identified (which IP address or hostname) on the network, and click the Next button to continue.

11. Finally, click the Install button to begin the installation.

When the Auto Deploy installation completes, open the vSphere Client and connect to vCenter Server where both the VMware Syslog Collector and Auto Deploy were just installed.

In the next section, you will learn how to configure both the Syslog Collector and Auto Deploy client plug-ins.

Enabling and Disabling vSphere Client Plug-ins

To verify that the Syslog Collector and Auto Deploy plug-ins are enabled, access the Plug-ins menu in the vSphere Client and choose the Manage Plug-ins option (see Figure 2.2).

If either the Syslog Collector or Auto Deploy plug-in is installed but shown as disabled, you will need to first enable the plug-in. To enable a plug-in, highlight the plug-in in the list of Installed Plug-ins and then right-click it and choose Enable from the context menu. This same procedure also works if you ever need to disable an enabled plug-in.

FIGURE 2.2   vCenter Plug-In Manager

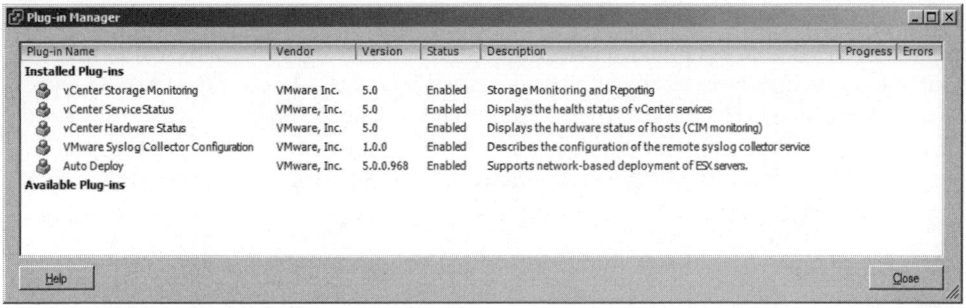

Once you have verified that all of the listed installed plug-ins are enabled, close the Plug-in Manager and browse to the Administration section of vCenter Server Home (see Figure 2.3). You will see that icons have been added for both Network Syslog Collector and Auto Deploy.

FIGURE 2.3   Syslog and Auto Deploy icons

At this point, you have installed the following items:

- vCenter Server Appliance
- vCenter Server
- vSphere Client
- vSphere Web Client (Server)
- Syslog Collector
- Auto Deploy

In the next section, I will cover licensing vCenter Server.

Licensing vCenter Server

Licensing in vSphere applies to vCenter Server, ESXi hosts, and solutions. Solutions are applications that extend the functionality or capabilities of vCenter Server and could include things like *VMware vCenter Operations* and *VMware vCenter Site Recovery Manager*.

Each vCenter Server, ESXi host, and solution will require a license after its evaluation period expires.

The actual licenses contain a given amount of capacity. License key capacity can vary and can be based on the number of processors in a host, the amount of vRAM in use, the number of asset instances, or the number of virtual machines. Two types of license limits are used to enforce licensing, and these are known as either *strong* or *soft*. Licenses with a strong limit will prevent operations that would result in exceeding the license capacity. Licenses with a soft limit will allow operations that would result in exceeding the license capacity but will trigger an alarm in vCenter Server.

 Major upgrades of vCenter and ESXi, such as upgrading from vSphere 4 to vSphere 5, as well as edition upgrades, such as from Enterprise to Enterprise Plus, will require obtaining new license keys.

You can obtain a license key from the VMware license portal at www.vmware.com/support/licensing. The license portal can be used to upgrade or downgrade license keys, combine or divide the capacity of keys, view the change history of license keys, and even find license keys. License keys consist of an alphanumeric sequence of 25 characters grouped in fives with dashes between each group, for example: A1B2C-3D4E5-G6H7I-8J9K0-L1M2N. License keys will contain information about the licensed product, expiration dates, license capacity, and more.

 If ESX/ESXi version 3.5 hosts will be managed with vCenter Server 5, a separate license server will be required to support these hosts.

vSphere license management is centralized, and the vSphere Client can be used to manage all licenses available in the license inventory of a vCenter Server or Linked Mode group. To view license information for a vCenter Server, follow these steps:

1. Log in to vCenter Server using the vSphere Client and select Home from the navigation bar.

2. Select Licensing, which is located in the Administration options.

3. You can view and manage license keys using the Management tab.

The Management tab displays available license keys listed by product, license key, or asset. Right-clicking any listed item allows you to add, assign, and remove license keys. Exercise 2.7 covers how to add a license key to vCenter Server.

To account for the fact that not everyone may have actual license keys, there will be a screenshot provided in this exercise that details the final steps of licensing. If you do not have valid license keys, work through the exercise as far as you can.

EXERCISE 2.7

Adding License Keys to vCenter in Evaluation Mode

1. Connect to a vCenter Server with the vSphere Client.

2. Select Home, and then select Licensing, which is located in the Administration options.

3. Verify that the Management tab is visible, and expand to Evaluation Mode ➢ (No License Key) ➢ vcenter.domain.com, as shown here.

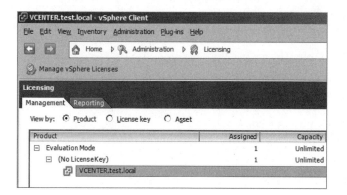

4. Right-click the vCenter Server name and choose the Change License Key option. An Assign License window will open.

5. Select the Assign A New License To This vCenter Server radio button, and then press the Enter Key button to continue.

6. When the Add New License Key dialog is presented, enter your vCenter Server license key. You can optionally enter a label for this key. In environments with many keys, these labels can be very useful. Click the OK button to close the Add New License Key window and continue. The Assign License dialog box will be updated with the key, as shown here.

(continued)

Assign License: VCENTER.test.local

○ Assign an existing license key to this vCenter Server

Product	Available
⊟ Evaluation Mode	
⊙ (No License Key)	

● Assign a new license key to this vCenter Server

| Enter Key... | A1B2C-3D4E5-G6H7I-8J9K0-L1M2N |

Product: vCenter Server 5 Standard
Capacity: Unlimited instances
Available: Unlimited instances
Expires: Never
Label: vCenter License - Quantity 1

Help   OK   Cancel

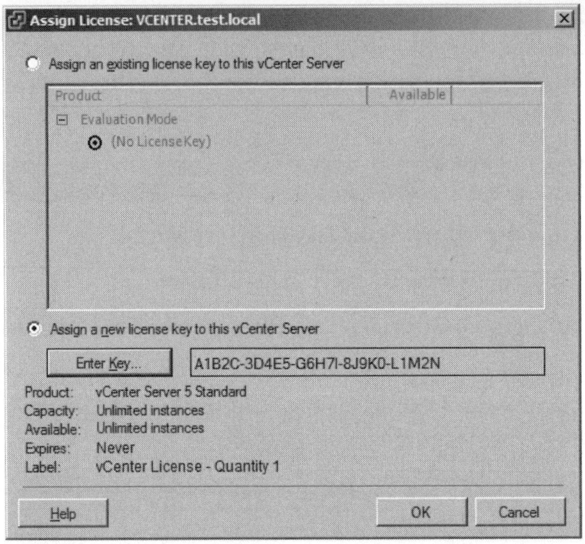

7. Press the OK button to assign the license.

8. Expand to vCenter Server 5 Standard ➢ vcenter.domain.com and verify that the license was added successfully.

Whether licenses are assigned or not, you can also manage licenses with the Manage vSphere Licenses Wizard. You can use the Manage vSphere Licenses Wizard to add, remove, or assign license keys. Figure 2.4 shows the Manage vSphere Licenses Wizard.

FIGURE 2.4   The Manage vSphere Licenses Wizard

Manage vSphere Licenses

Add License Keys
If you have recently purchased, upgraded, combined, or split keys, add them to your inventory now.

Add License Keys
Assign Licenses
Remove License Keys
Confirm Changes

Enter new vSphere license keys (one per line):

Enter optional label for new license keys:

Add License Keys

ℹ No new license keys have been added yet

Help   ≤ Back   Next ≥   Cancel

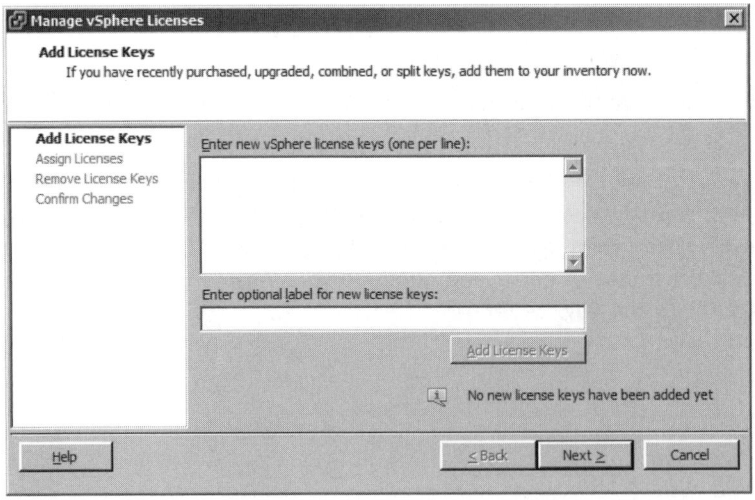

To access the Manage vSphere Licenses Wizard, right-click anywhere inside the product field on the Management tab in Licensing. There is also a Manage vSphere Licenses hyperlink, located at the top right of the Management tab in Licensing that will launch the Manage vSphere Licensing Wizard.

Now that I have covered vSphere licensing and how to license a vCenter Server, I will explain how to determine vCenter Server availability requirements.

Determining Availability Requirements for a vCenter Server in a Given vSphere Implementation

Depending on the vSphere implementation that you are working with, you may be required to provide additional availability options for vCenter Server. If vCenter Server is installed in a virtual machine, you are already on your way to providing higher availability.

Installing vCenter Server in a virtual machine allows the entire virtual machine to be backed up as an image. This backup image can be restored far more quickly than rebuilding a physical server. With the exception of vSphere Essentials, all editions of vSphere can leverage vSphere High Availability (HA) and vMotion to protect the vCenter Server virtual machine. The Enterprise and Enterprise Plus editions of vSphere can also leverage the VMware Distributed Resource Scheduler (DRS) to protect the vCenter Server virtual machine.

While *VMware Fault Tolerance* (FT) might first appear to be an attractive option for protecting vCenter Server, this is not possible due to the limitation to 1vCPU for FT protected VMs. vCenter Server requires a minimum of two vCPUs or one dual-core vCPU. Running vCenter Server on a VM with a single vCPU would be an unsupported configuration.

Clustering vCenter Server using Microsoft Cluster Services (MSCS) or Veritas Cluster Services (VCS) is another option that can provide high availability to a vCenter Server. The ability to cluster two physical servers, two virtual servers, or a combination of one physical server and one virtual server can also be an attractive option in some environments.

VMware does not certify third-party clustering solutions. VMware will offer support for vCenter Server installed on these solutions, but if the issue is determined to be related to the third-party software, you will likely be required to open a support request with the third-party vendor's support organization.

In the past, many virtual infrastructure administrators would keep a cold standby vCenter Server. This involved creating an image, typically a physical-to-virtual (P2V) conversion and having it ready to deploy in the event of an emergency. This strategy has risks associated with it, in that the consistency of the Active Directory Application Mode

(ADAM) database could not be guaranteed. vCenter Server uses ADAM, primarily for Linked Mode, but other information is stored there as well. Making a clone or P2V of vCenter Server may not properly copy the ADAM database. If you deploy this strategy, you should thoroughly test it. These risks may also hold true for certain image-based backups of vCenter Server.

The most attractive option, besides using HA, vMotion, and/or DRS, might be the VMware vCenter Server Heartbeat application. VMware vCenter Server Heartbeat is a Windows-based application that delivers high availability for VMware vCenter Server, protecting it from application, configuration, operating system, network, and hardware-related problems. VMware vCenter Server Heartbeat is used to protect vCenter Server and its database with failover failback on both physical and virtual platforms. Most importantly, VMware vCenter Server Heartbeat is a VMware product and is fully supported by VMware.

The best availability solution will be the one that fits the needs of the environment. Regardless of the approach taken, always make sure to have good consistent backups of the vCenter Server database.

Now that the options for providing a highly available vCenter have been discussed, it is time to discuss which vSphere Client should be used to access this highly available infrastructure.

Determining Use Case for vSphere Client and Web Client

The vSphere Client is the most-used application for managing both ESXi hosts and vCenter Server instances. The vSphere Client can only be locally installed on Windows operating systems and is the tool used for creating, managing, and monitoring virtual machines, their resources, and the ESXi hosts they reside on. It also used to provide console access for virtual machines and generally provides the full range of administrative functionality.

New in vSphere 5 is the vSphere Web Client. The vSphere Web Client is a cross-platform web application that runs in a supported web browser. However, the vSphere Web Client includes only a subset of the functionality provided by the vSphere Client, and it can connect only to vCenter Server, not ESXi hosts. The functionality provided by the vSphere Web Client is related to VM deployment and basic monitoring functions. It cannot be used to configure ESXi hosts, clusters, networks, datastores, or datastore clusters.

Deciding when to use the vSphere Client or the vSphere Web Client will ultimately be determined by the different requirements of the various IT staff in an organization. Virtual infrastructure administrators will use the vSphere Client for infrastructure configuration and specialized functions only available in the vSphere Client. If a virtual infrastructure administrator needs access to an ESXi host, he or she will have to use the vSphere Client. It is also probable that virtual infrastructure administrators will also use the vSphere Web Client for day-to-day operational tasks. Because of its reduced functionality, the vSphere Web Client is particularly well suited for help desk staff, operations center operators, virtual machine owners and non-Windows users. These types of users can use the vSphere Web Client from a supported web browser, without installing any software on their operating systems, simply by logging in to a website.

Real World Scenario

Using the vSphere Web Client

A company that has hundreds of virtual machines and thousands of employees has a small subset of employees responsible for administering certain virtual machines. Most of the virtual machine administrators also use Linux laptops. In the past, the vSphere Client was installed on a Windows desktop and made available to these users to administer their virtual machines.

With vSphere 5, these users can now use the vSphere Web Client to administer their virtual machines. Running Firefox on Linux allows these users to not rely on a separate Windows system and allows them to perform their virtual machine administration from their laptops with a fully supported configuration. There is no software for these users to install, and using the vSphere Web Client is as simple as visiting a website.

Now that installing and configuring vCenter Server has been covered in detail, you can next turn your attention toward installing and configuring ESXi. After all, vCenter Server just isn't nearly as interesting without ESXi hosts to manage.

Introduction to VMware ESXi

ESXi is VMware's bare-metal hypervisor that is used to run virtual machines on x86 hardware. ESXi abstracts the underlying hardware on these x86 servers and allows multiple virtual machines to share these resources. ESXi is offered in two editions. There is ESXi Installable, which is the version you download from VMware and install on your compatible x86 servers. There is also ESXi Embedded, which is installed on USB or SD cards in servers by the OEM. If you have used ESX up until now, there are going to be a few new things to learn. This is because starting with vSphere 5, ESX is no longer being offered as a hypervisor option.

Performing an Interactive Installation of ESXi

Performing an interactive installation of ESXi 5 is an essential part of any virtual infrastructure administrator's duties, and installing ESXi 5 interactively is a fairly straightforward task. Exercise 2.8 covers how to install ESXi 5 from the installation media.

EXERCISE 2.8

Performing an Interactive Installation of ESXi 5

1. Connect to a console session on the server that ESXi will be installed on.

2. In the server system's BIOS, verify that the server hardware clock is set to *UTC*. ESXi uses UTC and not time zones. Also, verify that VT-x or AMD-V are enabled and that the system will boot to the installation media you have available. If you need assistance with these steps, consult the documentation for your particular system.

3. Insert the optical or USB (or remote, if using out-of-band management) media that the ESXi installer is located on, and ensure that the ESXi Embedded edition is not already installed on this server. These two editions cannot coexist.

4. If you are using Fibre Channel or iSCSI SAN storage, you may want to disconnect the cables before proceeding. This can help prevent accidental installs of ESXi on to incorrect disks.

5. Restart the system or exit the BIOS so that the ESXi installer will boot. If you have never installed ESXi, you will immediately notice that there is no GUI installer like there was with ESX.

6. After reviewing the information on the Welcome screen, press the Enter key to continue.

7. Agree to the terms of the license agreement, and press the F11 key to accept the EULA and continue.

8. On the Select A Disk page, select the drive that ESXi will be installed on. You can press the F1 key for more information about the selected disk. Be absolutely certain that the correct disk is selected here before continuing.

```
                    Select a Disk to Install or Upgrade

    * Contains a VMFS partition

    Storage Device                                            Capacity
    ------------------------------------------------------------------
    Local:
       VMware,  VMware Virtual S (mpx.vmhba1:C0:T0:L0)         4.00 GiB
     * VMware,  VMware Virtual S (mpx.vmhba1:C0:T1:L0)         4.00 GiB
    Remote:
       (none)




       (Esc) Cancel    (F1) Details    (F5) Refresh    (Enter) Continue
```

9. Once you are certain you have selected the correct disk, press the Enter key to continue. If the disk you selected had data from a previous installation, a confirm disk selection dialog will appear. If you are sure you want to overwrite the disk, press the Enter key to continue.

10. Select a keyboard layout and press the Enter key to continue. The keyboard layout may be changed after the install from the ESXi console.

11. Enter a password, and then confirm the password. There is no minimum password length requirement. Press the Enter key to continue.

12. If any errors or warnings appear on the following screen, please review them and correct them if applicable. When you are ready to begin the ESXi installation, press the F11 key.

13. When installation completes, review the licensing and media removal information, and then press the Enter key to continue.

The interactive installation option is intended to be used for small deployments of fewer than five ESXi hosts.

Now that the interactive installation of ESXi is complete, you can turn your attention to using the Auto Deploy feature to deploy an ESXi host. Where interactive installations are intended for smaller environments, Auto Deploy can be used to scale to very large environments very quickly.

Deploying an ESXi Host Using Auto Deploy

Auto Deploy is used to provision ESXi hosts, using a vCenter Server. With Auto Deploy, the ESXi host will use the *Preboot Execution Environment* (PXE) at boot, and then vCenter Server will load the ESXi image directly into the host's memory. Auto Deploy stores no ESXi state on the host disk and allows diskless ESXi host configurations.

You installed Auto Deploy in Exercise 2.6, but the installation was only a small portion of making Auto Deploy work. The most time-consuming part of using Auto Deploy is configuring all the components required to make it work successfully. These configuration steps, at a minimum, include the following:

- Install vSphere Auto Deploy, which I covered in Exercise 2.6.

- Install the VMware PowerCLI, which includes the Auto Deploy cmdlets and the Auto Deploy snap-in.

- A *TFTP* server should be installed and available on the network to both the DHCP server and the vCenter Server system.

- The TFTP zip file should be downloaded from the Auto Deploy page in vCenter Server and extracted to a directory on the TFTP server.

- Set up your DHCP scope to include option 66 and to specify the TFTP server.

- Set up your DHCP scope to include option 67 and to specify a boot file named `undionly.kpxe.vmw-hardwired`.

- Set each ESXi host to be provisioned with Auto Deploy to PXE boot, following the manufacturer's instructions.

- Use *Image Builder* to create an image profile.

- Write rules that will assign an image profile and optional *host profile* to ESXi hosts provisioned with Auto Deploy.

Now that I have covered the minimal prerequisites for using Auto Deploy, you can move on to Exercise 2.9, which covers the steps to provision an ESXi host with Auto Deploy. Note that if Auto Deploy is not configured in your environment, this exercise will not work. Configuring Auto Deploy is outside the scope of the exam objectives and this book. Remember that for the VCP5 exam, you will be expected to know how to deploy an ESXi 5 host with Auto Deploy and not how to configure the various aspects of Auto Deploy.

EXERCISE 2.9

Deploying an ESXi Host Using Auto Deploy

1. Connect to a console session on the server that ESXi will be installed on.

2. In the server system's BIOS, verify that the server hardware clock is set to UTC. Also verify that the system will PXE boot. If you need assistance with these steps, consult the documentation for your particular system.

3. Reboot the server and watch as the system PXE boots; ESXi is loaded into memory and then starts.

4. When the ESXi host is up and running, use the vSphere Client to connect to it.

 There is an excellent Auto Deploy demo featured at VMware's official YouTube site: www.youtube.com/watch?v=G2qZ1-760yU. The configuration of Auto Deploy is also covered in detail in Scott Lowe's *Mastering VMware vSphere 5* (Sybex, 2011).

This exercise just scratches the surface of what Auto Deploy is capable of. Auto Deploy can be used in conjunction with host profiles to deliver fully configured ESXi hosts. Think of Auto Deploy as having the ability to add capacity on demand for a cluster, by simply powering on a server and letting it PXE boot. I have now covered the steps to deploy two ESXi hosts and will move on to configuring various settings on these hosts.

Configuring NTP on an ESXi Host

As mentioned earlier, ESXi uses UTC for system time. Time zones are not used in ESXi. To ensure that ESXi hosts have accurate system time, it is recommended that you configure ESXi hosts to use the Network Time Protocol (NTP).

Exercise 2.10 covers how to configure NTP on an ESXi host using the vSphere Client.

EXERCISE 2.10

Configuring NTP on an ESXi Host

1. Open the vSphere Client and connect to the ESXi host or vCenter Server that is managing the ESXi host.

2. From the inventory, select the ESXi host you want to configure NTP for and then click the Configuration tab in the right pane.

3. Choose the blue Time Configuration link in the Software panel.

4. Review the current configuration. Is the time correct? The NTP client should show a status of Stopped, and there should be no value shown for NTP Servers, as shown here.

5. To configure the NTP settings, click the blue Properties link in the top-right corner of the panel.

6. Manually set the time and date in the Date And Time section of the properties.

7. You will also want to set up this ESXi host to use NTP so that it will have consistently accurate time from this point forward. Start by selecting the NTP Client Enabled check box in the NTP Configuration settings. NTP is now enabled, but you will need to click the Options button to configure additional NTP settings.

8. When the NTP *Daemon* (ntpd) Options screen appears, select the NTP Settings option from the left column.

9. On the Settings screen, click the Add button to add an NTP server. This will be the NTP server that this ESXi host will sync its time with. There may be a standard NTP Server that the environment uses, and it may be located internally or externally.

10. After adding the NTP Server's IP address or fully qualified domain name (FQDN), click the OK button.

11. Select the Restart NTP Service To Apply Changes option and then select the General Settings option from the left column.

12. For the General Settings of the NTP Daemon (ntpd) Options screen, select the Start Automatically If Any Ports Are Open, And Stop When All Ports Are Closed option. This is the VMware-recommended option. Click the OK button to continue, and click the OK button again on the Time Configuration properties screen.

13. Review the current configuration. Is the time correct now? The NTP client should show a status of Running, and the NTP server you entered should now be listed beside the NTP servers.

NTP configuration is now complete. Repeat this process for any and all ESXi hosts running in the environment to ensure consistent and accurate timing in your virtual infrastructure. Next you will learn how to configure DNS and routing for an ESXi host.

Configuring DNS and Routing on an ESXi Host

An additional step in configuring ESXi hosts is the networking setup. Without accurate networking information, your ESXi hosts will surely run into issues in short order.

You will explore two different ways to configure DNS and routing on an ESXi host. Exercise 2.11 shows how to use the vSphere Client to configure DNS and routing for an ESXi host.

EXERCISE 2.11

Configuring DNS and Routing Using the vSphere Client

1. Open the vSphere Client and connect to the ESXi host or vCenter Server that is managing the ESXi host.

2. From the Inventory screen, select the ESXi host you want to configure DNS and routing for and then click the Configuration tab in the right pane.

3. Choose the blue DNS And Routing option from the Software panel.

4. Review the current information listed for Host Identification, DNS Servers, Search Domains, and Default Gateway. Is this information currently complete and correct? To modify the DNS and Routing settings, click the blue Properties link in the top-right corner of the panel. A DNS And Routing Configuration window will appear.

5. The DNS Configuration tab is shown first by default. Review the information contained in the DNS Configuration tab.

6. If changes need to be made to the Host Identification, DNS Servers, or Search Domain fields, make them on this tab. Once you've made the changes, click the Routing tab.

7. Verify that the default gateway listed is correct. If this information is incorrect, then you can modify it here.

8. Once you've made all the changes, click the OK button in the DNS And Routing window.

9. Depending on the changes made, an Update DNS Configuration task or an Update IP Route Configuration task may start. Wait for these tasks to complete and then review the DNS and routing information.

WARNING   Changing the ESXi hostname on an ESXi host that is being managed by vCenter Server can cause the ESXi host to become disconnected from vCenter Server. Make sure that DNS records are updated on the DNS servers in your environment as part of changing the ESXi hostname.

In Exercise 2.11, you configured DNS and routing for an ESXi host using the vSphere Client. In Exercise 2.12, you will learn how to configure DNS and routing from the ESXi DCUI. You will then return to the vSphere Client to view these changes.

EXERCISE 2.12

Configuring DNS and Routing from the ESXi DCUI

1. Obtain local console access to the ESXi host and press the F2 key to log in to the Direct Console User Interface (DCUI).

2. You will be presented with the System Customization menu.

3. Scroll down to the Configure Management Network option and review the hostname and IP address information shown on the right side of the screen. Press the Enter key to configure the management network. The Configure Management Network menu is shown here.

```
Configure Management Network


Network Adapters
VLAN (optional)

IP Configuration
IPv6 Configuration
DNS Configuration
Custom DNS Suffixes
```

(continued)

4. Scroll down to the IP Configuration item on the menu; press the Enter key to begin configuring the network settings for this ESXi host.

5. Review the current IP address, subnet mask, and default gateway information listed in the right pane. Press the Enter key to modify any of these settings. This will launch an IP Configuration window, as shown here.

```
 IP Configuration

 This host can obtain network settings automatically if your network
 includes a DHCP server. If it does not, the following settings must be
 specified:

 (o) Use dynamic IP address and network configuration
 ( ) Set static IP address and network configuration:

 IP Address                               [ 192.168.113.128  ]
 Subnet Mask                              [ 255.255.255.0    ]
 Default Gateway                          [ 192.168.113.1    ]

 <Up/Down> Select  <Space> Mark Selected        <Enter> OK  <Esc> Cancel
```

6. Use the up-arrow and down-arrow keys to toggle between the dynamic and static IP address settings. To select either option, make sure the line is highlighted and then press the spacebar on your keyboard.

7. To change the default gateway, or *routing* as it is referred to in the vSphere Client, you will have to select the static IP address option. Once the static IP address setting is selected, you can use the arrow keys to scroll down to the IP Address, Subnet Mask, and Default Gateway items and modify them as necessary.

8. Once you are satisfied with the changes, press the Enter key to exit the IP Configuration window. If you make any mistakes, simply press the Esc key to discard the changes.

9. You will return to the Configure Management Network menu options. Scroll down to the DNS Configuration option and review the DNS servers and ESXi hostname listed on the right. Press the Enter key to configure the DNS settings for this ESXi host. This will launch the DNS Configuration window, as shown here.

```
 DNS Configuration

 This host can only obtain DNS settings automatically if it also obtains
 its IP configuration automatically.


 ( ) Obtain DNS server addresses and a hostname automatically
 (o) Use the following DNS server addresses and hostname:

 Primary DNS Server        [ 192.168.113.2                        ]
 Alternate DNS Server      [ 192.168.113.4                        ]
 Hostname                  [ ESXi1.test.local                     ]


 <Up/Down> Select   <Space> Mark Selected         <Enter> OK   <Esc> Cancel
```

10. Just like in the IP Configuration window, you can use the up-arrow and down-arrow keys to toggle between the Obtain DNS Server and Use The Following DNS Server options. To select either option, make sure the line is highlighted and then press the spacebar.

11. To change the DNS servers, you will have to select the Use The Following DNS Server option. Once this setting is selected, you can use the arrow keys to scroll down to the Primary DNS Server, Alternate DNS Server, and Hostname items and modify them as necessary.

12. Once you are satisfied with the changes, press the Enter key to exit the DNS Configuration window. If you make any mistakes, simply press the Esc key to discard the changes.

13. You will return to the Configure Management Network menu options. Scroll down to the Custom DNS Suffixes option and review the information listed on the right. Press the Enter key to configure the Custom DNS Suffixes for this ESXi host. This will launch the Custom DNS Suffixes window.

14. Modify the Custom DNS Suffixes items as necessary. Once you are satisfied with the changes, press the Enter key to exit the Custom DNS Suffixes window. If you make any mistakes, simply press the Esc key to discard the changes.

15. You will now return to the Configure Management Network screen. Press the Esc key to exit. A Configure Management Network Confirmation screen will appear, as shown here.

(continued)

EXERCISE 2.12 *(continued)*

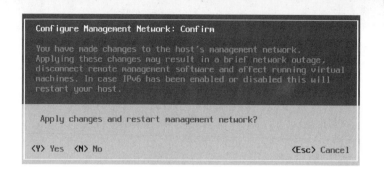

16. Press the Y key to save all the changes and exit the Configure Management Network screen. Press the N key to discard all changes and exit the Configure Network Management screen. You can also press the Esc key if you need to return to the Configure Management Network screen. For the purposes of this exercise, press the Y key.

17. You will return to the System Customization menu options, where you can use the Configure Management Network option to verify any changes you made. You can also use the Test Management Network option to verify that DNS and routing are working properly.

18. To test network connectivity, choose the Test Management Network option on the System Customization screen and then press the Enter key. The Test Management Network window will appear, as shown here.

```
Test Management Network

By default, this test will attempt to ping your default gateway
and DNS servers, and resolve your hostname.

Ping Address #0:       [ 192.168.113.1          ]
Ping Address #1:       [ 192.168.113.2          ]
Ping Address #2:       [                        ]
Resolve Hostname       [ ESXi1.test.local       ]

<Up/Down> Select              <Enter> OK  <Esc> Cancel
```

19. Use the up-arrow and down-arrow keys to enter values for the three ping addresses. Ensure that the ESXi hostname is listed in the Resolve Hostname field and press the Enter key to run the tests. The test will report a status of OK or Failed. Press the Enter key to exit the Testing Management Network window. Correct any failures before proceeding.

20. After verifying that the DNS and routing changes were successfully made, press the Esc key to exit the DCUI. Open the vSphere Client and connect to the ESXi host where DNS and routing were just configured or to the vCenter Server that manages this ESXi host.

21. Verify that the DNS and routing changes that were just performed in the DCUI are also reflected in the vSphere Client.

Restarting the management network can result in brief network outages. This could lead to service interruptions or unplanned downtime. Always proceed with caution when using this option. Even more important to remember is that if IPv6 is enabled or disabled, the ESXi host will be restarted automatically (without prompting) by the restart management network process.

Now that I have covered the steps required to configure DNS and routing from the vSphere Client and from the ESXi DCUI, you will learn how to configure hyperthreading on the ESXi host server.

Enabling, Configuring, and Disabling Hyperthreading

As it relates to vSphere, hyperthreading is an Intel-proprietary technology that is used to allow a processor to appear as two logical processors to the ESXi hypervisor. Before hyperthreading can be enabled in ESXi, it must first be enabled in the ESXi host system's BIOS. If you need assistance with enabling hyperthreading in your system's BIOS, consult the documentation for your particular system. Once the hardware is ready, the vSphere Client may be used to configure hyperthreading settings for ESXi.

Exercise 2.13 will cover the steps to configure hyperthreading for an ESXi host.

If you have an AMD processor, you are simply out of luck on this one.

EXERCISE 2.13

Enabling/Configuring/Disabling Hyperthreading

1. Open the vSphere Client and connect to the ESXi host or vCenter Server that is managing the ESXi host.

2. From the Inventory option, select the ESXi host you want to configure hyperthreading for and then click the Configuration tab in the right pane.

(continued)

EXERCISE 2.13 *(continued)*

3. Click the blue Processors link in the Hardware panel.

4. Review the current information. What is the current status of hyperthreading? To configure hyperthreading, click the blue Properties link in the top-right corner of the panel.

5. In the dialog box, you can turn hyperthreading off or on by selecting or deselecting the Enabled check box. Hyperthreading is turned on by default for host systems that fully support it, as shown here.

Processors	
General	
Hyperthreading	
☑ Enabled Physical Processors:	2
Logical Processors:	16
↺ Changes will not take effect until the system is restarted.	
OK Cancel Help	

6. Once hyperthreading is enabled or disabled, click the OK button to save the changes. While using the vSphere Client, you can review the hyperthreading status either in the Processors section of the Hardware Configuration screen or on the Summary tab for the ESXi host server.

Hyperthreading changes will not take effect until the ESXi host is rebooted.

Now that I've covered hyperthreading, I will move to the next objective of configuring the memory compression cache.

Enabling, Sizing, and Disabling Memory Compression Cache

When memory *overcommitment* is used, virtual machine performance can be improved through the use of memory compression. Memory compression works by compressing virtual pages and storing them in memory when an ESXi host becomes overcommitted. This is significantly faster than accessing the same pages from disk and can drive increased performance in overcommitted environments.

Like with many features in ESXi, you can customize the settings for the memory compression cache. Memory compression is enabled by default in ESXi, but it can be disabled using the vSphere Client. In Exercise 2.14, you will learn how to disable the memory compression cache and then enable it again.

EXERCISE 2.14

Enabling and Disabling the Memory Compression Cache

1. Open the vSphere Client and connect to the ESXi host or vCenter Server that is managing the ESXi host.

2. From the Inventory screen, select the ESXi host you want to configure the memory compression cache on and then click the Configuration tab in the right pane.

3. Choose the blue Advanced Settings link in the Software panel.

4. In the left pane of the Advanced Settings window, select Mem. Now locate the option titled Mem.MemZipEnable in the right pane.

(continued)

EXERCISE 2.14 *(continued)*

5. The Mem.MemZipEnable setting is used to enable or disable the memory com-
    pression cache. Notice the default value of 1. This means the memory compres-
    sion cache is enabled. Enter a value of 0 to disable the memory compression
    cache and click the OK button. An Update Option Values task will begin. When
    it completes, open the Advanced Settings window again and verify that the
    value of Mem.MemZipEnable has been changed to 0. The memory compression
    cache is now disabled.

6. Now change the value of Mem.MemZipEnable back to 1 to reenable the mem-
    ory compression cache; then verify that the value of Mem.MemZipEnable has
    been restored to 1.

7. Click OK to save the changes.

8. The memory compression cache is now disabled. Review the Mem.MemZip
    Enable value and verify that it is set to a value of 0.

9. Finally, change the Mem.MemZipEnable value to a value of 1 to leave it
    enabled. Unless you have a very robust test lab, the memory compression
    cache will likely be put to good use.

Exercise 2.14 covered how to turn the memory compression cache on and off. You can
next turn your attention toward sizing the compression cache. When virtual pages need to
be swapped, ESXi will first try to compress those pages instead. Compressed pages of 2KB
or less are then stored in the VM's compression cache. You can configure the maximum
size for the compression cache using the vSphere Client. Exercise 2.15 covers how to size
the memory compression cache.

EXERCISE 2.15

Sizing the Memory Compression Cache

1. Open the vSphere Client and connect to the ESXi host or vCenter Server that is
    managing the ESXi host.

2. From the Inventory screen, select the ESXi host you want to size the memory
    compression cache for and then click the Configuration tab in the right pane.

3. Choose the blue Advanced Settings link in the Software panel.

4. In the left pane of the Advanced Settings window, select Mem. Now locate the
    Mem.MemZipMaxPct option in the right pane.

    The value entered here determines the maximum size of the compression cache
    used for any individual virtual machine. This value represents a percentage

of the size of the virtual machine memory, and the value must be between 5 and 100. For example, if you enter **25** and a virtual machine's memory size is 1024MB, then the ESXi host can use up to 256MB of host memory to store the virtual machine's compressed pages.

5. Click OK to save the changes.

Now that I have covered the memory compression cache settings, I will move on to licensing an ESXi host.

Licensing an ESXi Host

Licensing in vSphere applies to vCenter Server, ESXi hosts, and solutions. Make sure to read the "Licensing vCenter Server" section earlier in this chapter on vCenter licensing, because the licensing information for ESXi is mostly a repeat of the information contained there. However, in the interest of covering this specific exam objective, Exercise 2.16 will walk you through the steps required to add a license key to an ESXi host.

 To account for the fact that you may not have actual license keys, there will be a screenshot provided in this exercise that details the final steps of licensing. If you do not have license keys, work through the exercise as far as you can.

EXERCISE 2.16

Adding License Keys to ESXi in Evaluation Mode

1. Connect to an ESXi host with the vSphere Client.

2. Select the ESXi host, and then select the Configuration tab from the right pane.

3. Choose the blue Licensed Features link in the Software panel.

4. Review the information presented on the screen, and then click the Edit link in the upper-right corner. An Assign License window will appear.

5. Select Assign A New License To This Host, and then press the Enter Key button to continue.

6. In the Add New License Key dialog, enter your ESXi host license key. Click the OK button to continue. The Assign License Dialog box will be presented.

(continued)

EXERCISE 2.16 *(continued)*

7. Click the OK button to assign the license.

8. Review the license information now shown in the vCenter Client to ensure that it is correct.

9. Next, obtain local console access to the ESXi host that was just licensed, and press the F2 key to log in to the DCUI.

10. When presented with the System Customization menu, scroll down to the View Support Information option and review the license serial number information.

Now that you have licensed an ESXi host with the vSphere Client and verified licensing with both the vSphere Client and the DCUI, I have covered all the steps of installing and configuring ESXi 5.

Up to this point, I have focused on new installations of vCenter Server and ESXi, but the final portion of this chapter will cover upgrading existing vCenter Server and ESXi installations.

Planning and Performing Upgrades of vCenter Server and VMware ESXi

Upgrading existing ESXi and vCenter Server systems is an important task for the virtual infrastructure administrator. vSphere has been around for quite some time, and the possibility of having to perform upgrades of existing vSphere environments is very real. I will start by identifying the upgrade requirements for ESXi hosts.

Identifying Upgrade Requirements for ESXi Hosts

The first step in upgrading ESXi hosts is to identify the upgrade requirements. It is important to be able to identify which hosts can be upgraded to ESXi 5 and to know which hosts will not be able to be upgraded to ESXi 5. Knowing the requirements for ESXi 5 is crucial in the upgrade process. The upgrade requirements include the following:

- A supported server platform that is listed on the VMware *Hardware Compatibility List* (HCL) at www.vmware.com/go/hcl

- 64-bit x86 CPUs

- Minimum of 2GB RAM

- One or more Gigabit or 10Gb Ethernet controllers listed in the VMware HCL

- A supported disk controller that is listed in the VMware HCL

 You can use the free VMware CPU Identification Utility to verify 64-bit capability with VMware. You can find it at www.vmware.com/download/shared_utilities.html.

It is also important to note that the following storage systems are supported for ESXi 5 installation and boot:

- SATA disk drives on supported SAS controllers

- SATA disk drives on supported onboard SATA controllers

- SAS disk drives

- Dedicated SAN disk on SAN (Fibre Channel or iSCSI)

- USB devices listed on the VMware HCL

ESXi can boot from disks larger than 2TB, provided that the system and controller card both support it.

In addition to the hardware requirements, it is also important to note the upgrade paths for existing vSphere 4.*x* implementations. Table 2.1 shows the upgrade paths to upgrade from ESX/ESXi 4.*x* to ESXi 5.

TABLE 2.1   ESXi 5 upgrade paths

Upgrade method	Upgrade from ESX/ESXi 4.*x* to ESXi 5
vSphere Update Manager	Yes
Interactive upgrade from media	Yes
Scripted upgrade	Yes
vSphere Auto Deploy	No
esxcli	No

 ESX/ESXi 3.*x* hosts are not supported for direct upgrade to ESXi 5. If you must upgrade ESX/ESXi 3.*x* hosts, you must first upgrade them to ESX/ESXi 4.*x*. It will typically be faster and easier to just perform a fresh install of ESXi 5 on these systems.

Now that I have covered the requirements and paths for upgrading existing ESXi hosts, I will next cover how to identify the steps required to upgrade a vSphere implementation.

Identifying Steps Required to Upgrade a vSphere Implementation

Many steps are required to upgrade a vSphere implementation, primarily because of the number of components involved. The first step is always to read the VMware vSphere 5 release notes for known issues. The release notes contain valuable information that can prevent you from wasting time with known issues. The vSphere 5 release notes are available here:

```
https://www.vmware.com/support/vsphere5/doc/vsphere-esx-vcenter-server-50-
release-notes.html
```

Once you've reviewed the release notes, it is time to take note of the ESXi hosts that will be upgraded. This includes the following items:

- Ensure that systems, and the components contained within, are all on the VMware HCL. Just because a server is on the HCL does not guarantee that all of its cards are going to be there as well. Always verify inclusion of all components in the VMware HCL.

- Ensure that server hardware for ESXi hosts is 64-bit.

- Ensure that the current ESX and ESXi versions are supported for upgrade to ESXi 5.

- Ensure that any plug-ins, agents, or scripts currently in use are compatible or available for ESXi 5.

- Run the vCenter Host Agent Pre-Upgrade Checker, available on the vCenter Server Installer media, to check for issues with existing agents on ESXi hosts.

For vCenter Server, a similar set of steps must be taken to ensure a successful upgrade. These include the following:

- Ensure that system requirements are met for all systems. This includes things such as having two processors in your vCenter Server.

- Ensure that the operating system used for vCenter Server is a supported version and that it is at the required patch level.

- Ensure that the database used for vCenter Server is a supported version and that it is at the required patch level.

- Ensure that a consistent full backup of the current vCenter Server database is available, prior to the vCenter upgrade.

- Ensure that the database permissions are set properly on the vCenter Server database.

- Ensure that the ODBC System DSN on the vCenter Server is using the proper driver and that it is a 64-bit DSN.

There are a few things to be aware of with vCenter upgrades, in relation to the 64-bit requirements introduced with vSphere 4.1:

- You can upgrade vCenter Server 4.*x* to vCenter Server 5 on the same machine if the vCenter Server 4.*x* instance is running on a 64-bit operating system.

- You cannot upgrade vCenter Server 4.*x* if it is running on Windows XP Professional x64, because vCenter Server 5 does not support Windows XP Professional x64.

- You can use the *Data Migration Tool* to upgrade to vCenter Server 5 if vCenter Server 4.*x* is installed on a 32-bit system.

- You can use the Data Migration Tool to upgrade to vCenter Server 5 if vCenter Server 2.5 U6 is installed on a 32-bit system.

- You can use the Data Migration Tool to migrate an existing SQL Server Express database from a previous vCenter Server 4.*x* install.

- You can use the native tools provided by the database manufacturer to move a locally installed database on a 32-bit vCenter Server 4.*x* instance to the 64-bit OS that will house the vCenter Server 5 instance.

After all the compatibility issues have been sorted out, the general sequence of events for upgrading a vSphere implementation is as follows:

1. Upgrade vCenter Server.

2. Upgrade vSphere Client.

3. Upgrade Update Manager (if applicable).

4. Upgrade ESX/ESXi hosts.

5. Upgrade VMware Tools in virtual machines.

6. Upgrade virtual hardware in virtual machines.

Again, this is the general sequence of events in a vSphere upgrade, and certain environments will likely have additional steps. An example of one of these additional steps could be "install new SAN multipathing agents" on the ESXi host. For any vSphere upgrade, a key component to success is the proper planning up front.

Now that I have discussed the sequence of events in a vSphere upgrade, I will discuss how to perform upgrades of vNetwork Distributed Switches and VMFS-3 datastores. These are important upgrades, in that they allow you to leverage some of the new features available only in vSphere 5.

Upgrading a vNetwork Distributed Switch

A version 4.0.0 or 4.1.0 vSphere *distributed switch* (dvSwitch) can be upgraded to the 5.0.0 version after the vCenter 5 and ESXi 5 upgrades are both complete. This is because the version 5.0.0 dvSwitch is compatible only with ESXi 5 and newer and will be available only after vCenter Server is running at version 5.

The dvSwitch upgrade will allow the distributed switch to take advantage of the latest set of features available in the vSphere 5 release. Exercise 2.17 details how to upgrade an existing version 4.0.0 dvSwitch to the 5.0.0 version. Note that virtual switches will be covered in great detail in Chapter 4, so this exercise may be more useful when revisited later.

EXERCISE 2.17

Upgrading a vNetwork Distributed Switch

1. Open the vSphere Client and connect to the vCenter Server 5 that is managing an ESXi 5 host with a version 4.0.0 or 4.1.0 dvSwitch.

2. From the vCenter Server inventory, select the Networking view.

3. Select a vSphere distributed switch from the inventory listed in the left pane.

4. On the Summary tab, locate the General section. Inside this box, there is a version listed for the dvSwitch. Beside the version, there will be a yellow icon and a link to upgrade the dvSwitch, as shown here.

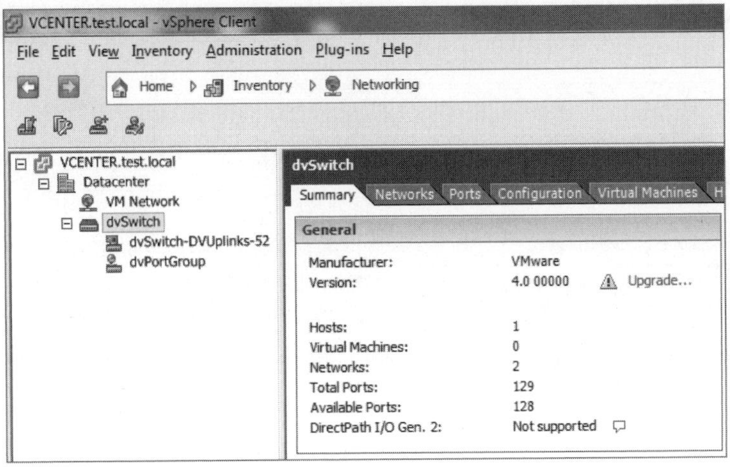

5. Click the Upgrade link to begin. The Upgrade vSphere Distributed Switch To Newer Version Wizard will launch, as shown here.

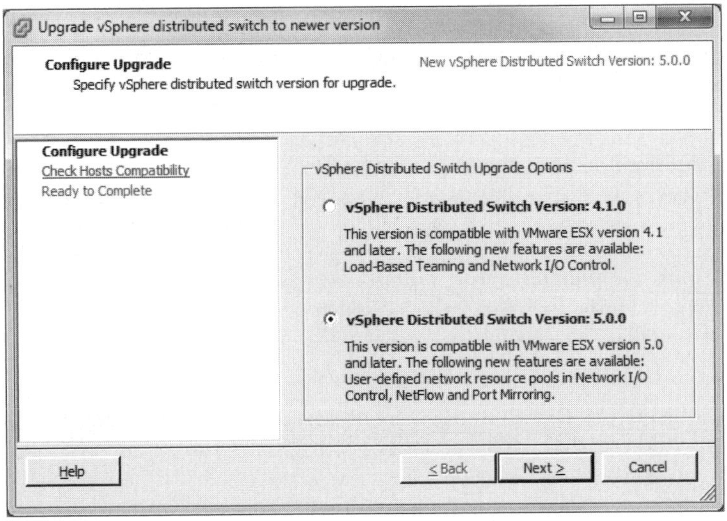

6. Review the information here that details the dvSwitch release information and new features. Select the vSphere Distributed Switch Version 5.0.0 option and click the Next button to continue.

7. The wizard will list the ESX/ESXi hosts associated with this dvSwitch and their compatibility with the selected dvSwitch version to be upgraded, as shown here.

(continued)

Upgrade vSphere distributed switch to newer version

Check Hosts Compatibility   New vSphere Distributed Switch Version: 5.0.0
Verify that hosts are compatible with the selected vSphere distributed switch version.

Configure Upgrade
Check Hosts Compatibility
Ready to Complete

Hosts Compatibility

Host	Compatibility with the new VDS version
esxi1.test.local	Compatible

All VMware ESX Server members of the vSphere distributed switch
are compatible with the new vSphere distributed switch version.
You may proceed with the upgrade.

Help   ≤ Back   Next ≥   Cancel

8. You can proceed with the upgrade only if all the listed hosts are compatible with the new dvSwitch version. Verify compatibility, and then click the Next button to continue.

9. Verify the information presented on the Ready To Complete screen, and then click the Finish button to perform the dvSwitch upgrade. A vSphere Distributed Switch Product Specification Operation task will begin.

10. When this task completes, review the General section of the Summary tab for the dvSwitch to verify that the new dvSwitch version is listed as 5.0.0.

vNetwork Distributed Switches cannot be downgraded to previous vSphere dvSwitch versions.

Now that I've covered upgrading a dvSwitch, I will cover the process to upgrade a datastore from VMFS-3 to VMFS-5.

Upgrading from VMFS-3 to VMFS-5

VMFS-5 is the latest version of VMware's *Virtual Machine File System* (VMFS). VMFS-5 is another major improvement in vSphere 5, and it will be covered in detail in Chapter 5. Chapter 5 will also cover the exam objective of upgrading a VMFS-3 datastore to VMFS-5, so for now Figure 2.5 shows a preview.

FIGURE 2.5   Upgrade to VMFS-5 dialog

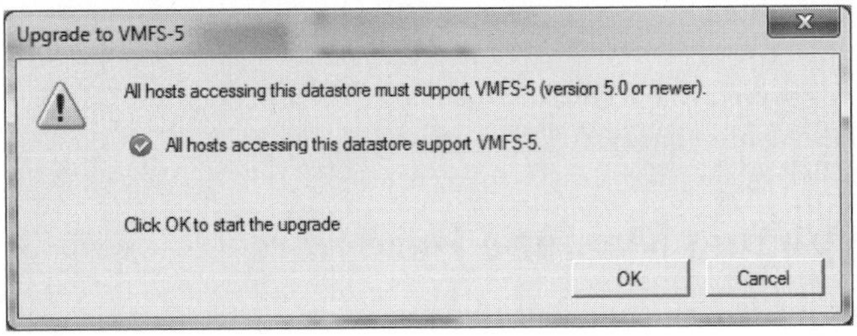

You can now turn your attention back to completing the updated sequence for a virtual infrastructure. Remembering the sequence, you have upgraded vCenter Server, the vSphere Client, and ESX/ESXi hosts, so now it is time to upgrade the VMware Tools in your virtual machines.

Upgrading VMware Tools

For any virtual infrastructure administrator, the process of updating *VMware Tools* should be a very familiar one. VMware Tools is used to enhance the performance of a VM's guest operating system but are not required for guest operating system functionality.

You can upgrade VMware Tools manually, or you can configure virtual machines to check and upgrade automatically during power cycles of the VM. You can also use Update Manager to upgrade VMware Tools. The procedure for installing VMware Tools manually is unchanged in vSphere 5 and consists of the following steps:

1. Open a console session to the VM.

2. Use the Guest ➤ Install/Upgrade VMware Tools menu option to mount the CD-ROM image containing VMware Tools.

3. On Windows guests, the setup will begin, or you will be prompted to run the installer. On Linux guests, you will extract the contents of the tar.gz file and then run the **./vmware-install.pl** command to begin the setup.

4. Follow the prompts, and customize as required.

VMware recommends upgrading VMware Tools to the latest release available for the best performance. The version of VMware Tools that is included with vSphere 5 is supported on both vSphere 4.*x* and vSphere 5 virtual machines. And of course, the version of VMware Tools included in vSphere 4.*x* is supported in vSphere 5. Since having VMware Tools is not a requirement for the guest OS, it is also not required that the vSphere 4.*x* version of VMware Tools be upgraded to the latest supported version.

VMware Tools included in releases prior to vSphere 4.x is not supported.

Now that I have covered the VMware Tools upgrade process, I will cover the steps to upgrade the virtual machine hardware.

Upgrading Virtual Machine Hardware

Virtual machines have hardware versions associated with them. This virtual machine hardware version indicates the hardware features available in the virtual machine and can include things like the BIOS or EFI, number of CPUs, maximum memory configuration, and more. When a virtual machine is created using the vSphere Client, you can use the Custom option to choose the version of the virtual hardware. By default new virtual machines will be created, with the latest version of the virtual hardware available on the host where the VM is being created.

vSphere 5 introduces the new virtual hardware version 8. ESXi 5 fully supports virtual hardware versions 8 and 7. This means that virtual hardware versions 8 and 7 can be created, edited, and run on vSphere 5. ESXi 5 also allows virtual hardware version 4 to be edited and run, but no new virtual hardware version 4 VMs can be created. Table 2.2 shows the ESX/ESXi host and virtual hardware version compatibility.

TABLE 2.2 ESX/ESXi host and virtual hardware compatibility

	Version 8	Version 7	Version 4	Compatible with vCenter Server version
ESXi 5	Create, edit, run	Create, edit, run	Edit, run	vCenter Server 5
ESX/ESXi 4.x	Not Supported	Create, edit, run	Create, edit, run	vCenter Server 4.x
ESX/ESXi 3.x	Not supported	Not supported	Create, edit, run	vCenter Server 2.x and newer

For those environments that may still have virtual hardware version 3 virtual machines, ESXi 5 allows these VMs to be upgraded to virtual hardware version 8.

A normal part of any ESX/ESXi host upgrade is to upgrade virtual machines to the new virtual hardware version. The process, much like the VMware Tools upgrade, is quite familiar to experienced virtual infrastructure administrators. The virtual hardware can be upgraded as a manual process, and Update Manager can also be used to perform orchestrated VMware Tools and virtual hardware upgrades.

To update the virtual hardware manually, follow these steps:

1. Right-click any eligible powered-off virtual machine in the ESXi or vCenter Server inventory and choose the Upgrade Virtual Hardware option. The Upgrade Virtual Hardware menu option will be missing if the virtual machine is powered on or already running virtual hardware version 8.

2. Review the confirmation screen and click Yes to begin the virtual hardware upgrade.

3. An Upgrade Virtual Hardware task will appear in the Recent Tasks list. When this task completes, verify that the VM is now reporting VM Version: 8 in the Summary tab for the VM.

The virtual hardware upgrade is an irreversible operation that can make the VM incompatible with previous versions of vSphere. VMware Converter is a useful tool for changing virtual hardware versions, if there is ever a later need to change virtual hardware versions.

The virtual machine hardware is typically the final item to be updated in a virtual infrastructure upgrade. This concludes your journey through upgrading a vSphere implementation. You will next learn how to use vCenter Update Manager to upgrade an existing ESXi host.

Upgrading an ESXi Host Using vSphere Update Manager

vSphere Update Manager is used for upgrading, migrating, updating, and patching clustered hosts, virtual machines, and guest operating systems. VMware recommends that those using vCenter Server also use vSphere Update Manager for host upgrades.

One item to be aware of when using vSphere Update Manager is that ESX hosts must have more than 350MB of free space in the /boot partition to support using Update Manager for the ESXi 5 upgrade. This will typically exclude ESX 4.*x* hosts that were upgraded from an ESX 3.*x* version; it could exclude some ESX 4.*x* hosts as well depending on the partitioning scheme that was used during installation. If this free space requirement is not met and Update Manager is not an option, you will have to use an interactive or scripted upgrade. These issues will not be present in Exercise 2.18, though, since you will be using Update Manager to upgrade an ESXi 4.1 host.

If you do not currently have access to Update Manager, it may be beneficial to review the Update Manager content in Chapter 9 or revisit this exercise at a later time.

If you are using vSphere Update Manager to upgrade or migrate an ESX/ESXi host to ESXi 5, static IP addresses are required for the hosts to be upgraded.

EXERCISE 2.18

Upgrading an ESXi Host Using vSphere Update Manager

1. Open the vSphere Client and connect to a vCenter Server 5 in which Update Manager 5 is registered.

2. Launch Update Manager from the Home page, under the Solutions And Applications section.

3. Once Update Manager loads, click the ESXi Images tab. In the upper-right corner locate the Import ESXi Image link and click it.

4. The Import ESXi Image Wizard will launch. Click the Browse button and then locate the ESXi 5 image (.ISO) file, as shown here.

5. Click the Next button to continue. The image will begin to upload, and a Security Warning window will appear.

   These warnings appear because a trusted certificate authority did not sign the certificates. If you trust these certificates, select the Install This Certificate check box and click the Ignore button to continue. An Import ESXi Image task will begin in vCenter, and the file upload progress will also be shown in the Import ESXi Image Wizard.

6. When the file upload completes, verify that the upload was successful. Click the Next button to continue.

7. Ensure that the Create A Baseline Using The ESXi Image check box is selected and give the baseline a name and description, as shown here.

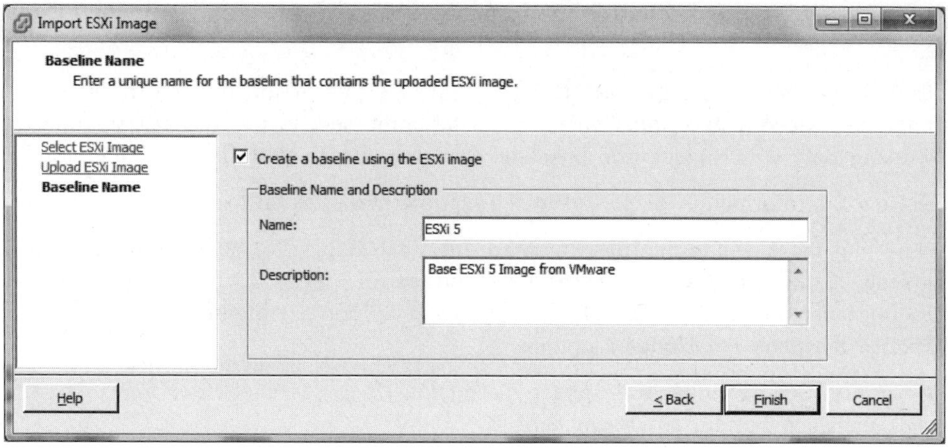

8. Click the Finish button to continue. Review the information under the Imported ESXi Images section of the ESXi Images tab in Update Manager and verify that everything is listed properly.

9. Next, select the Baselines And Groups tab and verify that the baseline you just created appears in the Baselines pane on the left.

10. To actually upgrade the ESXi 4.1 host with the ESXi 5 image you just uploaded, the next step is to create a host upgrade baseline. Select Home from the navigation bar and then choose Hosts And Clusters from the Inventory section.

11. Select the ESXi 4.1 host and then select the Update Manager tab.

12. Click the Attach link in the upper-right corner. Select the baseline you created in step 7 of this activity by selecting its check box, as shown here.

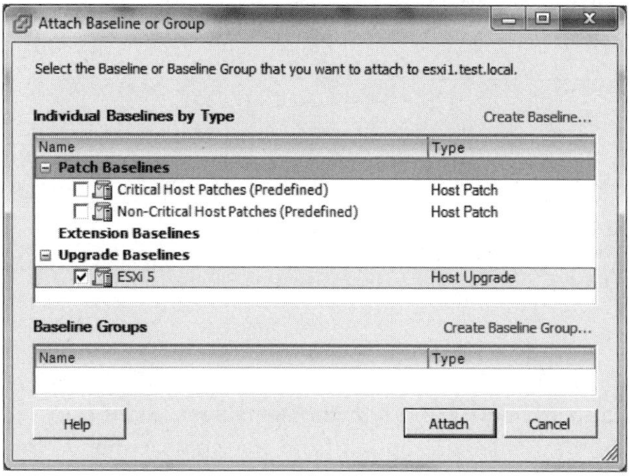

(continued)

EXERCISE 2.18 *(continued)*

13. Leave the Baseline Groups section blank, because this option is used to allow upgrade baselines and patch baselines to be combined. In this activity, you are working only with an upgrade baseline. Click the Attach button to continue.

14. Review the information displayed in the Update Manager tab.

15. Now that the baseline has been created, the next step is to manually initiate a scan of the ESXi 4.1 host. In the left pane, select the ESXi 4.1 host that will be upgraded to ESXi 5 and right-click it. From the context menu that appears, choose the Scan For Updates option.

16. A Confirm Scan window will appear. Select the Upgrades check box and then click the Scan button, as shown here.

17. A Scan Entity task will appear in the Recent Tasks list. When this task completes, review the scan results and noncompliance states shown in the Update Manager tab. The results will appear similar to those shown here.

18. The final step is to remediate the noncompliant host. Right-click the ESXi 4.1 host and choose the Remediate option from the context menu. The Remediate Wizard will begin.

19. On the Remediation Selection screen, choose the baseline created in step 7 of this activity, as shown here, and then click the Next button to continue.

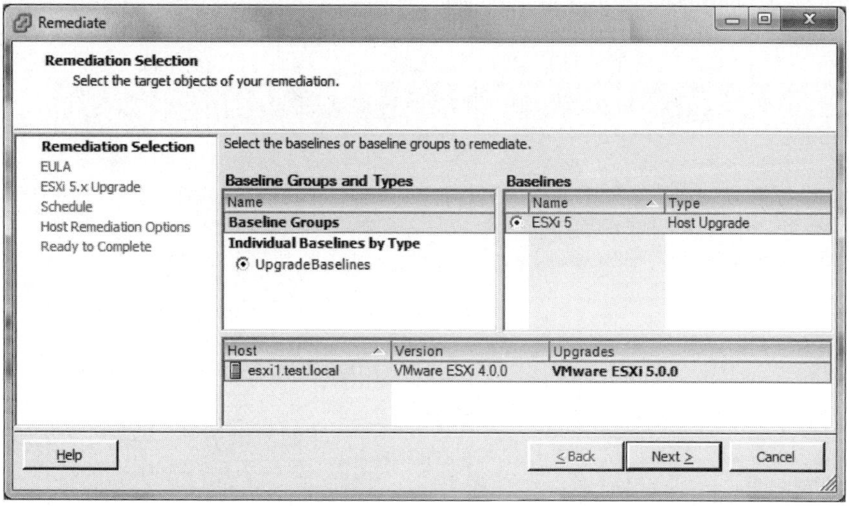

20. Review and accept the terms of the EULA. Select the I Accept The Terms And License Agreement check box and then click the Next button to continue.

21. On the next screen, check the option to ignore third-party software that is incompatible with the upgrade and click the Next button to continue. Note that if you omit this option and third-party software that is incompatible is installed on the hosts, the upgrade remediation will fail.

22. Give the task a name and description and choose a time for it to run. Click the Next button to continue.

The next two screens cover *maintenance mode* and cluster remediation options. The ESXi 5 upgrade will obviously require the ESXi 4.1 host to be put into maintenance mode. Depending on the feature set in use in your specific VMware environment, DRS and vMotion could be used to keep VMs up and running on other hosts during this upgrade. Base your decisions on the options presented in these screens around the specific features in use in your environment.

23. Click the Next button to continue.

24. Review the information presented in the summary for accuracy. If everything is correct, click the Finish button to begin the ESXi 5 upgrade.

25. A Remediate Entity task will appear in the Recent Tasks list. A series of other tasks will also appear in the Recent Tasks list while the upgrade takes place. When the Remediate Entity task completes, the upgrade is complete.

(continued)

EXERCISE 2.18 *(continued)*

26. Review the scan results and noncompliance states shown on the Update Manager tab. The results will appear similar to those shown here.

esxi1.test.local VMware ESXi, 5.0.0, 469512

| Summary | Virtual Machines | Resource Allocation | Performance | Configuration | Tasks & Events | Alarms | Permissio |

Name contains: [   ]   Clear   Scan...   Attach...   Help   Admin View

Attached Baseline Groups		Attached Baselines		Type	Host Compliance	# Hosts
✓ All Groups and Independent Baseli... ▶		✓ All	▶		🖥 All Applicable Hosts	1
		✓ ESXi 5		Upgr..	⊗ Non-Compliant	0
					⚠ Incompatible	0
					⊘ Unknown	0
					✓ Compliant	1

Compliant

All Groups and Independent Baselines -> All -> ⊗ Non-Compliant Hosts

Host Name	Patches	Upgrades	Extensions	Last Patch ...

[Hide Hosts]   🛡 Stage...   🛡 Remediate...

WARNING   In the event that the upgrade is unsuccessful, you cannot roll back to the previous ESX/ESXi 4.*x* instance. A fresh install would be the likely solution.

As you can see, vSphere Update Manager can simplify and automate much of the vSphere upgrade process. This capability alone makes it a very useful solution, especially when multiple ESXi hosts are involved. As good as Update Manager is, there may be times when an upgrade is simply just not the right choice. The next section will discuss determining when upgrades are appropriate.

Determining Whether an In-Place Upgrade Is Appropriate in a Given Upgrade Scenario

An in-place upgrade for ESXi is an upgrade performed on the same ESX/ESXi host on which a version of ESX/ESXi is already running. Sometimes an in-place upgrade may not be appropriate for a given vSphere environment. One scenario where this is true is for ESX/ESXi 3.*x* hosts. These hosts are not supported for direct upgrade to ESXi 5 and instead require a prerequisite upgrade to ESX/ESXi 4.*x*. In this scenario, it is likely easier and faster to just perform a fresh install of ESXi 5. It is also possible that the hardware these

ESX/ESXi 3.*x* systems are installed on may no longer be on the VMware HCL or meet the system requirements for ESXi 5.

Another scenario that may not be appropriate is for an ESX 4.*x* host that was upgraded from ESX 3.*x* with a partition layout that is incompatible with ESXi 5. In many cases, especially when changing from ESX to ESXi implementations, it is often easier and less complicated to perform a fresh install of ESXi 5.

Another consideration is to ensure compatibility of any VMware solutions or plug-ins before upgrading the vSphere environment. This is also true for items such as backup agents running on ESX hosts. Leveraging the new features of vSphere 5 at the cost of losing backup capability for VMs is not likely an acceptable solution. Every upgrade scenario will have its own unique set of requirements, and knowing when to upgrade or start fresh is an important part of the virtual administrator's responsibilities.

Summary

This chapter covered identifying the available vCenter Server editions, along with licensing, database sizing, and availability requirements for vCenter Servers. These topics are important in knowing how to plan and implement any vSphere environment.

You installed many VMware products in this chapter. This chapter was purposefully heavy on exercises; the reason for this is that you should be expected to have actual experience installing and using these VMware products. Knowing what these products do, and actually using the products, is key to doing well on the VCP5 exam.

This chapter also covered installing ESXi interactively and with Auto Deploy. You configured various settings on the ESXi hosts using the vSphere Client and the DCUI. Always be thinking about whether there are multiple ways to accomplish the same task in vSphere, and be sure you know those different ways.

Finally, this chapter covered upgrading vCenter Server and ESX/ESXi hosts. Identifying upgrade requirements for ESX/ESXi hosts and vCenter Servers is another key part of designing and building a virtual infrastructure. It also covered the sequence of events for upgrading a vSphere environment. This is important, because some components depend on other components. This chapter also covered how to upgrade to new versions of dvSwitches, VMFS, VMware Tools, and virtual machine hardware versions, because these are important parts of any upgrade to vSphere 5.

Exam Essentials

Know how to install vCenter Server 5, vCenter Server Appliance, vSphere Client, vSphere Web Client, and the various vCenter Support Tools. Understand the process of installing each of these products. Know the available vCenter Server editions and their differences. Know how to size the vCenter Server database. Know how to install/remove and enable/

disable vSphere Client plug-ins. Know how to license vCenter Server. Know how to determine availability requirements for a vCenter Server in a given vSphere implementation. Know how to determine use cases for the vSphere Client and the vSphere Web Client.

Know how to install and configure VMware ESXi.   Understand how to perform an interactive installation of ESXi. Know how to deploy an ESXi host using Auto Deploy. Know how to configure NTP, DNS and routing, hyperthreading, and the memory compression cache on an ESXi host. Know how to license an ESXi host.

Know how to plan and perform upgrades of vCenter Server and VMware ESXi.   Understand how to identify upgrade requirements for ESX/ESXi hosts. Know how to identify the steps required to upgrade a vSphere implementation. Know how to upgrade a vNetwork Distributed Switch, VMFS-3 volumes, VMware Tools, and virtual machine hardware. Know how to use Update Manager to upgrade an ESXi host to ESXi 5. Know how to determine whether an in-place upgrade is appropriate in a given upgrade scenario.

Review Questions

1. The version of VMware Tools included with vSphere 5 is supported on virtual machines in which vSphere versions? (Choose all that apply.)

    A. ESX 2.*x*

    B. ESX/ESXi 3.*x*

    C. ESX/ESXi 4.*x*

    D. ESX/ESXi 5

2. vCenter Server comes bundled with a Microsoft SQL Server 2008 R2 Express edition database. This bundled database is supported for up to how many hosts?

    A. 5

    B. 10

    C. 20

    D. Unlimited

3. When installing ESXi 5 interactively, the *root* user password is required to be how many characters?

    A. 6

    B. 7

    C. 8

    D. 0

4. A separate license server is required to manage which of the following hosts?

    A. ESXi 5

    B. ESX/ESXi 4.*x*

    C. ESX/ESXi 3.*x*

    D. All of the above

5. You plan to install vCenter Server 5 in a virtual machine. The vCenter Server will use a remote SQL database and will support 2 hosts and 15 virtual machines. How many vCPUs should you start with when building this VM? (Choose two.)

    A. One vCPU with two cores

    B. Two vCPUs with one core

    C. Three vCPUs with two cores

    D. Four vCPUs with one core

6. You have a three-node ESXi cluster that has recently been upgraded to use vCenter Server 5. After you upgrade the first host to ESXi 5, you notice the option to upgrade the dvSwitch to version 5.0.0. What must you do to upgrade the dvSwitch?

    A. Follow the upgrade procedure and upgrade the dvSwitch to the latest version.

> **B.** Upgrade one of the remaining two hosts to ESXi 5 and then follow the upgrade procedure to upgrade the dvSwitch to the latest version.
>
> **C.** Upgrade the remaining two hosts to ESXi 5 and then follow the upgrade procedure to upgrade the dvSwitch to the latest version.
>
> **D.** None of these are correct.

7. ESXi 5 can edit and run which virtual machine hardware versions? (Choose all that apply.)

   A. 8

   B. 7

   C. 4

   D. 3

8. What is the first item to be updated in the sequence of events in a vSphere upgrade?

   A. vCenter Server

   B. ESXi hosts

   C. Update Manager

   D. vSphere Client

9. What are two technologies that Auto Deploy relies on?

   A. RDP

   B. PXE

   C. DHCP

   D. SSL

10. ESXi 5 has a system requirement of a minimum of how many processor cores?

   A. 1

   B. 2

   C. 4

   D. 8

11. Which of the following can be used to apply license keys to an ESXi host? (Choose all that apply.)

   A. DCUI

   B. ESXi Shell

   C. vSphere Client

   D. vSphere Web Client

12. Which advanced setting is used to enable/disable the memory compression cache?

   A. Mem.BalancePeriod

   B. Mem.MemZipEnable

   C. Mem.ShareVmkEnable

   D. Mem.MemZipMaxPct

13. Which of the following can be used to configure DNS and routing settings for an ESXi host? (Choose all that apply.)

    A. vSphere Client

    B. vSphere Web Client

    C. Service Console

    D. DCUI

14. You have a virtual machine administrator who has Linux installed on her laptop. She needs to perform day-to-day operations of a Windows VM that she is responsible for. Which client application should she use?

    A. vSphere Client

    B. vCenter Client

    C. vSphere Web Client

    D. vCenter Remote Client

15. Which of the following vCenter Server Support Tools are available for install from the VMware vCenter installer? (Choose all that apply.)

    A. VMware ESXi Dump Collector

    B. VMware Syslog Collector

    C. VMware Auto Deploy

    D. VMware vSphere Authentication Proxy

16. VMware vCenter Server Standard is used in which of the following vSphere 5 Kits? (Choose all that apply.)

    A. Essentials Plus

    B. Standard

    C. Advanced

    D. Enterprise Plus

17. What is the minimum disk space required for the vCenter Server Appliance?

    A. 7GB

    B. 25GB

    C. 50GB

    D. 80GB

18. You right-click a VM in an ESXi 5 host and the Upgrade Virtual Hardware option is not available in the context menu. What are two possible reasons for this?

    A. The VM is running VM version 8.

    B. The VM is not running the latest VMware Tools version.

    C. The VM is powered on.

    D. The VM has an active snapshot.

19. Which of the following is a requirement for using Update Manager to update an existing ESX/ESXi host?

   A. The ESXi host must use dynamic IP addressing.

   B. Then ESXi host must use static IP addressing.

   C. vCenter Server Appliance needs to be installed.

   D. ESXi Dump Collector needs to be installed.

20. Which of the following utilities are supported for ESXi 5 upgrades from ESX/ESXi 4.*x* versions?

   A. `esxcli`

   B. `esxupdate`

   C. `vihostupdate`

   D. None of the above

Chapter 3

Secure vCenter Server and ESXi and Identify vSphere Architecture and Solutions

VCP5 EXAM OBJECTIVES COVERED IN THIS CHAPTER:

✓ **Secure vCenter Server and ESXi**

- Identify common vCenter Server privileges and roles
- Describe how permissions are applied and inherited in vCenter Server
- Configure and administer the ESXi firewall
- Enable/Configure/Disable services in the ESXi firewall
- Enable Lockdown Mode
- Configure network security policies
- View/Sort/Export user and group lists
- Add/Modify/Remove permissions for users and groups on vCenter Server inventory objects
- Create/Clone/Edit vCenter Server Roles
- Add an ESXi Host to a directory service
- Apply permissions to ESXi Hosts using Host Profiles
- Determine the appropriate set of privileges for common tasks in vCenter Server

✓ **Identify vSphere Architecture and Solutions**

- Identify available vSphere editions and features
- Explain ESXi and vCenter Server architectures
- Explain Private/Public/Hybrid cloud concepts
- Determine appropriate vSphere edition based on customer requirements

This chapter will cover the remaining two objectives of Section 1 of the VCP5 exam blueprint. Chapter 2 focused on planning, installing, configuring, and upgrading vCenter Server and VMware ESXi. This chapter will focus on securing vCenter Server and ESXi, in addition to identifying vSphere architecture and solutions. In other words, vCenter Server and ESXi are installed and running, and now you need to secure them and be able to identify which products and solutions you need.

   This chapter will cover identifying the common vCenter Server privileges and roles. It will also describe how permissions are applied and inherited in vCenter Server. Configuring and administering the ESXi firewall will be covered, including how to configure services. Configuring lockdown mode for ESXi hosts will be covered, along with configuring network security policies. It will cover how to view, sort, and export user and group lists in vCenter and how to apply permissions for users and groups on vCenter Server inventory objects. It will also cover how to work with vCenter Server roles, add an ESXi host to a directory service, and apply permissions to ESXi hosts using host profiles. Determining the appropriate set of privileges for common tasks in vCenter Server will also be covered.

   Finally, this chapter will cover identifying available vSphere editions and features. The ESXi and vCenter Server architectures will be explained, along with private, public, and hybrid cloud concepts. Determining the appropriate vSphere edition based on customer requirements will round out the chapter.

Securing vCenter Server and ESXi

Knowing how to secure ESXi hosts and vCenter Server is a very important part of any virtual administrator's responsibilities. VMware includes many features to protect ESXi and vCenter Server and all its inventory objects. These features include the ability to set granular permissions, a firewall, virtual switch layer 2 security, directory authentication mechanisms, and more. Knowing the capabilities of these features and how to use them is crucial for both the planning and ongoing maintenance of vSphere environments. The first features I will cover are the common vCenter Server privileges and roles. These roles and privileges can be used to secure the many inventory objects available in vCenter Server.

Identifying Common vCenter Server Privileges and Roles

When vCenter Server is installed, there will be a common set of *privileges* and *roles* available by default. Privileges define individual user rights, and roles are a collection of privileges. I will cover the roles first. There are three default system roles, and six sample roles included by default in vCenter Server, as shown in Figure 3.1.

FIGURE 3.1 System and sample roles

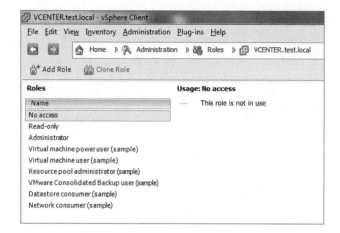

The three default system roles are as follows:

- No Access
- Read-Only
- Administrator

The three system roles are permanent, meaning they cannot be modified in any way. These three default system roles will likely be used in many environments. For example, No Access and Read-Only are very useful for quickly and effectively restricting user access.

The six default sample roles are as follows:

- Virtual Machine Power User
- Virtual Machine User
- Resource Pool Administrator
- VMware Consolidated Backup User
- Datastore Consumer
- Network Consumer

The default sample roles can be used as is or as guidelines for creating custom roles. Although it is possible to use the default sample roles, it is considered best practice not to modify them. If a sample role needs to be modified, consider cloning it instead. You can then modify the cloned sample role accordingly. The benefit of using this approach is that it allows the original sample role to be retained for future reference.

You can also create roles directly on ESXi hosts. However, these roles will not be accessible from within vCenter Server.

Now that I've explained the common roles, I will cover the privileges that each role can contain. Privileges define individual user rights. Figure 3.2 shows some of the available privileges that can be assigned to a role.

FIGURE 3.2   Privileges assignable to roles

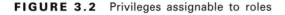

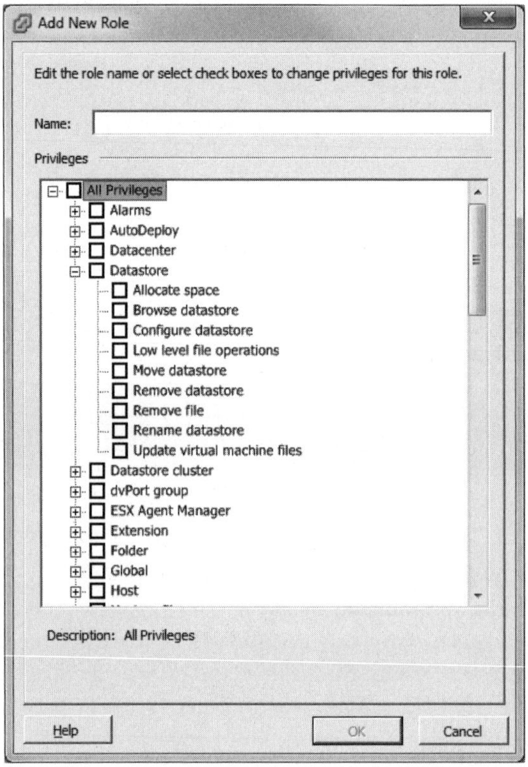

The number of privileges is quite large, and this can lead to some interesting capabilities for users. It is highly recommended that you take some time to review the available privileges that may be assigned to the sample or custom roles.

It is important to remember that privileges define individual user rights and that roles are collections of privileges. A *permission* is then created by pairing a role with a user or group and associating it with an object in the vCenter Server inventory. The next section will focus on how these permissions are applied and inherited in vCenter Server.

Describing How Permissions Are Applied and Inherited in vCenter Server

Now that you know how privileges and roles work in vCenter Server, you must next understand how permissions work in vCenter. If you happened to skip to this section without reading the preceding section on roles and privileges, it might be worthwhile to review the information there. If you have a good understanding of vCenter Server roles and privileges, then read on.

Permissions are applied in vCenter Server by pairing a user or group with a role. This pair is then associated with an object in the vCenter Server inventory to create the permission. In a default vCenter Server configuration, members of the local Windows Administrators group have the same permissions as a user who is assigned the Administrator role at the root vCenter level. A user with Administrator privileges must assign permissions to other non-Administrative users, because these users will by default have no permissions on any of the vCenter Server inventory objects.

Two forms of permissions apply to vCenter Server inventory objects: managed entities and global entities. Managed entities, which include clusters, datacenters, folders, and hosts, may have permissions assigned on them. Global entities, which include things such as licenses, roles, sessions, and custom fields, cannot have permissions assigned on them and instead will derive their permissions from the root vCenter level.

When permissions are assigned to inventory objects, permission inheritance or propagation must also be considered. When permissions are assigned to vCenter Server inventory objects, permission propagation is one of the configurable settings. In the Assign Permissions window, you can select the Propagate To Child Objects check box, as shown in Figure 3.3, to enable the propagation of permissions down the inventory hierarchy.

FIGURE 3.3   Propagate To Child Objects option

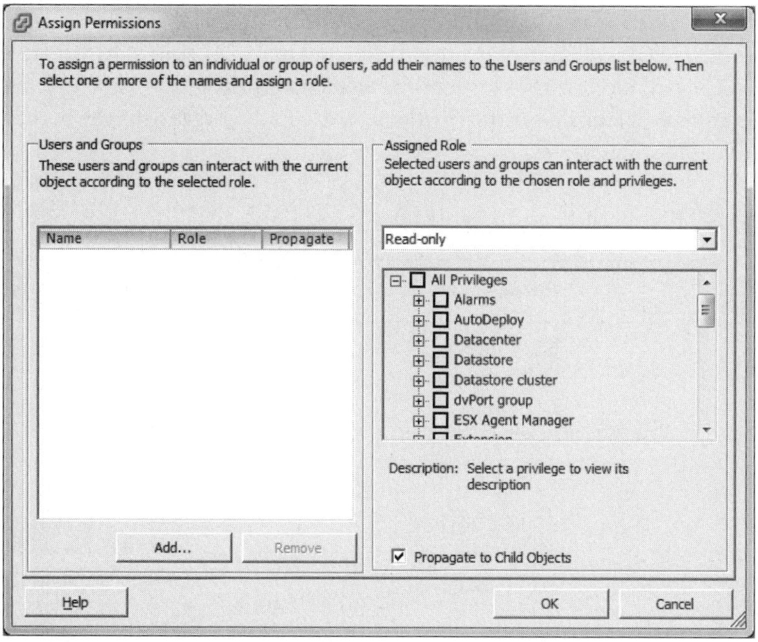

Every permission assigned will have the option to enable propagation, but it is important to remember that propagation is not universally applied. Any permission defined directly on a child object will override permissions propagated from parent objects.

Inventory objects can inherit permissions from multiple parent objects in the hierarchy, but objects can have only one permission for each user or group. For example, assume there is a user who is a member of two groups in Active Directory. Each of these Active Directory groups is given different permissions on a single virtual machine. This user will have the union of the permissions. This is because an inventory object, the virtual machine in this case, will inherit multiple permissions.

This same example would have seen a different outcome, if there had been a permission defined on the virtual machine for this user. Remember, user permissions take precedence over any group permissions.

WARNING   Before assigning a permission with a restrictive role to a group, verify that the group does not contain the Administrator account or any other accounts with administrative privileges.

Now that I have covered how permissions are applied and inherited in vCenter Server, you can turn your attention to securing ESXi via its firewall.

Configuring and Administering the ESXi Firewall

vSphere 5 includes a new firewall that sits between the ESXi host's management interface and the network. The access control is provided through a VMkernel network adapter (*vmknic*)–level firewall module that inspects packets against firewall rules. The firewall is enabled by default and blocks all traffic by default, except for traffic for the management services listed in Table 3.1.

TABLE 3.1   TCP and UDP port access in vSphere 5

Port	Purpose	Traffic type
22	SSH server	TCP in
53	DNS client	UDP in and out
68	DHCP client	UDP in and out
161	SNMP server	UDP in
80	HTTP access	TCP in
427	CIM client	UDP in and out

Port	Purpose	Traffic type
443	HTTPS access	TCP in
902	Authentication, provisioning, VM migration, VM consoles, heartbeat	TCP in and out UDP out
1234	Host-based replication	TCP out
1235	Host-based replication	TCP out
5988	CIM transactions over HTTP	TCP in
5989	CIM transactions over HTTPS	TCP in and out
8000	Requests from vMotion	TCP in and out
8100	vSphere Fault Tolerance (FT)	TCP and UDP in and out
8200	vSphere Fault Tolerance (FT)	TCP and UDP in and out

 The ESXi firewall also allows Internet Control Message Protocol (ICMP) traffic.

The vSphere Client is the preferred way to manage the ESXi firewall, but the `esxcli` command can also be used to administer the ESXi firewall. In Exercise 3.1, you will use the vSphere Client to configure the ESXi firewall and disable the NTP Client.

EXERCISE 3.1

Disabling the NTP Client in the ESXi Firewall

1. Connect to a vCenter Server with the vSphere Client.

2. Choose an ESXi host from the inventory and select it.

3. Click the Configuration tab for the ESXi host and then click the blue Security Profile link in the Software panel.

4. In the middle of the screen, there is a listing of the firewall connections. Click the blue Properties link in the right margin to view the ESXi firewall properties.

(continued)

5. Review the firewall properties. Services that are enabled have a check in the box. You can also review the incoming and outgoing ports used by the service, the protocol used by the service, and the status of the associated daemon (if applicable). You can also sort the services by clicking any column header.

6. For the purposes of this exercise, you are going to disable the NTP Client. To disable the NTP Client in the ESXi firewall, remove the check box beside the NTP Client entry. Click the OK button to continue.

7. A Block Firewall Ports task will begin. When this task completes, click the Properties link for the firewall.

8. Review the NTP Client status in the Firewall Properties window. Verify that the check box is unselected beside NTP Client and that the Daemon status shows Stopped.

This exercise walked through the steps to disable the NTP Client in the ESXi firewall. To enable the NTP Client again, you would simply reverse the steps and check the NTP Client check box. There is one other option that can be configured in the ESXi firewall, and that is the firewall settings. The firewall settings are used to specify which networks are allowed to connect to each service that is listed in the firewall properties. Exercise 3.2 will cover enabling the NTP Client and configuring allowed IP addresses for the NTP Client.

EXERCISE 3.2

Configuring Allowed IP Address Settings for the NTP Client in the ESXi Firewall

1. Connect to a vCenter Server with the vSphere Client.

2. Choose an ESXi host from the inventory and select it.

3. Click the Configuration tab for the ESXi host and then click the blue Security Profile link in the Software panel.

4. In the middle of the screen, there is a listing of the firewall connections. Click the blue Properties link in the right margin to view the ESXi firewall properties.

5. Select the NTP Client and select the check box. This will enable the NTP Client in the firewall again.

6. Now click the Firewall button at the bottom of the screen. A Firewall Settings window will appear.

Notice that by default connections are allowed from any IP address. Select the option to only allow connections from specific networks and enter the network that the vCenter Server management network is on. For example, if vCenter Server has an IP address of 10.10.10.10 and a subnet mask of 255.255.255.0, then enter **10.10.10.0/24**. You can list multiple networks here, using a comma as a separator. Click the OK button to continue.

7. Now click the OK button in the Firewall Properties window. An Update Allowed IP List For Firewall Ruleset task will begin. When this task completes, click the Properties link for the firewall.

8. Review the service properties in the bottom portion of the Firewall Properties window. Verify that the firewall settings include the allowed IP addresses you configured. 10.10.10.0/24 is shown here.

(continued)

EXERCISE 3.2 *(continued)*

Firewall Properties

Remote Access

By default, remote clients are prevented from accessing services on this host, and local clients are prevented from accessing services on remote hosts.

Select a check box to provide access to a service or client. Daemons will start automatically when their ports are opened and stop when all of their ports are closed, or as configured.

Label	Incoming Ports	Outgoing Ports	Protocols	Daemon
Required Services				
Secure Shell				
☑ SSH Server	22		TCP	Running
☐ SSH Client		22	TCP	N/A
Simple Network Management Protocol				
Ungrouped				
☑ DNS Client	53	53	UDP	N/A
☑ VMware vCenter Agent		902	UDP	Running
☑ NTP Client		123	UDP	Running
☑ Fault Tolerance	8100,8200	80,8100,8200	TCP,UDP	N/A

Service Properties

General

Service: NTP Client

Package Information: esx-base
                            This VIB contains all of the base functionality of vSphere ESXi.

Firewall Settings

Allowed IP Addresses: 10.10.10.0/24

[Firewall...] [Options...]

[OK] [Cancel] [Help]

The NFS Client rule set has a different behavior than other ESXi firewall rule sets. NFS Client settings are automatically configured by ESXi when NFS datastores are mounted or unmounted. This means any manual changes made to the NFS Client rule set will be overridden by ESXi whenever these NFS operations occur.

Now that you have configured the ESXi firewall, you can turn your attention to configuring the services in the ESXi firewall.

Enabling, Configuring, and Disabling Services in the ESXi Firewall

In addition to the firewall settings, the ESXi security profile also contains a list of services running on the ESXi host. These services can be configured to start based on the status of the firewall ports. This can be useful to control the behavior of certain services. Three startup policies are available for services:

Start Automatically If Any Ports Are Open, And Stop When All Ports Are Closed   This is the VMware-recommended setting. A service will attempt to start if any port is open and will continue to attempt to start until it successfully completes. The service will then be stopped when all ports are closed.

Start And Stop With Host   A service will start shortly after the host starts and close shortly after the host shuts down. It is similar to the first policy in that the service will regularly attempt to start until it is able to do so.

Start And Stop Manually   This setting is used to manually control the service state and does not take port availability into consideration. The service status will be preserved across ESXi host reboots.

These three startup policies for services can be changed using the vSphere Client. Exercise 3.3 covers the procedure for changing the startup policy.

EXERCISE 3.3

Configuring Startup Policies for ESXi Services

1. Connect to a vCenter Server with the vSphere Client.

2. Select an ESXi host from the inventory.

3. Click the Configuration tab for the ESXi host and then click the blue Security Profile link in the Software panel.

4. At the top of the screen, there is a listing of the services. Click the blue Properties link on the right margin to view the services properties.

5. Review information in the Services Properties window. You can sort this information by clicking any column header.

(continued)

EXERCISE 3.3 *(continued)*

Services Properties

Remote Access

By default, remote clients are prevented from accessing services on this host, and local clients are prevented from accessing services on remote hosts.

Unless configured otherwise, daemons will start automatically.

Label	Daemon
I/O Redirector(Active Directory Service)	Stopped
Network Login Server (Active Directory Service)	Stopped
NTP Daemon	Running
vpxa	Running
Local Security Authentication Server (Active Directory Service)	Stopped
ESXi Shell	Running
lbtd	Running
SSH	Running
Direct Console UI	Running
CIM Server	Running

Service Properties

General

Service: I/O Redirector (Active Directory Service)

Package Information: esx-base
                        This VIB contains all of the base functionality of vSphere ESXi.

Options...

OK   Cancel   Help

6. Select the NTP daemon from the list; then click the Options button at the bottom of the screen.

7. Notice that the default startup policy for the NTP daemon is set to Start Automatically If Any Ports Are Open And Stop When All Ports Are Closed.

8. Select the Start And Stop Manually option and then click the OK button. An Update Service Activation Policy task will begin. When this task completes, highlight NTP Daemon again in the Services Properties window and click the Options button at the bottom of the screen.

9. Verify that the Start And Stop Manually startup policy is selected, and then in the Service Commands section of this window, click the Stop button to stop the NTP daemon.

10. The Stop button will become grayed out, and the Start button will become active. A Stop Service task will also run and complete. Now click the OK button. Verify that NTP Daemon is listed as Stopped in the Services Properties window and then click the OK button.

11. Reboot the ESXi host.

12. When the ESXi host is again available in vCenter, return to the Configuration tab and select the Security Profile link in the Software panel. Click the blue Properties link for Services and verify that NTP Daemon is listed as Stopped.

13. Highlight the NTP Daemon and click the Options button. Using the Start button, start the NTP Daemon service and reboot the ESXi host once again.

14. When the ESXi host is again available in vCenter, return to the Configuration tab and select the Security Profile link in the Software panel. Click the blue Properties link for Services and verify that NTP Daemon is still listed as Running.

15. Highlight NTP Daemon one final time and click the Options button. Change the default startup policy for the NTP daemon back to Start Automatically If Any Ports Are Open And Stop When All Ports Are Closed.

This exercise showed how to set the startup policies for ESXi services. By setting the NTP daemon to the startup policy of Start And Stop Manually, you can control how the service behaves. A reboot of the ESXi host preserves these settings. This approach could be used to effectively disable a service. You also returned the NTP daemon to its default, and VMware-recommended, setting of Start Automatically If Any Ports Are Open, And Stop When All Ports Are Closed. This ensures that our ESXi host will use NTP and have accurate time moving forward.

Now that configuring ESXi services has been covered, you can turn your attention toward another security feature of ESXi. *Lockdown mode* is used to increase the security of ESXi hosts, by limiting the access allowed to the host.

Enabling Lockdown Mode

All operations performed against an ESXi host in lockdown mode must originate from the vCenter Server that is managing the ESXi host. *vSphere CLI* commands, *vSphere Management Assistant* (vMA), and the vSphere Client can no longer connect to an ESXi host once it is placed in lockdown mode. This makes vCenter Server an absolute requirement to use lockdown mode. The idea behind lockdown mode is to leverage the centralized roles and privileges and event auditing present in vCenter Server to increase security, provide greater availability, and simplify operations.

Lockdown mode does not affect the availability of the ESXi Shell, SSH, or the Direct Console User Interface (DCUI), if these services are enabled. For example, the root user can still log in to the DCUI when lockdown mode is enabled. Lockdown mode can be enabled when initially adding ESXi hosts to vCenter Server, as shown in Figure 3.4.

FIGURE 3.4   The Enable Lockdown Mode option

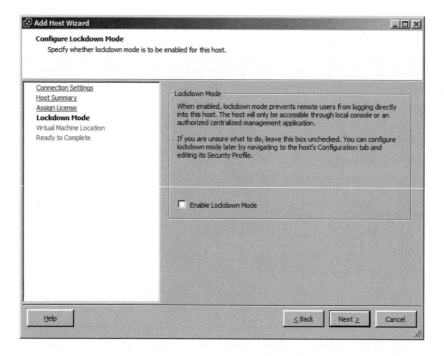

Lockdown mode can also be enabled with the DCUI, as shown in Figure 3.5.

Lockdown mode can also be configured with the vSphere Client. This will typically be the most common way that virtual infrastructure administrators enable or disable lockdown mode. Exercise 3.4 covers the steps to enable and disable lockdown mode using the vSphere Client.

FIGURE 3.5   Enabling Lockdown Mode with the DCUI

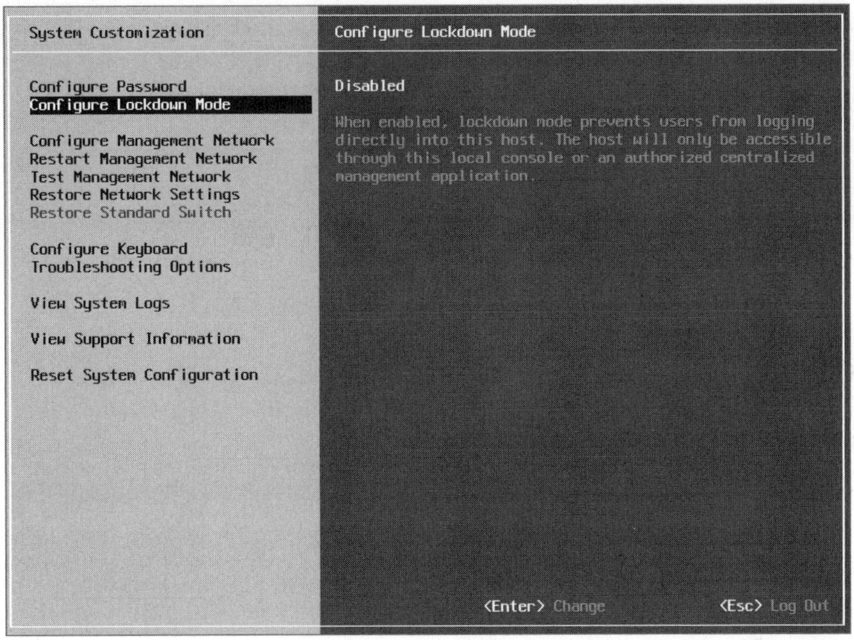

<table>
<tr><td>System Customization</td><td>Configure Lockdown Mode</td></tr>
</table>

Configure Password
Configure Lockdown Mode
Configure Management Network
Restart Management Network
Test Management Network
Restore Network Settings
Restore Standard Switch

Configure Keyboard
Troubleshooting Options

View System Logs

View Support Information

Reset System Configuration

Disabled

When enabled, lockdown mode prevents users from logging directly into this host. The host will only be accessible through this local console or an authorized centralized management application.

⟨Enter⟩ Change   ⟨Esc⟩ Log Out

EXERCISE 3.4

Enabling Lockdown Mode Using the vSphere Client

1. Connect to a vCenter Server with the vSphere Client.

2. Select the ESXi host you want to enable lockdown mode on in the right pane; then click the Configuration tab in the left pane.

3. Select the Security Profile link from the Software panel, and locate the Lockdown Mode section toward the bottom of the screen.

4. Click the Edit button to continue.

5. To enable lockdown mode, check the Enable Lockdown Mode box, as shown here.

(continued)

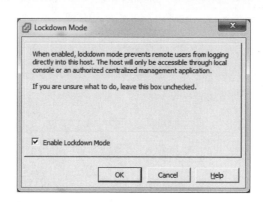

6. Click the OK button to enable lockdown mode.

7. An Enable Lockdown Mode task will start. When this task completes, the ESXi host will be in lockdown mode.

8. Verify that the ESXi host is reporting lockdown mode enabled in the vSphere Client.

9. Now log in to the ESXi host's DCUI and verify that lockdown mode also shows Enabled there.

This exercise covered the steps to enable lockdown mode for an ESXi host. To disable lockdown mode, simply repeat these steps and uncheck the Enable Lockdown Mode check box. Now that the process of enabling and disabling lockdown mode has been covered, you will learn how to configure network security policies.

Configuring Network Security Policies

Virtual switches are capable of enforcing security policies to protect virtual machines connected to them from impersonation and interception attacks. These policies can be configured at the vSwitch level or at the individual port group level in the vSwitch. Figure 3.6 shows the three different security policies and their default settings of Accept or Reject.

Promiscuous Mode policies allow a guest operating system with a NIC placed into promiscuous mode to observe all traffic on the same vSwitch or port group. Typically, this policy would be used only if you were running a packet sniffer or intrusion detection system on the guest operating system. When Promiscuous Mode is set to Accept, any guest operating system with a NIC placed into promiscuous mode can view traffic destined for other guests or hosts on the same network segment. Because this is an insecure mode of operation, the default setting for this policy is Reject.

FIGURE 3.6 vSwitch security policies

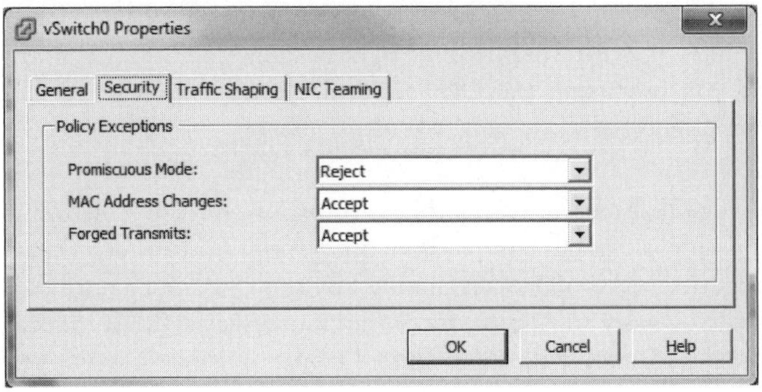

> **vSwitch0 Properties**
>
> General | Security | Traffic Shaping | NIC Teaming
>
> ┌ Policy Exceptions ─────────────────────────────┐
> │ Promiscuous Mode: [Reject   ▾]   │
> │ MAC Address Changes: [Accept   ▾]   │
> │ Forged Transmits: [Accept   ▾]   │
> └──┘
>
>   [OK]   [Cancel]   [Help]

To better understand how the MAC Address Changes and Forged Transmits policies function, I will first review some basic networking information. Each virtual network adapter in a virtual machine has its own unique MAC address. The MAC address is typically assigned when the adapter is created, but it can be changed or even hard-coded in the .vmx file.

 You can find the procedure for hard-coding a MAC address in VMware KB 219, "Setting a static MAC address for a virtual NIC," at http://kb.vmware.com/kb/219.

The MAC address specified in the virtual machine's .vmx file is known as the initial MAC address, and it cannot be changed by the guest operating system. Each virtual network adapter also has what is known as an effective MAC address. The guest operating system is responsible for setting the value of the effective MAC address, and it will typically match the initial MAC address. However, the initial and effective MAC addresses may be different. This is practically useful for virtual machines that were converted from physical hardware, where they may have been licensed to a specific MAC address. The downside to allowing the initial and effective MAC addresses to differ is that it introduces the opportunity for MAC address impersonation or spoofing. MAC address spoofing can allow network device impersonation or circumvention of access control lists. The MAC Address Changes and Forged Transmits policies work similarly, but there are a few subtle differences.

MAC Address Changes policies affect traffic that is received by a virtual machine. The MAC Address Changes policy is used to control how differentiation between the initial MAC address and the effective MAC address is handled by the vSwitch or port group. When the MAC Address Changes policy is set to Accept, the initial and effective MAC addresses can differ. In other words, the vSwitch will honor the MAC Address Change request. When the MAC Address Changes policy is set to Reject, the initial and effective MAC addresses must match or the vSwitch will disable the port the virtual machine's NIC is connected to. This virtual machine will no longer receive any traffic, until its initial MAC address and effective MAC address again match.

> If you are using the ESXi Software iSCSI initiator, be sure to set the MAC Address Changes option to Accept.

Forged Transmits policies affect traffic that is transmitted from a virtual machine. The Forged Transmits policy is used to control how differentiation between the initial MAC address and the effective MAC address is handled by the vSwitch or port group. When the Forged Transmits policy is set to Accept, the initial and effective MAC addresses can differ. In other words, the vSwitch will honor forged transmits since it won't even compare the MAC addresses. When the Forged Transmits policy is set to Reject, the initial and effective MAC addresses must match or the vSwitch will simply drop any packets received from the virtual machine.

> If Microsoft's Network Load Balancing is being used in unicast mode, set both the MAC Address Changes policy and the Forged Transmits policy to Accept.

Before you leave network security policies behind, keep in mind that the MAC Address Changes policy will affect traffic that is received to a virtual machine and that the Forged Transmits policy will affect traffic that is transmitted from a virtual machine. The vSwitch is the middleman in both operations. I will next cover how to view, sort, and export user lists from an ESXi host.

Viewing, Sorting, and Exporting User and Group Lists

There are two types of users in a vSphere environment: direct-access users and vCenter Server users. Direct-access (local) users are users who have accounts directly on an ESXi host. vCenter Server users have accounts used to access the vCenter Server. Each of these user types is entirely independent of each other. For example, a direct-access user on an ESXi host could have no access to the vCenter Server used to manage the same ESXi host. ESXi direct-access users are created on each ESXi host on a per-host basis. vCenter Server cannot be used to manage direct-access users on an ESXi host. Occasionally it will be necessary for a virtual infrastructure administrator to view the local users and groups on an ESXi host. This could possibly be for auditing purposes. These user and group lists may also be sorted and exported to HTML, XML, XLS, and CSV. Exercise 3.5 covers the procedure to view, sort, and export users and groups.

EXERCISE 3.5

Viewing, Sorting, and Exporting User and Group Lists from an ESXi Host

1. Connect to an ESXi host with the vSphere Client.

2. Click the Local Users & Groups tab. You can now use the Users and Groups buttons at the top of the panel to toggle between the Users and Groups views, as shown here.

ESXi1.test.local VMware ESXi, 5.0.0, 381646		
Getting Started \ Summary \ Virtual Machines \ Resource Allocation \ Performance \ Configuration \ Local Users & Groups		
View: Users Groups		
UID	User	Name
65534	nfsnobody	Anonymous NFS User
2	daemon	System daemons
0	root	Administrator
500	vpxuser	VMware VirtualCenter administration account
100	dcui	DCUI User

3. You can sort the Users view by UID, user, or name by simply clicking the column heading. The Groups view can be sorted by UID or group, using the same procedure of clicking the column heading. With the Users view selected, click the User column heading. The view is now sorted alphabetically by ESXi login.

4. To show or hide columns, right-click any of the column headings and use the check boxes to select or deselect the name of the column.

5. To export the user list, right-click anywhere in the Users view and choose the Export List option.

6. When the Save As dialog appears, enter a filename for the exported list and choose the desired file format using the Save As Type drop-down menu.

7. Open the exported file and verify its contents.

This exercise covered viewing, sorting, and exporting user lists from an ESXi host. Unlike ESXi, vCenter Server does not provide a user list for you to review. There is also no equivalent functionality in vCenter Server to manually create, remove, or otherwise change the vCenter Server users. Instead, the tools used to manage the Windows domain users or local user accounts database are used to manage vCenter Server users. vCenter Server does provide the ability to assign permissions for users and groups to inventory objects, and this will be the next topic discussed.

Adding, Modifying, and Removing Permissions for Users and Groups on vCenter Server Inventory Objects

In vSphere, a permission is a role plus the user or group name assigned to an inventory object. A permission grants the user or group the rights to perform the privileges specified in the role for the inventory object to which the role is assigned. Inventory objects include vCenter Server, datacenters, clusters, ESX/ESXi hosts, resource pools, *vApps*, virtual machines, datastore clusters, datastores, virtual switches, and folders. The procedure to add individual users or groups is nearly identical, and the procedure to add permissions for a user will be covered in Exercise 3.6. For the purposes of this exercise, you will begin with a work request to add the Read-Only role to a virtual machine for a domain user. Note that this exercise requires a working Active Directory domain. This exercise will reference a virtual machine named VM1, a user named Marshall, and a domain named TEST. You should make substitutions as required for your test environment.

EXERCISE 3.6

Adding Permissions for Users on vCenter Server Inventory Objects

1. Connect to a vCenter Server with the vSphere Client.

2. Select a virtual machine from the inventory.

3. Click the Permissions tab in the right pane to view the current permissions for the object.

4. To add a new permission, right-click anywhere in the Permissions view and choose the Add Permission option.

5. The Assign Permissions window will appear.

6. In the left pane, you can add a user or group permission by first clicking the Add button.

7. You can choose the domain and sort order for users and groups, and there is even a search function. Once the desired user name is found, select it and then click the Add button. This will place the user name in the Users field at the bottom of the screen.

   You can also skip directly to the Users field at the bottom of the screen and type in the username, in this case, **TEST\Marshall**. Use the Check Names button to verify the account. Once the desired username is added to the Users field, click the OK button to continue.

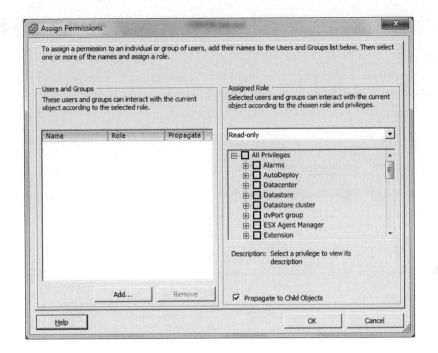

(continued)

8. Now that the domain user has been added, choose the Assigned Role drop-down menu and select the Read-Only role. You can also review the privileges this role has in the window below the drop-down menu for the role.

9. Since a virtual machine cannot have child objects, it does not matter whether the Propagate To Child Objects option is selected here. Click OK to add the permission to the virtual machine, and verify that the selected user is now listed on the Permissions tab of the selected virtual machine with the Read-Only role.

The domain user now has the Read-Only permission to the virtual machine, and the work request is closed. A couple of weeks pass by, and you receive another work request to make this same user an administrator of the virtual machine. Exercise 3.7 will modify the permissions for this virtual machine to change the user's role from Read-Only to Administrator.

EXERCISE 3.7

Modifying Permissions for Users on vCenter Server Inventory Objects

1. Connect to a vCenter Server with the vSphere Client.

2. Select the virtual machine used in the previous exercise from the inventory.

3. Click the Permissions tab in the right pane to view the current permissions for the object. Verify that the domain user account is listed with the Read-Only role.

4. To modify the permission for the domain user, right-click the permission, and choose the Properties option. You can also double-click the permission to obtain the properties.

5. A Change Access Rule window will open.

6. Review the information listed for accuracy, and then use the Select The New Role For This User Or Group drop-down menu to select the Administrator role. Click the OK button to continue.

7. Verify that the permission for the domain user has been changed and reflects the new role of Administrator on the Permissions tab of the virtual machine.

The domain user now has the Administrator role for the virtual machine, and the work request is closed. A couple of days pass by, and you receive another work request to remove all access to this virtual machine from this domain user. In Exercise 3.8, you will completely remove the domain user's permissions for the virtual machine.

EXERCISE 3.8

Removing Permissions for Users on vCenter Server Inventory Objects

1. Connect to a vCenter Server with the vSphere Client.

2. Select the virtual machine used in the previous exercise from the inventory.

(continued)

EXERCISE 3.8 *(continued)*

3. Click the Permissions tab in the right pane to view the current permissions. Verify that the domain user account is listed here and has the Administrator role.

4. To remove the permission for the domain user, right-click the permission, and choose the Delete option.

5. A Confirm Removal screen will appear.

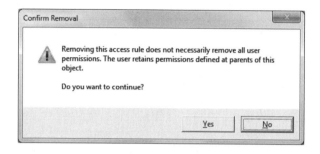

6. Review the information about permission inheritance and click the Yes button to confirm the removal of the user.

7. Verify that the domain user is no longer listed on the Permissions tab of the virtual machine.

The previous exercises focused on user permissions to a virtual machine. Group permissions are configured in the same basic manner and are nearly identical to set up. Generally speaking, it is considered better practice to use custom-defined Active Directory groups for permissions rather than user accounts.

WARNING   When working with Active Directory groups in vCenter, always be sure to use security groups and not distribution groups.

Now that I have covered establishing permissions for vCenter Server inventory objects, you will next learn about working with the vCenter Server roles that are used to define permissions in vCenter Server.

Creating, Cloning, and Editing vCenter Server Roles

Earlier in this chapter I discussed the three system roles and the six sample roles included in vCenter Server. While these default roles may be used, VMware recommends that unique roles be created to suit the specific access control needs of your environment. In the Exercise 3.9, you will follow this recommendation and create a new role.

EXERCISE 3.9

Creating a New Role in vCenter Server

1. Connect to a vCenter Server with the vSphere Client. Ensure that you are using an account with Administrator privileges.

2. On the Home page, click the Roles option.

3. The current roles are listed on the left in a column. Right-click anywhere in this left pane and choose the Add option from the context menu that appears.

4. The Add New Role window will appear.

5. Give the new role the name **Snapshot Taker**. Expand the list of privileges for Datastore and select the Allocate Space privilege's check box. Now scroll down to the Virtual Machine privileges and expand the list. Expand the State privileges and check the Create Snapshot privilege's box. The Add New Role window with the virtual machine privileges is shown here. Click OK to continue.

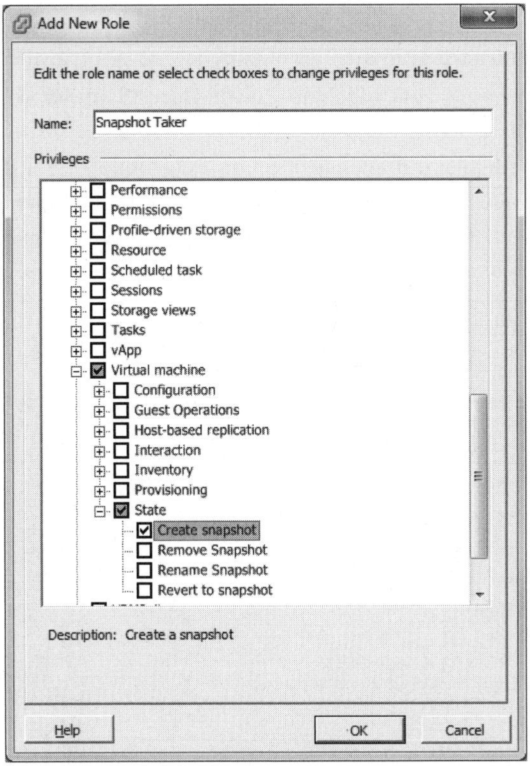

6. Click OK to create the role. Verify that the new role shows up in the list of roles.

This newly created role could be used to allow a user or group to have the ability to snapshot a virtual machine. Creating new roles is a fairly straightforward process, but understanding the required privileges can often be more difficult. The vSphere Security Guide and vSphere Virtual Machine Administration Guide both contain additional information about the required privileges for common tasks. This information can be quite valuable when creating your own custom roles.

It is sometimes easier to use one of the sample roles as a starting point for creating a custom role. VMware recommends that the default sample roles not be modified; the solution is to instead clone the default sample role. This will make an exact copy of the sample role that can then be modified for your own use. Exercise 3.10 will cover both cloning and editing a sample role.

EXERCISE 3.10

Cloning and Editing a Sample Role in vCenter Server

1. Connect to a vCenter Server with the vSphere Client. Ensure that you are using an account with Administrator privileges.

2. On the Home page, click the Roles option.

3. The current roles are listed on the left in a column. Select the Virtual Machine Power User (Sample) role and then right-click it and choose the Clone option.

4. The new role Clone of Virtual Machine Power User (Sample) will appear in the roles list. The clone is complete and ready for editing.

5. Right-click the cloned role and choose the Edit Role option from the context menu.

6. The Edit Role window will appear. Rename the role to **Virtual Machine Super Power User**. Deselect the Virtual Machine privilege. Now select the Virtual Machine privilege's check box and all of its subprivileges. The configuration should look similar to that shown here.

7. Click OK to save the changes made to the role.

I have now covered how to create, clone, and edit roles in vCenter Server. You will next focus on a security feature of ESXi, which is the ability to add an ESXi host to a directory service for authentication.

Adding an ESXi Host to a Directory Service

ESXi can be configured to use a directory service, like Microsoft's Active Directory, to manage users and groups. This is useful when users must have access to the ESXi host but maintaining a separate set of user accounts on the ESXi is also undesirable. A directory service like Active Directory can leverage existing user accounts and help simplify the administration and security of the ESXi hosts. To add an ESXi host to a directory service, there are several prerequisites, including the following:

- The Active Directory domain controllers and domain name must be resolvable in the ESXi host DNS server entries.

- Verify that the ESXi hostname is fully qualified with the domain name of the Active Directory forest, for example, esxi1.test.local.

- The time between the ESXi host and the directory service should be synchronized. This is most easily accomplished in ESXi by using NTP.

- There must be a group in Active Directory with the name ESX Admins. Place Active Directory user accounts that should have access to the ESXi host(s) in this group. The ESX Admins group is granted the Administrator role on the ESXi host(s).

You can use two methods to join an ESXi host to an Active Directory domain:

vSphere Authentication Proxy   The domain name of the Active Directory server and the IP address of the authentication proxy server are entered when joining an ESXi host to a domain. Using the vSphere Authentication Proxy allows you to not store Active Directory credentials on the ESXi host.

Active Directory Credentials   The Active Directory credentials and the domain name of the Active Directory server are entered when the ESXi host is joined to the domain.

In Exercise 3.11 you will add an ESXi host to an Active Directory domain using the Active Directory credentials method.

EXERCISE 3.11

Adding an ESXi Host to Active Directory

1. Connect to a vCenter Server with the vSphere Client.

2. Select an ESXi host and then click the Configuration tab. Click the blue Authentication Services link in the Software panel.

3. At the top of the page, there will be a Directory Services Configuration section. Click the blue Properties link in the top-right margin.

4. The Directory Services Configuration window will open. In the User Directory Service section, use the drop-down menu to select Active Directory.

5. Under the Domain Settings section, enter the domain name. The domain name can be entered in one of two ways:

   NAME.DOMAIN   For example, test.local. The computer account will be created under the default container in Active Directory.

   NAME.DOMAIN/CONTAINER/PATH   For example, test.local/NorthAmerica/ Richmond. The account is created under the Richmond organizational unit (OU) in Active Directory.

6. Once the domain name is entered, click the Join Domain button.

7. When prompted, enter a username and password that has permission to join a server to an Active Directory domain. The process for steps 4–7 will look similar to what is shown here.

8. After entering the Active Directory credentials, click the Join Domain button. A Join Windows Domain task will start. You can click the OK button in the Directory Service Configuration window now.

9. When the Join Windows Domain task completes, verify that the Directory Services Type is listed as Active Directory. Also verify in the domain settings that the domain is listed properly.

10. Now open the vSphere Client and connect to the ESXi host you just configured to use Active Directory. Enter the credentials for a user in Active Directory that is also a member of the ESX Admins group in Active Directory, as shown here.

11. Click the Permissions tab and then verify that TEST\esx^admins is listed with the Administrator role, as shown here.

Adding your ESXi hosts to Active Directory is a powerful security feature that allows you to leverage the capabilities of the directory service for authentication to your ESXi hosts. This capability can save the virtual administrator both time and effort, by avoiding the creation and maintenance of multiple local accounts. Now that I have covered adding ESXi hosts to Active Directory, you can turn your attention to applying permissions to ESXi hosts using host profiles.

Applying Permissions to ESXi Hosts Using Host Profiles

Host profiles help reduce the effort required to manually configure ESXi hosts, by capturing a blueprint of a reference host and then using this blueprint to ensure consistency across other ESXi hosts in the environment. To use host profiles, there must be an existing vSphere installation with at least one configured ESXi host that will be used as the reference host.

TIP   Host profiles are supported only for vSphere 4.0 or newer hosts and require the Enterprise Plus Edition of vSphere.

A host profile can be created from a configured ESXi reference host, and then the host profile can be attached to other ESXi hosts or a cluster in vCenter Server. The next step is to check ESXi hosts for compliance with the reference host profile. If the ESXi host is noncompliant, then the host profile can be applied to the ESXi host to remediate it. Exercise 3.12 will walk through the process of using host profiles to apply permissions to an ESXi host. For the purposes of this exercise, you will use only a single ESXi host. This will simplify the exercise and allow you to focus primarily on covering how to apply permissions using host profiles. Host profiles will be covered in great detail in Chapter 9, so you don't necessarily need to learn how this feature works here.

EXERCISE 3.12

Applying Permissions to an ESXi Host Using Host Profiles

1. Connect to a vCenter Server with the vSphere Client.

2. Select the ESXi 5 host that will be used as the reference host, and ensure that this ESXi host is configured to use the directory service of Active Directory.

3. A host profile can be created from the host profile's main view or from the ESXi host's context menu. Select the reference ESXi host and right-click it. Choose the Create Profile From Host option from the Host Profile menu, as shown here.

4. When the Create Profile From Wizard begins, give the host profile a descriptive name and a brief description. Click the Next button to continue.

5. Review the summary information. Click the Finish button, and a Create A Host Profile task will start. Wait for this task to complete before continuing to the next step.

6. The next step is to edit the profile to include the permission you want to apply to other ESXi hosts. This edit will also make the reference host noncompliant, but more on that in a moment.

7. Click the Home icon in the navigation bar at the top of the screen. Click the Host Profiles icon, located under the Management section. In the left pane, select the profile you just created. Right-click the profile and choose the Edit Profile option, as shown here.

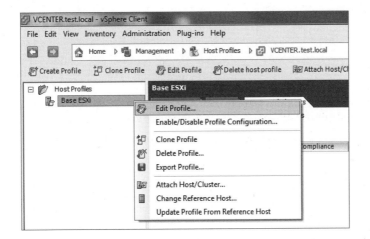

8. When the Edit Profile window launches, expand the Security configuration policy in the left pane. Right-click the Permission Rules folder and choose the Add Profile option. Now expand the Permission Rules folder and then expand the Permission Profile policy. Finally, select the permission item.

9. In the Configuration Details tab in the right pane, choose the Require A Permission Rule option from the drop-down menu. Another set of configuration options will appear. Enter an Active Directory group name in the form DOMAIN\GROUP and select the Name Refers To A Group Of Users box. Enter the nonlocalized assigned role name of **Admin** and select the Propagate Permission check box. The final configuration should look like the window shown here.

(continued)

10. Click the OK button in the Edit Profile window. Using the Home button on the navigation bar, return to the Hosts and Clusters view.

Now that you have created and edited a host profile, the next step is to attach the profile to an ESXi host.

11. Right-click the ESXi host and choose the Manage Profile option from the Host Profile menu.

12. In the Attach Profile window, choose the profile created in steps 3–5 in this exercise and click the OK button. An Attach Host profile task will start. When it completes, click the Summary tab for this ESXi host and verify that the correct host profile is listed in the General section. It should appear similar to what's shown here.

13. Right-click this ESXi 5 host again, and choose the Enter Maintenance Mode option from the context menu. ESXi hosts must be placed in maintenance mode to apply the profile.

Now that the profile is attached to the host, you will check the host for compliance with the profile.

14. Click the Home icon in the navigation bar at the top of the screen. Click the Host Profiles icon, located under the Management section. In the left pane, select the profile you just attached to your ESXi host. In the right pane, click the Hosts and Clusters tab.

```
esxi1.test.local VMware ESXi, 5.0.0, 381646
 Summary   Virtual Machines   Performance   Configuration   Tasks

 General

 Manufacturer:                    VMware, Inc.
 Model:                           VMware Virtual Platform
 CPU Cores:                       2 CPUs x 2.394 GHz
 Processor Type:                  Intel(R) Core(TM)2 Duo CPU
                                  P8600 @ 2.40GHz
 License:                         VMware vSphere 5 Enterprise
                                  Plus - Licensed for 2 physic...
 Processor Sockets:               2
 Cores per Socket:                1
 Logical Processors:              2
 Hyperthreading:                  Inactive
 Number of NICs:                  1
 State:                           Connected
 Virtual Machines and Templates:  0
 vMotion Enabled:                 No
 VMware EVC Mode:                 Disabled

 vSphere HA State                 N/A
 Host Configured for FT:          No

 Active Tasks:
 Host Profile:                    Base ESXi
```

15. Select the entity name of the ESXi host listed. If either the Host Profile Compliance or Compliance – Last Checked columns is empty or reports a status of Unknown, click the Check Compliance link in the top of the pane.

16. A Check Compliance task will start. Wait for this task to complete and verify that the Host Profile Compliance or Compliance – Last Checked column reports different values. The results should look similar to what's shown here.

```
Base ESXi
 Getting Started   Summary   Hosts and Clusters
 Select an entity below to view its compliance failures


 Entity Name              Host Profile Compliance      Compliance - Last Checked
 esxi1.test.local         ⊗ Noncompliant               8/25/2011 11:15:37 AM




 Compliance Failures
 Failures Against Host Profile
 A permission for user or group TEST\Finance-Admins does not exist
```

Now that you know the host is noncompliant, the final step is to apply the profile to the host.

(continued)

EXERCISE 3.12 *(continued)*

17. Select the ESXi host listed in the entity name list and click the Apply Profile link at the top of the screen, or right-click the ESXi host listed in the entity name and choose the Apply Profile option, as shown here.

18. The Apply Profile window will appear. If prompted, enter any required parameters for applying the profile. Review the changes listed, as shown here.

19. Click the Finish button. An Apply Host configuration task will start, followed closely by a Check Compliance task. Wait for both of these tasks to complete and then verify that the Host Profile Compliance is now reported as Compliant.

20. Exit maintenance mode on the ESXi host. Click the Permissions tab on the ESXi host that the host profile was applied to. Verify that the Active Directory group you added with the host profile is now listed.

Now that you have used host profiles to apply permissions to an ESXi host, you will next look at determining the appropriate set of privileges for common tasks in vCenter Server.

Determining the Appropriate Set Of Privileges for Common Tasks in vCenter Server

Part of the virtual administrator's responsibility is determining the appropriate set of privileges required by the various virtual infrastructure consumers. These will be the users who need to create and deploy virtual machines, use virtual machine consoles, or do any other number of administrative or operational tasks. With the number of privileges available in vCenter Server, the options for users are almost endless. I will cover the appropriate set of privileges for two different scenarios in this section. The first will be the privileges required for creating a new virtual machine, and the second will be for a virtual machine user who needs console access.

The minimum privileges required to create a new virtual machine are as follows:

- Virtual Machine.Inventory.Raw Create
- Virtual Machine.Configuration.Add New Disk (if new virtual disk(s) will be created)
- Virtual Machine .Configuration.Add Existing Disk (if an existing virtual disk will be used)
- Virtual Machine.Configuration.Raw Device (if an RDM or SCSI pass-through device is used)
- Resource.Assign Virtual Machine to Resource Pool
- Datastore.Allocate Space
- Network.Assign Network

To assign this set of privileges, you would use the roles feature in vCenter Server to create a new role. From here, you can add any number of additional privileges to expand the capabilities of this role. Another role that often is needed in the virtual infrastructure is for virtual machine users who need access to a local console of the virtual machine.

For example, say there is a virtual machine user who must have access to the virtual machine's console to monitor an application. This user could easily be granted the Administrator role, but this would give the user too much access to the virtual machine. Instead, a new role can be created to grant only console access to this user. The following is the minimum privilege required to give a user access to a virtual machine console:

- Virtual Machine.Interaction.Console interaction

As you can see, roles can contain a single privilege or multiple privileges. Understanding the required privileges can be difficult, and a good deal of experimentation with the privileges is the best way to learn them. As mentioned earlier in this chapter, both the vSphere Security Guide and the vSphere Virtual Machine Administration Guide contain additional information on required privileges for many common tasks. When these resources can't answer provide the solution, it becomes helpful to understand the privileges and how they work. This will allow you to create your own roles that provide only the required access.

The next section of this chapter will move away from securing ESXi and vCenter Server and move into identifying vSphere architecture and solutions.

Identifying vSphere Architecture and Solutions

As a VMware Certified Professional, you will be expected to know how VMware products are architected and work. You will also be expected to identify the appropriate solution for your business and clients. You will next look at the architecture of vSphere and its various editions and feature sets. I will also discuss the different cloud types and the role vSphere has in each of the cloud types.

Identifying Available vSphere Editions and Features

Many editions of vSphere are available, and for the exam it is important to know the differences between these versions. Figure 3.7 lists the vSphere editions and their associated features.

For the exam it is important to understand the features included in these editions and how these features can be implemented. I will now explain the ESXi and vCenter Server architectures, which are common across all vSphere editions.

Although knowing the editions and features listed in Figure 3.7 is helpful for the exam, it is equally important to understand what the features are and how the features are actually used. You are much more likely to see an implementation type of question on the VCP exam than you are to see a simple "What is the difference between these two editions?" type of question.

In addition to understanding the various vSphere editions and feature sets, it is also important to understand the architecture of both ESXi and vCenter Server. I will cover this topic next.

Explaining ESXi and vCenter Server Architectures

vSphere architecture is composed of three distinct layers:

Virtualization x86 servers with ESXi hypervisor

Management vCenter Server and associated services

Interface Solutions that provide additional functionality such as the vSphere Client or the vSphere CLI

TABLE 3.1 vSphere 5 editions and features

	Essentials Kit	Essentials Plus Kit	Standard Acceleration Kit	Enterprise Acceleration Kit	Enterprise Plus Acceleration Kit
Centralized Management	vCenter for Essentials	vCenter for Essentials	vCenter Standard	vCenter Standard	vCenter Standard
Included Entitlement	3 servers with up to 2 processors each	3 servers with up to 2 processors each	8 Processors - scalable with additional licenses	6 Processors - scalable with additional licenses	6 Processors - scalable with additional licenses
vRAM Entitlement	32 GB (192 GB total)	32 GB (192 GB total)	32 GB	64 GB	96 GB
vCPU Entitlement	8-way	8-way	8-way	8-way	32-way
SUSE Linux Enterprise Server for VMware			YES	YES	YES
Product Features					
Thin Provisioning	YES	YES	YES	YES	YES
Update Manager	YES	YES	YES	YES	YES
vStorage APIs for Data Protection	YES	YES	YES	YES	YES
Data Recovery		YES	YES	YES	YES
High Availability		YES	YES	YES	YES
vMotion		YES	YES	YES	YES
Virtual Serial Port Concentrator				YES	YES
Hot Add				YES	YES
vShield Zones				YES	YES
Fault Tolerance				YES	YES
Storage APIs for Array Integration				YES	YES
Storage APIs for Multipathing				YES	YES
Storage vMotion				YES	YES
Distributed Resources Scheduler (DRS)				YES	YES
Distributed Power Management (DPM)				YES	YES
Storage I/O Control					YES
Network I/O Control					YES
Distributed Switch					YES
Host Profiles					YES
Auto Deploy					YES
Storage DRS					YES
Profile-Driven Storage					YES

The virtualization layer consists of ESXi hosts, which abstract processor, memory, video, storage, and resources into virtual machines. ESXi hosts represent the aggregate resources of their underlying physical x86 hardware. For example, if a host has four quad-core 3GHz CPUs and 128GB RAM, then that host has 48GHz of processing resources and 128GB of RAM resources available.

ESXi hosts can also be placed into clusters, which aggregate the resources of all hosts in the cluster. Clusters typically have access to the same networks and storage resources and can be managed as a single entity. For example, if a cluster contained two ESXi hosts each with four quad-core 3GHz CPUs and 128GB RAM, then the cluster has 96GHz of processing and 256GB RAM resources available.

ESXi hosts or clusters can also use resource pools. Resource pools are created to partition resources of ESXi hosts or clusters containing multiple ESXi hosts. This can be useful when a certain group of virtual machines needs guaranteed resources. Resource pools can be dynamically changed, and their resources can also be shared when not in use.

⊕ Real World Scenario

Using Resource Pools

A customer is currently using a single ESXi host to run four virtual machines. Two of these virtual machines are used by R&D, and the other two virtual machines are used by HR staff. The R&D virtual machines have higher resource requirements than the HR virtual machines. The virtual infrastructure administrator needs to be able to ensure the R&D virtual machines get the resources they require.

The virtual infrastructure administrator creates two resource pools on the ESXi host and sets CPU Shares to High for the R&D resource pool and sets the CPU shares to Normal for the HR resource pool, as shown here.

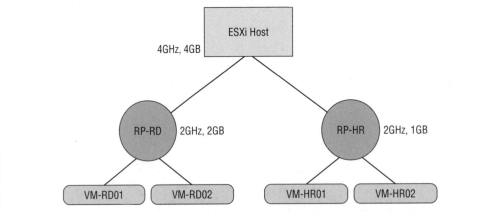

With this resource pool set up, the R&D group gets the resources required to run their workloads, while the HR resource pool also provides sufficient resources to these VMs to run their workloads.

Now that I've discussed the virtualization layer, I will describe the management layer. vCenter Server is a centralized management application used to manage ESXi hosts, but this statement does not accurately detail the extent of vCenter Server's capabilities. vCenter Server offers a single pane of glass interface that provides the following core services:

- Virtual machine provisioning
- Host and VM configuration
- Resources and virtual machine inventory management
- Statistics and logging
- Alarms and event management
- A task scheduler
- vApps

The capabilities of vCenter Server may be further extended with vCenter Server plug-ins. Certain plug-ins are included along with the base vCenter Server product, including the following:

- vCenter Storage Monitoring
- vCenter Hardware Status
- vCenter Service Status

There are also other vCenter Server plug-ins that can be installed separately, including the following:

- vSphere Update Manager (VUM)
- vShield Zones
- vCenter Orchestrator
- Data Recovery

vCenter Server also contains interfaces that integrate vCenter Server with third-party products and applications, including the following:

- ESXi server management
- VMware vSphere API
- Active Directory interface
- Database interface

Now that I have discussed the management layer, I will describe the interface layer. The management and virtualization layer can both be accessed through various interfaces. These interfaces include the following:

- vSphere Client
- vSphere Web Client

- vSphere PowerCLI
- vSphere SDK for Perl
- vSphere CLI (vCLI)
- vSphere SDK for .NET
- vSphere Web Services SDK

Understanding the architecture of ESXi and vCenter Server will be important for the exam, and it is important to know how these three layers interoperate with each other. Now that the ESXi and vCenter Server architectures have been described, I will next explain cloud concepts.

Explaining Private, Public, and Hybrid Cloud Concepts

The phrase *cloud computing* confuses many virtual infrastructure administrators. This could be because of factors such as differing vendor marketing strategies, but it is more likely that cloud computing is simply a paradigm shift in the way you traditionally deliver resources. Perhaps the simplest way to think of cloud computing is the consumption of a service without the responsibility of managing the service. For example, think of the electricity provided to your residence. I'm guessing that most of us didn't go out and build the infrastructure required to provide the electricity. Instead, we simply become consumers of a service offered by a local utility. We get to consume the service, while someone else is responsible for managing the infrastructure behind it.

Think back to the time before virtualization and the sequence of events required to deliver resources. If HR needed a new payroll application, a physical server would be quoted, shipped, unpackaged, racked, cabled, OS installed, apps installed, and so on. It could easily take weeks to deliver this service. With modern vSphere implementations, this old approach to resource delivery starts to sound similar to the task of building our own electrical infrastructure. It is these modern virtual infrastructures that are the foundation for cloud computing. Here are VMware's requirements for a cloud:

- It must be built on a pooled virtual infrastructure, including CPU, memory, storage, and networking resources.
- Applications must be easily moved between clouds.
- It should be open and interoperable.
- Consumers should pay only for resources they consume or commit to consuming.
- It should be a secure and trusted location.

- The option or ability to protect cloud-based workloads from data loss should be available.
- Maintenance of the infrastructure should be removed and completely transparent to the user.

Now that I have discussed what cloud computing is, I'll discuss the different types of clouds. The first is the private cloud. Simply put, the private cloud is what a lot of virtual infrastructure administrators are already using. vSphere is running in your datacenter, running on your hardware, and providing services to your internal customers, and you may or may not be charging your consumers for their usage.

A public cloud is the same basic model, but it is instead made available to the general public from large providers. Amazon's Elastic Compute Cloud (Amazon EC2) is an example of a public cloud. In the public cloud, you would pay for the consumption of resources from the third party delivering those resources.

There is also the hybrid cloud, which is a cloud infrastructure composed of two or more private or public clouds. These clouds remain unique entities, but there is virtual machine portability between the two. This model is useful for cloud bursting or load-balancing between clouds. Cloud bursting is the process of running certain workloads in another cloud when capacity has been reached in one cloud. For example, year-end procedures might require a significant amount of resources to complete. Instead of always having these costly resources available in a private cloud for this one-time use, the specific workload can be moved to a public cloud instead.

There is a common misconception that cloud computing directly implies the public cloud, but you should instead think of cloud computing as an approach rather than a location. Think about how resources are delivered and how each of these cloud environments could be leveraged to make your business more flexible and cost-effective. Now that I have covered cloud computing, I'll discuss how to determine the appropriate vSphere edition based on customer requirements.

Determining Appropriate vSphere Edition Based on Customer Requirements

Part of successfully designing any virtual infrastructure is determining which edition of vSphere will fit the specific requirements. Smaller businesses will often have an entirely different set of business requirements and budgets for their infrastructure than a large enterprise. Knowing how to leverage the correct edition of vSphere based on these requirements is important. Various factors can come into play here, such as virtual machine availability, leveraging advanced storage functionality, backup strategy, and even the number of virtual machines that will be powered on.

Real World Scenario

Choosing the Appropriate vSphere Edition for Customer Needs

A customer is currently using the free VMware vSphere Hypervisor on two x86 hosts to house five virtual machines. The customer has been using this setup for some time, but virtualization has been decided upon as the infrastructure of choice for the future. The customer plans to eliminate its remaining non-ESXi physical servers in the next year and is expecting to double the virtual infrastructure as a result. Virtual machine backups have been a pain point for this customer. The customer has an existing SAN and wants to leverage a centralized management solution for these ESXi hosts and to provide high uptime for the virtual machines in this environment.

Two editions of vSphere were immediately considered. The Essentials edition would allow the customer to meet the centralized management requirement with vCenter Server, but this edition would not adequately address the high availability requirements. The Essentials Plus edition would meet the centralized management requirement and could leverage the customer's SAN to provide HA and vMotion. Another value of the Essentials Plus edition is the inclusion of VMware Data Recovery, which would allow the customer to obtain image-level virtual machine backups.

The three other available editions of vSphere would have also worked for this customer, but the Essentials Plus edition currently best meets this customer's requirements. This solution also allows the customer room to grow and should serve them quite well in the future.

I have now covered how to determine the appropriate vSphere edition based on specific customer requirements. It is important to know the feature sets of each vSphere edition to ensure that you always choose the right solution.

Summary

This chapter covered securing vCenter Server and ESXi. Knowing how to secure the virtual infrastructure is extremely important. I covered vCenter Server privileges, roles, and permissions and understanding what each of these items is and how they relate to each other. I also covered securing ESXi with its built-in firewall, services, lockdown mode capability, and the layer 2 vSwitch security policies. I also covered user and group lists in ESXi and using permissions for users and groups in vCenter Server. The vCenter Server roles were covered, and I discussed best practices for roles. You learned how to add ESXi hosts to a directory service and applied permissions to an ESXi host using a host profile. I also covered determining the appropriate set of privileges for common tasks in vCenter Server.

Understanding how to secure both ESXi and vCenter and knowing how each relates to the other are key elements of the VCP exam.

The final part of this chapter focused on identifying vSphere architecture and solutions. Knowing the architecture of vSphere and other VMware solutions is helpful in designing your virtual infrastructure. I identified the available vSphere editions and features and explained the ESXi and vCenter Server architectures. I also discussed the differences between private, public, and hybrid cloud models. I wrapped up this chapter with determining the appropriate vSphere edition based on customer requirements with a case study. For the VCP exam, you will be expected to know what vSphere editions and features are available, when to use these features and editions, and how to secure them.

Exam Essentials

Know how to secure ESXi 5 and vCenter Server 5.   Understand the difference between a permission, a privilege, and a role. Be able to identify the common vCenter Server privileges and roles and know how to create, clone, and edit roles. Understand how permissions are applied and inherited in vCenter Server and know what permissions override others. Know how to configure and administer the ESXi firewall and ESXi services in the ESXi firewall. Understand what lockdown mode is used for and how to implement it. Be able to configure network security policies and understand when to use them. Know how to view, sort, and export user and group lists in vCenter, as well as how to add, modify, and remove permissions for users and groups on vCenter Server inventory objects. Know how to add an ESXi host to a directory service and why you would do so. Understand how to apply permissions to ESXi hosts using host profiles. Be able to determine the appropriate set of privileges for common tasks in vCenter Server.

Know how to identify vSphere architecture and solutions.   Understand the available vSphere editions and features, and be able to determine the appropriate vSphere edition based on specific customer requirements. Know both the ESXi and vCenter Server architectures and understand the concepts of private, public, and hybrid clouds.

Review Questions

1. How many default system roles are there in vCenter?

   A. 2

   B. 3

   C. 4

   D. 5

2. In vCenter Server, which of the following items defines individual user rights?

   A. Role

   B. Permission

   C. Privilege

   D. None of these

3. In vCenter Server, a role is a collection of _____.

   A. Roles

   B. Permissions

   C. Privileges

   D. User rights

4. What is created by pairing a vCenter Server role with a user or group and then associating it with an object in the vCenter Server inventory?

   A. Role

   B. Permission

   C. Privilege

   D. User right

5. In vCenter Server, which of the following statements are true about permission inheritance? (Choose two.)

   A. Any permission defined directly on a child object will override permissions propagated from parent objects.

   B. Any permission defined directly on a parent object will override permissions propagated from child objects.

   C. Virtual machines do not inherit multiple permissions.

   D. Virtual machines inherit multiple permissions.

6. Which of the following statements about the ESXi firewall is true?

   A. The firewall is disabled by default and must be enabled using the vSphere Client.

   B. The firewall is enabled by default and blocks all traffic by default, except for traffic for the default management services.

   C. The firewall is enabled by default, allows all outbound traffic, and blocks all inbound traffic.

   D. The firewall is disabled by default and must be enabled using the `esxcli` command.

7. Which of the following is the VMware-recommended startup policy for ESXi services?

   A. Start Automatically If Any Ports Are Open, And Stop When All Ports Are Closed.

   B. Start And Stop With Host.

   C. Start And Stop Manually.

   D. VMware does not specifically recommend any single startup policy.

8. Operations performed against an ESXi host in lockdown mode can originate from which of the following? (Choose all that apply.)

   A. vMA

   B. vSphere Client connected directly to ESXi host

   C. vCenter Server

   D. vSphere CLI commands

9. Which of the following vSwitch policy exceptions are set to the value of Accept by default? (Choose all that apply.)

   A. Promiscuous Mode

   B. MAC Address Changes

   C. Forged Transmits

   D. Traffic Shaping

10. To export the list of local ESXi users to an HTML file, which of the following approaches could be used?

   A. vSphere Client connected to a vCenter Server

   B. vSphere Client connected to ESXi host

   C. vSphere Client connected to either an ESXi host or to a vCenter Server

   D. vSphere Web Client

11. Which of the following is the preferred method to manage user permissions in vCenter Server?

   A. Using Local Windows groups

   B. Using Active Directory Distribution groups

   C. Using Active Directory Security groups

   D. Using Active Directory users

12. Which of the following is a true statement about the vCenter Server default system roles?

   A. They can be cloned.

   B. They can be edited.

    C. They can be removed.

    D. None of these.

13. Which of the following groups must be created in Active Directory, before an ESXi can successfully use Active Directory for authentication?

    A. ESXi Admin

    B. ESXi Admins

    C. ESX Admin

    D. ESX Admins

14. Which of the following are prerequisites for applying a permission change to a host using host profiles? (Choose all that apply.)

    A. vSphere 4.0 or newer hosts

    B. vSphere hosts configured for Active Directory authentication

    C. Enterprise Plus edition of vSphere

    D. vCenter Server

15. Which of the following privileges are required for a taking a virtual machine snapshot? (Choose all that apply.)

    A. Virtual Machine.State.Create Snapshots

    B. Virtual Machine.Provisioning.Allow Disk Access

    C. Datastore.Allocate Space

    D. Datastore.Update Virtual Machine Files

16. Which features of the Enterprise Plus Edition of vSphere are not included with the Enterprise Edition of vSphere? (Choose all that apply.)

    A. Storage APIs for Multipathing

    B. Storage I/O Control

    C. Storage vMotion

    D. Storage DRS

17. Which features of the Enterprise Edition of vSphere are not included with the Standard Edition of vSphere? (Choose all that apply.)

    A. Fault Tolerance

    B. Storage vMotion

    C. vShield Zones

    D. VAAI

18. The vSphere architecture is composed of which layers? (Choose all that apply.)

    A. Virtualization

    B. Client access

C. Management

D. Interface

19. You are running vSphere in the corporate datacenter. The datacenter servers are housed and managed on-site by your staff. Which type of cloud computing model are you using?

A. Private

B. Public

C. Hybrid

D. None of these

20. A customer needs to implement a virtual infrastructure that meets the following requirement: the customer wants to have both diskless and stateless ESXi hosts implemented. Which vSphere edition is required?

A. Enterprise Plus

B. Enterprise

C. Standard

D. None of the above

Chapter

4

Plan and Configure vSphere Networking

VCP5 EXAM OBJECTIVES COVERED IN THIS CHAPTER:

✓ **Configure vNetwork Standard Switches**

- Identify vNetwork Standard Switch (vSS) capabilities

- Create/Delete a vNetwork Standard Switch

- Add/Configure/Remove vmnics on a vNetwork Standard Switch

- Configure VMkernel ports for network services

- Add/Edit/Remove port groups on a vNetwork Standard Switch

- Determine use case for a vNetwork Standard Switch

✓ **Configure vNetwork Distributed Switches**

- Identify vNetwork Distributed Switch (vDS) capabilities

- Create/Delete a vNetwork Distributed Switch

- Add/Remove ESXi hosts from a vNetwork Distributed Switch

- Add/Configure/Remove dvPort groups

- Add/Remove uplink adapters to dvUplink groups

- Create/Configure/Remove virtual adapters

- Migrate virtual adapters to/from a vNetwork Standard Switch

- Migrate virtual machines to/from a vNetwork Distributed Switch

- Determine use case for a vNetwork Distributed Switch

✓ **Configure vSS and vDS Policies**

- Identify common vSS and vDS policies

- Configure dvPort group blocking policies

- Configure load balancing and failover policies

- Configure VLAN settings

- Configure traffic shaping policies

- Enable TCP Segmentation Offload support for a virtual machine

- Enable Jumbo Frames support on appropriate components

- Determine appropriate VLAN configuration for a vSphere implementation

This chapter will cover the objectives of Section 2 of the VCP5 exam blueprint. This chapter will focus completely on configuring vNetwork standard switches and vNetwork distributed switches in vSphere 5.

In addition, this chapter will cover identifying vNetwork standard switch capabilities, creating and configuring vNetwork standard switches, and determining the use case for vNetwork standard switches.

This chapter will also cover identifying vNetwork distributed switch capabilities, creating and configuring vNetwork distributed switches, and determining the use case for vNetwork distributed switches.

Finally, this chapter will cover identifying and configuring vNetwork standard switch and vNetwork distributed switch policies, as well as configuring load balancing and failover policies and VLAN settings. It will cover enabling TCP segmentation offload and jumbo frames. Determining the appropriate VLAN configuration for a vSphere implementation will round out the chapter.

Configuring vNetwork Standard Switches

Networking in vSphere is a key concept to understand for the VCP exam. Knowing how to configure networking helps establish highly available virtual machines via vMotion and FT. The networking configuration is also used to provide load-balanced and highly available virtual machine network traffic. Securing network storage communications, management interfaces, and virtual machines is another important aspect of networking, and if you recall, the security features of standard vSwitches were discussed in Chapter 3. The first topic I will cover in this chapter is identifying the capabilities of the vNetwork standard switch (vSS).

Identifying vNetwork Standard Switch Capabilities

vNetwork standard switches, or vSwitches, are software constructs of the local ESXi host that process layer 2 Ethernet headers. Figure 4.1 shows the architecture of a vSwitch. It is important to note that each ESXi host has its own set of vSwitches and maintains a separate configuration for each vSwitch located on the host.

You will see the terms *vNetwork standard switch*, *vSS*, and *vSwitch* throughout this chapter. It is important to remember that these terms are all referring to the same thing. For the sake of consistency, the term *vSwitch* will be used most often.

FIGURE 4.1   vSwitch architecture

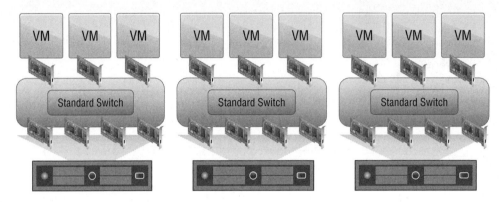

vSwitches are used in ESXi to provide two types of networking:

Virtual Machine   This connection type is used to allow virtual machines to communicate and applies exclusively to virtual machines.

VMkernel   This connection type is used for host-based connections such as ESXi management traffic, vMotion, FT, iSCSI, and NFS.

These two *connection types* are provided by *port groups* in the vSwitch. Port groups are listed on the Ports tab in the vSwitch properties, as shown in Figure 4.2.

You can obtain the properties for the vSwitch or the port group by selecting the vSwitch or port group and then clicking the Edit button. It is important to remember that properties defined on a port group will override properties defined on the vSwitch containing the port group.

> By default, a vSwitch has 120 ports. This can be changed to a maximum of 4,088.

One capability of a vSwitch is the ability to route virtual machine traffic internally. This means two VMs residing on the same ESXi host can communicate with their traffic not needing to leave the ESXi host. An additional capability of a vSwitch is that VMs can communicate to other external networks. vSwitches are also capable of supporting *VLANs* and 802.1Q VLAN encapsulation.

vSwitches can also be used to provide security via security policies. There are three security policies available:

- Promiscuous Mode
- MAC Address Changes
- Forged Transmits

These security policies are discussed in detail in Chapter 3, so any further review will be omitted.

Outbound traffic shaping is another capability of a vSwitch. ESXi can utilize traffic shaping policies to restrict network bandwidth available and allow bursts of traffic. These traffic shaping policies are applied to each VM network adapter connected to the standard switch. It is important to remember that ESXi can shape only outbound network traffic on vSwitches and that traffic shaping is disabled by default. Figure 4.3 shows the configurable options for traffic shaping.

FIGURE 4.2   vSwitch port groups

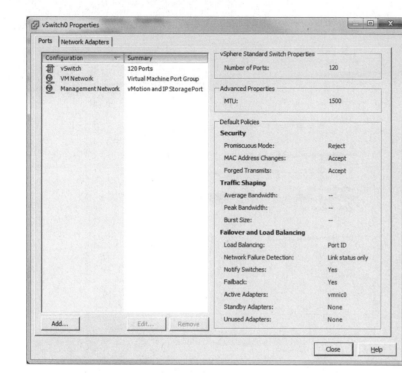

FIGURE 4.3   Options for traffic shaping

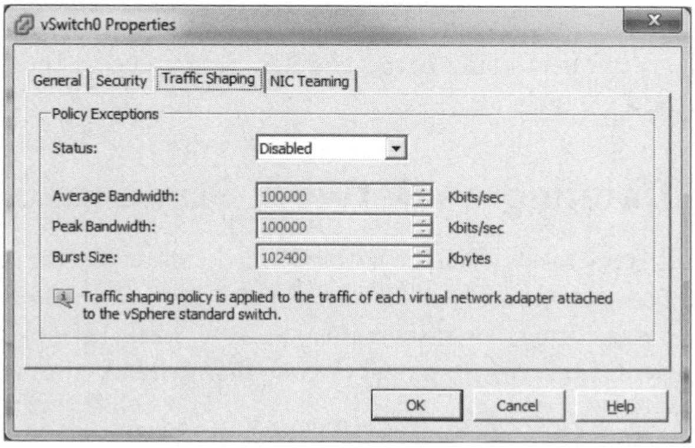

NIC teaming is another capability of a vSwitch. In ESXi, virtual machine network redundancy is provided by the vSwitch. Instead of the virtual machine having multiple network adapters set up in a teamed configuration, a vSwitch is set up to provide this fault tolerance. The options to configure this redundancy are found on the NIC Teaming tab of the vSwitch properties (Figure 4.4).

FIGURE 4.4 Options for NIC teaming

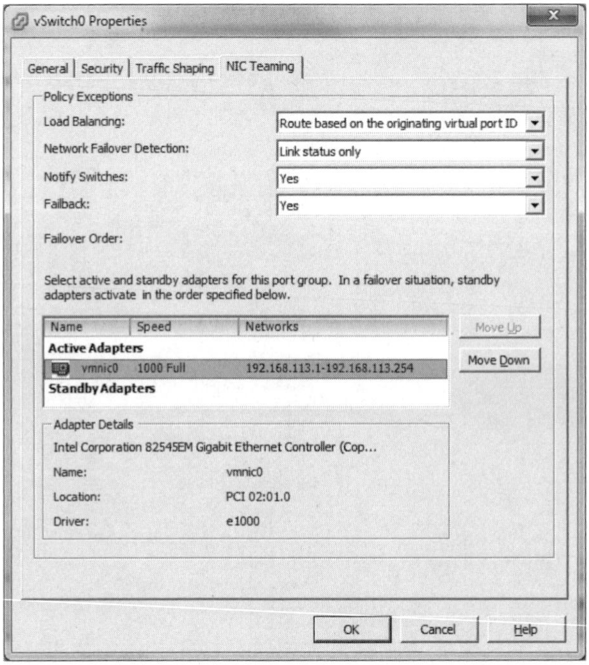

vSwitches also have the ability to use Cisco Discovery Protocol (CDP), which is Cisco's proprietary discovery protocol. CDP information can be obtained for peer devices connected to the network adapters on vNetwork standard switches by clicking the information icon beside the vSwitch, as shown in Figure 4.5.

vSwitches have many powerful capabilities, and many of the capabilities just covered will be discussed in much greater detail later in this chapter. Before I cover those details, I will cover how to create a vSwitch.

Creating and Deleting a vNetwork Standard Switch

When ESXi is installed interactively, a single vSwitch named vSwitch0 is created by default. This vSwitch contains two port groups: one for virtual machines and one for management. This default vSwitch will get you started, but at some point you will likely need to add additional networks. Exercise 4.1 will cover creating a new vSwitch that will be dedicated for virtual machine network traffic.

FIGURE 4.5 CDP information

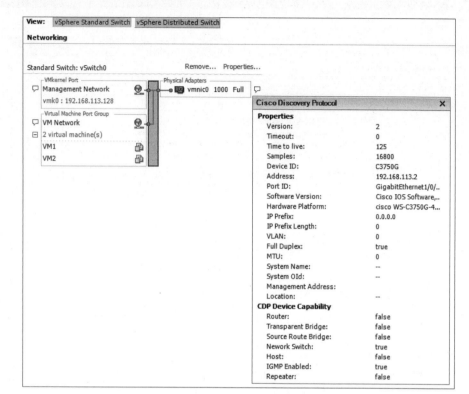

EXERCISE 4.1

Creating a vSwitch

1. Connect to an ESXi host with the vSphere Client.

2. Click the Configuration tab.

3. Click the blue Networking link in the Hardware panel.

4. Click the blue Add Networking link located in the upper-right corner. The Add Network Wizard will begin.

5. Select the Virtual Machine connection type and click the Next button to continue.

6. Choose the Create A vSphere Standard Switch option and select the NICs that will be used for the new virtual switch.

(continued)

EXERCISE 4.1 *(continued)*

7. Notice the Preview window at the bottom of the screen that shows what your choices will look like when implemented. Once the NICs are configured, click the Next button to continue.

8. Give the port group a network label. If using multiple ESXi hosts with vCenter and vMotion, make sure this network label is consistent across all of your ESXi hosts to ensure vMotion works properly. Choose a VLAN ID for this network if applicable and click the Next button to continue.

9. Review the preview information in the Summary screen and click the Finish button to add the vNetwork standard switch to the ESXi host.

10. An Update Network Configuration task will begin. When this task completes, review the switch information now shown for accuracy.

One part of this exercise that can be somewhat confusing is use of the terms *connection type* and *port group*. In step 5 of this exercise, you were asked to choose a connection type. In step 8, you were asked to provide a label for the port group. The connection type you choose will determine the type of port group that is created.

When adding a new vSwitch, a port group will be created by default. This is because a vSwitch without port groups would be like a physical switch without any ports.

It is always best to select at least two NICs for a vSwitch used for virtual machine network traffic in order to provide both redundancy and load balancing.

Now that you have created a new vSwitch, I will discuss the procedure for removing a vSwitch. Since you will build on the vSwitch you just created in future exercises in this chapter, I will describe only the steps to remove the vSwitch. To remove a vSwitch, locate the vSwitch in the Configuration tab and click the Remove link located directly above it. You will be prompted to confirm the removal of the vSwitch (Figure 4.6). Click the Yes button to continue.

FIGURE 4.6   Removing a vSwitch

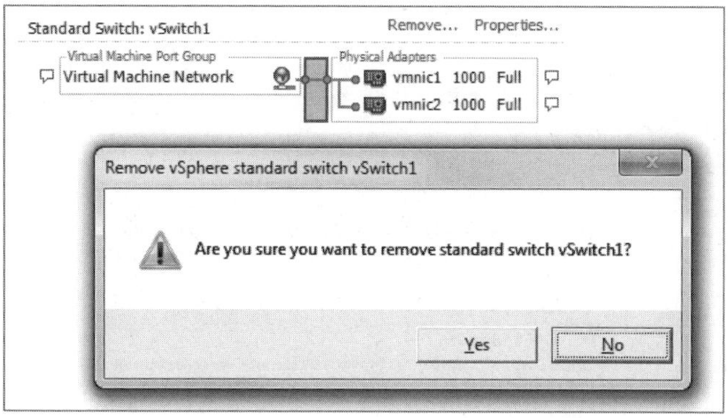

Attempting to delete a vSwitch will fail if virtual machines are actively using the vSwitch.

Now that I have covered creating and deleting vSwitches, I will next cover adding, configuring, and removing *vmnics* on a vSwitch.

Adding, Configuring, and Removing vmnics on a vNetwork Standard Switch

As your virtual environment grows, you will want to ensure that it can scale to meet these demands. In the event that virtual machine networking traffic were to approach capacity, it is possible to add additional physical NICs (vmnics) to the vSwitch. Exercise 4.2 will cover how to add an additional vmnic to an existing vSwitch and configure it.

EXERCISE 4.2

Adding a vmnic to a vSwitch and Configuring It

1. Connect to an ESXi host with the vSphere Client.

2. Click the Configuration tab.

3. Click the blue Networking link in the Hardware panel.

4. Locate the vSwitch created in Exercise 4.1 and click the blue Properties link for the vSwitch.

5. The vSwitch Properties window will appear. The Ports tab is shown by default. Click the Network Adapters tab.

6. Click the Add button at the bottom of the vSwitch Properties window. The Add Adapter Wizard will launch.

7. Select an unused vmnic from the Unclaimed Adapters list. Click the Next button to continue.

8. Review the policy failover order, as shown here.

9. Since the lead-in to this exercise discussed adding network capacity for virtual machines, ensure that all adapters are listed under Active Adapters.

   Standby adapters will be used only if the active adapters fail. If you want to make one or more adapters active and one or more standby, you can do so by selecting the vmnic and then using the Move Up and Move Down buttons.

10. Click the Next button to continue. Review the preview information in the Summary screen and click the Finish button to add the vmnic to the vSwitch.

11. An Update Virtual Switch task will begin. When this task completes, review the Network Adapters tab to ensure that the newly added vmnic is listed.

12. Click the Close button in the vSwitch Properties window.

At this point, the new NIC has been added to the vSwitch, and virtual machine network traffic will begin to use it. The addition of a vmnic is a nondisruptive action for virtual machines.

Another situation that you may encounter is the need to remove a vmnic from a vSwitch. This could happen when a vSwitch was built with too many NICs or is experiencing low utilization with the number of NICs currently available, and this capacity could now be better utilized on another vSwitch. Exercise 4.3 will cover how to remove a vmnic from an existing vSwitch.

EXERCISE 4.3

Removing a vmnic from a vSwitch

1. Connect to an ESXi host with the vSphere Client.

2. Click the Configuration tab.

3. Click the blue Networking link in the Hardware panel.

4. Locate the vSwitch you want to remove the vmnic from and click the blue Properties link for the vSwitch.

5. The vSwitch Properties window will appear. The Ports tab is shown by default. Click the Network Adapters tab.

6. Select the vmnic you want to remove and then click the Remove button at the bottom of the vSwitch Properties window.

7. You will be prompted to confirm the removal of the vmnic. Click the Yes button to continue.

8. An Update Virtual Switch task will begin. When this task completes, review the Network Adapters tab to ensure that the removed vmnic is no longer listed.

9. Click the Close button on the vSwitch Properties window.

At this point, the NIC has been removed from the vSwitch, and any virtual machine network traffic that was using this vmnic will be moved to an active vmnic in the vSwitch. The removal of a vmnic is a nondisruptive action for virtual machines.

Now that you have created, configured, and removed a vmnic from a vSwitch, it should be easier to see how vSwitches have the ability to scale with your environment. You can now turn your attention to configuring VMkernel ports for network services.

Configuring VMkernel Ports for Network Services

As mentioned in the beginning of this chapter, the VMkernel (vmknic) is used for host-based connections such as ESXi management traffic, vMotion, FT, iSCSI, and NFS. The process for configuring VMkernel ports differs from configuring virtual machine connection types in that an IP address is assigned to the VMkernel as part of the configuration. In Exercise 4.4, you will create a new vSwitch and configure a VMkernel port for vMotion use.

EXERCISE 4.4

Configuring a vSwitch with a VMkernel Port Group for vMotion

1. Connect to an ESXi host with the vSphere Client.

2. Click the Configuration tab.

3. Click the blue Networking link in the Hardware panel.

4. Click the blue Add Networking link in the upper-right corner. The Add Network Wizard will launch.

5. Select VMkernel from the Connection Types and click the Next button to continue.

6. Choose the Create A vSphere Standard Switch option and select the NICs that will be used for the new virtual switch.

(continued)

7. Click the Next button to continue.

8. In the Connection Settings step of the Add Network Wizard, give the VMkernel port group a network label. It is important to remember that this network label must be consistent across all ESX/ESXi hosts that vMotion will be used with.

9. If a VLAN ID is required, enter the VLAN ID.

10. Select the Use This Port Group For vMotion box. The final configuration should appear similar to what is shown here.

11. Click the Next button to continue.

12. In the IP Settings step of the Add Network Wizard, assign the VMkernel an IP address and subnet mask. For the purposes of this exercise, assume that the VMkernel used for vMotion will be on an isolated network. The final configuration should appear similar to what is shown here.

Add Network Wizard

VMkernel - IP Connection Settings
  Specify VMkernel IP settings

Connection Type
Network Access
☐ Connection Settings
  IP Settings
  Summary

○ Obtain IP settings automatically
◉ Use the following IP settings:

IP Address: 10 . 100 . 100 . 100

Subnet Mask: 255 . 255 . 255 . 0

VMkernel Default Gateway: 192 . 168 . 113 . 1   Edit...

Preview:

┌ VMkernel Port ─────────────┐   ┌ Physical Adapters ──┐
  vMotion2   vmnic4
  10.100.100.100   vmnic5

Help   ≤ Back   Next ≥   Cancel

13. Click the Next button to continue.

14. Review the Summary information and click the Finish button to save the changes.

15. An Update Network Configuration task will start. When this task completes, verify that the new vSwitch has been created and that a vMotion port group is listed.

As shown in step 12 of the previous exercise, a VMkernel default gateway may not always be required.

VMware best practices recommend that vMotion traffic be isolated on a separate network dedicated to vMotion. This is because the contents of the guest operating system's memory are transmitted over the network during a vMotion. Not isolating vMotion traffic could have serious security implications and should always be considered in network designs.

These same best practices of isolation generally apply for any VMkernel connection type. vMotion, storage, management, and FT traffic are all best configured in isolation. The previous exercise covered how to add a new vSwitch with a VMkernel port group used for vMotion, but a vMotion port group could have easily been configured on any existing vSwitch. The configuration for any VMkernel connection type, such as FT, iSCSI, NFS, and management traffic, is very similar; I will now discuss the setup for each VMkernel type.

In step 10 of Exercise 4.4, you selected the Use This Port Group For vMotion option. Figure 4.7 shows the available options.

FIGURE 4.7   VMkernel options

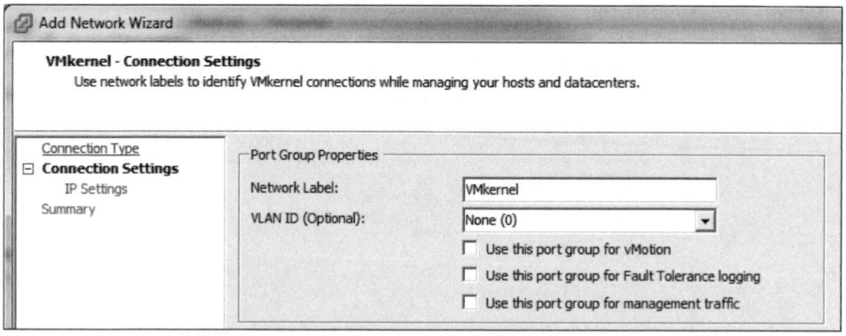

The use case for these three options is as follows:

Use This Port Group For vMotion   To enable vMotion traffic to be used with the port group

Use This Port Group For Fault Tolerance Logging   To enable FT traffic to be used with the port group

Use This Port Group For Management Traffic   To enable management traffic to be used with the port group

> To use the VMkernel for network storage (iSCSI or NFS), you would simply omit any of the options listed previously when configuring the VMkernel.

Now that I have covered configuring VMkernel port groups and some of the best practices, I will cover adding, editing, and removing port groups on a vSwitch.

Adding, Editing, and Removing Port Groups on a vNetwork Standard Switch

In Exercise 4.4 you created a vSwitch and a VMkernel port group to be used for vMotion. For Exercise 4.5, assume that you added this vMotion port group too soon, since you have only a single ESXi host. Also, assume that you need to add NFS storage to this ESXi host immediately. In Exercise 4.5, you will edit the vMotion port group to allow it to be used for accessing NFS storage instead.

EXERCISE 4.5

Editing a Port Group in a vSwitch

1. Connect to an ESXi host with the vSphere Client.

2. Click the Configuration tab.

3. Click the blue Networking link in the Hardware panel.

4. Locate the vSwitch created in Exercise 4.4 and click the blue Properties link for this vSwitch.

5. The vSwitch Properties window will appear. The Ports tab is shown by default.

6. Select the vMotion port group from the left pane and then click the Edit button. The Properties tab for the port group will open.

7. Change the Network Label to **NFS** and deselect vMotion Enabled, as shown here.

8. Click the OK button to continue. A Reconfigure Port Group task will begin. When this task completes, click the Close button on the vSwitch Properties window.

You have now edited what was a VMkernel port group configured for vMotion to instead be a VMkernel port group configured for NFS storage access.

Again, strictly for the purposes of Exercise 4.6, assume that you also need to configure your NFS appliance via its web management interface. The problem is that this management interface is sitting on the same network that you just set up a VMkernel connection type on to access the NFS volumes, but you can't use the VMkernel connection type for virtual machine networking. To get around this, you will temporarily create a virtual machine port group on this network. This will allow you to access the web management interface from a virtual machine. Exercise 4.6 will cover the steps to add and remove a virtual machine network port group to a vSwitch.

EXERCISE 4.6

Adding a Port Group in a vSwitch

1. Connect to an ESXi host with the vSphere Client.

2. Click the Configuration tab.

3. Click the blue Networking link in the Hardware panel.

4. Locate the vSwitch that was just modified in Exercise 4.5 and click the blue Properties link for this vSwitch.

5. The vSwitch Properties window will appear. The Ports tab is shown by default.

6. Click the Add button at the bottom of the window.

7. The Add Network Wizard will launch. Choose a Virtual Machine connection type and click the Next button to continue.

8. Give the virtual machine port group a network label, and enter a VLAN ID if required.

9. Click the Next button to continue and then review the information presented on the Summary screen.

10. Click the Finish button to add the virtual machine port group to the vSwitch. An Update Network Configuration task will begin.

11. When this task completes, verify that the virtual machine port group is listed in the vSwitch properties. Click the Close button to exit the vSwitch properties.

Now you have a virtual machine port group on the vSwitch used for the NFS storage network, and this virtual machine port group may be presented to any virtual machine on your ESXi host(s). This is accomplished through the virtual machine settings, as shown in Figure 4.8.

FIGURE 4.8   VM network labels

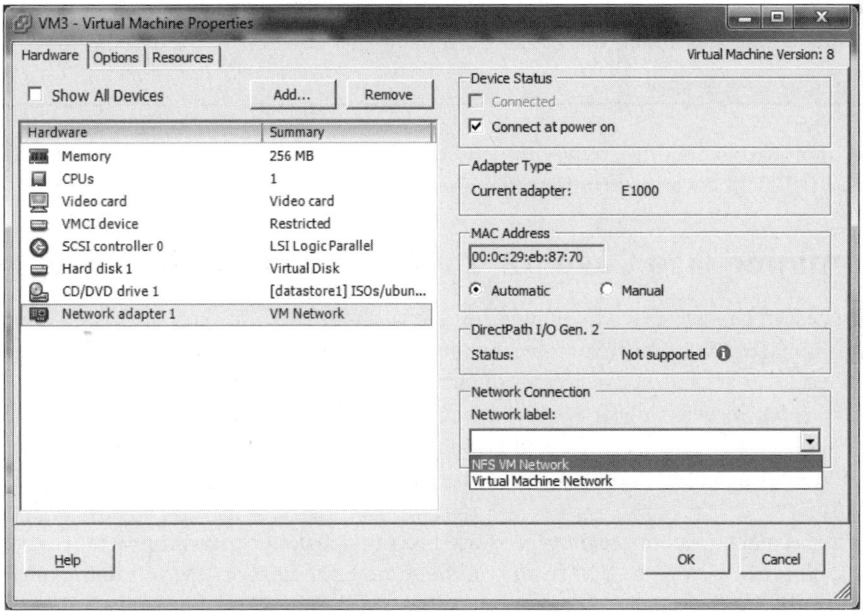

For the purposes of Exercise 4.7, assume that you are done using the virtual machine to configure the NFS server. Now for security purposes, you want to power off the virtual machine and remove this virtual machine network from the vSwitch. Exercise 4.7 will detail the procedure to remove this virtual machine port group from the vSwitch.

EXERCISE 4.7

Removing a Port Group in a vSwitch

1. Connect to an ESXi host with the vSphere Client.

2. Click the Configuration tab.

3. Click the blue Networking link in the Hardware panel.

4. Locate the vSwitch that was just modified in Exercise 4.6 and click the blue Properties link for this vSwitch.

5. The vSwitch Properties window will appear. The Ports tab is shown by default. Highlight the virtual machine port group created in Exercise 4.6 and then click the Remove button at the bottom of the window. You will be prompted to confirm removal of the port group. Click the Yes button to proceed. A Remove Port Group task will start.

6. When this task completes, verify that the port group is no longer listed in the vSwitch properties. Click the Close button on the vSwitch Properties window to continue.

I have now covered adding, removing, and editing port groups on vNetwork standard switches. I will next cover determining the use case for a vSwitch.

Determining Use Case for a vNetwork Standard Switch

I have discussed the use cases for vSwitches throughout the first part of this chapter, and I will now review them. vSwitches are software constructs of the local ESXi host that process layer 2 Ethernet headers. Since the vSwitch is a software construct of ESXi, a vCenter Server is never required to use a vSwitch. vSwitches are used to provide network services to the ESXi host and virtual machines. The two types of network services are virtual machine and VMkernel and are also known as connection types and port groups.

The virtual machine connection type is used to provide connections for virtual machines. This can be VM to VM traffic on the same ESXi host or VM to other external network traffic. Virtual machine connection types are the simpler of the two connection types, with the VLAN ID being the only unique configurable option.

VMkernel connection types are used to provide management network access, vMotion, FT, iSCSI, and NFS connections for ESXi hosts. These connection types have an IP address, whereas virtual machine connection types do not.

In summary, any virtual environment that needs networking capability could be a use case for a vSwitch. One exception to keep in mind is regarding *converged adapters* and 10 GbE adapters. If the ESXi host has a limited number of adapters, you may run into certain limitations when using vSwitches to manage multiple networks on fewer adapters. The next section of this chapter will move away from the vSwitch and focus on the vNetwork Distributed Switch (vDS), or dvSwitch.

Configuring vNetwork Distributed Switches

Understanding how to use and configure the vNetwork Distributed Switch is also a key requirement for the VCP5 exam. It will also be important to know the distinguishing capabilities of the dvSwitch. While many of the concepts are the same between vSwitch and dvSwitch, the dvSwitch adds many new features and functionalities that simply are not available with vSwitch. The first topic I will cover in this section is identifying the capabilities of the vNetwork Distributed Switch.

Identifying vNetwork Distributed Switch Capabilities

A vNetwork Distributed Switch (vDS) differs from a vNetwork standard switch (vSS) in that it allows a single virtual switch representation to span multiple ESXi hosts. This is a significant difference from the vSwitch, which relies on each ESXi host to have specific networking configured. Figure 4.9 shows the architecture of the dvSwitch. It is important to remember that in order to use dvSwitch, you are required to have both vCenter Server and the Enterprise Plus edition of vSphere.

You will see the terms *vNetwork Distributed Switch*, *vDS*, and *dvSwitch* throughout this chapter. It is important to remember that these terms are all referring to the same thing. For the sake of consistency, the term *dvSwitch* will be used most often.

FIGURE 4.9   dvSwitch architecture

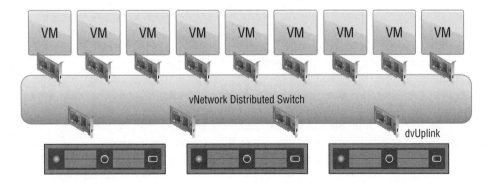

The dvSwitch includes all of the capabilities of the vSwitch, which I discussed earlier in this chapter, plus the following additional capabilities:

- Bidirectional virtual machine rate limiting (traffic shaping)
- Centralized vCenter administration and provisioning
- Cisco Nexus 1000V virtual switch (3rd party add-on)
- Dynamic adjustment for load-based NIC teaming
- Enhanced security and monitoring for vMotion traffic
- IEEE 802.1p tagging
- LLDP
- Netflow
- Network I/O Control
- Port mirror
- Private VLAN support

I will now cover each of these capabilities briefly. Where the vSwitch can shape only outbound (also known as *egress* or *TX*) traffic, the dvSwitch can shape also shape inbound (also known as *ingress* or *RX*) traffic. Traffic shaping is used when bandwidth limits need to be imposed on virtual machines.

dvSwitches are administered and provisioned from within vCenter, meaning that there is a single configuration to manage. This approach offers advantages over maintaining multiple vSwitch configurations on multiple ESXi hosts, especially in large environments.

Many of the features of the Enterprise Plus edition of vSphere are geared toward large environments. If you have never worked in a large environment, some of these features may not seem applicable to your situation. For the exam, it will be still be necessary to understand these features and their uses. You may have to think outside of your comfort zone to understand how powerful some of these features could be to an environment with hundreds of ESXi hosts and thousands of virtual machines.

The Cisco Nexus 1000V is a third-party dvSwitch that can be implemented inside your virtual infrastructure. This brings many enhancements such as the use of ACLs, port security, and more. But possibly the biggest change this technology brings is in the management of the virtual networks. With the Cisco Nexus 1000V, the network staff can manage a Cisco network device and realize the benefits of using a platform that they already understand how to use and are comfortable with.

Load-based NIC teaming uses a load-balancing algorithm to regularly check the load on teamed NICs. If one NIC is overloaded, a port-NIC mapping reassignment will occur to attempt to balance the load. This process can keep the load on teamed NICs balanced and is a significant improvement over how teaming is performed on the standard vSwitch.

Virtual machine networking state, including counters and port statistics, is tracked as virtual machines are migrated with vMotion from host to host in a dvSwitch. This provides a more consistent view of the virtual machine's network interfaces, regardless of the VM's location or migration history and simplifies the troubleshooting and network monitoring for virtual machines.

IEEE 802.1p tagging is a standard used to provide quality of service (*QoS*) at the media access control (MAC) level. This capability can be used to guarantee I/O resources and is applied to outbound network traffic.

vSphere 5 supports Link Layer Discovery Protocol (LLDP), which is a standards-based (IEEE 802.1AB) and vendor-neutral discovery protocol. Much like Cisco's proprietary discovery protocol CDP, LLDP is used to discover information about network devices.

Netflow is another new feature of the dvSwitch version available in vSphere 5. It allows the monitoring of application flows (or IP traffic). This NetFlow data helps in capacity planning and in ensuring that I/O resources are properly utilized in the virtual infrastructure.

Network I/O Control allows the creation of resource pools containing network bandwidth. Administrators can create new resource pools to associate with port groups and specify 802.1p tags, allowing different virtual machines to be in different resource pools. This allows a subset of virtual machines to be given a higher or lower share of bandwidth than the others.

Port mirroring is when a network switch sends a copy of network packets seen on switch ports, or an entire VLAN, to a network monitoring device connected to another switch port. This is also known as Switch Port Analyzer (SPAN) on Cisco switches. Port mirror is used for monitoring or troubleshooting.

A *Private VLAN (PVLAN)* is used to provide isolation between computers on the same IP subnet and can be useful in virtual environments. A PVLAN can be described as a nested VLAN, or a VLAN located within a VLAN. The first VLAN is known as the primary, while the nested VLANs are known as secondary. There are three types of PVLAN ports:

Promiscuous   Can communicate with all ports, including the isolated and community ports

Isolated   Can communicate with only promiscuous ports

Community   Can communicate with all ports in the same secondary PVLAN and the promiscuous PVLAN

As you can see, the dvSwitch offers many advanced capabilities that the vSwitch does not. While the dvSwitch may not be suitable for every environment, it is still important to know its capabilities for the exam. I will now cover how to create a dvSwitch and then cover how to leverage many of its capabilities.

Creating and Deleting a vNetwork Distributed Switch

dvSwitches can be created at the vCenter Server datacenter level. In vCenter Server 5, there are three versions of the dvSwitch that can be created:

vSphere Distributed Switch Version 4.0   This version is compatible with vSphere 4.0 and newer, but features supported by later versions of the dvSwitch will not be available.

vSphere Distributed Switch Version 4.1.0   This version is compatible with vSphere 4.1 and newer, and it introduces load-based teaming and Network I/O Control.

vSphere Distributed Switch Version 5.0.0   This version is compatible vSphere 5 and newer and introduces user-defined network resource pools in Network I/O Control, NetFlow, and port mirroring.

Now that I have reviewed the three versions of the dvSwitch available in vCenter Server 5, I will cover creating a version 5.0.0 dvSwitch in Exercise 4.8. The requirements for the exercises in the remainder of this chapter are vCenter Server 5 with Enterprise Plus licensing or running in *Evaluation Mode* and a minimum of two ESXi 5 hosts with two available/unassigned physical NICs. Also note that the exercises in the remainder of this chapter will build on each other sequentially, beginning with Exercise 4.8.

EXERCISE 4.8

Creating a dvSwitch

1. Connect to a vCenter Server with the vSphere Client.

2. Select the Home icon on the navigation bar and then click the Networking option located under Inventory.

3. Right-click a datacenter in the left pane. When the context menu appears, choose the New vSphere Distributed Switch option. If this option is grayed out, ensure that you are in the Networking view described in step 2.

4. The Create vSphere Distributed Switch Wizard will launch. Choose the vSphere Distributed Switch Version 5.0.0 option and click the Next button to continue.

5. Give the dvSwitch a name and accept the default value of 4 for the number of uplinks. The result should look similar to what's shown here.

    Uplink ports are used to connect the dvSwitch to physical NICs on ESXi hosts and represent the maximum number of per-host physical NICs that may be connected the dvSwitch.

6. Click the Next button to continue.

7. On the Add Hosts And Physical Adapters screen, select the Add Now option at the top. Then select a single ESXi 5 host from the list.

   You can also use the blue View Incompatible Hosts link at the top of the screen to verify whether the host you plan to use is compatible with the version of the dvSwitch you selected in step 4.

8. Once an ESXi 5 host has been selected, expand it to view the available network adapters. You can use the blue View Details link located beside each adapter to view the adapter details. For this exercise, select a single physical adapter from the list. The result should look similar to what's shown here.

(continued)

Create vSphere Distributed Switch

Add Hosts and Physical Adapters   vSphere Distributed Switch Version: 5.0.0
Select hosts and physical adapters to add to the new vSphere distributed switch.

Select VDS Version
General Properties
Add Hosts and Physical Adapters
Ready to Complete

When do you want to add hosts and their physical adapters to the new vSphere distributed switch?
○ Add now
○ Add later

Settings...   View Incompatible Hosts...

Host/Physical adapters	In use by switch	Settings	
☑ 🖳 esxi1.test.local		View Details...	
Select physical adapters			
☑ 🖳 vmnic4	--	View Details...	
☐ 🖳 vmnic5	--	View Details...	

Help   ≤ Back   Next ≥   Cancel

9. Click the Next button to continue. On the Ready To Complete screen, leave the Automatically Create a Default Port Group option selected and review the settings. Click the Finish button to create the dvSwitch.

10. A Create A vSphere Distributed Switch task and an Add dvPort Groups task will each begin. When both of these tasks have completed, verify that the dvSwitch is listed in the left pane in the Networking view.

At this point, the dvSwitch could be used, assuming that the uplink chosen in the exercise was physically connected and on the correct network. To test connecting to the dvSwitch, return to the Hosts And Clusters view. Right-click a virtual machine, and choose the Edit Settings option from the context menu that appears. Select a network adapter and then choose the dvPortGroup (dVS) from the network adapter drop-down menu, as in Figure 4.10. Click the OK button to save the changes, and then test the network connection from the VM.

You now have a single ESXi host configured to use your newly created dvSwitch, but the power of this feature is in having all of your ESXi hosts use it. In the next section, I will cover how to add and remove additional ESXi hosts to this dvSwitch.

FIGURE 4.10: VM network label

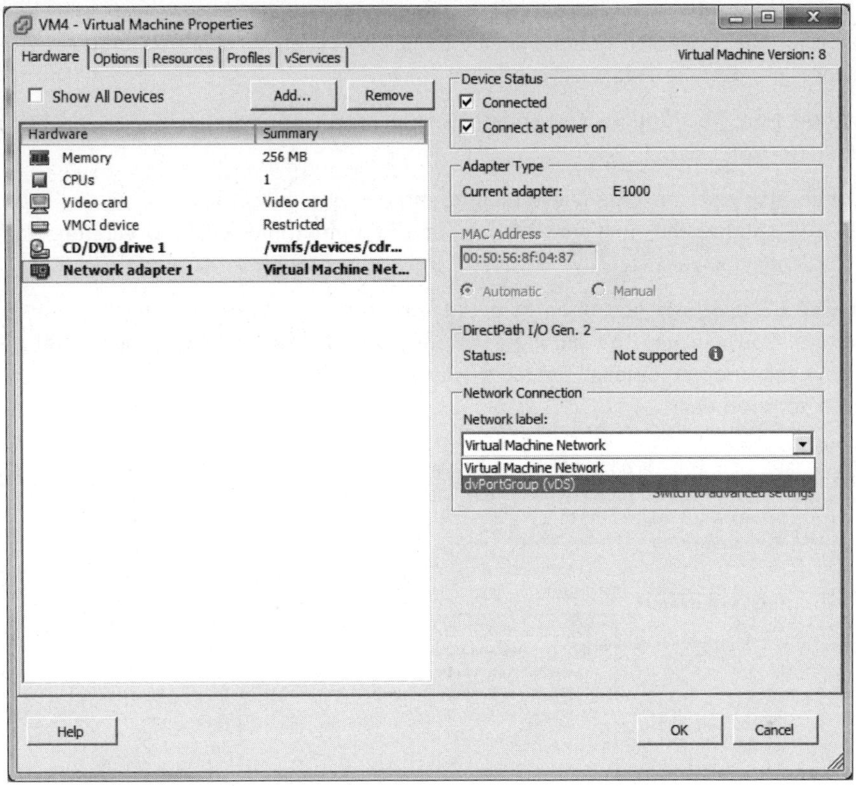

Adding and Removing ESXi Hosts to/from a vNetwork Distributed Switch

In Exercise 4.8, you learned that ESXi hosts can be added to a dvSwitch when the dvSwitch is created. Additional ESXi hosts can also be added or removed to a dvSwitch, after it has been created. Exercise 4.9 will cover adding ESXi hosts to the dvSwitch created in Exercise 4.8. The ESXi 5 host that will be added in Exercise 4.9 should be a different ESXi 5 host than the one used in Exercise 4.8.

EXERCISE 4.9

Adding an ESXi Host to a dvSwitch

1. Connect to a vCenter Server with the vSphere Client.

2. Select the Home icon on the navigation bar and then click the Networking option located under Inventory.

(continued)

3. Right-click the dvSwitch created in Exercise 4.8. When the context menu appears, choose the Add Host option.

4. The Add Host To vSphere Distributed Switch Wizard will begin. Select an ESXi 5 host from the list.

You can also use the blue View Incompatible Hosts link at the top of the screen to verify whether the host you plan to use is compatible with the version of the dvSwitch in use.

5. Once an ESXi 5 host has been selected, expand it to view the available network adapters. You can use the blue View Details link located beside each adapter to view the adapter details. Select a single adapter from this and click the Next button to continue.

6. On the Network Connectivity screen, leave any existing virtual adapters with the setting of Do Not Migrate. For now you just want to focus on adding the ESXi host to the dvSwitch. Click the Next button to continue.

7. On the Virtual Machine Networking screen, leave the option Migrate Virtual Machine Networking unchecked and click the Next button to continue.

8. Review the information presented in the Ready To Complete screen. Notice that the changes are highlighted in yellow.

(continued)

```
Add Host to vSphere Distributed Switch                                          ⊟ ⊡ X

  Ready to Complete
      Verify the settings for the new vSphere distributed switch.

  Select Host and Physical Adapters    vDS
  Network Connectivity
  Virtual Machine Networking
  Ready to Complete
                                    ⊕ dvPortGroup              ⊟ vDS-DVUplinks-171

                                    VLAN ID: --                  ⊟ 🔹 dvUplink1 (2 NIC Adapters)
                                    ⊞ Virtual Machines (1)            vmnic4 esxi1.test.local
                                                                      vmnic4 esxi2.test.local
                                                              ⊟ 🔹 dvUplink2 (0 NIC Adapters)
                                                                      New Port esxi2.test.local
                                                              ⊟ 🔹 dvUplink3 (0 NIC Adapters)
                                                                      New Port esxi2.test.local
                                                              ⊟ 🔹 dvUplink4 (0 NIC Adapters)
                                                                      New Port esxi2.test.local

      Help                                        ≤ Back    Finish      Cancel
```

9. Click the Finish button. A Reconfigure vSphere Distributed Switch task will begin. When this task completes, click the Hosts tab for the dvSwitch and verify that the ESXi 5 host just added appears in the list.

You have now added an additional ESXi host to your dvSwitch. The ESXi host can also be removed from the dvSwitch. You may recall from earlier in this chapter how a vSwitch cannot be removed if virtual machines are connected to it. This is also true when removing an ESXi host from a dvSwitch. Ensure that no virtual machines are connected to the dvSwitch before removing it or you will receive an error. Exercise 4.10 will cover removing an ESXi host from the dvSwitch.

Removing an ESXi host from a dvSwitch

1. Connect to a vCenter Server with the vSphere Client.

2. Select the Home icon on the navigation bar and then click the Networking option located under Inventory.

3. Select the dvSwitch used in Exercise 4.9 in the left pane. In the right pane, click the Hosts tab.

4. Right-click the ESXi host added Exercise 4.9, and when the context menu appears, choose the Remove From vSphere Distributed Switch option.

5. You will be prompted to confirm the removal of the dvSwitch. Click the Yes button to continue and remove the dvSwitch.

6. A Reconfigure vSphere Distributed Switch task will begin. When this task completes, verify that the ESXi host is no longer listed in the Hosts tab for the dvSwitch.

I have now covered adding and removing ESXi hosts to a dvSwitch. In the next section I will cover adding, configuring, and removing dvPort groups to a dvSwitch.

Adding, Configuring, and Removing dvPort Groups

Distributed port groups (*dvPort groups*) are similar to port groups in the vSwitch. They are used to provide networking for virtual machines and to the VMkernel in dvSwitches. However, the way in which dvPort groups are configured in the dvSwitch is different from the way in which port groups are configured in the vSwitch. To show these differences, Exercise 4.11 will add a dvPort group used for virtual machine traffic to a dvSwitch.

EXERCISE 4.11

Adding a dvPort Group to a dvSwitch

1. Connect to a vCenter Server with the vSphere Client.

2. Select the Home icon on the navigation bar and then click the Networking option located under Inventory.

3. Right-click the same dvSwitch used in Exercise 4.8 in the left pane. In the context menu that appears, choose the New Port Group option. The Create Distributed Port Group Wizard will begin.

4. Give the dvPort group a descriptive name and accept the default number of 128 ports. From the VLAN Type drop-down menu, choose the VLAN option. Assign a value to the VLAN in the VLAN ID field that appears.

(continued)

EXERCISE 4.11 *(continued)*

5. Click the Next button to continue and then review the information presented on the Ready To Complete screen. Click the Finish button to add the dvPort group to the dvSwitch.

6. An Add dvPort Group task will begin. When this task completes, verify that the new dvPort group is listed in the left pane. Review the information shown in the Summary tab.

In Exercise 4.11 there were four options for the VLAN type drop-down menu:

None   No VLAN will be used. This is the equivalent of leaving the optional VLAN ID field blank when creating a port group in a vSwitch.

VLAN   This is used to enter a VLAN ID with a value between 1 and 4094. This is the equivalent of setting a value for the optional VLAN ID when creating a port group in a vSwitch.

VLAN Trunking   This is used to enter a VLAN trunk range. This is different from a vSwitch in that a single dvPort group may be used to handle all of the trunked VLANs. A vSwitch would require a port group per VLAN to achieve the same result.

Private VLAN   This is used to select a private VLAN. If private VLANs have not been established, this option cannot be used. There is no equivalent functionality in the vSwitch.

🌐 Real World Scenario

Simplifying VLAN Trunking with dvSwitches

A customer has 250 VLANs that are being trunked to a vSwitch with 250 port groups. The customer is expecting to grow in the next 6 months and will need to add 50 VLANs to this trunk. As per the vSphere 5 Configuration Maximums, the maximum number of port groups per standard vSwitch is 256.

You meet with this customer to discuss how to plan for this change. You discover that this customer has Enterprise Plus licensing, and you discuss how moving from a vSwitch to a dvSwitch could solve this problem. A dvPort group can utilize a VLAN trunk range, which would allow the 256 limit present in the vSwitch to be exceeded. This will also simplify switch configuration and allow the customer to scale out for quite some time.

Once a dvPort group has been added to the dvSwitch, you also have the ability to configure additional options. In Exercise 4.12 you will configure additional options for the dvPort group added in Exercise 4.11.

EXERCISE 4.12

Configuring a dvPort Group

1. Connect to a vCenter Server with the vSphere Client.

2. Select the Home icon on the navigation bar and then click the Networking option located under Inventory.

(continued)

3. Select the dvPort group used in Exercise 4.11 in the left pane, and then click the Summary tab for the dvPort group in the right pane. To configure the dvPort group, you can use the blue Edit Settings link listed in the Commands section of the Summary tab for the dvPort group or right-click the dvPort group in the left pane and choose the Edit Settings option from the context menu.

4. The dvPort group Settings window will appear.

5. Review the information contained in the General section. Note the Port Binding drop-down menu at the bottom of this section and the default setting of Static Binding. Port binding will be discussed in detail at the conclusion of this exercise.

6. Click the Policies item in the left pane and review each of the items listed there. I will discuss and show how to configure these policies later in this chapter.

7. Click the Advanced item in the left pane and review the settings. By default both the Allow Override Of Port Policies and Configure Reset At Disconnect settings are enabled.

VLAN46 Settings

General
Policies
  Security
  Traffic Shaping
  VLAN
  Teaming and Failover
  Resource Allocation
  Monitoring
  Miscellaneous
Advanced

Advanced
☑ Allow override of port policies   Edit Override Settings...
☑ Configure reset at disconnect

Help   OK   Cancel

8. Click the blue Edit Override Settings link in the upper-right corner. The Port Group Override Settings window will appear. To allow all policies to be overridden at the port level, select the Yes option for all of the items listed in the Port Group Override Settings window.

Port Group Override Settings

Select individual port setting overrides.

Override Settings

Settings	**Overrides Allowed?**	
Block Port:	● Yes	○ No
Traffic Shaping:	● Yes	○ No
Vendor Configuration:	● Yes	○ No
VLAN:	● Yes	○ No
Uplink Teaming:	● Yes	○ No
Resource Allocation:	● Yes	○ No
Security Policy:	● Yes	○ No
NetFlow:	● Yes	○ No

Help   OK   Cancel

9. Click the OK button to save the port group override settings.

10. Click the OK button on the dvPort Group Settings window to save these changes. A Reconfigure dvPort Group task will begin.

The Allow Override Of Port Policies option is used to allow distributed port group policies to be overridden on a per-port level. This option is useful for making exceptions for given virtual machines while still maintaining a consistent set of policies for other virtual machines connected to the same dvPort group.

The Configure Reset At Disconnect option is used to restore the dvPort settings to those of the dvPort group when a dvPort is disconnected from a virtual machine. This ensures that no port with override settings is retained beyond disconnection from a virtual machine. This option is used to protect virtual machines from accidental use of a port with settings that have override values assigned.

You have now added a dvPort group and configured the override settings for it, but I still need to discuss port binding. *Port binding* determines when dvPorts in a dvPort group are assigned and unassigned to a virtual machine. There are three types of port binding:

- Static binding
- Dynamic binding
- Ephemeral binding

Static binding is the default port binding and is recommended by VMware for general use. With static binding, a dvPort is immediately assigned and reserved when the virtual machine is connected to the dvPort. This guarantees connectivity for the VM, and the dvPort is freed only when the virtual machine is removed from the dvPort group. With static binding, network statistics are kept when using vMotion or power cycling the virtual machine.

Dynamic binding is deprecated in vSphere 5 and was primarily used in situations where there were more virtual machines than available dvPorts but the number of available ports was not ultimately planned to be exceeded. An example of this would be an environment with 150 virtual machines connected to a dvPort group with 128 ports but where only 75 of these virtual machines would ever be powered on simultaneously. With dynamic binding, a dvPort is assigned only when a virtual machine is both powered on and has its NIC connected. The dvPort is freed when the virtual machine is powered off or its NIC is disconnected. With dynamic binding, network statistics are kept when using vMotion but lost if the virtual machine is powered off.

Ephemeral binding is more similar to the behavior of a vSwitch and can be managed either from vCenter Server or directly from the ESXi host. VMware recommends that ephemeral binding be used only for recovery purposes or situations where vCenter Server is unavailable. With ephemeral binding, a dvPort is created and assigned when a virtual machine is both powered on and has its NIC connected. The dvPort is deleted when the virtual machine is powered off or its NIC is disconnected. With ephemeral binding, network statistics are lost when using vMotion or power cycling the virtual machine.

Now that I have covered configuring a dvPort group and discussed port binding in detail, I will move to the next topic of removing a dvPort group. Exercise 4.13 will cover how to remove a dvPort group.

EXERCISE 4.13

Removing a dvPort Group

1. Connect to a vCenter Server with the vSphere Client.

2. Select the Home icon on the navigation bar and then click the Networking option located under Inventory.

3. Select the dvPort group used in the previous two exercises in the left pane. Right-click the dvPort group and choose the Delete option from the context menu.

4. You will be prompted to confirm deletion of the dvPort Group. Click the Yes button to continue.

5. A Delete dvPort Group task will begin. When this task completes, verify that the dvPort group is no longer listed under the dvSwitch.

I have now covered adding, configuring, and removing dvPort groups in dvSwitches. I also covered the override settings options in the advanced dvPort group settings and discussed how port binding works in the dvSwitch. In the next section, I will cover adding and removing uplink adapters to a dvSwitch.

Adding and Removing Uplink Adapters to dvUplink Groups

An uplink adapter is a physical network adapter used to provide external network connectivity to a dvSwitch. One uplink adapter on each ESXi host may be assigned to each uplink port on a dvSwitch. A Distributed Virtual Uplink (*dvUplink*) is used to provide a level of abstraction between the physical network adapters (vmnics) on the ESXi host and the dvSwitch. This allows ESXi hosts using the same dvSwitch to have differing vmnic configurations and still use the same teaming, load balancing, and failover policies.

Exercise 4.14 will cover adding and removing uplink adapters to a dvUplink group.

EXERCISE 4.14

Adding and Removing Uplink Adapters to dvUplink Groups

1. Connect to a vCenter Server with the vSphere Client.

2. Select Hosts and Clusters from the Inventory options and then select an ESXi 5 host in the left pane. This ESXi 5 host should be using the dvSwitch created in Exercise 4.8.

(continued)

EXERCISE 4.14 *(continued)*

3. Click the Configuration tab in the right pane and then select the blue Networking link in the Hardware panel.

4. The default view for this screen is the vSphere Standard Switch view. To change to the vSphere Distributed Switch view, click the gray button labeled vSphere Distributed Switch at the top of the tab. This button and the vSphere Distributed Switch view are shown here.

5. Click the blue Manage Physical Adapters link to begin. The Manage Physical Adapters window will open. Review the current configuration, and note that there are four uplink ports (dvUplink) available but only one physical adapter (vmnic). As shown here, dvUplink1 is used with vmnic4.

6. Click the blue Click To Add NIC link located under dvUplink2. The Add Physical Adapter window will appear. Select a vmnic from the list of Unclaimed Adapters on the left by highlighting it.

(continued)

EXERCISE 4.14 (continued)

7. Click the OK button to add the selected vmnic to the dvUplink. Notice on the Manage Physical Adapters screen that the vmnic just chosen is now listed under dvUplink2.

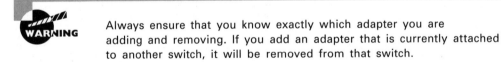

8. Click the OK button to continue and then verify that the uplink was added successfully on the vSphere Distributed Switch screen.

> **WARNING**   Always ensure that you know exactly which adapter you are adding and removing. If you add an adapter that is currently attached to another switch, it will be removed from that switch.

Now that I have covered adding and removing uplink adapters to dvUplink groups, I will cover creating, configuring, and removing virtual adapters in the dvSwitch.

Creating, Configuring, and Removing Virtual Adapters

In a dvSwitch, *virtual adapters* are used to provide VMkernel connections such as ESXi management traffic, vMotion, FT, iSCSI, and NFS. In Exercise 4.15, you will create a virtual adapter that will be used for vMotion traffic.

Adding a Virtual Adapter to a dvSwitch

1. Connect to a vCenter Server with the vSphere Client.

2. Select Hosts And Clusters from the Inventory options and then select an ESXi 5 host in the left pane. This ESXi 5 host should be using the dvSwitch created in Exercise 4.8.

3. Click the Configuration tab in the right pane and then select the blue Networking link from the Hardware panel.

4. The default view for this screen is the vSphere Standard Switch view. To change to the vSphere Distributed Switch view, click the gray button labeled vSphere Distributed Switch at the top of the tab.

5. Click the blue Manage Virtual Adapters link to begin. The Manage Virtual Adapters window will open. Since there are currently no virtual network adapters listed, click the blue Add link in the upper left of this screen.

6. The Add Virtual Adapter Wizard will begin. Choose the New Virtual Adapter option, as shown here.

(continued)

7. Click the Next button to continue. Choose the VMkernel Virtual Adapter Type and click the Next button to continue.

8. Use the drop-down menu beside the Select Port Group option to select the dvPortGroup from vSphere Distributed Switch vDS. Select the Use This Virtual Adapter For vMotion option. The final configuration should look as shown here.

9. Click the Next button to continue. Provide the VMkernel IP address in the Use The Following IP Settings area and then click the Next button to continue.

10. Review the information shown in the Ready To Complete screen. Note that changes to the dvSwitch are listed in yellow.

Add Virtual Adapter

Ready to Complete
Click Finish to confirm the new virtual adapter configuration.

Creation Type
Virtual Adapter Type
Connection Settings
Ready to Complete

vDS

dvPortGroup

VLAN ID: --
VMkernel Ports (1)
New Port : 10.100.100.100
Virtual Machines (0)

dvSwitch-DVUplinks-221

dvUplink1 (1 NIC Adapter)
dvUplink2 (1 NIC Adapter)
dvUplink3 (0 NIC Adapters)
dvUplink4 (0 NIC Adapters)

Help   ≤ Back   Finish   Cancel

11. Click the Finish button to add the virtual network adapter (VMkernel) to the dvSwitch. An Add Virtual NIC task will begin, followed by a Select Virtual NIC task. When these tasks complete, close the Manage Virtual Adapters window.

12. Expand the VMkernel ports item and verify that the information listed for the VMkernel is correct.

Only one vMotion port group per host can be enabled.

There are two options for adding a virtual adapter. In the previous exercise, the New Virtual Adapter option was chosen, but it is also possible to migrate an existing virtual adapter to a dvSwitch. The virtual adapter migration process will be covered in the next section of this chapter.

You have now added a virtual network adapter (VMkernel) interface to your dvSwitch. I will next cover how to configure this virtual adapter in Exercise 4.16.

EXERCISE 4.16

Configuring a Virtual Adapter

1. Connect to a vCenter Server with the vSphere Client.

2. Select Hosts And Clusters from the Inventory options and then select an ESXi 5 host in the left pane. This ESXi 5 host should be using the dvSwitch created in Exercise 4.8.

3. Click the Configuration tab in the right pane and then select the blue Networking link from the Hardware panel.

4. The default view for this screen is the vSphere Standard Switch view. To change to the vSphere Distributed Switch view, click the gray button labeled vSphere Distributed Switch at the top of the tab.

5. Click the blue Manage Virtual Adapters link to begin. The Manage Virtual Adapters window will open. Select vmk1 from the left pane and review the information shown. Note that you may also click the blue View Routing Table link to view the routing table for this virtual adapter.

6. To change any of the settings for the virtual adapter, vmk1 in this case, make sure the virtual adapter is highlighted and then click the blue Edit link at the top of the window.

7. An Edit Virtual Adapter vmk1 window will appear. Review the information in the General tab and then click the IP Settings tab.

8. Change the IP address of this virtual adapter and then click the OK button to continue.

9. An Update Virtual NIC task will begin. When this task completes, verify that the IP address was changed in the IP Settings section of the Manage Virtual Adapters window.

The virtual adapter can also be removed from the same Manage Virtual Adapters window where you just edited the virtual adapter. To remove a virtual adapter, make sure the virtual adapter is highlighted and then click the blue Remove link at the top of the window. You will be prompted to confirm removal by clicking a Yes or No button. Clicking the Yes button will start a Remove Virtual NIC task, and when this task completes, the virtual adapter will no longer be visible in the Manage Virtual Adapters window.

I have now covered adding a virtual adapter to a dvSwitch and also covered how to edit and remove this adapter. In the next section, I will cover how to migrate virtual adapters to and from a vSwitch.

Migrating Virtual Adapters to and from a vNetwork Standard Switch

Sometimes it may be necessary to migrate networking to and from a vSwitch. Exercise 4.17 will cover the steps involved in migrating a virtual adapter from a dvSwitch to an existing vSwitch and then back again.

EXERCISE 4.17

Migrating a Virtual Adapter to a vSwitch

1. Connect to a vCenter Server with the vSphere Client.

2. Select Hosts and Clusters from the Inventory options and then select an ESXi 5 host in the left pane. This ESXi 5 host should be using the dvSwitch created in Exercise 4.8.

(continued)

3. Click the Configuration tab in the right pane and then select the blue Networking link from the Hardware panel.

4. The default view for this screen is the vSphere Standard Switch view. Review the current vSwitch configuration for vSwitch0. It should appear similar to what's shown here.

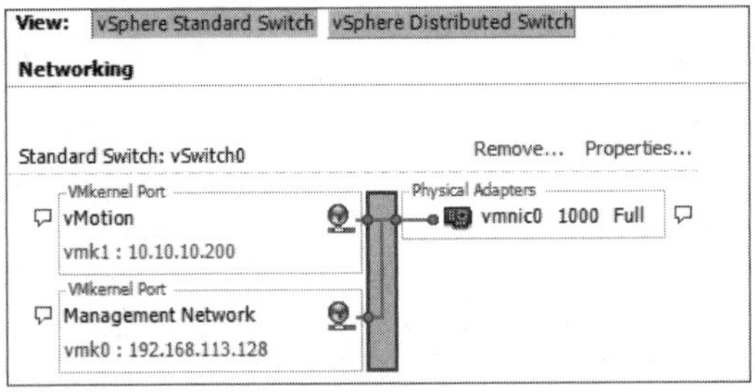

5. Change to the vSphere Distributed Switch view by clicking the gray button labeled vSphere Distributed Switch at the top of the Configuration tab.

6. Click the blue Manage Virtual Adapters link to begin. The Manage Virtual Adapters window will open. Select vmk1 from the left pane and review the information shown.

7. Click the blue Migrate link. The Migrate Virtual Adapter Wizard will begin. Highlight vSwitch0 and click the Next button to continue.

8. Give the port group a network label and VLAN ID, if required. Click the Next button to continue.

9. Review the information in the Ready To Complete screen and click the Finish button to migrate the virtual adapter. An Add Port Group task will begin, and it will be followed by an Update Virtual NIC task.

10. When both of these tasks are complete, verify that the virtual adapter vmk1 is no longer listed in the Manage Virtual Adapters list in the left pane.

11. Click the Close button on the Manage Virtual Adapters screen. Now click the vSphere Standard Switch button at the top of the Configuration tab and verify that the VMkernel was moved to vSwitch0.

(continued)

Depending on how your networking is set up, you may now have an invalid configuration. In the next set of steps, you will return the vMotion virtual adapter to the dvSwitch.

12. Change to the vSphere Distributed Switch view by clicking the gray button labeled vSphere Distributed Switch at the top of the Configuration tab.

13. Click the blue Manage Virtual Adapters link to begin. The Manage Virtual Adapters window will open. Click the blue Add link at the top of this screen.

14. The Add Virtual Adapter Wizard will begin. Select the Migrate Existing Virtual Adapters option and click the Next button.

15. Ensure that a check is placed in the box beside the vMotion virtual adapter. Also ensure that you choose a port group from the drop-down menu on the far right. Leave all other virtual adapters unchecked, since you want to move only the vMotion virtual adapter.

16. Click the Next button to continue. Review the information presented on the Ready To Complete screen and click the Finish button to migrate the virtual adapter back to the dvSwitch.

17. An Update Network Configuration task will begin. When it completes, verify that vmk1 is now listed in the Manage Virtual Adapters list in the left pane. Highlight it and verify the information presented in the right pane.

18. Click the Close button on the Manage Virtual Adapters screen and verify that the dvSwitch now has vmk1 listed under VMkernel ports.

I have now covered migrating virtual adapters to and from a vSwitch. In the next section, I will cover migrating virtual machines to and from a dvSwitch.

Migrating Virtual Machines to and from a vNetwork Distributed Switch

Sometimes it may also be necessary to migrate virtual machine networking to and from a vSwitch. In the following case study, you will examine a scenario where this capability would be useful.

Real World Scenario

Migrating Virtual Machine Networking to a dvSwitch

In an earlier case study in this chapter, you looked at a company that had outgrown an existing vSwitch implementation. The company had decided to use dvSwitches for their virtual machine networks and has performed the prerequisite work required for the move. It is now time to make the transition.

Migrating virtual machine networking will seamlessly allow this company to move all of their virtual machines on the current vSwitch to the new dvSwitch in a few simple steps. The migration is entirely automated, and there is no resulting virtual machine downtime as a result of this move.

Exercise 4.18 will cover the steps involved in migrating virtual machine networking from a dvSwitch to an existing vSwitch and then back again.

EXERCISE 4.18

Migrating Virtual Machines to and from a dvSwitch

1. Connect to a vCenter Server with the vSphere Client.

2. Select Hosts And Clusters from the Inventory options and then select an ESXi 5 host in the left pane. This ESXi 5 host should be using the dvSwitch created in Exercise 4.8.

(continued)

3. Click the Configuration tab and then click the blue Networking link in the Hardware panel. Ensure that the vSphere Standard Switch view is selected; then verify that there is an existing virtual machine network configured on a vSwitch listed here. If not, you will need to create one to complete this exercise. Also ensure that there is at least one virtual machine currently connected to this vSwitch.

```
Standard Switch: vSwitch1                    Remove...  Properties...
┌─ Virtual Machine Port Group ─┐     ┌─ Physical Adapters ─┐
  VM Network - vSwitch      ⊙──○ vmnic1 1000 Full
  1 virtual machine(s)
  VM2
```

VM2 - Virtual Machine Properties
Hardware	Options	Resources	Profiles	vServices

☐ Show All Devices   Add...   Remove

Hardware	Summary
Memory	256 MB
CPUs	1
Video card	Video card
VMCI device	Restricted
SCSI controller 0	LSI Logic SAS
Hard disk 1	Virtual Disk
CD/DVD drive 1	[datastore1] ISOs/ubun...
Network adapter 1	VM Network - vSwitch

4. Next, select the Home icon on the navigation bar and then click the Networking option located under Inventory.

5. Right-click a datacenter in the left pane. When the context menu appears, choose the Migrate Virtual Machine Networking option. The Migrate Virtual Machine Networking Wizard will launch.

6. For the Source Network selection, choose the Include All Virtual Machine Network Adapters That Are Connected To The Following Network option. Use the drop-down menu to match the virtual machine port group with the one from step 3 of this exercise.

7. In the Destination Network options at the bottom of the screen, choose a dvPort group from a dvSwitch.

8. Click the Next button to continue. On the Select VMs To Migrate screen, select All Virtual Machines. Click the Next button to continue.

9. Review the information on the Ready To Complete screen and click the Finish button to migrate the virtual machine networking to the dvSwitch. One or more Reconfigure Virtual Machine tasks will begin.

10. When these tasks are complete, select the dvPort group that the virtual machines were just moved to in the left pane of the Networking view. Click the Virtual Machines tab and verify that the virtual machines are now listed here.

11. Go to a virtual machine and choose the Edit Settings option to verify that the virtual network adapter is now connected to the dvPort group.

(continued)

In the remainder of this exercise, you will move the virtual machine networking back to the vSwitch.

12. In the Networking view, right-click a datacenter in the left pane. When the context menu appears, choose the Migrate Virtual Machine Networking option. The Migrate Virtual Machine Networking Wizard will launch.

13. For the Source Network selection, choose the Include All Virtual Machine Network Adapters That Are Connected To The Following Network option. Use the drop-down menu to select the dvPort group that the virtual machines are currently connected to.

14. In the Destination Network options at the bottom of the screen, choose a virtual machine port group from a vSwitch.

15. Click the Next button to continue. On the Select VMs To Migrate screen, select All Virtual Machines. Click the Next button to continue.

16. Review the information on the Ready To Complete screen and click the Finish button to migrate the virtual machine networking back to the vSwitch. One or more Reconfigure Virtual Machine tasks will begin.

17. When these tasks are complete, select the virtual machine port group that the virtual machines were just moved to in the left pane of the Networking view. Click the Virtual Machines tab and verify that the virtual machines are now listed here.

18. Go to a virtual machine and choose the Edit Settings option to verify that the virtual network adapter is now connected to the virtual machine port group on the vSwitch.

Note that in steps 6 and 7 of Exercise 4.18 you are choosing the options to move all virtual machines connected to the virtual machine port group on a vSwitch to a dvSwitch. In steps 13 and 14, you are choosing the options to move all virtual machines connected to the virtual machine port group on a dvSwitch to a vSwitch. In other words, you are reversing steps 6 and 7.

I have now covered migrating virtual machine networking to and from both a vSwitch and a dvSwitch. In the next section, I will discuss determining the use case for a dvSwitch.

Determining Use Case for a vNetwork Distributed Switch

The use case for dvSwitches could ultimately come down to the size of the environment. Larger environments will be more likely to benefit from many of the advanced features available only in the dvSwitch. To review from earlier, these features include the following:

- Bidirectional virtual machine rate limiting (traffic shaping)
- Centralized vCenter administration and provisioning
- Cisco Nexus 1000V virtual switch (3rd party add-on)
- Dynamic adjustment for load-based NIC teaming
- Enhanced security and monitoring for vMotion traffic
- IEEE 802.1p tagging
- LLDP
- Netflow
- Network I/O Control
- Port mirror
- Private VLAN support

Another use case for the dvSwitch is with converged adapters and 10 GbE adapters where there simply may not be enough physical NICs to effectively use the vSwitch and maintain proper network isolation. How the network is managed can be another determining factor for dvSwitch use. If the network team is going to manage the network, they may want to use the dvSwitch for its advanced capabilities.

In summary, any virtual environment with Enterprise Plus licensing and vCenter Server that needs networking capability could be a use case for the dvSwitch. It is also important to remember that hybrid configurations are entirely possible, and sometimes this mixture of both dvSwitches and vSwitches can be the best solution. The next section of this chapter will cover configuring vSwitch and dvSwitch policies.

Configuring vSS and vDS Policies

Policies may be set at the port group level on either a vSwitch or a dvSwitch. These policies apply to all of the port groups on a vSwitch or to ports in the dvPort group, but they may also be overridden. In the final section of this chapter, I will cover some of these policies, how they are used, and when to use them. The first topic I will cover in this section is identifying common vSwitch and dvSwitch policies.

Identifying Common vSwitch and dvSwitch Policies

The vSwitch and dvSwitch have four policies in common:

Failover And Load Balancing Policy   Used to determine how outbound network traffic will be distributed across network adapters and how to handle failed network adapters.

VLAN Policy   Used to establish VLAN ID for a network connection, but remember that private VLANs are not possible with vSwitches.

Security Policy   Used to establish layer 2 frame filtering policies.

Traffic Shaping Policy   Used to control the amount of bandwidth consumed. Remember that vSwitches offer this capability only on outbound traffic.

 While outbound traffic can be controlled with the vSwitch load balancing policy, it is important to remember that inbound traffic is controlled by the physical switch configuration.

It is important to remember that while these four policies are common across vSwitches and dvSwitches, there are still differences in their implementation. These differences will be important to understand for the exam. Now that I have covered the common policies between the vSwitch and the dvSwitch, I will next cover configuring dvPort group blocking policies.

Configuring dvPort Group Blocking Policies

Port blocking policies are used to selectively block ports from sending and receiving data and are available only in dvSwitches. In Exercise 4.19, you will configure dvPort group blocking policies.

EXERCISE 4.19

Configuring dvPort Group Blocking Policies

1. Connect to a vCenter Server with the vSphere Client.

2. Select the Home icon on the navigation bar and then click the Networking option located under Inventory.

3. Right-click a dvPort group in the left pane. Choose the Edit Settings option from the context menu that appears.

4. The dvPortGroup Settings window will appear. Select Policies in the left menu, and then select Miscellaneous.

5. Use the drop-down menu to change the value of Block All Ports to Yes and then click the OK button to save the changes.

6. A Reconfigure dvPort Group task will begin. When this task completes, click the Ports tab and verify that the State column reports Blocked for all connections listed there.

At this point, all connections using this dvPort group are blocked. If this is your only dvPort group or if you need these connections to work, go back through the exercise and undo the changes just made. Now that I have covered configuring dvPort group blocking policies, you can turn your attention to configuring load balancing and failover policies for vSwitches and dvSwitches.

Configuring Load Balancing and Failover Policies

Load balancing and failover policies are used to determine how network traffic will be distributed across network adapters and how to handle failed network adapters. The following options are configurable:

- Load Balancing
- Network Failover Detection
- Notify Switches
- Failback
- Failover Order

To view or configure these options for a vSwitch, use the blue Properties link on the Configuration tab, after selecting the Networking link listed under Hardware. Figure 4.11 shows the vSwitch properties.

FIGURE 4.11   vSwitch properties

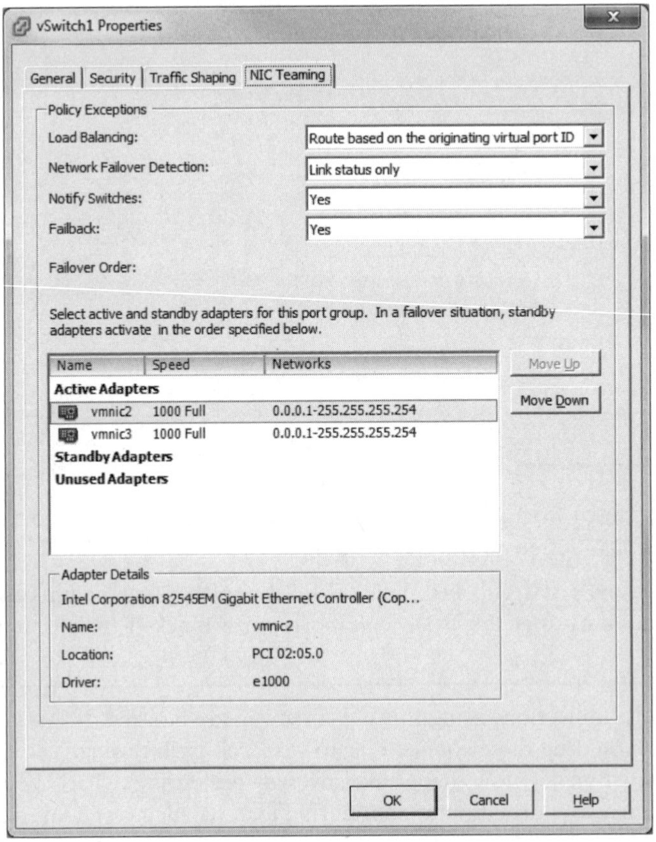

To view or configure these options for a dvSwitch, go to the Networking view, right-click a dvPort group listed in the left pane, and choose the Edit Settings option from the context menu. Choose the Policies section in the left pane and then the Teaming And Failover subsection. See Figure 4.12.

FIGURE 4.12   dvSwitch properties

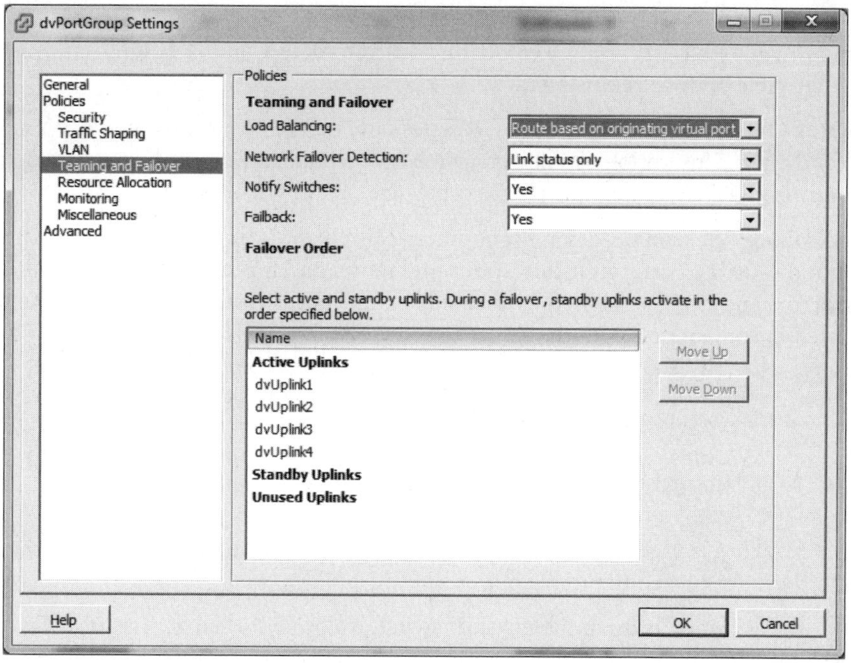

Now that I have listed the load balancing and failover policies and have shown where to find them, I will cover in more detail each of these policies and how they can be used.

The load-balancing policy is used to determine how ESXi hosts will use their uplink adapters; there are five configurable options in this policy:

Route Based On (The) Originating Virtual Port (ID)   The wording differs slightly between the vSwitch and the dvSwitch, but the meaning is the same. An uplink will be selected based on the virtual port where the traffic entered the switch. This is the default setting.

Route Based On IP Hash   An uplink will be selected based on a hash of the source and destination IP addresses of each packet.

Route based On Source MAC Hash   An uplink will be selected based on a hash of the source Ethernet.

Route Based On Physical NIC Load   An uplink will be selected based on the current load of the physical NICs. Note that this option is available only when using a dvSwitch.

Use Explicit Failover Order An uplink that is listed highest in the order of active adapters and passes failover detection criteria will be used.

> Route Based On IP Hash requires that etherchannel be configured on the physical switch, and etherchannel should be used only with the Route Based On IP Hash option.

Network Failover Detection is a mechanism used to detect uplink failures, and there are two configurable options in this policy:

Link Status Only As the name implies, it relies only on the link status provided by the network adapter. This option can detect switch failure and cable pulls but cannot detect configuration errors or cable pulls on the other side of a physical switch.

Beacon Probing Beacon probes are sent out and listened for on all NICs in the team. This information is used to determine link status and more, and it is capable of detecting configuration errors and cable pulls on the other side of a physical switch. Beacon probing should not be used in conjunction with the Route Based On IP Hash load-balancing policy and is most useful when three or more adapters are used in the teaming.

> Unless you have a very specific reason to use beacon probing, use the default option for network failover detection of link status only.

Notify Switches is used to notify switches in case of a failed uplink adapter on the ESXi host, and there are two configurable options in this policy:

Yes When this option is used, the physical switch is notified when a virtual NIC's location changes. This behavior is desirable most of the time, since it provides the lowest latencies.

No This option would typically be used only when connected virtual machines are using Microsoft Network Load Balancing (NLB) in unicast mode.

Failback is used to determine what an uplink adapter does after recovering from a failure, and there are two configurable options in this policy:

Yes The adapter is put back in service immediately after recovery, and the standby adapter returns to being a standby adapter. This is the default setting.

No The adapter is left out of service after recovery, until a time at which it is again needed.

The final configurable option is for the uplink adapter failover order. Note that the naming differs between the vSwitch, which uses the term *adapters*, and the dvSwitch, which uses the term *uplinks*. Aside from the naming differences, the three options in this policy perform the same way. The three options are as follows:

Active Adapters/Uplinks   These adapters will be used as long as network connectivity is available.

Standby Adapters/Uplinks   These adapters will be used if one of the active adapters loses connectivity.

Unused Adapters/Uplinks   These adapters will never be used.

 Do not configure standby adapters/uplinks when using the Route Based On IP Hash load-balancing policy.

The active, standby, and unused adapters/uplinks can be organized by clicking an adapter/uplink in the list to highlight it and then using the Move Up and Move Down buttons to place the adapter in the appropriate category.

I have covered configuring load balancing and failover policies for vSwitches and dvSwitches. I will now cover VLAN settings.

Configuring VLAN Settings

Both vSwitches and dvSwitches can be configured to use VLANs. Many of the vSwitch exercises earlier in this chapter covered how to configure the VLAN settings. The dvSwitch VLAN configuration was covered in Exercise 4.11, along with an explanation of the VLAN options. As a review, the VLAN settings for a port group in a vSwitch can be configured by obtaining the properties for the port group. This is shown in Figure 4.13, where VM Network has been assigned to VLAN 16.

FIGURE 4.13   VM port group VLAN settings

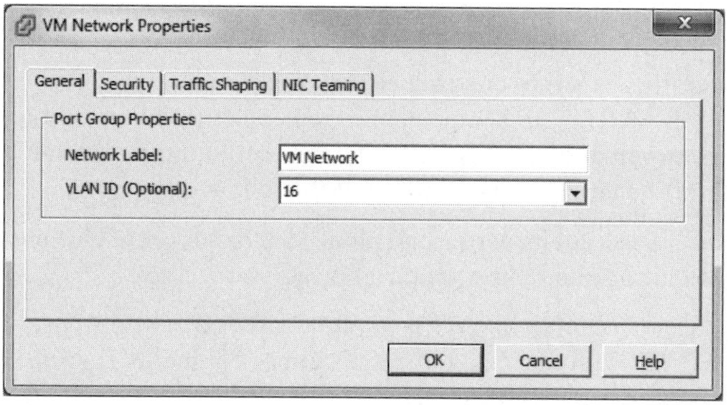

Similarly, the VLAN settings for a dvSwitch can be configured by obtaining the properties for the dvPort group. This is shown in Figure 4.14, where VM Network has been assigned to VLAN 16.

FIGURE 4.14 dvPort group VLAN settings

Now that I have reviewed configuring VLAN settings, I will move on to configuring traffic shaping policies in both vSwitches and dvSwitches.

Configuring Traffic Shaping Policies

Traffic shaping policies are used to control network bandwidth and can be configured in both vSwitches and dvSwitches. It is important to remember that only outbound traffic will be controlled on a vSwitch and that both inbound and outbound traffic will be controlled on a dvSwitch. A traffic shaping policy consists of the following:

Average Bandwidth The kilobits per second allowed across a port. This number is measured over a period of time and represents the allowed average load.

Peak Bandwidth The maximum kilobits per second allowed across a port. This number is used to limit the bandwidth during a burst and cannot be smaller than the average bandwidth number.

Burst Size The maximum kilobytes allowed in a burst. This option can allow a port that needs more bandwidth than what is specified in the average bandwidth value to gain a burst of higher speed traffic if there is bandwidth available.

Exercise 4.20 covers the steps to configure traffic shaping on a vSwitch.

EXERCISE 4.20

Configuring Traffic Shaping Policies on a vSwitch

1. Connect to a vCenter Server with the vSphere Client.

2. Select the Hosts And Clusters view from the inventory.

3. Select an ESXi host from the left pane and then click the Configuration tab in the right pane.

4. Click the blue Networking link in the Hardware panel.

5. Select a vSwitch from the vSphere Standard Switch view and then click the blue Properties link beside it.

6. On the Ports tab, select the vSwitch by clicking it and then click the Edit button at the bottom of the list.

7. A vSwitch<Number> window will open. Click the Traffic Shaping tab.

8. Note that the Status value in the drop-down menu is by default set to Disabled. Change the value to Enabled, using the drop-down menu.

9. Set the Average Bandwidth value to a smaller value than the Peak Bandwidth value. The final configuration should appear similar to what's shown here.

10. Click the OK button to save these changes. An Update Virtual Switch task will begin. When it completes, verify the traffic shaping values are listed in the vSwitch Properties window.

11. On the Ports tab, select a port group by clicking it and then click the Edit button at the bottom of the list.

12. Click the Traffic Shaping tab.

(continued)

13. Note that the status is Enabled and the values for Average Bandwidth, Peak Bandwidth, and Burst Size are inherited from the vSwitch setting.

14. To disable traffic shaping policies for this port group, place select the Status field and use the drop-down menu to change the status to Disabled.

15. The traffic shaping policy has now been overridden for this port group, and the values for Bandwidth and Burst Size are grayed out.

	VM Network Properties		
General	Security	**Traffic Shaping**	NIC Teaming

Policy Exceptions

To override a policy defined by the switch, check the box below.

Status: ☑ Disabled ▼

Average Bandwidth:	12288	Kbits/sec
Peak Bandwidth:	16384	Kbits/sec
Burst Size:	3072	Kbytes

ℹ Traffic shaping policy is applied to the traffic of each virtual network adapter attached to the port group.

OK Cancel Help

16. Click the OK button to save these changes. A Reconfigure Port Group task will begin. When it completes, verify that traffic shaping values do not exist for the port group.

17. Click the Close button to exit the vSwitch Properties window.

The ability to override particular traffic shaping policies on the port group level provides additional granularity to the vSwitch configuration. This can be particularly useful if limits are needed on certain networks and other networks need to run as fast as possible.

When a traffic shaping policy is applied, it will be applied to each vmnic attached to the port group and not to the vSwitch as a whole.

Now that I have covered traffic shaping policies in the vSwitch, I will move on to configuring traffic shaping policies in the dvSwitch. This will be covered in Exercise 4.21.

```
EXERCISE 4.21
```

Configuring Traffic Shaping Policies on a dvSwitch

1. Connect to a vCenter Server with the vSphere Client.

2. Select the Home icon on the navigation bar and then click the Networking option located under Inventory.

3. Right-click a dvPort group in the left pane. Choose the Edit Settings option from the context menu that appears.

4. The dvPortGroup Settings window will appear. Select Traffic Shaping in the left menu.

5. Use the drop-down menu to change the Status field for both Ingress (network into VM) and Egress (VM out to network) to Enabled. Enter the same values for the Average Bandwidth, Peak Bandwidth, and Burst Size that you used in Exercise 4.20 when configuring traffic shaping on the vSwitch.

Note that Ingress and Egress do not have to be enabled as a pair. You can pick either one individually or both together.

6. Click the OK button to save these changes. A Reconfigure dvPort Group task will begin.

(continued)

7. To disable traffic shaping policies for a dvPort, select the dvSwitch that this port group belongs to in the left pane. Click the Ports tab in the right pane.

8. Highlight a port that has a value in the Connectee column. Now right-click the port and choose the Edit Settings option from the context menu that appears.

   Note that for the remaining steps to be successful, a VM will need to be connected to the dvSwitch, and the port group override settings must allow traffic shaping to be overridden. Exercise 4.12 covered the override settings, if you need a reference.

9. For the Ingress Traffic Shaping setting, select Override and then use the drop-down menu to change the status to Disabled.

10. Repeat these steps for the Egress Traffic Shaping setting. Notice that the Bandwidth and Burst Size values are grayed out once the drop-down menu is set to Disabled. The final configuration should look like this:

11. Click the OK button to save the changes. A Reconfigure dvPort task will begin. When this task completes, the dvPort is configured to override the traffic shaping policies implemented on the dvPort group.

Just like with the vSwitch in the previous exercise, the ability to override particular traffic shaping policies on a dvPort level provides additional granularity to the dvSwitch configuration.

I have now covered the traffic shaping policies for both the vSwitch and the dvSwitch. I will next cover enabling TCP segmentation offload support (TSO) for a VM.

Enabling TCP Segmentation Offload Support for a Virtual Machine

TCP segmentation offload (TSO) reduces the CPU overhead required by TCP/IP communications and improves network I/O performance. By default, TSO is enabled on VMkernel interfaces, but it must be enabled on virtual machines by using the *VMXNET 2* or *VMXNET 3* network adapter types. The virtual machine must also use a supported guest operating system. For a complete updated list of the supported operating systems that can be used with the VMXNET 2 and VMXNET 3 network adapters, visit http://kb.vmware.com/kb/1001805.

Exercise 4.22 will cover the steps to enable TSO for a VM.

EXERCISE 4.22

Enabling TSO for a Virtual Machine

1. Connect to a vCenter Server with the vSphere Client.

2. Select the Hosts And Clusters view from the inventory.

3. Right-click a powered-off virtual machine in the left pane. Choose the Edit Settings option from the context menu. The Virtual Machine Properties window will appear.

4. Highlight a network adapter. Review the adapter properties in the right pane. Verify that the virtual machine's adapter type is not listed as VMXNET 2 (Enhanced) or VMXNET 3. If either of these adapters is in use, then no further action is required to enable TSO for this virtual machine.

5. If the network adapter is not VMXNET 2 or VMXNET 3, then take note of the virtual machine's MAC address and the current network label. In the next step you will remove this adapter, and you may need this information again.

6. Make sure that the network adapter is highlighted, and then click the Remove button at the top of the screen. The current network adapter will change to a strikethrough font, and the Summary column will state Removed.

7. Click the Add button. The Add Hardware Wizard will begin. Select Ethernet Adapter by clicking it and then click the Next button to continue.

(continued)

8. For the Adapter Type, choose either VMXNET 2 (Enhanced) or VMXNET 3 from the drop-down menu. Make the network label match the previous setting from the removed adapter, and make sure that the Connect At Power On box has a check in it. The final configuration should look similar to what's shown here.

9. Click the Next button and then review the information presented on the Ready To Complete screen. Click the Finish button to add the network adapter to the VM.

10. Click the OK button on the Virtual Machine Properties window to save the settings changes. A Reconfigure Virtual Machine task will begin. When the task completes, power up the virtual machine. You should also update VMware Tools to the latest version, if necessary.

11. In Windows guests, you can verify TSO support by typing the following command at a command prompt:

```
netsh int ip show offload
```

You have now enabled TSO support for a virtual machine. The next topic I will cover is enabling jumbo frames support.

Enabling Jumbo Frames Support on Appropriate Components

A jumbo frame is an Ethernet frame with a payload size greater than 1,500 bytes and less than or equal to 9000 bytes. This size is also known as the maximum transmission unit (MTU). Like TSO, jumbo frames can improve network I/O performance and use fewer CPU resources. Jumbo frames must be supported on the network end-to-end, meaning that the ESXi host, the destination, and any and all physical switches between the two must support jumbo frames.

In Exercise 4.23, you will create a new vSwitch with a VMkernel connection type that could be used for iSCSI or NFS traffic. You will also configure the vSwitch to use jumbo frames.

EXERCISE 4.23

Enabling Jumbo Frames for a vSwitch

1. Connect to a vCenter Server with the vSphere Client.

2. Select Hosts and Clusters from the Inventory options and then select an ESXi 5 host in the left pane.

3. Click the Configuration tab, and under the Hardware section click the blue Networking link. Ensure that the vSphere Standard Switch view is selected.

4. Click the blue Add Networking link and create the new vSwitch by adding a new VMkernel port group named NFS. I covered vSwitch creation in Exercise 4.1 and VMkernel port creation in Exercise 4.4, if you need a reference for these steps.

5. Click the blue Properties link above the vSwitch that was just created. The vSwitch Properties window will appear.

6. On the Ports tab, highlight the vSwitch in the left pane and click the Edit button at the bottom of the screen. A second vSwitch Properties window will appear.

7. On the General tab, change the Advanced Properties MTU value to 9000.

(continued)

8. Click the OK button on the vSwitch Properties screen. An Update Virtual Switch task will begin. When this task completes, verify that the MTU value is reported as 9000 in the vSwitch Properties window.

   You have now configured the vSwitch to use jumbo frames, but the VMkernel is not configured to use the same MTU size. In the following steps, you will change the VMkernel port group MTU size to match that of the vSwitch.

9. On the vSwitch Properties window's Ports tab, highlight the NFS port group created in step 4 and click the Edit button at the bottom of the screen. An NFS Properties window will appear.

10. Change the MTU value to 9000, as shown here.

11. Click the OK button. An Update Virtual NIC task will begin, and a Reconfigure Port Group task will also begin. When these tasks complete, verify that the MTU value for the NFS port group is reported as 9000 in the vSwitch Properties window.

12. Click the Close button to exit the vSwitch Properties window.

The new vSwitch with a VMkernel port group has now been configured to use jumbo frames. However, jumbo frames must still be enabled for all devices connected to this vSwitch. This includes the physical switch, the NAS device, and any other physical or virtual machines that will be connected to this network.

I discussed a use case in Exercise 4.6, where a virtual machine might be used to connect to an isolated storage network running an NFS server. In the case of a jumbo frame–configured network, like the one you just built in Exercise 4.23, you would also need to make changes to the virtual machine to allow it to use jumbo frames on this network.

The process to enable a virtual machine to use jumbo frames is partially the same as the process used to enable TSO. I covered enabling TSO in Exercise 4.22, which involved adding a VMXNET 2 or VMXNET 3 network adapter to the virtual machine. In addition to using a VVMXNET 2 or VMXNET 3 network adapter, the following items are also required to use jumbo frames in a virtual machine:

- The VMXNET 2 or VMXNET 3 network adapter must be connected to a virtual machine port group on a vSwitch with jumbo frames enabled.

- Ensure that all physical switches and other devices connected to the virtual machine support jumbo frames. Remember that jumbo frames must be supported end-to-end.

- The guest OS must also be configured to support jumbo frames. In Windows guests, this is accomplished by changing the MTU setting in the network adapter properties, as shown in Figure 4.15.

FIGURE 4.15   Jumbo frames in Windows

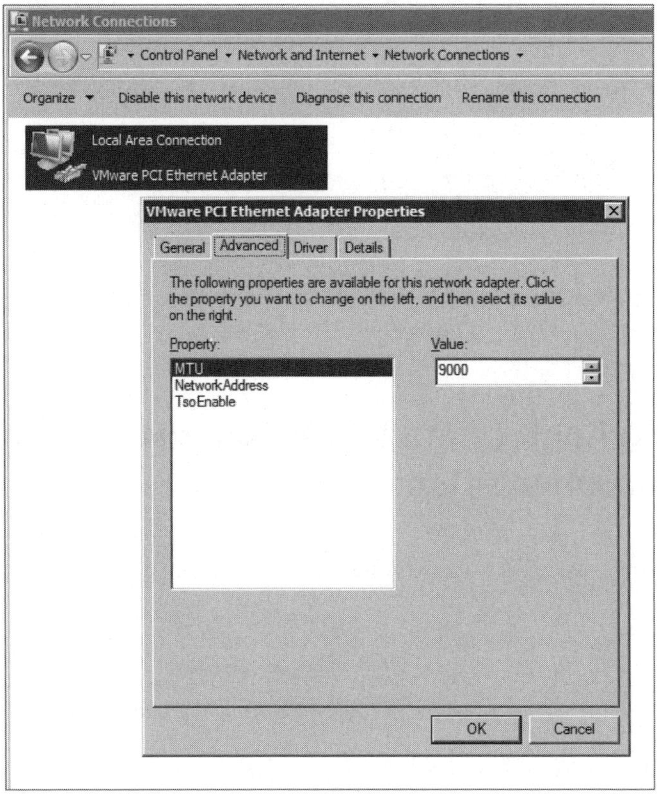

Jumbo frames can also be configured on a dvSwitch. This is accomplished by using the Edit Settings option for the dvSwitch. On the Properties tab, choose the Advanced option. The MTU size may be changed in the right pane, as shown in Figure 4.16.

FIGURE 4.16 dvSwitch jumbo frames

I have now covered enabling jumbo frames on a vSwitch, a dvSwitch, and a virtual machine. I will next cover determining when to use VLANs in a vSphere implementation.

Determining Appropriate VLAN Configuration for a vSphere Implementation

A virtual local area network (VLAN) is used to segment a single physical network into multiple logical networks. VLANs are used in vSphere implementations for the following reasons:

- Simplifies ESXi host integration
- Improves network security
- Reduces network congestion
- Isolates network traffic

To support VLANs in vSphere, either the physical or virtual switch must tag the Ethernet frames with an 802.1Q tag. This tag is also known as the VLAN ID. Three configuration modes can be used to tag and untag the packets for virtual machine frames:

External Switch Tagging (EST)   The physical switch performs all VLAN tagging. ESXi host network adapters are connected to access ports on the physical switch.

Virtual Switch Tagging (VST)   The vSwitch (or dvSwitch) performs all VLAN tagging. ESXi host network adapters must be connected to trunk/tagged ports on the physical switch. This is the most common implementation.

Virtual Guest Tagging (VGT)   An 802.1Q VLAN trunking driver installed in the virtual machine performs all VLAN tagging. ESXi host network adapters must be connected to trunk ports on the physical switch. VLAN ID 4095 is specified in the port group or dvPort group with this configuration.

Determining the appropriate VLAN configuration for a vSphere implementation will often come down to understanding both the requirements and the available infrastructure. VLAN configuration is part of the vSphere design, and there will likely always be some sort of retrofit involved to integrate vSphere into existing environments.

Keep in mind that VST is the most commonly used VLAN implementation. This is because VST can utilize trunked VLANs and that nothing has to be configured in the guest OS. Using trunked VLANs cuts down on the number of physical NICs required in the ESXi hosts, and not having to configure each guest OS lowers administrative effort and cuts down on complexity.

Summary

This chapter covered networking in vSphere 5. Knowing how to network with vSwitches and dvSwitches and when to use each is extremely important for the exam. I discussed vSwitches and identifying their capabilities. I also covered creating and deleting vSwitches. I covered adding, configuring, and removing vmnics on vSwitches. Configuring VMkernel ports on vSwitches for network services was covered, in addition to adding, editing, and removing port groups in the vSwitch. I also covered determining the use case for a vSwitch.

After I covered vSwitches, I covered dvSwitches. I discussed dvSwitches and identified their capabilities. I also covered creating and deleting dvSwitches and adding and removing ESXi hosts to dvSwitches. I covered adding, configuring, and removing dvPort groups and how to add and remove uplink adapters to dvUplink groups. Creating, configuring, and removing virtual adapters were all covered. I covered migrating virtual adapters and virtual machines to and from a dvSwitch. I also covered determining the use case for a dvSwitch.

The final part of this chapter focused on configuring vSwitch and dvSwitch policies. I identified the common policies they share. I also covered configuring dvPort group blocking policies, load-balancing polices, and failover policies. I discussed VLAN settings and traffic shaping policies. I also covered how to enable TSO and jumbo frames. I wrapped up this chapter with determining the appropriate VLAN configuration for a vSphere implementation. For the VCP exam, you will be expected to know what vSwitch and dvSwitch features are available, when to use these features, and how to use them.

Exam Essentials

Know how to configure vSwitches. Be able to identify the capabilities of a vSwitch. Understand how to create and delete vSwitches. Know how to add, configure, and remove vmnics on a vSwitch. Understand how to configure VMkernel ports for different network services. Be able to add, edit, and remove port groups on a vSwitch. Be able to determine the use case for a vSwitch.

Know how to configure dvSwitches. Be able to identify the capabilities of a dvSwitch. Understand how to create and delete dvSwitches. Know how (and when) to add and remove ESXi hosts from a dvSwitch. Know how to add, configure, and remove dvPort groups in a dvSwitch. Understand how uplink adapters work and how to add and remove them to dvUplink port groups. Be able to create, configure, and remove virtual adapters. Know how to migrate virtual adapters to/from a dvSwitch. Also know how to migrate virtual machine networking to/from a dvSwitch. Be able to determine the use case for a dvSwitch.

Know how to configure vSwitch and dvSwitch policies. Be able to identify common policies that are shared between the vSwitch and the dvSwitch. Understand how to configure dvPort group blocking policies, load-balancing polices, and failover policies. Know how to configure VLAN settings and traffic shaping policies. Understand how and when to enable TSO and jumbo frames. Be able to determine the appropriate VLAN configuration for a vSphere implementation.

Review Questions

1. In a vSwitch, which of the following can be used to obtain information for peer network devices?

   A. Beacon probing

   B. LLDP

   C. CDP

   D. PVLANs

2. What are the two connection types available when creating a new vSwitch?

   A. Virtual machine

   B. Management

   C. LAN

   D. VMkernel

3. Which of the following policies are common across vSwitches and dvSwitches? (Choose all that apply.)

   A. Failover and Load Balancing Policy

   B. VLAN Policy

   C. Security Policy

   D. Traffic Shaping Policy

4. Which of the following VLAN tagging configurations require trunk/tagged ports to be configured on a physical switch? (Choose two.)

   A. EST

   B. VST

   C. VGT

   D. EXT

5. Which of the following is a use case for a vSwitch? (Choose all that apply.)

   A. Environment with ESXi hosts and no vCenter Server

   B. Environment with ESXi hosts and vCenter Server with Standard Licensing

   C. Environment with ESXi hosts and vCenter server with Enterprise Licensing

   D. Environment with ESXi hosts and vCenter Server with Enterprise Plus Licensing

6. Which load-balancing policy is available only with the dvSwitch?

   A. Route Based On IP Hash

   B. Route Based On Physical NIC Load

   C. Route Based On MAC Hash

   D. Use Explicit Failover Order

7. You need to remove one of the two physical adapters from a vSwitch that has a virtual machine port group with 25 connected virtual machines. What sequence of events should you use to accomplish this task?

   A. Leave all VMs on the ESXi host. Remove the vmnic from the vSwitch.

   B. Leave all VMs on the ESXi host. Remove the vSwitch.

   C. Migrate all VMs to another ESXi host using vMotion. Remove the vmnic from the vSwitch. Move the VMs back to this ESXi host.

   D. Migrate all VMs to another ESXi host using vMotion. Remove the vSwitch. Move the VMs back to this ESXi host.

8. You have a customer that requires Network I/O Control and NetFlow. Which version of the dvSwitch must be used?

   A. 4.0.0

   B. 4.1.0

   C. 4.1.1

   D. 5.0.0

9. When creating a dvSwitch, what are the options for adding ESXi hosts? (Choose all that apply.)

   A. Add now

   B. Add one

   C. Add later

   D. Add all

10. When adding a dvPort group to a dvSwitch, you use the VLAN Trunking option. How many dvPort groups will be required to support three trunked VLANS?

   A. 0

   B. 1

   C. 2

   D. 3

11. A customer has a NFS server implemented on a dedicated and isolated network. The ESXi hosts connect to this NFS server through a vSwitch configured with a VMkernel port group. You need to connect a virtual machine to the management interface on the NFS server. What are the steps you need to take?

   A. Create a virtual machine port group on the vSwitch. Connect a virtual machine to this port group. Give the VM an IP address on the storage network. Connect to and use the management interface on the NFS server. Disconnect the VM from this port group and remove the virtual machine port group.

   B. Create a virtual machine port group on a new vSwitch. Connect a virtual machine to this port group. Give the VM an IP address on the new network. Connect to and use the management interface on the NFS server.

C. Connect the virtual machine to the VMkernel port group. Give the VM an IP address on the storage network. Connect to and use the management interface on the NFS server. Disconnect the VM from the VMkernel port group and remove the VMkernel port group.

D. Create a virtual machine port group on the vSwitch. Connect a virtual machine to this port group. Give the VM an IP address on the storage network. Connect to and use the management interface on the NFS server. Disconnect the VM from this port group.

12. Which of the following statements are true about etherchannel and load-balancing policies? (Choose two.)

A. Route Based On IP Hash requires etherchannel.

B. Route Based On MAC Hash requires etherchannel.

C. Do not configure standby adapters/uplinks when using the Route Based On MAC Hash load-balancing policy.

D. Do not configure standby adapters/uplinks when using the Route Based On IP Hash load-balancing policy.

13. Which of the following network adapters are required for virtual machines to utilize TSO? (Choose all that apply.)

A. e1000

B. vlance

C. VMXNET 2 (Enhanced)

D. VMXNET 3

14. What types of traffic can a vmknic be used for? (Choose all that apply.)

A. vMotion

B. Virtual Machine

C. iSCSI

D. Management

15. Which of the following is a use case for the dvSwitch? (Choose all that apply.)

A. Environment with ESXi hosts and no vCenter Server

B. Environment with ESXi hosts and vCenter Server with Standard licensing

C. Environment with ESXi hosts and vCenter server with Enterprise licensing

D. Environment with ESXi hosts and vCenter Server with Enterprise Plus licensing

16. What is used to allow ESXi hosts using the same dvSwitch to have differing vmnic configurations and still use the same teaming, load-balancing, and failover policies?

A. dvPort group

B. dvUplink

C. Uplink adapters

D. dvPort

17. You have a customer that requires the use of virtual machine traffic shaping on both inbound and outbound connections. Which of the following solutions provide this capability?

A. dvSwitch

B. vSwitch

C. Both of these

D. None of these

18. Which of the following are required to use jumbo frames in a virtual machine?

A. VMXNET 2

B. Guest OS configuration changes

C. Ensuring that all devices on the network segment support jumbo frames

D. dvSwitch

19. Which statement best describes static port binding?

A. A dvPort is created and assigned when a virtual machine is created.

B. A dvPort is created and assigned when a virtual machine is both powered on and has its NIC connected.

C. A dvPort is immediately assigned and reserved when the virtual machine is connected to the dvPort.

D. A dvPort is immediately assigned and reserved when the dvSwitch is created.

20. Which of the following describes the use for virtual adapters in the dvSwitch? (Choose all that apply.)

A. Used to provide virtual machine connections

B. Used to provide vMotion traffic

C. Used to provide FT traffic

D. Used to provide NFS traffic

Plan and Configure vSphere Storage

VCP5 EXAM OBJECTIVES COVERED IN THIS CHAPTER:

✓ **Configure Shared Storage for vSphere**

- Identify storage adapters and devices

- Identify storage naming conventions

- Scan/Rescan storage

- Enable/Configure/Disable vCenter Server storage filters

- Describe zoning and LUN masking practices

- Identify use cases for FCoE

- Identify hardware/dependent hardware/software iSCSI initiator requirements

- Determine use case for hardware/dependent hardware/ software iSCSI initiator

- Configure/Edit hardware/dependent hardware initiators

- Enable/Disable software iSCSI initiator

- Configure/Edit software iSCSI initiator settings

- Configure iSCSI port binding

- Enable/Configure/Disable iSCSI CHAP

- Compare and contrast array thin provisioning and virtual disk thin provisioning

- Determine use case for and configure array thin provisioning

✓ **Create and Configure VMFS and NFS Datastores**

- Identify VMFS-5 capabilities

- Create/Rename/Unmount/Delete a VMFS Datastore

- Identify VMFS Datastore properties

- Extend/Expand VMFS Datastores

- Upgrade a VMFS-3 Datastore to VMFS-5

- Place a VMFS Datastore in Maintenance Mode

- Determine appropriate Path Selection Policy for a given VMFS Datastore

- Select the Preferred Path for a VMFS Datastore

- Disable a path to a VMFS Datastore

- Create an NFS share for use with vSphere

- Connect to a NAS device

- Mount/Unmount an NFS Datastore

- Identify NFS Datastore properties

- Determine use case for multiple VMFS/NFS Datastores

✓ **Configure the VMware vSphere Storage Appliance**

- Determine use case for deploying the VSA

- Define Storage vSphere Storage Appliance (VSA) architecture

- Determine appropriate ESXi host resources for the VSA

- Configure ESXi hosts as VSA hosts

- Configure the storage network for the VSA

- Deploy/Configure the VSA Manager

- Administer VSA storage resources

This chapter will cover the objectives of section 3 of the VCP5 exam blueprint. This chapter will focus completely on configuring storage in vSphere 5.

This chapter will first cover identifying storage adapters and devices. Identifying storage naming conventions will also be covered. I will cover how to scan and rescan for storage, as well as how to enable, configure, and disable vCenter Server storage filters. Zoning and LUN masking practices will be discussed, and I will also identify the use cases for FCoE. I will cover identifying requirements and use cases for dependent hardware iSCSI adapters, independent hardware iSCSI adapters, and software iSCSI adapters. How to configure and edit the dependent hardware iSCSI adapter will be covered. Enabling and disabling the software iSCSI adapter will also be covered, along with configuring and editing the software iSCSI adapter settings. I will discuss how to configure iSCSI port binding and enabling, configuring, and disabling iSCSI CHAP. I will compare and contrast array thin provisioning and virtual disk thin provisioning and determine the use case for array thin provisioning.

I will next identify VMFS-5 capabilities and create, rename, delete, and unmount a VMFS datastore. I will also identify VMFS datastore properties and extend and expand VMFS datastores. Upgrading a VMFS-3 datastore to VMFS-5 will be covered, along with placing a VMFS datastore in maintenance mode. I will also cover selecting the preferred path for a VMFS datastore, disabling a path to a VMFS datastore, and determining the appropriate path selection policy for a given VMFS datastore. NFS will be covered, and you will connect to a NAS device and create an NFS share for use with vSphere. I will cover how to mount and unmount NFS datastores and how to identify NFS datastore properties. I will also determine the use case for multiple VMFS/NFS datastores.

Finally, this chapter will cover configuring the VMware vSphere Storage Appliance (VSA). I will determine the use case for deploying the VSA and will define its architecture. Determining the appropriate ESXi host resources for the VSA will be discussed, along with how to configure ESXi hosts as VSA hosts. I will cover how to configure the storage network for the VSA and how to deploy and configure the VSA Manager. Administering VSA storage resources will complete the chapter.

Configure Shared Storage for vSphere

Knowing how to configure shared storage for a vSphere environment is a very important part of the virtual infrastructure administrator's duties. Many of the advanced features of vSphere, including HA, DRS, vMotion, Storage vMotion, and FT all rely on shared storage. This shared storage can be in the form of VMFS datastores on a SAN, raw device mappings on a storage area network (*SAN*), or Network File System (*NFS*) volumes on networked-attached storage (*NAS*) devices. The first topic in this chapter is identifying storage adapters and devices in ESXi.

Identifying Storage Adapters and Devices

ESXi abstracts physical storage from virtual machines and uses storage adapters to provide connectivity between ESXi hosts and storage. The connected storage is also known as a *target*. SCSI, iSCSI, RAID, Fibre Channel, Ethernet, and Fibre Channel over Ethernet (FCoE) are all supported adapter classes used to provide storage connectivity in ESXi. The storage adapters are accessed by ESXi through device drivers in the VMkernel. In ESXi, a device is simply storage space on a target. A device may often be referred to as a *LUN*.

 Not all storage adapters are supported by ESXi. Always check the HCL for device compatibility, and never assume that a device will work.

The vSphere Client can be used to identify both storage adapters and connected devices. Exercise 5.1 covers how to use the vSphere Client to identify storage adapters and how to obtain information about the devices connected through these storage adapters.

EXERCISE 5.1

Identifying Storage Adapters and Devices in ESXi

1. Connect to a vCenter Server with the vSphere Client.

2. Select an ESXi host from the inventory.

3. Click the Configuration tab for the ESXi host and then click the blue Storage Adapters link in the Hardware panel.

4. In the upper part of this screen, review the list of storage adapters. Click each entry in the list and then review the details listed below it. In the image shown here, the local disks in the ESXi server are listed for vmhba1.

Storage Adapters

Device	Type	WWN
PIIX4 for 430TX/440BX/MX IDE Controller		
vmhba0	Block SCSI	
vmhba32	Block SCSI	
53c1030 PCI-X Fusion-MPT Dual Ultra320 SCSI		
vmhba1	SCSI	

Details

vmhba1
Model: 53c1030 PCI-X Fusion-MPT Dual Ultra320 SCSI
Targets: 2   Devices: 2   Paths: 2

View: Devices Paths

Name	Runtime Name	Operational State	Type	Transport	Capacity
Local VMware, Disk (mpx.vmhba1:C0:T1:L0)	vmhba1:C0:T1:L0	Mounted	disk	Parallel SCSI	4.00 GB
Local VMware, Disk (mpx.vmhba1:C0:T0:L0)	vmhba1:C0:T0:L0	Mounted	disk	Parallel SCSI	4.00 GB

Any storage adapters that are present in the system, such as HBA cards, DVD-ROM drives, and RAID cards, will be listed under the Storage Adapters section. Also remember that certain adapters, such as software iSCSI and FCoE, must first be enabled before they will be visible in the Storage Adapters list.

5. Once you've selected a storage adapter, you can use the two gray buttons labeled Devices and Paths in the Details portion of the screen to toggle between these two different views. By default the Devices view is selected.

6. In the previous image, note the devices listed for vmhba1. Properties included are the Name, Operational State, Capacity, and more. Like other listings in vSphere, the columns can be customized by right-clicking any column header.

7. Click the Paths button to view the path information for a chosen storage adapter. Review the information presented for details about the paths to the devices.

In the last step of Exercise 5.1, you looked at viewing the path information for a device. In the next section, I will discuss the storage device naming conventions used.

Identifying Storage Naming Conventions

In ESXi, each device is identified by a device identifier. The device identifiers are as follows:

- SCSI INQUIRY
- Path-based
- Legacy
- Runtime Name

I will now go into detail about each of these device identifiers. With SCSI INQUIRY, the storage system generates an identifier for the device that is both persistent and unique. The prefixes *eui*, *naa*, and *t10* are used with this identifier. Table 5.1 shows the naming convention and examples for the SCSI INQUIRY device identifiers.

TABLE 5.1   SCSI INQUIRY identifier naming convention and example

Naming convention	Example
eui.<EUI>:<Partition>	eui.5577bd49251ddb52
naa.<NAA>:<Partition>	naa.6006016094602800e07ff528b73ae011:2

In Table 5.1, the eui example is using the entire device, so the unique part of this identifier is 5577bd49251ddb52. The naa example is also shown with its own unique part of the identifier, but it is using a specific partition (partition 2) on the device.

With the Path-based identifier, the ESXi host generates an identifier for devices that do not provide eui, naa, or t10 data. This identifier is not unique or persistent. The prefix *mpx* is used with this identifier. Table 5.2 shows the naming convention and an example for the Path-based device identifier.

TABLE 5.2   Path-based identifier naming convention and example

Naming convention	Example
mpx.vmhba<Adapter>:C<Channel>:T<Target>: L<LUN> :<Partition>	mpx.vmhba2:C0:T0:L0

In Table 5.2, the example is using storage adapter 2, storage channel number 0, target number 0, and LUN 0, and no partition is specified.

With the Legacy identifier, the ESXi host issues an identifier that includes a series of unique digits. The prefix *vml* is used with this identifier. Table 5.3 shows the naming convention and an example for the Legacy device identifier.

TABLE 5.3   Legacy identifier naming convention and example

Naming convention	Example
vml.<VML>:<Partition>	vml.02000600006006016094602800364ce2 2e3825e011524149442030:1

In Table 5.3, the example is shown with its own unique part of the identifier, but it is also using a specific partition (partition 1) on the device.

Runtime Name is an identifier used exclusively to identify the name of the first path to a device. It is not reliable or persistent. Table 5.4 shows the naming convention and an example for the Runtime Name path identifier.

TABLE 5.4   Runtime name identifier naming convention and example

Naming convention	Example
vmhba<Adapter>:C<Channel>:T<Target>:L<LUN>	vmhba1:C0:T1:L0

In Table 5.4, the example is using storage adapter 1, storage channel number 0, target number 1, and LUN 0.

To help you better understand these naming conventions, some important terms are defined here:

vmhba<Adapter>   The name of the storage adapter used by the ESXi host.

C<Channel>   The number of the storage channel.

T<Target>   The target number, as determined by the ESXi host.

L<LUN>   The number that shows the position of the LUN within the target. Note that if a target has only a single LUN, the LUN number will always be 0.

Now that the naming conventions used in ESXi have been covered, you can turn your attention to scanning and rescanning for storage devices.

Scanning and Rescanning Storage

Adding and modifying storage are common events in any virtual environment. While certain operations on VMFS datastores and RDMs are discovered by automatic rescans, sometimes a manual rescan is required. For example, manual rescans are required for any of the following changes:

- A new disk array is zoned on a SAN.
- A new device (LUN) is created on a SAN.
- The path masking on a host is changed.
- A cable is reconnected.
- CHAP settings in iSCSI environments are modified.
- Static or dynamic address in iSCSI environments are modified.

The rescan options are used any time these types of changes are made. The rescan operation allows ESXi hosts to have up-to-date and accurate information about storage devices. Exercise 5.2 will cover how to use the rescan functions.

EXERCISE 5.2

Rescanning Storage in ESXi

1. Connect to a vCenter Server with the vSphere Client.

2. Select an ESXi host from the inventory.

3. Click the Configuration tab for the ESXi host and then click the blue Storage link in the Hardware panel.

4. In the default Datastores view, notice the blue Rescan All link located at the top right. Click this link, and a Rescan window will appear, as shown here.

(continued)

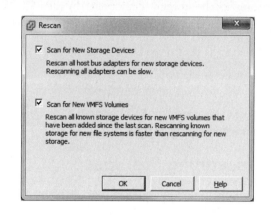

5. By default, both the Scan For New Storage Devices and Scan For New VMFS Volumes options are selected. Accept these defaults; then click the OK button to begin the rescan operations.

6. A Rescan All HBAs task will begin, and it will be immediately followed by a Rescan VMFS task.

    In steps 5–6, the Scan For New Storage Devices option rescanned all *HBAs* in the host for new storage devices. When this task completed, the Scan For New VMFS Volumes task began to scan all known storage devices for new VMFS volumes. There may be times when you simply need to scan a single HBA for new devices, without scanning every single HBA in the system.

7. On the Configuration tab, click the blue Storage Adapters link under the Hardware settings.

8. Select a single HBA by clicking it. Now right-click the HBA and choose the Rescan option from the context menu that appears.

9. A Rescan HBA task will begin, and it will be immediately followed by a Rescan VMFS task.

    In steps 7–8, the Rescan option rescanned a single HBA and then immediately scanned for VMFS volumes. You also may need to scan many hosts for new devices and VMFS volumes.

10. In the left pane of the vSphere Client, right-click a datacenter, cluster, or folder that contains ESXi hosts and select the Rescan For Datastores option from the context menu that appears.

11. A Rescan For Datastores Warning window will appear, as shown here.

Rescan for Datastores Warning

⚠ Rescanning hosts can take a long time. During this time, vMotion migrations might not be operable and some datastore operations may be disallowed.

Click OK to rescan.

☐ Do not show this message again

OK   Cancel

12. Review the warning information to understand the implications of this operation. Click the OK button. This will launch the same Rescan window seen in step 4 of this exercise.

13. By default, both the Scan For New Storage Devices and Scan For New VMFS Volumes options are selected. Accept these defaults; then click the OK button to begin the rescan operations.

14. For each host contained in the datacenter, cluster, or folder you chose, a Rescan All HBAs task will begin. This task will be immediately followed by a Rescan VMFS task for each host.

VMFS datastores are also referred to as VMFS volumes. In this book, the term VMFS *datastores* will be used most often, because this is consistent with the naming convention used in the VCP5 exam blueprint.

Exercise 5.2 covered three distinct rescan operations performed with the vSphere Client. First it covered scanning all HBAs in a single ESXi host for new storage devices and VMFS volumes. It next covered how to rescan a single HBA, and the exercise concluded with how to rescan all HBAs in multiple ESXi hosts. Now that I have covered scanning for devices and VMFS volumes, you can turn your attention to enabling, configuring, and disabling vCenter Server storage filters.

Enabling, Configuring, and Disabling vCenter Server Storage Filters

Storage filters are used in vCenter Server to help prevent storage corruption and performance issues caused by the unsupported use of storage devices. In essence, the storage filters will allow only particular types of devices to be listed for particular operations. Table 5.5 lists the four storage filters and their associated keys.

TABLE 5.5   vCenter Server storage filters and keys

Filter name	Key
VMFS Filter	config.vpxd.filter.vmfsFilter
RDM Filter	config.vpxd.filter.rdmFilter
Same Host and Transports Filter	config.vpxd.filter.SameHostAndTransportsFilter
Host Rescan Filter	config.vpxd.filter.hostRescanFilter

The VMFS Filter is used to filter out devices that are already in use as VMFS datastores on any host managed by vCenter Server. These devices will not be allowed to be reused as new VMFS volumes or RDMs. In other words, when a scan for new devices operation is performed, existing VMFS volumes will not be listed. This prevents the accidental reuse of VMFS volumes.

The RDM Filter is used to filter out devices that are already in use as RDM devices on any host managed by vCenter Server. These devices will not be allowed to be reused as new VMFS volumes or different RDMs. In other words, when a scan for new devices operation is performed, existing RDMs will not be listed.

The Same Host and Transports Filter is used to filter out devices that have some type of incompatibility. For example, adding an extent when the device is not exposed to all hosts or adding a Fibre Channel extent to a VMFS datastore on local storage would be prevented and thus filtered.

The Host Rescan Filter is used to automatically rescan for VMFS datastores after datastore management operations are performed.

 You should consult with the VMware support team before making any changes to the storage filters. Exercise 5.3 should definitely not be performed in any production environment.

The vCenter Server storage filters have very specific use cases and will most likely be used in conjunction with VMware support. With that being said, the Host Rescan Filter is the least likely of the four filters to cause problems. In Exercise 5.3, you will disable, configure, and then enable the Host Rescan Filter storage filter.

EXERCISE 5.3

Disabling, Configuring, and Enabling vCenter Server Storage Filters

1. Connect to a vCenter Server with the vSphere Client.

2. Choose Home in the navigation bar; then choose the vCenter Server Settings option from the Administration options.

3. The vCenter Server Settings window will appear. Click the Advanced Settings option in the left pane.

4. Scroll through the list of keys and verify whether any of the vCenter Server storage filter keys in Table 5.5 are listed. By default, all four filters are enabled but not listed.

5. If the config.vpxd.filter.hostRescanFilter key is already listed in the list of keys, skip to step 8.

6. Enter the text **config.vpxd.filter.hostRescanFilter** in the Key field at the bottom of the screen and enter the text **false** in the Value field. The final configuration is shown here.

vCenter Server Settings			
Advanced Settings			
Configure advanced server settings			

Key	Value	Summary
config.alert.log.enabled	true	
config.level[CpuFeatures].logLevel	info	
config.level[CpuFeatures].logName	CpuFeatures	
config.level[VmCheck].logLevel	info	
config.level[VmCheck].logName	VmCheck	
config.log.compressOnRoll	true	
config.log.level	info	
config.log.maxFileNum	30	
config.log.maxFileSize	52428800	
config.log.memoryLevel	verbose	
config.task.minCompletedLifetime	60	
config.vmacore.cacheProperties	true	
config.vmacore.ssl.useCompression	true	
config.vmacore.threadPool.TaskMax	90	
config.vmacore.threadPool.threadN...	vpxd	
config.vpxd.filterOverheadLimitIssues	true	
event.maxAge	180	Maximum age in days an ev...
event.maxAgeEnabled	false	Remove events older than t...
instance.id	30	Unique instance identifier for...
LicenseServer.matchHostToVirtualC...	true	When adding a host, make t...
log.level	Information	Amount of detail collected in...
mail.sender		Email address for email alerts...
mail.smtp.port	25	SMTP server port number. T...

Left pane:
Licensing
Statistics
Runtime Settings
Active Directory
Mail
SNMP
Ports
Timeout Settings
Logging Options
Database
Database Retention Policy
SSL Settings
Advanced Settings

Key: config.vpxd.filter.hostRescanFilter   Value: false   Add

Help   OK   Cancel

7. Click the Add button to disable the Host Rescan Filter storage filter. Verify that the new key has been added in the list of keys on the screen and then click the OK button to close the vCenter Server Settings window. Skip to step 9.

(continued)

8. If the config.vpxd.filter.hostRescanFilter key was already listed, simply highlight this key and then click the Value field. Change the text to the value **false** and then click the OK button on the vCenter Server Settings window.

    The Host Rescan Filter is now disabled, and datastore management operations will no longer result in automatic VMFS rescans. Because having the Host Rescan Filter disabled is not a recommended practice, you will now change the setting back.

9. Return to the vCenter Server Settings window and click the Advanced Settings option in the left pane.

10. Scroll through the list of keys and locate this key:

    config.vpxd.filter.hostRescanFilter

11. Highlight the config.vpxd.filter.hostRescanFilter key and then click the Value field. Change the text to the value **true** and then click the OK button on the vCenter Server Settings window. The Host Rescan Filter is now enabled again.

Note that it is not possible to remove these keys once they have been added to the Advanced Settings section of the vCenter Server Settings window. If the keys have been added, then their behavior must be controlled with the true and false values. Remember, the value of false will turn off the filter, and the value of true will turn on the filter.

Regardless of the value specified in the config.vpxd.filter.hostRescanFilter key, an ESXi host will automatically rescan when a new device is presented to it.

Now that I have covered vCenter Server storage filters, I will describe zoning and LUN masking practices.

Describing Zoning and LUN Masking Practices

Zoning and LUN masking are used to secure devices located on Fibre Channel (FC) SANs. Zoning is a process used at the switch level in FC SANs to define which HBAs can connect to which controllers on the SAN. Another way to think of zoning is as an access control for device communications. In a typical vSphere environment, a zone would be created for each ESXi host's HBA initiator and all of the storage controller ports (targets).

LUN masking is a process performed at the SAN storage processors level that makes LUNs hidden from certain hosts. LUN masking can also be used to reduce the number of devices presented to an ESXi host, which would make rescan operations faster.

Now that I have covered zoning and LUN masking, I will identify the use cases for Fibre Channel over Ethernet (FCoE).

Identifying Use Cases for FCoE

Fibre Channel over Ethernet can be used to allow ESXi hosts to access Fibre Channel storage over 10Gb lossless Ethernet. The FCoE protocol works by encapsulating Fibre Channel frames into Ethernet frames. This can mean that the need for Fibre Channel HBAs no longer exists in your ESXi hosts.

ESXi must have one of two types of FCoE adapters in order to use FCoE:

Converged Network Adapter (CNA)   Also known as hardware FCoE. These adapters combine both network and Fibre Channel functionality onto a single card. With a CNA, the ESXi host can use both components. The hardware FCoE adapter does not need to be configured in order to use it.

NIC with FCoE Support   Also known as software FCoE. These adapters use the native FCoE stack in ESXi. The software FCoE adapter first requires networking configuration and activation in order to use it.

 A maximum of four software FCoE adapters per ESXi 5 host is supported.

One obvious use case for FCoE is in blade environments. With the many networks that an ESXi host is expected to support, some blades may simply lack the I/O slots required to add redundant Fibre Channel HBAs.

Another use case for FCoE could be the consolidation of the network infrastructure. If FCoE is used, then the SAN switches could also be eliminated along with the HBAs in the ESXi host. This consolidation can simplify management and also cut down on the number of devices and cabling required to support Fibre Channel. Think of the cabling difference when comparing five ESXi hosts, each with two Fibre Channel HBAs plus eight 1GbE NICs, to five ESXi hosts, each with just two converged network adapters.

Now that I have covered FCoE and its use cases, I will move on to *Internet Small Computer System Interface* (iSCSI) and identifying the iSCSI initiator requirements in vSphere.

Identifying Hardware/Dependent Hardware/Software iSCSI Initiator Requirements

Similar to the behavior of the FCoE protocol just discussed, an iSCSI initiator encapsulates SCSI commands into Ethernet packets. This allows ESXi hosts to communicate with an iSCSI-capable SAN over standard Ethernet cabling. In ESXi 5, there are two types of iSCSI initiators. These are known as the software iSCSI adapter and the hardware iSCSI adapter.

With the software iSCSI adapter, the initiator code is included as part of the VMkernel. This allows any standard network adapter to be used, and the processing involved in the iSCSI encapsulation is performed by the ESXi host. This can be more resource intensive for the ESXi host, but it does not require the purchase of a hardware iSCSI adapter to obtain iSCSI connectivity.

With the hardware iSCSI adapter, an actual piece of hardware is used to perform both the networking and iSCSI offload functionality (or in some adapters just the iSCSI offload functionality). Offloading means removing the CPU load required to process iSCSI off your ESXi host. With the hardware adapter, the iSCSI processing will be performed on the adapter. These adapters will almost always require additional up-front costs. The hardware iSCSI adapters are further broken down into two additional categories:

Dependent Hardware iSCSI Adapter   This is an adapter that performs the iSCSI processing but relies on the VMkernel for networking access. Again, as the name suggests, the dependent hardware iSCSI adapter depends on VMware software interfaces for networking, configuration, and management operations. An example of this type of adapter is the Broadcom 5709 NIC.

Independent Hardware iSCSI Adapter   This is an adapter that performs both the iSCSI processing and networking. This adapter is also known as an iSCSI HBA. This adapter implements its own interfaces for networking, configuration, and management and does not depend on VMware software to provide them. An example of this type of adapter is the QLogic QLA4052 adapter.

Dependent hardware iSCSI adapters may sometimes be included in servers, but these adapters often require separate licensing. Always check with your server vendor to determine whether there are additional costs associated with the provided dependent hardware iSCSI adapters.

Now that I have discussed the two types of iSCSI initiators in ESXi, I will cover determining the use case for them.

Determining Use Case for Hardware/Dependent Hardware/Software iSCSI Initiator

Part of designing an iSCSI environment for the virtual infrastructure involves knowing when to use which type of initiator. Determining the use case for the different iSCSI initiators is often about finding the right balance between performance and cost.

The software iSCSI adapter typically requires the least initial investment, because any standard NIC can be used. This is useful in situations where the environment is smaller, cost matters significantly, or the ESXi hosts have sufficient processing to spare.

The dependent hardware iSCSI adapter will typically require a larger initial investment than a standard NIC. This is because these adapters have the ability to offload the iSCSI processing from the ESXi host. This adapter is useful in situations where there may not be processing to spare on the ESXi hosts. These adapters are also useful in that they can be used as standard NICs as well, so they provide flexibility. There are several things that need to be remembered about the dependent hardware iSCSI adapter. Because the iSCSI traffic bypasses the regular network stack, performance reporting may be inaccurate for the NIC. Broadcom adapters also do not support jumbo frames or IPv6 and should be used with *flow control* enabled. Consider these limitations when planning which iSCSI adapter to choose.

The independent hardware iSCSI adapter will typically require the largest initial investment. This is because the adapters have the ability to both offload the iSCSI processing from the ESXi host and provide networking. This adapter is useful in situations where the host cannot be expected to provide processing for iSCSI traffic. This adapter is the most efficient in terms of the resource consumption on the ESXi host.

Now that I have covered determining the use case for the iSCSI initiators, I will cover configuring the dependent hardware iSCSI adapter.

Configuring and Editing Hardware/Dependent Hardware Initiators

The dependent hardware iSCSI adapter depends on VMware software to provide both networking and iSCSI configuration and management interfaces. Although the iSCSI engine of the dependent hardware iSCSI adapter will appear on the list of storage adapters as a vmhba, additional configuration must be performed before it can be used. Exercise 5.4 will cover the steps required to configure and edit a dependent hardware iSCSI adapter. This exercise will assume an iSCSI target exists in your lab. If not, you can still follow along up until the final steps of the exercise.

EXERCISE 5.4

Configuring and Editing a Dependent Hardware iSCSI Adapter

1. Connect to a vCenter Server with the vSphere Client.

2. Select an ESXi host from the inventory.

3. Click the Configuration tab for the ESXi host and then click the blue Storage Adapters link in the Hardware panel.

4. If a dependent hardware iSCSI adapter is installed, it will appear in the Storage Adapters list.

5. Select a dependent hardware iSCSI adapter and click the blue Properties link located in the Details box.

6. An iSCSI Initiator (vmhba<Number>) Properties window will appear. Review the details of the selected adapter in the General tab. Remember which storage adapter (vmhba<Number>) you select here.

(continued)

7. Click the Network tab and notice that the VMkernel Port Bindings information is empty. Click the Add button. A Bind With VMkernel Network Adapter window will appear, as shown here.

8. The vmnic listed under the Physical Adapter column is the network adapter associated with this storage adapter. In the previous image, vmnic9 was used. Click the Cancel button to continue.

   Now that you know which physical network adapter is used with the storage adapter, the next step is to configure VMkernel networking. Remember, dependent hardware adapters rely on vSphere to provide networking.

9. Using the vmnic number from steps 7 and 8, create a VMkernel port group or dvPort group that uses this vmnic. The steps to create this networking were covered in Exercises 4.4 and 4.11 in Chapter 4, if you need a reference. Give the VMkernel an IP address on the same subnet as your iSCSI storage system.

10. After the VMkernel networking has been created, return to the Storage Adapter properties window and click the Network tab.

11. Click the Add button. If the VMkernel networking is configured correctly, the virtual switch you created should be listed in the Port Group column, and a VMkernel adapter number should also be present.

12. Click the OK button to bind the VMkernel network adapter. Review the information on the Network tab for accuracy.

At this point, the dependent hardware iSCSI adapter is essentially configured. The only remaining step is to add and configure an iSCSI target. For this exercise, you will configure Dynamic Discovery with no authentication, since *CHAP* configuration will be covered in Exercise 5.9.

13. Click the Dynamic Discovery tab. Click the Add button and enter the IP address and port number for the iSCSI target.

14. Click the Close button to save the changes.

15. When prompted to rescan the HBA, click the Yes button. A Rescan HBA task will begin. When it completes, check for new storage devices (if applicable).

I have now covered how to configure and edit a dependent hardware iSCSI adapter. In the next section, I will cover how to enable and disable the software iSCSI initiator.

Enabling and Disabling Software iSCSI Initiator

In the previous exercise, you learned how to configure and edit a dependent hardware iSCSI adapter. Some environments may not have dependent hardware iSCSI adapters or independent hardware iSCSI adapters and will instead leverage a standard NIC for iSCSI access. The software iSCSI initiator is used in this case. Exercise 5.5 will cover how to enable the software iSCSI initiator.

EXERCISE 5.5

Enabling the Software iSCSI Initiator

1. Connect to a vCenter Server with the vSphere Client.

2. Select an ESXi host and then click the Configuration tab. Click the blue Storage Adapters link in the Hardware panel.

3. Click the blue Add link located in the upper-right part of the Configuration tab. Review the list of storage adapters and verify that the iSCSI Software Adapter is not listed.

    If iSCSI Software Adapter is already listed here and you are comfortable with this process, then skip to step 6. It is important to note that only a single software iSCSI adapter can be added to each ESXi host.

4. An Add Storage Adapter window will appear, as shown here.

5. Ensure that the Add Software iSCSI Adapter option is selected and then click the OK button. Review the information presented in the next window and click the OK button to continue. A Change Software Internet SCSI Status task will begin.

6. When this task completes, select the vmhba<Number> adapter that is listed under iSCSI Software Adapter. Review the information on the details screen at the bottom of the Configuration tab and then click the blue Properties link located on the right of the Details section.

7. An iSCSI Initiator (vmhba<Number>) Properties window will appear. Verify that the Software Initiator Properties Status value is set to Enabled, as shown here.

Take note of the other tabs in the iSCSI Initiator (vmhba<Number>) Properties window. You will be using each of these tabs later in this chapter, as you continue to configure iSCSI. At this point, the software iSCSI initiator is enabled and ready to be configured for use. The software iSCSI initiator can also be disabled, if there is a point in the future when it is no longer required.

Exercise 5.6 will cover how to disable the software iSCSI initiator. It is important to note that disabling the software iSCSI adapter will require an ESXi host reboot. If you do not want to reboot your host, then you may simply want to read through this exercise.

EXERCISE 5.6

Disabling the Software iSCSI Initiator

1. Connect to a vCenter Server with the vSphere Client.

2. Select an ESXi host and then click the Configuration tab. Choose the blue Storage Adapters link in the Hardware panel.

3. Select the vmhba<Number> adapter that is listed under the iSCSI Software Adapter. Review the information in the details screen at the bottom of the Configuration tab and then click the blue Properties link located on the right of the Details section.

4. An iSCSI Initiator (vmhba<Number>) Properties window will appear. Verify that the Software Initiator Properties Status value is set to Enabled.

5. Click the Configure button on the lower right of the screen. A General Properties window will appear.

(continued)

EXERCISE 5.6 *(continued)*

6. In the Status section of the General Properties window, remove the check mark beside Enabled. The contents of the window will become disabled. Click the OK button.

7. A Change Software Internet SCSI Status task will begin. When this task completes, a Reboot Required window will appear.

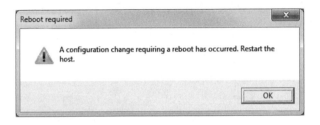

8. Note that it is safe to click the OK button here, because this is just an informational message.

9. In the iSCSI Initiator (vmhba<Number>) Properties window, verify that the Software Initiator Properties Status value now reports Disabled.

10. Click the Close button in the iSCSI Initiator (vmhba<Number>) Properties window.

11. Reboot the host.

12. When the host is available again, verify that the Software iSCSI initiator is no longer listed in the Storage Adapters list. The absence of the iSCSI Software Adapter in the Storage Adapters list confirms that the software iSCSI initiator is disabled.

I have now detailed how to enable and disable the software iSCSI initiator. In the following section, you can turn your attention to configuring and editing additional software iSCSI initiator settings.

Configuring and Editing Software iSCSI Initiator Settings

Once the software iSCSI initiator has been enabled, the next step is to configure it. In Exercise 5.7, you will configure and edit additional software iSCSI initiator settings.

EXERCISE 5.7

Configuring and Editing the Software iSCSI Initiator Settings

1. Connect to a vCenter Server with the vSphere Client.

2. Select an ESXi host and then click the Configuration tab. Click the blue Storage Adapters link in the Hardware panel.

3. Select the vmhba<Number> adapter that is listed under the iSCSI Software Adapter. Review the information on the details screen at the bottom of the Configuration tab and then click the blue Properties link located on the right of the Details section.

4. An iSCSI Initiator (vmhba<Number>) Properties window will appear.

5. On the General tab in the iSCSI Initiator (vmhba<Number>) Properties window, click the Configure button. A General Properties window will appear, as shown here.

Note the two additional iSCSI properties of iSCSI Name and iSCSI Alias. The descriptor entered for the iSCSI Alias is simply a friendly name that can be safely modified.

6. Enter a friendly name for the iSCSI Alias and click the OK button to save the changes. An Update Internet SCSI Alias task will begin. When this task completes, verify that the alias is listed in the iSCSI Initiator (vmhba<Number>) Properties window.

7. Click the Advanced button in the iSCSI Initiator (vmhba<Number>) Properties window to view the Advanced Settings window. These options are not normally used and would be more likely used in conjunction with VMware support. Click the Cancel button to close the Advanced Settings window.

8. Click the CHAP button on the iSCSI Initiator (vmhba<Number>) Properties window to view the CHAP Credentials window. I will discuss these options later in this chapter.

You have now configured your software iSCSI initiator settings and will next configure iSCSI port binding.

Configuring iSCSI Port Binding

iSCSI port binding is the process of associating an iSCSI storage adapter with a VMkernel adapter used for networking. The software iSCSI adapter and the dependent hardware iSCSI adapter both require a VMkernel connection type to be established, before configuring iSCSI port binding. You performed port binding for the dependent hardware iSCSI adapter in Exercise 5.4 and will now perform port binding for the software iSCSI adapter in Exercise 5.8.

EXERCISE 5.8

Configuring iSCSI Port Binding on the Software iSCSI Initiator

1. Connect to a vCenter Server with the vSphere Client.

2. Select an ESXi host and then click the Configuration tab. Click the blue Storage Adapters link in the Hardware panel.

3. Select the vmhba<Number> adapter that is listed under the iSCSI Software Adapter. Click the blue Properties link located on the right of the Details section.

4. An iSCSI Initiator (vmhba<Number>) Properties window will appear. Click the Network Configuration tab and then click the Add button.

5. A Bind With VMkernel Network Adapter window will appear, as shown here.

6. Select the virtual switch created prior to the start of this exercise by clicking or selecting it. Click the OK button to bind the selected VMkernel adapter with the iSCSI adapter. An Add Virtual NIC To iSCSI Adapter task will begin.

7. Review the information in the iSCSI Initiator (vmhba<Number>) Properties window. It should appear similar to the image shown here.

iSCSI Initiator (vmhba33) Properties

General | Network Configuration | Dynamic Discovery | Static Discovery |

VMkernel Port Bindings:

Port Group	VMkernel Adapter	Port Group Policy	Path Status	Physical Network Adapter
iSCSI (vSwitch2)	vmk1	Compliant	Not Used	vmnic5 (1000, Full)

Add...   Remove

VMkernel Port Binding Details:

Virtual Network Adapter

VMkernel:	vmk1
Switch:	vSwitch2
Port Group:	iSCSI
Port Group Policy:	Compliant
IP Address:	10.10.10.128
Subnet Mask:	255.255.255.0

Physical Network Adapter

Name:	vmnic5
Device:	Intel Corporation 82545EM Gigabit Ethernet Controller (Copper)
Link Status:	Connected
Configured Speed:	1000 Mbps (Full Duplex)

Close   Help

8. Click the Close button in the iSCSI Initiator (vmhba<Number>) Properties window.

9. A Rescan window will appear asking whether a rescan of the host bus adapter is desired. Click the No button, because there are no devices that a rescan operation will detect at this point.

The NIC that is used in port binding must be on the same subnet as the iSCSI target, or the ESXi host will not be able to establish sessions to it.

I have now covered nearly all of the configuration steps for the different iSCSI adapters, but there is still one final configuration item remaining. In the following section, I will cover how to enable, configure, and disable iSCSI CHAP options for iSCSI traffic.

Enabling, Configuring, and Disabling iSCSI CHAP

Challenge Handshake Authentication Protocol (CHAP) is used to provide security in iSCSI environments. CHAP utilizes a three-way handshake algorithm that is based on a CHAP secret that both the initiator and the target are aware of. Instead of sending the secret over the wire, a hash of the secret is used. CHAP is supported at the adapter level in ESXi. For greater security, per-target CHAP authentication is also supported for the dependent hardware iSCSI adapter and the software iSCSI adapter.

The two CHAP authentication methods supported in ESXi are described here:

One-Way CHAP   The target (storage system) authenticates the iSCSI adapter (initiator). This is also known as *unidirectional*.

Mutual CHAP   The target (storage system) authenticates the iSCSI adapter (initiator), and the iSCSI adapter also authenticates the target. This is also known as *bidirectional*. Mutual CHAP is supported for dependent hardware iSCSI adapters and software iSCSI adapters only.

A security level is specified for CHAP during configuration. Table 5.6 shows the CHAP security levels.

TABLE 5.6   CHAP security levels

CHAP security level	Description	Supported
Do not use CHAP.	CHAP connections are not used by the host. This setting is used to disable CHAP.	Software iSCSI Dependent hardware iSCSI Independent hardware iSCSI
Do not use CHAP unless required by target.	Non-CHAP connections are preferred by the host, but a CHAP connection can be used if the target requires it.	Software iSCSI Dependent hardware iSCSI
Use CHAP unless prohibited by target.	CHAP connections are preferred by the host, but a non-CHAP connection can be used if the target does not support it.	Software iSCSI Dependent hardware iSCSI Independent hardware iSCSI
Use CHAP.	CHAP connections are required by the host.	Software iSCSI Dependent hardware iSCSI

Each storage array's implementation of CHAP will be specific. Always consult the array documentation for the supported CHAP configurations before you specify the CHAP security level in ESXi.

Exercise 5.9 covers how to enable, configure, and disable iSCSI CHAP. In the interest of using an adapter that you most likely have access to, this exercise will focus on configuring CHAP for the software iSCSI adapter.

Enabling, Configuring, and Disabling iSCSI CHAP on the Software iSCSI Adapter

1. Connect to a vCenter Server with the vSphere Client.

2. Select an ESXi host and then click the Configuration tab. Click the blue Storage Adapters link in the Hardware panel.

3. Select the vmhba<Number> adapter that is listed under the iSCSI Software Adapter. Click the blue Properties link located on the right of the Details section.

4. An iSCSI Initiator (vmhba<Number>) Properties window will appear. Click the CHAP button located at the bottom of this window. The CHAP Credentials window will appear, as shown here.

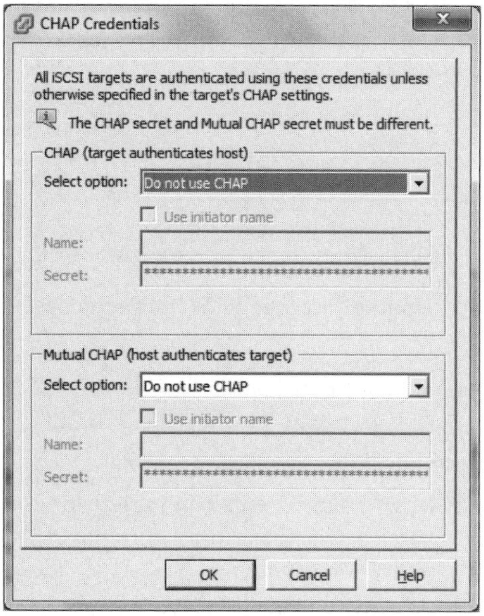

Notice that the default option is Do Not Use CHAP for both the CHAP and Mutual CHAP settings. As shown in Table 5.6, this setting means that CHAP is currently disabled. In the following steps, you will enable CHAP and configure one-way CHAP.

(continued)

5. In the CHAP (Target Authenticates Host) settings, use the Select Option drop-down menu to select the Use CHAP option. The three options located below the drop-down menu will become active.

6. Select the Use Initiator Name box. The Name field will become disabled. Enter a secret, and the final configuration should look similar to the image shown here.

7. Click the OK button. An Update Internet SCSI Authentication Properties task will start.

8. When this task completes, click the Close button in the iSCSI Initiator (vmhba<Number>) Properties window. You will be prompted to rescan the host bus adapter. Click the No button.

   At this point, CHAP has been enabled and configured for one-way CHAP. The remaining steps of the exercise will focus on returning CHAP to its default state of disabled.

9. Open the CHAP properties for the Software iSCSI Adapter, and in the CHAP (Target Authenticates Host) settings, use the Select Option drop-down menu to select the Do Not Use CHAP option. The three options located below the drop-down menu will become inactive.

10. Click the OK button in the CHAP Credentials window. An Update Internet SCSI Authentication Properties task will start.

11. When this task completes, click the Close button in the iSCSI Initiator (vmhba<Number>) Properties window. You will be prompted to rescan the host bus adapter. Click the No button.

 Although this exercise focused on the software iSCSI adapter, the process for configuring CHAP is the same for all of the iSCSI adapters.

I have now covered CHAP and configuring CHAP for your iSCSI connections. In the following section, I will move away from iSCSI and cover the differences between thin provisioning when implemented at the virtual disk and the array level.

Comparing and Contrasting Array Thin Provisioning and Virtual Disk Thin Provisioning

Thin provisioning is the process of provisioning storage but not actually using all of the provisioned space. This can take place on SAN and NAS devices at the storage level or at the virtual disk level. Both of these approaches offer similar benefits, and both will require additional monitoring to be used with success.

With virtual disk thin provisioning in ESXi, a virtual disk is provisioned upon creation. The size is chosen as one of the options, and then the VMDK is created with this provisioned size. With this approach, the VMDK starts small and grows as necessary. For example, a virtual machine is created with a single 50GB thin-provisioned hard disk. An operating system and several applications are then installed on this VM. The provisioned storage value will report 50GB, and the Used Storage value might report 25GB. This disk is saving 25GB of space on the storage system.

 Thin-provisioned virtual disks cannot be used with VMware FT.

With array thin provisioning, the concept is basically the same. Space is allocated as devices (volumes or LUNs) are created on the storage device, but the consumption of this space is only as required. Storage array thin provisioning requires ESXi 5 and a storage device with a firmware version that supports T10-based Storage APIs: Array Integration (Thin Provisioning).

Both of these approaches allow for the over-provisioning of storage resources. This can be a powerful feature and can provide cost savings, but it must be used with caution. If a thin-provisioned storage device runs out of space, the results are never good. Because of this, monitoring is essential with both forms of thin provisioning.

Determining Use Case for and Configuring Array Thin Provisioning

Thin provisioning allows for the over-provisioning of storage and allows for greater flexibility in predicting growth. The type of disks used in your virtual machines can often help determine the use case for array thin provisioning. There are three different disk types for the virtual machines:

Thin Provisioned   These disks grow as required.

Flat Disk   These disks have all space allocated when created, but the space on the disk is not zeroed.

Thick Provisioned   These disks have all space allocated when created, and the space is also zeroed out upon creation.

I will discuss these disk types in more detail in Chapter 6, but it is also useful to know some of this information now as it pertains to array thin provisioning.

If your virtual machines use mostly thin-provisioned and flat-disk formats, then array thin provisioning can save consumed space on the SAN. If you use thick-provisioned disks, thin provisioning on the SAN will be limited. Keep in mind that VMware FT and certain clustering solutions will also require thick-provisioned disks, so array thin provisioning is often not a good fit with these solutions.

Raw device mappings are often a great use case for array thin provisioning, because the file systems on these volumes will have room for growth factored into their size upon creation and will also require free space for the file system.

Many NAS servers will typically use a default allocation policy of thin, and if you are using one of these units, then thin provisioning is a guaranteed use case. Another interesting new feature in vSphere 5 is NFS reserve space, which allows thick disks on the NAS server. Check with your NAS vendor to see whether it supports thick disks or whether thin provisioning is the only option.

The process for configuring array thin provisioning will differ from vendor to vendor and system to system, so always consult the documentation provided by your storage device vendor for the configuration and best practices.

 The configuration of thin provisioning on storage devices is not supported in ESXi. You will have to use the vendor's management tools for this.

Now that I have covered thin provisioning, I will cover creating and configuring VMFS and NFS datastores.

Create and Configure VMFS and NFS Datastores

As a VMware Certified Professional, you will be expected to know how to add and use VMFS and NFS datastores. In this section, I will cover how to create and configure them. You will also explore many of the operational tasks involved with both VMFS and NFS datastores.

Identifying VMFS-5 Capabilities

Virtual Machine File System (VMFS) was created by VMware as a purpose-built and optimized clustered file system that provides storage virtualization. VMFS provides many capabilities, each of which is described here:

Clustered File System   VMFS is a clustered file system that allows concurrent access from multiple hosts.

Encapsulation   Virtual machines that are housed on VMFS datastores have all of their files encapsulated in directories on VMFS.

Simplified Administration   Typically, large VMFS datastores are created on storage devices in ESXi. This simplifies interactions between virtualization administrators and storage administrators, because the virtual administrator has a pool of storage that can be used for virtual machines.

Dynamic Growth   VMFS can be expanded or extended, allowing flexibility and scalability. This process can happen while VMs are running on the datastore. VMDK files can also be expanded on VMFS volumes, while the virtual machines they are assigned to are running.

Advanced Feature Enablement   When combined with shared storage from a SAN, VMFS also allows advanced vSphere features such as vMotion, DRS, HA, and FT to be used.

Thin Provisioning   VMFS supports thin-provisioned VMDK files, allowing for over-allocated VMFS datastores.

Backup and Recoverability   VMFS allows proxied backups of virtual machines, while the VM is in use.

RDMs   Support for RDM devices.

VMFS-5 is the version of VMFS included with vSphere 5. This version includes the following enhancements:

Unified 1MB File Block Size   For newly created VMFS-5 volumes, the previous 1MB, 2MB, 4MB, or 8MB file block sizes have been replaced with a single block size of 1MB.

Using this 1MB block size, VMFS-5 can support VMDK files of 2TB minus 512 bytes. It should be noted that a single VMDK file is still limited to a size limit of 2TB minus 512 bytes.

Large Single Extent Volumes   Storage devices greater than 2TB are now supported for use as VMFS datastores. The new limit in VMFS-5 is 64TB.

Large Physical RDMs   RDMs in physical compatibility mode now have a maximum size of 64TB.

Online In-Place Upgrades   VMFS-3 datastores can be upgraded to VMFS-5 without service interruption to hosts or virtual machines.

Smaller Sub-blocks   These blocks are sized at 8KB, as compared to 64KB in previous versions. This means files sized between 1KB and 8KB will consume only 8KB, rather than 64KB.

Small File Support   Used for files less than or equal to 1KB. With these small files, the file descriptor location will be stored in the VMFS metadata rather than file blocks. If these files ever grow beyond 1KB, then the files will start using 8KB blocks. The idea with both smaller sub-blocks and small file support is to reduce the amount of disk space consumed in the VMFS datastore by small files.

Large File Numbers   VMFS-5 introduces support for approximately 130,690 files on the VMFS datastore. (VMFS-3 supports approximately 30,720 files.)

ATS Enhancement   Hardware assisted locking, also known as Atomic Test & Set (ATS), is now used for file locking on storage devices that support hardware acceleration.

Although VMFS-5 supports 64TB volumes, always consult your storage vendor to ensure that sizes this large are supported on the storage device.

Now that I have covered the capabilities of VMFS and the specifics of VMFS-5, I will cover creating and performing operations on a VMFS datastore.

Creating, Renaming, Unmounting, and Deleting a VMFS Datastore

If you installed ESXi on disk, a default VMFS volume was likely created as part of the install. The local VMFS volume is also likely small and is not shared storage. One of the capabilities of VMFS is to be used with shared storage to provide the framework for the advanced features of vSphere. Exercise 5.10 will detail creating and renaming a VMFS datastore. While this exercise can be performed with any available storage device, the examples used will show an iSCSI disk.

EXERCISE 5.10

Creating and Renaming a VMFS Datastore

1. Connect to a vCenter Server with the vSphere Client.

2. Select an ESXi host and then click the Configuration tab. Click the blue Storage link in the Hardware panel.

3. Click the blue Add Storage link at the top of the Configuration panel. The Add Storage Wizard will appear.

4. Choose the Disk/LUN option in the Storage Type section and click the Next button to continue.

5. On the Select Disk/LUN screen, select the appropriate device from the list by highlighting it. This should appear similar to the image shown here.

Note the search function available on this screen, and remember that columns can be sorted and customized here.

6. Once the appropriate device has been selected, click the Next button to continue.

(continued)

EXERCISE 5.10 *(continued)*

7. Choose the VMFS version to be used. If this is a stand-alone host or an all–ESXi 5 host environment, choose the VMFS-5 option. If you have legacy, meaning pre–ESXi 5, hosts, then choose the VMFS-3 option. Once the selection has been made, click the Next button to continue.

8. Review the current disk layout. It is generally a good idea to look for the text The Hard Disk Is Blank in this screen. If you're certain that this disk is suitable, click the Next button to continue.

9. Enter a datastore name and click the Next button to continue.

10. In the Capacity section, choose the Maximum Available Space option and click the Next button to continue.

11. Review the information on the Ready To Complete screen and click the Finish button to create the datastore.

12. A Create VMFS Datastore task will begin. When this task completes, verify that the new datastore appears in the list of datastores shown on the Configuration tab.

    You have now created a VMFS datastore, and it is ready to be used. In the next part of this exercise, you will rename the VMFS datastore.

13. Select the datastore just created by clicking it in the Datastores view. Review the details shown at the bottom of the screen under Datastore Details. Click the blue Properties link located on the right side of the Datastore Details section. A <Datastore> Properties window will appear, as shown here.

14. Click the Rename button at the top of the screen. A Rename <Datastore> window will appear. Enter a new name for the datastore and click the OK button. A Rename Managed Entity task will begin.

15. When this task completes, verify that the new datastore name is reflected in the <Datastore> Properties window. Click the Close button on the <Datastore> Properties window.

16. Now highlight the datastore that was just renamed at the top of the Datastores view on the Configuration tab. Right-click the datastore and choose Rename from the context menu that appears. A text box will appear over the datastore allowing you to rename it. Press the Enter key to save the changes. A Rename Managed Entity task will begin.

17. Now hover the mouse cursor over the datastore name and click. A text box will appear over the datastore allowing you to rename it. Press the Enter key to save the changes. A Rename Managed Entity task will begin.

You have now renamed the VMFS datastore you created in three different ways. If this VMFS datastore was accessible to multiple ESXi hosts being managed by vCenter, then the new name would be reflected on each of these hosts.

When creating VMFS datastores, it is important to maintain a one-to-one relationship between each VMFS datastore and LUN.

Additional operations that can be performed on VMFS datastores include unmounting and deleting them. Unmounting a datastore will not destroy the datastore but will simply make the datastore inaccessible to the ESXi host(s). If other ESXi hosts have this datastore mounted, they may continue to access the datastore as usual. The unmount operation has several prerequisites:

- Virtual machines and templates may not reside on the datastore.
- *ISOs* located on the datastore must be removed from virtual machines.
- Mapping files for RDMs on the datastore must be removed.
- The datastore cannot be part of a *datastore cluster.*
- The datastore must not be managed by Storage DRS.
- Storage I/O Control must be disabled for the datastore.
- The datastore must not be used for vSphere HA heartbeat.
- No operations, including those from scripts or third-party utilities, that would result in I/O to the datastore can be used while the unmount operation is in progress.

VMFS datastores can be unmounted one at a time, or you can choose the hosts that the VMFS datastore should be unmounted from. Exercise 5.11 will detail the steps for both of these approaches.

EXERCISE 5.11

Unmounting a VMFS Datastore

1. Connect to a vCenter Server with the vSphere Client.

2. Select an ESXi host and then click the Configuration tab. Click the blue Storage link in the Hardware panel.

3. Select the VMFS datastore created in Exercise 5.10 by clicking it.

4. Right-click the datastore and choose the Unmount option from the context menu that appears.

View:	Datastores	Devices		
Datastores				
Identification	▽	Status	Device	Drive Type
🗄 VMFS-VOL1				

Browse Datastore...

Alarm ▶

Assign User-Defined Storage Capability...

Rename

Unmount

Delete

Open in New Window... Ctrl+Alt+N

Refresh

Properties...

Copy to Clipboard Ctrl+C

5. A Confirm Datastore Unmount window will appear that lists any issues found with the prerequisites. If problems are discovered, the OK button will be disabled. If no issues are reported, click the OK button to continue.

6. An Unmount VMFS task will begin. When the task completes, verify that the datastore is now listed as Inactive in the Datastores view on the Configuration tab.

View:	Datastores	Devices
Datastores		
Identification	▲	
🗄 VMFS-VOL1 (inactive)...		

If this VMFS datastore was being shared by other ESXi hosts, check the status of the VMFS datastore that was just unmounted on one of these other hosts now. You will find that the VMFS datastore is still mounted and accessible. It is also worth noting that this VMFS datastore can easily be mounted again, simply by right-clicking the datastore and choosing the Mount option from the context menu that appears.

7. To unmount VMFS datastores on multiple ESXi hosts simultaneously, first click the Home icon in the navigation bar. Choose the Datastores and Datastore Clusters icon from the Inventory objects and then click the Datastores And Datastore Clusters tab.

8. Review the list, and pick a VMFS datastore that will be unmounted from multiple ESXi hosts by clicking it. Now right-click the datastore and choose the Unmount option from the context menu that appears.

9. The Unmount Datastore Wizard will appear, as shown here.

10. Notice that by default all ESXi hosts are selected in the Remove Access column. Deselect at least one host by removing the check mark for the host name and click the Next button to continue.

11. On the Check Prerequisites screen, review any issues found with the prerequisites. If problems are discovered, they will be listed with circular red X icons. You will not be able to continue until these issues are resolved. If no issues are reported, click the Next button to continue.

12. Review the information on the Ready To Complete screen and click the Finish button. An Unmount VMFS Volume task will begin for each ESXi host that was selected in the second step of the wizard.

13. When these tasks complete, verify that the VMFS datastore is listed as Inactive on the Datastores And Datastore Clusters tab.

As with the single unmount operation covered in the beginning of this exercise, the Mount Datastore Wizard can be launched by right-clicking the inactive VMFS datastore and choosing the Mount option from the context menu that appears. This will allow the mounting of a VMFS datastore to multiple ESXi hosts in a few simple steps.

I have now covered creating, renaming, unmounting, and mounting VMFS datastores. The remaining operation that needs to be covered is how to delete VMFS datastores.

WARNING Deleting a VMFS datastore will destroy the datastore and its contents, and the VMFS datastore will be removed from any host that has access to it.

To delete a VMFS datastore, all virtual machines should be removed prior, and other ESXi hosts should no longer be accessing the VMFS datastore. Exercise 5.12 will cover the steps to delete a VMFS datastore. Proceed with caution, and if a test VMFS datastore isn't available, it may be best to just read through this exercise.

EXERCISE 5.12

Deleting a VMFS Datastore

1. Connect to a vCenter Server with the vSphere Client.

2. Select an ESXi host and then click the Configuration tab. Click the blue Storage link in the Hardware panel.

3. Select the VMFS datastore to be deleted by clicking it.

4. Right-click the datastore and choose the Delete option from the context menu that appears.

5. A Confirm remove datatore prompt will appear, as shown here.

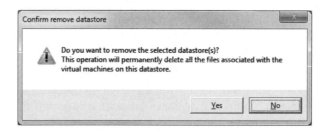

6. Review this information and click the Yes button to continue.

7. A Remove Datastore Task will start, and it will be immediately followed by a Rescan VMFS task. When these tasks complete, verify that the VMFS datastore is no longer listed on the Configuration tab.

I have now covered the VMFS datastore operations of create, rename, unmount, and delete. Next, I will cover how to identify VMFS datastore properties.

Identifying VMFS Datastore Properties

There are several places where VMFS datastore properties can be obtained. On the Configuration tab, after choosing the Storage option from the Hardware panel, the Datastores view contains many VMFS properties. Like many of the views in vCenter Server, the visible columns can be customized. Figure 5.1 shows the VMFS datastore properties available in the Datastores view.

FIGURE 5.1 VMFS datastore properties in the Datastores view

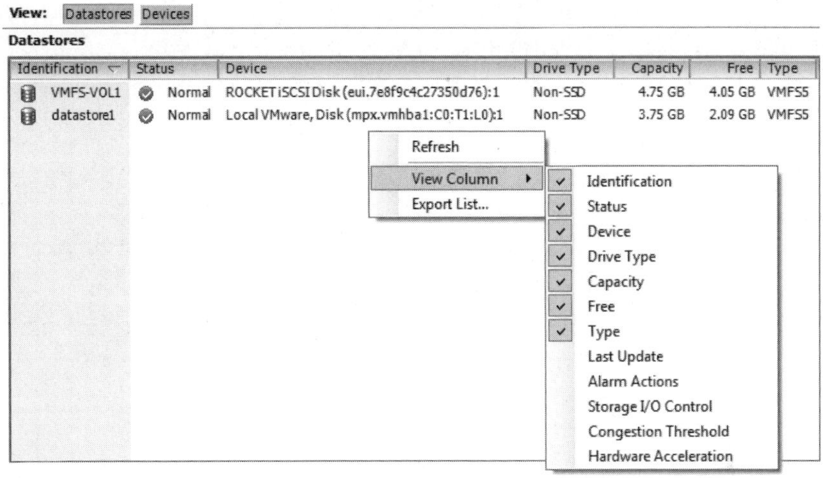

By selecting a VMFS datastore in Datastores view, additional VMFS properties are available in the Datastore Details field at the bottom of the screen. Some of the additional information available here includes free space on the VMFS datastore, the VMFS version, and the block size used. Figure 5.2 shows all of the information available in the Datastore Details field.

FIGURE 5.2: VMFS datastore properties in Datastore Details field

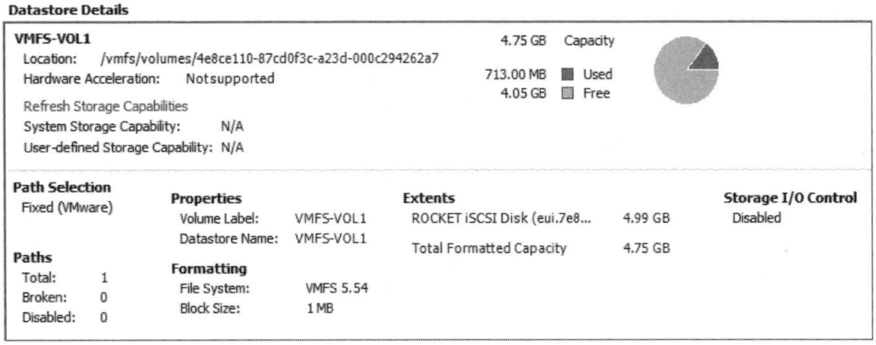

Right-clicking a VMFS datastore and choosing the Properties option from the context menu is one more option to view various VMFS datastore properties. Alternately, you can launch the VMFS datastore properties by clicking the blue Properties link to the right of the Datastore Details field on the Configuration tab. Figure 5.3 shows all of the information available in the VMFS properties.

FIGURE 5.3 VMFS datastore properties

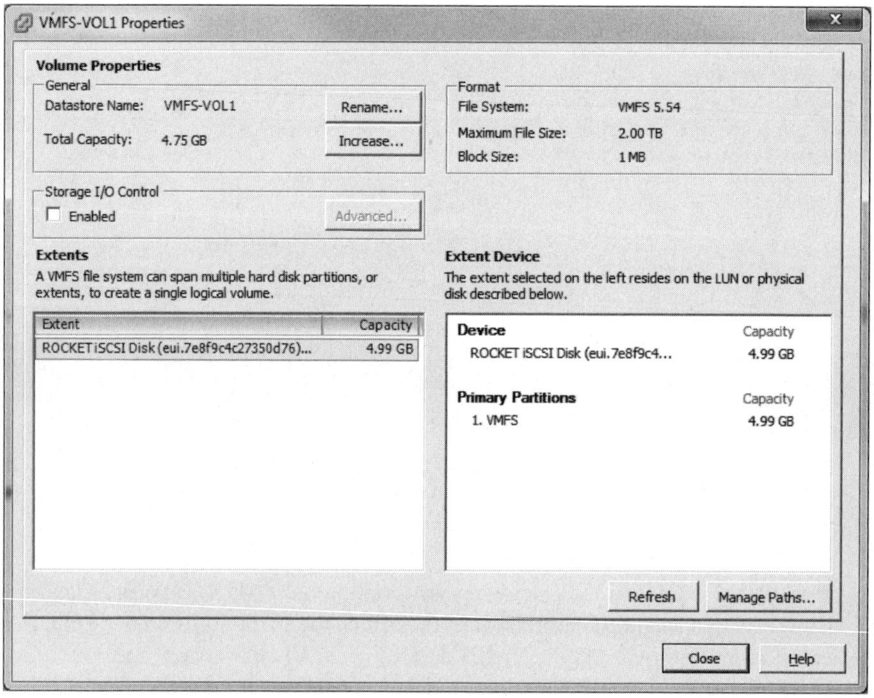

In the VMFS Properties window, there are additional configuration items as well. These include the ability to rename the VMFS datastore, to increase the size of the VMFS datastore, and to manage the paths used to access the VMFS datastore. Storage I/O Control can also be enabled here.

> **TIP** Various VMFS datastore properties are obtained in many different locations, so make sure you know your way around the vSphere Client.

One of the options in the VMFS datastore properties shown in Figure 5.3 was the ability to increase the VMFS datastore size. In the next section, I will discuss this topic.

Extending and Expanding VMFS Datastores

Expanding VMFS datastores is sometimes necessary. This can be because of circumstances like a VMFS datastore not being sized adequately or a VM that has experienced unexpected growth. To handle these situations, VMFS datastores can be increased dynamically. There are two methods used to increase the size of VMFS datastores:

Add Extent   This is also known as *extending* the VMFS datastore. This is where another storage device is coupled with the original storage device to extend a VMFS datastore that spans the devices.

Grow Extent   This is also known as *expanding* the VMFS datastore. This is where the storage device backing the VMFS datastore is increased in size, and the VMFS datastore is then expanded to fill this space. This method is very similar to the functionality often used in VMware and Windows environments to increase a VMDK and then expand the NTFS volume to use this new space.

Exercise 5.13 covers growing an extent in a VMFS datastore. A prerequisite for this exercise is that the device backing the VMFS datastore must have already been expanded. This expansion operation will need to be performed on your storage system through its appropriate management function. If you have a VMware Workstation lab, you will have a simple task to expand a VMDK file.

EXERCISE 5.13

Growing an Extent in a VMFS Datastore

1. Connect to a vCenter Server with the vSphere Client.

2. Select an ESXi host and then click the Configuration tab. Click the blue Storage link in the Hardware panel.

3. Select the VMFS datastore to be grown by clicking it.

4. Right-click the datastore and choose the Properties option from the context menu that appears.

5. A <Datastore> Properties window will appear, as shown here.

(continued)

EXERCISE 5.13 *(continued)*

6. In the lower-right quadrant of this screen, verify that the device is showing a capacity greater than the listed capacity of the primary partition.

7. To grow the VMFS datastore, click the Increase button in the upper-left quadrant of this screen.

8. An Increase Datastore Capacity Wizard will launch.

9. Select the appropriate extent device from the list, and verify that the Expandable column reports a value of Yes.

    Remember, if the Expandable column isn't visible, you can easily add it by right-clicking any column header. Also notice that once you select an extent device that is expandable, an informational message will appear at the bottom of the screen. This message simply informs you that the datastore will be expanded (grown).

10. Once the correct extent device has been selected, click the Next button to continue.

11. Review the information under Current Disk Layout and verify that free space will be used to expand the VMFS datastore. Click the Next button to continue.

12. For the Extent Size option, select Maximum Available Space and then click the Next button to continue.

13. Review the information presented on the Ready To Complete screen and click the Finish button to grow the VMFS datastore.

(continued)

14. A Compute Disk Partition Information For Resize task will begin, and it will be immediately followed by an Expand VMFS Datastore task.

15. When these tasks complete, verify in the <Datastore> Properties window that the Primary Partition shows the new value. Also note that the Total Capacity value is updated and correct.

Now that I have covered growing or expanding a VMFS datastore, Exercise 5.14 will cover adding a new extent to, or extending, a VMFS datastore. A prerequisite for this exercise will be an additional device that can be used as an extent. This will require additional configuration on your storage system and again will be easily accomplished by those using a VMware Workstation lab.

EXERCISE 5.14

Adding an Extent in a VMFS Datastore

1. Connect to a vCenter Server with the vSphere Client.

2. Select an ESXi host and then click the Configuration tab. Click the blue Storage link in the Hardware panel.

3. Select the VMFS datastore that the extent will be added to by clicking it.

4. In the lower to middle right side of the screen, click the blue Properties link.

5. In the <Datastore> Properties window that appears, click the Increase button.

6. An Increase Datastore Capacity Wizard will launch.

7. Select the appropriate extent device from the list, and verify that the Expand-able column reports a value of No. As in the previous exercise, also note the informational message that appears at the bottom of the screen after you select the device extent.

8. Once the correct extent device has been selected, click the Next button to continue.

9. Review the information under Current Disk Layout and verify that a partition will be created and used to extend the VMFS datastore. Click the Next button to continue.

10. For the Extent Size option, select Maximum Available Space and then click the Next button to continue.

11. Review the information presented in the Ready To Complete screen and click the Finish button to grow the VMFS datastore.

12. An Extend Datastore task will begin. When it completes, verify in the <Datas-tore> Properties window that the Total Capacity reflects the new value.

If any other ESXi hosts are accessing a VMFS datastore that an extent is added to, the datastores will need to be refreshed on each of these hosts. This is necessary to ensure all hosts display accurate information.

I have now covered how to expand and extend VMFS datastores. In the next section, I will cover how to upgrade a VMFS-3 datastore to VMFS-5.

Upgrading a VMFS-3 Datastore to VMFS-5

To leverage the new features of VMFS-5, current VMFS-3 datastores can be upgraded to VMFS-5. Upgraded VMFS-3 datastores will retain their given block sizes, and these datastores can be upgraded while VMs are running on them. In the VMFS-3 to VMFS-5 upgrade process, the ESXi file-locking mechanism will ensure that no processes are accessing the VMFS datastore. The ESXi 5 host will preserve all files on the VMFS datastore during the upgrade. Here are a few other points to remember:

- It is recommended that backups of all virtual machines on the VMFS datastore be taken prior to the upgrade.

- It is also important to know that the VMFS-3 to VMFS-5 upgrade is a one-way process. There is no rollback option.

- All hosts accessing the VMFS-3 datastore being upgraded must be ESXi 5 or newer. Any host connected to this VMFS-3 datastore that doesn't support VMFS-5 will lose connectivity to the datastore after the upgrade to VMFS-5 completes.

- Remove any partitions that ESXi does not recognize from the storage device, or the upgrade will fail.

Once you have ensured that the VMFS-3 datastore is ready to be upgraded to VMFS-5, you can proceed with the upgrade. Exercise 5.15 will cover upgrading an existing VMFS-3 datastore to the VMFS-5 format. If the ESXi hosts in your lab do not have an existing VMFS-3 datastore, then you can simply create a new VMFS-3 datastore in ESXi 5 for use in this exercise.

EXERCISE 5.15

Upgrading a VMFS-3 Datastore to VMFS-5

1. Open the vSphere Client and connect to an ESXi host or the vCenter Server that is managing the ESXi host with a VMFS-3 datastore.

2. Select the Configuration tab from the right pane and then select Storage from the Hardware panel.

3. In the list of datastores, select a datastore that currently uses the VMFS-3 format. After the datastore has been selected, review the datastore details, as shown here.

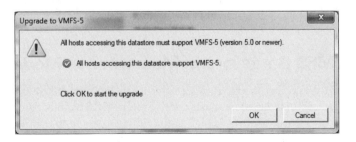

4. Notice the Formatting: File System value for the VMFS volume. You will also notice a blue link titled Upgrade To VMFS-5. Click the blue Upgrade To VMFS-5 link to begin.

5. A warning message will appear stating that all hosts accessing this datastore must support VMFS-5. The status of all hosts connected to the datastore is also listed, as shown here.

6. If there are no compatibility issues listed, click the OK button to start the VMFS-5 upgrade.

7. An Upgrade VMFS task will appear in the Recent Tasks list. When this task completes, verify that the datastore is now using VMFS-5 in the Type column of the Datastores view. Also take note of the Formatting: File System value in the Datastore Details section.

ESXi 5 offers complete read-write support for both VMFS-3 and VMFS-5 datastores, but VMFS-2 is not supported in ESXi 5. VMFS-2 datastores must first be upgraded to VMFS-3 in order to upgrade them to VMFS-5.

Now that I have covered how to upgrade a VMFS-3 datastore to VMFS-5, there are a few caveats worth mentioning for these datastores:

- Upgraded VMFS-5 datastores continue to use the previous block size of the VMFS-3 datastore.

- Upgraded VMFS-5 datastores can use the 1KB small-files feature.

- Upgraded VMFS-5 datastores can be grown to 64TB, exactly like newly created VMFS-5 datastores.

- Upgraded VMFS-5 datastores have all of the *VAAI* Atomic Test & Set (ATS) improvements, exactly like newly created VMFS-5 datastores.

- Upgraded VMFS-5 datastores will continue to use 64KB sub-blocks and not the new 8K sub-blocks.

- Upgraded VMFS-5 datastores will continue to have a file limit of 30,720 files. Newly created VMFS-5 datastores can contain approximately 130,690 files.

- Upgraded VMFS-5 datastores will continue to use the master boot record (MBR) type of partition. When the upgraded VMFS-5 datastore grows beyond 2TB, it will automatically switch from MBR to GUID Partition Table (GPT) with no impact to your running VMs.

- Upgraded VMFS-5 datastores continue to have their partition starting at sector 128. Newly created VMFS-5 datastores have their partition starting at sector 2048.

Now that I have shown how to upgrade a VMFS-3 datastore to VMFS-5 and discussed the caveats of doing so, you can turn your attention to placing a VMFS datastore in maintenance mode.

Placing a VMFS Datastore in Maintenance Mode

Similar to how ESXi hosts can be placed in a cluster with DRS enabled, shared VMFS datastores can be placed in a datastore cluster with Storage DRS enabled. Storage DRS is one of the exciting new features of vSphere 5, and it will be covered in detail in Chapter 8. Chapter 8 will also cover the exam objective of placing a VMFS datastore in maintenance mode, so for now a preview is shown in Figure 5.4.

I will next cover how to select the preferred path for a VMFS datastore.

Determining Appropriate Path Selection Policy for a Given VMFS Datastore

Multipathing, as its name implies, is a technique used to provide multiple paths from an ESXi host to storage devices. This is done both to increase performance and to provide fault tolerance. Multipathing is managed in ESXi through a collection of VMkernel APIs known as Pluggable Storage Architecture (PSA). Figure 5.5 provides an overview of the Pluggable Storage Architecture.

FIGURE 5.4   Enter SDRS maintenance mode

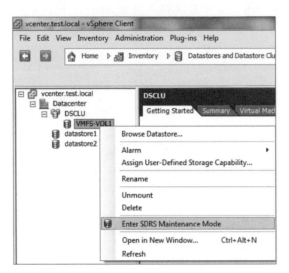

FIGURE 5.5   Pluggable Storage Architecture

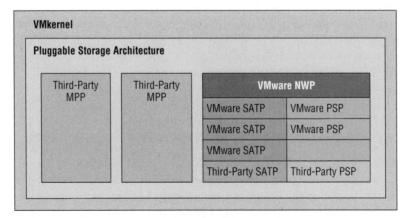

When ESXi starts up or an adapter is rescanned, the PSA uses *claim rules* to determine which multipathing plug-in (MPP) to use. The MPP will be responsible for both claiming and managing the multipathing for the device. MPPs are extensible and can be provided by third parties. ESXi also includes a Native Multipathing plug-in (NMP) by default that typically supports storage systems listed on the VMware HCL. If third-party MPPs are used, they replace the functionality included with the NMP. The NMP manages two types of sub-plug-ins:

Storage Array Type Plug-in (SATP)   The SATP is responsible for performing array-specific functions in a failover situation, monitoring the health, and reporting changes of each physical path.

Path Selection Plug-in (PSP)   The PSP deals with path selection for a given device.

A PSP is assigned for each logical device by the VMware NMP. This PSP is based on information obtained by the SATP. By default, there are three PSPs, each of which is explained here:

VMW_PSP_FIXED   The ESXi host will use the first working path discovered, or it may use a designated preferred path if manually configured this way. This is used by most active-active storage devices and is displayed as Fixed (VMware) for the path selection policy in the vSphere Client.

VMW_PSP_MRU   The ESXi host will use the most recently used path. If this path becomes unavailable, an alternate path will be used. With MRU, there is no preferred path. This is used by most active-passive storage devices and is displayed as Most Recently Used (VMware) for the path selection policy in the vSphere Client.

VMW_PSP_RR   The ESXi host will use rotating paths. For active-active storage devices, this rotation will occur through all available paths. For active-passive storage devices, this rotation will occur through all active paths. This is used with both active-active and active-passive storage devices and is displayed as Round Robin (VMware) for the path selection policy in the vSphere Client.

As mentioned earlier, ESXi hosts will automatically select the path selection policy based on the information contained in the claim rules when ESXi starts up or an adapter is rescanned. Typically, the path selection policy will not need to be modified. If in doubt, check with your storage vendor to determine whether the appropriate path selection policy is being used by your VMFS datastores.

Now that I have covered the PSA and how multipathing works in ESXi, I will cover how to select the preferred path for a VMFS datastore.

Selecting the Preferred Path for a VMFS Datastore

The vSphere Client can be used to view the path information for a VMFS datastore and to modify the path(s) used by the VMFS datastore. Exercise 5.16 will cover the steps required to select the preferred path for a VMFS datastore. It is recommended that you use either an empty VMFS datastore or a VMFS datastore with no running VMs on it for this exercise.

EXERCISE 5.16

Selecting the Preferred Path for a VMFS Datastore

1. Open the vSphere Client and connect to an ESXi host or the vCenter Server that is managing the ESXi host with an existing VMFS datastore.

2. Select the Configuration tab from the right pane and then select Storage from the Hardware panel.

3. Select a VMFS datastore. Right-click this VMFS datastore and choose the Properties option that appears on the context menu.

4. The Datastore Properties window will appear. Click the Manage Paths button located in the lower-right corner.

5. A <DeviceName> Properties window will appear, as shown here.

6. If your path is currently set to Fixed, as it is in the previous image, you will notice that the Preferred column will have an asterisk in it.

7. Use the Path Selection drop-down menu to change the path selection policy for this VMFS datastore.

(continued)

EXERCISE 5.16 *(continued)*

Any third-party PSP that is installed on the ESXi host you are working on will also appear in the drop-down menu for the path selection policy, so there could be more choices here than the default three provided.

8. If you are changing to the Fixed path selection policy, right-click one of the available paths and choose the Preferred option from the context menu that appears.

9. Once all changes have been made, click the Change button located to the right of the Path Selection drop-down menu.

10. A Set Logical Unit Policy task will begin, and the <DeviceName> Properties window will refresh to show the new path selection policy and path(s) information.

Remember that the path information typically will not need to be changed. Consult with your storage provider or VMware before making these types of changes, especially in production environments.

I have now detailed how to change the path selection policy for a VMFS datastore. Next I will cover how to disable a path to a VMFS datastore.

Disabling a Path to a VMFS Datastore

Certain maintenance operations might require the disabling of a path to a VMFS datastore. Exercise 5.17 will cover the steps required to disable a path to a VMFS datastore. As with the previous exercise, you are encouraged to use either an empty VMFS datastore or a VMFS datastore with no running VMs on it for this exercise.

EXERCISE 5.17

Disabling a Path to a VMFS Datastore

1. Open the vSphere Client and connect to an ESXi host or the vCenter Server that is managing the ESXi host with an existing VMFS datastore.

2. Select the Configuration tab from the right pane and then select Storage from the Hardware panel.

3. Select a VMFS datastore. Click the blue Properties link in the lower-right corner of the screen.

4. The Datastore Properties window will appear. Click the Manage Paths button located in the lower-right corner.

5. A <DeviceName> Properties window will appear.

6. Right-click a path and choose the Disable option, as shown here.

Paths					
Runtime Name	Target	LUN	Status	Preferred	
vmhba39:C0:T0:L0	iqn.2001-05.com...	0	◆ Active (I/O)		
vmhba39:C1:T0:L0	iqn.2001-05.com...	0	◇ Active (I/O)		

Disable
Preferred
Copy path to clipboard

Refresh

7. A Disable Multipath task will begin. When it completes, verify that the path has been disabled.

I have now covered how to disable a path for a VMFS datastore. The same warnings and caveats that applied to changing the path selection policy apply here. Proceed with caution when disabling paths to VMFS datastores. I will next move away from VMFS and cover the configuration of NAS and NFS for ESXi.

Creating an NFS Share for Use with vSphere

The Network File System (NFS) can be used by ESXi hosts to create datastores or to create ISO and template repositories. ESXi includes a built-in NFS client for this purpose. Creating an NFS share for use with ESXi has several caveats:

- The network-attached storage device should be listed on the VMware HCL.

- NFS version 3 over TCP must be used.

- A file system must be created on the NAS device and exported. Ensure that all VMkernel interfaces are listed in this export list.

- ESXi hosts must be able to access the NFS server in read-write mode.

- Read-write access must be allowed for the root system account.

- The NFS export must use the no_root_squash option.

- VMkernel networking over a standard physical NIC is required. Multiple NICs can be used, as long as the vSwitches/dvSwitches and physical switches are configured accordingly.

- Always check with your NAS vendor and use their recommended best practices for NFS in VMware environments.

The specifics of configuring an NFS share will vary from vendor to vendor. Always consult with your specific vendor for their specific instructions on configuring an NFS share for use with vSphere. These documents will often include additional best practices, and their use is always highly recommended.

I have now covered how to create NFS shares for use with vSphere. Next I will cover how to connect to a NAS device and use the NFS share.

Connecting to a NAS Device

Network-attached storage is a storage device that can use different protocols to make files available. One of these protocols is NFS v3, which ESXi can use as a datastore. In Exercise 5.18, you will connect to a NAS device and mount an NFS volume. This exercise will require a properly configured NAS device to complete. If your test environment is lacking a NAS device, you may want to just read through this exercise.

EXERCISE 5.18

Connecting to a NAS Device

1. Open the vSphere Client and connect to an ESXi host or the vCenter Server that is managing the ESXi host.

2. Ensure that a VMkernel connection has already been created on the same subnet that the NAS server is located on.

3. Select the Configuration tab from the right pane and then select Storage from the Hardware panel.

4. Click the blue Add Storage link in the upper-right corner of the screen. The Add Storage Wizard will appear.

5. Choose the Network File System option for the Storage Type and click the Next button to continue.

6. In the Locate Network File System window, enter the NFS server's DNS name, IP address, or NFS UUID. Provide the mount point folder name in the Folder field, and provide the NFS share with a datastore name to be used in ESXi. The final setup should look similar to the image shown here.

Add Storage

Locate Network File System
Which shared folder will be used as a vSphere datastore?

NAS
   Network File System
   Ready to Complete

Properties

Server: `192.168.113.154`

Examples: nas, nas.it.com, 192.168.0.1 or
FE80:0:0:0:2AA:FF:FE9A:4CA2

Folder: `/mnt/nfs/export/nfs001`

Example: /vols/vol0/datastore-001

☐ Mount NFS read only

⚠ If a datastore already exists in the datacenter for this NFS share and you
intend to configure the same datastore on new hosts, make sure that you
enter the same input data (Server and Folder) that you used for the original
datastore. Different input data would mean different datastores even if the
underlying NFS storage is the same.

Datastore Name

`NFS-1`

Help   ≤ Back   Next ≥   Cancel

The Mount NFS Read Only option is often useful for ISO repositories but not
for datastores. This exercise pertains to datastores, so you can leave this option
unchecked.

7. Review the information presented on the Summary screen and click the Finish
    button to add the NFS share to the ESXi host.

8. A Create NAS Datastore task will begin. When this task completes, verify that
    the NFS datastore is listed on the Configuration tab under the Datastores view.

Unlike VMFS datastores, NFS datastores must be manually added to
each ESXi host that will connect to them. It is also crucial that the
server and folder names entered in the Add Storage Wizard are identical across all ESXi hosts. If the server and folder names don't match,
ESXi hosts will see these NFS mounts as being different datastores.

I have now covered the steps required to connect to a NAS device and mount an NFS
volume. The actual operation of connecting to a NFS share is typically quite simple, in
comparison to the setup required on the NAS device. In the next section, I will cover
identifying NFS datastore properties.

Identifying NFS Datastore Properties

Once an NFS datastore is mounted, the properties for the datastore can be obtained in the Datastore Details field of the Configuration tab. Select Storage from the Hardware panel and then select the NFS datastore. The Datastore Details field at the bottom of the screen will show the properties for the NFS datastore. Figure 5.6 shows the NFS datastore properties.

FIGURE 5.6 NFS datastore properties in Datastore Details

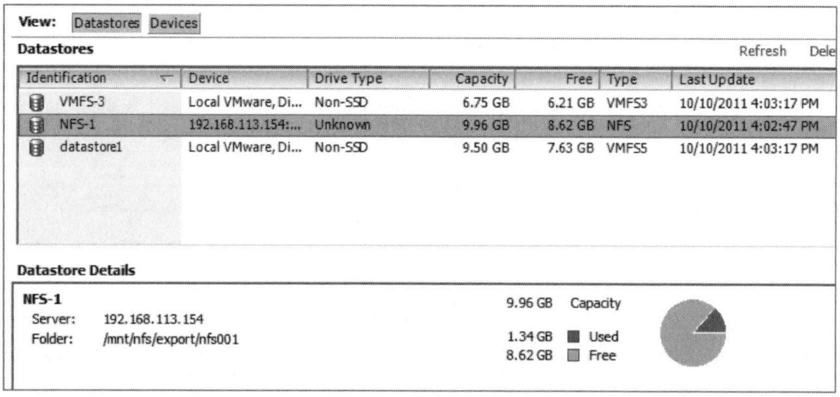

I have now covered obtaining the properties for NFS datastores. In the next section, I will cover unmounting and mounting the NFS datastore you mounted in Exercise 5.18.

Mounting and Unmounting an NFS Datastore

Once an NFS datastore is mounted, it can also be unmounted. Unmounting a datastore will not destroy the datastore but will simply make the datastore inaccessible to the ESXi host(s). If other ESXi hosts have this datastore mounted, they can continue to access the datastore as usual.

The operation to unmount an NFS datastore is quite simple. In the Datastores view on the Configuration tab, right-click the NFS datastore and choose the Unmount option from the context menu that appears.

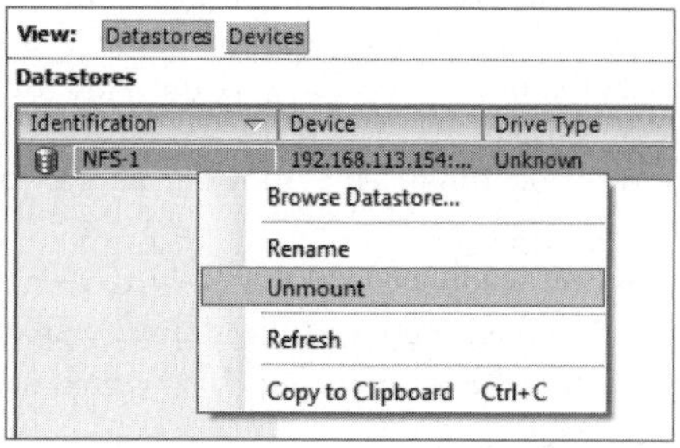

If there are running VMs located on an NFS datastore, you cannot unmount it.

Unlike a VMFS datastore, which will stay listed in the Datastores view as Inactive, when an NFS datastore is unmounted, it is removed from the Datastore view. To mount an unmounted NFS datastore again, you will need to repeat the NFS mount that was covered in Exercise 5.18.

I have now covered mounting NFS datastores, obtaining NFS datastore properties, and unmounting NFS datastores. In the next section, I will cover determining the use case for multiple VMFS and NFS datastores.

Determining the Use Case for Multiple VMFS/NFS Datastores

Multiple datastores in ESXi can serve many purposes, some of which include the following:

Load Distribution   Multiple datastores can be backed by various physical disk configurations. This allows tiering of VMFS datastores and could also be leveraged by Storage DRS.

Departmental or Political   The HR or finance department may have purchased a NAS or SAN and want this storage to be dedicated to their virtual machines.

Higher Availability   Mixing SANs or NAS devices can lead to higher availability, specifically around planned maintenance. If the capacity is available, then VMs could be consolidated onto one storage system for the maintenance period.

NAS and SAN Additions   Adding and retiring new storage systems could require new datastores to be added.

Differing Workloads   Desktops can have a much different set of requirements and capabilities than servers, and things such as deduplication may want to be leveraged on certain backend storage systems.

ISO or Template Repositories   Certain ISOs and templates will likely be available in the virtual environment.

Dynamic Disk Mirroring   Windows can use dynamic disks to span a boot volume across two datastores. This could make a VM more resilient to the loss of a single datastore.

Storage vMotion   Storage vMotion will require a minimum of a source and destination datastore.

VMFS-5   Certain environments may want to add new datastores for VMFS-5 volumes, as opposed to upgrading them in place.

Replication   Certain datastores can be used with VMware SRM or other replication solutions. Having multiple datastores allows the placement of only replicated VMs on a VMFS datastore that will be replicated.

I have covered multiple use cases for multiple VMFS and NFS datastores. Storage is abstracted from VMs through the use of datastores, and there is a lot of flexibility because of this. There are likely many more use cases available. See whether you can identify at least one before continuing to the next section. I will now leave NFS and VMFS behind and cover another one of the new features of vSphere 5: the VMware vSphere Storage Appliance.

Configure the vSphere Storage Appliance

One of the bigger new announcements in vSphere 5 was for the VMware vSphere Storage Appliance (VSA). The VSA is targeted toward the SMB market or to those who otherwise would not have shared storage in their vSphere environments. The VSA is a software solution that transforms the internal storage from two to three ESXi hosts into a protected shared storage resource.

Determining the Use Case for Deploying the VSA

The VSA is clearly targeted at small and medium-size business (*SMB*) customers. Therefore, the predominant use case for the VSA is smaller environments without NAS and SAN currently in use.

🌐 Real World Scenario

A Use Case for the VSA

A small business has been using the VMware *vSphere Hypervisor* to run its development and test virtual machines. Management has been impressed with the benefits that virtualization has delivered, and they are now ready to roll out production systems on ESXi.

One of the requirements of this implementation is the ability to use vMotion for the virtual machines. The environment has no NAS or SAN, and the customer does not plan on acquiring any storage hardware for this project. The reasons for this are a small budget and minimal staff that already has too much to manage, without introducing storage hardware.

The customer decides to use the VSA for this project, because it fits well with their environment. A supported storage solution may be implemented in software that requires minimal staff involvement and will allow the customer to use vMotion.

Now that I have covered the use case for the VSA, I will cover its architecture.

Defining vSphere Storage Appliance (VSA) Architecture

A VSA cluster is composed of three parts: physical servers with local storage, ESXi 5, and the VSA virtual machines. The VSA can be deployed in either a two-node or three-node configuration on ESXi 5 hosts. Figure 5.7 shows the architecture of the two-node VSA configuration. Each ESXi host will have a VSA instance, which is a virtual machine, deployed to it. This VM will use the available local storage space on the ESXi host to create and present a mirrored NFS volume to all ESXi hosts.

FIGURE 5.7   Two-node VSA configuration

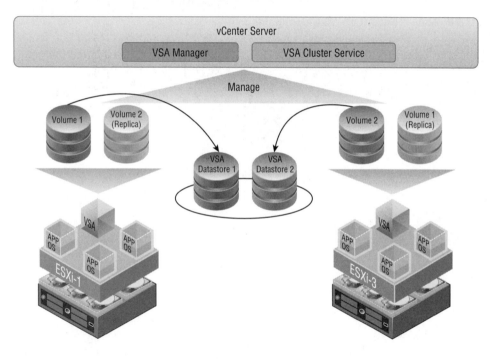

In a two-node VSA cluster, the local storage in the ESXi hosts is used by the VSA to create two equally sized volumes. One of these is exported as an NFS share, and the other is used for replication of the NFS share on the other ESXi host. Therefore, a two-node VSA cluster will have two total datastores and two total replicas. In a two-node cluster, the use of an additional service, installed on the vCenter Server along with the VSA Manager, is required. This service is named the VMware VSA Cluster Service, and it participates as a third member of the VSA cluster but does not provide any storage. This is because a VSA cluster requires that more than half of its members stay online. If a single node in a two-node cluster fails, the VMware VSA Cluster Service will allow the VSA cluster to satisfy this requirement and stay online.

In a three-node cluster, which is the largest VSA cluster available, the architecture and operation are slightly different than the two-node VSA cluster. Figure 5.8 shows the architecture of the three-node VSA configuration.

With the three-node VSA cluster, the local storage in the ESXi hosts is still used to create two equally sized volumes. One of these is exported as an NFS share, and other is used for replication with one other ESXi host in the VSA cluster. Therefore, a three-node VSA cluster will have three total datastores and three total replicas. In the three-node VSA cluster, the use of the VMware VSA Cluster Service is not required. Note that the VMware VSA Cluster Service is still installed on the vCenter Server when the VSA Manager is installed, but it will not be used.

FIGURE 5.8 Three-node VSA configuration

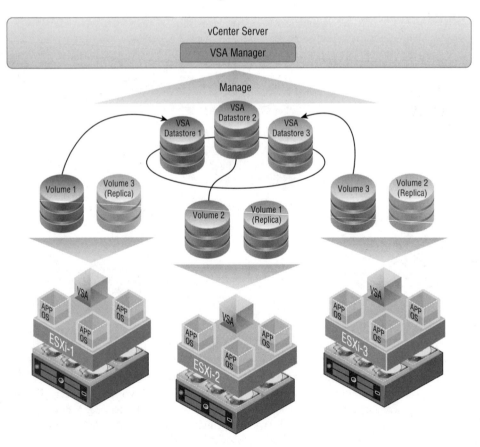

It is important to note that the VSA is not included with any edition of vSphere but is licensed as a separate product.

The architecture of the VSA provides resiliency and offers simplicity in its operation. The use case and architecture of the VSA have now both been covered. I will now cover the resources required from your ESXi hosts to run the VSA.

Determining Appropriate ESXi Host Resources for the VSA

Because the VSA is a set of virtual machines, the ESXi hosts must have certain resources available to the VSA. Table 5.7 contains the ESXi hardware requirements for the VSA.

TABLE 5.7 ESXi hardware requirements for VSA

Hardware	VSA cluster requirements
Configuration	The two or three ESXI hosts must have a homogeneous hardware configuration.
CPU	64-bit x86 CPUs. 2GHz or higher per core.
Memory	6GB, minimum. 24GB, recommended. 72GB, maximum supported and tested with VSA 1.0. 1TB, maximum supported by ESXi 5.0.
Network	Four NIC ports minimum. Supported configurations include the following: Four single-port NICs Two dual-port NICs Two single-port NICs and one dual-port NIC One quad-port NIC (introduces a single point of failure)
Hard disk	The following are supported configurations: Four, six, or eight hard disks of the same model and with the same capacity 2TB maximum capacity per hard disk, supported 180GB minimum total hard disk space per ESXi host, required All SATA disks or all SAS disks
RAID	VMware recommends a RAID5, RAID6, or RAID10 configuration.

There are also software requirements for the VSA. Table 5.8 contains the ESXi software requirements for the VSA.

TABLE 5.8 ESXi software requirements for VSA

Hardware	VSA cluster requirements
ESXi Version	5 and newer.
ESXi Licensing	vSphere Essentials Plus edition or higher.
Cluster Configuration	The ESXi hosts may not participate in any other cluster.
vSphere Networking	Only the vSwitches and port groups created during installation can exist. The ESXi hosts must have static IP addresses that are located in the same subnet as the vCenter Server.
VMs	No VMs must be deployed on the ESXi hosts in the VSA cluster.

Looking at the software requirements makes it a bit more obvious that the VSA is intended to be deployed as part of a new vSphere implementation.

 vCenter Server cannot be deployed as a VM on one of the ESXi hosts that will participate in the VSA cluster. Keep this in mind when designing for SMB environments, where there will likely be resource constraints.

I have now covered determining the appropriate ESXi host resources for deploying and using the VSA. I will now cover configuring our ESXi hosts as VSA hosts.

Configuring ESXi Hosts as VSA Hosts

In addition to the software requirements listed in Table 5.8, ESXi hosts also need to have minimal configuration performed on them prior to becoming VSA hosts. These configuration tasks include the following:

Password The ESXi hosts must have a password assigned to the root account. Use the DCUI to assign a password to root.

IP Address The ESXi hosts must have static IP addresses that are located in the same subnet as the vCenter Server.

VLAN ID It is recommended to use an isolated management network for the ESXi hosts. If a VLAN is used for this purpose, then assign the same VLAN ID to each ESXi host.

DNS   Ensure that ESXi hosts are configured to use DNS servers. Adding DNS entries to ESXi hosts was covered in Chapter 2 in Exercises 2.11 and 2.12.

Connectivity   Test the Management Network in the DCUI and ensure that connectivity and name resolution work properly.

If the ESXi software requirements have been met, completing the previous configuration tasks on each ESXi host will have these hosts ready for VSA installation.

Configuring the Storage Network for the VSA

The storage network used by the VSA consists of a recommended two GbE switches and the minimum requirement of four NICs installed in each of the ESXi hosts participating in the VSA cluster. Figure 5.9 shows the recommended network redundancy setup for a three-node cluster.

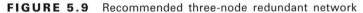

FIGURE 5.9   Recommended three-node redundant network

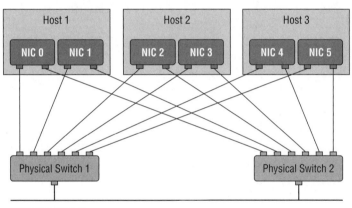

The four required NICs in the ESXi host are used for two types of traffic called frontend and backend. Frontend traffic consists of the following communications:

- VSA cluster member and VSA Manager
- ESXi hosts and VSA volumes
- VSA member cluster and VSA Cluster Service

Backend traffic consists of the following communications:

- Volume and its replica on another ESXi host (replication)
- VSA cluster member to VSA cluster member
- vMotion between ESXi hosts

The VSA Installer will automatically create and configure the networking for the ESXi hosts in the VSA cluster. The key is to have the physical networking set up properly. Figure 5.10 shows the logical network architecture of a VSA cluster member.

Now that I have covered the configuration of the storage network for the VSA, I will cover deploying and configuring the VSA Manager.

Deploying and Configuring the VSA Manager

Once all of the prerequisites have been covered, the next step in building the VSA cluster is to deploy the VSA Manager on the vCenter Server. The VSA Manager is a plug-in for vCenter Server that will be used to both create and manage the VSA cluster. The installation of VSA Manager will also install the VSA Cluster Service.

FIGURE 5.10 Logical network architecture of a VSA cluster member

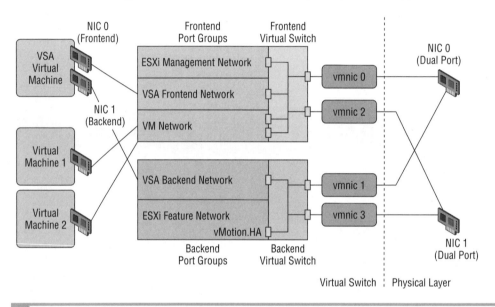

 The VSA Manager can be installed only on 64-bit systems running vCenter Server 5.

Exercise 5.19 will cover the steps to install the VSA Manager on vCenter Server. You may complete this lab regardless of whether you have the ESXi prerequisites covered. You will need to have the VSA media downloaded and available to the vCenter Server.

EXERCISE 5.19

Deploying and Configuring the VSA Manager

1. Connect to a console session on the vCenter Server 5 and log on with an Administrator account.

    If using the ISO for the VSA media, do not use autorun.exe.

2. Browse the mounted ISO or the extracted files from the VSA media and locate the following installer file: X:\installers\VMware-VSAManager\VMware-vsaman-ager.exe.

3. Launch this application.

4. When the installation starts, first select the language and then click the OK button.

5. On the Welcome screen, click the Next button.

6. On the End-User Patent Agreement screen, click the Next button.

7. Agree to the terms of the license agreement, and click the Next button.

8. The vCenter Server IP address or hostname will be prepopulated on the next screen, as shown here:

9. VMware recommends that the port number not be changed. Verify that the vCenter Server IP address or hostname is correct and click the Next button.

10. On the License Information screen, enter a vCenter Server license key that includes the VSA as a feature. If you do not have a license key, the VSA will run in evaluation mode. Click the Next button.

11. Click the Install button to install the VSA Manager.

12. Click the Finish button.

    The VSA Manager is now installed. In the remainder of this exercise, the VSA will be configured.

    (continued)

EXERCISE 5.19 *(continued)*

13. Open the vSphere Client and connect to the vCenter Server that the VSA Manager was just installed on.

14. Select the Plug-ins menu and then choose the Manage Plug-ins menu option.

15. Verify that the VSA Manager is listed in the Installed Plug-ins list and has a status of Enabled.

16. Next, select a datacenter from the vCenter Server inventory and click the VSA Manager tab. This tab is shown here:

| Summary | Virtual Machines | Hosts | IP Pools | Performance | Tasks & Events | Alarms | Permissions | Maps | Storage Views | VSA Manager |

VSA Installer   ✕

Welcome

Welcome to the VSA Installer wizard. The wizard provides step-by-step instructions to create or recover a VSA cluster.

Welcome
vSphere Features
Select Datacenter
Select Hosts
Configure Network
Format Disks
Verify Configuration
Install Features

VSA Installer

VMware vSphere® Storage Appliance is a distributed shared storage solution that uses the local disks of several hosts. The product abstracts the storage resources from two or more hosts and presents them as replicated datastores that are accessible by those hosts. The solution enables VMware vSphere® vMotion and VMware vSphere® High Availability without provisioning and managing a separate shared storage solution.

⦿ **New Installation**

Install a new VSA cluster.

○ **Recover VSA Cluster**

Recover an existing VSA cluster.

Help   Logs   < Back   Next >   Cancel

After installing the VSA Manager and verifying that it is listed in the Installed Plug-ins, the VSA Manager tab may not display any content. If this is the case, verify that Adobe Flash Player is installed on the system that you are running the vSphere Client on.

The VSA Manager has now been deployed to your vCenter Server and configured. In the next section, I will cover administering VSA storage resources.

Administering VSA Storage Resources

The actual installation of the VSA is not covered in the exam blueprint, but VCPs are expected to know how to administer the VSA. To bridge this gap, I will cover how to install the VSA. Installing a new VSA cluster is actually a great way to learn more about both how the VSA is designed and how it works.

 A VSA Offline Demo available in the VMware Communities guides you through the steps of installing the VSA Manager, manually installing a new VSA cluster, and administering VSA resources. This can be a very valuable tool for those who do not have the hardware required to run the VSA in a lab setting. The VSA Offline Demo is available at http://communities.vmware.com/thread/326302.

Exercise 5.20 will cover the steps to manually install a new VSA cluster using the VSA Manager plug-in in the vSphere Client.

EXERCISE 5.20

Installing a New VSA Cluster Using VSA Manager

1. Open the vSphere Client and connect to the vCenter Server that the VSA Manager was just installed on.

2. Select a datacenter from the vCenter Server inventory and click the VSA Manager tab.

3. On the Welcome screen, choose the New Installation option. Click the Next button to continue.

4. Review the feature list and click the Next button to continue.

5. Select the datacenter that the VSA cluster will be installed in by highlighting it. Click the Next button to continue.

6. Select the ESXi hosts that the VSA cluster will be installed on. When two or three hosts have been selected, the red circular icon with the X in it will change to a green circular icon with a check mark.

(continued)

If you are using unsupported hardware, you are allowed to proceed, but you will receive a warning dialog first. Simply click the OK button, and remember that an unsupported hardware configuration should never be used in production environments.

7. Click the Next button to continue.

8. Under the VSA Management options, enter the VSA Cluster IP Address. This IP address will be used by the VSA cluster member that controls the cluster. This address must not be in the 192.168/16 private subnet.

9. If using a two-node cluster, you will also have to provide the VSA Cluster Service with an IP address. Again, do not use the 192.168/16 private subnet for this address.

10. Click the blue link that contains the hostname of one of the ESXi servers selected in step 6. This will expand the server settings.

Take note of how the Management IP Address and NFS IP Address fields are prepopulated with incremental IP addresses taken from the IP address you provided to the VSA Cluster IP address. The following fields are configured here:

Management IP Address   Used for the management network of the VSA cluster member

Datastore IP Address   Used for the VSA NFS datastore

Feature IP Address   Used by vMotion

VLAN ID   Used to set the VLAN ID for the management network

(continued)

Back-end IP Address   Used for replication and clustering and must be on the 192.168/16 subnet

Back-end VLAN ID   Used to set the VLAN ID for the backend network

11. Verify whether these addresses and are acceptable and give vMotion a static IP address. Change the VLAN ID as required for your environment.

12. Repeat steps 10–11 for each of the remaining hosts. When all hosts have been configured, click the Next button to continue.

13. Choose the Format Disks On First Access option and click the Next button to continue.

14. Verify the configuration settings and click the Install button. You will be prompted to confirm data deletion of all existing data on the local ESXi hosts. Click the Yes button to continue.

15. The screen will display results as it moves through the configuration, and when complete, you will see a screen like the one shown here.

VSA Installer   ✕

Install Features
The installer will deploy a vSphere Storage Appliance on the hosts and create a VSA cluster.

Welcome
vSphere Features
Select Datacenter   VSA Installer will now install and configure the vSphere Storage Appliance
Select Hosts   on the hosts. This process might take several minutes to complete if you
                           selected the option to format disks on first access and up to a few hours if
Configure Network   you selected the option to format disks immediately.
Format Disks
Verify Configuration
Install Features

                        ✓   Configuring VSA cluster network

                        ✓   Deploying vSphere Storage Appliance

                        ✓   Installing VSA cluster

                        ✓   Mounting the datastores

                   ✓   All features are now installed and configured.

[Help]   [Logs]   [Close]

16. Also, take note of the new configuration listed in the left pane, because a new cluster and virtual machines are now present. The configuration should appear similar to what is shown here.

17. Click the Close button to exit the VSA Installer and review the VSA cluster properties in the VSA Manager tab.

18. Notice the three available views of Datastores, Appliances, and Map on the VSA Manager tab. These views can be selected to obtain additional properties about both the datastores and the appliances.

I have now covered installing a new VSA cluster and can focus on some of the administration tasks that VCPs will be expected to know how to perform with the VSA Manager.

One of the administrative tasks that will need to be performed on a VSA cluster is to placing the VSA cluster in maintenance mode. This is useful when any component of the VSA cluster needs to have maintenance performed on it. Exercise 5.21 will cover the steps to enter VSA cluster maintenance mode, again using the VSA Manager plug-in in the vSphere Client.

EXERCISE 5.21

Entering VSA Cluster Maintenance Mode

1. Open the vSphere Client and connect to the vCenter Server.

2. Locate the powered-on virtual machines in the VSA HA Cluster and power them all off, with the exception of the VSA virtual machines.

3. Select a datacenter from the vCenter Server inventory and click the VSA Manager tab.

4. Click the blue Enter VSA Cluster Maintenance Mode link at the top of the VSA Manager tab. A dialog box will appear asking you to confirm the maintenance mode operation. Click the Yes button to continue.

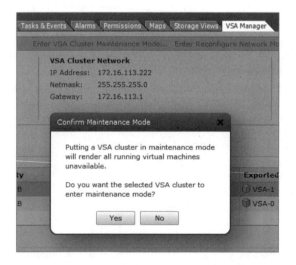

5. A dialog box will appear that shows the maintenance mode status. When the VSA cluster has successfully entered maintenance mode, click the Close button.

6. Take note of the status in the VSA Cluster Properties panel and in the Datastore view Status column. The value of Maintenance should be listed for both, as shown here.

At this point, the maintenance task would be performed on the host, datastore, network, or other infrastructure component. Once the maintenance tasks have been completed, the VSA cluster will need to come back online. The remaining steps will cover this procedure.

7. Click the blue Exit VSA Cluster Maintenance Mode link at the top of the VSA Manager tab. A dialog box will appear and show the progress of the operation. When it completes, click the Close button to continue.

8. Verify that VSA Cluster Status reports Online. Also verify that the Datastores view reports Online for all of its Status fields.

9. Once the VSA cluster is online, power on the virtual machines in the VSA cluster.

In addition to placing the entire VSA cluster in maintenance mode, a single cluster member can be placed in maintenance mode. This would allow maintenance to be performed on the host that the cluster node was running on and would not require downtime for the maintenance. Exercise 5.22 will cover the steps to place a VSA cluster member in maintenance mode.

EXERCISE 5.22

Entering Appliance Maintenance Mode

1. Open the vSphere Client and connect to the vCenter Server.

2. Select a datacenter from the vCenter Server inventory and click the VSA Manager tab.

3. Select the Appliances view by clicking the Appliances button.

4. Select a VSA cluster member and right-click it. Choose Enter Appliance Maintenance Mode from the context menu that appears. You may also click the blue Enter Appliance Maintenance Mode link on the right of the screen, just below the list of appliances.

5. A dialog box will appear asking you to confirm the maintenance mode operation. Click the Yes button to continue.

6. A dialog box will appear that reports the status, and a Power Off Virtual Machine task will start.

7. Wait for the status of the appliance to report Maintenance. It may be necessary to refresh the page.

8. Click the Datastores button to switch to the Datastores view, where you will see something similar to what is shown here.

VSA Cluster Status	
Name:	vStorage Cluster
Status:	✓ Online
VSA Cluster Service IP Address:	172.16.113.224
VSA Cluster Service Status:	✓ Online

View: [Datastores] [Appliances] [Map]

Name ▲	Status	Capacity
VSADs-0	◆ Degraded	97.99 GB
VSADs-1	◆ Degraded	97.99 GB

Datastore Properties

Name:	VSADs-0
Status:	◆ Degraded
Exported By:	VSA-1
Datastore Path:	//172.16.113.225/exports/a4ffec9a-b547-4fea-b089-fddecf2af1b5

▼ VSADs-0	◆ Degraded
▼ VSA-1	✓ Online
Replica	✓ Online
▼ VSA-0	▨ Maintenance
Replica	⊘ Offline

9. Note that VSA Cluster Status reports Online but that there are items degraded and in maintenance mode.

   The status of the datastore is degraded, because the replica is no longer online. This is the expected behavior while a VSA cluster member is in maintenance mode. As in the previous exercise, the applicable maintenance task would be performed, and then the VSA cluster member will need to come back online. The remaining steps will cover this procedure.

10. Click the Appliances button to change back to the Appliances view. Right-click the offline VSA cluster member and choose the Exit Appliance Maintenance Mode option from the context menu that appears.

11. A dialog box will appear showing the progress, and a Power On Virtual Machine task will start. Several other tasks may also begin, including one or more VSA Storage Data Synchronization tasks. This task can take some time to complete, so be patient.

12. When the VSA cluster member has completed exiting maintenance mode, click the Close button in the dialog box.

13. Click the Datastores button to switch back to the Datastores view and verify that all items are now reporting Online.

I have now covered installing a VSA cluster, placing the VSA cluster in maintenance mode, and placing an individual VSA cluster member in maintenance mode. This concludes the section on the VSA and this chapter.

Summary

This chapter covered planning and configuring vSphere storage. Knowing how to use the different storage options is an important part of any virtual infrastructure administrator's duties. This chapter covered how to identify storage adapters and devices. Storage naming conventions were covered along with scanning and rescanning for storage devices. The chapter covered vCenter Server storage filters and described zoning and LUN masking practices. The chapter also identified use cases for FCoE. It covered identifying the different iSCSI adapters and their requirements, along with determining the use case for each. The software iSCSI initiator was covered, including how to enable, disable, and configure it. Port binding was covered for dependent hardware iSCSI adapters and software iSCSI adapters. The chapter also discussed CHAP and how to configure it. The first part of this chapter concluded with thin provisioning and determining its use cases.

The second part of the chapter focused on VMFS and NFS datastores. The capabilities of VMFS-5 were discussed, and you created, renamed, unmounted, and deleted a VMFS datastore. Identifying VMFS datastore properties was covered, along with the options for increasing the size of VMFS datastores. I showed how to upgrade a VMFS-3 datastore to

VMFS-5 and discussed the caveats around the upgraded datastores. Path selection policies, preferred paths, and disabling paths were all covered as well. How to create NFS shares for use with ESXi was detailed, along with connecting to NAS devices. You mounted and unmounted NFS datastores, identified NFS datastore properties, and determined the use case for multiple VMFS/NFS datastores.

The final part of this chapter focused on the vSphere Storage Appliance. The use case for the VSA was discussed, along with its architecture. The resources required by the ESXi hosts and how to configure those ESXi hosts as VSA hosts were both covered as well. I discussed configuring the storage network for the VSA and deploying the VSA Manager. I concluded this chapter with some common VSA administration tasks. The VSA is an exciting new feature of vSphere, and a third of this chapter was devoted to it. Be sure to know the VSA objectives for the VCP5 exam.

Exam Essentials

Know how to configure shared storage for vSphere 5.   Be able to identify storage adapters and devices. Know the storage naming conventions and their formats. Be able to scan and rescan for storage devices. Know the vCenter Server storage filters and how to enable, configure, and disable them. Know what zoning and LUN masking are and what they are used for. Be able to identify the use cases for FCoE. Know the three types of iSCSI adapters, their requirements, and when to use each of them. Be able to configure and edit the three types of iSCSI adapters. Understand how to use port binding in the vSphere Client. Understand what CHAP is, why it is used, and how to use it. Understand the differences between array thin provisioning and virtual disk thin provisioning. Be able to determine the use case for array thin provisioning and know that vSphere cannot manage storage array thin provisioning.

Know how to create and configure VMFS and NFS datastores.   Be able to identify the capabilities of VMFS-5. Know how to create, rename, unmount, and delete VMFS datastores. Know the various locations that VMFS properties can be obtained. Understand the two ways that VMFS datastores may be increased in size and the differences in these two approaches. Be able to upgrade VMFS-3 volumes to VMFS-5 and know the caveats associated with upgrading them. Know how to place a VMFS datastore in maintenance mode. Be able to determine the appropriate path selection policy for a VMFS datastore, and know how to select the preferred path for a VMFS datastore. Also know how to disable a path to a VMFS datastore. Know the requirements for NFS shares created on NAS devices, and know how to connect to the NAS device and mount an NFS datastore. Also know how to unmount an NFS datastore and understand the operation for mounting it again. Be able to identify NFS datastore properties. Understand the use cases for multiple VMFS/NFS datastores.

Know how to configure the vSphere Storage Appliance.   Be able to determine the use case for deploying the VSA and understand the VSA architecture. Know how to determine appropriate ESXi host resources for the VSA and how to configure ESXi hosts as VSA hosts. Be able to configure the storage network for the VSA and know how to deploy and configure the VSA Manager. Understand how to administer VSA storage resources.

Review Questions

1. You select the Configuration tab for an ESXi host and choose the Storage Adapters link from the Hardware panel, but the iSCSI Software Adapter is not listed. What could be the problem?

   A. The software iSCSI adapter must be installed.

   B. The software iSCSI adapter is not enabled.

   C. The software iSCSI adapter can be viewed only from the DCUI.

   D. The software iSCSI adapter must have VMkernel networking set up before it is visible in the Storage Adapters list.

2. Which of the following is an example of a SCSI INQUIRY device identifier?

   A. eui.5577bd49251ddb52

   B. mpx.vmhba2:C0:T0:L0

   C. vml.02000600006006016094602800364ce22e3

   D. vmhba1:C0:T1:L0

3. For ESXi hosts that will participate in a VSA cluster, which of the following NIC configurations are both supported and do not introduce a single point of failure? (Choose all that apply.)

   A. Four single-port NICs

   B. Two dual-port NICs

   C. Two single-port NICs and one dual-port NIC

   D. One quad-port NIC

4. You create a new VMFS-5 datastore for one of your ESXi hosts. What is the largest VMDK file that can be created on this datastore?

   A. 1TB

   B. 2TB minus 512 bytes

   C. 2TB

   D. 64TB

5. Which of the following are default path selection policies in ESXi? (Choose all that apply.)

   A. Fixed (VMware)

   B. Dynamic (VMware)

   C. Most Recently Used (VMware)

   D. Round Robin (VMware)

6. You have a customer that requires that the target (storage system) authenticates the iSCSI adapter (initiator) and that the iSCSI adapter also authenticates the target. Which CHAP authentication method should be used?

A. One-way CHAP

B. Mutual CHAP

C. Three-way CHAP

D. None of these

7. You have a customer that is deploying ESXi and will be using iSCSI storage. The customer wants the iSCSI implementation to use the least amount of the ESXi host resources as possible. Which of the following storage adapters would be the best choice for this set of requirements?

A. Software iSCSI adapter

B. Dependent hardware iSCSI adapter

C. Independent hardware iSCSI adapter

D. FCoE adapter

8. How many ESXi hosts can participate in a VSA cluster? (Choose all that apply.)

A. Two

B. Three

C. Four

D. Six

9. A customer wants to deploy three ESXi hosts and use the VSA to provide shared storage. The customer also wants to run vCenter Server in a virtual machine. Which of the following solutions can you propose to the customer? (Choose all that apply.)

A. Run vCenter in a virtual machine on one of these three ESXi hosts.

B. Run vCenter in a physical machine.

C. Run vCenter Server on an ESXi host that is not part of the VSA cluster.

D. None of these.

10. What are two ways that VMFS datastores can be enlarged after their initial creation? (Choose two.)

A. Inflate

B. Extend

C. Expand

D. Zeroed

11. Which of the following are vCenter Server storage filters? (Choose all that apply.)

A. VMFS Filter

B. RDM Filter

> **C.** Same Host and Transports Filter
>
> **D.** Host Rescan Filter

12. You upgraded a VMFS-3 volume with a block size of 8MB to VMFS-5. What is the block size of the VMFS-5 volume?

> **A.** 8MB
>
> **B.** 4MB
>
> **C.** 2MB
>
> **D.** 1MB

13. Which of the following statements are correct about the VSA Manager? (Choose all that apply.)

> **A.** It is installed as a vCenter plug-in.
>
> **B.** It is available only when accessed from the datacenter object in the vSphere Client.
>
> **C.** It can be used to install a new VSA cluster.
>
> **D.** It can be used to recover an existing VSA cluster.

14. Which of the following information is required when adding an NFS share to be used as a datastore? (Choose all that apply.)

> **A.** NFS server name, IP address, or NFS UUID
>
> **B.** Path to the NFS share
>
> **C.** NFS server credentials
>
> **D.** NFS datastore name

15. Which of the following are use cases for FCoE? (Choose two.)

> **A.** Blade servers
>
> **B.** Rackmount servers
>
> **C.** Network consolidation
>
> **D.** Network expansion

16. As part of routine maintenance, you unmounted an NFS datastore from an ESXi host. What do you need to do to mount this NFS datastore again, when the maintenance window is complete?

> **A.** Reboot the ESXi host.
>
> **B.** Right-click the inactive datastore and choose the Mount option from the context menu that appears.
>
> **C.** Use the Add Storage Wizard to mount it.
>
> **D.** Rescan the ESXi host's HBAs.

17. Which of the following storage adapters performs both the iSCSI processing and the networking for iSCSI traffic?

> **A.** Software iSCSI adapter
>
> **B.** Dependent hardware iSCSI adapter

C. Independent hardware iSCSI adapter

D. FCoE adapter

18. You create a VM with a single 50GB thin-provisioned virtual disk, and your storage array also uses thin provisioning. You later decide to protect this VM with VMware FT. How much space does this VM's single virtual disk consume on the storage array?

A. Greater than 50GB.

B. 50GB.

C. Less than 50 GB.

D. It depends on the amount of data in the VMDK.

19. Which of the following iSCSI adapters can be used to access the storage resources in a VSA cluster?

A. iSCSI software adapter

B. Dependent hardware iSCSI adapter

C. Independent hardware iSCSI adapter

D. None of these

20. You have a 10-node ESXi cluster, and you just presented new devices to all 10 ESXi hosts. You need to quickly scan the adapters on all 10 hosts to find the new device. What option is the fastest?

A. In the vSphere Client, rescan each individual storage adapter on each ESXi host.

B. Write a script to perform this operation.

C. In the vSphere Client, use the Rescan For Datastores option from the context menu that appears on the vCenter Server root object.

D. In the vSphere Client, use the Rescan For Datastores option from the context menu that appears on the cluster object.

Chapter

6

Create and Deploy Virtual Machines and vApps

VCP5 EXAM OBJECTIVES COVERED IN THIS CHAPTER:

✓ **Create and Deploy Virtual Machines**

- Identify capabilities of virtual machine hardware versions
- Configure and deploy a Guest OS into a new virtual machine
- Place Virtual Machines In Selected ESXi Hosts/Clusters/ Resource Pools
- Identify methods to access and use a virtual machine console
- Install/Upgrade/Update VMware Tools
- Identify VMware Tools device drivers
- Configure virtual machine time synchronization
- Identify virtual machine storage resources
- Configure/Modify disk controller for virtual disks
- Configure appropriate virtual disk type for a virtual machine
- Create/Convert thin/thick provisioned virtual disks
- Configure disk shares
- Determine appropriate datastore locations for virtual machines based on application workloads
- Configure/Modify virtual CPU and Memory resources according to OS and application requirements
- Configure/Modify virtual NIC adapter and connect virtual machines to appropriate network resources

- Convert a physical machine using VMware Converter
- Import a supported virtual machine source using VMware Converter
- Modify virtual hardware settings using VMware Converter

✓ **Create and Deploy vApps**

- Determine when a tiered application should be deployed as a vApp
- Create a vApp
- Add objects to an existing vApp
- Identify and Edit vApp settings
- Configure IP pools
- Suspend/Resume a vApp
- Clone and Export a vApp

This chapter will cover the objectives of sections 4.1 and 4.2 of the VCP5 exam blueprint. It will focus on creating and deploying virtual machines and vApps.

This chapter will first cover identifying the capabilities of virtual machine hardware versions. Configuring and deploying a guest OS into a new VM will also be covered. Identifying methods to access the console of a VM will be covered. The chapter will cover how to install and upgrade VMware Tools and how to identify VMware Tools device drivers. Configuring VM time synchronization will be covered. It will cover how to identify VM storage resources and how to modify the disk controller for virtual disks. The chapter will also cover how to configure the appropriate virtual disk type for a virtual machine. Creating and converting thin and thick provisioned virtual disks and configuring disk shares will be covered. The chapter will also cover placing virtual machines in selected ESXi hosts, clusters, and resource pools.

The chapter will cover converting a physical machine (P2V) and importing a supported VM source using VMware Converter. Modifying VM hardware settings using VMware Converter will also be covered. It will also cover configuring and modifying vCPU and memory resources according to OS and application requirements, in addition to configuring and modifying virtual NIC adapters and connecting VMs to appropriate network resources. Determining appropriate datastore locations for virtual machines based on application workloads will also be discussed.

The final section of this chapter will cover determining when a tiered application should be deployed as a vApp. It will cover how to create, clone, and export vApps. Configuring IP pools for vApps will be covered, as well as editing vApp settings. The chapter will also cover how to add objects to an existing vApp and suspend and resume a vApp.

Creating and Deploying Virtual Machines

Everything covered thus far in this book has been about getting to this point. The virtual infrastructure exists in its entirety to run virtual machines. Knowing how to create and deploy VMs is an essential task for any virtual infrastructure administrator. The first topic covered is identifying the capabilities of virtual machine hardware versions.

Identifying Capabilities of Virtual Machine Hardware Versions

A virtual machine hardware version is used to designate the features of the virtual hardware. The virtual machine hardware version indicates the hardware features available in the virtual machine and can include things such as the BIOS or EFI, number of CPUs, maximum memory configuration, and more. When a virtual machine is created using the vSphere Client, you can use the Custom option to choose the version of the virtual machine hardware. By default, new virtual machines will be created with the latest version of the virtual hardware available on the host where the VM is being created. In vSphere 5, this will be virtual machine hardware version 8.

Virtual machine hardware version 8 includes the following capabilities:

- 32 vCPU support
- 1TB memory support
- Virtual NUMA (vNUMA) support
- Enhanced graphics, including 3D support
- USB 3.0 device support
- Client-connected USB devices
- *EFI BIOS*
- Smart card reader support
- Support for Mac OS X Server v10.6

The capabilities of virtual machine hardware version 8 are an improvement over the capabilities of virtual machine hardware version 7, which was included with vSphere 4. The capabilities of virtual machine hardware version 7 included support for eight vCPUs and 255GB memory. Comparing virtual machine hardware version 7 with virtual machine hardware version 4, which included support for four vCPUs and 64GB minus 4MB memory, makes it somewhat easier to see the evolution of the virtual machine hardware versions.

Virtual machines using virtual machine hardware versions prior to version 8 can still be run on ESXi 5 hosts but will not have all of the features of virtual machine hardware version 8. Table 6.1 shows the ESX/ESXi host and virtual hardware compatibility.

TABLE 6.1   ESX/ESXi Host and virtual hardware compatibility

	Version 8	Version 7	Version 4	Compatible with vCenter Server Version
ESXi 5.0	Create, edit, run	Create, edit, run	Edit, run	vCenter Server 5.0
ESX/ESXi 4.x	Not Supported	Create, edit, run	Create, edit, run	vCenter Server 4.x
ESX/ESXi 3.x	Not Supported	Not Supported	Create, edit, run	vCenter Server 2.x and newer

If you want to use the latest features included in virtual machine hardware version 8, you must also use ESXi 5.

Virtual machine hardware versions can be upgraded; this process was covered in Chapter 2 of this book.

Now that I have covered the capabilities of virtual machine hardware versions, I will cover configuring and deploying a guest operating system into a new virtual machine.

Configuring and Deploying a Guest OS into a New Virtual Machine

There are two different ways to configure and deploy a virtual machine in vSphere 5. If you are familiar with vSphere 4, you will undoubtedly be comfortable with the process of configuring and deploying VMs from the vSphere Client, and with vSphere 5 this process is the same. Exercise 6.1 will cover configuring and deploying a new virtual machine.

EXERCISE 6.1

Configuring and Deploying a New VM with the vSphere Client

1. Connect to a vCenter Server with the vSphere Client.

2. Choose a datacenter, host, cluster, resource pool, or virtual machine folder and right-click it. Select the New Virtual Machine option from the context menu that appears.

3. The Create New Virtual Machine Wizard will launch.

4. Choose the Custom option in the Configuration section and click the Next button.

   The Typical option can also be used here, but this will limit the number of choices you get to make when creating the VM. Specifically, one of the options that will be skipped is the virtual machine hardware version, which will default to the latest version supported on the ESXi host you deploy the VM to.

5. Give the virtual machine a unique name of up to 80 characters in length and specify an inventory location. Click the Next button to continue.

   Additional information on initial virtual machine placement will be presented in the next section of this chapter.

6. If resource pools are configured on the destination host, choose a resource pool for the new VM and click the Next button. If resource pools are not configured on the destination host, then the wizard will simply skip this step.

7. Select a datastore that suits the workload requirements of the VM and that is large enough to hold the entire contents of the VM. Click the Next button to continue.

(continued)

If you are using either *VM storage profiles* or Storage DRS, then there are additional options presented on this screen. If either of these options is appropriate for your environment, select them now. Storage DRS is covered in Chapter 8 of this book.

8. Keeping in mind the virtual machine hardware version compatibility listed in Table 6.1, choose virtual machine hardware version 8. If there will be compatibility issues with virtual machine hardware version 8, choose virtual machine hardware version 7 instead. Click the Next button to continue.

9. Select the guest operating system of Microsoft MS-DOS, as shown here.

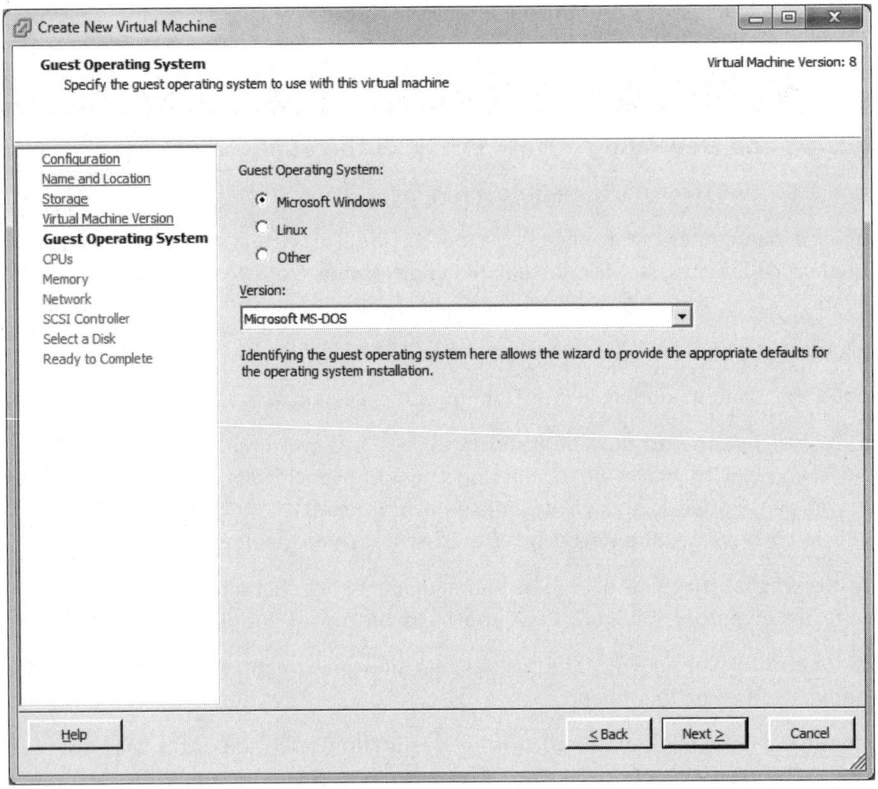

It is important to remember that the guest operating system that is selected here will impact the remaining choices presented in the Create New Virtual Machine Wizard. A simple demonstration of this will now be presented.

10. Click the Next button. Because MS-DOS supports only a single processor, the wizard will skip the CPU step of the wizard and go straight to the Memory step. Take note of the prepopulated Memory Size field value here.

11. Click the Back button. Change the Guest Operating System Version to Microsoft Windows Server 2008 R2 (64-bit) and then click the Next button.

12. Because Windows 2008 Server R2 supports multiple processors, you will now be presented with the option to select the number of virtual sockets and the number of cores per virtual socket. Leave both of these values at the default of 1 and click the Next button to continue.

13. On the Memory screen, note that the prepopulated memory size value has been changed to reflect the VMware-recommended value specific to this guest OS. Again, accept the default value and click the Next button.

14. Choose the number of NICs that this virtual machine will have and assign them to the appropriate network. Also, use the drop-down menus to choose the appropriate network, adapter type, and whether the adapter will be in a connected state at power on. In the image shown here, the VM is assigned a single VMXNET3 adapter that will be connected to the VM Network (dvSwitch) at power on.

(continued)

15. After the networking for the virtual machine has been configured, choose the SCSI controller to use for the virtual machine. Unless you have a specific use case, use the default selected controller. Click the Next button to continue.

    The virtual network adapters and the SCSI controllers in the previous two steps will be discussed in detail later in this chapter.

16. Choose the Create A New Disk option and click the Next button. Note that there are options available to use an existing disk or to omit the disk entirely.

17. Provide the capacity for the new virtual disk using the options at the top of the screen. Select the Thin Provision option for Disk Provisioning, and use the Store With The Virtual Machine option for Location.

    It is important to coordinate the virtual disk sizing with the datastore selected in step 7 earlier in this exercise. If you attempt to create a 200GB virtual disk on a datastore with 100GB of free space, you will receive an error. The disk provisioning options will be discussed later in this chapter.

18. After the virtual disk has been sized, click the Next button.

19. Accept the default value of SCSI 0:0 for Virtual Device Node and leave the Independent Mode option unchecked.

    The Virtual Device Node setting identifies which SCSI controller will be used. In step 15 of this exercise, a controller type was selected. The disk you created in steps 16–17 will be attached to this controller as the first disk.

20. Click the Next button to continue and review the information presented in the Ready To Complete screen.

Create New Virtual Machine

Ready to Complete
Click Finish to start a task that will create the new virtual machine

Virtual Machine Version: 8

Configuration
Name and Location
Storage
Virtual Machine Version
Guest Operating System
CPUs
Memory
Network
SCSI Controller
Select a Disk
Create a Disk
Advanced Options
Ready to Complete

Settings for the new virtual machine:

Name:	NewVM
Host/Cluster:	esxi2.test.local
Datastore:	VMFS-VOL
Guest OS:	Microsoft Windows Server 2008 R2 (64-bit)
CPUs:	1
Memory:	4096 MB
NICs:	1
NIC 1 Network:	VM Network (dvSwitch)
NIC 1 Type:	VMXNET 3
SCSI Controller:	LSI Logic SAS
Create disk:	New virtual disk
Disk capacity:	40 GB
Disk provisioning:	Thin Provision
Datastore:	VMFS-VOL
Virtual Device Node:	SCSI (0:0)
Disk mode:	Persistent

☐ Edit the virtual machine settings before completion

⚠ Creation of the virtual machine (VM) does not include automatic installation of the guest operating system. Install a guest OS on the VM after creating the VM.

Help   ≤ Back   Finish   Cancel

21. Take note of the Edit Virtual Machine Settings Before Completion option, which if checked will allow you to make additional changes to the VM's settings before creating the VM. Omit this option for now.

Also take note of the informational text at the bottom of the screen. This is a reminder that the Create New Virtual Machine Wizard will not install a guest operating system into the virtual machine. The guest OS must be installed, as a separate process just like with a physical machine, after the VM is created.

22. Click the Finish button to begin creating the new VM. A Create Virtual Machine task will begin. When it completes, the new VM will be listed in the inventory.

Virtual machines that use the EFI firmware have a minimum RAM requirement of 96MB, or they will not stay powered on.

I have now covered configuring and deploying a new VM with the vSphere Client. The other method for deploying a new VM in vSphere 5 is to use the vSphere Web Client. Exercise 6.2 will cover deploying a new virtual machine with the vSphere Web Client.

EXERCISE 6.2

Configuring and Deploying a New VM with the vSphere Web Client

1. Open a web browser and connect to the FQDN of the vCenter Server that will be used for this exercise.

2. Click the blue Log In To vSphere Web Client link.

3. When the vSphere Web Client loads, enter your credentials. These can be the same credentials used in the vSphere Client.

4. Choose a datacenter, host, cluster, resource pool, or virtual machine folder in the left pane. In the upper-right margin of the right pane, look for two icons. One is blue with a small green plus sign, and the other is a gray gear with a downward-facing arrow beside it.

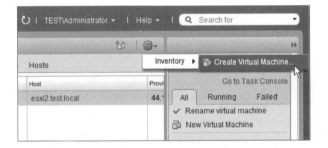

5. Click the blue icon with the small green plus sign or click the gear and choose the Create Virtual Machine option from the Inventory menu. This will launch the Provision Virtual Machine Wizard.

6. Highlight the Create A New Virtual Machine option in the center of the screen by clicking it and then click the Next button to continue.

7. Give the virtual machine a unique name of up to 80 characters in length and specify an inventory location.

8. Select a folder or datacenter where the VM will be located. You can also search for the folder or datacenter using the provided search function. Click the Next button to continue.

   Additional information on initial virtual machine placement will be presented in the next section of this chapter.

9. Select a cluster, ESXi host, vApp, or resource pool that will provide resources to this virtual machine. Click the Next button to continue.

10. Select a datastore that suits the workload requirements of the VM and that is large enough to hold the entire contents of the VM. Ensure that the green circular icon with an arrow (compatibility check) is present at the bottom of the screen before continuing.

The following datastores are accessible by the destination you've selected. Select the destination datastore for the virtual machine configuration files and all of the virtual disks.

Name	Capacity	Provisioned	Free	Type	Storage
VMFS	1.75 GB	536.00 MB	1.23 GB	VMFS	

Compatibility:

✓ Compatibility checks succeeded.

[Back] [Next] [Finish] [Cancel]

11. Click the Next button to continue.

12. Keeping in mind the virtual machine hardware version compatibility listed in Table 6.1, choose virtual machine hardware version 8. If there will be compatibility issues with virtual machine hardware version 8, choose virtual machine hardware version 7 instead. Click the Next button to continue.

13. Choose Guest OS Family of Windows and Guest OS Version of Microsoft Windows Server 2008 R2 (64-bit) and click the Next button to continue.

14. On the Customize Hardware screen, review the settings for this new virtual machine. The settings will appear similar to what's shown here.

(continued)

Virtual Hardware	VM Options		
▸ ☐ CPU	Cores: 1 ▾ ⓘ		
▸ ▦ Memory	RAM: 4096 ▾ MB ▾ Maximum: 1011 GB		
▸ ▤ New Hard disk	40 ▴▾ GB ▾		
▸ ⊙ New SCSI controller	LSI Logic SAS		
▸ ▦ New Network	VM Network (dvSwitch) ▾	☑ Connect...	
▸ ◉ New CD/DVD Drive	Client Device ▾	☐ Connect...	
▸ ▤ New Floppy drive	Client Device ▾	☐ Connect...	
▸ ▢ Video card	Specify custom settings ▾		
▸ ⚙ VMCI device	☐ Enable VMCI between VMs		
▸ Other Devices			

New device: ——— Select ——— ▾ Add   Virtual Machine Version: 8

Back   Next   Finish   Cancel

15. Use the drop-down menus to change the value for the New Network field and ensure that a check mark appears in the Connect box.

16. Click the right-pointing gray arrow that is located beside the New Hard Disk option to expand the new hard disk options. Locate the Disk Provisioning field in the left pane and then select the Allocate And Commit Space On Demand (Thin Provisioning) check box. The result should look like this.

Virtual Hardware	VM Options

▼ 💾 New Hard disk	40 ⬍	GB ▾
Maximum Size	216.05 GB	
Location	Store with the virtual machine ▾	
Disk Provisioning	☑ Allocate and commit space on demand (Thin Provisioning)	
	☐ Flat pre-initialized	
Shares	Normal ▾	1000
Limit - IOPs	Unlimited ▾	
Virtual Device Node	⦿ SCSI(0:0) New Hard disk ▾	
	○ IDE(0:0) ▾	
Disk Mode	⦿ Dependent	
	Dependent disks are included in snapshots.	
	○ Independent - Persistent	
	Changes are immediately and permanently written to disk.	
	Persistent disks are not affected by snapshots.	
	○ Independent - Nonpersistent	
	Changes to this disk are discarded when you power off or	
	revert to the snapshot.	

New device: ——— Select ——— ▾ [Add]   Virtual Machine Version: 8

[Back] [Next] [Finish] [Cancel]

After the thin provisioning has been selected, take a few moments to explore the rest of the disk options. Also, take some time to explore the remaining screens and view the available options in the vSphere Web Client. Note that both a Virtual Hardware view and a VM Options view are available, and these views can be toggled using the buttons at the top of the screen.

17. After reviewing the options in the Customize Hardware portion of the wizard, click the Next button to continue configuring and deploying this virtual machine.

18. You will be presented with the Review Settings screen. Verify the information presented here is correct and click the Finish button to deploy the new VM.

19. A Notification window will appear in the lower-right corner reporting a task in progress. A Create New Virtual Machine task will also appear in the Recent Tasks list in the vSphere Client.

20. When the VM has been deployed, the vSphere Web Client view will refresh to show the new virtual machine.

(continued)

EXERCISE 6.2 *(continued)*

NewVM   ▷ ■ 🖨 🖨 | ⚙-

Summary Monitor Resource Management

▼ **Status**	☐
Overall	⊘ Normal

▼ **Guest OS Details**	☐
Power State	Powered Off
Guest OS	Microsoft Windows Server 2008 R...
IP Addresses	
DNS Name	
VMware Tools	◆ Not running (Not Installed)
Console	
	Launch console

▼ **Annotations**	☐
Notes	

▼ **VM Hardware**	
▸ CPU	1 CPU(s), 0 MHz used
▸ Memory	4096 MB, 0 MB used
▸ Hard disk 1	40.00 GB
▸ Network adapter 1	disconnected
◉ CD/DVD drive 1	Disconnected
🖫 Floppy drive 1	Disconnected
▸ Other	Additional Hardware
HW Version	8

Edit Settings...

▼ **Related Items**	
Storage	VMFS
Networks	VM Network
Host	esxi1.test.local
Resource Pool	esxi1.test.local

◀ | :: | ▶

---

21. Review the virtual machine settings in the vSphere Web Client for accuracy. Leave the vSphere Web Client open, because it will be used in the next exercise.

Just like with the vSphere Client, deploying a VM will not install an operating system on the VM. Use the same procedures for installing an OS that you would use for physical hardware.

I have now covered configuring and deploying a new virtual machine in the vSphere Client and the vSphere Web Client. In the next section, I will discuss in more detail the placement of virtual machines.

Placing Virtual Machines in Selected ESXi Hosts/ Clusters/Resource Pools

When the virtual machines were created in Exercises 6.1 and 6.2, part of the process was to identify the inventory location. Figure 6.1 shows this step when using the vSphere Web Client.

FIGURE 6.1 VM placement options

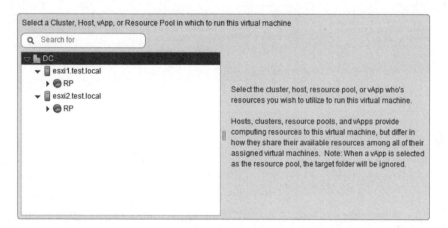

The cluster, ESXi host, and resource pool can each be selected when the virtual machine is created. The available options will depend on how the virtual infrastructure is designed. For example, a cluster without DRS enabled will not have the resource pools as an option. The decision you make for the initial placement is in no way permanent, and virtual machines can move about the virtual infrastructure either through manual processes such as vMotion or through automated migrations from DRS.

Now that I have shown how to build virtual machines and discussed the options for their initial placement, I will cover identifying the methods used to access a virtual machine console.

Identifying Methods to Access and Use a Virtual Machine Console

Unlike physical machines, virtual machines don't have a keyboard, monitor, and mouse that an individual can physically sit down in front of and use to manage the VM. However, the virtual machine console can still be accessed. Several methods can be used to access virtual machine consoles. Applications such as Remote Desktop (RDP) and VNC can be used to access consoles, and vSphere also includes two built-in options. The vSphere Client and the vSphere Web Client both include the ability to access a virtual machine console.

To access the virtual machine console from the vSphere Client, simply right-click any virtual machine in the inventory and choose the Open Console option from the context menu that appears, as shown in Figure 6.2.

FIGURE 6.2 Accessing the virtual machine console with the vSphere Client

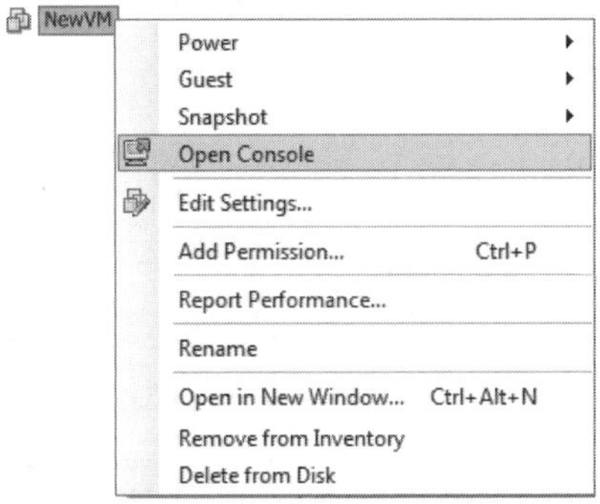

The vSphere Web Client can also be used to access a virtual machine console, but the process is a bit more detailed. Exercise 6.3 will cover the steps required to access a virtual machine console using the vSphere Web Client.

EXERCISE 6.3

Accessing a Virtual Machine Console with the vSphere Web Client

1. Open a web browser and connect to the FQDN of the vCenter Server that will be used for this exercise.

2. Click the blue Log In To vSphere Web Client link.

3. When the vSphere Web Client loads, click Download Client Installation Plug-in located in the bottom-left corner of the screen.

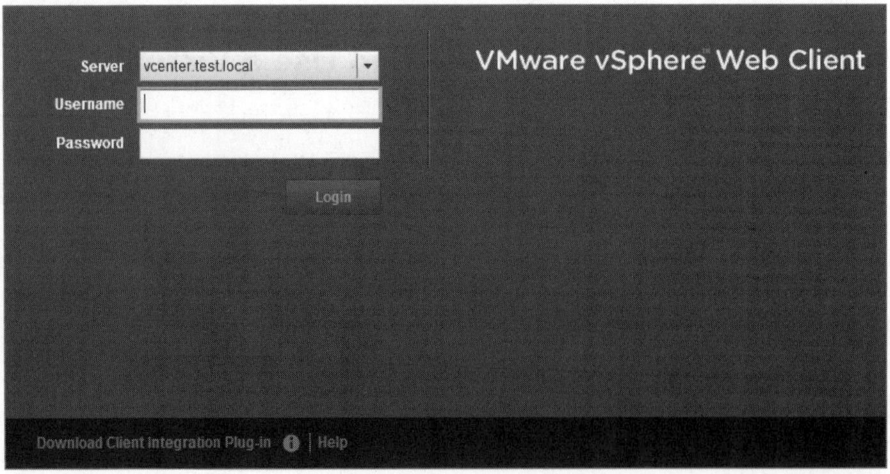

4. Use the procedure appropriate for your web browser to launch the VMware Remote Console Plug-in application.

5. When the VMware Remote Console Application launches, click the Next button to begin. Select the boxes for the web browsers on which you want to install the plug-in.

6. You may be prompted to close your web browser(s) before continuing. Click the Install button to begin the installation of the VMware Remote Console Application.

7. Click the Finish button when the installation completes. Open your web browser and return to the vSphere Web Client login screen.

8. After logging in, expand the objects in the left pane and locate a virtual machine. Select a virtual machine in the left pane by clicking it.

9. In the center of the screen in the Guest OS Details pane, click the blue Launch Console link.

10. The Console window will open in a new tab in the browser window.

For working in the console window, using the vSphere Web Client, here are some helpful commands:

- Pressing Ctrl+Alt will release the cursor from the console window.
- Pressing Ctrl+Alt+Enter will exit full screen mode.

Now that I have covered identifying the various methods used to access virtual machine consoles, you can turn your attention to installing, upgrading, and updating the VMware Tools.

Installing, Upgrading, and Updating VMware Tools

Although never required for guest OS functionality, VMware Tools enhance the performance of a VM's guest operating system and provide additional management functionalities for the VM. VMware Tools can be installed manually using the vSphere Client, and the procedure will be covered in Exercise 6.4 for a Windows guest operating system.

EXERCISE 6.4

Installing VMware Tools Using the vSphere Client

1. Open a console session to a virtual machine.

2. From the VM menu option, choose the Guest submenu and then select the Install/Upgrade VMware Tools option.

3. An Install VMware Tools dialog will be presented. Review this information and click the OK button to continue.

4. The CD-ROM image will be mounted, and if enabled, autorun.exe will launch Setup. If autorun.exe does not begin installation, browse the contents of the mounted CD-ROM and start the installation manually.

5. Click the Next button on the VMware Tools Welcome screen.

6. Choose the Custom option and click the Next button to continue.

7. In the left pane, expand the VMware Device Drivers and review the list of device drivers that will be installed. The complete list of device drivers is shown here.

8. Note that the installation directory can be changed by using the Change button. Click the Next button to continue.

9. Click the Install button to install the VMware Tools.

10. When the installation is complete, click the Finish button. You will then be prompted to reboot the guest OS. Click the Yes button to reboot the VM now.

Now that I have covered installing VMware Tools in a virtual machine, I will cover upgrading and updating the VMware Tools. Upgrading and updating the VMware Tools is likely also a familiar process for most virtual infrastructure administrators, because it is a VMware-recommended best practice to keep the VMware Tools at the latest release available.

As mentioned in Chapter 2, VMware Tools can be upgraded manually, or virtual machines can be configured to check and upgrade automatically during power cycling of the VM. Update Manager is another option for upgrading the VMware Tools. An interesting fact is that the upgrade is actually an uninstall of the old VMware Tools followed immediately by an install of the latest version of the VMware Tools. Exercise 6.5 will cover the steps for upgrading an existing VMware Tools installation on Windows Server 2008 R2 to the latest version.

EXERCISE 6.5

Upgrading VMware Tools Using the vSphere Client

1. Open a console session to a virtual machine.

2. From the VM menu option, choose the Guest submenu and then select the Install/Upgrade VMware Tools option.

3. An Install/Upgrade Tools dialog will appear.

(continued)

EXERCISE 6.5 *(continued)*

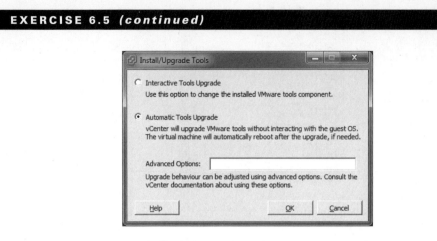

4.   Choose the Automatic Tools Upgrade option and click the OK button.

The Automatic Tools Upgrade option will uninstall the old VMware Tools, install the new version of the VMware Tools with no interaction, and then reboot the guest OS if necessary.

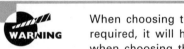 When choosing the Automatic Tools Upgrade option, if a reboot is required, it will happen without prompting. Be sure to remember this when choosing the option you will use to upgrade the VMware Tools.

One other option that is occasionally required is to update the VMware Tools. This can be useful in situations where a particular device driver needs to be added or removed from the installation. The process for updating the VMware Tools is nearly identical to the upgrade process. The difference will be covered in Exercise 6.6, where the steps to remove Virtual Printing will be covered.

EXERCISE 6.6

Updating VMware Tools Using the vSphere Client

1.   Open a console session to a virtual machine.

2.   From the VM menu option, choose the Guest submenu and then select the Install/Upgrade VMware Tools option.

3.   An Install/Upgrade Tools dialog will be presented.

4.   Choose the Interactive Tools Upgrade option and click the OK button.

5.   The CD-ROM image will be mounted, and if enabled, autorun.exe will launch Setup. If autorun.exe does not begin installation, browse the contents of the mounted CD-ROM and start the installation manually.

6. The VMware Tools installer will launch. Click the Next button on the Welcome screen to begin.

7. Choose the Modify option and click the Next button to continue.

8. In the left pane, expand the VMware Device Drivers item and locate Virtual Printing. Select Virtual Printing and choose This Feature Will Not Be Available, as shown here.

VMware Tools   ×

Custom Setup   **vmware**
Select the program features you want installed.

Click on an icon in the list below to change how a feature is installed.

	Feature Description
⊞ Toolbox	Enable automatic printing to host
⊟ VMware Device Drivers	computer's printers
Record/Replay Driver	
Paravirtual SCSI	
Virtual Printing	

  This feature will be installed on local hard drive.
  This feature, and all subfeatures, will be installed on local hard drive.
  This feature will not be available.

C:\Program Files\VMware\VMware Tools\

Help	< Back	Next >	Cancel

9. The Virtual Printing icon will now have a red *X* to its left. Click the Next button to continue.

10. Click the Modify button to begin the update of the VMware Tools.

11. Click the Finish button when the update completes and click the Yes button on the restart prompt.

The version of VMware Tools included with vSphere 5 is supported on both vSphere 4.*x* and vSphere 5 virtual machines. The version of VMware Tools included with vSphere 4.*x* is also supported in vSphere 5.

I have now covered installing, upgrading, and updating the VMware Tools. In the next section, I will cover the device drivers that are included with the VMware Tools.

Identifying VMware Tools Device Drivers

The VMware Tools provide device drivers for the mouse, sound, graphics, networking, and more, but the device drivers that are installed in a typical VMware Tools installation will depend on the guest operating system. Performing a custom installation of VMware Tools, or a modify operation of an existing installation, will allow you to choose which device drivers are installed in the guest OS. Table 6.2 lists the VMware Tools device drivers that could be included in a VMware Tools installation and a brief description of each.

 Windows Vista and newer guest operating systems will use the VMware SVGA 3D (Microsoft – WDDM) driver, instead of the SVGA driver. This driver is used to add support for Windows Aero.

Now that I have covered the VMware Tools device drivers, I will move on to configuring virtual machine time synchronization.

Configuring Virtual Machine Time Synchronization

The VMware Tools have the ability to synchronize the time of the guest OS with the time of the ESXi host that the guest is running on. This feature is known as *periodic time synchronization*. When this feature is enabled, VMware Tools will check once a minute to determine whether the clocks are synchronized. If the clocks are not in sync, the time will be adjusted in the guest OS accordingly. The VMware Tools will move the time ahead for guests that have fallen behind and will slow down the clock on guests that have become ahead of the current host time.

In most cases, the native functions (Win32Time, NTP) used in operating systems will be more accurate than periodic time synchronization and should be used instead to guarantee accurate time in the guest OS. Regardless of the approach taken, only a single method of time synchronization should ever be used.

TABLE 6.2 VMware Tools device drivers

Device driver	Description
Record/Replay	Used to enable recording and replaying of virtual machines.
Paravirtual SCSI	Used to provide increased performance for paravirtualized SCSI devices.
Virtual Printing	Used to allow guests to access the host's printers.
Memory Control	Used to provide enhanced memory management functionality.

Device driver	Description
Mouse	Used to smooth mouse movement in the guest OS.
SVGA	Used to enable 32-bit displays, greater display resolutions, and improved graphics performance.
Audio	Used to provide audio for virtual sound cards.
SCSI	Used when the BusLogic adapter is specified for a virtual machine.
VMXNet NIC	Used to provide increased performance for network devices.
Volume Shadow Copy Service Support	Used to enable VSS support for Windows Vista or Windows Server 2003 or newer. Older versions of Windows will use the FileSystem Sync driver instead.
VMCI	Used to enable VM-to-VM or VM-to-host communications using datagrams and shared memory.
Wyse Multimedia Support	Used to enhance remote desktop multimedia experience.
LSI	Used to provide enhanced drivers for LSI controllers.

Exercise 6.7 will cover the steps used to determine whether VMware Tools periodic time synchronization is in use. I will also cover how to enable and disable periodic time synchronization. This exercise will use a Windows Server 2008 R2 guest OS and will use the command-line tools. As a reminder, vSphere 5 will be the final vSphere release to support the VMware Tools GUI.

EXERCISE 6.7

Configuring Periodic Time Synchronization in a Virtual Machine

1. Obtain a console session to a virtual machine with a Windows 2008 R2 guest OS and log in.

2. Open a command prompt and type the following command:

```
cd "C:\Program Files\VMware\VMware Tools"
```

(continued)

EXERCISE 6.7 *(continued)*

Note that on different Windows operating systems, this path may vary. On Linux and Solaris the path will be /usr/sbin and will vary on other operating systems as well.

3. At the command prompt, type the following command:

VmwareToolboxCmd.exe timesync status

Note that on Linux, Solaris, and FreeBSD the command is as follows:

vmware-toolbox-cmd

4. The results of this command are shown here.

5. In this example, time synchronization is disabled. To enable time synchronization, the following command would be entered:

VmwareToolboxCmd.exe timesync enable

6. If time synchronization is disabled, the following command would be entered to enable it:

VmwareToolboxCmd.exe timesync disable

At this point, periodic time synchronization has been disabled. Certain operations will trigger the VMware Tools to synchronize time in the virtual machine:

- Starting VMware Tools service/daemon (reboot or power on)
- Resuming a VM from a suspend operation
- Reverting to snapshot
- Shrinking a disk

 To completely disable all VMware Tools–initiated time synchronization functionality for a VM, the virtual machine's .vmx file must be modified.

Now that I have covered time synchronization, I will cover identifying virtual machine storage resources.

Identifying Virtual Machine Storage Resources

In Exercise 6.1 you configured and deployed a virtual machine. Part of the configuration was the creation of a virtual disk for the virtual machine. Now that the VM has been deployed, I will identify its storage resources. Figure 6.3 shows the storage resources used by a virtual machine.

Four areas are listed for the selected storage resource. The first field is Disk File and shows the path information of the virtual disk. The Disk File field includes the datastore, the VM directory name, and the virtual disk name.

The second area listed is Disk Provisioning. The Type value is listed first in the Disk Provisioning area and shows the disk format used by the virtual disk. The next item listed in the Disk Provisioning area is Provisioned Size. This shows the amount of disk space provisioned for the virtual disk. The final item listed is the Maximum Size (GB) value, which represents the maximum size the VMDK file can grow to.

FIGURE 6.3   Virtual machine storage resources

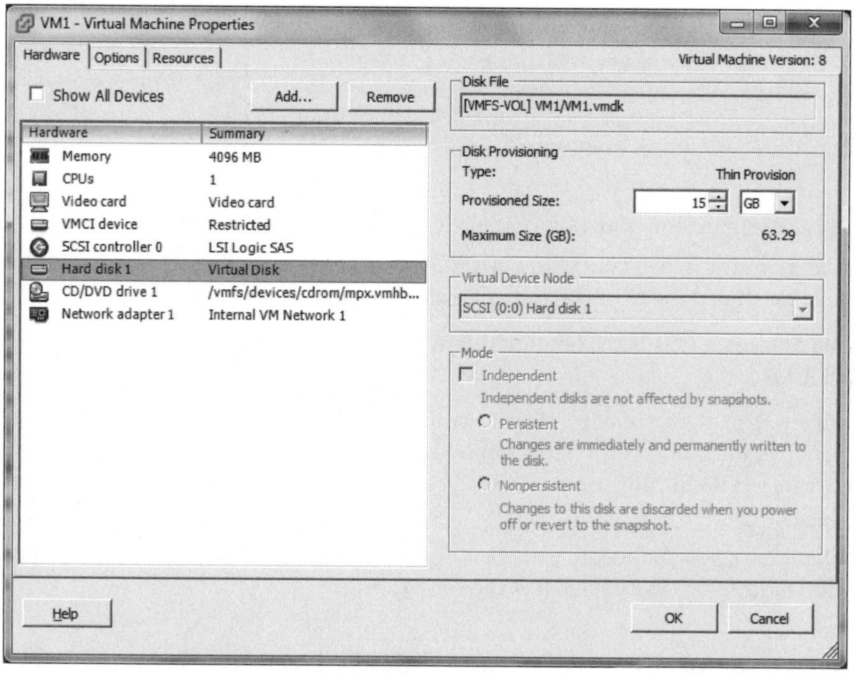

The third area is Virtual Device Node. This represents the SCSI controller and the drive number. In Figure 6.3, SCSI 0:0 is used, meaning SCSI controller 0 and disk 0. Note that this value is grayed out for powered-on virtual machines.

The final area is Mode. This is where independent disks can be configured. As with the virtual device node, the disk mode field is also grayed out for powered-on virtual machines. Independent disks are excluded from snapshot operations. Two modes can be used with independent disks:

Independent Persistent   This disk behaves just like a normal disk, and all writes are committed to disk.

Independent Nonpersistent   All changes to this type of independent disk are lost at VM power off or reset.

There is one other location to obtain information about virtual machine storage resources. In the Resources panel on the Summary tab for the virtual machine there are three fields, as shown in Figure 6.4.

FIGURE 6.4   Virtual machine storage resources

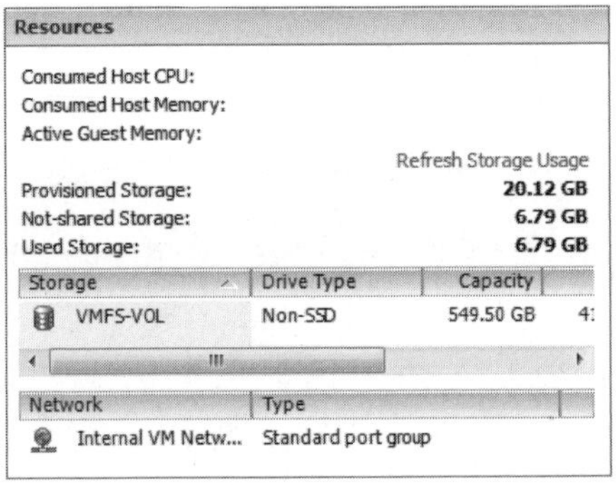

The storage resource information presented here consists of the following:

Provisioned Storage   This value represents the provisioned size of all virtual disks in the virtual machine plus the size of the virtual machine's swap file.

Not-shared Storage   This is the amount of storage used only by the VM and not shared with other VMs.

Used Storage   This is the amount of space consumed by all of the files that make up the virtual machine, including swap files, config files, and snapshots. For thin provisioned disks, this value will typically report a value less than the value reported for the Provisioned Storage field.

Now that I have covered identifying virtual machine storage resources, I will cover configuring and modifying disk controllers for virtual disks.

Configuring and Modifying Disk Controller for Virtual Disks

Virtual SCSI controllers are used by virtual machines to access their virtual disks. When you create a virtual machine, the default controller for the guest operating system you selected will be provided. This controller type will seldom need to be changed. The virtual SCSI controller types are described here:

BusLogic Parallel   This is an emulated version of a hardware storage adapter from BusLogic. This adapter is typically used with older operating systems that include the BusLogic driver by default.

LSI Logic Parallel   This is an emulated version of a hardware storage adapter from LSI. This adapter is typically used with newer operating systems that include the LSI driver by default.

LSI Logic SAS   This controller was introduced with vSphere 4 and is intended to provide increased performance over the BusLogic and LSI Logic Parallel controllers. It is available only for VMs that are using virtual machine hardware version 7 or newer. As some vendors phase out support for parallel SCSI, the LSI Logic SAS adapter could also be a wise choice to ensure future compatibility. Check with your OS vendor for more information.

VMware Paravirtual   This storage controller was also introduced with vSphere 4 and is intended to provide high performance with lower CPU utilization. It is intended for use with high I/O and high-performance storage and is not supported by all operating systems. Check the following VMware KB article to ensure operating system compatibility with the VMware Paravirtual SCSI (PVSCSI) adapter:

    http://kb.vmware.com/kb/1010398

    Virtual disks cannot be reassigned to a different controller type.

In addition to specifying the disk controller type, you can also configure the SCSI bus sharing type to be used with the controller. SCSI bus sharing allows different virtual machines to access the same virtual disk(s) simultaneously and is useful in clustering solutions. The three types of SCSI bus sharing are as follows:

None   This is the default setting and does not allow the virtual disks to be shared.

Virtual   This setting allows virtual disks to be shared by virtual machines located on the same ESXi host.

Physical   This setting allows virtual disks to be shared by virtual machines located on any ESXi host.

The available operations for SCSI controllers are adding, removing, and changing the type, as well as setting the bus sharing options. In Exercise 6.8 you will add an additional disk controller and configure the SCSI bus sharing options for it. The exercise will begin with a Windows 2008 R2 guest OS on a virtual machine with a single LSI Logic SAS controller and virtual disk.

EXERCISE 6.8

Configuring and Modifying a Disk Controller in the vSphere Client

1. Connect to a vCenter Server with the vSphere Client.

2. Right-click a powered-off virtual machine from the inventory. Choose the Edit Settings option from the context menu that appears.

3. The Virtual Machine Properties editor will appear, as shown here.

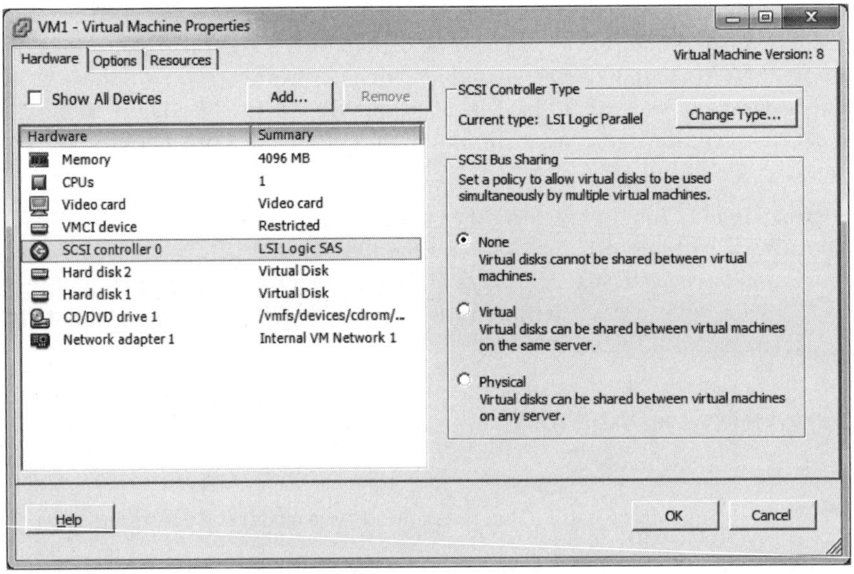

The first step is to add an additional controller to the virtual machine.

4. Click the Add button located at the top of the Hardware tab. The Add Hardware window will appear. Select Hard Disk from the list of devices in the middle of the screen and click the Next button to continue.

5. On the Select A Disk screen, choose the Create A New Virtual Disk option and click the Next button.

6. Give the disk a capacity of 1GB and choose the Thick Provision option for Disk Provisioning. Click the Next button to continue.

7. On the Advanced Options screen, use the drop-down menu to change Virtual Device Node to 1:0, as shown here.

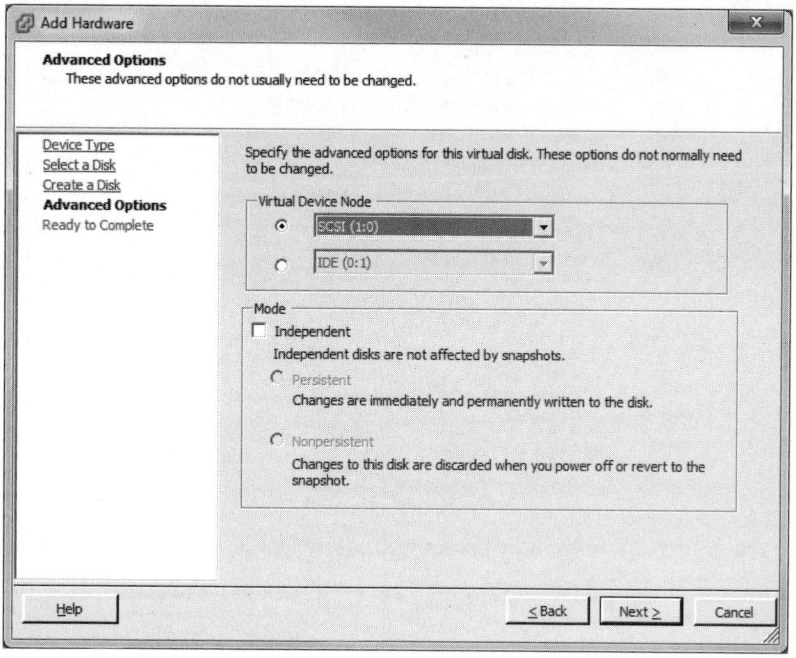

Choosing virtual device node 1:0 will create a new virtual disk controller, since the default disk added to the VM upon creation is typically on virtual device node 0:0.

8. Click the Next button to continue. On the Ready To Complete screen, click the Finish button.

9. Notice that in the Virtual Machine Properties window, there are new bold entries for the controller and disk you just added. Select the New SCSI Controller (Adding) item.

10. Note the SCSI Controller Type listed in the top right of this screen. Click the Change Type button.

(continued)

11. A Change SCSI Controller Type window will appear.

Change SCSI Controller Type

⚠ Changing the SCSI Controller Type:

- Will replace the existing controller with a new selected controller.
- Will copy the common settings to the new controller.
- Will reassign all SCSI devices from the old controller to the new one.

Warning: Changing the controller type for the virtual machine's boot disk will prevent the virtual machine from booting properly.

SCSI Controller Type
- ○ BusLogic Parallel (not recommended for this guest OS)
- ○ LSI Logic Parallel
- ○ LSI Logic SAS
- ● VMware Paravirtual

[OK]   [Cancel]

12. Review the warning information presented before proceeding.

13. Change the SCSI Controller Type option to VMware Paravirtual and click the OK button.

14. Now notice that in the Virtual Machine Properties window, the LSI Logic SAS controller has been changed to Paravirtual.

   At this point, the disk controller has been changed, but you still need to change the SCSI Bus Sharing options. The remainder of this exercise will cover the steps required to change the SCSI Bus Sharing options.

15. In the Virtual Machine Properties window, click the Virtual option listed under SCSI Bus Sharing.

16. Click the OK button to save the changes.

17. A Reconfigure Virtual Machine task will start. When this task completes, the virtual machine is ready to be powered on and used.

Disk controllers can also be added, removed, modified, and have their SCSI bus sharing options changed using the vSphere Web Client.

Now that I have covered configuring and modifying a disk controller, I will move on to showing how to configure the appropriate virtual disk type for a virtual machine.

Configuring Appropriate Virtual Disk Type for a Virtual Machine

As you saw in Exercise 6.8, when virtual disks are created, certain properties can be specified. These properties include the size of the disk, the type of provisioning to use, the location to store the disk, the virtual device node, and the disk mode. In this section, the different virtual disk types will be discussed.

Virtual disk types, disk provisioning, and format are all used to refer to the type of virtual disk used in a virtual machine. The three types of virtual disks are flat disk, thick provision, and thin provision.

A flat disk, which is also known as a Thick Provision Lazy Zeroed disk, is a VMDK file that is created and all of the space is provisioned immediately. While the space is provisioned immediately, the space is actually zeroed on command. A virtual disk that is created as 20GB will consume 20GB of space on the datastore, regardless of the actual disk usage in the guest OS.

 Zeroed or *zeroing* is the process where disk blocks are overwritten with zeroes. This process is performed to ensure that no prior data is still on the volume that might cause problems with the VMDK.

A thick provisioned disk, which can also be known as a Thick Provision Eager Zeroed disk, is a VMDK file that is created and all of the space is provisioned immediately. With this type of VMDK, the space is also zeroed at the time of creation. This type of disk takes the longest to create and is required for certain features like VMware FT. A virtual disk that is created as 20GB will consume 20GB of space on the datastore, regardless of the actual disk usage in the guest OS. There is a slight performance increase with this format, since the zeroing does not have to happen at runtime like it does with the other two formats.

A thin provisioned disk is a VMDK file that is created with a zero size, and it will grow on demand as required. A virtual disk that is 20GB will consume approximately the actual space used by the guest operating system.

In addition to virtual disks, raw device mappings can be used in virtual machines. A raw device mapping (RDM) file can be used to store virtual machine data directly on the SAN, as opposed to storing it in a VMDK file on a VMFS datastore. This can be useful if SAN snapshots are required, if applications that are SAN aware are used, or if Microsoft Cluster Service (MSCS) is used.

Adding an RDM to a virtual machine will create an RDM file that points to the raw device. This RDM file will have a .vmdk extension and will even report the size of the raw device in the Datastore Browser, but this file contains only the mapping information. Two compatibility modes can be used with RDMs:

Physical This compatibility mode allows the guest OS to access the raw device directly and is used for SAN-aware applications running in a virtual machine. Snapshots are not possible with this compatibility mode.

Virtual   This compatibility mode allows the guest OS to treat the RDM more like a virtual disk and can be used with snapshots.

In Exercise 6.9, I will cover the steps to add an RDM to a virtual machine using the vSphere Client. Note that for this exercise you will need to have a raw device configured on your SAN.

EXERCISE 6.9

Adding an RDM to a Virtual Machine with the vSphere Client

1. Connect to a vCenter Server with the vSphere Client.

2. Right-click a virtual machine in the inventory. Choose the Edit Settings option from the context menu that appears.

3. The Virtual Machine Properties window will appear.

4. Click the Add button located at the top of the Hardware tab. The Add Hardware window will appear. Select Hard Disk from the list of devices in the middle of the screen and click the Next button to continue.

5. On the Select A Disk screen, choose the Raw Device Mappings option and click the Next button.

Note that if no applicable storage devices are available, the Raw Device Mappings option will be grayed out and unavailable.

6. Choose the LUN to use by selecting it from the list and click the Next button.

7. Select the default Store With Virtual Machine option and click the Next button.

8. Select the Compatibility Mode for the RDM and click the Next button.

```
┌──────────────────────────────────────────────────────────────────────┐
│ 🖭 Add Hardware                                                    [ X ]│
├──────────────────────────────────────────────────────────────────────┤
│   Select Compatibility Mode                                            │
│     Which compatibility mode do you want this virtual disk to use?     │
│                                                                        │
│   Device Type        The compatibility mode you choose will apply only │
│   Select a Disk      to this virtual disk and will not                 │
│   Select Target LUN  affect any other disks using this LUN mapping.    │
│   Select Datastore   ┌─ Compatibility ──────────────────────────────┐ │
│   Compatibility Mode │                  Allow the guest operating    │ │
│   Advanced Options   │  ⦿ Physical      system to access the         │ │
│   Ready to Complete  │                  hardware directly. Taking a  │ │
│                      │                  snapshot of this virtual     │ │
│                      │                  machine will not include     │ │
│                      │                  this disk.                   │ │
│                      │                  Allow the virtual machine to │ │
│                      │  ○ Virtual       use VMware snapshots and     │ │
│                      │                  other advanced functionality.│ │
│                      └───────────────────────────────────────────────┘ │
│                                                                        │
│     Help                            ≤ Back   Next ≥      Cancel        │
└──────────────────────────────────────────────────────────────────────┘
```

9. Review the Virtual Device Node information and modify it if necessary. Click the Next button.

10. Review the information on the Ready To Complete screen and click the Finish button to add the RDM to the virtual machine.

11. Verify that New Hard Disk is listed and reported as Mapped Raw LUN in the Summary column.

12. Click the OK button on the Virtual Machine Properties window. A Reconfigure Virtual Machine task will begin. When this task completes, the RDM has been added.

13. To configure the RDM, use the native disk management tools in the guest OS to scan for new devices and to format the disk appropriately.

When configuring an RDM disk in the guest OS, make sure that the partition is aligned properly.

Configuring the appropriate virtual disk type for a virtual machine will depend on a variety of factors in your environment. Some of these factors could include the following:

Storage Consumption   If space or the ability to over-allocate storage is a primary concern in an environment, then thin provisioned disks would be appropriate.

Fault Tolerance (FT)   If VMware FT is required, then thick provisioned disks would be appropriate.

Performance   If absolute performance is a concern, then thick provisioned disks would also be appropriate.

Storage Support   If your storage is NFS and doesn't support the *VAAI* NAS extensions, then thin provisioning would be the only option.

Clustering   Clustering solutions will often require thick provisioned disks and/or RDMs.

Disk Operations   While all VMs are encapsulated and generally very portable, RDMs can be easily moved or attached to other virtual or physical servers in the same SAN fabric.

Now that I have covered configuring appropriate virtual disk types for virtual machines, I will cover creating and converting both thin and thick virtual disks.

Creating and Converting Thin/Thick Provisioned Virtual Disks

As you have seen in previous exercises, the virtual disk formats are typically chosen upon virtual machine creation. The format chosen here is in no way permanent, and the conversion of any disk format to another disk format is easily accomplished. Exercise 6.10 will cover the steps to convert a thin disk, in a powered-off virtual machine, to a thick disk.

EXERCISE 6.10

Converting a Thin Disk to a Thick Disk

1. Connect to a vCenter Server with the vSphere Client.

2. Select a powered-off virtual machine with a thin provisioned disk from the inventory. You created one of these in Exercise 6.1.

3. Right-click the virtual machine and choose the Edit Settings option from the context menu that appears.

4. When the Virtual Machine Properties window appears, select the hard disk from the list of devices.

5. In the right side of the Virtual Machine Properties window, verify that the Disk Provisioning Type value is reported as Thin Provision.

6. Also note the path to the virtual disk, as shown in the Disk File field at the top right of the Virtual Machine Properties window.

7. Click the Cancel button to exit the Virtual Machine Properties window.

8. Select the Summary tab for this virtual machine, and locate the datastore that houses this virtual machine's virtual disk in the Resources panel under the Storage listing.

9. Right-click the datastore and choose the Browse Datastore option that appears in the context menu.

10. The Datastore Browser will open. Navigate into the directory that is named the same as the VM.

11. Inside this directory, locate the virtual disk file using the path information obtained in step 6. Note the reported values for the virtual disk in both the Size and Provisioned Size columns.

12. Right-click the virtual disk file and choose the Inflate option from the context menu that appears, as shown here.

13. An Inflating window will appear that provides the progress of the inflate operation. This task may take some time to complete for large VMDK files. An Inflate Virtual Disk task will also be listed in the Recent Tasks in the vSphere Client.

14. When the Inflate Virtual Disk task completes, verify the value reported for the virtual disk in the Size column matches what was reported in step 11 for the provisioned size.

15. Open the vSphere Client and select the hard disk from the list of devices.

16. In the right side of the Virtual Machine Properties window, verify that the Disk Provisioning Type value is now reported as Thick Provision.

As shown in Exercise 6.10, the inflate operation will convert a thin provisioned disk to a thick provisioned disk. The vmkfstools command, Storage vMotion, and VMware Converter could each be used to accomplish this same task.

Now that I have discussed converting thin disks to thick, you can turn your attention to configuring disk shares for a virtual machine.

Configuring Disk Shares

In vSphere, shares are used to specify the relative importance of a virtual machine as it pertains to a specific resource. Shares can be configured for CPU, memory, or disk. Disk shares are used to prioritize disk access for virtual machines that access the same datastores.

It is important to note that disk shares are applicable only on a per-host basis and cannot be pooled across a cluster. Shares may have the values of Low, Normal, High, and Custom. Each of these values will be compared to the sum of all shares for all VMs on the host. Virtual machines with the highest share values will have higher throughput and lower latency than virtual machines with lower share values.

An input/output operations per second (IOPs) limit can also be set for a virtual machine. This will limit the number of disk I/O operations per second for the virtual machine.

Exercise 6.11 will cover the steps required to configure disk shares for a virtual machine using the vSphere Web Client. This exercise will set the shares value to High and the IOPs limit to Unlimited, which would give this VM a very high priority.

EXERCISE 6.11

Configuring Disk Shares for a Virtual Machine Using the vSphere Web Client

1. Open a web browser and connect to the FQDN of the vCenter Server and then log in to the vSphere Web Client.

2. Select a virtual machine from the left pane, and then choose the blue Edit Settings link in the VM Hardware panel.

3. An Edit VM window will appear. In the default Virtual Hardware view, click the arrow icon to the left of the hard disk you want to configure shares for. The hard disk item will be expanded to reveal configuration options.

4. Using the drop-down menu to the right of the Shares field, change the value to High. Leave the Limit – IOPs set to unlimited.

Edit VM NewVM   ⑦ ▸▸

| Virtual Hardware | VM Options |

▼ 💾 *Hard disk 1 | 40   ▲▼ | GB ▼ |

    Maximum Size   216.05 GB

    Type   Thick

    Disk File   [esxi2-dsVMFS] New Virtual
                Machine/New Virtual Machine.vmdk

    Shares (*) | High   ▼ | 2000 |

    Limit - IOPs | Unlimited   ▼ |

    Virtual Device Node | SCSI(0:0) Hard disk 1   ▼ |

    Disk Mode   ⦿ Dependent
                Dependent disks are included in snapshots.
                ○ Independent - Persistent

New device: | ----- Select ----- ▼ | Add   Virtual Machine Version: 8

OK   Cancel

5. Click the OK button to save the changes.

The vSphere Client can also be used to configure disk shares for a virtual machine.

Now that I have covered configuring disk shares for a virtual machine, I will cover determining the appropriate datastore locations for virtual machines based on application workloads.

Determining Appropriate Datastore Locations for Virtual Machines Based on Application Workloads

When adding virtual disks to virtual machines, two options are available in the Add Hardware Wizard for choosing the location used to store the virtual disk files:

Store With The Virtual Machine This option will store the virtual disk file in the virtual machine directory, along with the virtual machine's configuration and log files. This approach is generally easy to manage, since all of the virtual machine's files are in a single location.

Specify A Datastore Or Datastore Cluster This option will allow the virtual machine disk file to be stored on a separate datastore or datastore cluster. This approach can add complexity to the management of the VM.

Having multiple datastores and the ability to distribute virtual disks across multiple datastores can offer many advantages. Determining the appropriate datastore location will often come down to looking at the physical storage that is backing the datastore. Certain workloads will require specific disk configurations, and knowing the capabilities of the disks behind the datastore will be beneficial in determining which datastore to use.

Microsoft SQL Server is commonly configured to use both RAID5 and RAID1+0 disk configurations. With multiple datastores on differing RAID sets, this capability can easily be provided for SQL Server or other servers that have similar requirements.

If replication is being used at the storage level, any virtual machine could have its page file placed on a different virtual disk in a different datastore. This could allow very fast page file access, in addition to excluding this constantly changing disk from replication.

Applications that are read-intensive will likely perform extremely well on a datastore backed by storage that is utilizing *SSD* disks.

Virtual desktops can be placed on datastores backed by storage that supports *deduplication.*

The key thing to remember when determining the appropriate datastore location is that you will need to understand both the application's requirements and the capability of the storage system backing the datastore. In the next section, I will cover configuring and modifying vCPU and memory resources for specific application requirements.

Configuring and Modifying Virtual CPU and Memory Resources According to OS and Application Requirements

Different virtual machines will require different resources for both CPU and memory, just as physical servers have different configurations. Although it may initially seem like a good idea to give your VMs maximum memory and maximum CPU resources, it is actually a best practice to start small and grow as required. This approach both conserves resources and creates a more scalable environment.

The first step in building out a virtual machine is to look at the system requirements for the guest OS. Windows Server 2008 R2 has the following recommended system requirements:

- Processor: Single 2GHz or faster
- Memory: 2GB

At this point, you know the virtual machine needs a single vCPU and 2GB of RAM. As the second step in sizing your virtual machine, let's look at the system requirements for the application. For this example, let's look at vCenter Server, which has the following system requirements:

- Processor: Two 64-bit CPUs or one 64-bit dual-core processor
- Memory: 4GB

At this point, you know the virtual machine needs two vCPUs or a single dual-core vCPU and 4GB RAM. As the final step in sizing the virtual machine, you would add up any additional system requirements for things such as antivirus or other standard applications that will be installed on the server. Once the final number is totaled, the virtual machine may be sized accordingly using the Virtual Machine Properties Editor in the vSphere Client.

Virtual machines have the ability to grow, and even shrink if required, in a dynamic fashion. If additional applications need to be added to a server, the system requirements can be calculated and adjusted. There is no need to oversize virtual machines, when the environment is this flexible. The final step in sizing is the ongoing performance monitoring of the virtual machine. As problems are found or as the system grows beyond its original capacity, the virtual machine can continue to evolve with the workload.

Now that I have covered sizing the CPU and memory for a virtual machine, you can turn your attention to configuring and modifying network connections for virtual machines.

Configuring and Modifying Virtual NIC Adapter and Connecting Virtual Machines to Appropriate Network Resources

Configuring and modifying virtual NIC adapters is an important part of maintaining the virtual infrastructure. In many environments, there are multiple networks, and some environments will even have DMZ or external-facing networks connected to their ESXi hosts. Because of this, it is very important to understand the networking setup in a given vSphere environment. Configuring networking for a virtual machine involves selecting a network adapter type, a network connection, and the connection options. Before you configure a virtual NIC, take a look at the supported NIC types:

E1000   This is an emulated version of the Intel 82545EM Gigabit Ethernet NIC. Drivers are available in most Linux versions 2.4.19 and newer, Windows XP Professional (64-bit) and newer, and Windows Server 2003 (32-bit) and newer.

Flexible   This adapter identifies itself as a Vlance adapter at boot but can function as a VMXNET adapter if the VMware Tools are installed.

Vlance   This is an emulated version of the AMD 79C970 PCnet32 LANCE NIC. Drivers are available in most 32-bit guests but not for Windows Vista and newer.

VMXNET   This adapter is built for virtual machines and requires the VMware Tools to provide a driver.

VMXNET 2 (Enhanced)   This adapter is based on the VMXNET adapter but offers jumbo frames and hardware offload support. This adapter is available for limited guest operating systems running on ESX/ESXi 3.5 and newer and requires the VMware Tools to provide a driver.

VMXNET 3   This adapter is a paravirtualized NIC designed for performance. VMXNET 3 offers jumbo frames, hardware offloads, support for multiqueue, IPv6 offloads, and MSI/ MSI-X interrupt delivery. It is important to note that VMXNET 3 is a completely different adapter than either VMXNET or VMXNET 2, and it requires the VMware Tools to provide a driver.

Now that I have covered the available virtual NIC adapters, Exercise 6.12 will cover the steps required to add and configure a virtual NIC to a virtual machine and connect the virtual machine to a network. Note that this exercise will remove the currently configured NIC for the virtual machine and replace it. Use a virtual machine that can lose network connectivity, and document the current networking information for this VM. Also ensure that this VM has the latest version of the VMware Tools installed.

EXERCISE 6.12

Adding, Configuring, and Connecting a Virtual NIC Adapter Using the vSphere Client

1. Connect to a vCenter Server with the vSphere Client.

2. Right-click a virtual machine in the left pane. Choose the Edit Settings option from the context menu that appears.

3. The Virtual Machine Properties window will appear. Select the listed network adapter. Take note of the Device Status options and the Network Label value.

4. With the network adapter still selected, click the Remove button at the top of the Hardware tab. Note how the network adapter is now in a strikethrough font and the Summary tab reports Removed.

5. Click the Add button at the top of the Hardware tab. The Add Hardware Wizard will launch.

6. Select Ethernet Adapter from the list of devices in the center of this screen and click the Next button.

7. Using the drop-down menu, change Adapter Type to VMXNET 3. Using the drop-down menu, change Network Label to the value from step 3 in this exercise. And using the check box for the Device Status, match the previous setting from step 3. Click the Next button.

8. Review the information on the Ready To Complete screen and click the Finish button.

9. The final configuration should look like the image shown here.

VM1 - Virtual Machine Properties

Hardware | Options | Resources

Virtual Machine Version: 8

☐ Show All Devices [Add...] [Remove]

Hardware	Summary
Memory	4096 MB
CPUs	1
Video card	Video card
VMCI device	Restricted
SCSI controller 0	LSI Logic SAS
Hard disk 1	Virtual Disk
CD/DVD drive 1	/vmfs/devices/cdrom/...
~~Network adapter 1 (removing)~~	Removed
New NIC (adding)	**VM Network**

Device Status
☐ Connected
☑ Connect at power on

Adapter Type
Current adapter: VMXNET 3

MAC Address
[   ]
◉ Automatic   ○ Manual

DirectPath I/O Gen. 2
Status: --

Network Connection
Network label:
[VM Network   ▼]

[Help]   [OK]   [Cancel]

10. Click the OK button to save these changes. A Reconfigure Virtual Machine task will begin. When this task completes, the configuration is complete.

11. Because the NIC was replaced with a new one, the network configuration in the guest OS will need to be reconfigured, before the VM can be used on the network again. Follow the procedures specific to your OS for this step.

NOTE   There is a field provided to specify the MAC address for a virtual NIC, but there are some fairly strict rules around this operation. Refer to the following VMware KB article for more information:

    http://kb.vmware.com/kb/219

I have now covered configuring virtual NIC adapters in your virtual machines. In the following section, I will cover converting physical servers with VMware Converter.

Converting a Physical Machine Using VMware Converter

VMware Converter is an application provided by VMware that can be used to convert physical servers to virtual machines (P2V), convert virtual machines to virtual machines (V2V), reconfigure virtual machines, and import various image formats and convert them to virtual machines. In vSphere 5, VMware Converter is now a standalone application, and the VMware vCenter Converter plug-in for vSphere Client is no more. It should also be noted that Converter Standalone 4.3 and newer do not support cold cloning.

Cold cloning is the process of booting a physical or virtual machine to VMware Converter media and running the conversion from it. This approach allows for consistent images, because the operating system and applications would all be powered off. In VMware Converter Standalone 5, hot cloning is used. Hot cloning converts the physical server or virtual machine while it is running the guest OS and applications. To ensure consistency with hot clones, it is recommended you stop all services and applications while the conversion is in process. This will ensure that the applications and data are consistent when the conversion is complete.

The cloning process will copy data over the network. There are two primary modes used for the cloning process:

Volume Based   This mode will be used if volumes are resized to a smaller size, and it will simply copy each file on the source over the network to the destination.

Disk Based   This mode will be used if volumes remain the same size or are increased in size, and it will copy the disk blocks. This mode is much faster than the volume based mode.

 Converter Standalone cannot detect any source volumes and file systems that are located on physical disks larger than 2TB.

It is also important to note that Ethernet controllers will change as part of the conversion process. After a P2V operation, networks will have to be reconfigured on the guest OS. The conversion and the change of the underlying hardware can also have implications for software that is licensed on MAC addresses or some other aspect of physical hardware.

VMware Converter Standalone 5 can be installed on a physical server or virtual machine either as a local installation or as a client-server installation. In Exercise 6.13, you will install VMware Converter Standalone 5 on a Windows 2008 R2 virtual machine as a local install and then use it to convert a physical server to a virtual machine.

EXERCISE 6.13

Installing VMware Converter Standalone and Converting a Physical Server to a Virtual Machine

1. Open a web browser and enter the following URL:

   http://www.vmware.com/go/getconverter

2. Log in or register and then download the VMware vCenter Converter Standalone 5 binary.

3. Verify the checksum for the downloaded file and then launch the executable to begin Setup.

4. Using the drop-down menu, choose the desired Language option, and click the OK button.

5. Click the Next button on the Welcome screen and the Patent screen. Agree to the legal terms and click the Next button.

6. Select the desired installation directory and click the Next button to continue.

7. Choose Local Installation for Setup Type and click the Next button.

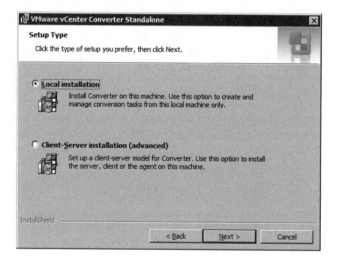

8. Click the Install button. When the installation completes, make sure the Run Client Now option is checked and click the Finish button.

9. The VMware vCenter Converter Standalone application will launch. Click the Convert Machine button located in the upper-left corner of the screen, or use the File menu to choose New and Convert Machine.

(continued)

10. A Conversion Wizard will launch. Using the drop-down menu, choose the Powered-on Machine option from the Select Source Type options.

11. Specify a remote machine in the lower portion of the screen and enter the IP address or FQDN of the physical server to be converted. Also, enter a user-name and password that has Administrative access to the physical server. Choose the appropriate OS family, using the drop-down menu. The final configuration should look similar to the image shown here.

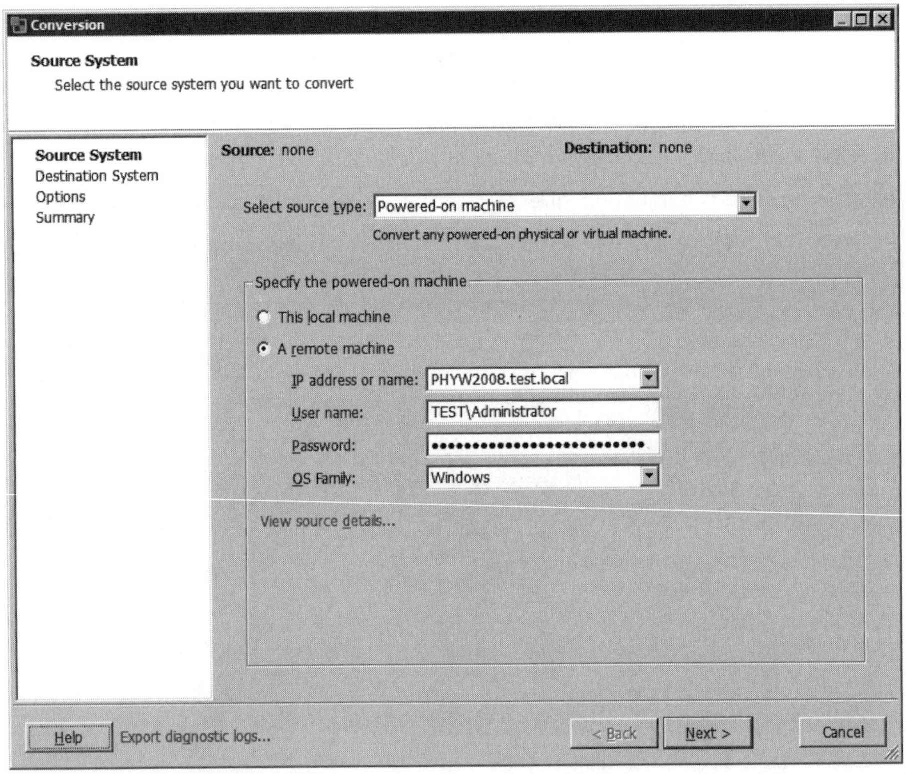

12. Click the blue View Source Details link. You will be prompted to install the VMware vCenter Converter Standalone agent. Choose the Automatically Uninstall The Files When Import Succeeds option and click the Yes button to continue.

13. The status of the agent deployment will be shown on the same window, and when complete, a Machine Details window will appear. Review the details here and click the Close button.

Machine Details for PHYW2008.test.local   ☒

Name:	PHYW2008.test.local
Machine type:	Physical machine
Operating system:	Windows 2008 R2 (64 bit)
Total size:	1,115.5 GB
Number of vCPUs:	4 (2 sockets * 2 cores)
RAM:	4092 MB
Network:	Nic1
	Nic2

Source disks/volumes layout:

Disk 1 - 557.75 GB

System Reserved (\\?\Volume{cb3f8b8d-c91e-11e0-b329-806e6f6e6963}\) - 28 MB use

(C:) - 13.99 GB used / 49.9 GB total <NTFS>

(D:) - 500.1 GB used / 507.75 GB total <NTFS>

[Close]

14. On the Destination System screen, select the default Destination Type of VMware Infrastructure Virtual Machine. Enter the FQDN for the vCenter Server that this virtual machine will be managed by, and enter the appropriate credentials for the vCenter Server.

Conversion   _□×

Destination System

Select a host for the new virtual machine

Source System
Destination System
Destination Virtual Machine
Destination Location
Options
Summary

Source: PHYW2008.test.local   **Destination:** none

Select destination type: | VMware Infrastructure virtual machine   ▾ |

Creates a new virtual machine for use on a VMware Infrastructure product.

VMware Infrastructure server details

Server:	vcenter.test.local ▾
User name:	TEST\Administrator
Password:	••••••••••••••••••••

[Help] Export diagnostic logs...   [< Back] [Next >]   [Cancel]

(continued)

15. Click the Next button to continue.

16. At the top of the Destination Virtual Machine screen, name the new virtual machine. Choose an inventory location for the new virtual machine and click the Next button to continue.

17. Now select the cluster or host that the virtual machine will be hosted on from the Inventory option in the middle of the screen. Use the drop-down menu to select a datastore and virtual machine hardware version. Click the Next button to continue.

18. On the Options screen, make any changes necessary. This can include reducing the number of vCPUs, changing which disks are copied, resizing the disks that are copied, connecting and disconnecting networks, and more.

Note that any settings that are modified will have a blue diamond located in front of them. When all of the changes have been made, click the Next button.

19. Review the information on the Summary screen and click the Finish button. A task will be listed in the VMware Converter Standalone window that shows the source, destination, progress, and more.

Task ID	Job ID	Source	Destination	Status
1	1	PHYW2008.test.local	vcenter.test.local/PHYW2008	1%

20. Selecting the task will populate the Summary and Task Progress tabs at the bottom of the screen. These tabs provide more detail on the progress.

21. When this task completes, open the vSphere Client and locate the converted server in the inventory. Power it on and watch it boot from a console session.

Converting a physical machine to a virtual machine involves much more than just running the VMware Converter. Any hardware agents, hardware management applications, and vendor-specific device drivers will need to be removed. Networking will need to be reconfigured, and some time will likely need to be spent with the system logs to ensure that everything is working properly. Only after this cleanup is complete should the applications on the converted virtual machine be started.

Now that I have covered converting a physical machine to a virtual machine using VMware vCenter Converter Standalone 5, I will cover how to import a supported VM source using VMware Converter.

Importing a Supported Virtual Machine Source Using VMware Converter

VMware Converter can also convert a variety of other sources into vSphere environments. Some of these sources include the following:

- Acronis True Image Echo
- Acronis True Image Home
- Symantec Backup Exec System Recovery
- Symantec LiveState Recovery
- Norton Ghost
- Parallels
- StorageCraft ShadowProtect Desktop
- StorageCraft ShadowProtect Server

- VMware Workstation
- VMware Fusion
- VMware Player
- vCenter Server
- ESX/ESXi
- Hyper-V

Exercise 6.14 will cover the steps to import a powered-off Hyper-V virtual machine into a vSphere environment using VMware Converter. Not all test environments will have a Hyper-V virtual machine. If you have any of the other supported sources, you may substitute them as necessary in this exercise or just follow along.

EXERCISE 6.14

Importing a Hyper-V VM Using VMware Converter

1. Open the VMware vCenter Converter Standalone application.

2. Click the Convert Machine button located in the upper-left corner of the screen, or use the File menu to choose New and Convert Machine.

3. A Conversion Wizard will launch. Using the drop-down menu, choose the Hyper-V Server option for Source Type.

4. Enter the FQDN of the Hyper-V Server in the Server field. Enter the appropriate credentials for this Hyper-V Server and click the Next button to continue.

5. Click the Next button, and you will be prompted to install the VMware vCenter Converter Standalone agent on the remote Hyper-V host. Choose the Automatically Uninstall The Files When Import Succeeds option and click the Yes button to continue.

6. The status of the agent deployment will be shown in the same window. When the agent is deployed, the Source Machine screen will be displayed.

7. Select a powered-off Hyper-V virtual machine from the list and click the Next button.

8. Using the drop-down menu, ensure that a destination type of VMware Infrastructure Virtual Machine is selected and enter the FQDN and credentials for the vCenter Server.

(continued)

EXERCISE 6.14 *(continued)*

9. Click the Next button. At the top of the Destination Virtual Machine screen, name the destination virtual machine. Choose an inventory location for this virtual machine and click the Next button to continue.

10. Now select the cluster or host that the virtual machine will be hosted on from the Inventory option in the middle of the screen. Use the drop-down menu to select a datastore and virtual machine hardware version. Click the Next button.

11. On the Options screen, make any changes necessary. This can include reducing the number of vCPUs, changing which disks are copied over, resizing the disks that are copied over, connecting and disconnecting networks, and more.

12. Click the Next button and review the information presented on the Summary screen. Click the Finish button to begin importing the Hyper-V source.

13. A task will be listed in the VMware Converter Standalone window that shows the source, destination, progress, and more.

14. Selecting the task will populate the Summary and Task Progress tabs at the bottom of the screen. These tabs provide more detail on the progress.

15. When this task completes, open the vSphere Client and locate the converted server in the inventory. Power it on and watch it boot from a console session.

Now that I have covered importing a virtual machine from Hyper-V Server into a vSphere environment, I will use VMware Converter to show how to modify the virtual hardware settings of a virtual machine.

Modifying Virtual Hardware Settings Using VMware Converter

So far, I have covered two ways to use VMware Converter. I showed how to perform a P2V and import a Hyper-V Server source. Another useful function that can be performed by VMware Converter is a V2V conversion within the vSphere environment. Using VMware Converter for a V2V operation is particularly useful in two situations:

- Shrinking disks
- Downgrading the virtual machine hardware version

Although virtual disks can be easily expanded, shrinking them is not as easily accomplished. Likewise, there is no mechanism in place to easily downgrade the virtual machine hardware version. A V2V operation can solve both of these problems.

Real World Scenario

Using VMware Converter for V2V Conversions

A virtual infrastructure administrator recently upgraded the virtual machine hardware version on a virtual machine in the production environment. Several days later an incident is reported by the owner of the application running on this virtual machine. The application owner reports that problems began immediately following the virtual machine hardware version upgrade.

The virtual infrastructure administrator decides to use VMware Converter to perform a V2V of the virtual machine. The V2V conversion will allow the virtual machine hardware version to be changed back to the prior version. The converted version of the application can then be loaded offline or on a test network to verify whether it functions correctly with the previous version of the virtual machine virtual hardware.

In Exercise 6.15, you will use VMware Converter to perform a V2V conversion on an existing powered-off virtual machine with virtual machine hardware version 8. You will convert this virtual machine to virtual machine hardware version 7, and you will also shrink the OS volume on this virtual machine in the process of the conversion.

EXERCISE 6.15

Performing a V2V Conversion to Modify Virtual Hardware Settings Using VMware Converter

1. Open the VMware vCenter Converter Standalone application.

2. Click the Convert Machine button located in the upper-left corner of the screen, or use the File menu to choose New and Convert Machine.

3. A Conversion Wizard will launch. Using the drop-down menu, choose the VMware Infrastructure Virtual Machine option for Source Type.

4. Enter the FQDN of the vCenter Server where the virtual machine that will be converted is located. Provide appropriate credentials for the vCenter Server and click the Next button.

5. Depending on how your environment is configured, a Converter Security Warning dialog may appear. If you trust this certificate, click the Ignore button to continue.

6. On the Source Machine screen, select the host, cluster, folder, or resource pool that the VM to be converted is located in. Once the VM is located in the right pane, select it by clicking it. Click the Next button.

7. On the Destination System screen, select the default destination type of VMware Infrastructure Virtual Machine. Enter the FQDN for the vCenter Server that this converted virtual machine will be managed by, and enter the appropriate credentials for the vCenter Server.

   The vCenter Server selected in step 7 can be the same vCenter Server that was specified in step 4 of this exercise, but it could also be another vCenter Server. The remainder of this exercise will assume that the same vCenter Server was chosen.

8. Click the Next button, and then you may be presented with another Converter Security Warning dialog. As in step 5, you can choose Ignore if you trust your environment.

9. At the top of the Destination Virtual Machine screen, name the new virtual machine. Choose an inventory location for the new virtual machine and click the Next button to continue.

   The V2V operation will create a copy of the source, so the destination VM will need to have a different name if the same vCenter Server is being used.

10. Now select the cluster or host that the virtual machine will be hosted on from the Inventory option in the middle of the screen, and use the drop-down menu to select an appropriate datastore. Change the virtual machine hardware version to Version 7 using the drop-down menu. The final configuration should look like the image shown here.

(continued)

EXERCISE 6.15 *(continued)*

Choosing virtual machine hardware version 7 in the previous step was one objective of this exercise. In the remaining steps, you will resize the C: source volume to achieve the other objective of shrinking a virtual disk.

11. Click the Next button.

12. On the Options screen, click the blue Edit link to the right of the Data To Copy item. Using the drop-down menu for Data Copy Type, change the value to Select Volumes To Copy. The screen will refresh to show a new set of options.

13. In the row where the C: source volume is listed, locate the Destination Size column. Using the drop-down menu here, review the current size and the minimum size values.

14. Decide on a new smaller size for the C: source volume and then pick the <Type Size In GB> option from the drop-down menu. The drop-down menu will now allow you to enter this value. Enter the number only and then press the Enter key on the keyboard. The drop-down menu will now update to reflect the value you just entered. The final configuration will look like this.

15. Review the information on the Summary screen and click the Finish button to begin the V2V conversion.

16. A task will be listed in the VMware Converter Standalone window that shows the source, destination, progress, and more.

17. Selecting the task will populate the Summary and Task Progress tabs at the bottom of the screen. These tabs provide more detail on the progress.

18. When this task completes, open the vSphere Client and locate the converted virtual machine in the inventory. Right-click it and choose the Edit Settings option from the context menu that appears.

19. Verify that the virtual machine hardware version has been downgraded and that the virtual disk has been resized.

I have now covered three ways to use VMware Converter in your vSphere environment. You can now move on to the next section of this chapter, which covers creating and deploying vApps.

Create and Deploy vApps

Besides virtual machines, vSphere can also be used as a platform for running applications. This is accomplished with vApp, which is a container that consists of one or more virtual machines. These virtual machines are treated as a group in the vApp, and properties such as start order and shutdown order can be configured for the group. In this section, I will discuss vApps and how to create and use them.

Determining When a Tiered Application Should Be Deployed as a vApp

By design, a tiered application is logically separated across multiple servers. An example three-tier application in vSphere might include a web frontend running on a virtual machine, a middleware application running on another virtual machine, and a database running in yet another virtual machine. The tiered architecture has certain dependencies, and this is true in both physical and virtual environments. For example, the web server must be able to communicate with the middleware application, which must be able to communicate with the database server. These dependencies are typically covered with documentation and operational procedures.

vApp is an approach that can be used to simplify the dependencies of tiered applications, particularly when all tiers of the application are virtual machines. vApps may have specified start orders for the virtual machines they contain. This allows a tiered application to be encapsulated and treated as a unit rather than its parts. For example, a vApp can be powered up as a unit.

🌐 Real World Scenario

Using vApps

A new project has been requested from the R&D department of a customer's business. They want to create an external web-based customer portal and have requested a set of virtual machines for this project. The list of servers includes a domain controller, a database server, an application server, and a web server. They want this environment to be self-contained and have no connectivity to any of the other networks in the company.

It is decided that a vApp will be used for this project. The virtual machines will be added to the vApp, and it will function as a unit. Start order will be used to ensure the environment is both powered up and shut down in the proper sequence. Using a vApp will simplify both administrative and operational overheads, by treating the entire set of virtual machines as an application.

Now that I have discussed when a tiered application should be deployed as a vApp, I will cover creating a vApp.

Creating a vApp

Before a vApp can be used, it has to be created. vCenter Server is a requirement to use vApps. A vApp can be created in the vCenter Server datacenter object from a DRS-enabled cluster with at least one host. This is shown in Figure 6.5 with vApp1. vApps can also be created on a stand-alone ESX 3.0 or newer host. This is shown in Figure 6.5 with vApp2.

FIGURE 6.5   vApp location options

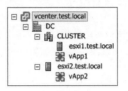

 If you plan to deploy a vApp on a DRS-enabled cluster, remember that DRS requires either the Enterprise or Enterprise Plus edition of vSphere.

Exercise 6.16 will cover the steps required to create a vApp.

EXERCISE 6.16

Creating a vApp Using the vSphere Web Client

1. Open a web browser and connect to the FQDN of the vCenter Server and then log in to the vSphere Web Client.

2. Expand the inventory objects in the left pane and find a valid parent object for the vApp. Right-click this object and choose the Inventory ➤ New vApp option from the context menu that appears. In the image shown here, the cluster object was used as the starting point.

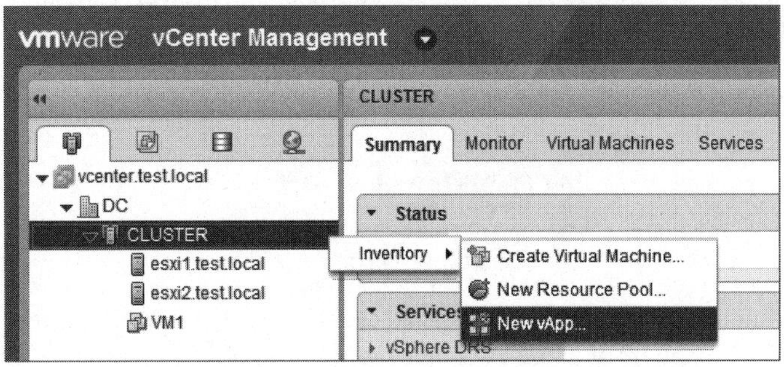

(continued)

EXERCISE 6.16 *(continued)*

3. A New vApp Wizard will launch. Give the vApp a unique name in the vApp Name field and select a datacenter or folder in which to deploy it. Click the Next button.

4. Configure the CPU and Memory Resources settings as necessary for your environment, or simply click the Next button to accept the default values.

5. Review the information on the Ready To Complete screen and click the Finish button.

6. After the vApp is created, verify that the vApp is listed in the left pane.

vApps can also be created with the vSphere Client.

You have now created a vApp. At this point, it isn't really useful, so you will next add objects (like tiered applications) to it.

Adding Objects to an Existing vApp

Objects that can be added to a vApp include virtual machines, resource pools, and other vApps. There are two options that can be used to add objects. To add new objects, using the vSphere Client, right-click the vApp and select one of the New options from the context menu. These options are shown in Figure 6.6.

FIGURE 6.6 Adding a new object to a vApp

The other option is to add existing objects to the vApp. This is easily accomplished in the vSphere Client or vSphere Web Client, by dragging the objects into the vApp. For example, dragging an existing virtual machine into a vApp will happen without any prompting as long as the move is allowed.

Objects can also be easily removed from a vApp by dragging them to a new location.

Using either the vSphere Client or the vSphere Web Client, take some time now and create at least one new virtual machine or add an existing virtual machine to the vApp created in Exercise 6.16. Once the vApp has been populated with objects, you will start identifying settings for the vApp.

Identifying and Editing vApp Settings

Now that you have created a vApp and added objects to it, you can identify and edit the vApp settings. Exercise 6.17 will cover identifying the various vApp settings and editing the start order options. The vSphere Client will be used for this exercise.

EXERCISE 6.17

Identifying vApp Settings

1. Connect to a vCenter Server with the vSphere Client.

2. Right-click a vApp in the left pane. Choose the Edit Settings option from the context menu that appears.

3. An Edit vApp Settings window will appear, as shown here.

(continued)

The Options tab's Resources setting is displayed by default. The Resources setting is used to specify CPU and memory resources for the vApp. Configuring these options is similar to configuring the options for a resource pool, which will be covered in Chapter 8.

4.   On the Options tab, click the Properties option in the left pane. This will display any properties that have been defined for the vApp.

5.   Click the IP Allocation Policy option in the left pane. This will display the IP allocation policy that the vApp uses. This option will be discussed later in this chapter.

6.   Click the Advanced option in the left pane. This will display any information that has been entered about the vApp. There are also two options at the lower part of this screen that can be used to assign advanced properties or the IP address allocation scheme that is used in the IP Allocation Policy option.

7.   Click the Start Order tab. This tab displays the order in which the virtual machines in this vApp will be both started and shut down.

Notice that in this image there are two groups. The first group, Group 1, contains a DNS server. No virtual machines in Group 2 will be powered on until the DNS server is first powered up. Then in Group 2, the database server will first be powered up. It will be followed by the application server and finally the web server.

8. Select a virtual machine in the left pane. In the Startup Action section on the right, select the VMware Tools Are Ready check box.

   This option will allow the subsequent virtual machines to start up sooner than the 120-second delay if the VMware Tools start sooner. The VMware Tools starting is generally a good sign that the VM is up and running.

9. In the Shutdown Action section on the right, use the drop-down menu to change the default Operation to Guest Shutdown. When this change has been made, the Shutdown Sequence timer becomes enabled.

   These changes can be made or customized for each virtual machine in the list. This allows finer control over how the vApp starts up.

10. Now click the vServices tab and note that there are no dependencies defined.

    vServices are used to provide access to a service across a network, and a vService Dependency can be used to make a VM or vApp dependent on a vService before starting.

11. Click the OK button on the Edit vApp Settings window to save the changes made to the Start Order in steps 8–9.

12. An Update vApp Configuration task will begin.

I have now covered identifying the various vApp settings and editing the Start Order Startup and Shutdown actions. In the next section, I will cover configuring IP pools for a vApp.

Configuring IP Pools

An IP pool is a network configuration stored in vCenter. The IP pool is associated with one or more virtual machine port groups and can be used to provide IP addresses to virtual machines in a vApp.

 An IP pool does not provide the same functionality as a DHCP server. Leveraging IP pools for addressing requires some type of support inside the guest OS of the VMs that make up the vApp.

Exercise 6.18 will cover the steps required to configure an IP pool and set up a vApp to use it.

EXERCISE 6.18

Configuring an IP Pool and vApp

1. Connect to a vCenter Server with the vSphere Client.

2. Select the Hosts and Clusters view and select the datacenter that contains the vApp. In the right pane, click the IP Pools tab.

3. Click the blue Add link at the top of the IP Pools tab. A New IP Pool Properties window will appear.

4. Enter a value for the IP Pool Name, at the top of the IP Pool Properties window.

5. Using either the IPv4 or IPv6 tab, enter the appropriate subnet and gateway information. Select the Enable IP Pool box and then enter the ranges. An example of the setup for IPv4 is shown here.

Note that the range is a starting IP address, a number sign (#), and a number that represents the value of the range. In the previous image, the range starts at 172.16.0.2 and includes the next 253 addresses. The gateway and broadcast address are always excluded from the range.

6. You can also click the blue View link at the end of the Ranges text box to view the addresses that would be available in the range.

7. Click the DHCP tab. Select the IPv4 DHCP Present box. This option will be discussed in more detail later in this exercise.

8. Click the DNS tab. Populate these fields as appropriate for your environment.

9. Click the Proxy tab. Enter the server name and port number for an HTTP proxy server, if your environment has one.

10. Click the Associations tab. Select at least one of the virtual machine port groups listed here. Click the OK button to save the IP Pool.

11. The IP Pool will now be listed in the IP Pools list in the left pane, and its details appear in the right pane.

| Summary | Virtual Machines | Hosts | IP Pools | Performance | Tasks & Events | Alarms |

IP Pools: Remove   Add...   **Details:**

Pool172

IPv4 Configuration
Subnet:	172.16.0.0
Netmask:	255.255.255.0
Gateway:	172.16.0.1
IP Pool:	Enabled
	172.16.0.2#253
DHCP Present:	Yes
DNS Servers:	172.16.0.1

IPv6 Configuration
Subnet:	Not Configured
Netmask:	ffff:ffff:ffff:ffff:ffff:ffff::
Gateway:	Not Configured
IP Pool:	Disabled
DHCP Present:	No
DNS Servers:	Not Configured

Other Network Properties
DNS Domain:	test.local
Host Prefix:	Not Configured
DNS Search Path:	test.local
HTTP Proxy:	Not Configured
Associated Networks:	Internal VM Network

At this point the IP pool has been created and is ready to be used. The remainder of this exercise will show how to associate the vApp with this IP pool.

12. Locate the vApp in the left pane and expand its contents. Verify that each VM is connected to a virtual machine port group that you associated the IP pool with in step 10.

13. Select the vApp and right-click it. Choose the Edit Settings option from the context menu that appears. An Edit vApp Settings window will appear.

14. On the Options tab, select Advanced from the left pane. Click the IP Allocation button in the bottom-right corner. An Advanced IP Allocation window will appear.

15. Select the OVF Environment box. Use the drop-down menu in the IP Protocol section to select one of the three options of IPv4, IPv6, or Both.

(continued)

In the Advanced IP Allocation window, the DHCP option could have also been selected. Selecting this option would allow the vApp to use the DHCP Server entered on the DHCP tab of the IP Pool configuration from step 7 of this exercise. This exercise covers IP pools, so you will use only the OVF Environment option.

16. Click the OK button on the Advanced IP Allocation window to save these changes.

17. In the Edit vApp Settings window, select the IP Allocation Policy option in the left pane. Select the Transient IP Allocation policy.

Note that the DHCP option is grayed out. If the DHCP option had been selected in step 15 of this exercise, then the DHCP option would be available as an option in this screen. Again, this configuration would be used to utilize DHCP and not an IP pool.

18. Click the OK button to save the changes. An Update vApp task will begin. When this task completes, configuration of the IP pool and the vApp is complete.

Before I leave IP pools behind, I will review the IP allocation policies for a vApp. The three available policies are as follows:

Fixed   This policy is used when the virtual machines in the vApp are configured with static IP addresses.

Transient   This policy is used when the virtual machines in the vApp are configured to use IP pools.

DHCP   This policy is used when the virtual machines in the vApp are configured to use a DHCP server to acquire IP addresses.

Now that I have covered IP pools, I will discuss suspending and resuming a vApp.

Suspending and Resuming a vApp

Like virtual machines, vApps can also be suspended and resumed. To suspend a vApp, using the vSphere Client, right-click the vApp and choose the Suspend option from the context menu that appears. You will then be prompted to confirm suspension of the vApp. Virtual machines are suspended based on the reverse start order, and this order can be confirmed by viewing the tasks listed in the Recent Tasks pane in the vSphere Client. Figure 6.7 shows the suspend option in the vSphere Client.

FIGURE 6.7   Suspending a vApp with the vSphere Client

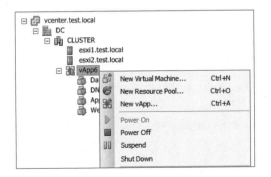

To resume a vApp, using the vSphere Client, right-click the vApp and choose the Power On option from the context menu that appears. Virtual machines will be resumed as specified in the start order, and this order can be confirmed by viewing the tasks listed in the Recent Tasks pane in the vSphere Client. Figure 6.8 shows the Power On option in the vSphere Client.

FIGURE 6.8   Resuming a vApp with the vSphere Client

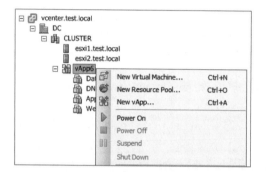

I have now covered suspending and resuming a vApp; next I will cover cloning and exporting a vApp.

Cloning and Exporting a vApp

vApps can be cloned and exported, just as virtual machines can. Exercise 6.19 will cover the steps required to clone a vApp using the vSphere Client.

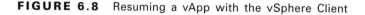

EXERCISE 6.19

Cloning a vApp Using the vSphere Client

1. Connect to a vCenter Server with the vSphere Client.

2. Right-click the vApp in the left pane. Choose the Clone option from the context menu that appears.

3. The Clone vApp Wizard will launch. Select a destination host, cluster, or resource pool for the cloned vApp and click the Next button.

4. Provide the cloned vApp with a unique name and select an inventory location for it. Click the Next button.

5. Select a datastore for the cloned vApp and click the Next button.

6. Select the appropriate disk format and click the Next button.

7. Review the information presented on the Ready To Complete screen and click the Finish button to begin the vApp clone.

8. A Clone vApp task will begin. When this task completes, verify that the cloned vApp is listed in the inventory.

You have now cloned a vApp. Cloning vApps is useful in instances where a copy of a vApp is needed, perhaps for a new test or development environment.

Exporting a vApp is often useful in the same instances that cloning a vApp is useful, but exported vApps can also be imported on different systems in different locations. Exercise 6.20 will cover the steps required to export a vApp.

EXERCISE 6.20

Exporting a vApp Using the vSphere Client

1. Connect to a vCenter Server with the vSphere Client.

2. Locate the vApp in the left pane and select it. Use the File menu in the vSphere Client to choose the Export option and then choose the Export OVF Template option.

3. The Export OVF Template window will appear.

4. Provide a descriptive name for the OVF template. This will be the name of the file, used in the directory in the next field.

5. Choose a directory with adequate free space to hold the OVF template. The directory chosen here is where the OVF template will be saved to on the same system that the vSphere Client is being run from.

6. Using the drop-down menu, choose the Single File (OVA) format option.

    Two options are available here:

    Folder Of Files (OVF) This option is used to package the OVF template as a set of files (.ovf, .vmdk, and .mf).

    Single File (OVA) This option is used to package the OVF template into a single .ova file.

7. Provide a description for the OVF template.

    If any virtual machines in the vApp are connected to an ISO file or floppy image, there will be an option allowing you to include these image files as part of the OVF template.

8. If applicable, choose whether to include image files.

(continued)

EXERCISE 6.20 *(continued)*

9. The final configuration should look similar to the image shown here.

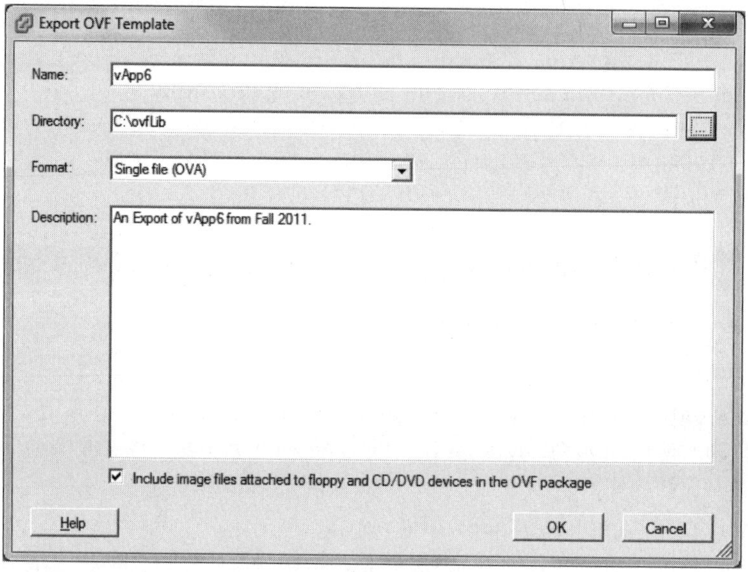

10. Click the OK button. An Export OVF Template task will begin, and a dialog box will appear that provides the progress of the export operation.
11. When this task completes, verify that the vApp was exported to the location you selected on the local file system.

Now that you have cloned and exported a vApp, this chapter is complete. In the next chapter, you will continue to work with virtual machines.

Summary

This chapter covered creating and deploying virtual machines. Knowing how to create and deploy virtual machines is absolutely essential for any virtual infrastructure administrator. In this chapter, I covered identifying the capabilities of the different virtual machine hardware versions and configuring and deploying a virtual machine. How to place VMs in selected ESXi hosts, resource pools, and clusters was covered. I also discussed the various methods that can be used to access and use a virtual machine console. Installing, upgrading, and updating the VMware Tools and the VMware Tools device drivers were covered. I covered configuring virtual machine time synchronization and identifying virtual machine storage resources. I configured disk controllers for virtual disks, appropriate virtual disk types, and disk shares and discussed creating and converting thin and thick provisioned virtual disks. I covered determining appropriate datastore locations for virtual machines based on application workloads. I also covered configuring and modifying vCPU and memory resources according to OS and application requirements. Configuring and modifying virtual NIC adapters and connecting VMs to appropriate network resources were also covered. The first part of this chapter concluded with using VMware Converter to perform a P2V conversion, import a Hyper-V virtual machine, and perform a V2V to modify virtual hardware settings.

The final part of this chapter focused on creating and deploying vApps. Determining when a tiered application should be deployed as a vApp was discussed. I covered creating a vApp and adding objects to an existing vApp. I also covered identifying and editing the settings of a vApp. I configured an IP pool for the vApp and covered suspending and resuming a vApp. I concluded this chapter by covering how to clone and export a vApp.

Exam Essentials

Know how to create and deploy virtual machines.   Be able to identify the capabilities of virtual machine hardware versions. Know how to configure and deploy a guest OS into a new virtual machine and how to place the VM in ESXi hosts, clusters, and resource pools. Be able to identify the methods used to access virtual machine consoles. Know how to install, upgrade, and update the VMware Tools and be able to identify the different VMware Tools device drivers. Be able to configure virtual machine time synchronization and identify virtual machine storage resources. Know how to configure and modify disk controllers, virtual disk types, and disk shares. Understand how to create and convert thin provisioned virtual disks. Be able to determine appropriate datastore locations for virtual machines based on application workloads. Know how to configure and modify vCPU and memory resources according to OS and application requirements. Understand how to configure and modify virtual NIC adapters and connect virtual machines to the appropriate network resources. Understand the P2V process using VMware Converter. Know how to import a supported VM source using VMware Converter, and know how to perform a V2V with VMware Converter to modify virtual hardware settings.

Know how to create and deploy vApps.   Be able to determine when a tiered application should be deployed as a vApp. Know how to create a vApp and add objects to it. Be able to identify and edit vApp settings. Understand how to configure and use IP pools. Know how to suspend and resume a vApp, in addition to how to clone and export a vApp.

Review Questions

1. You updated the virtual machine hardware version for a virtual machine from version 7 to version 8. Several days later an application on this virtual machine is being reported as no longer working. You need to return the virtual machine back to the previous virtual hardware version. How do you do this?

    A. Use the vSphere Client to change the version.

    B. Use the vSphere Web Client to change the version.

    C. Use VMware Converter to change the version.

    D. None of these is correct.

2. Which of the following methods can be used to configure and deploy a new virtual machine? (Choose all that apply.)

    A. vMA

    B. vSphere Client

    C. vSphere Web Client

    D. vApp

3. You have a virtual machine with a single 20GB thin disk with 40 percent free space. The virtual machine needs to have a SAN-aware application installed that will consume 100MB of additional disk space. What type of disk should you add to this virtual machine?

    A. Physical Compatibility Mode RDM.

    B. Virtual Compatibility Mode RDM.

    C. No disk needs to be added.

    D. None of these is correct.

4. Which of the following are VMware device drivers loaded by the VMware Tools? (Choose all that apply.)

    A. Mouse

    B. VMCI

    C. VMXNet

    D. Memory Control

5. Which editions of vSphere include the VMware vCenter Converter plug-in? (Choose all that apply.)

    A. Essentials

    B. Enterprise

    C. Enterprise Plus

    D. None of these

6. Which of the following can be used to clone a vApp?

    A. VMware Converter

    B. vSphere Client

    C. vSphere Web Client

    D. vMA

7. Which type of SCSI bus sharing allows virtual disks to be shared by virtual machines located on the same ESXi host?

    A. None

    B. Local

    C. Physical

    D. Virtual

8. Which of the following DHCP servers can be specified in the IP pools of a vApp?

    A. Either IPv4 or IPv6 DHCP servers

    B. Both IPv4 and IPv6 DHCP servers

    C. Only IPv4 DHCP servers

    D. Only IPv6 DHCP servers

9. Which of the following NICs are paravirtualized?

    A. vlance

    B. VMXNET

    C. VMXNET 2

    D. VMXNET 3

10. Which of the following objects may be added to an existing vApp? (Choose all that apply.)

    A. Virtual machines

    B. Resource pools

    C. vApps

    D. Folders

11. Which of the following statements are correct about the VMware Tools? (Choose two.)

    A. The VMware Tools are required for virtual machines.

    B. The VMware Tools are required only for advanced functionality in virtual machines.

    C. An automatic VMware Tools upgrade can reboot the guest OS without prompting.

    D. An interactive VMware Tools upgrade can reboot the guest OS without prompting.

12. Which of the following statements are true about the start order for the virtual machines in a vApp? (Choose two.)

    A. Each group is started at the same time, and virtual machines in the groups are started in the order listed.

    B. Each virtual machine in the same group is started in the order listed, before the next group begins.

    C. Shutdown is performed in reverse order of the start order.

    D. Shutdown is performed as a simultaneous operation against all virtual machines in the vApp.

13. Which disk mode results in a disk that loses all changes at virtual machine power-off or reset?

    A. Independent Persistent

    B. Dependent Persistent

    C. Independent Nonpersistent

    D. Dependent Nonpersistent

14. You want to use VMware Converter to import a Hyper-V hosted virtual machine into your vSphere 5 environment. Which of the following is the correct way to perform this operation?

    A. Run VMware Converter with the Hyper-V virtual machine running.

    B. Power off the Hyper-V virtual machine and run VMware Converter.

    C. Power off the Hyper-V virtual machine and copy its files to the system where VMware Converter is installed. Then import the Hyper-V VM locally.

    D. Use the vSphere Client with the VMware vCenter Converter plug-in to import the Hyper-V virtual machine.

15. You plan to deploy a vApp on a DRS-enabled cluster. Which editions of vSphere will you be able to accomplish this with? (Choose all that apply.)

    A. Essentials Plus

    B. Standard

    C. Enterprise

    D. Enterprise Plus

16. Which of the following are capabilities of virtual machine hardware version 8? (Choose two.)

    A. 32 vCPU

    B. 64 vCPU

    C. 512GB RAM

    D. 1TB RAM

17. What are the three options available for choosing the location used to store the virtual disk files? (Choose three.)

    A. With the virtual machine

    B. In a datastore different from the virtual machine

    C. In a datastore cluster

    D. In a resource pool

18. Which of the following methods can be used to convert a thin disk to a thick disk? (Choose all that apply.)

    A. The Datastore Browser Inflate option

    B. Storage vMotion

    C. VMware Converter

    D. vmkfstools

19. Which of the following options can be used to disable periodic time synchronization? (Choose two.)

    A. `VmwareToolboxCmd.exe`

    B. `vmware-toolbox-cmd`

    C. vSphere Client

    D. vSphere Web Client

20. Which of the following methods can be used to obtain virtual machine console access? (Choose all that apply.)

    A. vSphere Client

    B. vSphere Web Client

    C. ESXi Shell

    D. VMware Converter

Chapter

7

Manage and Administer Virtual Machines and vApps

VCP5 EXAM OBJECTIVES COVERED IN THIS CHAPTER:

✓ **Manage Virtual Machine Clones and Templates**

- Identify Cloning and Template options

- Clone an existing virtual machine

- Create a template from an existing virtual machine

- Deploy a virtual machine from a template

- Update existing virtual machine templates

- Deploy virtual appliances and/or vApps from an OVF template

- Import and/or Export an OVF template

- Determine the appropriate deployment methodology for a given virtual machine application

- Identify the vCenter Server managed ESXi hosts and Virtual Machine maximums

✓ **Administer Virtual Machines and vApps**

- Identify files used by virtual machines

- Identify locations for virtual machine configuration files and virtual disks

- Configure virtual machine options

- Configure virtual machine power settings

- Configure virtual machine boot options

- Configure virtual machine troubleshooting options

- Identify common practices for securing virtual machines

- Determine when an advanced virtual machine parameter is required

- Hot Extend a virtual disk

- Adjust virtual machine resources (shares, limits and reservations) based on virtual machine workloads

- Assign a Storage Policy to a virtual machine

- Verify Storage Policy compliance for virtual machines

This chapter will cover the objectives of sections 4.3 and 4.4 of the VCP5 exam blueprint. This chapter will focus on managing and administering virtual machines and vApps.

This chapter will first cover identifying the cloning and template options, and you will learn how to clone an existing virtual machine. The chapter will also cover how to create a template from an existing VM and how to deploy a VM from a template. Updating existing templates will also be covered. The chapter will cover how to deploy virtual appliances and vApps from an OVF template. How to import an OVF template will also be covered. Determining the appropriate deployment methodology for a given virtual machine application will be covered. The first section of this chapter will end with covering the configuration maximums for ESXi hosts and virtual machines.

In the final section of this chapter, I will identify the files used by virtual machines and the locations for VM configuration files and virtual disks. I will cover configuring virtual machine options, power settings, boot options, and troubleshooting options. I will identify common practices for securing VMs and cover how to determine when an advanced VM parameter is required. The steps to hot extend a virtual disk will be explained. How to adjust a virtual machine's resources based on workload will also be covered. The chapter will end with assigning a storage policy to a virtual machine and verifying VM storage policy compliance.

Managing Virtual Machine Clones and Templates

Virtual infrastructure administrators can use clones and templates to both save time and ensure consistency of deployed virtual machines. Knowing how to manage virtual machine clones and templates is an essential task for any virtual infrastructure administrator. The first topic I will cover in this chapter is identifying cloning and template options.

Identifying Cloning and Template Options

Cloning in vCenter Server is the process of creating an exact copy of a virtual machine, including the virtual hardware and the guest OS. A clone can be taken of a powered-on or powered-off virtual machine. Clones are often useful for testing purposes. For example, a production server could be cloned while online, and then the clone could be used in a test environment. The cloned virtual machine is its own virtual machine and in no way depends on the original.

A virtual machine can also be converted to a template in vCenter Server, and once converted, the templates cannot be powered on or have their configurations changed. Templates can be used in vCenter Server to provide simplified provisioning of virtual machines. A typical use for templates is to set up a master image of a frequently deployed server operating system, for example Windows Server 2008 R2. This virtual machine can be modified to form a standard build for your environment, and then all future Windows Server 2008 R2 servers can be deployed from this virtual machine template. An additional feature of deployment from a template is the ability to customize the guest operating system. Using templates both simplifies builds and nearly eliminates mistakes in the process.

Many different options can be specified during either a clone operation or when deploying from a template:

- You can select a datacenter.
- You can select a cluster or an ESXi host.
- You can select a resource pool.
- You can select a virtual disk format.
- You can select a datastore.
- You can select a storage profile.
- You can select whether to disable Storage DRS.
- You can select whether to *customize the guest OS*.
- You can select whether to power on the VM after creation.

Both vCenter Server and the vSphere Client are required to use cloning and templates.

Now that I have identified cloning and template options, I will cover each in more detail. First I will cover cloning an existing virtual machine.

Cloning an Existing Virtual Machine

In Exercise 7.1, you will use the vSphere Client to clone an existing Windows Server 2008 R2 virtual machine. For the purpose of the exercise, I will assume that this Windows Server 2008 R2 virtual machine is your master image that is used for deploying new virtual machines.

EXERCISE 7.1

Cloning an Existing Virtual Machine

1. Connect to a vCenter Server with the vSphere Client.

2. Locate the virtual machine and right-click it. Select the Clone option from the context menu that appears. The Clone Virtual Machine Wizard will launch.

3. Provide the new virtual machine with a unique name and choose an inventory location. Click Next.

4. Choose the host or cluster that will be used to run the virtual machine. Review any issues reported in the Compatibility window before proceeding. Click Next.

5. If your environment has resource pools, pick a resource pool. Click Next.

6.   Using the drop-down menu, select a virtual disk format for the cloned virtual machine. By default, the selection is Same Format As Source. Choose a datastore to store the virtual machine on. Click Next.

7.   On the Guest Customization screen, leave the Power On This Virtual Machine After Creation option unchecked. This will give you the chance to review and modify the virtual hardware settings after the clone completes.

8.   Select the Customize Using The Customization Wizard option and click Next.

Choosing the Do Not Customize option would clone the virtual machine, creating an exact replica of it. The Customize Using An Existing Customization Specification option could be used, if there were an existing customization specification available. The option chosen in step 8, Customize Using The Customization Wizard, will allow you to both customize the virtual machine and create a customization specification. You will use the customization specification you create in this exercise later in this chapter.

The vSphere Client Windows Guest Customization window will appear.

9.   Fill in the Name and Organization fields and click Next.

10.   Provide a NetBIOS computer name for the guest OS to use. You can also utilize the Use The Virtual Machine Name option here, if you want the computer name and the virtual machine names to match. Click Next to continue.

(continued)

EXERCISE 7.1 *(continued)*

11. Enter the Windows Product Key and choose the appropriate options for the Server License Mode. Click Next to continue.

12. Provide the password for the local Windows Administrator account and confirm it. Click Next to continue.

13. Select the time zone and click Next.

14. Click Next on the Run Once screen.

15. Choose the Typical Settings option for networking and click Next to continue.

16. Fill in the Windows Server Domain or Workgroup fields appropriate for your environment. If you choose to add the guest OS on this virtual machine to the domain, you will need to provide a username and password of a user with authority to join machines to the domain. Click Next.

17. Unless you have a very specific reason not to, leave the Generate New Security ID (SID) option checked and click Next to continue.

18. Ensure that the Save This Customization Specification For Later Use box is selected. Give the customization specification a unique name and a description. The final configuration should look like this.

19. Click Next and review the information presented on the Ready To Complete Screen.

20. Click Finish to save the customization specification information.

21. On the Clone Virtual Machine screen, review the information presented on the Ready To Complete screen.

Note the Edit Virtual Hardware (Experimental) option on the Ready To Complete screen. Experimental options are those that may find their way into future versions of the product, but there is no guaranteed support from VMware for them. It is not recommended that you use experimental features on production systems.

22. Click Finish to begin the clone process.

23. A Clone Virtual Machine task will begin. When this task completes, locate the new virtual machine in the inventory. Right-click it and choose the Edit Settings option from the context menu. Verify the settings and power it on, if you want.

24. On the vSphere navigation bar at the top of the screen, click the Home icon. Under the Management section, click the Customization Specifications Manager icon.

25. The customization specification you saved in step 20 is listed here and should look like this.

Name	Guest OS	Description	Date Saved	
Win2008R2-Base	Windows	Base Windows 2008 R2 Image	10/23/2011 4:05:03 PM	

26. Right-click the customization specification and choose the Edit option from the context menu that appears, if you ever need to make changes to it.

You can also schedule clone operations using the Scheduled Tasks feature in vCenter Server.

I just covered cloning a virtual machine and how to use the customization specifications included in vCenter Server. In the following section, I will cover creating a template from an existing virtual machine.

Creating a Template from an Existing Virtual Machine

In the previous exercise, you cloned a master virtual machine in order to deploy a new virtual machine from it. This process works and is acceptable, but what if another administrator were to power on the master image and make changes to it? One solution to the problem of keeping master images from being modified is to convert these virtual machines to templates.

Once a virtual machine is converted to a template, it cannot be powered on in vCenter Server. When a virtual machine is converted to a template, the .vmx file extension changes to .vmtx. The .vmtx file extension designates a template VM. This is shown in Figure 7.1.

FIGURE 7.1 Template VM in Datastore Browser

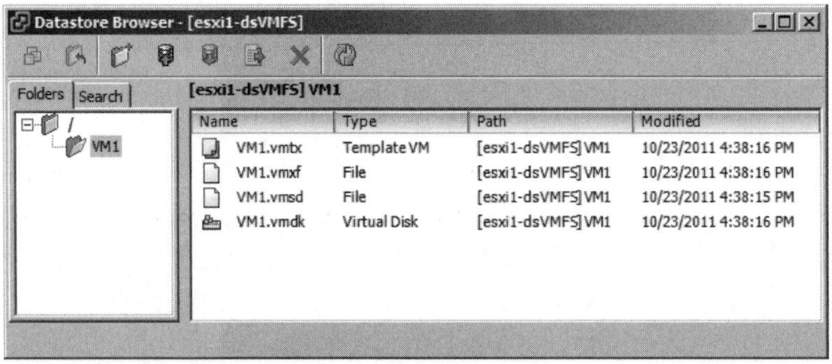

Templates are also not visible in the Hosts and Clusters view in the vSphere Client. Converting virtual machines to templates is a simple process in vCenter Server. In Exercise 7.2, you will create a template from an existing virtual machine. For the purpose of the exercise, I will assume that the same Windows Server 2008 R2 virtual machine from Exercise 7.1 will be used as your master image.

EXERCISE 7.2

Creating a Template from an Existing VM

1. Connect to a vCenter Server with the vSphere Client.

2. Select Hosts And Clusters.

3. Locate the powered-off virtual machine in the left pane. Take note of which ESXi host it is located on. Right-click the virtual machine and select Template ➢ Convert To Template.

4. A Mark Virtual Machine As Template task will begin. When this task completes, the virtual machine will disappear from the Hosts and Clusters view.

5. Select the ESXi host that the virtual machine was located on. Click the Virtual Machines tab. Locate the template in the list. It will now have a template icon, which should make it easier to identify.

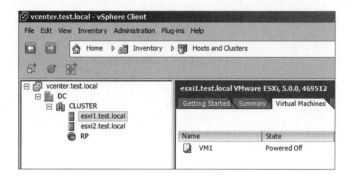

6. In the navigation bar at the top of the screen, click the Home icon and then click the VMs And Templates icon located in the Inventory list.

7. Locate the template.

The template is now ready to use. In the next section, you will learn how to deploy a virtual machine from the template you just created.

Deploying a Virtual Machine from a Template

The process of deploying a virtual machine from a template is very similar to the process of cloning a virtual machine. In Exercise 7.3, you will deploy a virtual machine from the template created in Exercise 7.2.

EXERCISE 7.3

Deploying a VM from a Template

1. Connect to a vCenter Server with the vSphere Client.

2. Locate the template created in Exercise 7.2, using the Virtual Machines tab for a selected ESXi host or the VMs And Templates option from the inventory.

3. Right-click the template and review the options that appear in the context menu.

(continued)

EXERCISE 7.3 *(continued)*

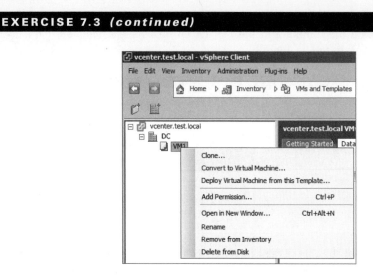

Note that the available operations for templates include cloning, adding permissions, renaming, removing from the inventory, and deleting.

4. Choose the Deploy Virtual Machine From This Template option. The Deploy Template Wizard will launch.

5. Provide the new virtual machine with a unique name and choose an inventory location. Click Next to continue.

6. Choose the host or cluster that will be used to host the virtual machine. Review any issues reported in the Compatibility window before proceeding. Click Next to continue.

7. If your environment has resource pools, pick a resource pool. Click Next to continue.

8. Using the drop-down menu, select a virtual disk format for the virtual machine. By default, the selection is Same Format As Source. Choose a datastore to store the virtual machine on. Click Next.

9. On the Guest Customization screen, leave the Power On This Virtual Machine After Creation option unchecked. This will give you the chance to review and modify the virtual hardware settings after the virtual machine is deployed.

10. Select the Customize Using An Existing Customization Specification option. A Customization Specification Manager window will appear on the bottom of the screen.

11. Select the customization specification created in Exercise 7.1 by clicking it. Note there is also an option presented to allow the customization specification to be adjusted, but leave this option unchecked for now.

12. Click Next and then review the information presented on the Ready To Complete screen.

13. Click Finish to begin deploying the new virtual machine from a template.

14. A Clone Virtual Machine task will begin. When it completes, locate the new virtual machine in the inventory.

I just covered deploying a virtual machine from a template. In the next section, I will cover how to update templates.

Updating Existing Virtual Machine Templates

After a virtual machine is converted to a template, it is not able to be powered on. Although this provides a degree of protection for the master virtual machine image, over time this template will certainly become stale. Build guides may change, vendor-supplied updates will likely need to be applied, and any number of changes will need to happen to get the master virtual machine image compliant with the current standards.

To address these issues, a template can simply be converted back to a virtual machine. Once the template is converted to a virtual machine, it is able to be powered on and updated as necessary. Exercise 7.4 will cover the steps required to convert a template to a virtual machine so that it can be updated.

EXERCISE 7.4

Updating Virtual Machine Templates

1. Connect to a vCenter Server with the vSphere Client.

2. Locate the template created in Exercise 7.2, using the Virtual Machines tab for a selected ESXi host or the VMs And Templates option from the inventory.

3. Right-click the template and choose the Convert To Virtual Machine option that appears in the context menu.

4. The Convert Template to Virtual Machine Wizard will begin.

5. Choose the host or cluster that will be used to host the virtual machine. Review any issues reported in the Compatibility window before proceeding. Click Next to continue.

6. If your environment has resource pools, pick a resource pool. Click Next to continue.

7. Review the information presented on the Ready To Complete screen and click Finish to convert the template to a virtual machine.

8. A Mark As Virtual Machine task will begin. When this task completes, locate the virtual machine in the inventory.

At this point, the template is no more. Browsing the datastore would reveal that the .vmtx file has been replaced with a .vmx file. The virtual machine is now visible again in the Hosts and Clusters view. Because you are now working with a virtual machine, its configuration can be edited. The virtual machine can also be powered on, and updates can be applied to the guest OS. When all of these changes have been made, the virtual machine can be powered off and again converted to a template.

You have now learned how to update templates. In the next section, I will discuss how to deploy virtual appliances and vApps from an OVF template.

Deploying Virtual Appliances and vApps from an OVF Template

Virtual appliances are preconfigured and ready-to-use virtual machines that include an operating system and/or applications. VMware provides a virtual appliance marketplace at www.vmware.com/appliances where virtual appliances can be downloaded. Virtual appliances offer convenience and portability and are often optimized for virtual infrastructures.

⊕ **Real World Scenario**

Virtual Appliances

A virtual infrastructure administrator has learned that his company has just acquired another company. As part of this acquisition, his company will become responsible for more than 100 virtual machines, including 10 virtual machines with Ubuntu desktop running as the guest OS. The virtual infrastructure administrator is some-what apprehensive about this, because he has no experience with Linux. He decides to get an early jump on learning how Ubuntu works and plans to build a virtual machine that will run the Ubuntu guest operating system.

The virtual infrastructure administrator downloads the Ubuntu installation media, and when it completes, he creates a new virtual machine. He boots the virtual machine to the installation media and gets through the basic installation. Next he spends several hours configuring the operating system and getting the VMware Tools installed. At the end of the day, he tells a co-worker about his Ubuntu experience and how long it took to get everything working. The co-worker asks him why he didn't just use a virtual appliance instead.

The virtual infrastructure administrator had never heard of virtual appliances and was surprised to hear that he could have downloaded a prebuilt virtual machine with the Ubuntu guest OS and VMware Tools already installed. Using a virtual appliance would have allowed the entire project to be completed in a fraction of the time.

Virtual appliances may sound similar to an exported vApp, which was covered in Exercise 6.20, and that is because they are. vApps are built on an industry-standard format, the Open Virtualization Format (OVF). This is the same format used for the vast majority of the virtual appliances in the VMware virtual appliance marketplace.

Deploying a virtual appliance is a simple task. If you think back to the very first exercise in this book, then you may recall that you have already deployed a virtual appliance. In Exercise 2.1, you deployed the vCenter Server Appliance. The vCenter Server Appliance was packaged in the "folder of files" format, where the OVF template consisted of a set of files.

If you don't recall Exercise 2.1, don't go back there just yet. In the next section, I will cover importing OVF templates, and the procedure is exactly the same as deploying virtual appliances.

Importing and Exporting an OVF Template

In Exercise 6.20 from Chapter 6, you exported an OVF template for a vApp. There is no import function in the vSphere Client, and an exported OVF template is simply imported using the Deploy OVF Template function in the vSphere Client.

There is no difference in the operation of deploying a virtual appliance and importing an exported vApp. Both are OVF templates, and both are imported into the vSphere environment by using the Deploy OVF Template function in the vSphere Client.

In Exercise 7.5, you will import the OVF template you created in Exercise 6.20.

EXERCISE 7.5

Importing an OVF Template

1.   Connect to a vCenter Server with the vSphere Client.

2.   Use the File menu and choose the Deploy OVF Template option.

3.   The Deploy OVF Template Wizard will launch. Browse to the location of the exported vApp from Exercise 6.20 and choose the OVA file. Once the OVA file has been selected, it will appear in the Deploy From A File Or URL field. Click Next to continue.

4.   Verify the OVF template details for accuracy and click Next to continue.

5.   Specify a name and location for the deployed template. This name will be the name of the deployed VM. Click Next to continue.

6.   Select a host or cluster to run the virtual machine. Click Next to continue.

7.   If you have resource pools configured in your environment, choose a resource pool. Click Next to continue.

8.   Choose a datastore to store the vApp. Click Next to continue.

9.   Choose the Thin Provision option and click Next to continue.

10. Choose the appropriate network for the vApp and click Next to continue.

11. Review the information presented on the Ready To Complete screen and click Finish to begin deploying the vApp.

12. A Deploy OVF Template task will begin, and a progress window will appear. Verify that the task completes in the vSphere Client and then locate the vApp in the inventory.

I have now covered using the Deploy OVF Template Wizard to import a vApp. I will next discuss how to determine the appropriate deployment methodology for a given VM application.

Determining the Appropriate Deployment Methodology for a Given Virtual Machine Application

Determining the appropriate deployment methodology for the virtual machines in your environment will be determined by a variety of factors. Another phrase that can be used to describe the deployment methodology is *virtual machine provisioning.* Table 7.1 covers the provisioning methods and use cases.

TABLE 7.1   Deployment methodology for VMs

Provisioning	Use cases
On-demand	One-off deployments Small environments with few VMs Specific configurations used for testing Initially creating a VM to be used as a template
Clones	Making copies for testing Avoiding repetition of tasks
Templates	Deploying multiple consistent images from a protected virtual machine
OVF/virtual appliances	Using preconfigured virtual machines or vApps Creating portable/packaged applications

Now that I have covered determining the appropriate deployment methodology for a given virtual machine application, I will move on to identifying the vCenter Server–managed ESXi and virtual machine configuration maximums.

Identifying the vCenter Server–Managed ESXi Hosts and Virtual Machine Maximums

Knowing the configuration maximums is an important part of working in a vSphere environment. The configuration maximums are used to determine the maximum supported values for a variety of different components in the ESXi hosts and the virtual machines. Table 7.2 lists some of the ESXi and virtual machine configuration maximums.

TABLE 7.2   ESXi host configuration maximums

Item	Maximum
Logical CPUs per ESXi host	160
vCPUs per ESXi host	2,048
RAM per ESXi host	2TB

TABLE 7.2   ESXi host configuration maximums *(continued)*

Item	Maximum
Virtual disks per ESXi host	2,048
iSCSI LUNs per ESXi host	256
Fibre Channel LUNs per ESXi host	256
NFS mounts per ESXi host	256
VMFS volumes per ESXi host	256
e1000 1Gb Ethernet ports (Intel PCI-x) per ESXi host	32
e1000e 1Gb Ethernet ports (Intel PCI-e) per ESXi host	24
Combination of 10Gb and 1Gb Ethernet ports per ESXi host	Six 10Gb and four 1Gb ports
Total virtual network switch ports per ESXi host (vDS and vSS)	4,096
vCPUs per VM	32
RAM per VM	1TB
Virtual SCSI adapters per virtual machine	4
Virtual disk size	2TB minus 512 bytes
Virtual NICs per virtual machine	10
USB devices connected to a VM	20

This list is just a small sampling of the information contained in the vSphere 5 "Configuration Maximums" document. This document is an essential reference for the VCP 5 exam, and you can download it here:

www.vmware.com/pdf/vsphere5/r50/vsphere-50-configuration-maximums.pdf

The "Configuration Maximums" document is the definitive source for finding the supported maximums of a configuration for either an ESXi host or a virtual machine running on the ESXi host. The document also includes maximums for vCenter Server, VMware FT, vCenter Update Manager, and more.

Simple questions from the "Configuration Maximums" document are not likely to appear on the VCP5 exam. It is much more likely that you will receive a question where knowing one of these values is a prerequisite to knowing how to answer the question correctly.

Now that I have covered identifying the configuration maximums for ESXi hosts and the virtual machines running on them, you can move to the next section of this chapter. In this section, I will cover administering virtual machines and vApps.

Administering Virtual Machines and vApps

Once virtual machines are deployed, they will need to be administered. Administering virtual machines and administering vApps are among the more common tasks that most virtual infrastructure administrators perform on the job. Knowing how to administer virtual machines and vApps is an important set of skills to have for any virtual infrastructure administrator and is equally important for the VCP5 exam. In the following section, I will discuss administering virtual machines and vApps.

Identifying Files Used by Virtual Machines

Virtual machines consist of a set of files stored on a storage device. The minimum files required for a virtual machine are a configuration file (VMX), a virtual disk file (VMDK), and an NVRAM file (BIOS or EFI). While these three files alone can constitute a virtual machine, there are many more file types that may be visible in a virtual machine's directory on a datastore. Some of these additional files are described in Table 7.3.

TABLE 7.3 Virtual machine files

File	Description
.vmx	Virtual machine configuration file. This file contains every aspect of the virtual machine, including the virtual hardware assigned to it.
.vmxf	Virtual machine supplemental configuration file.
.vmdk	Virtual disk characteristics. This is a small text file that contains descriptive data about the -flat.vmdk file.

TABLE 7.3   Virtual machine files *(continued)*

File	Description
-flat.vmdk	Virtual disk contents. This is the actual contents of the virtual hard disk and will be significantly larger than the VMDK file.
-delta.vmdk	Snapshot delta files. These files can also be referred to as *delta links*, *redo logs*, and *child disks*. Note that when viewed from the ESXi Shell, snapshot delta files will also be visible with the -00000#-delta.vmdk extension.
.nvram	Virtual machine BIOS or EFI configuration file.
.vmsd	A database that stores information and metadata about snapshots for a virtual machine.
.vmsn	Stores the memory state at the time of the snapshot.
.vswp	The virtual machine's swap file.
.vmss	Virtual machine suspend file.
.log	The current virtual machine log file.
-#.log	Archived (rotated) virtual machine log files.
-ctk.vmdk	Holds change block tracking (CBT) information for a corresponding VMDK file.
-aux.xml	Snapshot manifest metadata file. In vSphere 5, this file is no longer required but is still created. The .vmsd file is now used instead.
.vmtx	Virtual machine template configuration file.
.hlog	vCenter marker file for a vMotion operation.
.psf	Persistent state file, used with vSphere Replication feature of SRM 5 to keep pointers for changed blocks.

It is also important to note that when viewing file types in the Datastore Browser, the virtual disk file information is abstracted. Figure 7.2 shows a listing of the files for VM1, as viewed in the Datastore Browser.

Notice that there is a single VMDK file listed that represents both the .vmdk and -flat.vmdk files. To view both of these actual files and their attributes, you can use the ESXi Shell. Figure 7.3 shows the listing of .vmdk files for the virtual machine VM1.

FIGURE 7.2   Virtual disks viewed in Datastore Browser

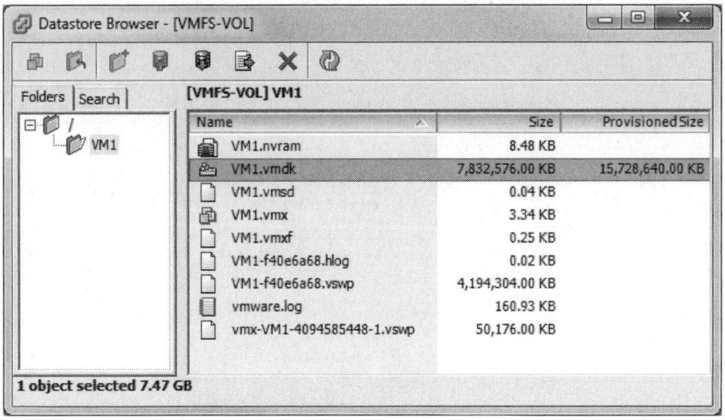

FIGURE 7.3   Virtual disks viewed in ESXi Shell

Note that in this listing the .vmdk and -flat.vmdk files are both visible. Always be aware of the level of abstraction present in the Datastore Browser when working with virtual disks.

Now that I have identified the various files used by virtual machines, I will cover identifying locations for virtual machine configuration files and virtual disks.

Identifying Locations for Virtual Machine Configuration Files and Virtual Disks

When a virtual machine is created, using any of the available methods, one of the options is to select destination storage for the virtual machine files. This location will be a VMFS or NFS datastore in your vSphere environment. The files used by the virtual machine will be stored on this datastore in a directory specified during the creation and will typically have the same name as the virtual machine. However, it is possible to store the virtual machine swap file and virtual disks in different directories.

The virtual machine swap (.vswp) file is created when a virtual machine is powered on. This file is used only if the ESXi host runs out of physical memory and is used to allow overcommitment of virtual memory for virtual machines running on the ESXi host. Initially, the .vswp file will be equal to the amount of virtual machine–assigned memory minus the memory reservation set for the VM. These files can be large, and in some cases, like when troubleshooting or using replication, it is better to have them on their own storage locations and not in the same *working location* as the virtual machine. (The working location is the directory where the virtual machine's configuration files are stored.) Figure 7.4 shows the virtual machine working location field.

FIGURE 7.4 Virtual machine working location

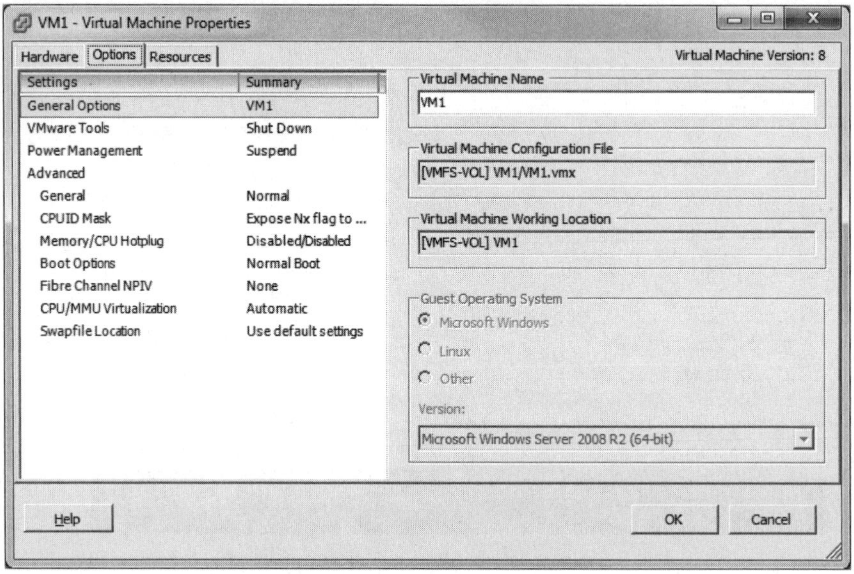

Virtual machine swap files can be placed in the following locations:

Default Selecting this option will store the virtual machine swap file at the default location, as defined in the host or cluster where the VM currently resides.

Always Store With The Virtual Machine Selecting this option will store the virtual machine swap file in the working location. This is the same location where the VM's configuration file is stored.

Store In The Host's Swapfile Datastore Selecting this option will store the virtual machine swap file in the swap file datastore as defined on the host or cluster where the VM currently resides. Otherwise, the virtual swap file will be stored in the virtual machine's working location.

> **NOTE** Configuring virtual machine swap file locations will be covered in detail in Chapter 9.

In addition to the virtual machine swap file, the virtual disks for a virtual machine can be stored in different datastores. When a new virtual disk is added to a virtual machine, the virtual disk location can be specified as part of the process. It is also possible to add virtual disks to a virtual machine from an existing directory, which would allow virtual disks to be in different datastores. Cold migrating or using Storage vMotion are two supported ways that a virtual disk could be moved to different datastores.

Now that the locations for virtual machine configuration files and virtual disks have been identified, I will cover configuring virtual machine options.

Configuring Virtual Machine Options

Virtual machine options are used to configure a variety of additional virtual machine properties. These options are accessed using the Options tab of the Virtual Machine Properties editor. You might recall that the Options tab was shown in Figure 7.4, where the virtual machine working location was identified. The properties that can be configured on the Options tab include the following:

- Virtual machine name
- Guest operating system
- VMware Tools
- Power management
- Logging, debugging, and statistics
- Configuration parameters
- CPUID mask
- Memory hot add and CPU hot plug
- BIOS and/or EFI
- *NPIV*
- Virtual machine monitor execution modes
- Swap file location

In Exercise 7.6, you will modify a virtual machine's configuration file (.vmx) by using the Configuration Parameters functionality in the Options tab. In this exercise, you will add two configuration parameters intended to limit the number and size of the virtual machine log files.

EXERCISE 7.6

Configuring Virtual Machine Options

1. Connect to a vCenter Server with the vSphere Client.

2. Select a powered-off virtual machine from the inventory and right-click it. Choose the Edit Settings option from the context menu that appears.

3. The Virtual Machine Properties window will appear. Click the Options tab.

4. Under the Advanced section in the left pane, select the General option by clicking it. Note in the Settings area at the top of the screen that the Enable Logging option is enabled by default. This option will enable logging to a single virtual machine log file in the working location of the VM.

(continued)

EXERCISE 7.6 *(continued)*

5. In the lower-right pane, click the Configuration Parameters button. The Configuration Parameters window will appear, as shown here.

6. Click the Add Row button at the bottom of the window. A new row will be created in the list of configuration parameters. In the Name column, enter the following value: **log.rotateSize**.

7. Press the Tab key and enter the following value in the Value column in the same row: **1000**.

   This configuration parameter ensures that a new log file will be created when the current log file reaches the size of 1000 bytes. This size is purposefully small for this exercise and would normally be much larger. In the next steps, you will configure log rotation settings.

8. Click the Add Row button again. Another new row will be created in the list of configuration parameters. In the Name column, enter the following value: **log.keepOld**.

9. Press the Tab key on the keyboard and enter the following value in the Value column in the same row: **10**.

   This configuration parameter ensures that no more than 10 log files will be maintained. Older log files will be deleted as necessary.

10. The configuration parameters just entered should look like this.

log.keepOld	10
log.rotateSize	1000

11. Click OK in the Configuration Parameters window and then click OK in the Virtual Machine Properties window to save these changes.

12. A Reconfigure Virtual Machine task will start. When this task completes, browse to the working location of this virtual machine using the Datastore Browser.

13. Expand the directory for the virtual machine and locate the virtual machine's configuration file. This is the file that ends with the .vmx extension.

14. Right-click the .vmx file and choose the Download option from the context menu that appears. Save the file to a convenient location.

15. Open the file with WordPad or your favorite text editor. (Do not use Notepad, because it will not format the file properly.)

16. Locate the following lines in the .vmx file:

```
log.keepOld = "10"
log.rotateSize = "1000"
```

These two lines are the formatted result of the two rows you added in steps 6 to 10.

17. Leave the Datastore Browser open and power on this virtual machine.

18. Return to the Datastore Browser and refresh the contents of the working location of this VM by clicking the green Refresh button in the toolbar.

19. Note that the directory contents now include 10 log files. Note the names of the log files. Shut down the virtual machine and refresh the datastore contents again. Take note of the names of the log files now, because they should have been rotated and include new names.

Now that I have covered configuring advanced options by using the configuration parameters function, I will cover configuring additional options for the virtual machine. I will start with the power settings.

Configuring Virtual Machine Power Settings

A virtual machine has power options that are used to determine whether the virtual machine is suspended or left powered on when the guest OS is placed in standby mode. It is important to note that these options are not applicable to all guest operating systems and that *Wake on LAN* is supported only for Windows guest operating systems. Figure 7.5 shows the guest power management settings for a virtual machine running a 64-bit CentOS 5 guest operating system.

FIGURE 7.5 Wake on LAN Absent for CentOS VM

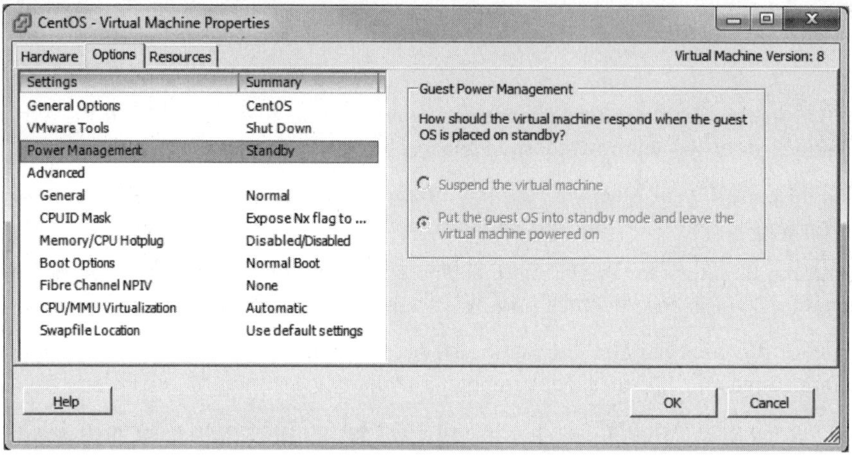

CentOS - Virtual Machine Properties

Hardware	Options	Resources		Virtual Machine Version: 8

Settings	Summary
General Options	CentOS
VMware Tools	Shut Down
Power Management	**Standby**
Advanced	
General	Normal
CPUID Mask	Expose Nx flag to ...
Memory/CPU Hotplug	Disabled/Disabled
Boot Options	Normal Boot
Fibre Channel NPIV	None
CPU/MMU Virtualization	Automatic
Swapfile Location	Use default settings

Guest Power Management

How should the virtual machine respond when the guest OS is placed on standby?

○ Suspend the virtual machine

◉ Put the guest OS into standby mode and leave the virtual machine powered on

Help   OK   Cancel

In addition to only supporting Windows guests, Wake on LAN also has the following NIC requirements:

- Flexible (VMware Tools required)
- vmxnet
- Enhanced vmxnet
- vmxnet 3

Wake on LAN can resume only those VMs that are in an S1 sleep state. S1 means the processor caches have been flushed and the CPUs have ceased all execution of instructions, but power to the CPUs and RAM is maintained. Therefore, suspended, hibernated, or powered-off VMs cannot be resumed via Wake on LAN.

In Exercise 7.7, you will configure the power settings for a powered-off virtual machine. Powering the VM off is a prerequisite to changing the power settings.

EXERCISE 7.7

Configuring Virtual Machine Power Management Settings

1. Connect to a vCenter Server with the vSphere Client.

2. Select a powered-off virtual machine from the inventory and right-click it. Choose the Edit Settings option from the context menu that appears.

3. The Virtual Machine Properties window will appear. Click the Options tab.

4. In the left pane, click the Power Management option.

5. Choose the Put The Guest OS Into Standby Mode option and select the appropriate network adapter. The final configuration should look like this.

```
VM1 - Virtual Machine Properties                                    [_] [□] [X]

Hardware  Options  Resources                          Virtual Machine Version: 8

Settings              Summary            ┌─ Guest Power Management ──────────────────────┐
General Options       VM1                │                                                │
VMware Tools          Power Off          │ How should the virtual machine respond when the guest
Power Management      Standby            │ OS is placed on standby?                        │
Advanced                                 │                                                │
  General             Normal             │ ○  Suspend the virtual machine                 │
  CPUID Mask          Expose Nx flag to… │                                                │
  Memory/CPU Hotplug  Disabled/Disabled  │ ⊙  Put the guest OS into standby mode and leave the
  Boot Options        Normal Boot        │    virtual machine powered on                  │
  Fibre Channel NPIV  None               │                                                │
  CPU/MMU Virtualization  Automatic      │    Wake on LAN for virtual machine traffic on: │
  Swapfile Location   Use default settings│                                               │
                                         │    ☐  Network adapter 1 (VM Network)           │
                                         │    ☑  Network adapter 2 (Admin Network)        │
                                         └────────────────────────────────────────────────┘

Help                                                        OK          Cancel
```

6. Click OK to save these changes.

7. A Reconfigure Virtual Machine task will begin. When this task completes, the power settings have been modified successfully.

Unsupported virtual network adapters might appear in the list of Wake on LAN options but will not work. Always verify that the virtual adapters listed on the Hardware tab of the virtual machine properties are supported for Wake on LAN before configuring Wake on LAN support.

Now that I have covered configuring the power settings for a virtual machine, I will cover configuring the virtual machine boot options.

Configuring Virtual Machine Boot Options

You can use the virtual machine boot options to control how a virtual machine starts. These options can be useful for obtaining access to a virtual machine's BIOS or EFI settings or for providing additional time to press the Esc key in order to obtain a boot menu. The virtual machine boot options can be configured using either the vSphere Client or the vSphere Web Client. In Exercise 7.8, you will configure the boot options for a powered-off virtual machine using the vSphere Web Client.

EXERCISE 7.8

Configuring Virtual Machine Boot Options Using the vSphere Web Client

1. Open a web browser and connect to the FQDN of the vCenter Server that will be used for this exercise.

2. Click the blue Log In To vSphere Web Client link.

3. Log in to the vSphere Web Client.

4. Select the powered-off virtual machine in the inventory in the left pane.

5. Click the blue icon with the yellow pencil on it located at the top right of the toolbar to edit the virtual machine settings.

6. An Edit VM window will appear. The default view is the Virtual Hardware tab. Click the VM Options tab at the top of the window.

7. In the VM Options view, expand the boot options by clicking Boot Options.

8. The boot options will now be displayed. Take a moment to review the options available here.

9. Select the Force BIOS Setup check box.

10. Click OK to save this change.

11. A Reconfigure Virtual Machine notification will appear. When the task completes, click the green Play icon on the top toolbar to power on the virtual machine.

12. Click the Launch Console link in the Guest OS Details pane and verify that the virtual machine successfully entered the BIOS setup.

Now that I have covered how to configure a virtual machine's boot options, I will cover how to configure troubleshooting options for virtual machines.

Configuring Virtual Machine Troubleshooting Options

As reliable as virtual machines are, occasionally it is necessary to troubleshoot them. Fortunately, several options are available for configuring virtual machine troubleshooting. One of these options was covered in Exercise 7.6, where you ensured that virtual machine logging was enabled. Just as the virtual machine logging options were configured in the virtual machine properties' Options tab, the other available troubleshooting options are also located here. These options, as shown in the vSphere Client, are shown in Figure 7.6.

In addition to logging, the other item in the Settings field is the Disable Acceleration option. You can use this option to slow down a virtual machine if there is a problem running or installing software in the virtual machine. If the problem with the software is then resolved, you can turn off the Disable Acceleration option.

FIGURE 7.6   Virtual machine troubleshooting options

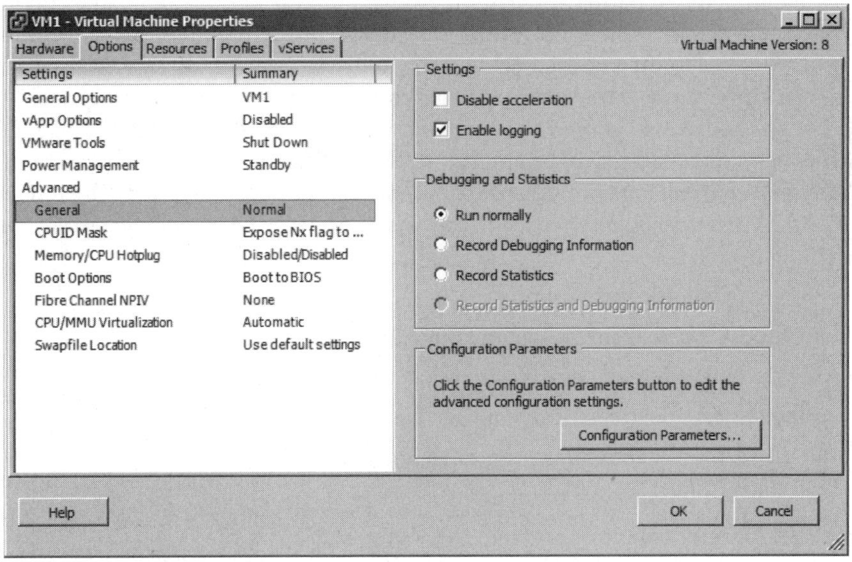

In the Debugging And Statistics section, you can configure virtual machines to obtain additional debugging or statistical information. These options are typically used when working with VMware support.

I have now covered configuring troubleshooting options for virtual machines and will next cover identifying common practices for securing virtual machines.

Identifying Common Practices for Securing Virtual Machines

Because the virtual infrastructure can encompass so much of the physical infrastructure, securing virtual machines can seem like a daunting task. Consider that securing a virtual machine can involve all of the following items:

- Guest operating systems
- Virtual machine
- ESXi hosts
- Storage units connected to ESXi hosts
- Networks connected to the ESXi hosts
- vCenter Server or other management applications
- Backup servers or applications

Securing virtual machines is in many ways no different from securing physical machines. Operations such as hardening the guest operating systems, installing periodic guest operating system updates, and updating antivirus and other applications are all good examples of this. Beyond the practices used to protect the guest OS, there are some specific protections that must be provided to the virtual machines themselves.

Virtual machines can be hardened in many additional ways. Earlier in this chapter, in Exercise 7.6, you added log rotation to a virtual machine. This is an example of one of the many hardening practices that can be applied to virtual machines. These options can be found in the most current version of the vSphere Security Hardening Guide. The following are some of the virtual machine–specific hardening options that can be added to the virtual machine configuration file:

- Preventing virtual disk shrinking
- Preventing other users from spying on administrator remote consoles
- Ensuring that unauthorized devices are not connected (unless needed/required)
- Preventing unauthorized removal, connection, and modification of devices
- Disabling VM-to-VM communication through VMCI
- Limiting VM log file size and number
- Limiting informational messages from the VM to the VMX file
- Disabling certain unexposed features
- Disabling remote operations within the guest
- Not sending host performance information to guests
- Controlling access to VMs through VMsafe

The ESXi hosts also need to be protected in order to protect the virtual machines. ESXi hosts should be patched and hardened using the information contained in the vSphere Security Hardening Guide. ESXi hosts also include a firewall, which should be configured properly. ESXi hosts should use a syslog server and persistent logging and should also be configured for NTP to ensure accurate time. Management consoles should be on isolated networks dedicated to server management. The security of the virtual machines on the ESXi host is only as good as the security on the ESXi hosts used to run them. Much like with physical servers, if local access is obtained to the ESXi host, then the security battle is already lost.

> At the time this book was written, the most current version of the vSphere Security Hardening Guide was still applicable to vSphere versions up to 4.1. This guide will certainly be updated for vSphere 5, but a lot of the content will remain the same. To find the most current vSphere Security Hardening Guide, check the VMTN Security and Compliance community:
>
> http://communities.vmware.com/community/vmtn/server/security?view=doc

In addition to the ESXi hosts, the storage and networks attached to them need to be secured to protect virtual machines. vMotion traffic is sent over the network in clear text, so to protect virtual machines, this traffic should be isolated. Hosts may have access to multiple networks, and understanding these networks is important in ensuring that virtual machines are not misconfigured. Virtual switch security should also be configured appropriately to minimize risks. Ethernet-based storage networks should use authentication mechanisms and be isolated. Fibre Channel SAN environments should make use of zoning and LUN masking practices to ensure that only authorized hosts have access to the storage devices.

Management applications, like vCenter Server, will also need to be secured to protect the virtual machines. By default vCenter Server installed on a Windows server puts the local Administrators group in the Administrator role for vCenter Server. If a standard default password is used for the local Administrator account in Windows, then more people may have potential access to your VMs than you think. VM sprawl can be another problem for virtual machine security. As virtual machines are deployed and then not tracked or not placed in life-cycle management systems, there could be VMs that are forgotten. Giving virtual infrastructure operations personnel the least amount of privileges can also be helpful in securing virtual machines. This can prevent operators from performing actions such as connecting VMs to the wrong networks, attaching disks, or worse.

One final consideration for securing virtual machines is to look at the backup applications or scripts that are used to back up complete virtual machine images. A backup of a complete system is a truly portable copy of a complete working system. Encryption or other methods of protecting the backups can be useful in protecting systems with sensitive data. For systems that utilize a Windows proxy server, it is also critical that the proper precautions are taken to ensure that Windows does not write signatures to your VMFS volumes. In addition, backup operators and other administrators who use this machine need to understand these implications.

Now that I have covered securing virtual machines, I will cover determining when an advanced virtual machine parameter is required.

Determining When an Advanced Virtual Machine Parameter Is Required

In the previous section, I covered the virtual machine configuration file security hardening options. If any of the virtual machine hardening best practices listed in the vSphere Security Hardening Guide were to be applied to a virtual machine, then it could be accomplished by adding advanced configuration parameters to the virtual machine. In Exercise 7.6, you added two of these advanced configuration parameters to a virtual machine. Figure 7.7 shows the two advanced configuration parameters that were added in Exercise 7.6.

Another time when advanced configuration parameters might be added to a virtual machine is when working with VMware support. Advanced parameters can also be used to gain access to experimentally supported features and to create unsupported configurations. Those that have built a vSphere environment in a VMware Workstation lab have likely used some of these unsupported options to be able to test advanced features of vSphere.

FIGURE 7.7   Advanced configuration parameters

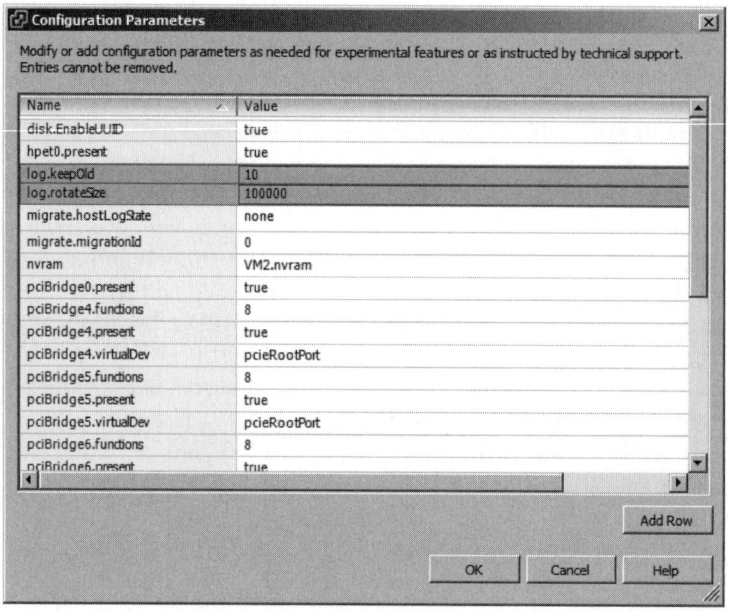

> ### 🌐 Real World Scenario
>
> #### Virtual Machine Templates and Configuration Parameters
>
> A virtual infrastructure administrator has decided that she wants to harden her virtual machines with certain configuration parameters contained in the vSphere Security Hardening Guide. Her vSphere environment is relatively new and contains only five virtual machines. She has manually updated these virtual machines but is looking for a solution to include these configuration parameters on all virtual machines she deploys in the future.
>
> The virtual infrastructure administrator has two templates that she has used to deploy her five virtual machines. She decides that she will add the advanced configuration parameters to the templates so that all newly deployed virtual machines will include these settings by default. She converts her templates to virtual machines, adds the configuration parameters, and then converts the virtual machines back to templates. Now any new virtual machines deployed from these templates will automatically include the security-hardening parameters.

Now that I have covered determining when advanced virtual machine configuration parameters are required, I will move on to hot extending a virtual disk.

Hot Extending a Virtual Disk

Hot extending a disk means increasing its capacity while the guest OS is running. Hot extending a virtual disk is a task that every virtual infrastructure administrator has probably already performed. This process is simple, and end users appreciate this capability as much as the virtual infrastructure administrator does. In Exercise 7.9, the steps to hot extend a virtual disk using the vSphere Web Client will be covered. This exercise will use a Windows Server 2008 R2 virtual machine.

EXERCISE 7.9

Hot Extending a Virtual Disk Using the vSphere Web Client

1. Open a web browser and connect to the FQDN of the vCenter Server that will be used for this exercise.

2. Click the blue Log In To vSphere Web Client link.

3. Log in to the vSphere Web Client.

(continued)

4. Locate the VM in the inventory in the left pane and select it.

5. Click the blue icon with the yellow pencil on it located at the top right of the toolbar to edit the virtual machine settings.

6. An Edit VM window will appear. The default view is the Virtual Hardware tab. Locate the hard disk that will be extended.

7. Note the currently listed size shown to the right of the selected hard disk. Enter the new larger value for the hard disk and then click the OK button.

8. A Reconfigure Virtual Machine notification will appear. When the task completes, the disk has been extended.

    At this point, the virtual disk has technically been hot extended. Until the guest OS has been reconfigured to utilize this new space, there is no real benefit to simply hot extending the disk. The remainder of this exercise will show how to extend the disk in Windows Server 2008 R2.

9. Click the Launch Console link in the Guest OS Details pane and log in to the Windows Server 2008 R2 VM.

10. Typically when logging in to Windows Server 2008 R2, Server Manager will start automatically. If Server Manager does not automatically start, locate it in the Start menu under Administrative Tools.

11. Expand the Storage item in the left pane. Select the Disk Manager.

12. In the right pane, review the information for the extended disk. The space that was added to the virtual disk should be visible and reported as Unallocated to the right of the current volume.

    If the extended space is not visible, right-click the Disk Management icon in the left pane and choose the Rescan Disks option from the context menu that appears.

13. Right-click the volume to be extended and choose the Extend Volume option from the context menu that appears.

14. The Extend Volume Wizard will launch. Click Next to begin.

15. Review the information on the Select Disks screen and click Next to continue. By default, the extend operation will use all of the available space.

16. Click Finish to extend the volume in Windows.

17. On the Disk Management screen, verify that the volume was extended and is reporting the new size.

NOTE   Different operating systems have different support for hot extending disks. Check with your OS vendor to see whether hot extend is supported. If hot extend is supported, the vendor should have specific instructions available.

It is also important to remember that virtual disks may not be hot extended if the virtual machine has an active snapshot, and the disk options will even be grayed out in the Virtual Machine Properties editor. Now that I have covered hot extending a disk, I will show how to adjust virtual machine resources based on virtual machine workloads.

Adjusting Virtual Machine Resources (Shares, Limits, and Reservations) Based on Virtual Machine Workloads

Sometimes a virtual machine needs additional resources; for example, at month end, the finance application may require significantly more CPU and memory resources. Fortunately, there are ways to adjust the virtual machine resources for these types of situations.

You might recall the section on configuring disk shares in Chapter 6. Shares are used to specify the relative importance of a virtual machine as it pertains to a specific resource. In addition to the disk, the other two resources that may be configured for the virtual machine are CPU and memory. Just like disk shares, both CPU and memory resources can be adjusted on the Resources tab of the Virtual Machine Properties editor. This tab is shown in Figure 7.8. I will briefly define each of these resource types, and I will cover this subject in great detail in Chapter 8.

FIGURE 7.8   Resources tab for virtual machine

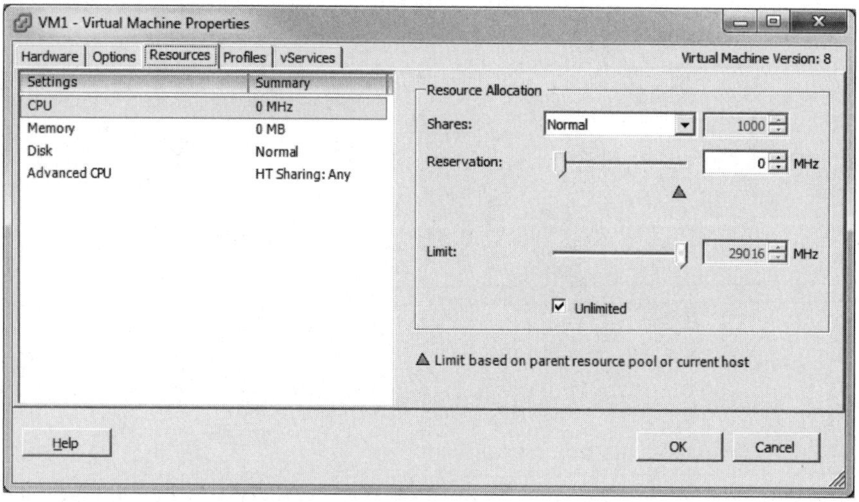

As discussed in the previous chapter, shares are used to specify relative importance of specific resources. Shares can have the values of Low, Normal, High, and Custom. Each of these values will be compared to the sum of all shares for all VMs on the host. Virtual machines with the highest share values will be able to consume more resources in periods of resource contention on the ESXi host.

In addition to shares, reservations can be used to guarantee a minimum allocation of CPU and memory for a virtual machine. This setting is used to claim a specific amount of the resource for the virtual machine so that these resources will always be available. Memory reservations can also be used to avoid overcommitment of physical memory resources. Memory reservations are required for virtual machines running in a vSphere Storage Appliance cluster, for example.

Limits are used to set an upper bound for resources. This prevents a virtual machine from using more resources than specified. This setting is by default set to Unlimited for both CPU and memory. Using this setting will ensure that the virtual machine uses close to the vCPU and memory allocations it has been granted.

Exercise 7.10 will cover the steps required to adjust virtual machine resources using the vSphere Client. For the purpose of this exercise, assume that the workload requires memory reservations to be set.

EXERCISE 7.10

Adjusting Virtual Machine Resources

1. Connect to a vCenter Server with the vSphere Client.

2. Locate a powered-off virtual machine in the inventory and select it. Right-click the virtual machine and choose the Edit Settings option from the context menu that appears.

3. A Virtual Machine Properties window will appear. Click the Resources tab.

4. Select Memory in the left pane, and note that values can be specified for Shares, Reservation, and Limit. Select the Reserve All Guest Memory (All Locked) box. The available options will all be grayed out after making this selection.

(continued)

EXERCISE 7.10 *(continued)*

VM1 - Virtual Machine Properties

Hardware | Options | Resources   Virtual Machine Version: 8

Settings	Summary
CPU	0 MHz
Memory	8192 MB (All locked)
Disk	Normal
Advanced CPU	HT Sharing: Any
Advanced Memory	NUMA Nodes: 2

Resource Allocation

☑ Reserve all guest memory (All locked)

Shares: Normal   81920

Reservation: 0   MB

Limit: 45228   MB

☑ Unlimited

⚠ Limit based on parent resource pool or current host

Help   OK   Cancel

5. Click OK to save these changes. A Reconfigure Virtual Machine task will begin. When this task completes, power on the virtual machine, and it will have a memory reservation.

Configuring shares, reservations, and limits on individual virtual machines can be time-consuming and even confusing to keep track of. Resource pools are generally the preferred way of guaranteeing resources to your virtual machines. I will discuss resource pools in the next chapter.

Now that I have covered adjusting virtual machine resources, I will next cover assigning a storage policy to a virtual machine.

Assigning a Storage Policy to a Virtual Machine

Profile-driven storage is used to provide guaranteed service levels to virtual machines. This works by using storage capabilities and VM storage profiles. Storage capabilities are divided into two types:

System-Defined   When storage systems use vSphere Storage APIs – Storage Awareness (*VASA*), the systems will inform vCenter Server of their capabilities.

User-Defined   When storage systems do not use VASA, user-defined capabilities may be provided by the vSphere administrator to inform vCenter Server of the capabilities of the storage.

Where the storage capabilities define the capabilities of the storage, VM storage profiles are used to define different levels of storage requirements for virtual machines.

 Profile-driven storage does not support RDMs and is available only in the Enterprise Plus edition of vSphere.

Exercise 7.11 will cover the steps required to prepare the virtual infrastructure to use storage profiles.

EXERCISE 7.11

Implementing Storage Profiles

1. Connect to a vCenter Server with the vSphere Client.

2. Select VM Storage Profiles from the Management options.

3. Click the Manage Storage Capabilities button located under the navigation bar. The Manage Storage Capabilities window will appear.

![Manage Storage Capabilities window. Text reads: Storage capabilities are a group of parameters that a datastore guarantees. Capabilities can be system-defined and user-defined. Supported storage systems assign system-defined capabilities to datastore and you cannot modify them. You can add, remove, and edit user-defined storage capabilities, and associate them with datastores. Columns: Name, Description, Type. Buttons: Add..., Remove, Edit..., Help, Close.]

You have now verified whether system-defined storage capabilities are listed in the Manage Storage Capabilities window. Next you will add a user-defined storage capability and associate it with a datastore.

4. Click the Close button in the Manage Storage Capabilities window. Click the Home icon in the navigation bar and then select Datastores And Datastore Clusters from the Inventory options.

5. Right-click a datastore and choose the Assign User-Defined Storage Capability option from the context menu that appears.

6. An Assign User-Defined Storage Capability window will appear, as shown here.

(continued)

7. Click the New button. An Add Storage Capability window will appear. Enter **Gold** for the Name field and provide a description if desired. Click OK.

8. Ensure that Gold is selected in the drop-down menu in the Assign User-Defined Storage Capability window and click OK to continue.

9. Click the Summary tab for this datastore, and verify that User-Defined Storage Capability reports Gold. Click the blue information icon located to the right of Gold to view the storage capability details, as shown here.

At this point, a user-defined capability has been created and associated with a datastore. Before storage profiles can be used, you must enable them.

10. Click the Home icon in the navigation bar and then select VM Storage Profiles from the Management options.

11. Click the Enable VM Storage Profiles button located under the navigation bar. The Enable VM Storage Profiles window will appear.

12. Select a cluster or host with a VM Storage Profile Status of Unknown.

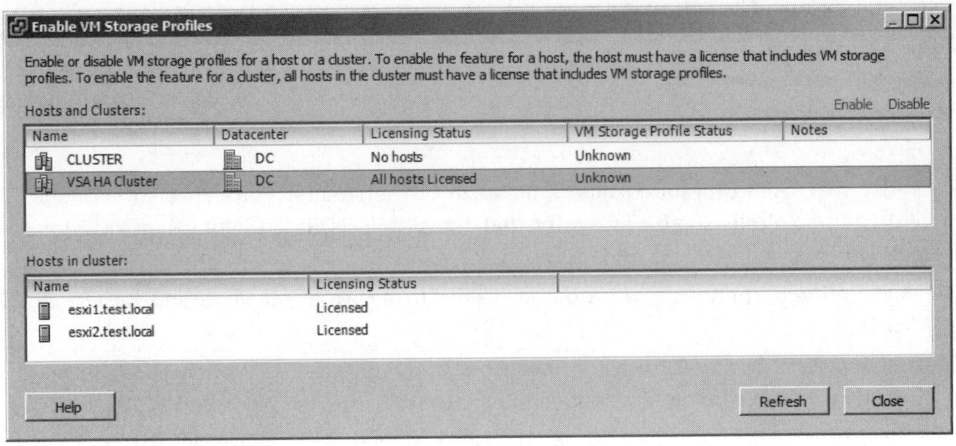

13. Click the blue Enable link located at the top right of this window. A Reconfigure Cluster or Reconfigure Host task will begin. When this task completes, the VM Storage Profile Status column should now report a status of Enabled.

14. Click the Close button in the Enable VM Storage Profiles window.

   At this point, storage profiles are created and enabled. The next step is to create a VM storage profile that will be later used to define the storage requirements for a virtual machine and its virtual disks.

15. Right-click the VM Storage Profiles item in the left pane and choose the Create VM Storage Profile option from the context menu that appears. The Create New VM Storage Profile Wizard will appear.

16. Enter **Gold-Storage-Profile** for the Name filed and provide a description if desired. Click Next to continue.

17. Select the Gold user-defined storage capability box, as shown here.

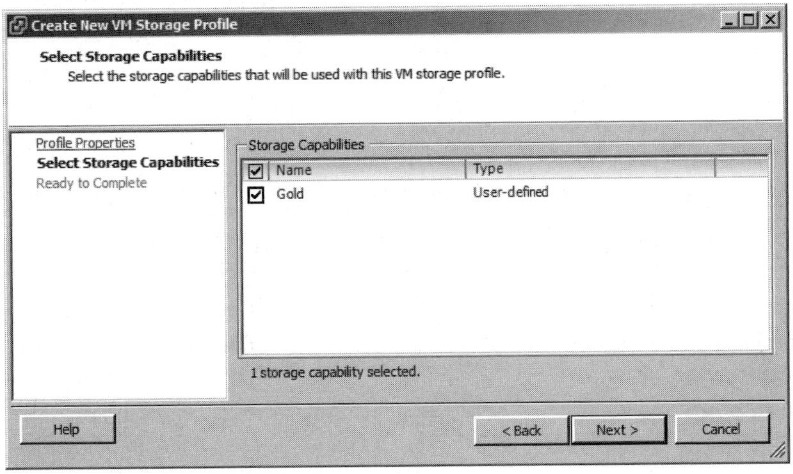

(continued)

18. Click Next to continue.

19. Review the information presented in the Ready To Complete screen and click Finish.

20. Verify that Gold-Storage-Profile is listed in the left pane. You can also click the VM Storage Profiles tab and verify that the profile is listed. Note that VM storage profiles can also be edited and deleted here.

Next you will apply this VM storage profile to a virtual machine and its virtual disks.

21. Pick a virtual machine from the inventory and right-click it. Choose Edit Settings from the context menu that appears.

22. The Virtual Machine Properties window will appear. Click the Profiles tab.

23. Change the Home VM Storage Profile option to Gold-Storage-Profile using the drop-down menu. Note in the field below that the virtual hard disk has no VM storage profile associated with it.

24. Click the Propagate To Disks button and note how the VM storage profile is applied to the virtual hard disks for the virtual machine.

25. Click OK to save these changes. A Reconfigure Virtual Machine task will begin. When this task completes, locate the VM Storage Profiles panel on the Summary tab for the VM.

26. Ensure that the profile and its compliance are listed. You may need to click the blue Refresh button to refresh the panel, if there is no information displayed.

27. Click the Home icon in the navigation bar and then select VM Storage Profiles from the Management options.

28. Select VM Storage Profiles in the left pane and then select the VM Storage Profiles tab. Click the blue Refresh link located at the top of the tab. Verify that the Associated VMs and Associated Virtual Disks columns report the correct values.

I have now covered assigning a storage policy to a virtual machine. In the next section, I will cover the steps to verify storage policy compliance for a virtual machine.

Verifying Storage Policy Compliance for Virtual Machines

After establishing VM storage policies, it is often necessary to check virtual machines for compliance to the policy. In step 26 of the previous exercise, I covered how to check an individual virtual machine for VM storage profile compliance. In Exercise 7.12, I will cover the steps to determine whether all virtual machines and their virtual disks are using datastores that are compliant with their associated VM storage profile.

EXERCISE 7.12

Verifying VM Storage Policy Compliance

1. Connect to a vCenter Server with the vSphere Client.

2. Select VM Storage Profiles from the Management options on the Home screen.

3. Select the Gold-Storage-Profile item that you created in the previous exercise in the left pane. Click the Virtual Machines tab.

4. Review the list of virtual machines and virtual disks. Ensure that the Compliance Status column reports a value of Compliant and shows a green circular icon with a check mark, as shown here.

5. If the date shown in the Last Checked column is old, you can click the blue Check Compliance Now link at the top of the Virtual Machines tab to force a compliance check.

If any virtual machines or virtual disks report a status of Non-Compliant, the corrective action would be to use cold migration or Storage vMotion to move these items to compliant datastores.

I have now covered how to check virtual machine compliance for VM storage profiles, and with that, this chapter is complete.

Summary

This chapter covered managing and administering virtual machines. Knowing how to manage and administer virtual machines is essential knowledge for any virtual infrastructure administrator. Also in this chapter, I identified the different cloning and template options. You cloned an existing virtual machine and created a template from a virtual machine. Deploying virtual machines from templates was covered, in addition to updating existing virtual machine templates. I covered deploying virtual appliances and vApps from an OVF template. Importing and exporting OVF templates were each covered. I discussed how to determine the appropriate deployment methodology for a given virtual machine application. Identifying the vCenter Server–managed ESXi hosts and virtual machine maximums wrapped up the first section of this chapter.

The second part of this chapter focused on administering virtual machines and vApps. The files that make up virtual machines were identified, along with the locations where these files can be stored. I covered configuring different virtual machine options, including power settings, boot options, and troubleshooting options. Common practices for securing virtual machines were discussed. Determining when advanced configuration parameters are required was also covered. Hot extending a virtual disk was covered. Adjusting virtual machine resources was discussed. This chapter concluded with assigning a storage policy to a virtual machine and verifying the compliance of the storage policy.

Exam Essentials

Know how to manage virtual machine clones and templates.   Be able to identify the different cloning and template options. Know how to clone a virtual machine and create a template from a virtual machine. Understand how to deploy a new VM from a template and how to update existing templates. Be able to deploy virtual appliances and vApps from an OVF template. Know how to import and export an OVF template. Be able to determine the appropriate deployment method for a given virtual machine. Know the vSphere configuration maximums.

Know how to administer virtual machines and vApps.   Be able to identify the files used by a virtual machine and know the locations where the various files can be stored. Be able to configure virtual machine options, power settings, boot options, and troubleshooting options. Understand common practices for securing virtual machines and when advanced configuration parameters are required. Be able to hot extend a disk. Know how to adjust virtual machine resources on a per-VM basis. Understand storage profiles, including how to assign them and how to check virtual machines for storage profile compliance.

Review Questions

1. Which of the following items are listed as options on the context menu when right-clicking a template in the vSphere Client? (Choose all that apply.)

    A. Clone

    B. Add Permission

    C. Rename

    D. Convert to Virtual Machine

2. Which of the following configuration maximums are 2TB? (Choose all that apply.)

    A. RAM per ESXi host

    B. RAM per virtual machine

    C. Virtual disk size

    D. Virtual compatibility mode RDM size

3. You work in a 100 percent Windows virtual machine environment. You need to deploy four Linux VMs for a project. Which deployment methodology would be the least amount of work?

    A. Create four virtual machines one at a time.

    B. Create one virtual machine and clone it three times.

    C. Create one virtual machine and then convert it to a template. Deploy the remaining VMs from this template.

    D. Create a vApp.

4. You want to add several items listed in the vSphere Security Hardening Guide to a virtual machine configuration file. How will you most easily accomplish this task?

    A. Power off the virtual machine and add the options to the VM using the Configuration Parameters button in the virtual machine properties.

    B. Add the options to the VM using the Security Parameters button in the virtual machine properties.

    C. Power off the virtual machine and clone it. Specify these options as part of the cloning process.

    D. Clone the virtual machine and specify these options as part of the cloning process.

5. A particular application is having a problem with installation. Which of the following options can be used to slow down a virtual machine in hopes of allowing the install to complete?

    A. Disable Acceleration

    B. Limit

    C. Shares

    D. Reservation

6. Which of the following are the two types of storage capabilities used with profile-driven storage? (Choose two.)

   A. System-defined

   B. Storage-defined

   C. Profile-defined

   D. User-defined

7. vApps are built on which industry-standard format?

   A. OVA

   B. OVF

   C. OVT

   D. OVX

8. Which of the following options can be modified in the virtual machine properties while the virtual machine is powered on?

   A. Guest Operating System

   B. Force BIOS Setup

   C. CPUID Mask

   D. Power Management

9. Which of the following is the correct sequence for updating existing virtual machine templates?

   A. Using the vSphere Client, convert the template to a virtual machine, power on the virtual machine, make changes to the virtual machine as required, power off the virtual machine, and convert the virtual machine to a template.

   B. Using the vSphere Client, power on the virtual machine template, make changes to the virtual machine as required, and power off the virtual machine template.

   C. Using the vSphere Client, rename the virtual machine template using the Datastore Browser, power on the virtual machine, make changes to the virtual machine as required, power off the virtual machine template, and rename the virtual machine using the Datastore Browser.

   D. Using the vSphere Client, convert the template to a virtual machine using VMware Converter, power on the virtual machine, make changes to the virtual machine as required, power off the virtual machine, and convert the virtual machine to a template.

10. You have found that several virtual machines have a VM storage profile compliance status of noncompliant. What action can you take to fix this problem? (Choose all that apply.)

    A. Use Storage vMotion to move the virtual machines to compliant datastores.

    B. Cold migrate the virtual machines to compliant datastores.

    C. vMotion these virtual machines to new hosts in the cluster.

    D. Power cycle the virtual machine.

11. Which of the following items need to be secured in order to properly secure virtual machines? (Choose all that apply.)

   A. Virtual machine configuration files

   B. vMotion network(s)

   C. vCenter Server permissions

   D. ESXi hosts

12. Which of the following virtual machine resources can be adjusted on the Resources tab of the Virtual Machine Properties editor? (Choose all that apply.)

   A. Shares

   B. Limits

   C. Reservations

   D. Allocations

13. What is the file extension for a virtual machine configuration file when the virtual machine has been converted to a template?

   A. .vmx

   B. .vmxf

   C. .vmtx

   D. .vmsd

14. A virtual machine owner is reporting that she is out of disk space on a virtual machine with a single disk running Windows Server 2008 R2. The guest OS has one volume only. What steps do you take to most quickly solve this problem?

   A. Add another virtual disk to the virtual machine and instruct the virtual machine owner to move some of her data to it.

   B. Hot extend the virtual disk in the vSphere Client and then extend the volume in Windows using the Disk Manager.

   C. Instruct the user to schedule downtime and power down the virtual machine's guest OS. Hot extend the disk.

   D. Clone the virtual machine and resize the disk.

15. You are trying to use the setup option for the BIOS of a virtual machine; however, the virtual machine starts up too fast for you to access the setup option. Which virtual machine boot options can be used to solve this problem? (Choose all that apply.)

   A. Specify a different boot firmware.

   B. Set a Power On Boot Delay value.

   C. Select the Force BIOS Setup option.

   D. Set a Failed Boot Recovery value.

16. Which of the following file types can be moved outside the working location of a virtual machine? (Choose two.)

A. VSWP

B. LOG

C. VMX

D. VMDK

17. Which of the following files is a database that stores information and metadata about snapshots for a virtual machine?

A. .vmss

B. .vmsn

C. .vswp

D. .vmsd

18. Which of the following can be used to create clones and templates? (Choose all that apply.)

A. vCenter Server

B. vSphere Client

C. vSphere Web Client

D. VMware Converter

19. Which of the following combinations are supported for Wake on LAN functionality? (Choose two.)

A. Windows guest OS and vmxnet

B. Windows guest OS and vmxnet 2

C. Windows guest OS and vmxnet 3

D. Linux guest OS and vmxnet 3

20. Which of the following can be deployed in the vSphere Client by using the Deploy OVF Template option from the File menu? (Choose all that apply.)

A. Virtual appliances

B. Virtual disks

C. vTeam

D. vApps

Chapter

8

Establish Service Levels with Cluster, Fault Tolerance, and Resource Pools

---

VCP5 EXAM OBJECTIVES COVERED IN THIS CHAPTER:

✓ **Creating and Configuring VMware Clusters**

- Determine appropriate failover methodology and required resources for an HA implementation

- Describe DRS virtual machine entitlement

- Create/Delete a DRS/HA Cluster

- Add/Remove ESXi Hosts from a DRS/HA Cluster

- Add/Remove virtual machines from a DRS/HA Cluster

- Enable/Disable Host Monitoring

- Configure admission control for HA and virtual machines

- Enable/Configure/Disable virtual machine and application monitoring

- Configure automation levels for DRS and virtual machines

- Configure migration thresholds for DRS and virtual machines

- Create VM-Host and VM-VM affinity rules

- Configure Enhanced vMotion Compatibility

- Monitor a DRS/HA Cluster

- Configure Storage DRS

✓ **Planning and Implementing VMware Fault Tolerance**

- Determine use case for enabling VMware Fault Tolerance on a virtual machine

- Identify VMware Fault Tolerance requirements

- Configure VMware Fault Tolerance networking
- Enable/Disable VMware Fault Tolerance on a virtual machine
- Test an FT configuration

✓ **Creating and Administering Resource Pools**

- Describe the Resource Pool hierarchy
- Define the Expandable Reservation parameter
- Create/Remove a Resource Pool
- Configure Resource Pool attributes
- Add/Remove virtual machines from a Resource Pool
- Determine Resource Pool requirements for a given vSphere implementation
- Evaluate appropriate shares, reservations and limits for a Resource Pool based on virtual machine workloads
- Clone a vApp

This chapter will cover the objectives of sections 5.1, 5.2, and 5.3 of the VCP5 exam blueprint. This chapter will focus on clusters, VMware Fault Tolerance (FT), and resource pools.

This chapter will first cover discussing HA implementation resources and failover methodologies. I will cover describing virtual machine entitlement, along with some basic information about DRS and HA. I will cover the steps required to create and delete a DRS/HA cluster, as well as how to add and remove ESXi hosts from a DRS/HA cluster. I will also cover the steps to monitor a DRS/HA cluster. I will show how to enable and disable host monitoring in a cluster and cover how to configure admission control for HA and VMs. Virtual machine and application monitoring will be covered, along with automation levels for DRS and virtual machines. Configuring the migration thresholds for DRS and virtual machines will be covered. I will cover how to create VM-Host and VM-VM affinity rules. EVC compatibility and monitoring clusters will also be covered. This section will conclude with configuring Storage DRS.

The second section of this chapter will cover the VMware Fault Tolerance feature. I will cover determining the use cases for VMware FT and identifying the requirements to implement FT in a vSphere environment. I will also cover how to create networking for the Fault Tolerance logging traffic. I will cover the steps to enable and disable FT and to test it.

The final section of this chapter will focus on resource pools. The resource pool hierarchy will be described, and the Expandable Reservation parameter will be discussed. I will show how to create and remove resource pools, configure their attributes, and add and remove virtual machines to a resource pool. I will also cover how to determine the resource pool requirements for a given vSphere implementation. I will evaluate appropriate shares, reservations, and limits for a resource pool, based on VM workloads. This chapter will conclude with reviewing the procedure for cloning a vApp.

Creating and Configuring VMware Clusters

In vSphere, a cluster is a collection of ESXi hosts and the virtual machines associated with them that have shared resources and are managed by vCenter Server. Clusters are used to enable some of the more powerful features in vSphere, such as DRS, HA, FT, and vMotion. The first topic I will cover in this chapter is determining the appropriate failover methodology and required resources for an HA implementation.

Determining the Appropriate Failover Methodology and Required Resources for an HA Implementation

As you will see later in this chapter, creating clusters and configuring clusters in vCenter Server are both relatively simple tasks. Like many aspects of vSphere, creating a cluster involves proper up-front planning. Part of this planning is determining how you want the cluster to function. Will the cluster have both DRS and HA enabled, or perhaps just one and not the other? The answers to these questions will impact the way the cluster is designed. Remember that DRS provides load balancing and HA provides high availability. While these two features complement each other well, they serve different functions and don't always have to be used in unison.

For clusters that will use HA, determining the resources that will be required is in part determined by how failures in the cluster will be handled. For example, are all virtual machines required to have a certain amount of uptime? If you have a two-node cluster, with each ESXi host running at 80 percent capacity of memory and processing, then a single host failure will not likely allow you to achieve the virtual machine availability requirements. The failover behavior is handled by admission control policies in the HA cluster and will be discussed later in this chapter.

Knowing your environment's specific availability requirements will determine the appropriate failover methodology and help you determine the resources required for an HA implementation. In the next section, I will describe DRS virtual machine entitlement.

Describing DRS Virtual Machine Entitlement

While each ESXi host has its own local scheduler, enabling DRS on a cluster will create a second layer of scheduling architecture. Figure 8.1 shows this architecture.

FIGURE 8.1: Global and local schedulers

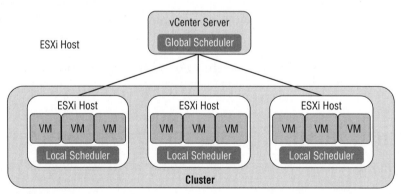

Both of these schedulers compute resource entitlement for virtual machines. This resource entitlement is based on both a static and dynamic entitlement. The static entitlement consists of a virtual machine's shares, reservations, and limits. The dynamic entitlement for the virtual machine consists of metrics such as estimated active memory and CPU demand.

If the DRS cluster is not overcommitted, then the virtual machine entitlement will be the same as the resource allocation for the virtual machine. In periods of contention, DRS will use the virtual machine entitlement to determine how to best distribute resources.

Now that I have described the virtual machine entitlement, I will cover how to create and delete a cluster.

Creating and Deleting a DRS/HA Cluster

Once the planning and design work is done, creating a cluster is simple. Exercise 8.1 will cover the steps to use the vSphere Client to create a new cluster with HA and DRS enabled.

EXERCISE 8.1

Creating a New Cluster with HA and DRS Enabled

1. Connect to a vCenter Server with the vSphere Client.

2. Switch to the Hosts and Clusters view. Right-click a datacenter object and choose the New Cluster option from the context menu that appears. The New Cluster Wizard will launch.

3. Provide the cluster with a descriptive and unique name and select both the Turn On vSphere HA and Turn On vSphere DRS options.

(continued)

4. Click Next.

5. Set Automation Level to Manual and click Next to continue.

6. Leave the Power Management option at its default setting of Off and click Next.

7. Deselect the Enable Host Monitoring option. Change the Admission Control option to Disable. Choosing this option will gray out the Admission Control Policy settings.

8. Click Next.

9. Accept the default settings for the Virtual Machine Options settings and click Next to continue.

10. Accept the default settings for the VM Monitoring settings and click Next to continue.

11. Accept the default settings for VMware EVC and click Next to continue.

12. Accept the default setting for the VM Swapfile Location settings and click Next to continue.

13. Review the information presented on the Ready To Complete screen.

New Cluster Wizard

Ready to Complete
Review the selected options for this cluster and click Finish.

- Cluster Features
- vSphere DRS
- vSphere HA
- VMware EVC
- VM Swapfile Location
- **Ready to Complete**

The cluster will be created with the following options:

Cluster Name:	TESTER
vSphere DRS:	Enabled
vSphere DRS Automation Level:	Manual
vSphere DRS Migration Threshold:	Apply priority 1, priority 2, and priority 3 recommendations.
vSphere HA Host Monitoring:	Suspended
Admission Control:	Disabled
VM Restart Priority:	Medium
Host Isolation Response:	Leave powered on
vSphere HA VM Monitoring:	Disabled
Monitoring Sensitivity:	High
VMware EVC Mode:	Disabled
Virtual Machine Swapfile Location:	Same directory as the virtual machine

Help   < Back   Finish   Cancel

14. Click Finish to create the cluster.

15. A Create Cluster task will begin. When this task completes, verify that the new cluster has been created in the left pane of the Hosts and Clusters view.

16. Right-click the cluster and choose the Edit Settings option that appears in the context menu. The cluster properties window will appear. Look through the available options and then click Cancel when done.

The cluster has been created, and DRS and HA have both been enabled.

NOTE   This exercise focused on creating a cluster, and I will revisit all of the options presented in the New Cluster Wizard later in this chapter.

The newly created cluster likely has a warning, because of the lack of shared storage. Clusters can exist without shared storage, but nearly all of the functionality they provide will require shared storage. Before proceeding, please add shared storage to any ESXi hosts that will be added to the cluster you just created. If you need assistance, check Chapter 5 where I showed how to configure shared storage. The remainder of the exercises in this chapter will assume that the same shared storage is available for each ESXi host in the cluster created in Exercise 8.1.

Another configuration that should exist in each ESXi host in the cluster is VMkernel networking for vMotion traffic. Having vMotion configured enables DRS to migrate virtual machines to different hosts. Exercises 4.4 and 4.15 in Chapter 4 covered configuring vMotion networking, if you need assistance with this step. The remainder of the exercises in this chapter will also assume that vMotion has been configured for each ESXi host in the cluster created in Exercise 8.1.

Occasionally, you might need to delete a cluster. The steps to delete a cluster are simple and consist of right-clicking a cluster in the left pane of the vSphere Client and choosing the Remove option from the context menu that appears. A Remove Cluster confirmation dialog will appear, and clicking the Yes button will delete the cluster.

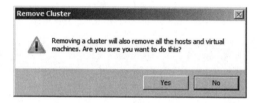

The steps to create and delete a DRS- and HA-enabled cluster have been covered. However, a cluster with no ESXi hosts is not very functional, so in the next section I will cover how to add ESXi hosts to this cluster.

Adding and Removing ESXi Hosts from a DRS/HA Cluster

Like vCenter Server, a cluster isn't nearly as interesting until ESXi hosts have been added to it. In the previous exercise, I created a new cluster with DRS and HA enabled. In Exercise 8.2, two ESXi hosts will be added to this cluster. This exercise will assume that there is one host already present in the same datacenter as the cluster and that the second host will be added to the cluster as a new host.

EXERCISE 8.2

Adding and Removing ESXi Hosts to and from a Cluster

1.   Connect to a vCenter Server with the vSphere Client.

2.   Select Hosts And Clusters.

3.   In the left pane, locate an ESXi host that will be added to the cluster. As shown here, esxi1.test.local is used.

4. Click this host and drag it into the cluster. The Add Host Wizard will launch.

5. Accept the default option for the virtual machine resources.

    Choosing the default option here will put all of the ESXi host's virtual machines in the cluster's root resource pool and will delete any resource pools currently defined on the ESXi host.

6. Click Next and review the information presented on the Ready To Complete screen.

7. Click Finish to add this ESXi host to the cluster.

8. A Move Host Into Cluster task will begin, as will a Configuring vSphere HA task. When these tasks complete, verify that the ESXi host is now a member of the cluster by expanding the cluster in the left pane.

    You have now added an existing ESXi host from your datacenter into a new cluster. The remainder of the exercise will cover the steps to add a host that was not already being managed by a vCenter Server.

9. Right-click the cluster and choose the Add Host option from the context menu that appears. The Add Host Wizard will launch.

10. Enter the *FQDN* of the ESXi host and provide administrative credentials to log in to this host.

Add Host Wizard   _ □ ×

Specify Connection Settings
Type in the information used to connect to this host.

Connection Settings
Host Summary
Choose Resource Pool
Ready to Complete

Connection

Enter the name or IP address of the host to add to vCenter.

Host: esxi2.test.local

Authorization

Enter the administrative account information for the host. vSphere Client will use this information to connect to the host and establish a permanent account for its operations.

Username: root

Password: *****************

Help   < Back   Next >   Cancel

(continued)

EXERCISE 8.2 *(continued)*

11. Click Next to continue. A Security Alert window will appear. Click the Yes button if you trust the ESXi host in your lab environment.

12. Review the information on the Host Summary screen and click Next.

13. If you have licenses and want to use them, assign them on the Assign License screen. Otherwise, use the Evaluation Mode option. Click Next to continue.

14. Leave the Lockdown Mode option unchecked and click Next.

15. As in step 5, choose the default option for the virtual machine resources. Click Next to continue.

16. Review the information presented on the Ready To Complete screen and click Finish to add this ESXi host to the cluster.

17. An Add Host task will begin, as will a Configuring vSphere HA task. When these tasks complete, verify that the ESXi host is now a member of the cluster by expanding the cluster in the left pane.

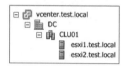

The ESXi hosts have now been added to the cluster. The remainder of this exercise will cover the steps to delete an ESXi host from the cluster. Just as I added the first ESXi host by dragging it, an ESXi host can be removed from a cluster by dragging it into a new supported location.

18. Select one of the two ESXi hosts that were just added to the cluster and right-click it. Choose the Enter Maintenance Mode option from the context menu that appears.

19. A Confirm Maintenance Mode window will appear. Review this information and click Yes to proceed.

20. An Enter Maintenance Mode task will begin. When this task completes, the icon for the ESXi host will change to indicate that it is in maintenance mode.

21. Click this ESXi host and drag it into the datacenter object.

22. A Move Entities task will begin. When this task completes, verify that the ESXi host is now listed in the datacenter.

Moving forward, you will need to have at least two ESXi hosts in the cluster, so move the ESXi host back into the cluster now. Once it is back in the cluster, exit maintenance mode on the ESXi host.

You have now added two ESXi hosts to the cluster. Any virtual machines that were already present on either of these two ESXi hosts are now automatically part of the cluster. In the next section, I will cover adding and removing new virtual machines to the cluster.

Adding and Removing Virtual Machines to/from a DRS/HA Cluster

The process of adding a virtual machine to a cluster is very similar to the process of adding a virtual machine to a host or vApp. In chapters 6 and 7 I covered adding virtual machines to ESXi hosts and vApps, deploying OVF templates, and moving machines with VMware Converter. Each of these deployment options allows you to choose a cluster, so adding a virtual machine to a cluster should certainly be familiar ground by now.

To create a new VM that will be a member of a cluster, simply right-click the cluster and choose the New Virtual Machine option from the context menu that appears. One difference when using the Create New Virtual Machine Wizard to add a virtual machine to a cluster is that the option to pick a host or cluster is no longer presented in the configuration options. This is shown in Figure 8.2.

FIGURE 8.2 No host/cluster option for VM

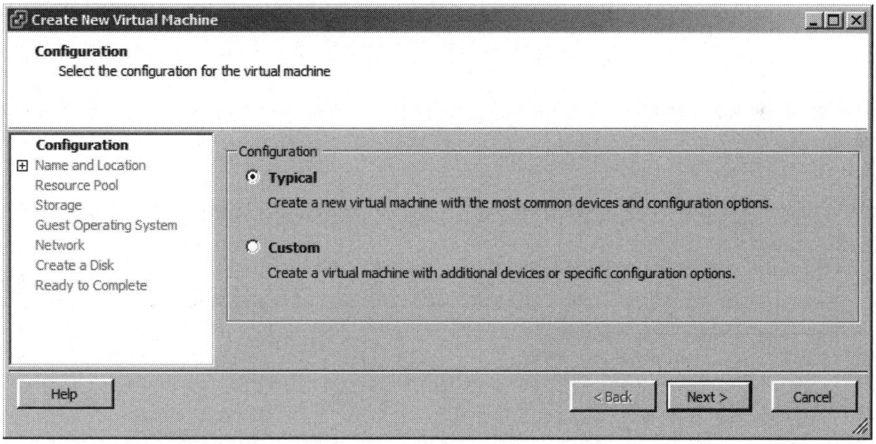

Virtual machines running on ESXi hosts in the same datacenter but not in the cluster can also be added to the cluster. This could be used for a VM that was in a testing or pilot program but is now ready to be moved into production and benefit from DRS and HA. In Exercise 8.3, the steps to move a powered-on VM from another host to a cluster will be covered. This exercise will require an additional ESXi host that is not part of the cluster and, as mentioned earlier in this chapter, assumes that a vMotion network and shared storage exist for all of the ESXi hosts.

EXERCISE 8.3

Adding a VM from an Existing ESXi Host to a Cluster

1. Connect to a vCenter Server with the vSphere Client.

2. Locate a powered-on virtual machine. Right-click it and choose the Migrate option from the context menu that appears.

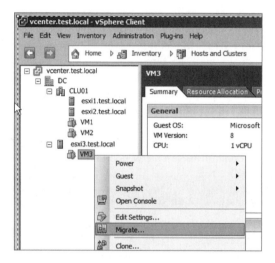

3. The Migrate Virtual Machine Wizard will launch. Choose the Change Host option and click Next.

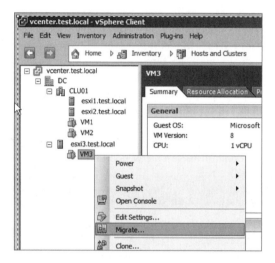

4. Choose the High Priority Option and click Next.

5. Review the information on the Ready To Complete screen and click Finish to move the VM to the cluster.

6. A Migrate Virtual Machine task will begin. When this task completes, verify that the virtual machine is now a member of the cluster.

 If a vMotion network were not available between the two ESXi hosts used in the previous exercise, the powered-off virtual machine could still be cold migrated to the cluster.

Removing a virtual machine is accomplished in much the same way that a virtual machine is added to a cluster. vMotion can be used to migrate a powered-on VM from a cluster to another host with access to both the vMotion network and the same shared storage. If the vMotion network and shared storage requirements are not met, then the VM can be *cold migrated* from the cluster to an ESXi host.

You have now created a cluster, added ESXi host(s) to it, and added virtual machines to it. Next I will begin to explore some of the options available in the cluster settings.

Enabling and Disabling Host Monitoring

In Exercise 8.1, you created a DRS/HA cluster, and there were two HA settings that were modified from the default settings. These changes were to disable host monitoring and to disable admission control. Changing these settings initially allowed the cluster to be more flexible for a lab-type environment. Now that the cluster is built and hosts and VMs are running in it, I will configure the HA settings. First I will cover enabling host monitoring.

To begin, right-click the cluster object and choose the Edit Settings option from the context menu that appears. Select vSphere HA in the left pane. Figure 8.3 shows the vSphere HA settings.

The first field is used to enable and disable host monitoring. Enable host monitoring here by selecting the Enable Host Monitoring option. Click OK to save the changes.

Enabling host monitoring will allow ESXi hosts in the cluster to exchange network heartbeats via the HA agents over their management networks. To understand how this works, it is first necessary to discuss how HA works in vSphere 5. HA is completely redesigned in vSphere 5 and now utilizes a master-slave host design. In this design, a single member of the cluster is the master host, while all other hosts are slaves. For network heartbeating, the master host monitors the status of the slave hosts.

If the master host stops receiving network heartbeats from a slave host, it must determine whether the host is failed, isolated, or partitioned. To determine which type of event has occurred, the master host will try to exchange heartbeats with a datastore. This is known as *datastore heartbeating* and allows the master host to better determine the true state of the slave host(s).

FIGURE 8.3 vSphere HA options

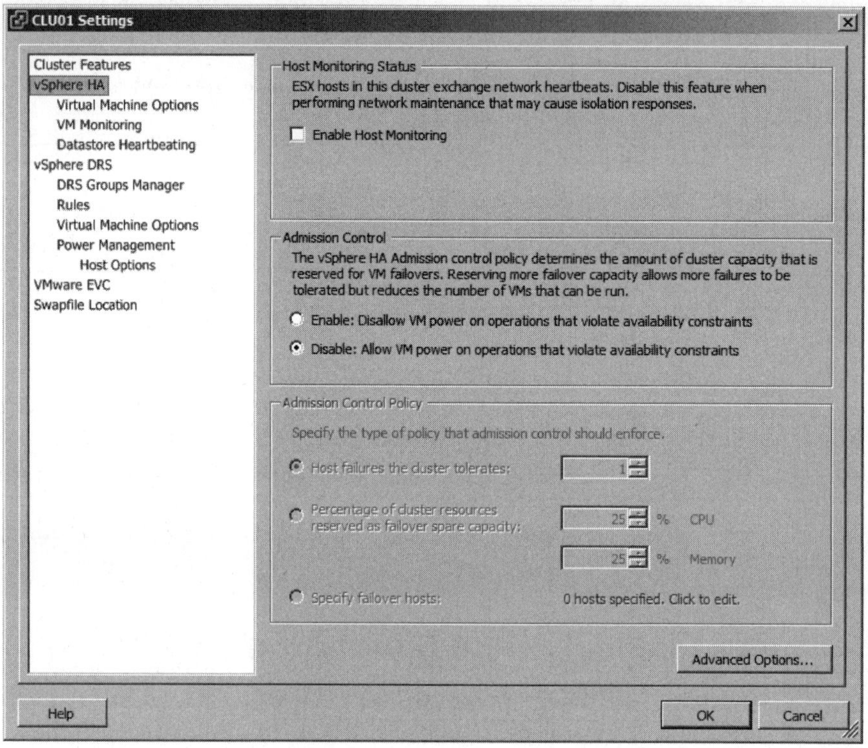

If the master host can no longer receive heartbeats via the HA agent on the slave host, the slave host is not responding to pings, and the datastore heartbeats are not occurring from the slave host, then the slave host is considered failed. HA will restart the virtual machines that were running on the slave host.

If a slave host is still running but network heartbeats are not being received via the HA agents, the master host will attempt to ping the cluster isolation address. If this ping operation fails, the slave host is considered isolated. The master host will now utilize the host isolation response to determine what action to take with the virtual machines.

If a slave host is no longer receiving network heartbeats from the master host but is able to communicate with other slave hosts, then the slave host is considered partitioned. An election process will take place among the slave hosts in the partition to determine a new master host. This is considered a degraded protection state but will allow the hosts in the cluster to resume the ability to detect failed hosts or isolated hosts so that the correct HA action can be taken.

vSphere HA will restart VMs and does not provide stateful application-level fault tolerance.

Host monitoring can be disabled for network or ESXi host maintenance in lab settings or other configurations where you would not want HA to function as normal, such as when first building out the cluster. Now that I have covered host monitoring, I will cover admission control and configuring the admission control policy.

Configuring Admission Control for HA and Virtual Machines

Admission control is used to guarantee that capacity exists in the cluster to handle host failure situations. The current available resources of the cluster are used by admission control to calculate the required capacity, so this value will be dynamic. Placing a host in maintenance mode or experiencing a host failure will change the capacity calculations for the cluster. Admission control attempts to ensure that resources will always be available on the remaining hosts in the cluster to power on the virtual machines that were running on a failed or unavailable host. The recommended configuration for admission control is to enable it. This will allow the cluster to reserve the required capacity and keep you out of host resource saturation situations.

Admission control is further configured by selecting the admission control policy. These policies are used to further define how admission control will ensure capacity for the cluster. The three policies are as follows:

- Host failures the cluster tolerates

- Percentage of cluster resources reserved as failover spare capacity

- Specify failover hosts

Each of these three options will now be discussed in more detail, but also keep in mind that HA is a complex subject and that multiple chapters could easily be devoted to it.

Host Failures the Cluster Tolerates   With this policy, a user-specified number of hosts may fail, and vSphere HA will reserve resources to fail over the virtual machines running from this number of failed hosts. The calculation used for this is based on a slot size, which is the amount of memory and CPU assigned to powered-on virtual machines. The slot size is compared to the capacity of the hosts in the cluster to determine how many total slots are available. vSphere HA will then attempt to reserve enough resources to be able to satisfy the number of needed slots.

Percentage of Cluster Resources Reserved as Failover Spare Capacity   With this policy, a user-specified percentage of the cluster's aggregate CPU and memory resources are reserved for recovery from ESXi host failures. CPU and memory percentages can be configured separately, and the CPU and memory reservation values of the virtual machine are used in the calculation by vSphere HA.

Specify Failover Hosts   With this policy, a user-specified number of hosts are reserved strictly for failover. The failover host(s) cannot have powered-on virtual machines, because the failover host(s) will be used only for an HA event. In an HA event, vSphere HA will attempt to start the virtual machines on the failover host. If the specified failover host is not available or is at capacity, then vSphere HA will attempt to use other hosts in the cluster to start virtual machines.

Now that I have briefly discussed admission control and the admission control policies, I will show how to configure both in Exercise 8.4.

EXERCISE 8.4

Configuring Admission Control and Admission Control Policies

1. Connect to a vCenter Server with the vSphere Client.

2. Locate a cluster in the inventory. Right-click it and choose the Edit Settings option from the context menu that appears.

3. Select vSphere HA in the left pane in the cluster settings window.

4. Ensure that the Enable Host Monitoring option is selected in the Host Monitoring Status section.

5. In the Admission Control section, ensure that the Enable option is selected.

    If admission control was previously disabled, selecting the Enabled option will make the admission control policy section active.

6. Select the admission control policy of Percentage Of Cluster Resources Reserved As Failover Spare Capacity.

7. Change the values to 35% for each.

8. Select the Specify Failover Hosts option. Notice how the previous values stay the same but are now grayed out.

9. Click the blue 0 Hosts Specified link. A Specify Failover Hosts window will appear.

10. Move at least one of your two ESXi hosts from the Available Hosts pane on the left into the Failover Hosts pane on the right by using the arrow buttons located between the two panes.

The final configuration should look like this.

11. Click OK in the Specify Failover Hosts window to save these changes.

12. Note that the blue link has now been updated to indicate that one host is specified for failover.

13. Click OK to save the admission control settings. A Reconfigure Cluster task will begin.

14. When this task completes, locate the vSphere HA panel on the Summary tab for the cluster. Verify that a value of 1 is listed for Current Failover Hosts and click the blue information icon to view the hostname.

(continued)

15. Power on a virtual machine in the cluster. Attempt to migrate it with vMotion to the failover host. You will receive an error message stating that the operation cannot be performed.

One other item that needs to be addressed is the virtual machine options for vSphere HA. These options are also listed in the cluster settings and are contained in the vSphere HA options. Figure 8.4 shows the Virtual Machine Options screen.

FIGURE 8.4   Virtual Machine Options screen for HA

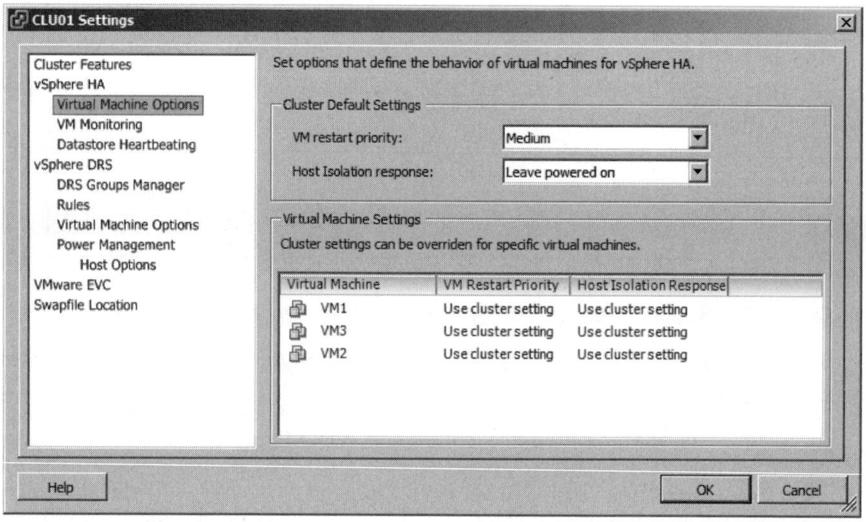

The Virtual Machine Options section of the cluster settings is used to specify the restart priority and host isolation response for both the cluster and the individual virtual machines. The virtual machine restart priority is used to specify the start order for virtual machines, if an HA event occurs. VMs with the highest restart priority are restarted first. This setting can be used to ensure that important virtual machines get powered on first. It is also useful in cases where cluster resources become exhausted in an HA event, to ensure that the more important VMs are powered on.

If you recall the vApp start order options I discussed in Chapter 6, VM restart priority can be used in a somewhat similar way. In an application with a three-tiered architecture, the database server could have a High restart priority, the application server could have a Medium priority, and the web server frontend could have a Low priority. While there will be no guarantees, like with a vApp, it is still a sound approach. There are four settings for virtual machine priority:

- Disabled
- Low

- Medium
- High

The Disabled option can be used to disable HA for virtual machines. This could be useful for clusters that include nonessential virtual machines.

Host isolation response is used configure the behavior of the ESXi host when it has lost its management network connection but has not failed. When a host is no longer able to communicate with the HA agents running on other ESXi hosts in the cluster and is also unable to ping its isolation address, it is considered isolated. Once isolated, the host will execute the isolation response. The isolation responses are as follows:

- Leave powered on
- Power off
- Shut down

These options are self-explanatory, but do know that the shutdown isolation response requires that the guest operating systems have the VMware Tools installed. Now that I have discussed vSphere HA options for virtual machines, I will show how to configure them in Exercise 8.5.

EXERCISE 8.5

Configuring VM Options for vSphere HA

1. Connect to a vCenter Server with the vSphere Client.

2. Locate a cluster in the inventory. Right-click it and choose the Edit Settings option from the context menu that appears.

3. Select Virtual Machine Options listed under vSphere HA in the left pane in the cluster settings window.

4. Using the VM Restart Priority drop-down menu, change the option to Low.

5. Using the Host Isolation Response drop-down menu, change the option to Shut Down.

   These two options have now changed the default behavior for the cluster as a whole. In the remainder of the exercise, I will show how to modify individual virtual machine settings. The remainder of the exercise will also work off the three-tiered application I discussed earlier. If you don't have a three-tiered application, complete the exercise with existing virtual machines instead.

6. Using the drop-down menu beside the virtual machine that houses the database, change VM Restart Priority to High by clicking the current value. Clicking the current value will present a drop-down menu. Ensure Host Isolation Response is set to the Use Cluster Setting option.

   These options will configure HA to shut down the database cleanly and then restart this virtual machine with a high priority. Note that individual virtual machine priority settings will override those of the cluster.

(continued)

EXERCISE 8.5 *(continued)*

7. Using the drop-down menu beside the virtual machine that houses the middleware, change VM Restart Priority to Medium. Ensure Host Isolation Response is set to the Use Cluster Setting option.

   These options will configure HA to shut down the middleware virtual machine and then restart it with a medium priority. Note again that individual virtual machine priority settings will override those of the cluster.

8. Using the drop-down menu beside the virtual machine that houses the web server, change VM Restart Priority to Low. Ensure Host Isolation Response is set to the Use Cluster Setting option.

   These options will configure HA to shut down the web server frontend for the application and then restart it with a low priority.

   The final configuration should appear similar to what is shown here.

9. Click OK to save these changes.

10. A Reconfigure Cluster task will begin. When this task completes, the virtual machine options for HA will be set.

I have now covered admission control, covered admission control policies, and configured admission control for a cluster with DRS and HA enabled. I also discussed and configured the virtual machine options within HA. Enabling, configuring, and disabling virtual machine and application monitoring will be covered next.

Enabling, Configuring, and Disabling Virtual Machine and Application Monitoring

VM monitoring is used to provide high availability for individual virtual machines. Where vSphere HA can restart virtual machines when a host fails or becomes isolated, VM monitoring can restart individual virtual machines when they have failed or become unresponsive. Application monitoring works in much the same way, except that a specific application is monitored rather than the virtual machine.

VM monitoring works by monitoring VMware Tools heartbeats and I/O activity from the VMware Tools process running in the guest OS. If VMware Tools heartbeats stop for the duration of the failure interval, the last 120 seconds of disk I/O activity will be checked. If there is no disk I/O in this period, the virtual machine will be reset.

Virtual machine monitoring sensitivity can also be configured for the cluster and for individual VMs. This allows you to fine-tune the monitoring sensitivity both to obtain rapid resolution and to avoid false positives. Table 8.1 shows the VM monitoring sensitivity values for the cluster setting.

TABLE 8.1   VM monitoring sensitivity settings

Setting	Failure interval	Reset period
High	30 seconds	1 hour
Medium	60 seconds	24 hours
Low	120 seconds	7 days

 You can also use the Custom option for VM Monitoring Sensitivity, if the defaults do not provide the functionality required for your environment.

Virtual machines can be configured individually so that an individual VM can have settings that override those of the cluster. These options are configured in the VM Monitoring section of the cluster settings and will be discussed in more detail in Exercise 8.6.

Application monitoring performs similarly to VM monitoring. It differs in that it uses heartbeats from a specific application and thus requires the application to be customized to utilize VMware application monitoring.

In Exercise 8.6, I will show how to enable and configure VM and application monitoring.

EXERCISE 8.6

Enabling and Configuring VM Monitoring and Application Monitoring

1. Connect to a vCenter Server with the vSphere Client.

2. Locate a cluster in the inventory. Right-click it and choose the Edit Settings option from the context menu that appears.

3. Select VM Monitoring listed under vSphere HA in the left pane in the cluster settings window.

4. Using the drop-down menu beside VM Monitoring, change the value to VM And Application Monitoring.

   Note that by default VM Monitoring is set to Disabled. To disable the VM Monitoring option after this exercise is complete, simply change the value here.

5. Using the slider menu in the center of the screen, change Monitoring Sensitivity to Low.

   Note that this will enable the VM to be restarted if no heartbeat or I/O is detected within a two-minute interval. The virtual machine can be restarted up to three times within the reset period of seven days. If the VM fails a fourth time within the reset period, vSphere HA will take no further action. The remainder of this exercise will again make use of the three-tiered application example. Replace these virtual machines with those in your own lab as necessary.

6. Change the VM Monitoring value for the database server to Disabled. Note that the Application Monitoring column will gray out once this selection is made.

   The database server has now been excluded from VM and application monitoring.

7. Change the Application Monitoring value for the Middleware server to Custom. A Custom VM Monitoring Settings window will appear, as shown here.

8. Change one value here and then click OK to accept the custom values. Leave the Application Monitoring value at Include.

9. Change the Application Monitoring value for the web server to Exclude and note how the value for VM Monitoring changes automatically to Low.

10. The final configuration should look like this.

11. Click OK to save these changes. A Reconfigure Cluster task will begin. When this task completes, the virtual machine and application monitoring options for HA will be set.

I have now covered enabling and configuring virtual machine and application monitoring for vSphere HA. Next I will move on to DRS and configuring automation levels for DRS and virtual machines.

Configuring Automation Levels for DRS and Virtual Machines

Since DRS is responsible for both the initial placement of virtual machines and migrations using vMotion, automation levels can be configured to help control how involved the distributed resource scheduler will actually be. Table 8.2 shows the available automation levels and a description of each.

TABLE 8.2 VM monitoring sensitivity settings

Automation level	Description
Manual	No action will be taken, and vCenter Server will inform of suggested virtual machine migrations.
Partially automated	vCenter Server will inform of suggested virtual machine migrations and place the virtual machines on ESXi hosts at VM startup.
Fully automated	vCenter Server will use vMotion to optimize resource usage in the cluster and place the virtual machines on ESXi hosts at VM startup.

The automation level can be set for the entire DRS cluster, but virtual machines may have their individual automation levels set to override the cluster settings. In Exercise 8.7, I will set the automation level for a cluster and set a virtual machine's individual automation level to differ from the cluster settings.

EXERCISE 8.7

Configuring Automation Level for Cluster and a VM

1. Connect to a vCenter Server with the vSphere Client.

2. Locate a cluster in the inventory. Right-click it and choose the Edit Settings option from the context menu that appears.

3. Select vSphere DRS the left pane in the cluster settings window. The automation level will be shown in the right pane.

   In Exercise 8.1 when I showed how to create the cluster, the automation level was set to Manual. In the following steps, you will change the automation level to Fully Automated.

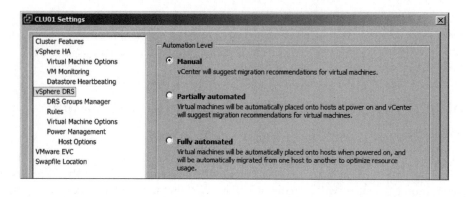

4. Select the Fully Automated option and accept the default migration threshold option. Click OK to save these changes.

   The migration threshold settings will be covered in detail in the next section of this chapter.

5. A Reconfigure Cluster task will begin. When this task completes, the DRS automation level has been changed for the cluster.

   Changing the automation level for the cluster was the first part of this exercise, and the remainder of the exercise will focus on changing the automation level for an individual virtual machine in the cluster.

6. Obtain the cluster settings again and choose the Virtual Machine Options item listed under vSphere DRS in the left pane.

7. Ensure that Enable Individual Virtual Machine Automation Levels is selected. Removing this check mark from the check box will disable individual automation levels and gray out the virtual machine options below.

8. Select a virtual machine from the list and click the value listed beside it in the Automation Level column.

9. In the drop-down menu that appears, change Automation Level to Disabled for this virtual machine.

   Disabling the automation level will prevent vCenter from making or performing migration recommendations for it. Disabling the automation level is also known as *pinning* a virtual machine to a host.

   The final configuration should look like this.

   (continued)

EXERCISE 8.7 *(continued)*

```
CLU01 Settings                                                    [x]

Cluster Features
vSphere HA                      ☑ Enable individual virtual machine automation levels.
    Virtual Machine Options
    VM Monitoring
    Datastore Heartbeating       Set individual automation level options for virtual machines in the cluster.
vSphere DRS
    DRS Groups Manager                 Virtual Machine or Automation Level contains: ▾ [            ]    Clear
    Rules
   [Virtual Machine Options]     Virtual Machine            Automation Level
    Power Management               Webserver                Default (Fully Automated)
        Host Options               Middleware               Default (Fully Automated)
VMware EVC                         Database                 Disabled
Swapfile Location




        Help                                                        OK        Cancel
```

10. Click OK to save these changes.

   A Reconfigure Cluster task will begin. When this task completes, the DRS automation level has been changed for the virtual machine.

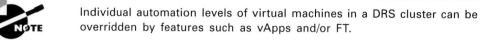 Individual automation levels of virtual machines in a DRS cluster can be overridden by features such as vApps and/or FT.

I have now covered configuring the automation level for a DRS cluster and individual virtual machines that are running in the cluster. In the next section, I will configure migration thresholds for DRS and virtual machines.

Configuring Migration Thresholds for DRS and Virtual Machines

In the previous exercise of configuring the cluster automation level, the default migration threshold was accepted. The migration threshold is used to specify which recommendations are generated or applied, depending on the selected cluster automation level. For example, the manual and partially automated automation levels will result only in vMotion recommendations being generated. The migration threshold can be adjusted using the slider provided in the DRS automation-level settings.

Moving the migration threshold slider to the left will make DRS more conservative or minimize the number of recommendations or operations performed by DRS. Moving the slider to the right will make DRS more aggressive and will result in more recommendations or operations in the cluster. Like many of the options in vSphere, the key is to find the migration threshold setting that works best in your particular environment. In Exercise 8.8, I will cover the steps for configuring the migration threshold for DRS.

EXERCISE 8.8

Configuring the Migration Threshold for DRS

1. Connect to a vCenter Server with the vSphere Client.

2. Locate a cluster in the inventory. Right-click it and choose the Edit Settings option from the context menu that appears.

3. Select vSphere DRS the left pane in the cluster settings window. The automation level will be shown in the right pane.

4. In Exercise 8.7 the automation level was set to Fully Automated, and the default setting was accepted for the migration threshold.

5. Slide the Migration Threshold slider to the far left. Review the information displayed below the slider. This information will change each time the slider is moved to explain the effect of the current position.

6. Move the slider one position to the right and review the information displayed below it. Repeat these steps until the slider has reached the far-right side.

7. Move the slider to its default position in the middle and click the Cancel button.

The migration threshold is applied to the cluster as a whole, and there is no option to change the migration threshold for an individual virtual machine. The closest setting that can be used to exclude virtual machines from the migration threshold setting is the individual virtual machine automation level. As I covered in the previous exercise, the individual virtual machine automation level can be either changed or disabled.

> Disabling the individual automation level of a virtual machine that vCenter Server is running on is often used to ensure that vCenter Server is always located, or "pinned," on a single ESXi host.

Now that I have covered setting the migration threshold for a DRS cluster, I will cover how to create VM-Host and VM-VM affinity rules.

Creating VM-Host and VM-VM Affinity Rules

Affinity rules are used in clusters to control the placement of virtual machines. Two types of relationships can be established with affinity rules:

Affinity   Used to keep VMs together

Anti-affinity   Used to keep VMs separated

For example, an affinity rule can be used to ensure that two virtual machines run on the same ESXi host. This is often used for performance reasons, because all of traffic between virtual machines will be localized. An anti-affinity rule might be used when there are redundant virtual machines established as part of a fault-tolerant design. Keeping these VMs separated could provide protection from unplanned application downtime in the event of an ESXi host failure.

In addition to the two types of relationships established with affinity rules, there are two different types of affinity rules:

VM-Host   Used with a group of VMs and a group of hosts

VM-VM   Used between individual virtual machines

The key thing to remember with the two types of affinity rules are that the VM-Host rules apply to groups and they will utilize the DRS Groups Manager. VM-VM rules apply to individual virtual machines and do not utilize the DRS Groups Manager.

> Affinity rules in DRS are not the same thing as the CPU scheduling affinity that can be specified for a VM in the Virtual Machine Properties editor.

Now that I have discussed what affinity rules are and the relationships that can be established with them, Exercise 8.9 will cover the steps required to create a VM-Host affinity rule. As mentioned previously, VM-Host affinity rules are used to group virtual machines and hosts. Both of these groups must be created as DRS groups before any VM-Host affinity rules can be created.

EXERCISE 8.9

Creating a VM-Host Affinity Rule

1. Connect to a vCenter Server with the vSphere Client.

2. Locate a cluster in the inventory. Right-click it and choose the Edit Settings option from the context menu that appears.

3. Select DRS Groups Manager from beneath the vSphere DRS option in the left pane in the cluster settings window.

4. In the Virtual Machines DRS Groups section, click the Add button. A DRS Group window will appear.

5. Give the DRS group a descriptive name in the Name field.

   The left pane lists the virtual machines that are not in this DRS group. This should be all virtual machines in the cluster, since there are currently no DRS groups created. It is important to remember that a virtual machine may be in more than one DRS group.

6. Move one or more virtual machines from the left pane into the right pane using the arrow buttons located between the panes.

   The right pane represents virtual machines that will be contained in the DRS group.

7. Once all of the applicable virtual machines have been moved into the right pane, the result should look like this.

(continued)

EXERCISE 8.9 *(continued)*

8. Click OK and verify that the virtual machine DRS group is now listed.

9. In the Host DRS Groups section, click the Add button. A DRS Group window will appear. This window is identical to the one used in steps 5 to 8 but will contain ESXi hosts instead of virtual machines.

10. Give the DRS group a descriptive name and add a single ESXi host to the group. The configuration should look like this.

11. Click OK and verify that both a Virtual Machine DRS Group and a Host DRS Group are each listed in their respective sections in the cluster settings window.

12. Click OK to save these groups. A Reconfigure Cluster task will begin.

At this point, the DRS groups required to create a VM-Host affinity rule have been created. The remainder of the exercise will cover creating the actual affinity rule.

13. Return to the cluster properties window and select Rules from beneath the vSphere DRS option in the left pane in the cluster settings window.

14. Click the Add button in the lower-right pane to create a new rule. A Rule window will appear.

Note that the Rule tab is the default tab in the Rule window. Also note that the DRS Groups Manager can be accessed from the DRS Groups Manager tab. This is provided as a convenient option.

15. Provide the rule with a descriptive name.

16. Using the drop-down menu located under the Type field, choose the Virtual Machines To Hosts option.

17. Note that a DRS Groups section appears after making this change.

Three options are available here, and these three components are what actually make up an affinity rule.

18. Using the drop-down menu located under the Cluster VM Group field, verify that the VM group created earlier in this exercise is selected.

19. Using the drop-down menu located under the Cluster Host Group field, verify that the Host group created earlier in this exercise is selected.

Both of these drop-down menus should contain only a single entry, since only a single VM group and host group were created. If multiple groups had been created, the drop-down menus would contain them all.

20. In the unlabeled drop-down menu located between the Cluster VM Group and Host Group menus, choose the Must Run On Hosts In Group option.

The final configuration should look like this.

(continued)

EXERCISE 8.9 *(continued)*

Rule

Rule | DRS Groups Manager

Give the new rule a name and choose its type from the menu below. Then, select the entities to which this rule will apply.

Name
```
Tier3App-SingleHost
```

Type
```
Virtual Machines to Hosts
```

DRS Groups

Cluster Vm Group:
```
3TieredApp
```

```
Must run on hosts in group
```

Cluster Host Group:
```
2NodeSplit-Host1
```

Virtual machines that are members of the Cluster DRS VM Group 3TieredApp Must run on hosts in group 2NodeSplit-Host1.

OK   Cancel

21. Click OK to add the rule.

22. The rule will now be listed in the cluster settings window. Expand the rule to view its components.

CLU01 Settings

Cluster Features
vSphere HA
    Virtual Machine Options
    VM Monitoring
    Datastore Heartbeating
vSphere DRS
    DRS Groups Manager
    Rules
    Virtual Machine Options
    Power Management
      Host Options
VMware EVC
Swapfile Location

Use this page to create rules for virtual machines within this cluster. Rules will apply to virtual machines only while they are deployed to this cluster and will not be retained if the virtual machines are moved out of the cluster.

Name	Type	Defined by
Tier3App-SingleHost	Run VMs on Hosts	User
3TieredApp	Cluster VM Group	
2NodeSplit-Host1	Cluster Host Group	

Add...   Remove   Edit...   Details...

Help   OK   Cancel

23. Click the Details button at the bottom of the screen and review the information presented in the Details window. Click the Close button to exit the Details window.

24. Click the Edit button at the bottom of the screen and notice that the Rule window will appear. This is the same window that was used to create the rule, but the fields are prepopulated with the name and components of the rule.

25. Click Cancel to close the Rule window.

Note that there is a check box listed to the left of the rule name. Removing the check mark from this check box will disable the rule. This can be useful for troubleshooting purposes and will prevent you from having to delete and re-create individual rules.

26. Click OK in the cluster settings window. A Reconfigure Cluster task will begin. When this task completes, the VM-Host affinity rule will become active.

 Virtual machines that are removed from a cluster will lose their DRS group affiliations, and returning the virtual machine to the cluster will not restore them.

In step 20 of the previous exercise, four options are available when creating the VM-Host affinity rule. These options are as follows:

Must Run On Hosts In Group   VMs in the specified VM group are required to run on ESXi hosts in the specified host group.

Should Run On Hosts In Group   VMs in the specified VM group are preferred to run on ESXi hosts in the specified host group.

Must Not Run On Hosts In Group   VMs in the specified VM group are required to never run on ESXi hosts in the specified host group.

Should Not Run On Hosts In Group   VMs in the specified VM group are preferred to not run on ESXi hosts in the specified host group.

There are also a few caveats that need to be mentioned about VM-Host affinity rules:

- If multiple VM-Host affinity rules exist, they are applied equally.
- VM-Host affinity rules are not checked for compatibility with each other.
- DRS and HA will not violate affinity rules, so affinity rules could actually affect cluster functionality.

The best practice is to use VM-Host affinity rules sparingly and to consider using the preferential options in rules. This allows more flexibility.

Now that I have covered VM-Host affinity rules, I will move on to VM-VM affinity rules. Where VM-Host affinity rules are used to specify relationships between VM groups and host groups, a VM-VM affinity rule applies only to individual virtual machines. In Exercise 8.10, I will cover the steps for creating a VM-VM affinity rule.

EXERCISE 8.10

Creating a VM-VM Affinity Rule

1. Connect to a vCenter Server with the vSphere Client.

2. Locate a cluster in the inventory. Right-click it and choose the Edit Settings option from the context menu that appears.

3. Select Rules from beneath the vSphere DRS option in the left pane in the cluster settings window.

4. In the right pane, you will see the rule created in the previous exercise. Remove the check box from this rule, before proceeding, to disable the rule.

5. Click the Add button at the bottom of the screen to create a new VM-VM anti-affinity rule.

6. A Rule window will appear. Provide the rule with a descriptive name.

7. Using the drop-down menu located under the Type field, choose the Separate Virtual Machines option.

8. Click the Add button at the bottom of the Rule window to add the virtual machines to this rule.

9. Select two virtual machines that should not run on the same host. The final configuration should look like this.

The example image assumes that two web servers are being used to provide application redundancy, and the VM-VM anti-affinity rule is used to keep them on different hosts.

10. Click OK to add the rule.

11. The rule will now be listed in the Cluster Settings window. Expand the rule to view its components.

12. Select the rule and click the Details button at the bottom of the screen. Review the information presented in the Details window. Click the Close button to exit the Details window.

13. Click the Edit button at the bottom of the screen and notice that the Rule window will appear. This is the same window that was used to create the rule, but the fields are prepopulated with the name and components of the rule.

14. Click Cancel to close the Rule window.

15. Note that VM-VM rules can also be disabled by removing the check mark from the check box beside the rule name.

16. Click OK in the cluster settings window. A Reconfigure Cluster task will begin. When this task completes, the VM-VM anti-affinity rule will become active.

Just like the VM-Host affinity rules, there is a caveat for VM-VM affinity rules. If VM-VM affinity rules conflict with each other, the newer of the conflicting rules will be disabled. For example, in the previous exercise, I covered how to create an anti-affinity rule. If an affinity rule were to be added with the same two virtual machines, the result would look similar to what is shown in Figure 8.5.

FIGURE 8.5   Conflicting VM-VM affinity rules

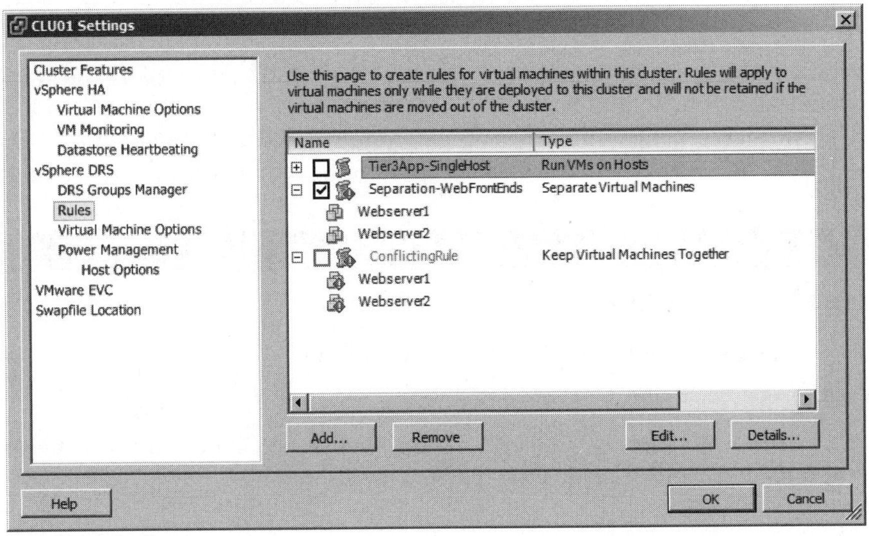

In Figure 8.5, a new rule was added with the name Conflicting Rule that attempted to keep the two web server virtual machines together. Also note that DRS places higher priority on preventing violations of anti-affinity rules than it does on preventing violations of affinity rules. Now that I have covered VM-VM affinity rules, I will cover how to configure Enhanced vMotion Compatibility for a cluster.

Configuring Enhanced vMotion Compatibility

Enhanced vMotion Compatibility (EVC) can be used in a cluster to allow greater vMotion compatibility for the different ESXi hosts in the cluster. Configuring EVC for a cluster allows the ESXi host processors to present a baseline processor feature set known as the EVC mode. The EVC mode will be equal to the host in the cluster that contains the smallest feature set.

Only processor features that affect vMotion will be masked by EVC. It has no effect on processor speeds or vCPU counts.

Enabling EVC for a cluster is a simple operation, but it is important to know that the following requirements exist for enabling EVC on a cluster:

- All hosts in the cluster must have only Intel or only AMD processors. Mixing Intel and AMD processors is not allowed.

- ESX/ESXi 3.5 update 2 or newer is required for all hosts in the cluster.

- All hosts in the cluster must be connected to the vCenter Server that is used to manage the cluster.

- vMotion networking should be configured identically for all hosts in the cluster.

- CPU features, like hardware virtualization support (AMD-V or Intel VT) and AMD No eXecute (NX) or Intel eXecute Disable (XD), should be enabled consistently across all hosts in the cluster.

In Exercise 8.11, the steps to configure EVC on a cluster will be covered. In the interest of covering all lab environments, I will create a new cluster with no ESXi hosts for this exercise. This way, if you are using nested ESXi in your lab, you can complete the exercise. It will also allow me to cover how to enable EVC when the cluster is created.

EXERCISE 8.11

Enabling EVC for a Cluster

1. Connect to a vCenter Server with the vSphere Client.

2. Switch to the Hosts and Cluster view.

3. Select a datacenter object in the inventory and right-click it. Choose the New Cluster option from the context menu that appears.

4. Give the cluster a descriptive and unique name. Do not enable DRS or HA for the cluster. Click Next to continue.

5. Select the Enable EVC For Intel Hosts option. Accept the default value in the drop-down menu of Intel "Merom" Gen. (Xeon Core 2) and click Next to continue.

6. Accept the default value for Swapfile Policy For Virtual Machines and click Next to continue.

7. Review the information presented on the Ready To Complete screen and click Finish to create the EVC-enabled cluster.

   At this point, a cluster has been created with EVC enabled. The remainder of this exercise will focus on the steps required to change the EVC mode.

8. Locate the cluster you just created in the inventory. Right-click it and choose the Edit Settings option from the context menu that appears.

9. Select VMware EVC from the left pane. Review the current VMware EVC Mode status at the top of the information presented in the right pane.

10. In the lower right of the screen, click the Change EVC Mode button.

(continued)

11. The Change EVC Mode window will appear.

12. Using the drop-down menu to the right of VMware EVC Mode, change the selection to Intel Sandy Bridge Generation. The Compatibility window should report Validation Succeeded, since there are no ESXi hosts in this cluster.

13. Click OK in the Change EVC Mode window and then verify that the VMware EVC Mode reports Intel Sandy Bridge Generation in the cluster settings window.

14. Click OK to save the changes. A Reconfigure Cluster task and a Configure Cluster EVC task will both start. When these tasks complete, the EVC mode has been changed successfully.

In the previous exercise, there were no ESXi hosts in the cluster. This allowed flexibility in creating and changing the EVC mode. In the real world, where clusters will have hosts, it is important to understand how EVC mode impacts these hosts.

Lowering the EVC mode for a cluster involves moving from a greater feature set to a lower feature set. This is often useful when introducing ESXi hosts on newer hardware into an existing cluster. It is important to remember that any virtual machines running on ESXi hosts with newer features than the EVC mode supports will need to be powered off, before lowering the EVC mode.

Raising the EVC mode for a cluster involves moving from a lower feature set to a greater feature set. This is often useful when hardware refreshes of ESXi hosts have raised the CPU baseline capability. It is important to remember that any running virtual machines may continue to run during this operation. The VMs simply will not have access to the newer CPU features of the EVC mode until they have been powered off. Also note that a reboot will not suffice, and a full power cycle of the virtual machine is required.

The following two VMware KB articles are helpful for determining both EVC compatibility and processor support:

- http://kb.vmware.com/kb/1005764

- http://kb.vmware.com/kb/1003212

Now that I have covered configuring EVC mode for a cluster, I will cover how to monitor a DRS/HA cluster.

Monitoring a DRS/HA Cluster

There are many options for monitoring a DRS cluster, and having the vSphere Client open is a great start. If there are significant problems, the cluster item in the inventory will display an alert or warning icon. A warning condition is shown for a cluster in Figure 8.6.

FIGURE 8.6   Cluster with warning condition

In Figure 8.6 an ESXi host in the cluster was abruptly powered off to simulate a host failure. The cluster went into a warning status, and the ESXi host is listed with an alert status. This real-time information can be quite valuable.

A great deal of additional real-time information can be obtained about a cluster by simply viewing its Summary tab in the vSphere Client. Five panels are available on the Summary tab, and much of the information contained here is the same information found in the cluster settings properties window. Figure 8.7 shows the five panels available for viewing in the cluster Summary tab.

FIGURE 8.7   Cluster's Summary tab

General

vSphere DRS:	On
vSphere HA:	On
VMware EVC Mode:	Disabled
Total CPU Resources:	10 GHz
Total Memory:	16.00 GB
Total Storage:	460.94 GB
Number of Hosts:	2
Total Processors:	4
Number of Datastore Clusters:	0
Total Datastores:	4
Virtual Machines and Templates:	4
Total Migrations using vMotion:	2

Commands

New Virtual Machine	New Datastore Cluster
Add Host	Edit Settings
New Resource Pool	

vSphere HA

Admission Control:	Enabled
Current CPU Failover Capacity:	100 %
Current Memory Failover Capacity:	100 %
Configured CPU Failover Capacity:	25 %
Configured Memory Failover Capacity:	25 %
Host Monitoring:	Enabled
VM Monitoring:	Disabled
Application Monitoring:	Disabled
Cluster Status	
Configuration Issues	

vSphere DRS

Migration Automation Level:	Fully Automated
Power Management Automation Level:	Off
DRS Recommendations:	0
DRS Faults:	0
Migration Threshold:	Apply all recommendations.
Target host load standard deviation:	<= 0.05
Current host load standard deviation:	0 (✓ Load balanced)
View Resource Distribution Chart	
View DRS Troubleshooting Guide	

Storage

Storage resources	Status	Drive Type	Capacity
esxi1-dsVMFS	✓ Normal	Non-SSD	217.00 GB
esxi2-dsVMFS	✓ Normal	Non-SSD	217.00 GB
NFS	✓ Normal	Unknown	13.47 GB
NFS2	✓ Normal	Unknown	13.47 GB

The General panel shows the status of DRS and HA and the current EVC mode of the cluster. There is also information on the CPU, memory, and storage resources available to the cluster. Inventory information about hosts, processors, datastores, VMs, and vMotion operations are also available in the General panel.

Located under the General panel is the Commands panel, which provides convenient access to many of the same options available in the context menu for the cluster.

The vSphere HA panel is located on the top right and contains information on admission control and admission control policies. Host, VM, and application monitoring information are also available in this panel. At the bottom of the vSphere HA panel, there are two blue links provided for the cluster status and configuration issues. Figure 8.8 shows the vSphere HA Cluster Status window.

FIGURE 8.8   vSphere HA Cluster Status window

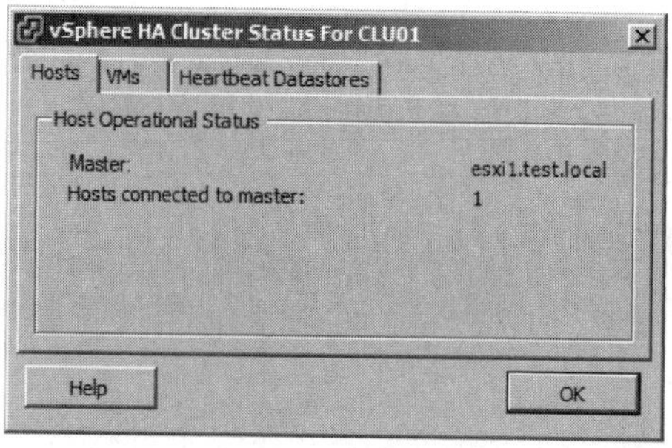

The vSphere HA Cluster Status window defaults to the Hosts tab, where the master node is identified and the number of slave nodes connected to the master node are listed. The VMs tab provides information on the number of VMs protected and unprotected by vSphere HA. The Heartbeat Datastores tab provides information on the datastores used for heartbeating.

The other blue link provided in the vSphere HA panel is to identify configuration issues in the cluster. Clicking this link will open the Cluster Configuration Issues window, where any problems with the cluster will be listed.

The next panel is the vSphere DRS panel, which lists the automation level, DRS recommendations and faults, migration threshold setting, and load standard deviation information. There are also two blue links included in the vSphere DRS panel. The lowest blue link titled View DRS Troubleshooting Guide will launch the help file. The other blue link titled View Resource Distribution Chart is one of the more useful tools for monitoring your cluster's resource consumption. Figure 8.9 shows the DRS Resource Distribution window.

The default view in the DRS Resource Distribution window is for CPU resources. Using the gray % and MHz buttons at the top of the window will allow the view to be toggled between utilization views. Each ESXi host in the cluster will be listed in the left column, and each of the colored boxes represents either a single virtual machine or a group of what are essentially idle virtual machines. Green boxes are good to see here! The legend at the bottom of the window shows that green means 100 percent of the entitled resources are being delivered for the VM. Any other color means the VM is not receiving all of its entitled resources. By hovering the cursor over any of these colored boxes, you can obtain the name of the virtual machine and information about its current resource usage.

FIGURE 8.9   DRS Resource Distribution window

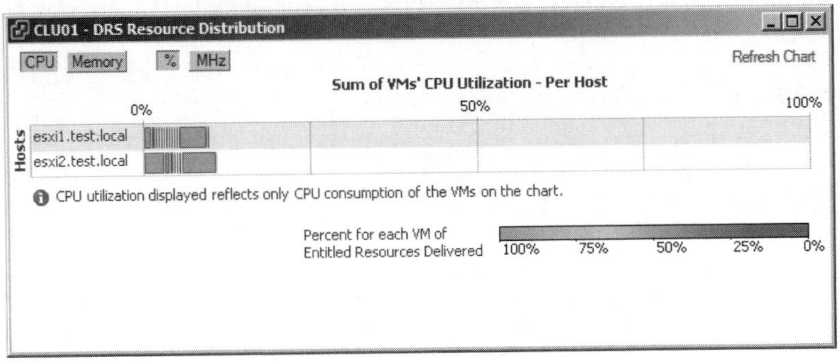

The memory settings for the cluster are also available in the DRS Resource Distribution window, and this view can be selected by clicking the gray Memory button at the top of the window. Figure 8.10 shows the memory view.

FIGURE 8.10   DRS memory utilization view

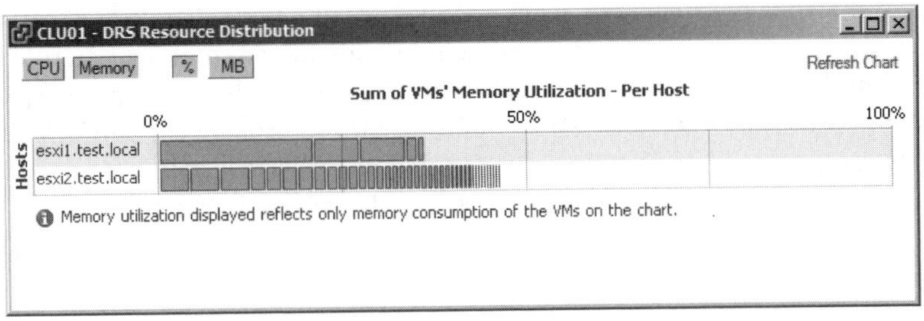

Using the gray % and MB buttons at the top of the window will allow the view to be toggled between utilization views. Each ESXi host in the cluster will be listed in the left column, and each of the gray boxes represents a single virtual machine. Just like with the CPU resources, hovering the cursor over any of these gray boxes will allow you to obtain the name of the virtual machine and information about its current resource usage.

As you can see, the information presented in the DRS Resource Distribution window provides a quick and easy way to see whether your hosts are load balanced and can often be revealing about which VMs are using the most resources. The information presented here also allows you to view more closely how DRS actually load balances.

Another option that can be used to monitor the cluster is the DRS tab that is visible when the cluster is selected in the left pane. The DRS tab default view of Recommendations lists the DRS properties and recommendations, if configured with either the partially automated or manual automation level. The Faults view can be used to view faults that prevented the application of a DRS recommendation. The final view is the History view, which can be used to review historical information for DRS actions.

The Resource Allocation tab, Performance tab, Tasks & Events tab, and Alarms tab can each also be used to monitor a cluster. Alarms can also be configured in vCenter Server to help monitor your cluster. Figure 8.11 shows the default vSphere HA alarm definitions.

FIGURE 8.11   vCenter alarms for vSphere HA

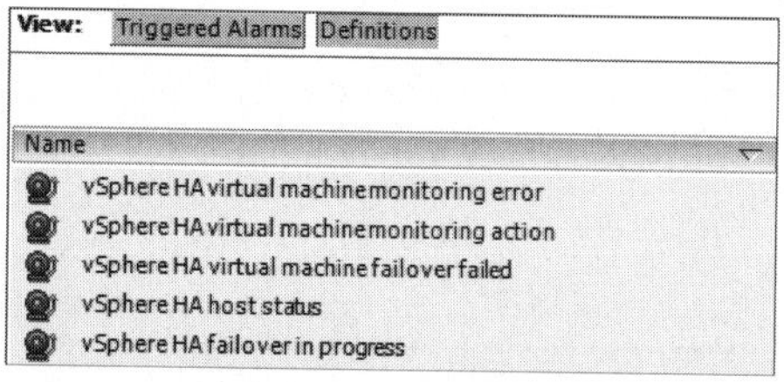

vCenter Server alarms will be covered in detail in Chapter 11, and many of the monitoring topics will also be revisited in Chapter 10 when troubleshooting HA/DRS clusters will be covered.

In addition to the included functionality in vCenter Server, there are additional options like VMware vCenter Operations or any number of third-party solutions that can be used to monitor your clusters. These products can provide additional insight into your virtual infrastructure and are often already deployed in many environments. Operational staff members are also typically trained in using these solutions. Leveraging these existing monitoring solutions can add additional monitoring capabilities for your DRS/HA clusters.

Now that I have covered monitoring a cluster, I will cover how to configure Storage DRS.

Configuring Storage DRS

Storage DRS is a new feature in vSphere 5. Storage DRS offers to datastores what a DRS-enabled cluster offers to ESXi hosts. When a virtual machine is deployed, it can be deployed into a cluster, and DRS will take care of the initial placement of the VM on an ESXi host. DRS can also move the virtual machine to a different host, as necessary, in order to provide the VM its entitled resources. Storage DRS provides both virtual machine placement and load balancing based on I/O and/or capacity. The goal of Storage DRS is to lessen the administrative effort involved with managing datastores by representing a pool of storage as a single resource.

🌐 Real World Scenario

Goodbye to Spreadsheets

A virtual infrastructure administrator has multiple datastores in her infrastructure. Her environment has datastores located on a SAN, but none of these datastores is consistent in their configuration. There is one disk group with fifteen SATA drives, one disk group with six 15k FC drives, and many other groups that vary in number, capacity, and drive speed. Until now, the virtual infrastructure administrator has kept spreadsheets to keep up with these disk configurations and virtual machine placements.

She also spends a lot of time dealing with complaints of slowness, identifying the latencies, and manually correcting them with Storage vMotion. Of course, after this, she has to update the spreadsheets to help her make sense of it all.

After the virtual infrastructure administrator upgrades her environment to vSphere 5, she decides that she will implement datastore clusters and use Storage DRS. Storage DRS will monitor her environment for capacity and I/O performance issues and correct them automatically. The virtual infrastructure administrator was relieved to be able to say goodbye to both her manual processes and the spreadsheets.

Storage DRS is made possible by the new datastore cluster object, which is simply a collection of datastores with shared resources and management. There are several requirements to use datastore clusters:

- Only ESXi 5 hosts can be attached to any of the datastores in a datastore cluster.
- Mixing NFS and VMFS datastores is not allowed in the same datastore cluster.
- A datastore cluster cannot contain datastores shared across multiple datacenters.
- VMware recommends as a best practice that datastores with hardware acceleration enabled not be used with datastores that do not have hardware acceleration enabled.

Configuring Storage DRS starts with creating a datastore cluster. Exercise 8.12 covers the steps to create a datastore cluster and configure Storage DRS.

EXERCISE 8.12

Configuring Storage DRS

1. Connect to a vCenter Server with the vSphere Client.

2. Switch to the Datastores and Datastore Clusters view.

(continued)

EXERCISE 8.12 *(continued)*

3. Right-click a datacenter object in the left pane and choose the New Datastore Cluster option from the context menu that appears.

4. The New Datastore Cluster Wizard will launch.

5. Provide a unique and descriptive name in the Datastore Cluster Name field. Ensure that the Turn On Storage DRS option is selected.

6. Click Next to continue.

7. Choose the default Automation Level option of No Automation (Manual Mode).

   The Storage DRS automation level is very similar to the automation level setting in DRS. The obvious exception is that there are only two settings available with Storage DRS. Manual is used when no automation is desired, and virtual machine placement and load balancing migration recommendations will only be suggested by vCenter Server.

8. Click Next to continue.

   The following image can be used as a reference for steps 9 to 14 of this exercise.

9. In Storage DRS Runtime Rules, ensure that the Enable I/O Metric For SDRS Recommendations option is selected.

   Enabling this option will allow vCenter Server to consider I/O metrics when making Storage DRS recommendations or automated migrations. In other words, this option enables I/O load balancing for the datastore cluster.

10. Leave the default values selected for Storage DRS Thresholds.

    The Storage DRS thresholds are similar to the migration threshold setting used in DRS. A percentage of space utilization and a millisecond value of I/O latency can each be configured to trigger Storage DRS to make a recommendation or take an automated action.

11. Click the blue Show Advanced Options link.

12. Leave the slider at the default value of 5% for the No Recommendations Until Utilization Difference Between Source And Destination Is option.

    This option is configured to ensure that a capacity-based recommendation is worthwhile. In other words, if the source datastore is 94 percent full and the target is 90 percent full, then don't make the move. The difference in these 2 percentages is the value 4. The default value of 5 percent would not allow this move to occur.

13. Using the drop-down menu, change the Check Imbalances Every value to a different value.

    This setting is used to determine the frequency that Storage DRS will check capacity and load.

14. Leave the I/O Imbalance Threshold slider at its default value.

    This setting is also similar to the migration threshold used in DRS. It is used to configure the amount of I/O imbalance that Storage DRS should tolerate.

15. Click Next.

16. On the Select Hosts and Clusters screen, select a cluster to add the datastore cluster to. Click Next to continue.

17. Select datastores to add to the datastore cluster, keeping in mind the requirements listed before the exercise.

Available Datastores:		Show Datastores:	Connected to all hosts			

System Capability or User-defined Capability contains: ▾ [   ]   Clear

Name	Host Connection Status	Capacity	Free Space	System Capability	User-defined Capability	Type
☑ NFS1	⊘ All Hosts Connected	135 GB	124 GB	N/A	N/A	NFS
☑ NFS2	⊘ All Hosts Connected	135 GB	124 GB	N/A	N/A	NFS

2 datastores selected

(continued)

18. Click Next to continue.

19. Review the information presented on the Ready To Complete Screen and click Finish to create the datastore cluster.

20. A Create A Datastore Cluster task will begin. Also, a Move Datastores Into A Datastore Cluster task will begin, and a Configure Storage DRS task will begin. When these tasks complete, verify that the datastore cluster is listed in the left pane. Expand it to view the datastores it contains.

21. Select the datastore cluster in the left pane and then select the Summary tab in the right pane.

22. The datastore cluster is now created, and existing virtual machines can be migrated to it with Storage vMotion.

You have now created a datastore cluster and enabled Storage DRS on it. This concludes the first section of this chapter on creating and configuring VMware clusters. In the next section, I will cover VMware Fault Tolerance.

Planning and Implementing VMware Fault Tolerance

As a VMware Certified Professional, you will be expected to know when and how to use VMware Fault Tolerance (FT). FT is used to provide higher levels of virtual machine availability than what is possible with vSphere HA. VMware FT uses VMware *vLockstep* technology to provide a replica virtual machine running on a different ESXi host. In the event of an ESXi host failure, the replica virtual machine will become active with the entire state of the virtual machine preserved. In this section, I will cover use cases and requirements for VMware FT, as well as how to configure it.

Determining Use Cases for Enabling VMware Fault Tolerance on a Virtual Machine

VMware FT can provide very high availability for virtual machines, and it is important to understand which applications are candidates for using VMware FT. There are several use cases for VMware FT:

- Applications that require high availability, particularly applications that have long-lasting client connections that would be reset by a virtual machine restart.

- Applications that have no native capability for clustering.

- Applications that could be clustered but clustering solutions want to be avoided because their administrative and operational complexities.

- Applications that require protection for critical processes to complete. This is known as *on-demand fault tolerance.*

🌐 Real World Scenario

On-Demand Fault Tolerance

A manufacturing company has an application that was developed in-house that is used four times a year. This application is used to provide specific quarter-end reports to the finance department. There is one report in particular that is notorious for taking many hours to complete. Recently the physical server housing this application had a motherboard failure while the report was running. As a result of this failure and the time required to repair it, the report was significantly delayed. Finance was able to complete their work on time, but many of the staff had to work through the night to make it happen.

A meeting was called between various members of IT and the business to discuss a solution for this problem. Specifically, the finance department did not want a hardware failure to delay them like this again. The virtual infrastructure administrator was present and suggested that the server be converted to a virtual machine and protected with VMware FT on an on-demand basis. This would allow the virtual machine to run as a normal virtual machine and gain the benefit of being protected with HA for normal day-to-day operations. During the four times a year that the key reports are run, the virtual infrastructure administrator enables FT for this virtual machine. The virtual machine is now protected from a physical server failure and consumes the extra resources required to provide this protection only four times a year.

It is important to remember that VMware FT will not protect virtual machines from guest OS and/or application failures. If either the guest operating system or the applications running in the guest OS fail, then the secondary VM will fail identically. It is also important to note that VMware FT has both resource and licensing implications. If the primary VM uses 2GB of RAM, the secondary VM will also use 2GB of RAM, and both of these RAM allocations will count toward the vRAM total. Now that I have covered the use cases for enabling VMware FT on virtual machines, I will identify some of the requirements for using it.

Identifying VMware Fault Tolerance Requirements

The actual number of requirements to use VMware FT is rather large, and for the VCP exam it would be unreasonable to expect you to know all of them. For this section, only the requirements specifically listed in the vSphere Availability Guide have been included. There are many requirements for using VMware FT at the cluster, host, and virtual machine levels. For the cluster, these requirements include the following:

- Host certificate checking must be enabled in the vCenter Server settings.

- A minimum of two FT-certified ESXi hosts with the same FT version or host build number must be used.

- The ESXi hosts in the cluster must have access to the same datastores and networks.

- The ESXi hosts must have both Fault Tolerance logging and vMotion networking configured.

- vSphere HA must be enabled on the cluster.

In addition to the cluster requirements, the ESXi hosts have their own set of requirements:

- The ESXi hosts must have processors from an FT-compatible processor group.

- Enterprise or Enterprise Plus licensing must be in place.

- ESXi hosts must be certified for FT in the VMware HCL.

- ESXi hosts must have hardware virtualization (HV) enabled in the BIOS.

For information on processors and guest operating systems that are supported with VMware FT, refer to the following VMware KB article: http://kb.vmware.com/kb/1008027

There are also requirements for the virtual machines that will be used with VMware FT:

- Eager zeroed thick provisioned virtual disks and RDMs in virtual compatibility mode must be used in the virtual machine.

- Virtual machines must be on shared storage.

- The guest OS installed on the virtual machine must be on the list of supported operating systems that can be used with VMware FT.

You should also note that only virtual machines with a single vCPU are compatible with Fault Tolerance. *vSMP* is not supported. Unsupported devices, such as USB devices, parallel ports, or serial ports, cannot be attached to the virtual machine; also, incompatible features such as snapshots, Storage vMotion, and *linked clones* must not be used on virtual machines that will be protected with VMware FT.

The VMware FT requirements listed previously are not all-inclusive, and the requirements and limitations could easily consume an entire chapter. For a comprehensive and constantly updated list of the requirements and limitations of VMware FT, check my blog at http://communities.vmware.com/blogs/vmroyale/2009/05/18/vmware-fault-tolerance-requirements-and-limitations.

Now that I have covered the requirements to use VMware FT, I will move on to configuring networking for the fault tolerance logging traffic.

Configuring VMware Fault Tolerance Networking

To use VMware FT, there are two networking requirements that must be met. The first of these requirements is a vMotion network to be used by ESXi hosts in the cluster. vMotion is required, because the secondary VM is initially created by a vMotion of the primary VM to a different ESXi host in the cluster. Because of this design, it is also recommended to have separate 1GbE NICs for vMotion and fault tolerance logging traffic.

The fault tolerance logging traffic is the second network requirement for VMware FT. This is also a VMkernel connection type that is used to move all nondeterministic events from the primary VM to the secondary VM. Nondeterministic events include network and user input, asynchronous disk I/O, and CPU timer events. This is the connection that is used to keep the primary and secondary virtual machines in lockstep.

In Exercise 8.13, I will create a baseline networking setup that will include both vMotion and fault tolerance logging networking. This exercise will use a standard vSwitch and will require two available NICs in each ESXi host in the cluster. If you already have a vSwitch created for vMotion, you can omit the sections of this exercise that pertain to creating the vMotion network.

EXERCISE 8.13

Configuring VMware FT Logging Traffic

1. Connect to a vCenter Server with the vSphere Client.

2. Choose an ESXi host that is a member of a cluster and select the Configuration tab for this ESXi host.

3. Click the blue Networking link in the Hardware panel.

4. Click the blue Add Networking link.

5. When the Add Network Wizard launches, select the VMkernel connection type and click Next to continue.

6. Select an available vmnic on the correct network segment and click Next to continue.

7. Provide a unique and consistent network label for the port group. Enter a VLAN ID if necessary, and select the Use This Port Group For vMotion option.

(continued)

EXERCISE 8.13 *(continued)*

8. Click Next to continue.

9. Provide a static IP address and appropriate subnet mask to the VMkernel that will be used for vMotion traffic and click Next to continue.

10. Review the information on the Ready To Complete screen and click Finish to create the new vSwitch and the vMotion port group.

11. An Update Network Configuration task will begin, and a Select Virtual NIC task will also begin. When these tasks complete, verify that the new vSwitch is listed on the Configuration tab.

    At this point, the new vSwitch contains a single port group that will be used for vMotion traffic. In the next part of this exercise, another NIC will be added to this vSwitch.

12. On the Configuration tab, click the blue Properties tab for the vSwitch that was just created.

13. The vSwitch Properties window will appear with the default view of the Ports tab. Select the Network Adapters tab.

14. Click the Add button located in the lower-left corner.

15. The Add Adapter Wizard will launch. Select a check box for an unclaimed adapter. Click Next to continue.

16. For Policy Failover Order, ensure that both adapters are placed in the Active Adapters list at the bottom of the screen. It should look like this.

```
┌─────────────────────────────────────────────────────────────────────┐
│ 🔲 Add Adapter Wizard                                      _ □ ×     │
├─────────────────────────────────────────────────────────────────────┤
│   Adapter Selection                                                   │
│      New adapters may be taken from a pool of unused ones, or transferred from an existing │
│      vSphere standard switch.                                         │
│                                                                       │
│  ┌──────────┐  Policy Failover Order:                                 │
│  │ Adapter  │  Select active and standby adapters for this port group. During a │
│  │ NIC Order│  failover, standby adapters activate in the order specified below. │
│  │ Summary  │                                                         │
│  │          │  ┌───────────────────┬──────────────────┐              │
│  │          │  │ Configuration     │ Summary          │              │
│  │          │  ├───────────────────┼──────────────────┤              │
│  │          │  │ vSwitch           │ 128 Ports        │              │
│  │          │  └───────────────────┴──────────────────┘              │
│  │          │                                                         │
│  │          │  ┌────────┬──────────┬───────────────────┐  ┌────────┐ │
│  │          │  │ Name   │ Speed    │ Networks          │  │Move Up │ │
│  │          │  ├────────┴──────────┴───────────────────┤  └────────┘ │
│  │          │  │ Active Adapters                        │  ┌────────┐ │
│  │          │  │ 🔲 vmnic1   1000 Full   168.0.0.1-175.255.255.2... │ │Move Down│ │
│  │          │  │ 🔲 vmnic3   1000 Full   168.0.0.1-175.255.255.2... │ └────────┘ │
│  │          │  │ Standby Adapters                       │            │
│  └──────────┘                                                         │
│                                                                       │
│  ┌──────┐                          ┌──────┐ ┌────────┐ ┌────────┐    │
│  │ Help │                          │< Back│ │ Next > │ │ Cancel │    │
│  └──────┘                          └──────┘ └────────┘ └────────┘    │
└─────────────────────────────────────────────────────────────────────┘
```

17. Click Next to continue.

18. Review the information presented on the Summary screen, and then click Finish to add the vmnic.

19. An Update Virtual Switch task will begin. When this task completes, verify that there are now two vmnics listed on the Network Adapters tab.

You have now added a second NIC to your vSwitch. In the next part of this exercise, I will show you how to add the fault tolerance logging port group to the vSwitch.

20. Click the Ports tab in the vSwitch Properties window.

21. Click the Add button located in the lower-left corner.

22. When the Add Network Wizard launches, again select the VMkernel connection type and click Next to continue.

23. Provide a unique and consistent network label for the port group. Enter a VLAN ID, if necessary, and select the Use This Port Group For Fault Tolerance Logging option.

(continued)

24. Click Next to continue.

25. Provide a static IP address and appropriate subnet mask to the VMkernel that will be used for fault tolerance logging traffic and click Next to continue.

26. Review the information on the Ready To Complete screen and click Finish to create the new vSwitch and the fault tolerance logging port group.

27. An Update Network Configuration task will begin, and a Select Virtual NIC task will also begin. When these tasks complete, verify that the new port group is listed on the Ports tab of the vSwitch Properties window.

   You have created a vSwitch with two physical uplinks and two port groups. The final configuration of the vSwitch will separate the port groups onto different vmnics. This will ensure that vMotion uses one physical uplink and that fault tolerance logging will use the other physical uplink. In the event that a single physical uplink associated with this vSwitch fails, this configuration will provide fault tolerance.

28. On the Ports tab of the vSwitch Properties window, select the vSwitch item listed at the top of the list.

29. On the right side, in the Failover And Load Balancing section, locate the Active Adapters information. Verify that both network adapters that were added to the vSwitch are listed and that Standby Adapters has a value of None.

30. Select the vMotion port group in the left pane. On the right side, review the information for Active Adapters and Standby Adapters. This information matches the vSwitch properties and lists two active adapters.

31. Select the FTlog port group in the left pane and verify that it too has the same active and standby adapters listed as the vSwitch and the vMotion port group.

32. Select the vMotion port group in the left pane and click the Edit button at the bottom of the window.

33. The Port Group Properties window will appear. Review the information presented on the General tab, and then select the NIC Teaming tab.

34. In the Failover Order option, select the Override Switch Failover Order option. This will activate the lower portion of the window.

35. Select the lower numbered vmnic and then click the Move Down button until this vmnic is listed under the Standby Adapters section. The final configuration should look like this.

36. Click OK to save these changes. A Reconfigure Port group task will start. When this task completes, make sure that the vMotion port group is selected in the left pane.

37. On the right side, in the Failover And Load Balancing section, locate the Active Adapters information. Verify that both the higher-numbered vmnic is listed as an active adapter and that the lower-numbered vmnic is listed as a standby adapter.

38. Select the FTlog port group in the left pane, and click the Edit button at the bottom of the window.

39. The Port Group Properties window will appear. Review the information presented on the General tab and then select the NIC Teaming tab.

40. For the Failover Order option, select the Override Switch Failover Order option. This will activate the lower portion of the window.

41. Select the higher-numbered vmnic and then click the Move Down button until this vmnic is listed under the Standby Adapters section. The final configuration should look like this.

(continued)

Failover Order:

☑ Override switch failover order:

Select active and standby adapters for this port group. In a failover situation, standby adapters activate in the order specified below.

Name	Speed	Networks
Active Adapters		
vmnic1	1000 Full	168.0.0.1-175.255.255.254
Standby Adapters		
vmnic3	1000 Full	168.0.0.1-175.255.255.254
Unused Adapters		

Move Up

Move Down

42. Click OK to save these changes. A Reconfigure Port group task will start. When this task completes, make sure that the FTlog port group is selected in the left pane.

43. On the right side, in the Failover And Load Balancing section, locate the Active Adapters information. Verify that both the lower-numbered vmnic is listed as an active adapter and that the higher-numbered vmnic is listed as a standby adapter.

44. Click Close in the vSwitch Properties window and review the vSwitch settings shown on the Configuration tab.

45. Select the Summary tab. Review the information presented in the General pane. vMotion Enabled and Host Configured For FT should both show a value of Yes.

esxi2.test.local VMware ESXi, 5.0.0, 469512

Summary | Virtual Machines | Performance | Configuration | Tasks

General

Manufacturer:	Cisco Systems Inc
Model:	R210-2121605W
CPU Cores:	8 CPUs x 2.666 GHz
Processor Type:	Intel(R) Xeon(R) CPU E5640 @ 2.67GHz
License:	Evaluation Mode -
Processor Sockets:	2
Cores per Socket:	4
Logical Processors:	16
Hyperthreading:	Active
Number of NICs:	6
State:	Connected
Virtual Machines and Templates:	6
vMotion Enabled:	Yes
VMware EVC Mode:	Disabled
vSphere HA State	Connected (Slave)
Host Configured for FT:	Yes

46. Repeat this exercise for each ESXi host in the cluster.

WARNING Fault tolerance logging traffic is unencrypted and contains guest network data, guest storage I/O data, and the guest's memory contents. Because of this, fault tolerance logging traffic should always be isolated.

I have now covered configuring the network for fault tolerance logging to be used with VMware FT. Next I will show how to enable and disable VMware FT on a virtual machine.

Enabling and Disabling VMware Fault Tolerance on a Virtual Machine

Once all of the VMware FT prerequisites are met, the actual process of enabling FT for a virtual machine is incredibly simple. Exercise 8.14 covers the steps to enable FT for a virtual machine.

EXERCISE 8.14

Enabling FT for a Powered-Off Virtual Machine

1. Connect to a vCenter Server with the vSphere Client. The vSphere Web Client cannot be used for this operation.

2. Locate a powered-off virtual machine that belongs to a cluster with ESXi hosts that have been configured for FT.

3. Right-click the virtual machine and choose the Fault Tolerance ➢ Turn On Fault Tolerance option from the context menu that appears.

   Depending on the disk configuration of the virtual machine, you will next be presented with one of two dialogs. Each of these dialogs contains the same information, but one of them presents additional information about the virtual machine's disks. This additional information would be presented if the virtual disks are not in the thick provisioned eager zeroed format. The dialog with the additional disk information is shown here.

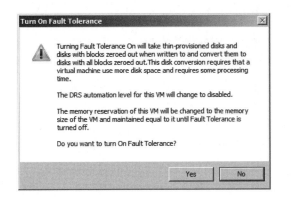

(continued)

EXERCISE 8.14 *(continued)*

4. Review the information presented in the Turn On Fault Tolerance dialog and click the Yes button to continue.

   If the virtual disks were not in the thick provisioned eager zeroed format, the disks will need to be converted to the proper format before FT can be enabled. This disk conversion operation cannot be performed if the virtual machine is powered on. If the virtual disks in the virtual machine were already in the thick provisioned eager zeroed format, then the disk information would not have been present in the Turn On Fault Tolerance dialog.

5. A Turn On Fault Tolerance task will begin. When this task completes, take note of the icon for the FT-protected VM in the left pane. It has now changed to a darker shade of blue.

6. Power on the FT-protected virtual machine.

7. Select the Summary tab for the FT-protected virtual machine. Locate the Fault Tolerance pane and verify the information presented there. This information should look like this.

Fault Tolerance	
Fault Tolerance Status:	**Protected**
Secondary Location:	esxi1.test.local
Total Secondary CPU:	186 MHz
Total Secondary Memory:	768.00 MB
vLockstep Interval:	0.015 seconds
Log Bandwidth:	15 KBps

8. Select the cluster that the FT-protected virtual machine is running in and then select the Virtual Machines tab.

9. Notice that the FT-protected virtual machine is listed and that there is also a secondary virtual machine listed.

CLU01

Summary | Virtual Machines | Hosts | DRS | Resource Allocation

Name	State	Status
FTVM	Powered On	Normal
FTVM (secondary)	Powered On	Normal

Now that the steps to protect a VM with FT have been covered, I will cover the steps to disable FT for a VM that has been protected with it. Virtual machines protected with FT can have FT either disabled or turned off. Turning off FT for a VM will delete the second-ary VM and all historical performance data. The virtual machine's DRS automation level will also be set at the cluster default settings. This option is used when FT will no longer be used for a virtual machine. Examples of this would be when a virtual machine has had its SLA modified or is due for scheduled maintenance and a snapshot is desired as part of the process.

Disabling FT for a VM will preserve the secondary VM, the configuration, and all his-torical performance data. Disabling FT would be used if VMware FT might be used again in the future for this virtual machine. An example of this would be when using on-demand fault tolerance for a virtual machine. Exercise 8.15 covers the steps to disable FT for a vir-tual machine that is currently protected with it.

EXERCISE 8.15

Disabling FT for a Powered-Off Virtual Machine

1. Connect to a vCenter Server with the vSphere Client. The vSphere Web Client cannot be used for this operation.

2. Locate a powered-off virtual machine that belongs to a cluster with ESXi hosts that have been configured for FT.

3. Right-click the virtual machine and choose the Fault Tolerance ➢ Disable Fault Toler-ance option from the context menu that appears.

4. A Disable Fault Tolerance dialog box will appear. Review the information presented here, and click the Yes button to continue.

5. A Disable Fault Tolerance task will begin. When this task completes, verify the fault tolerance status in the Fault Tolerance pane of the virtual machine's Summary tab.

6. Also notice that a Warning icon has been placed over the virtual machine. Click the Alarms tab to view the warning information.

(continued)

7. Right-click the triggered alarm and choose the Acknowledge Alarm option from the context menu that appears. Right-click the triggered alarm again and choose the Clear option from the context menu that appears.

8. In the left pane, note that the warning icon has now been removed from the virtual machine but that the VM icon still maintains the darker blue color.

   At this point, the VM is no longer protected by FT. If there was a time where FT protection was again required, the following steps could be used to enable FT on the virtual machine.

9. Right-click this same virtual machine and choose the Fault Tolerance ➢ Enable Fault Tolerance option from the context menu that appears.

10. An Enable Fault Tolerance task will begin. When this task completes, verify the Fault Tolerance Status in the Fault Tolerance pane of the virtual machine's Summary tab.

Now that I have covered enabling and disabling VMware FT, I will cover the steps required to test an FT configuration.

Testing an FT Configuration

Now that FT has been configured and a virtual machine is being protected by it, the only remaining item is verifying that FT works as expected. The only way to know whether FT will work as expected is to test failover using the built-in functions in vCenter Server or to manually fail a host.

Testing via manually failing a host is easily accomplished. If your ESXi hosts are physical servers, then you could simply pull the power cable on the host that the FT primary VM is running on. If your ESXi hosts are virtual machines, then simply power off the ESXi host that the FT primary VM is running on. Either one of these approaches will guarantee an ESXi host failure. If you have many running virtual machines or simply aren't comfortable powering off your ESXi host this way, then you can also use the FT Test Failover functionality from the Fault Tolerance menu in the vSphere Client. This testing approach is preferred, since it is both fully supported and noninvasive. Exercise 8.16 will cover the steps to test your FT configuration.

EXERCISE 8.16

Testing Failover of FT

1. Connect to a vCenter Server with the vSphere Client. The vSphere Web Client cannot be used for this operation.

2. Locate a powered-off virtual machine that belongs to a cluster with ESXi hosts that have been configured for FT.

3. Select the Summary tab for the virtual machine and review the information presented in the Fault Tolerance pane. Take note of the fault tolerance status and the Secondary Location values. An example is shown here.

Fault Tolerance	
Fault Tolerance Status:	**Protected**
Secondary Location:	esxi2.test.local
Total Secondary CPU:	106 MHz
Total Secondary Memory:	0.00 MB
vLockstep Interval:	0.014 seconds
Log Bandwidth:	15 KBps

4. Right-click the virtual machine and choose the Fault Tolerance ➢ Test Failover option from the context menu that appears.

5. A Test Failover task will begin, and an alert icon will appear on the VM in the left pane. The Fault Tolerance pane will display results similar to what is shown here.

Fault Tolerance	
Fault Tolerance Status:	⚠ **Not protected**
	Starting
Secondary Location:	esxi1.test.local
Total Secondary CPU:	N/A
Total Secondary Memory:	N/A
vLockstep Interval:	N/A
Log Bandwidth:	N/A

6. When the secondary VM has again been restarted, the alert icon will be removed from the virtual machine in the left pane. The Fault Tolerance pane will display results similar to what are shown in the following image.

Fault Tolerance	
Fault Tolerance Status:	**Protected**
Secondary Location:	esxi1.test.local
Total Secondary CPU:	106 MHz
Total Secondary Memory:	10.00 MB
vLockstep Interval:	0.014 seconds
Log Bandwidth:	15 KBps

Note that the VM has changed ESXi hosts in this testing.

Now that I have covered testing an FT configuration, the VMware FT coverage is complete. In the next section of this chapter, I will cover creating and administering resource pools.

Creating and Administering Resource Pools

As a VMware Certified Professional, resource pools are a topic you should be very familiar with. Resource pools are used to partition the CPU and memory resources of ESXi hosts. They offer a convenient way to separate resources along requirements or political boundaries and also offer a way to control the resource usage of multiple virtual machines at once. This offers significant advantages over setting individual virtual machine limits, reservations, and shares. In this section, I will cover how resource pools work and how to configure and use them.

Describing the Resource Pool Hierarchy

Each ESXi host or DRS-enabled cluster has a hidden root resource pool. This root resource pool is the basis for any hierarchy of shared resources that exist on stand-alone hosts or in DRS-enabled clusters. In Figure 8.12, the CLUSTER object represents the root resource pool.

FIGURE 8.12   Resource pool hierarchy

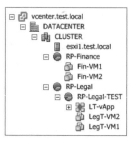

The root resource pool is hidden, since the resources of the ESXi host or cluster are consistent. Resource pools can contain child resource pools, vApps, virtual machines, or a combination of these objects. This allows for the creation of a hierarchy of shared resources. Objects created at the same level are called siblings. In Figure 8.12, RP-Finance and RP-Legal are siblings. Fin-VM1 and Fin-VM2 are also siblings.

When creating child resource pools below an existing resource pool, the resource pool at a higher level is called a parent resource pool. In Figure 8.12, RP-Legal is a parent resource pool for the child resource pool of RP-Legal-TEST.

Each resource pool can have shares, limits, and reservations specified, in addition to specifying whether the reservation is expandable. The Expandable Reservation parameter will now be defined.

You will typically not want to use resource pools to organize your virtual machines. Also use caution with resource pools, because each additional child resource pool added will make the environment increasingly more difficult to understand and manage properly.

Defining the Expandable Reservation Parameter

The Expandable Reservation parameter can be used to allow a child resource pool to request resources from its parent or ancestors if the child resource pool does not have the required resources. This allows greater flexibility when creating child resource pools. The expandable reservation is best shown in action, so Exercise 8.17 will demonstrate how the expandable reservation works.

EXERCISE 8.17

Configuring and Testing Expandable Reservations

1. Connect to a vCenter Server with the vSphere Client.

2. Select a cluster from the inventory and right-click it. Choose the New Resource Pool option from the context menu that appears.

3. When the Create Resource Pool window appears, enter the name **Parent Resource Pool** and use the slider to set CPU Reservation to 1000MHz.

4. Deselect the Expandable Reservation setting in the CPU Resources section. The final configuration of the CPU Resources should look like this.

Create Resource Pool			
Name:	Parent Resource Pool		
CPU Resources			
Shares:	Normal	4000	
Reservation:	⎯⎮⎯⎯⎯	1000	MHz
	△		
	☐ Expandable Reservation		
Limit:	⎯⎯⎯⎯⎮	8054	MHz
	☑ Unlimited		

5. Accept the defaults for all other settings and click OK to create the resource pool.

(continued)

EXERCISE 8.17 *(continued)*

6. A Create Resource Pool task will begin. When this task completes, verify that the new resource pool is listed under the cluster.

   The parent resource pool has been created with a 1000MHz reservation, and the Expandable Reservation parameter was not selected. This setting creates a parent resource pool that has a static 1000MHz of CPU resources. In the following steps, a child resource pool will be created.

7. Right-click the Parent Resource Pool resource pool created in steps 2 to 5. Choose the New Resource Pool option from the context menu that appears.

8. When the Create Resource Pool window appears, enter the name **Child Resource Pool** and use the slider to set CPU Reservation to 500MHz.

9. Deselect the Expandable Reservation setting in the CPU Resources section. The final configuration of the CPU Resources should look like this.

10. Accept the defaults for all other settings, and click OK to create the resource pool.

11. A Create Resource Pool task will begin. When this task completes, verify the new resource pool is listed under the first resource pool.

    The child resource pool has been created with a 500MHz reservation, and the Expandable Reservation parameter was not selected. This setting creates a resource pool that has a static 500MHz of CPU resources. In the following steps, a VM will be created and powered on.

12. Right-click the Child Resource Pool resource pool and choose the New Virtual Machine option from the context menu that appears.

13. Create any virtual machine configuration you like in the Create New Virtual Machine Wizard. When the VM has been created, right-click it and choose the Edit Settings option from the context menu that appears.

14. Click the Resources tab and select the CPU item in the left pane. Using the slider, configure the VM to have a CPU Reservation setting of 750MHz.

Resource Allocation

Shares: Normal ▼   1000

Reservation: ═╪═════════   750 MHz

                    △

Limit: ════════════╪═   8054 MHz

                ☑ Unlimited

15. Click OK and power up the virtual machine once the Reconfigure Virtual Machine task completes.

You should be presented with the error shown here.

Initialize powering On

❌   Insufficient resources.

Time: **11/7/2011 1:55:36 PM**

Target: **DATACENTER**

vCenter Server: **vcenter.test.local**

Close

Since this virtual machine has a reservation of 750MHz and the resource pool it belongs to has a reservation of only 500MHz, resource pool admission control prevents the virtual machine from being powered on. In the next set of steps, I will cover how to configure the Child Resource Pool to use the Expandable Reservation option.

16. Right-click the Child Resource Pool object and choose the Edit Settings option from the context menu that appears.

17. Select the Expandable Reservation option in the CPU Resources section and click OK.

18. An Update Resource Pool Configuration task will begin. When this task completes, power on the same virtual machine that generated an error in step 15.

You should now be presented with a running virtual machine, as shown here.

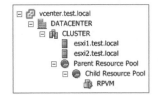

The expandable reservation allowed Child Resource Pool to pull the required resources from Parent Resource Pool to satisfy the CPU reservation of the virtual machine.

Now that I have defined and discussed the Expandable Reservation parameter, I will cover the steps required to create a resource pool using the vSphere Web Client.

Creating and Removing a Resource Pool

As shown in Exercise 8.17, the actual task of creating resource pools is very simple. Options like the expandable reservation illustrate that the more difficult task is in understanding how resource pools work and how they will be used in your environment. Exercise 8.18 details the steps to create a resource pool using the vSphere Web Client.

EXERCISE 8.18

Creating a Resource Pool

1. Open a web browser and connect to the FQDN of the vCenter Server that will be used for this exercise.

2. Click the blue Log In To vSphere Web Client link.

3. When the vSphere Web Client loads, enter your credentials.

4. Right-click a cluster in the left pane and choose the Inventory ➢ New Resource Pool option from the context menu that appears.

5. Give the resource pool the name **RP-Legal** and use the drop-down menu to change the Shares value to High for both the CPU and memory.

6. Ensure that the Reservation Type field's Expandable box is selected. The final configuration should look exactly like this.

7. Click OK to create the resource pool. A Create Resource Pool task will begin. When this task completes, the resource pool is ready to be used.

8. Right-click the same cluster in the left pane and choose the Inventory ➢ New Resource Pool option from the context menu that appears.

9. Give the resource pool the name **RP-Finance** and accept the defaults for all of the settings.

10. Click OK to create the resource pool. A Create Resource Pool task will begin. When this task completes, the resource pool is ready to be used

In this exercise, two resource pools were created. Assume that the cluster used in this exercise had a combined 6GHz of CPU and 30GB of RAM. In periods of resource contention, the RP-Legal resource pool will receive 4GHz of CPU and 20GB of memory, while the RP-Finance resource pool will receive 2GHz of CPU and 10GB of memory. In periods of no resource contention, the expandable reservation allows either resource pool to have more resources.

The task to delete a resource pool is also very simple. Keep in mind the implications of deleting a resource pool when working with child resource pools. Any virtual machines that are in the resource pool will be moved automatically to the parent resource pool or the root resource pool. To delete a resource pool, right-click it in the vSphere Web Client and choose the Inventory ➢ Remove option from the context menu. You will be prompted to remove the resource pool, as shown in Figure 8.13.

FIGURE 8.13   Remove Resource Pool prompt

Click the Yes button to remove the resource pool. A Delete Resource Pool task will begin. When this task completes, verify that any virtual machines in the resource pool were moved as expected.

Now that I have covered creating and removing resource pools, I will next cover how to configure resource pool attributes.

Configuring Resource Pool Attributes

Resource pools can be modified after their creation by configuring their attributes. This is useful in situations where the resource pool requirements have changed. The shares, reservation, and limit can each be modified for the resource pool. Shares, reservations, and limits were discussed in Chapter 7, but they will be reviewed again.

Resource pool shares can be specified with respect to the total resources of the parent resource pool. Sibling resource pools will share the parent's resource, based on their specified share values. Virtual machines in resource pools with the highest share values will be able to consume more resources in periods of resource contention on the ESXi host.

In addition to shares, reservations can be used to guarantee a minimum allocation of CPU and memory for the resource pool. This setting is used to claim a specific amount of the resource for the virtual machine so that these resources will always be available. Memory reservations can also be used to avoid overcommitment of physical memory resources.

Limits are used to set an upper bound for memory and CPU resources. This prevents a virtual machine in the resource pool from using more resources than specified. This setting is by default set to Unlimited for both CPU and memory. Using this setting will ensure that the virtual machine uses close to the vCPU and memory allocations it has been granted.

To edit a resource pool in the vSphere Client, right-click it and choose the Edit Settings option that appears in the context menu. The resource pool attributes will be shown and should look similar to what is shown in Figure 8.14.

FIGURE 8.14   Resource pool attributes

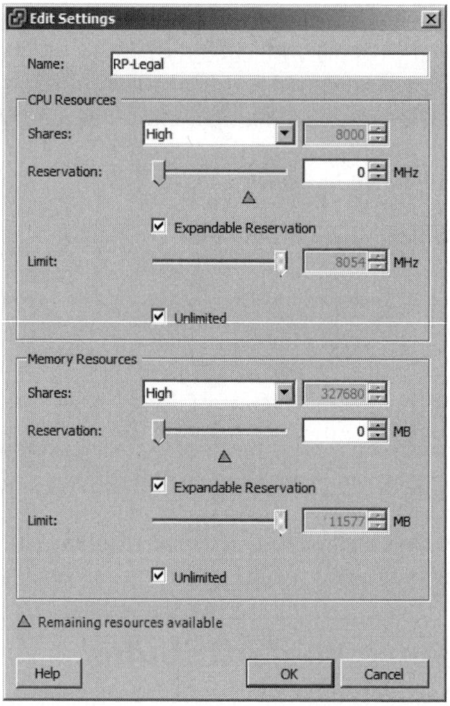

I have now covered how to configure resource pool attributes and will now cover how to add and remove virtual machines to/from a resource pool.

Adding and Removing Virtual Machines to/from a Resource Pool

Objects that can be added to a resource pool include other resource pools, vApps, and virtual machines. There are multiple options that can be used to add virtual machines to a resource pool. In Exercise 8.17, a virtual machine was added to a resource pool by right-clicking the resource pool and selecting the New Virtual Machine option from the context menu.

Virtual machines can also be added to resource pools, while powered on or off, by dragging and dropping them in the vSphere Client. Many virtual machine operations and tasks will also allow you to choose the resource pool as part of the operation. These operations include the following:

- Creating a new virtual machine at the host, cluster, or datacenter level
- Migrating a virtual machine using vMotion or cold migration
- Deploying OVF templates
- Cloning a virtual machine
- Deploying a VM from a template
- P2V conversions with VMware Converter

There are several caveats that must be covered for adding virtual machines to a resource pool:

- If the virtual machine is powered on and the resource pool does not have adequate resources to guarantee its reservations, admission control will not allow the move to complete.
- Virtual machine–configured reservations and limits will not change.
- Virtual machine shares of high, medium, or low will be adjusted to reflect the total number of shares in the new resource pool.
- Virtual machine shares configured with a custom value will retain the custom value. A warning will appear if a significant change in total share percentage would occur.

The operations that can be used to remove a virtual machine from a resource pool are similar to the operations for adding a virtual machine to a resource pool. Virtual machines can be dragged and dropped out of resource pools, while powered on or off, using the vSphere Client. vMotion, cold migrations, removing a virtual machine from inventory, and deleting a virtual machine are additional ways to remove it from a resource pool.

Virtual machine operations will often provide the ability to select a resource pool, but this option will appear only if and when the resource pools are already configured.

Now that the operations for adding and removing virtual machines to resource pools have been covered, I will cover how to determine the resource pool requirements for a given vSphere implementation.

Determining Resource Pool Requirements for a Given vSphere Implementation

Determining the resource pool requirements for a given vSphere implementation involves knowing or predicting what your environment will require for resources. The requirements will depend on a variety of factors:

- Knowing the characteristics and requirements of workloads or planned workloads
- Knowing the specific terms of SLAs or other agreements that dictate performance
- Knowing whether the resources will be divided along workload, business, or even political boundaries
- Knowing whether the applications would benefit from expandable reservations in resource pools
- Knowing who will own and administer the resource pools
- Knowing whether child resource pools will be created and used
- Knowing whether resource pools or the workloads running in them would benefit from using reservations or limits
- Knowing whether VMware DRS will be used and the vSphere editions (Enterprise and Enterprise Plus) required
- Knowing whether VMware HA will be used
- Knowing whether VMware FT will be used

This is not an all-inclusive list, and each implementation will be different. The key is to know the workloads, the infrastructure layout, licensing, and how the business or organization works. Political factors or budget control may determine the design in many cases, regardless of the technical factors.

Now that I have covered determining the resource pool requirements for a given vSphere implementation, I will move on to evaluating appropriate shares, reservations, and limits for a resource pool based on virtual machine workloads.

Evaluating Appropriate Shares, Reservations, and Limits for a Resource Pool Based on Virtual Machine Workloads

Much like determining the resource pool requirements, evaluating the appropriate settings really means knowing your workloads. In some cases, the workloads themselves may change or have new requirements. In Exercise 8.19, I will evaluate memory reservation settings for a virtual machine that has a new requirement of being protected with VMware FT.

EXERCISE 8.19

Evaluating Memory Reservations for a FT VM

1. Connect to a vCenter Server with the vSphere Client.

2. Select a cluster from the inventory and right-click it. Choose the New Resource Pool option from the context menu that appears.

3. When the Create Resource Pool window appears, give it a unique name. Accept the defaults for CPU Resources.

4. Using the slider, set Memory Reservation to 1024MB.

5. Deselect the Expandable Reservation setting in the Memory Resources section.

6. Click OK to create the resource pool. A Create Resource Pool task will begin.

   You have now created the new resource pool that will be used for this exercise. The next step is to add a virtual machine to it.

7. Move an existing powered-off virtual machine that is configured with a memory size of 1024MB into the resource pool or create a new virtual machine with a memory size of 1024MB. Ensure that a guest OS that is supported for use with VMware FT is used.

8. In the Virtual Machine Properties editor, select the Resources tab. Configure the virtual machine to have a memory reservation of 1024MB.

(continued)

EXERCISE 8.19 *(continued)*

You have now added a virtual machine to the resource pool, and the virtual machine's memory reservation equals that of the resource pool.

9. Power on the virtual machine. You should receive an Insufficient Resources error message like the one shown here.

This error has occurred because the resource pool has a 1024MB static memory reservation. The resource pool is not allowed to borrow resources from the root resource pool, and this virtual machine is configured to use 1024MB of RAM. To be able to power on this virtual machine, the resource pool must have the required memory resources. This task has failed, because the virtual machine memory overhead has not been allocated in the resource pool. Each virtual machine has a memory overhead that is based on the number of vCPUs and memory in the VM. In the previous image, you can see the Memory Overhead value of 67.18MB listed. In the next steps, you will configure the resource pool to have the required resources to power on the virtual machine.

10. Select the virtual machine and obtain the Memory Overhead value from the General pane in the Summary tab. Round this number to the nearest whole number.

11. Right-click the resource pool and choose the Edit Settings option from the context menu that appears. Add the rounded virtual machine memory overhead value from the previous step to the current Reservation value in the Memory Resources section.

12. Click OK to save the changes. An Update Resource Pool Configuration task will begin. When this task completes, power on the virtual machine.

13. When the guest OS has finished loading, select the resource pool in the left pane. Click the Resource Allocation tab and review the information presented in the Memory section in the upper portion of the screen.

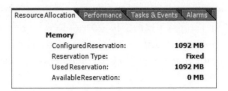

14. Shut down the virtual machine. Review the information on the resource pool Resource Allocation tab again.

    You have now created a resource pool, added a virtual machine to it, and configured the reservation of the resource pool to allow the virtual machine to be powered on. Next FT will be enabled for this virtual machine.

15. Right-click the powered-off virtual machine and choose the Fault Tolerance ➤ Turn On Fault Tolerance option.

16. Review the information presented on the Turn On Fault Tolerance screen and click Yes.

17. A Turn On Fault Tolerance task will begin. When this task completes, power on the virtual machine. The same Insufficient Resources error message received in step 9 will appear.

    Enabling FT failed, because creating the secondary VM requires the same number of resources from the resource pool as the primary VM requires. The primary virtual machine was powered on, but the secondary was unable to be powered on because the lack of available resources. In the next steps of this exercise, I will adjust the resource pool memory reservation to account for this requirement.

18. Right-click the resource pool and choose the Edit Settings option from the context menu that appears. Take the current Reservation value in the Memory Resources section and double it. Enter this new value in the Reservation field.

19. Click OK to save these changes. An Update Resource Pool Configuration task will begin. When this task completes, enable FT for the virtual machine again.

20. The same Insufficient Resources error message received in steps 9 and 17 will appear one more time.

The insufficient resources error appeared again, because VMware FT has an additional overhead that ranges from 5 to 20 percent depending on the workload. You will now adjust the resource pool reservation to account for this 5 to 20 percent overhead. Note that adding 20 percent should guarantee success in the final steps of this exercise.

21. Right-click the resource pool and choose the Edit Settings option from the context menu that appears. Take the current Reservation value in the Memory Resources section and add 20 percent to it. Round this value to the nearest whole number, if necessary.

```
┌─Memory Resources──────────────────────────────────┐
│                                                    │
│   Shares:        [Normal          ▼] [  163840 ⬍]  │
│                                                    │
│   Reservation:   ──▭───────────── [  2621 ⬍] MB    │
│                            △                       │
│                                                    │
│                  ☐ Expandable Reservation          │
│                                                    │
│   Limit:         ─────────────────▯ [ 11579 ⬍] MB  │
│                                                    │
│                  ☑ Unlimited                       │
│                                                    │
└────────────────────────────────────────────────────┘
```

22. Click OK to save these changes. An Update Resource Pool Configuration task will begin. When this task completes, enable FT for the virtual machine again.

23. When the Start Fault Tolerance Secondary VM task completes, select the resource pool in the left pane. Click the Resource Allocation tab and review the information presented in the Memory section in the upper portion of the screen.

```
┌──────────────────────────────────────────────────────┐
│ Resource Allocation \ Performance \ Tasks & Events \ Alarms │
│                                                        │
│   Memory                                               │
│     Configured Reservation:        2621 MB             │
│     Reservation Type:                 Fixed            │
│     Used Reservation:              2310 MB             │
│     Available Reservation:          311 MB             │
└──────────────────────────────────────────────────────┘
```

24. The 20 percent value was likely too high, and you can review the value shown under Available Reservation to determine this.

This exercise could be considered a review of the entire chapter, but its main purpose was to cover the steps to evaluate appropriate reservations for a resource pool based on a virtual machine workload. Next I will briefly review cloning a vApp.

Cloning a vApp

Cloning a vApp was discussed in Chapter 6, and Exercise 6.19 covered the steps necessary to clone a vApp using the Clone vApp Wizard. As a reminder, Figure 8.15 shows the Ready To Complete screen of this wizard.

FIGURE 8.15   Clone vApp Wizard

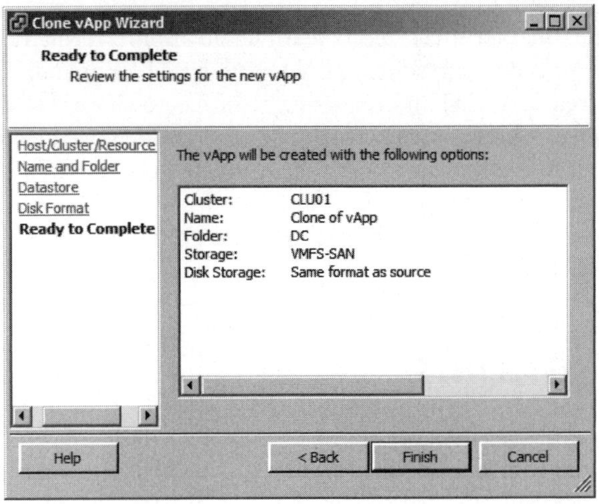

This concludes this chapter on clusters, FT, and resource pools.

Summary

The first part of this chapter focused on creating and configuring VMware clusters. This chapter began with determining the appropriate failover methodology and required resources for an HA implementation. DRS virtual machine entitlement was described, and I showed how to create and delete a cluster. I covered adding and removing ESXi hosts to/from a cluster, along with adding and removing virtual machines to/from the cluster. How to enable and disable host monitoring and how to configure admission control were covered. I covered virtual machine and application monitoring. Configuring automation levels for DRS and virtual machines was covered, along with configuring migration thresholds for DRS and individual virtual machines. I created VM-Host and VM-VM affinity rules.

I discussed EVC and the steps to configure it. Monitoring a DRS/HA cluster was covered, and the first section concluded with configuring Storage DRS.

The second part of this chapter focused on planning and implementing VMware Fault Tolerance. Determining the use case for enabling VMware Fault Tolerance on a virtual machine was discussed first. I then moved on to identifying VMware Fault Tolerance requirements. Configuring VMware Fault Tolerance logging networking was covered. I enabled and disabled VMware Fault Tolerance on a virtual machine and concluded this section with testing FT configurations.

The final part of this chapter focused on creating and administering resource pools. This section began with describing the resource pool hierarchy. The Expandable Reservation parameter was discussed. Creating and removing resource pools were both covered, along with configuring resource pool attributes. I added and removed virtual machines to a resource pool and discussed determining the resource pool requirements for a given vSphere implementation. I covered evaluating appropriate shares, reservations, and limits for a resource pool based on virtual machine workloads, and I concluded this chapter with a review of cloning a vApp.

Exam Essentials

Know how to create and configure VMware clusters.   Be able to determine the appropriate failover methodology and required resources for an HA implementation. Know how to describe DRS virtual machine entitlement. Understand how to create and delete a DRS/HA cluster. Be able to add and remove ESXi hosts and virtual machines from a DRS/HA cluster. Know how to enable and disable host monitoring. Be able to configure admission control for HA and virtual machines. Know how to enable, configure, and disable virtual machine and application monitoring. Understand how to configure automation levels and migration thresholds for DRS and virtual machines. Know how to create VM-Host and VM-VM affinity rules. Be able to configure EVC. Understand the different ways that a DRS/HA cluster can be monitored. Be able to configure Storage DRS.

Know how to plan and implement VMware FT.   Be able to determine the use case for enabling VMware Fault Tolerance on a virtual machine. Know the requirements and limitations of VMware FT. Be able to configure fault tolerance logging networking. Understand how to enable and disable FT for a virtual machine. Know the different ways to test an FT configuration.

Know how to create and administer resource pools.   Be able to describe the resource pool hierarchy. Understand the Expandable Reservation parameter. Be able to create and remove resource pools. Know how to configure resource pool attributes. Understand the different ways to add and remove virtual machines from a resource pool. Be able to determine resource pool requirements for a given vSphere implementation. Know how to evaluate appropriate shares, reservations, and limits for a resource pool based on virtual machine workloads. Be able to clone a vApp.

Review Questions

1. Which of the following are ESXi host requirements for VMware FT? (Choose all that apply.)

   A. Enterprise or Enterprise Plus licensing must be in place.

   B. ESXi hosts must be certified for FT in the VMware HCL.

   C. ESXi hosts must have hardware Virtualization (HV) enabled in the BIOS.

   D. ESXi hosts must have EVC mode enabled.

2. Which of the following are true statements about Storage DRS? (Choose two.)

   A. ESXi 4.1 and newer hosts are required.

   B. ESXi 5 and newer hosts are required.

   C. Mixing NFS and VMFS datastores is not allowed.

   D. Mixing NFS and VMFS datastores is allowed.

3. What condition must be first met to remove an ESXi host from a cluster?

   A. The host must have host monitoring disabled.

   B. The host must be in maintenance mode.

   C. The host must be disconnected from vCenter Server.

   D. None of these.

4. Which of the following are considered best practices for setting up the fault tolerance logging network? (Choose two.)

   A. Single shared 1GbE NIC for vMotion and fault tolerance logging traffic

   B. Single dedicated 1GbE NIC for fault tolerance logging traffic only

   C. Isolating the fault tolerance logging traffic

   D. Routing the fault tolerance logging traffic

5. A virtual machine has its host isolation response set to Shut Down, but this virtual machine does not have the VMware Tools installed. What will happen to this virtual machine, if the ESXi host it is running on becomes isolated?

   A. It will shut down.

   B. Nothing.

   C. It will be powered off.

   D. It will be suspended.

6. You need to create an affinity rule to require a set of virtual machines to run on a specific ESXi host. Which of the following do you need to create?

   A. VM-Host affinity rule

   B. VM-Host anti-affinity rule

    C. VM-VM affinity rule

    D. VM-VM anti-affinity rule

7. When implementing VMware FT, what is the overhead percentage that is required?

    A. 5 to 10 percent

    B. 10 percent

    C. 5 to 20 percent

    D. 20 percent

8. Which of the following schedulers exist in a DRS-enabled cluster? (Choose two.)

    A. Priority scheduler

    B. Global scheduler

    C. Entitlement scheduler

    D. Local scheduler

9. Which of the following statements best describes the Expandable Reservation parameter?

    A. The Expandable Reservation parameter can be used to allow a child resource pool to request resources from its parent.

    B. The Expandable Reservation parameter can be used to allow a child resource pool to request resources from its parent or ancestors.

    C. The Expandable Reservation parameter can be used to allow a parent resource pool to request resources from its child.

    D. The Expandable Reservation parameter can be used to allow a parent resource pool to request resources from a sibling.

10. When raising the EVC mode for the cluster, which of the following statements is true? (Choose two.)

    A. Raising the EVC mode for cluster involves moving from a greater feature set to a lower feature set.

    B. Raising the EVC mode for cluster involves moving from a lower feature set to a greater feature set.

    C. Running virtual machines will need to be powered off during this operation.

    D. Running virtual machines may continue to run during this operation.

11. When using vMotion to migrate a virtual machine, the option to select a resource pool was not available for the destination. What could be a reason for this?

    A. The VM has an individual memory reservation set.

    B. vMotion does not allow this operation.

    C. Changing resource pools is not allowed.

    D. No resource pools exist in the destination.

12. In which of the following automation levels will vCenter Server inform of suggested virtual machine migrations and place the virtual machines on ESXi hosts at VM startup?

    A. Manual

    B. Partially automated

    C. Fully automated

    D. None of these

13. Which of the following admission control policies will result in an ESXi host in the cluster that is unable to run virtual machines until a failover situation occurs?

    A. Host failures the cluster tolerates

    B. Percentage of cluster resources reserved as failover spare capacity

    C. Specify failover hosts

    D. None of these

14. Which of the following are configurable resource pool attributes? (Choose all that apply.)

    A. Shares

    B. Reservation

    C. Priority

    D. Name

15. A master host has stopped receiving heartbeats from a slave host. What are the possible conditions that the slave host could be in? (Choose all that apply.)

    A. Failed

    B. Unprotected

    C. Isolated

    D. Partitioned

16. Which of the following can be used to enable and disable VMware FT for a virtual machine that contains a single eager zeroed thick provisioned disk? (Choose all that apply.)

    A. The vSphere Client for the powered-on virtual machine

    B. The vSphere Client for the powered-off virtual machine

    C. The vSphere Web Client for the powered-on virtual machine

    D. The vSphere Web Client for the powered-off virtual machine

17. You need to test the FT configuration in your environment. Which of the following approaches is both supported and noninvasive?

    A. Pull the power cables from an ESXi host that is running VMs with FT enabled.

    B. Use the vSphere Client and right-click the secondary virtual machine. Choose the Delete From Disk option.

    C. Put an ESXi host with FT VMs running on it in maintenance mode.

    D. Use the vSphere Client and right-click a virtual machine that has FT enabled on it. Choose the Fault Tolerance Test Failover option from the context menu that appears.

18. You want DRS to use the most aggressive setting possible for the migration threshold. How do you accomplish this?

    A. Move the slider for the automation level to the far left in the DRS settings.

    B. Move the slider for the migration threshold to the far left in the DRS settings.

    C. Move the slider for the automation level to the far right in the DRS settings.

    D. Move the slider for the migration threshold to the far right in the DRS settings.

19. Which of the following is a use case for VMware FT? (Choose all that apply.)

    A. Application that requires high availability

    B. Application that has no native capability for clustering

    C. Application that requires protection for critical processes to complete

    D. Application that has persistent and long-standing connections

20. Which of the following options can be used to restart individual virtual machines when they have failed or become unresponsive?

    A. VMware FT

    B. VM monitoring

    C. Application monitoring

    D. None of these

Chapter

9

Maintain Service Levels

VCP5 EXAM OBJECTIVES COVERED IN THIS CHAPTER:

✓ **Migrate Virtual Machines**

- Migrate a powered-off or suspended virtual machine

- Identify ESXi host and virtual machine requirements for vMotion and Storage vMotion

- Identify Enhanced vMotion Compatibility CPU requirements

- Identify snapshot requirements for vMotion/Storage vMotion migration

- Configure virtual machine swap file location

- Migrate virtual machines using vMotion/Storage vMotion

- Utilize Storage vMotion techniques (changing virtual disk type, renaming virtual machines, etc.)

✓ **Backup and Restore Virtual Machines**

- Identify snapshot requirements

- Create/Delete/Consolidate virtual machine snapshots

- Install and Configure VMware Data Recovery

- Create a backup job with VMware Data Recovery

- Perform a test and live full/file-level restore with VMware Data Recovery

- Determine appropriate backup solution for a given vSphere implementation

✓ **Patch and Update ESXi and Virtual Machines**

- Identify patching requirements for ESXi hosts and virtual machine hardware/tools

- Create/Edit/Remove a Host Profile from an ESXi host

- Attach a Host Profile to an ESXi host or cluster

- Performing Compliance Scanning, Applying Host Profiles And Remediating An ESXi Host Using Host Profiles

- Install and Configure vCenter Update Manager

- Configure patch download options

- Create/Edit/Delete an Update Manager baseline

- Attach an Update Manager baseline to an ESXi host or cluster

- Scan and remediate ESXi hosts and virtual machine hardware/tools using Update Manager

- Stage ESXi host updates

This chapter will cover the objectives of sections 5.4, 5.5, and 5.6 of the VCP5 exam blueprint. This chapter will focus on migrating, backing up, and restoring virtual machines, in addition to patching ESXi hosts and updating the virtual machine hardware and the VMware Tools.

This chapter will first cover migrating virtual machines. I will cover migrating a powered-off or suspended virtual machine. The ESXi and virtual machine requirements for vMotion and Storage vMotion will be identified. The CPU requirements for EVC will be identified, along with virtual machine snapshot requirements for use with vMotion and Storage vMotion. I will cover how to configure the virtual machine swap file location and discuss the impact this can have on vMotion and Storage vMotion operations. Migrating virtual machines using vMotion and Storage vMotion will be covered, along with using Storage vMotion to change virtual disk types, renaming virtual machines, and more.

The second section of this chapter will cover backing up and restoring virtual machines. Snapshot requirements will be identified. The procedure to create, delete, and consolidate snapshots will be covered. I will cover installing and configuring VMware Data Recovery, along with creating backup jobs and restores with VMware Data Recovery. Determining the appropriate backup solution for a given vSphere implementation will also be discussed.

The final section of this chapter will focus on patching and updating ESXi and virtual machines. Patching requirements for ESXi hosts and virtual machine hardware and the VMware Tools will be identified. I will show how to create, edit, and remove a host profile from an ESXi host, attach/apply a host profile to a cluster, and perform compliance scanning and remediation of an ESXi host using host profiles. vSphere Update Manager will be installed and configured, and the patch download options will be configured. I will show how to create, edit, and delete an Update Manager baseline and attach an Update Manager baseline to a cluster. Scanning and remediating ESXi hosts and virtual machine hardware and the VMware Tools using Update Manager will be covered, along with staging ESXi host updates.

Migrating Virtual Machines

The ability to migrate virtual machines is a feature that all virtual infrastructure administrators can appreciate. Migration is defined as the process of moving a VM from one ESXi host or datastore to another. Migration allows the virtual infrastructure to be both more dynamic and highly available. The first topic I will cover in this chapter is migrating powered-off or suspended virtual machines.

Migrating a Powered-Off or Suspended Virtual Machine

Before the steps to migrate a powered-off virtual machine are covered, the different types of migration need to be covered. Four types of migration are possible in vCenter Server, as described in Table 9.1.

TABLE 9.1 VM migration options

Migration type	Description
Cold migration	Used to migrate a powered-off virtual machine to a new host and/or datastore. Cold migration can be used to move VMs to different datacenters.
Migrate a suspended VM	Used to migrate a suspended virtual machine to a new host and/or datastore. Suspended VMs can be migrated to different datacenters.
vMotion migration	Used to migrate a powered-on virtual machine to a new host with no disruption. vMotion cannot be used to move VMs to different datacenters.
Storage vMotion migration	Used to migrate the virtual disk files of a powered-on virtual machine to a new datastore with no disruption.

Migration means "move." Do not confuse migrate with copy operations such as cloning, where a new virtual machine will be created.

Exercise 9.1 covers the steps to migrate a powered-off virtual machine.

EXERCISE 9.1

Migrating a Powered-Off Virtual Machine Using the vSphere Client

1. Connect to a vCenter Server with the vSphere Client.

2. Locate a powered-off virtual machine.

3. Right-click it and choose the Migrate option from the context menu that appears.

4. The Migrate Virtual Machine Wizard will launch.

5. Select the Change Host option and click Next to continue.

6. Select a cluster and a host to move this virtual machine to and click Next to continue.

7. If applicable, select a resource pool and click Next.

8. Review the information on the Ready To Complete screen and click Finish.

9. A Relocate Virtual Machine task will begin.

10. When this task completes, verify on the virtual machine's Summary tab that the new ESXi host is listed in the Host field.

The process to migrate a suspended virtual machine is similar to the process used to migrate a powered-off virtual machine. Exercise 9.2 covers the steps to migrate a suspended virtual machine.

EXERCISE 9.2

Migrating a Suspended Virtual Machine Using the vSphere Web Client

1. Open a web browser and connect to the FQDN of the vCenter Server that will be used for this exercise.

2. Click the blue Log In To vSphere Web Client link.

3. When the vSphere Web Client loads, enter your credentials.

4. Locate a suspended virtual machine in the left pane.

5. Right-click it and choose the Inventory ➤ Migrate option from the context menu that appears.

6. The Migrate VM Wizard will launch.

(continued)

7. Select the Change Both Host And Datastore option and click Next to continue.

   If the virtual machine is powered on, the option to choose both the host and datastore will be grayed out.

8. Select a cluster or resource pool and click Next.

9. Select a destination host and click Next to continue.

10. Select a different datastore for the virtual machine. Verify that the Compatibility field lists Compatibility Checks Succeeded. Click Next to continue.

The following datastores are accessible by the destination you've selected. Select the destination datastore for the virtual machine configuration files and all of the virtual disks.

Name	Capacity	Provisioned	Free	Type	Storage
esxi1-dsVMFS	217.00 GB	975.00 MB	216.05 GB	VMFS	
VMFS-SAN	9.75 GB	8.96 GB	812.00 MB	VMFS	
DSCLU01	26.94 GB	2.09 GB	24.86 GB		Enabl

Advanced >>

Compatibility:

✔ Compatibility checks succeeded.

[Back] [Next] [Finish] [Cancel]

11. Choose the Same Format As Source option for the disk format. These options will be covered in detail later in this chapter. Click Next to continue.

12. Review the information presented in the review and click Finish to migrate the suspended virtual machine to a new ESXi host and datastore.

13. A Relocate Virtual Machine task will begin.

14. When this task completes, verify on the virtual machine's Summary tab that the new ESXi host is listed in the Host field and that the new datastore is listed.

15. Right-click the virtual machine in the left pane and choose the Power ➤ Power On option.

16. Open the virtual machine console and verify that it is operating properly.

Suspended virtual machines must be able to resume execution on the target host using an equivalent instruction set. The Migrate Virtual Machine Wizard includes a compatibility check and will not allow incompatible migrations to proceed.

Now that I have covered migration and migrating powered-off and suspended virtual machines, I will move on to using vMotion. However, I will first identify the ESXi host and VM requirements for vMotion and Storage vMotion.

Identifying ESXi Host and Virtual Machine Requirements for vMotion and Storage vMotion

Before you can use vMotion or Storage vMotion, the ESXi hosts must satisfy several requirements:

- ESXi hosts must be licensed to use vMotion.
- ESXi hosts must have access to the same shared storage.
- ESXi hosts must have VMkernel networking established for the vMotion traffic.
- ESXi hosts must be licensed to use Storage vMotion.

⊕ Real World Scenario

Using Storage vMotion Without a License

A virtual infrastructure administrator is building a new environment. The environment will consist of an iSCSI SAN, three ESXi servers, vCenter Server in a virtual machine, and vSphere Essentials Plus licensing. The servers have arrived, but the SAN has been delayed. The virtual infrastructure administrator notices that the ESXi servers each contain two 300GB SAS drives.

The virtual infrastructure administrator decides to go ahead and get an early start on building out the environment. He installs ESXi on each of the three servers. He then creates a new virtual machine to install vCenter Server on and stores the virtual machine on the local storage of one of the ESXi hosts. When he installs vCenter Server, he does not enter his Essentials Plus license keys and instead elects to run the environment in evaluation mode for 60 days. He deploys another server to be used for vSphere Update Manager and also deploys the vSphere Management Appliance. All three of these virtual machines are on local storage on different ESXi hosts.

The SAN arrives a few days later, and the virtual infrastructure administrator configures the VMkernel networking for it and gets each of the three hosts connected to this shared storage. He then uses Storage vMotion to move his vCenter Server, vSphere Update Manger, and vMA virtual machines to the shared storage. Once these Storage vMotion operations are complete, he enters his vSphere Essentials Plus licensing information in vCenter Server. The 60-day evaluation mode option chosen during the vCenter Server installation allowed him to use features he was not licensed for and ultimately complete his work without waiting for the SAN to arrive.

Just as there are requirements to use vMotion and Storage vMotion on the ESXi hosts, there are also virtual machine requirements for vMotion and Storage vMotion:

- Virtual machines that use raw disks for clustering cannot be migrated.

- Virtual machines that use a virtual device backed by a device that is not accessible on the destination host cannot be migrated.

- Virtual machines that use a virtual device backed by a device on the client computer cannot be migrated.

- Virtual machines that use USB pass-through devices can be migrated, but only if the devices are enabled for vMotion.

- Virtual machines that use NPIV are not supported with Storage vMotion.

- You can vMotion virtual machines that utilize NPIV, only if the RDM files are all located on the same datastore.

- Virtual machine disks must be in persistent mode or be RDMs for Storage vMotion.

- Virtual machines in the process of having a VMware Tools upgrade cannot be migrated.

Now that I have identified the ESXi host and virtual machine requirements for vMotion and Storage vMotion, I will identify the EVC CPU requirements.

Identifying Enhanced vMotion Compatibility CPU Requirements

The EVC requirements were discussed in Chapter 8. As a review, the following requirements exist for EVC CPUs:

- All hosts in the cluster must have only Intel or only AMD processors. Mixing Intel and AMD processors is not allowed.

- CPU features, such as hardware virtualization support (AMD-V or Intel VT) and AMD No eXecute (NX) or Intel eXecute Disable (XD), should be enabled consistently across all hosts in the cluster.

- All of the ESXi hosts in the cluster must contain supported CPUs for the desired EVC mode.

For more information on EVC processor support, check the VMware KB article "Enhanced VMotion Compatibility (EVC) processor support" at http://kb.vmware.com/kb/1003212.

Now that I have reviewed the EVC CPU requirements, I will identify the snapshot requirements for vMotion and Storage vMotion.

Identifying Snapshot Requirements for vMotion/Storage vMotion Migration

There are currently no requirements for using virtual machine snapshots with vMotion or Storage vMotion in a homogeneous vSphere 5 environment. As long as the virtual machine is located on an ESXi 5 host and the vSphere environment meets the vMotion or Storage vMotion requirements, either of these two approaches can be used to migrate powered-on virtual machines with snapshots.

 If your vSphere environment has a mix of ESX or ESXi hosts running different versions, then Storage vMotion can be used only for virtual machines with snapshots if these virtual machines are running on an ESXi 5 host. For more information, check VMware KB 1035550.

I have now identified the snapshot requirements for vMotion and Storage vMotion. In the next section, I will configure the virtual machine swap file location.

Configuring Virtual Machine Swap File Location

Virtual machine swap files were discussed in detail in Chapter 7. Before the steps to configure the virtual machine swap file location are covered, a brief review will be provided.

The virtual machine swap (.vswp) file is created when a virtual machine is powered on. This file is used only if the ESXi host runs out of physical memory and is used to allow overcommitment of virtual memory for virtual machines running on the ESXi host. Initially the .vswp file will be equal to the amount of virtual machine–assigned memory minus the memory reservation set for the VM. These files can be large, and in some cases, such as when troubleshooting or using replication, it is better to have them in their own storage locations and not in the same working location as the virtual machine. The working location is the directory where the virtual machine's configuration files are stored.

Virtual machine swap files can be placed in the following locations:

Default   Selecting this option will store the virtual machine swap file at the default location as defined in the host or cluster where the VM currently resides.

Always Store With The Virtual Machine   Selecting this option will store the virtual machine swap file in the working location. This is the same location where the VM's configuration file is stored.

Store In The Host's Swapfile Datastore   Selecting this option will store the virtual machine swap file in the swap file datastore as defined on the host or cluster where the VM currently resides. Otherwise, the virtual swap file will be stored in the virtual machine's working location.

The virtual machine swap file location is important in migrations with vMotion, because it affects vMotion compatibility. For example, in migrations between ESX/ESXi 3.5 and newer hosts, if the swap file is located in a different location on the destination host, the swap file must be copied to this new location. This can slow down vMotion operations.

The virtual machine swap file location can be configured in up to three separate locations. These locations are the cluster, host, and virtual machine. In Exercise 9.3, the steps to configure the virtual machine swap file location for each of these locations will be covered. I will begin with setting the swap file location at the cluster level and will then change the swap file location on an ESXi host that is a member of the cluster. Finally, a virtual machine will have its swap file location modified.

EXERCISE 9.3

Configuring the Virtual Machine Swap File Location

1. Connect to a vCenter Server with the vSphere Client.

2. Select an ESXi host that is a member of a cluster from the left pane. Select the Configuration tab in the right pane.

3. Click the blue link for Virtual Machine Swapfile Location located in the Software panel.

4. Review the information presented for the Virtual Machine Swapfile Location. Note that the Edit link is grayed out.

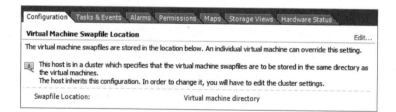

Also note that the default configuration is for the cluster to define the virtual machine swap file location.

5. Select the cluster that this ESXi host is a member of in the left pane and right-click it. Select the Edit Settings option from the context menu that appears. The Cluster Settings window will appear.

6. Select the Swapfile Location item in the left pane. The default, and recommended, setting is to store the swap file in the same directory as the virtual machine. Change this option to Store The Swapfile In The Datastore Specified By The Host.

7. Click OK to save this change. A Reconfigure Cluster task will begin.

You have now changed the virtual machine swap file location for the cluster. The ESXi hosts will now need to have a datastore configured to store swap files.

8. Select the same ESXi host that was used in step 2 and return to the Virtual Machine Swapfile Location.

9. Notice that now the Edit link is blue and active. Click it.

10. A Virtual Machine Swapfile Location window will appear.

11. Select a datastore and click OK to continue. An Update Local Swap Datastore task will begin.

12. Verify on the Configuration tab that the datastore selected is listed in the Swapfile Location field.

    The virtual machine swap file location has now been configured at the ESXi host level. In the next set of steps, I will verify that this change works as expected.

13. Locate a powered-off virtual machine that is a member of the cluster and that is located on the ESXi host used in the previous steps.

14. On the virtual machine's Summary tab, locate the datastore listed in the Resources pane.

15. If this is the same datastore that was selected in step 11, a different virtual machine or use Storage vMotion to migrate the VM to a different datastore before proceeding.

16. Power on the virtual machine. Note in the Resources pane that the datastore configured in step 11 is now listed as a second datastore.

17. Right-click this datastore and choose the Browse Datastore option from the context menu that appears.

18. The virtual machine's swap file will be listed in the root of the datastore, as shown here.

(continued)

EXERCISE 9.3 *(continued)*

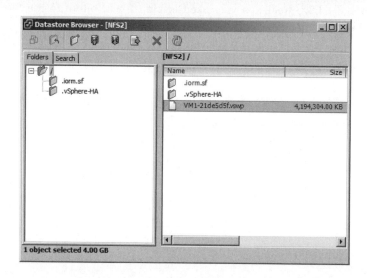

19. Close the datastore browser and shut down this virtual machine.

    You will now change the virtual machine's individual swap file location setting. This setting will override the swap file location setting specified at either the ESXi host or cluster level.

20. Right-click the virtual machine and choose the Edit Settings option from the context menu that appears.

21. Click the Options tab and select the Swapfile Location item listed in the left pane. Review the information presented in the right pane.

22. Change the Swapfile Location to the Always Store With The Virtual Machine option.

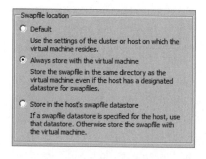

23. Click OK in the Virtual Machine Properties editor to save the swap file location change. A Reconfigure Virtual Machine task will begin.

24. Power on the virtual machine again.

25. Note in the Resources pane that the datastore configured in step 11 is now no longer listed.

26. Right-click the remaining datastore and choose the Browse Datastore option from the context menu that appears.

27. The virtual machine's swap file will be listed in the virtual machine's working location, as shown here.

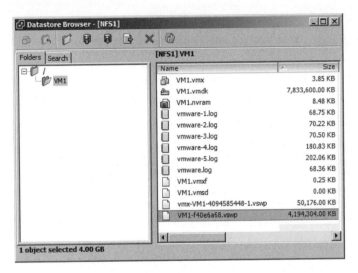

28. As a final step, restore all virtual machine swap file location settings to their defaults, which are the recommended settings from VMware.

As noted per the Virtual Machine Swapfile Location setting in the Configuration tab for the ESXi host, an individual virtual machine swap file location setting will override the setting specified on an ESXi host or cluster.

Now that I have covered configuring the virtual machine swap file location, I will cover migrating virtual machines using vMotion and Storage vMotion.

Migrating Virtual Machines Using vMotion/Storage vMotion

Migrating virtual machines with vMotion is a relatively simple operational task. Most virtual infrastructure administrators have surely performed a migration with vMotion, as VMware reports that 80 percent of its customers have vMotion in use in production environments. Exercise 9.4 covers the steps to migrate a powered-on virtual machine with vMotion using the vSphere Web Client.

EXERCISE 9.4

Migrate a Virtual Machine with vMotion Using the vSphere Web Client

1. Open a web browser and connect to the FQDN of the vCenter Server that will be used for this exercise.

2. Click the blue Log In To vSphere Web Client link.

3. When the vSphere Web Client loads, enter your credentials.

4. Locate a powered-on virtual machine in the left pane and select it. Note in the Summary tab the ESXi host that this VM is running on.

5. Right-click the virtual machine and choose the Inventory ➤ Migrate option from the context menu that appears.

6. The Migrate <Virtual Machine Name> Wizard will launch.

7. Select the Change Host option and click Next to continue.

8. Select a cluster or resource pool. Verify the compatibility status and also note that there is a check box located at the bottom of the screen that allows a specific ESXi host to be selected. Selecting this check box will add another step to the wizard.

9. Select the Allow Host Selection Within This Cluster option, and click Next to continue.

10. Select a host by clicking it. Review any compatibility messages that appear in the lower portion of the window and click Next.

11. Accept the default and recommended vMotion priority of Reserve CPU For Optimal vMotion Performance.

   The Perform With Available CPU Resources can be useful if the environment is currently CPU constrained.

12. Click Next to continue.

13. Review the information in the summary and click Finish to begin the vMotion migration.

14. A Relocate Virtual Machine task will begin. When this task completes, verify that the virtual machine has been moved to a different host on the virtual machine's Summary tab.

Migrating a virtual machine using Storage vMotion is another relatively simple task. Exercise 9.5 covers the steps to migrate a virtual machine with Storage vMotion using the vSphere Client.

EXERCISE 9.5

Migrate a Virtual Machine With Storage vMotion Using the vSphere Client

1. Connect to a vCenter Server with the vSphere Client.

2. Locate a powered-on virtual machine in the left pane and select it. Note in the Summary tab the datastore that this virtual machine is stored on.

3. Right-click the virtual machine and choose the Migrate option from the context menu that appears.

4. The Migrate Virtual Machine Wizard will launch.

5. Select the Change Datastore option and click Next to continue.

6. Leave Select A Virtual Disk Format at the default. Select a datastore and verify that the compatibility field at the bottom of the screen reports Validation Succeeded.

(continued)

EXERCISE 9.5 *(continued)*

7. Click Next to continue.

8. Review the information on the Ready To Complete screen and click Finish.

9. A Relocate Virtual Machine task will begin.

10. When this task completes, verify on the virtual machine's Summary tab that the new datastore is listed in the Datastore field.

Additional advanced options can also be used with the Migrate Virtual Machine Wizard when migrating a virtual machine to a new datastore. In the next section, I will cover these advanced options.

Utilizing Storage vMotion Techniques

The advanced options available when performing a Storage vMotion can allow the virtual disk format to be changed, a storage profile to be changed, and disks and configuration files to be divided into separate datastores.

In prior versions of vSphere, it was possible to rename a virtual machine and then cold migrate or perform a Storage vMotion migration to another datastore to update both the directory and filenames. This behavior has changed in vSphere 5, and at the time this book was written, only the directory will be renamed with this operation. The result is shown in Figure 9.1, where VM1 was renamed VM199 and then migrated.

FIGURE 9.1   Renamed and migrated VM

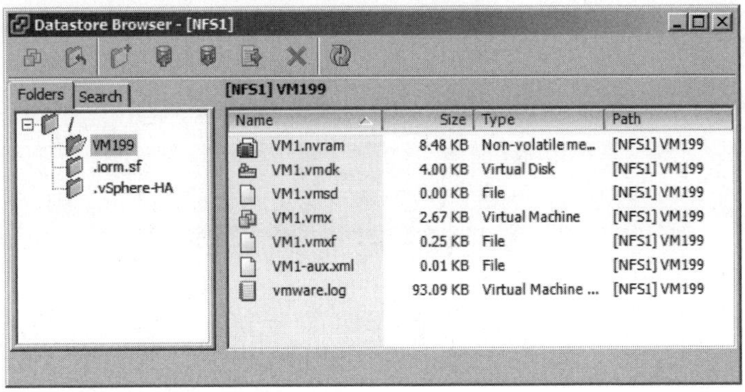

Exercise 9.6 covers the advanced options that can be used to migrate a virtual machine with Storage vMotion. This exercise will use the vSphere Client, but you can also use the vSphere Web Client. To simplify this exercise, use a virtual machine that has a single virtual disk assigned to it.

EXERCISE 9.6

Performing a Storage vMotion with Advanced Techniques

1. Connect to a vCenter Server with the vSphere Client.

2. Locate a powered-on virtual machine in the left pane and select it. Note in the Summary tab the datastore that this virtual machine is stored on.

3. Right-click this virtual machine and choose the Edit Settings option from the context menu that appears.

4. The Virtual Machine Properties editor will appear. Select Hard Disk 1 from the left pane. Review the Disk Provisioning information in the right pane to determine the disk type. The disk type will be reported as either Thin Provision, Thick Provision Lazy Zeroed, or Thick Provision Eager Zeroed. Remember the type of virtual disk, because you will need it later in this exercise.

5. Close the Virtual Machine Properties editor.

6. Right-click the virtual machine and choose the Migrate option from the context menu that appears.

7. The Migrate Virtual Machine Wizard will launch.

8. Select the Change Datastore option and click Next to continue.

(continued)

EXERCISE 9.6 *(continued)*

9. The next step of the Migrate Virtual Machine Wizard is to select the destination storage. To access the advanced options, click the Advanced button located toward the lower-right side of the window.

   The view will change and look similar to this.

10. Select the virtual disk file by clicking it.

11. Click in the Disk Format column in the highlighted row to access a drop-down menu. Change the virtual disk format to a different type than what was shown in step 4 of this exercise.

   Setting this option will change the virtual disk format as part of the migration. Note that the configuration file is listed as N/A, since it is a .vmx file and not a .vmdk file.

12. Click in the Datastore column. A Select A Datastore Or Datastore Cluster window will appear. The datastore that the virtual machine is currently located on will be selected by default.

13. Pick a new datastore for this virtual disk file to be moved to by clicking the datastore. Once the new datastore is highlighted, click OK.

    The datastore column will update to reflect the new location. The final configuration should appear similar to this.

14. Click Next and then review the information on the Ready To Complete screen. Click Finish to begin the Storage vMotion.

15. A Relocate Virtual Machine task will begin. When this task completes, verify that there are two datastores listed on the Summary tab in the Resources pane.

16. Browse each datastore and verify that the contents are as expected.

Changing the virtual disk format with NFS servers may not always be possible. If the NFS server supports the *VAAI NAS extensions* that enable reserve space, then thick-provisioned disks on NFS are possible. If not, then the option to change virtual disk formats will be grayed out.

The various forms of migration have now been covered. In the next section of this chapter, I will move on to backing up and restoring virtual machines.

Backing Up and Restoring Virtual Machines

As a VMware Certified Professional, you will be expected to know how to back up and restore virtual machines using VMware Data Recovery. VMware Data Recovery is VMware's backup appliance that is included in all editions of vSphere except the Essentials edition. Another common operational task that virtual infrastructure administrators must know is how and when to use VMware snapshots. In this section, I will cover snapshots and VMware Data Recovery and discuss how to determine appropriate backup solutions.

Identifying Snapshot Requirements

Snapshots are used in vSphere to preserve state and data in a virtual machine. A virtual machine snapshot will preserve the following:

- Virtual machine settings
- Power state
- Disk state
- Memory state (optional)

Snapshots are very useful for short-term protection from changes made to a virtual machine. For example, a virtual machine can be placed in snapshot mode prior to software upgrades, operating system updates, or any virtual machine configuration changes. If the upgrade, update, or other change were to fail or otherwise be found unsuitable, then the virtual machine could be quickly and easily returned to its previous state. The key thing to remember with VMware snapshots is that they are intended for short-term use only. They are not a replacement for backups, and snapshot *delta disks* alone may not be used as backups.

To better understand why snapshots are not suitable replacements for backups, it helps to understand how snapshots work. When a snapshot is taken, a delta disk is created for the virtual disk(s) in the virtual machine. This delta disk is used for all disk writes, since the original VMDK file is placed in read-only mode to preserve its state. If the memory is also preserved in the snapshot, then an additional file will be created that contains the memory and power state. These delta disks are also referred to as *differencing* disks, and they contain only the differences between the original virtual disk or parent snapshot (if multiple snapshots are being used). This is why snapshot files cannot be used as backups. Another key thing to understand about delta disks is that they expand with each disk write and can grow to the same size as the original virtual disk. Know that there is also a performance penalty when using snapshots. This penalty will depend on the workload, the number of snapshots used, and the duration of the snapshot(s).

 Taking a snapshot will create VMDK, -00000#-DELTA-VMDK, VMSD, and VMSN files. These files are detailed in Table 7.3 in Chapter 7.

When used with VMware Tools, snapshots also provide the ability to provide varying degrees of consistency for powered-on virtual machines running certain versions of the Window OS. Table 9.2 shows these abilities.

TABLE 9.2   VM snapshot consistency abilities

Guest OS	VMware Tools driver	Consistency
Windows XP 32-bit Windows 2000 32-bit	Sync Driver	File-system consistent
Windows Vista 32-bit/64-bit Windows 7 32-bit/64-bit	VMware VSS	File-system consistent
Windows 2003 32-bit/64-bit	VMware VSS	Application consistent
Windows 2008 32-bit/64-bit Windows 2008 R2	VMware VSS	Application consistent

Windows 2008 snapshots will be application consistent only when the following conditions are met:

- ESX 4.1 or newer hosts are used
- The UUID attribute is enabled
- SCSI disks are used in the virtual machine
- Dynamic disks are not supported

The VMware Tools provide drivers to allow running applications to have their I/O paused during snapshot operations. This feature, also known as *quiescing*, can be used to ensure at least some level of consistency for virtual machines that will have snapshots applied. Most backup applications leverage snapshots as part of image-level backups of virtual machines. The level of consistency achieved will vary, and it is extremely important to understand your workloads, their VSS support capability, and their specific behaviors when using them with virtual machines that will utilize snapshots. Just as you would with backup jobs, you will always want to test the consistency of applications when used with powered-on virtual machine snapshots. I will revisit consistency at the conclusion of this section on backups.

In addition to understanding how snapshots work, there are several restrictions when using snapshots:

- Raw disks, physical compatibility mode RDM disks, or *iSCSI initiators* being used inside a guest OS are not supported.
- PCI vSphere Direct Path I/O devices are not supported.
- Independent disks are not supported, unless the virtual machine is powered off.
- Virtual machines that use bus sharing are not supported.
- Machines protected with VMware FT are not supported.
- Sufficient free space in the datastore is required for delta files.

There is also some overhead involved when using snapshots. The overhead is approximately 2GB per 256GB. Table 9.3 lists the overheads and the resulting maximum VMDK sizes that can be used with snapshots.

TABLE 9.3 Snapshot overheads

Max VMDK size	Max overhead	Max VMDK size less overhead
256GB to 512 bytes	~ 2GB	254GB (VMFS-3 only)
512GB to 512 bytes	~ 4GB	508GB (VMFS-3 only)
1024GB to 512 bytes	~ 8GB	1016GB (VMFS-3 only)
2048GB to 512 bytes	~ 16GB	2032GB (VMFS-3, VMFS-5)

Because of these overheads, VMware recommends that the maximum size of any VMDK be based on a value that adjusts for the overhead involved. Not following this recommendation could lead to VMDK files that cannot be placed in snapshot mode or failed operations that depend on the use of snapshots.

For more information on snapshot overheads, refer to VMware KB http://kb.vmware.com/kb/1012384.

Now that I have covered snapshots and identified the requirements for using them, I will move on to creating, deleting, and consolidating virtual machine snapshots.

Creating, Deleting, and Consolidating Virtual Machine Snapshots

Creating snapshots is a simple operational task that can be performed with either the vSphere Client or the vSphere Web Client. In most cases, Snapshot Manager is the tool that you will use to create, delete, and review snapshots for a virtual machine. Exercise 9.7 covers the steps to create and revert to a snapshot.

EXERCISE 9.7

Creating a Virtual Machine Snapshot and Then Revert To It

1. Connect to a vCenter Server with the vSphere Client.

2. Select a powered-on virtual machine that has the VMware Tools installed from the left pane and right-click it. Choose the Snapshot ➢ Take Snapshot option from the context menu that appears.

3. Snapshot Manager will open.

4. Provide the snapshot with a descriptive name and description.

5. Ensure that the Snapshot The Virtual Machine's Memory option is selected.

6. Ensure that the Quiesce Guest File System (Needs VMware Tools Installed) option is selected.

7. Click OK to create the snapshot. A Create Virtual Machine Snapshot task will begin.

8. When this task completes, open Snapshot Manager again by right-clicking the virtual machine and choosing the Snapshot ➢ Snapshot Manager option from the context menu that appears.

(continued)

EXERCISE 9.7 *(continued)*

9. Review the information shown in Snapshot Manager and then close Snapshot Manager.

A snapshot has now been created for this virtual machine. In the next part of this exercise, you will make changes to both the virtual machine configuration and the guest OS file system.

10. Open the console to the virtual machine and create a directory on the root file system. Name this directory **SNAPSHOT**.

11. Open the Virtual Machine Properties editor and click the Options tab.

12. Select the Boot Options item in the left pane.

13. Select the Force BIOS Setup option.

14. Click OK and wait for the Reconfigure Virtual Machine task to complete.

In the remainder of the exercise, assume that the changes made to this VM were unsuccessful and you would now like to return the virtual machine to its prior state.

15. Open Snapshot Manager again by right-clicking the virtual machine and choosing the Snapshot ➤ Revert To Current Snapshot option from the context menu that appears.

A dialog box will appear prompting you to confirm this action.

16. Click Yes to revert to the current snapshot.

17. A Revert To Current Snapshot task will begin. When this task completes, open the console of the virtual machine. Verify that the directory created in step 10 is not there.

18. Open the Virtual Machine Properties editor and click the Options tab.

19. Select the Boot Options item in the left pane.

20. Verify that the Force BIOS Setup option is no longer selected.

21. Open Snapshot Manager and verify that the snapshot still exists.

I have now shown how to create a snapshot for a powered-on virtual machine and covered how to revert to the snapshot. Exercise 9.8 covers the steps to delete this snapshot.

EXERCISE 9.8

Deleting a Virtual Machine Snapshot

1. Connect to a vCenter Server with the vSphere Client.

2. Open the console of the virtual machine used in the previous exercise and create a directory on the root file system. Name this directory SNAPSHOT.

3. Open the Virtual Machine Properties editor and click the Options tab.

4. Select the Boot Options item in the left pane.

5. Select the Force BIOS Setup option.

6. Click OK and wait for the Reconfigure Virtual Machine task to complete.

    These are essentially the same steps performed in the previous exercise, but this time assume that the changes made to this VM were successful. The remainder of this exercise will cover the steps to commit the current state of the virtual machine by deleting the snapshot.

7. Open Snapshot Manager by right-clicking the virtual machine and choosing the Snapshot ➢ Snapshot Manager option from the context menu that appears.

8. Snapshot Manager will open. Verify that the snapshot from the previous exercise is listed and selected.

9. Click the Delete button at the bottom of the Snapshot Manager window.

    A dialog box will appear prompting you to confirm this action.

(continued)

EXERCISE 9.8 *(continued)*

10. Click Yes to delete the snapshot.

11. A Remove Snapshot task will begin. Wait for this task to complete, and do not close Snapshot Manager.

12. When the Remove Snapshot task completes, verify that the snapshot is no longer listed in Snapshot Manager. Close Snapshot Manager.

    Deleting the snapshot will commit the current state of the virtual machine. The remainder of this exercise will verify that the changes made to the virtual machine were committed successfully.

13. Open the console of the virtual machine and verify that the SNAPSHOT directory exists on the root file system.

14. Open the Virtual Machine Properties editor and click the Options tab.

15. Select the Boot Options item in the left pane.

16. Verify that the Force BIOS Setup option is selected.

You have now deleted a snapshot for a powered-on virtual machine. If the delete operation is successful, then no further action is required. In most cases, snapshot commit operations work as expected, but there can sometimes be problems. An example of this is if there was inadequate datastore free space during a snapshot commit. In the past, these failed operations required either workarounds with new snapshots and the Delete All option in Snapshot Manager or placing support calls to VMware. One of the new features in vSphere 5 is the consolidate option for snapshots. The consolidate functionality essentially provides a way to notify virtual infrastructure administrators to this failed commit condition and provide a method to handle any failed snapshot commits. If a snapshot commit operation fails, a message will appear on the virtual machine's Summary tab. Figure 9.2 shows this message.

FIGURE 9.2   Snapshot consolidation warning

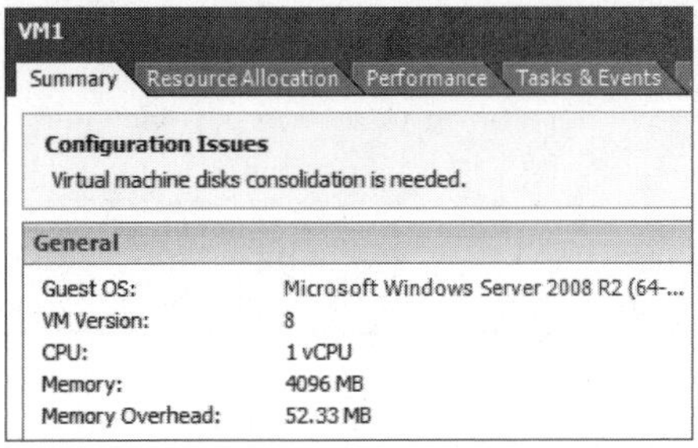

Exercise 9.9 covers the steps to consolidate virtual machine snapshots. This exercise will utilize the Windows PowerShell v2 and the vSphere PowerCLI in order to create the consolidate condition. The consolidate operation can be performed with either the vSphere Client or the vSphere Web Client.

EXERCISE 9.9

Consolidating Virtual Machine Snapshots

1. Connect to a vCenter Server with the vSphere Client.

2. Locate a powered-on virtual machine in the left pane and right-click it. Choose the Snapshot ➢ Take Snapshot option from the context menu that appears.

3. When Snapshot Manager opens, take a snapshot of the VM.

    You have now created a snapshot of the virtual machine. In the following steps, you will install the vSphere PowerCLI. The PowerCLI will be used to force a snapshot consolidate condition.

4. Ensure that you have Windows PowerShell v2 on the system that the vSphere PowerCLI will be installed on.

5. Download version 5 or newer of the vSphere PowerCLI from http://downloads.vmware.com/downloads/download.do?downloadGroup=PCLI50.

6. Once the download completes, launch the setup file.

(continued)

EXERCISE 9.9 *(continued)*

7. A dialog box may appear stating that the VMware VIX will be installed automatically. If so, click OK to continue.

You may also receive a message about the PowerShell execution policy, as shown here.

8. Review this information and then click the Continue button.

9. On the Welcome screen, click Next to begin.

10. Click Next on the Patents screen.

11. Accept the terms of the license agreement and click Next to continue.

12. Choose the destination folder and click Next to continue.

13. Click the Install button to install the vSphere PowerCLI.

14. When the installation completes, click Finish.

15. Using the newly created VMware vSphere PowerCLI icon on the Windows desktop, launch the vSphere PowerCLI.

The first thing that needs to be addressed is the execution policy. This was pointed out by the installer in step 7 of this exercise. In the following steps, you will set the PowerShell execution policy to require that downloaded scripts and configuration files be signed. This is a security feature of PowerShell.

16. When the vSphere PowerCLI opens, enter the following command:

```
Set-ExecutionPolicy RemoteSigned
```

17. Review the information presented and then press the Y key. Press Enter to continue.

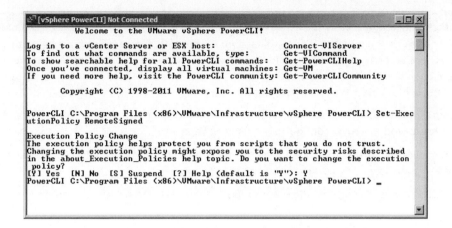

Now that the execution policy is set, you will use the vSphere PowerCLI to remove the snapshot but not commit the changes. This will result in a condition where consolidation is needed. Note that the following steps would be used only to simulate this exact condition.

18. Type the following command, to connect to the vCenter Server used in step 1 of this exercise:

Connect-VIServer

19. At the Server[0] prompt, enter the FQDN of the vCenter Server and press Enter.

20. At the Server[1] prompt, press Enter.

21. Type the following command, replacing <VM-Name> with the name of the virtual machine used in step 3 of this exercise:

$VM = get-VM <VM_Name> | Get-View

22. Enter the following command to remove the snapshot listing in the Snapshot Manager but leave the delta disks in the virtual machine's working location.

$VM.RemoveAllSnapshots(0)

23. Open Snapshot Manager and verify that the snapshot taken in step 3 of this exercise is not listed.

24. Browse the datastore that the virtual machine is located in, and confirm that there are still delta disks present for this virtual machine.

(continued)

EXERCISE 9.9 *(continued)*

You have now simulated a failed snapshot commit. In the remaining steps of this exercise, you will use the Consolidate function to clean up the delta disks that were left behind. This is the important part of this exercise, because all of the previous steps only created the error condition.

25. Locate the virtual machine that you have been working with in the left pane and select it. Verify that a configuration issue is reported.

26. Right-click the virtual machine in the left pane and choose the Snapshot ➢ Consolidate option from the context menu that appears.

27. A Confirm Consolidate window will appear. Click the Yes button to continue.

```
┌─────────────────────────────────────────────────────┐
│ Confirm Consolidate                              [X]  │
├─────────────────────────────────────────────────────┤
│                                                       │
│   ⚠   This operation will consolidate all redundant   │
│       redo logs on your VM.                           │
│       Are you sure you want to continue?              │
│                                                       │
│                                                       │
│                          [   Yes   ]   [   No   ]     │
└─────────────────────────────────────────────────────┘
```

28. A Consolidate Virtual Machine Disk Files task will begin. When this task completes, verify that the message on the virtual machine's Summary tab is no longer present.

29. Open Snapshot Manager and confirm that there are no snapshots listed.

30. Open the datastore browser and navigate to the virtual machine's directory. Verify that the delta disk files have been removed.

In a real consolidation scenario, always investigate the virtual machine's datastore(s) to ensure that adequate free space is available before performing the consolidation operation.

Now that snapshots have been covered, I will move on to installing and configuring VMware Data Recovery.

Installing and Configuring VMware Data Recovery

VMware Data Recovery is a disk-based backup and recovery solution provided by VMware in all editions of vSphere except for Essentials. VMware Data Recovery supports deduplication stores of up to 1TB in size, which allows for space savings on these disk-based backups. Three components make up the VMware Data Recovery solution:

- vSphere Client plug-in, installed on a Windows system
- Backup appliance, installed on ESXi host
- File Level Restore client, installed in supported VM guest OS

Before you can begin to install any of the VMware Data Recovery components, you need to meet the following system requirements:

- vCenter Server is required.

- The vSphere Client is required.

- ESX/ESXi 4 or newer hosts are required.

- The ESXi host that the backup appliance runs on must be managed by vCenter Server.

- You must use supported storage, such as NAS, SAN, or CIFS.

- You need storage space equal to the used space in all VMDKs that are intended to be backed up.

- You need a minimum of 10GB of free space, and VMware highly recommends 50GB of free space. Unless your environment is very small, you will very likely need more than 50GB to actually use VMware Data Recovery.

- The backup appliance must have access to vCenter Server web services (ports 80 and 443).

- The VMware Data Recovery client plug-in and File Level Restore (FLR) client both connect to the backup appliance on port 22024.

- The backup appliance connects to ESX/ESXi hosts on port 902.

- The ESX/ESXi host names must be resolvable in DNS.

- Appropriate security credentials must be used by each of the VMware Data Recovery components.

- CIFS shares on servers that have other roles, like the vCenter Server, should not be used.

- CIFS shares connected to a virtual machine should not be used.

- The same CIFS shares should not be used on multiple backup appliances.

 Each VMware Data Recovery backup appliance can back up 100 virtual machines, but only 8 virtual machines can be backed up simultaneously.

The first component that will be installed is the VMware Data Recovery Client plug-in; Exercise 9.10 covers the required steps.

EXERCISE 9.10

Installing the VMware Data Recovery Client Plug-in

1. Connect to a system that the VMware Data Recovery client plug-in will be installed on and obtain console access. This is a system that already has the vSphere Client installed.

2. Insert or mount the VMware Data Recovery media and launch the Data Recovery Installer.

(continued)

EXERCISE 9.10 *(continued)*

3. Click the blue Data Recovery Client Plug-In link on the installer screen to begin.

4. On the setup splash screen, click Next to begin.

5. On the Welcome screen, click Next.

6. On the Patent screen, click Next.

7. Accept the terms of the license agreement and click Next.

8. Click Next to begin the install.

9. Review the information on the Installation Complete screen and click the Close button.

10. Open the vSphere Client and connect to a vCenter Server.

11. Select the Plug-ins menu and choose the Manage Plug-ins option.

12. The Plug-in Manager will launch.

Plug-in Name	Vendor	Version	Status
Installed Plug-ins			
VMware Data Recovery	VMware, Inc.	2.0.0.50	Enabled
VMware vCenter Storage Monitoring Service	VMware Inc.	5.0	Enabled
vCenter Hardware Status	VMware, Inc.	5.0	Enabled
vCenter Service Status	VMware, Inc.	5.0	Enabled
VSA Manager	VMware, Inc.	1.0.0.6	Disabled
Available Plug-ins			

13. Verify that the VMware Data Recovery plug-in is listed and shows a status of Enabled.

14. Close the Plug-in Manager and click the Home icon in the navigation bar.

15. Verify that a VMware Data Recovery icon appears in the Solutions And Applications section.

The VMware Data Recovery client plug-in and backup appliance versions must match.

Now that the VMware Data Recovery client plug-in is installed, the backup appliance needs to be installed. Exercise 9.11 covers the steps to deploy the VMware Data Recovery backup appliance.

EXERCISE 9.11

Installing the VMware Data Recovery Backup Appliance

1. Connect to a vCenter Server with the vSphere Client.

2. Insert or mount the VMware Data Recovery media.

3. Select File ➢ Deploy OVF Template.

4. Click the Browse button and then locate the VMwareDataRecovery_OVF10.ovf file in the VMwareDataRecovery-ovf-x86_64 directory on the VMware Data Recovery media.

5. Click Next on the Source screen of the Deploy OVF Template Wizard.

6. Review the OVF Template Details and click Next.

7. Click the Accept button to accept the license agreement and then click Next to continue.

8. Provide a unique and descriptive name for the VMware Data Recovery appliance and select an inventory location. Click Next to continue.

9. Choose the appropriate cluster, host, and/or resource pool and click Next to continue.

10. Select a storage destination for the virtual appliance and then click Next.

(continued)

EXERCISE 9.11 *(continued)*

If a VMFS datastore is chosen and VMFS-3 datastores are in use in the environment, be sure to select a VMFS datastore that uses the largest VMFS block size currently in use in the environment.

11. Select the virtual disk format for the VMware Data Recovery backup appliance and click Next to continue.

12. Select a network mapping and click Next to continue.

These network mappings can be changed after deployment by using the Virtual Machine Properties editor. The backup appliance has two NICs by default, with the intention of using one for management and one for network storage access. You may or may not require this second NIC in your environment.

13. Accept the default time zone of UTC for the Timezone Setting option. Click Next to continue.

14. Review the information on the Ready To Complete screen and click Finish to deploy the VMware Data Recovery backup appliance.

15. When the backup appliance is deployed, select it in the left pane. Review the information on the Summary tab for the backup appliance.

General	
Product:	VMware Data Recovery
Version:	2.0.0.1861 (2.0.0.1861 Build 433157)
Vendor:	VMware, Inc.
Guest OS:	CentOS 4/5/6 (64-bit)
VM Version:	7
CPU:	2 vCPU
Memory:	2048 MB
Memory Overhead:	37.24 MB
VMware Tools:	② Running (3rd-party/Independent)
IP Addresses:	172.16.113.199 View all
DNS Name:	vdr.test.local
EVC Mode:	N/A
State:	Powered On
Host:	esxi2.test.local
Active Tasks:	
vSphere HA Protection:	② Protected

WARNING   The deployed VMware Data Recovery backup appliance's Summary tab will have the annotation of VMware Data Recovery Module. It is essential that this annotation not be modified in any way, because the backup appliance is recognized by this annotation.

The VMware Data Recovery backup appliance has now been installed, but it still needs a storage location to use for the backups. Adding virtual hard disks to the backup appliance is a quick and easy way to provide this storage. VMware recommends the use of virtual disks or RDMs for deduplication stores, instead of CIFS shares.

> **TIP**
>
> Deduplication stores are limited to 1TB for virtual disks and RDMs. Deduplication stores are limited to 500GB for CIFS network shares.

Exercise 9.12 covers how to add a virtual hard disk to the backup appliance.

EXERCISE 9.12

Adding a Virtual Disk to the VMware Data Recovery Backup Appliance

1. Connect to a vCenter Server with the vSphere Client.

2. Locate the backup appliance in the left pane. Right-click it and choose the Edit Settings option from the context menu that appears.

3. On the Hardware tab, click the Add button. The Add Hardware Wizard will appear.

4. Select Hard Disk from the list of devices and click Next.

5. Choose the Create A New Virtual Disk option and click Next.

6. Give the disk a capacity suitable for your environment and choose the Thick Provision Lazy Zeroed option for Disk Provisioning. Click Next to continue.

7. Set the Virtual Device Node to the value of 1:0, as shown here.

(continued)

EXERCISE 9.12 (continued)

8. Click Next to continue.

9. Review the information presented on the Ready To Complete screen and click Finish to add the virtual disk to the backup appliance.

10. Click OK in the Virtual Machine Properties editor and wait for the Reconfigure Virtual Machine task to complete.

> This virtual disk can be easily extended later, using the Virtual Machine Properties editor. There is a single-click option in the VMware Data Recovery backup appliance to complete the disk extend.

The VMware Data Recovery backup appliance is now installed, and a virtual disk has been added to it. The final component of VMware Data Recovery, the File Level Restores (FLR) client, will now be installed. The term *install* is a misnomer, though, because the FLR client consists of a single file. This file is copied from the VMware Data Recovery media to the supported guest operating system running in the virtual machine. The supported guest operating systems include the following:

- Red Hat Enterprise Linux (RHEL) 5.4/CentOS 5.4
- Red Hat 4.8/CentOS 4.8
- Ubuntu 8.04
- Ubuntu 8.10
- Ubuntu 9.04
- Windows XP
- Windows Vista
- Windows 7
- Windows Server 2003
- Windows Server 2008

Installing the FLR client in a Windows guest OS is as simple as copying a single file. Browse the VMware Data Recovery media and locate and then copy the file \WinFLR\ VMwareRestoreClient.exe to a location on the supported guest OS. Note that the FLR client on Windows requires the .NET Framework 2.0 or newer.

> VMs that use GUID partition tables (GPTs) will not work with FLR.

The steps to install the FLR client in a Linux guest operating system are a bit more involved. In either 32-bit or 64-bit supported Linux guest operating systems, the FLR client has the following requirements:

- 32-bit version of FUSE 2.5 or newer

- LVM

These utilities must be available and added to PATH. Once these prerequisites are covered, the FLR client can be installed. Exercise 9.13 covers these steps using Ubuntu.

EXERCISE 9.13

Installing the FLR Client in Ubuntu

1. Connect to the virtual machine via console, SSH, or your preferred method of access.

2. Mount the VMware Data Recovery ISO to the virtual machine.

3. In either a terminal window or the local console, enter the following command:

`cd /media/VMwareDataRecovery/LinuxFLR`

4. Create a directory for the FLR client on the local filesystem:

`mkdir ~/vDR-FLR`

4. Copy the archive file to the local filesystem, with the following command:

`cp VMwareRestoreClient.tgz ~/vDR-FLR`

5. Change to the directory the VMwareRestoreClient.tgz file was copied to with the following command:

`cd ~/vDR-FLR`

6. Enter the following command to extract the files from the archive:

`tar xvzf VMwareRestoreClient.tgz`

7. Change into the extracted file directory with the following command:

`cd VMwareRestoreClient`

8. Issue the following command to view the files in this directory:

`ls`

   Note the two filenames of vdrFileRestore and VdrFileRestore. Remember that Linux is case-sensitive and these are two separate files. The VdrFileRestore file is the one that will be used later in this chapter to restore files to a virtual machine.

With the setup of the FLR client complete, all three of the VMware Data Recovery components are now installed. I will now move on to configuring the VMware Data Recovery backup appliance.

Exercise 9.14 covers the steps to configure the VMware Data Recovery backup appliance.

EXERCISE 9.14

Configuring the VMware Data Recovery Backup Appliance

1. Connect to a vCenter Server with the vSphere Client.

2. Locate the backup appliance in the left pane. Right-click it and choose the Open Console option from the context menu that appears.

3. When the console window opens, power on the backup appliance.

4. When the backup appliance loads, be sure that the console window has focus and then press Enter to log in.

5. Enter the username **root** and press Enter.

6. Enter the password **vmw@re** and press Enter.

7. Once logged in, enter the command **passwd**.

8. Enter the new password for the root account.

9. Reenter the new password for the root account.

10. Once the root password has been changed, enter the command **exit**.

11. You will be returned to the VMware Data Recovery backup appliance configuration screen.

12. If you have DHCP running on the network segment that the VMware Data Recovery backup appliance is running on, then note the URL on the configuration screen and skip to step 26. Note that you should consider using a static address for the VMware Data Recovery backup appliance.

13. If you do not have DHCP running on the network segment that the VMware Data Recovery backup appliance is running on, then the networking will need to be configured.

14. On the configuration screen, select the Configure Network option and press Enter.

15. You will first be prompted to configure an additional IPv6 address. Press the n key and press Enter.

16. You will next be prompted to choose between DHCP and static IP addressing. Press n and press Enter.

17. Enter the IP address for the backup appliance and press Enter.

18. Enter the appropriate subnet mask and press Enter.

19. Enter the gateway address and press Enter.

20. Enter the first DNS server address and press Enter.

21. Enter the second DNS server address and press Enter.

22. Provide a hostname and press Enter.

23. You will be prompted to specify whether an IPv4 proxy server is necessary to reach the Internet. Choose the appropriate response and press Enter to continue.

24. You will be prompted to review the information just entered and confirm whether it is correct. If the information is correct, press y and then press Enter on keyboard.

```
CHANGE NETWORK CONFIGURATION for eth0

          Please enter the desired network parameters.
                 To exit, type q at any prompt.

This machine may receive an IPv6 SLAAC address when the network provides one.
Configure an additional IPv6 address? y/n [n]: n

Use a DHCPv4 Server instead of a static IPv4 Address? y/n [n]: n

IPv4 Address []: 172.16.113.199
Netmask []: 255.255.255.0
Gateway []: 172.16.113.1
DNS Server 1 [10.17.47.1]: 172.16.113.2
DNS Server 2 [10.17.47.65]: 172.16.113.3
Hostname [localhost.localdom]: vdr.test.local
Is an IPv4 proxy server necessary to reach the Internet? y/n [n]: n


IPv4 Address:     172.16.113.199
Netmask:          255.255.255.0
Gateway:          172.16.113.1
Proxy Server:
DNS Servers:      172.16.113.2, 172.16.113.3
Hostname:         vdr.test.local

Is this correct? y/n [y]: y
```

(continued)

EXERCISE 9.14 *(continued)*

25. The networking will be reconfigured, and you will be returned to the configuration screen. Verify that the URL field is now populated with the correct address.

26. Enter this URL in a web browser and verify that you can connect and log in to the VMware Data Recovery backup appliance via its web management interface.

27. Take some time and explore this management interface.

You have now changed the password, configured networking, and spent some time exploring the web management interface for the backup appliance. Exercise 9.15 will cover the steps to connect the backup appliance to a vCenter Server.

EXERCISE 9.15

Connecting the VMware Data Recovery Backup Appliance to vCenter Server

1. Connect to a vCenter Server with the vSphere Client.

2. In the vSphere Client, click the Home icon in the navigation bar.

3. Choose the VMware Data Recovery icon from the Solutions And Applications section at the bottom of the screen.

4. Expand the inventory list in the left pane and select the appropriate backup appliance. The name of the virtual appliance will be populated into the drop-down menu in the right pane.

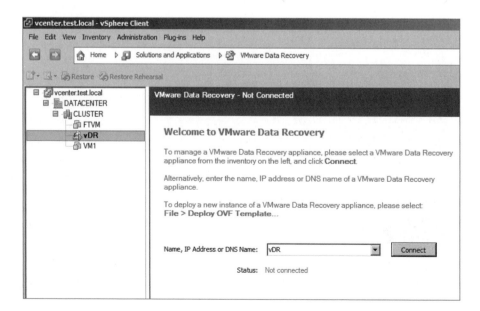

5. Click the Connect button.

6. You will be prompted to provide the password for the account you are currently signed into vCenter Server with. Enter the password and click OK.

These credentials will be stored and used to connect to vCenter Server to perform backup and restore operations. You may want to consider creating and using a service account or be mindful of the password expiration settings used on this account.

7. Since this is the first time a vSphere Client has connected to the backup appliance, the Getting Started Wizard will be launched.

8. Verify that the current credentials are reported as valid. If not, enter an appropriate set of credentials. Click Next to continue.

9. Review the backup destinations. Specifically, look for the virtual disk that was added to the backup appliance in Exercise 9.12. Use the blue Refresh link at the top of the window if the disk is not visible.

10. Click the disk to highlight it. Click the blue Format link at the top of the window to format this disk. A Format warning window will appear. If you are sure that the correct disk is selected, click OK to format this disk.

11. Monitor the progress of the format status in the Status column. When the format is complete, the device name will change to SCSI-1:0, and the Status column will change to Mounted.

(continued)

EXERCISE 9.15 *(continued)*

Getting Started Wizard

Backup Destinations

Data Recovery requires a backup destination such as a virtual disk, RDM or a network share. A virtual disk needs to be properly formatted and mounted. Add backup destinations to be used during backup operations.

Credentials

Backup Destinations

Configuration Complete

Destinations: Refresh   Add Network Share...   Format...   Mount

Name △	Comments	Type	Status	Capacity	Free
/SCSI-1:0/		Local Volume	Mounted	149 GB	149 GB

Help   < Back   Next >   Close

12. Click Next to continue.

13. Review the information on the Ready To Complete screen. Remove the check from the Create A New Backup Job After Completion option and click the Close button to complete the Getting Started Wizard.

14. Click the Configuration tab and then click the blue Set vCenter Server Or ESXi Host Credentials link. A Set vCenter Server Or ESXi Host Credentials window will appear. If the credentials ever need to be modified, this is the location to make the change.

Set vCenter Server or ESX Host Credentials

The Backup Appliance needs to connect to either a vCenter Server or an ESX host. Please enter the User Name and Password to be used by the Backup Appliance, and then click on Apply to use the new settings.

IP address / Name: vcenter.test.local

User name: TEST\Administrator

Password: ****************

Apply   Cancel

WARNING   Regardless of the VMware Tools status reported for the VMware Data Recovery backup appliance, do not update the VMware Tools on this appliance.

Now that the steps to install and configure the VMware Data Recovery backup appliance have been covered, I will now cover the steps required to create a backup job with it.

Creating a Backup Job with VMware Data Recovery

Backup jobs can be created using the VMware Data Recovery client plug-in from the vSphere Client. These backup jobs can specify the virtual machine(s), the destination, and the retention period. Exercise 9.16 covers the steps to create a backup job with VMware Data Recovery. For this exercise, choose a guest OS that the FLR client is supported on. This virtual machine will be used in additional exercises in this chapter. The supported guest operating systems for use with the FLR client were listed earlier in this chapter.

EXERCISE 9.16

Creating a Backup Job with VMware Data Recovery

1. Connect to a vCenter Server with the vSphere Client.

2. In the vSphere Client, click the Home icon in the navigation bar.

3. Choose the VMware Data Recovery icon from the Solutions And Applications section at the bottom of the screen.

4. Expand the inventory list in the left pane and select the appropriate backup appliance. Click the Connect button in the right pane.

5. Click the Backup tab in the right pane.

6. Click the blue New link located in the upper-right section of this tab.

7. A Backup Job # – Backup Wizard will launch. Provide the backup job with a descriptive name and click Next.

8. Select a single virtual machine from the inventory and click Next to continue.

(continued)

Note that you can also use the Virtual Machine Name filtering options at the top to help locate virtual machines. Entering characters in this text box will filter the virtual machines listed below in real time. This is a perfect example of a feature that would be extremely useful in an environment with hundreds or thousands of virtual machines.

9. Select a destination to store the backup and click Next. Notice the blue Add Network Share link, which can be used to add a CIFS destination.

Make sure you select a virtual machine that will fit on the disk added to the backup appliance when making the choice here.

10. Review the default schedule. Accept the default options for the backup window and click Next to continue.

11. Review the default and available options for retention. Accept the default options for the retention policy and click Next to continue.

Backup Job - Backup Wizard

Backup Job: Retention Policy

The retention policy determines how many backups to keep and for how long to keep them. Older backups not protected by the retention policy are deleted as needed to make room for new backups. Select a pre-defined retention policy or create a custom policy.

Name
Virtual Machines
Destination
Backup Window
Retention Policy
Ready to Complete

Retention Policy:
○ Few
◉ More
○ Many
○ Custom

Description:
This policy saves more virtual machine backups than the Few option. Choose this policy if you need to retain more than just the most recent backups.

More Policy Details:

Number of recent backups to retain: 7

Older backups to retain:
8 Weekly backup(s)
6 Monthly backup(s)
4 Quarterly backup(s)
1 Yearly backup(s)

Help   ≤ Back   Next ≥   Cancel

12. Review the information on the Ready To Complete screen and click Finish to add the backup job.

13. The backup job should run immediately, and if it does, you can skip step 14.

14. If the backup job doesn't start immediately, then right-click the backup job and choose the Backup Now ➢ All Sources option from the context menu that appears. Verify that the backup job begins.

15. Ensure that the backup job completes before moving on to the next exercise.

The Reports tab in the right pane of the VMware Data Recovery application interface in the vSphere Client can be used to verify when backup jobs have completed.

Now that I have covered creating a backup job with VMware Data Recovery, I cover how to perform both a test and live full and file-level restore.

Performing a Test and Live Full/File-Level Restore with VMware Data Recovery

Once VMware Data Recovery creates a backup job, restores of the entire virtual machine or individual files are possible. It is also possible to clone a backup to a new virtual machine. Exercise 9.17 covers the steps to restore an individual file to a virtual machine. This exercise will use the virtual machine backed up in Exercise 9.16 and will cover a Windows guest OS.

EXERCISE 9.17

Performing an Individual File-Level Restore Using the FLR Client

1. Connect to the console of the virtual machine that was backed up in Exercise 9.16. Be sure you have Administrator privileges on this virtual machine.

2. Browse the VMware Data Recovery media and copy the file \WinFLR\ VMwareRestoreClient.exe to the virtual machine.

3. Launch VMwareRestoreClient.exe and wait for the VMware Data Recovery Restore Client window to open. Enter the IP address of the VMware Data Recovery backup appliance.

   Note the Advanced check box in the lower-left corner of this screen. The Advanced Mode of FLR can be used to access restore points from multiple virtual machines. The Standard Mode of FLR will only allow the virtual machine to see its own restore points.

4. Select the Advanced option. Additional login options will now become available.

5. Enter the FQDN of the vCenter Server and provide appropriate credentials. Click the Login button to continue.

6. Locate the same virtual machine that you are currently logged in to in the list and expand it to show the restore points. Select a restore point by clicking it.

(continued)

EXERCISE 9.17 (continued)

7. Click the Mount button located in the upper-left corner. The Status column will begin reporting Mounting. Wait for the Status column to update and show a value of Mounted. The path to the mount will also be shown in the Status column, as shown here.

8. Select a virtual disk file listed below the restore point and then click the Browse button on the top toolbar to browse to the path of the mount.

9. Locate the file(s) to be restored.

10. The file(s) may simply be copied from this path to the desired location.

11. When all files have been restored, return to the VMware Data Recovery Restore Client window and click the Unmount All button.

12. The Status column will no longer report any value, and the Mount button will again be active in the top toolbar.

13. Close the VMware Data Recovery FLR client.

I have now covered file-level restores for a Windows guest OS. While file-level restores may often solve a problem, sometimes an entire virtual machine may need to be restored.

Exercise 9.18 covers the steps to restore a virtual machine. This exercise will overwrite an existing virtual machine, so please make sure to use a test system.

EXERCISE 9.18

Restoring a VM with VMware Data Recovery

1. Connect to a vCenter Server with the vSphere Client.

2. In the vSphere Client, click the Home icon in the navigation bar.

3. Choose the VMware Data Recovery icon from the Solutions And Applications section at the bottom of the screen.

4. Expand the inventory list in the left pane and select the appropriate backup appliance. Click the Connect button in the right pane.

5. Click the Restore tab in the right pane.

6. Click the blue Restore link located at the top of the right pane. The Virtual Machine Restore Wizard will launch.

7. Locate the virtual machine to be restored and expand its contents by clicking the plus sign in the box located to the left of the VM name. Locate the desired restore point and select it.

8. Click Next to continue.

9. On the Destination Selection screen, there are many options and items that need to be discussed. The right pane of the Destination Selection screen is shown here.

(continued)

EXERCISE 9.18 *(continued)*

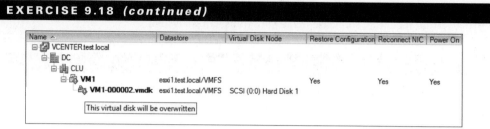

Name △	Datastore	Virtual Disk Node	Restore Configuration	Reconnect NIC	Power On
VCENTER.test.local					
DC					
CLU					
VM1	esxi1.test.local/VMFS		Yes	Yes	Yes
VM1-000002.vmdk	esxi1.test.local/VMFS	SCSI (0:0) Hard Disk 1			

This virtual disk will be overwritten

The first things to note are the alerts overlaying the virtual machine icons. Hovering the mouse over the alert state items produces the text *This virtual disk will be overwritten* shown in the previous image. Note that the Datastore, Virtual Disk Node, Restore Configuration, Reconnect NIC, and Power On columns can all be changed by clicking the values. Clicking these values will produce a drop-down menu where you can specify the available options. You can also right-click the virtual machine to rename it or move it to a different location. The virtual disk(s) on this screen can also be right-clicked to change the restore location.

10. Accept the defaults for all of the available options and click Next to continue.

11. Review the information presented on the Ready To Complete screen and pay particular attention to the notes listed at the bottom of this screen. These notes will look similar to what is shown here.

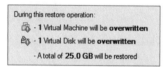

During this restore operation:
- **1** Virtual Machine will be **overwritten**
- **1** Virtual Disk will be **overwritten**
- A total of **25.0 GB** will be restored

12. Click the Restore button to begin the restore operation. The Reports tab will now be shown in the right pane.

13. A series of tasks will be launched in vCenter Server, and the progress of the restore can be monitored in the Reports tab.

Backup	Restore	**Reports**	Configuration		

Report Name △	Items	Warnings, Errors
Events	16	0, 0
Running Tasks	1	0, 0
Virtual Machines	9	0, 0
Warnings and Errors	0	0, 0

Running Tasks

Start Time ▽	Description	Warnings, Errors	Progress
11/18/2011 10:12:41 AM	VM1		7%

Execution Progress Details

Name:	**VM1**	Status:	**Restoring Virtual Machine "VM1"...**
Sources:	**/SCSI-1:0/**	Progress:	**1.81 GB of 25.0 GB**
Destination:	**VM1**	Stop	

14. When the restore operation completes, verify that the virtual machine is working as expected.

I have now covered the steps to restore a virtual machine using VMware Data Recovery. With any backup software, it is good to know that the backups can be restored. Testing restoration is, or should be, common practice in most environments. This ensures that when it is time to restore a virtual machine, there will be no surprises or unexpected behaviors. VMware Data Recovery provides a built-in way to test the restore process, known as *restore rehearsal from last backup*. Exercise 9.19 covers the steps to perform this operation.

EXERCISE 9.19

Testing the Restore of a VM with VMware Data Recovery

1. Connect to a vCenter Server with the vSphere Client.

2. In the vSphere Client, click the Home icon in the navigation bar.

3. Choose the VMware Data Recovery icon from the Solutions And Applications section at the bottom of the screen.

4. Expand the inventory list in the left pane and select the appropriate backup appliance. Click the Connect button in the right pane.

5. Locate a virtual machine in the left pane and right-click it.

6. Choose the Restore Rehearsal From Last Backup option from the context menu that appears.

7. The Virtual Machine Restore Wizard will launch.

8. Locate the virtual machine to be restored and expand its contents by clicking the plus sign in the box located to the left of the VM name. Locate the desired restore point and select it.

9. Click Next to continue.

10. On the Destination Selection screen, right-click the virtual machine name and select Rename from the context menu that appears. Rename it as appropriate for your environment.

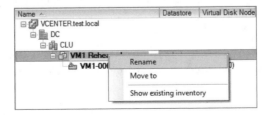

11. In the Datastore column, click the --SELECT-- text to choose the desired datastore for the virtual machine's VMX and VMDK file(s).

(continued)

12. Note that the default option for the Reconnect NIC is No. Ensure that this is selected and also change the value of Power On to No.

13. Review the information presented on the Ready To Complete screen.

Name ⌃	Restore Point	Datastore	Restore Configuration	Reconnect NIC	Power On
⊟ 🗐 VCENTER.test.local					
⊟ 🖳 DC					
⊟ 🗐 CLU					
⊟ 🗐 **VM2**	11/18/2011 9:29:23 AM	esxi1.test.local/VMFS	Yes	No	No
🗁 **VM1-000002.vmdk**	11/18/2011 9:29:23 AM	esxi1.test.local/VMFS			

During this restore operation:

🗐 - **1** Virtual Machine will be **created**

🗁 - **1** Virtual Disk will be **created**

   - A total of **25.0 GB** will be restored

14. Click the Restore button to begin the restore operation. The Reports tab will now be shown in the right pane.

15. A series of tasks will be launched in vCenter Server, and the progress of the restore can be monitored in the Reports tab.

16. When the restore operation completes, open the Virtual Machine Properties editor for the virtual machine.

17. Verify that the virtual machine's configuration was restored properly by comparing it to the original virtual machine. Also ensure that the virtual machine's NIC is not set to Connect At Power On.

18. Power on the virtual machine and verify that the virtual machine works as expected.

I have now covered how to perform a test restore, or a restore rehearsal from last backup, using VMware Data Recovery. In the next section, I will cover determining an appropriate backup solution for a given vSphere implementation.

Determining Appropriate Backup Solution for a Given vSphere Implementation

Determining the appropriate backup solution for a given vSphere implementation will ultimately come down to understanding the workloads, the business requirements, and many more environment-specific factors. There are a multitude of questions that should be asked:

- Will disk-based backup, tape backup, or both be used?
- If disk-based backup is used, is deduplication a requirement?
- How much data must be backed up?
- What is the estimated annual growth of backed-up data?
- With what frequency must the data be backed up?
- What are the data retention requirements?
- Is there a requirement to encrypt the backup data?
- What are the characteristics of the backup window?
- Are there SLAs in place that dictate TTR or RPO objectives?
- Is the backup solution for both VMs and physical servers?
- Are remote systems in need of backup?
- How many virtual machines must be backed up?
- How many VMs must be backed up simultaneously?
- Is vCenter Server in the environment?
- Which edition of vSphere is in use?
- What level of consistency is required for each workload?
- Are backup agents desired or required for certain workloads?
- Are the applications running in the VMs VSS aware?
- Is VMware FT in use in the environment?
- Are file-level restores required?
- Which operating systems and versions are in the environment?
- Do any virtual machines use iSCSI initiators in the guest OS?
- Is the ability to replicate backups required?
- Are multiple definable restore points required?
- Can or should existing backup software be leveraged?
- Is the IT staff already trained in a particular backup product?
- What is the budget for the backup solution?
- Are their snapshot solutions provided by the storage vendor?
- How will the backup software be accessed and by whom?

> **🌐 Real World Scenario**
>
> **Choosing Backup Software**
>
> A virtual infrastructure administrator is looking for a backup solution for her new virtual infrastructure. The environment currently contains multiple virtual machines with Windows 2000, SQL Server 6.5, and a custom in-house developed application running in them. These virtual machines were *P2V* converted from older hardware that was failing, and while not an ideal situation, these VMs are used in production. The business requires consistent backups of these virtual machines. Currently the virtual machines are backed up with a third-party application that utilizes an agent to get consistent SQL Server backups.
>
> The virtual infrastructure administrator wants to use a backup solution that can capture a complete and application-consistent image of these virtual machines. She has investigated VMware Data Recovery but discovered that application consistency was not possible for these virtual machines. She investigates the capabilities of the third-party backup application and discovers that it too will not be able to provide application-consistent image-level backups of these virtual machines.
>
> The virtual infrastructure administrator ultimately decides to continue to use the existing third-party backup application for daily backups of the data in these virtual machines. She also decides to use the third-party software to capture an image-level backup of the virtual machine. This image-level backup will be performed monthly, during a scheduled maintenance window. This image-level backup will be taken with the application and SQL Server services stopped in order to provide an application-consistent image-level backup. This approach allows her to recover the server to within 30 days but have much more current data.

Just like with many aspects of virtualization, there is no single backup solution that will fit every environment. Finding the right solution is more about understanding the particular requirements of the environment and delivering a backup/recovery solution that can meet those exact needs.

Patching and Updating ESXi and Virtual Machines

As a VMware Certified Professional, you will be expected to know how to patch and update ESXi hosts. Another item you will be expected to know is how to update the virtual machine hardware and the VMware Tools. Both of these practices are important in ensuring a highly available and highly performing virtual infrastructure. In this section, I will cover how to keep ESXi hosts up-to-date and how to keep the VMware Tools and virtual machine hardware up-to-date.

Identifying Patching Requirements for ESXi Hosts and Virtual Machine Hardware/Tools

Patching ESXi 5 hosts can be accomplished in different ways, but the two most common methods are the following:

- Using vSphere Update Manager
- Manually with the `esxcli` command

Regardless of the method used to patch an ESXi 5 host, the process is basically the same. The host will need to be placed in maintenance mode, and the patch or patches need to be applied and then verified. vSphere Update Manager can automate this multistep process, which can be quite helpful.

When patching ESX/ESXi hosts, vSphere Update Manager has the following requirements:

- Only ESX/ESXi 3.5 and newer hosts are supported.
- Upgrades/migrations require ESX/ESXi 4 and newer.
- vCenter Server is required.
- vSphere Update Manager requires its own database.

The `esxcli` command can be used from the ESXi Shell, the vMA, the vSphere PowerCLI, or the vSphere CLI. The requirements for patching ESXi hosts with the `esxcli` command are to ensure that you have both the access and the proper permissions to the ESXi host being patched.

Updating the VMware Tools and virtual machine hardware versions can also be accomplished in a variety of ways. These include the following:

- Using vSphere Update Manager
- Manually using the vSphere Client or the vSphere Web Client

Regardless of the method used to update the virtual machine hardware or the VMware Tools, the process is the same. Windows guests will have the VMware Tools uninstalled, a new version of the VMware Tools will be installed, and then a reboot will be required. As discussed in the upgrade sequence in Chapter 2, the VMware Tools upgrade should happen prior to the virtual machine hardware upgrade. This sequence ensures that any new virtual machine hardware will already have drivers available. The virtual machine hardware upgrade will also require both a shutdown and a subsequent reboot for Windows guests.

vSphere Update Manager has the following requirements to update virtual machine hardware versions and the VMware Tools:

- ESX/ESXi 4 and newer hosts are supported.
- Virtual machine patch operations are not supported.

When manually updating the virtual machine hardware or the VMware Tools with either the vSphere Client or the vSphere Web Client, the requirements are to have the appropriate privileges at the virtual machine level and the guest OS level.

While host profiles cannot be used to apply patches to ESXi hosts, they can be used to update settings on ESXi hosts. You may recall applying permissions to ESXi hosts in Exercise 3.12 in Chapter 3. There are a variety of settings that can be configured and checked for compliance. Using host profiles can be a powerful solution for updating configuration changes to multiple ESXi hosts. Host profiles have the following requirements, when patching ESX/ESXi hosts:

- Only ESX/ESXi 4 and newer hosts are supported.
- Enterprise Plus licensing is required.

Now that the requirements for patching ESX/ESXi hosts and virtual machine hardware and the VMware Tools have been covered, I will cover how to create, edit, and remove a host profile from an ESXi 5 host.

Creating, Editing, and Removing a Host Profile from an ESXi Host

The first step in using host profiles to monitor compliance for your ESXi hosts is to create a host profile. Exercise 9.20 covers the steps to create an ESXi host profile.

EXERCISE 9.20

Creating an ESXi Host Profile

1. Connect to a vCenter Server with the vSphere Client. Ensure that Enterprise Plus licensing is available or that the vCenter Server is running in evaluation mode.

2. Select the reference ESXi host and right-click it. Choose the Host Profile ➢ Create Profile From Host option from the context menu that appears.

3. When the Create Profile From Wizard begins, give the host profile a descriptive name and a brief description. Click Next to continue.

4. Review the summary information on the Ready To Complete The Profile screen and click Finish. A Create A Host Profile task will start. Wait for this task to complete before continuing.

5. Leave the vSphere Client open, because it will be used in the next exercise.

You have now created a host profile, but you need to edit some of its settings. For the purpose of this exercise, assume that the NTP server in your environment has been changed. I will cover how to edit the NTP settings of the host profile to reflect this change in exercise 9.21.

EXERCISE 9.21

Editing an ESXi Host Profile

1. Click the Home icon in the navigation bar at the top of the screen in the vSphere Client. Click the Host Profiles icon, located under the Management section.

2. In the left pane, select the profile that was created in the previous exercise. Right-click the profile and choose the Edit Profile option.

3. When the Edit Profile window launches, expand the Date And Time Configuration policy in the left pane. Select the Time Settings item in the right pane and verify the information presented in the Configuration Details tab.

   If the NTP settings have been previously configured, then the drop-down menu will show Configure A Fixed NTP Configuration and show the configured NTP server. If no NTP server was previously configured for the reference ESXi host, then the drop-down menu will show User Must Explicitly Choose The Policy Option.

4. Ensure that the drop-down menu is set to Configure A Fixed NTP Configuration and enter the new NTP server address.

Configuration Details	Compliance Details	
What should be the time settings?		
Configure a fixed NTP configuration	▼	Revert
*List of time servers, specified as either IP addresses or fully qualified domain names (FQDNs).	172.16.113.16	

5. Click the Compliance Details tab. Ensure that the Validate That List Of NTP Servers Isoption is selected. You can click the blue server link to view the configured NTP server(s).

   Choosing this option ensures that a compliance check will verify this setting.

6. Click OK to save these changes to the host profile.

7. An Update Host Profile task will begin. When this task completes, the policy is ready to be used.

To remove a host profile, simply right-click the host profile and choose the Delete Profile option from the context menu that appears. You will be prompted to confirm the delete.

Now that creating, editing, and removing host profiles have each been covered, the next step is to attach the host profile to an ESXi host.

Attaching and Applying a Host Profile to an ESXi Host or Cluster

Once a host profile is created, it needs to be attached to another ESXi host or cluster. Exercise 9.22 will cover the steps to attach the host profile you created to the reference ESXi host.

EXERCISE 9.22

Attaching a Host Profile to an ESXi Host

1. Connect to a vCenter Server with the vSphere Client. Ensure that Enterprise Plus licensing is available or that the vCenter Server is running in evaluation mode.

2. Right-click the ESXi host and choose the Host Profile ➢ Manage Profile option from the Host Profile menu.

3. In the Attach Profile window, choose the profile created in Exercise 9.20 and click OK.

4. An Attach Host Profile task will start. When it completes, click the Summary tab for this ESXi host and verify that the correct host profile is listed in the General section.

   Since the host profile was edited after you initially created it, the host profile now needs to be applied to the reference ESXi host. This will ensure that the reference ESXi host will be compliant in the next exercise.

5. ESXi hosts must be in maintenance mode to have a host profile applied, so right-click the reference ESXi host and choose the Enter Maintenance Mode option from the context menu that appears.

6. Once the ESXi host is in maintenance mode, right-click the ESXi host and choose the Host Profile ➢ Apply Profile option from the Host Profile menu.

7. The Apply Profile window will appear. Wait for the configuration change to load and then review the change listed in the Apply Profile window.

> **Apply Profile: esxi1.test.local**
>
> The following configuration changes will be applied on the host.
>
> Configuration Tasks
>
> Configure time servers to be 172.16.113.16
> Update the firewall configuration

8. Click Finish to apply the host profile.

9. Check the Time Configuration in the Configuration tab to see that the NTP server information is updated.

You have now attached and applied the modified host profile to the reference ESXi host. In the next section, you will check a second ESXi host for compliance and remediate it.

Performing Compliance Scanning and Remediating an ESXi Host Using Host Profiles

Now that you have attached and applied the host profile to your reference host, you are set to leverage the power of host profiles. This power is in one configuration change to the host profile that can then be applied to many ESXi hosts. Although changing multiple ESXi hosts is possible, Exercise 9.23 covers the steps to check a single ESXi host for compliance and remediate it.

EXERCISE 9.23

Compliance Scanning and Remediating an ESXi Host

1. Connect to a vCenter Server with the vSphere Client. Ensure that Enterprise Plus licensing is available or that the vCenter Server is running in evaluation mode.

2. Right-click a second ESXi host and choose the Host Profile ➢ Manage Profile option from the Host Profile menu.

3. In the Attach Profile window, choose the profile created in Exercise 9.20 and click OK.

4. An Attach Host Profile task will start. When it completes, click the Summary tab for this ESXi host and verify that the correct host profile is listed in the General section.

5. Place this ESXi host in maintenance mode.

6. Now that the profile is attached to the host, you will check the host for compliance with the profile. Click the Home icon in the navigation bar at the top of the screen. Click the Host Profiles icon, located under the Management section.

7. In the left pane, select the profile you just attached to the ESXi host. In the right pane, click the Hosts And Clusters tab.

(continued)

EXERCISE 9.23 *(continued)*

Baseline Update			
Getting Started	Summary	Hosts and Clusters	
Select an entity below to view its compliance failures			Apply Profile...
			Entity Name, Host Profile Compliance or Compliance
Entity Name	Host Profile Compliance	Compliance - Last Checked	Profile
esxi1.test.local	Unknown		Baseline Update
esxi2.test.local	Unknown		Baseline Update

8. Select each of the two ESXi hosts listed by clicking them while holding down the Ctrl key. Click the Check Compliance link in the top of the pane.

9. A Check Compliance task will start for each host. Wait for these tasks to complete and verify that the Host Profile Compliance or Compliance – Last Checked columns report different values. The results should look similar to this.

Baseline Update			
Getting Started	Summary	Hosts and Clusters	
Select an entity below to view its compliance failures			Apply Profile...
			Entity Name, Host Profile Compliance or Compliance
Entity Name	Host Profile Compliance	Compliance - Last Checked	Profile
esxi1.test.local	Compliant	11/19/2011 6:09:31 PM	Baseline Update
esxi2.test.local	Noncompliant	11/19/2011 6:07:41 PM	Baseline Update

10. Now that you know the second host is noncompliant, the final step is to apply the profile to the host.

11. Select the noncompliant ESXi host listed in the Entity Name column and click the blue Apply Profile link at the top of the screen.

12. The Apply Profile window will appear. Review the changes listed and click Finish.

13. An Apply Host Configuration task will start, followed closely by a Check Compliance task. Wait for both of these tasks to complete and then verify that the Host Profile Compliance is now reported as Compliant for both ESXi hosts.

Baseline Update			
Getting Started	Summary	Hosts and Clusters	
Select an entity below to view its compliance failures			Apply Profile...
			Entity Name, Host Profile Compliance or Compliance
Entity Name	Host Profile Compliance	Compliance - Last Checked	Profile
esxi1.test.local	Compliant	11/19/2011 6:09:31 PM	Baseline Update
esxi2.test.local	Compliant	11/19/2011 6:17:41 PM	Baseline Update

You have now checked an additional ESXi host for compliance to the host profile and then remediated it. Remember that the power in host profiles is in maintaining consistency across multiple ESXi hosts from a much fewer number of host profiles. Now that I have covered configuration consistency, I will move on to maintaining patch levels for ESXi hosts and updates for virtual machine hardware and the VMware Tools.

Installing and Configuring VMware vSphere Update Manager

VMware vSphere Update Manager is an automated patch management solution used to simplify the management of VMware vSphere environments. Update Manager can automate patches for ESXi hosts, virtual machine hardware, and the VMware Tools.

Before installing Update Manager, first verify membership in the Administrators group on the system and verify that the Update Manager system requirements are met. It's recommended to have a separate drive or volume to store the downloaded patch files. Other prerequisites are as follows:

- vCenter Server installation media should be available.
- The .NET Framework 3.5 SP1 or newer is required.
- vCenter Server should be installed and working properly.
- An Oracle or Microsoft SQL Server database should be used. Environments smaller than 5 hosts and 50 VMs can use the bundled SQL Server 2008 R2 Express database.
- A 64-bit Windows system is required for installation.
- A 32-bit DSN is required for database connectivity, if not using the bundled SQL Express database.
- vSphere Update Manager 5 is compatible only with vCenter Server 5.
- The Update Manager server and client plug-ins must be running the same version.
- Update Manager, vCenter Server, and the vSphere Client must be running compatible versions.

 While vSphere Update Manager and vCenter Server can use the same database, VMware recommends that separate databases be used.

Once the prerequisites have been met for Update Manager, installation can begin. Exercise 9.24 will cover the steps to install vSphere Update Manager.

EXERCISE 9.24

Installing vSphere Update Manager

1. Connect to a console session on any supported Windows client or server and log on with an Administrator account.

   Note that vSphere Update Manager can be installed on the vCenter Server or its own dedicated server.

2. Launch the vCenter Server Installer and select VMware vSphere Update Manager from the list of VMware Product Installers.

3. Click the Install button to begin.

4. When the installation wizard starts, select the desired language and click OK.

5. On the Welcome screen, click Next to begin.

6. Click Next on the End-User Patent Agreement screen to continue.

7. Accept the terms of the license agreement and click Next.

8. Deselect the Download Updates From Default Sources Immediately After Installation option, as shown here.

9. Click Next to continue.

10. On the vCenter Server Information screen, enter valid credentials for vSphere Update Manager to use to connect to vCenter Server. Ensure that the vCenter Sever name and port information are both correct. Click Next to continue.

11. Choose the appropriate database/credentials; note that if you use a stand-alone Oracle or SQL database, a 32-bit DSN is required.

12. Use the drop-down menu to specify the network interface that will be used for vSphere Update Manager and select the Yes, I Have Internet Connection And I Want To Configure Proxy Settings Now option.

13. Click Next to continue.

14. Configure the proxy server as necessary and click Next to continue. If you do not have a proxy server, simply deselect the Configure Proxy Settings option and click Next.

15. Select the destination folder for the Update Manager installation and the location for downloading patches. Click Next to continue.

Note that a best practice is to change the location for patch downloads to a different volume than where the operating system is installed. This practice can help prevent OS volume disk full errors from occurring. This location can be changed after installation by manually editing the <patchStore> information contained in the C:\Program Files (x86)\VMware\Infrastructure\Update Manager\vci-integrity.xml file.

16. Review the information on the Ready To Complete screen and click the Install button to install vSphere Update Manager.

17. Click Finish when the installation completes.

vSphere Update Manager has now been installed, but the vSphere Client plug-in still needs to be configured. The remaining steps of this exercise will cover enabling this plug-in.

18. Connect to a vCenter Server with the vSphere Client.

19. Select the Plug-ins menu and then choose the Manage Plug-ins menu option. The Plug-in Manager window will appear.

(continued)

EXERCISE 9.24 *(continued)*

20. The VMware vSphere Update Manager Extension is listed under the Available Plug-ins section. Click the blue Download And Install link in the Status column. The Status value will change to Downloading while the file is downloaded locally.

21. When the installer launches, select the desired language and click OK to continue.

22. On the Welcome screen, click Next.

23. Accept the terms of the license agreement and click Next.

24. Click the Install button to begin the install.

25. Click Finish on the Installation Complete screen.

26. Verify that the VMware vSphere Update Manager Extension is now listed under the Installed Plug-ins section of the Plug-in Manager.

27. You will also be prompted with a certificate warning. Handle this as appropriate for your environment.

28. Close the Plug-in Manager.

29. Click the Home icon in the navigation bar of the vSphere Client.

30. Verify that Update Manager is now listed under Solutions And Applications.

31. Click this icon to open Update Manager; review the interface options available.

Now that I have covered installing the vSphere Update Manager, I will cover how to configure its network settings in Exercise 9.25.

EXERCISE 9.25

Configuring vSphere Update Manager Network Settings

1. Connect to a vCenter Server using a vSphere Client with the vSphere Update Manager plug-in installed.

2. Click the Home icon in the navigation bar of the vSphere Client.

3. Click the Update Manager icon located in the Solutions And Applications section.

4. Click the Configuration tab.

5. The Network Connectivity settings are displayed by default. Review the current settings, as shown here.

Update Manager Administration for VCENTER							
Getting Started	Baselines and Groups	**Configuration**	Events	Notifications	Patch Repository	ESXi Images	VA Upgrades

Settings

- ▸ Network Connectivity
- Download Settings
- Download Schedule
- Notification Check Schedule
- Virtual Machine Settings
- ESX Host/Cluster Settings
- vApp Settings

Network Connectivity

┌─ Client Communication with the Update Manager Server ─────────
│
│   SOAP port: `8084`
└──

┌─ Update Manager patch store used by the ESX and ESXi hosts ──
│
│   Server port (range: 80, 9000–9100):   `9084`
│
│   IP address or host name for the patch store: `VUM` ▼
└──

⚠ For client communication, the vSphere Client must be able to access the specified ports on the Update Manager server. For patch transfers, ESX hosts must be able to access the specified ports on the Update Manager server. VMware vSphere Update Manager restart is required for these changes to take effect.

If there are any firewalls, they must be configured to allow traffic through these ports.

Apply

6. If the IP Address Or Host Name For The Patch Store option has a value other than an IP address, use the drop-down menu to change this value to the IP address of the system where vSphere Update Manager is installed.

   VMware recommends using an IP address here. Also note that IPv6 is not supported for scanning and/or remediation of virtual machines or virtual appliances.

7. After changing the value of the Address Or Host Name For The Patch Store option to the IP address of the vSphere Update Manager system, click the Apply button to save the change.

8. When the Apply button is grayed out, the change has been saved.

The network settings have now been configured, and I will next cover configuring the virtual machine settings. Note that the download settings will be covered in detail in the next section of this chapter.

The virtual machine settings are used to enable and disable the snapshot functionality and to define the retention period. By default, a snapshot will be taken of virtual machines before the updates are applied. This feature can be used to protect individual virtual machines in the event that an update causes a problem. By default, this snapshot will also be set to allow unlimited growth. As discussed earlier in this chapter, use caution with this default setting, because it could lead to very large snapshot files and the problems associated with them.

vSphere Update Manager can take snapshots of virtual machine hardware version 4 and newer only.

Exercise 9.26 will cover the steps to configure the virtual machine settings.

EXERCISE 9.26

Configuring vSphere Update Manager Virtual Machine Settings

1. Connect to a vCenter Server using a vSphere Client with the vSphere Update Manager plug-in installed.

2. Click the Home icon in the navigation bar of the vSphere Client.

3. Click the Update Manager icon located in the Solutions And Applications section.

4. Click the Configuration tab.

5. Click the blue Virtual Machine Settings link in the Settings panel on the left.

Update Manager Administration for VCENTER

| Getting Started | Baselines and Groups | Configuration | Events | Notifications | Patch Repository | ESXi Images | VA Upgrades |

Settings

- Network Connectivity
- Download Settings
- Download Schedule
- Notification Check Schedule
- ▸ Virtual Machine Settings
- ESX Host/Cluster Settings
- vApp Settings

Virtual Machine Settings

Specify the remediation rollback options. If enabled, rollback will take a snapshot of the virtual machine before remediation.

☑ Take a snapshot of the virtual machines before remediation to enable rollback.

    ○ Keep for [18] hours

    ◉ Do not delete snapshots

🛈 Snapshots reduce the performance of the virtual machine. Delete the snapshots as soon as the remediation is validated.

[Apply]

6. Select the Keep For Hours option and enter an acceptable value for your environment. This will not allow snapshots to grow forever and is a good best practice to
   implement.

7. Click the Apply button to save these changes. When the Apply button is grayed
   out, the changes have been saved.

You have now configured the snapshot behavior for virtual machines used with vSphere
Update Manager. I will next cover the ESXi host and cluster settings in Update Manager.

The ESXi host and cluster settings are used to control the maintenance mode behavior of
ESXi hosts, cluster settings, and boot settings for ESXi hosts that utilize PXE boot. These
settings can be configured to allow vSphere Update Manager to perform updates to ESXi
hosts that are members of a cluster with DRS and/or HA enabled.

Figure 9.3 shows the default maintenance mode settings.

FIGURE 9.3   Update Manager ESXi host settings

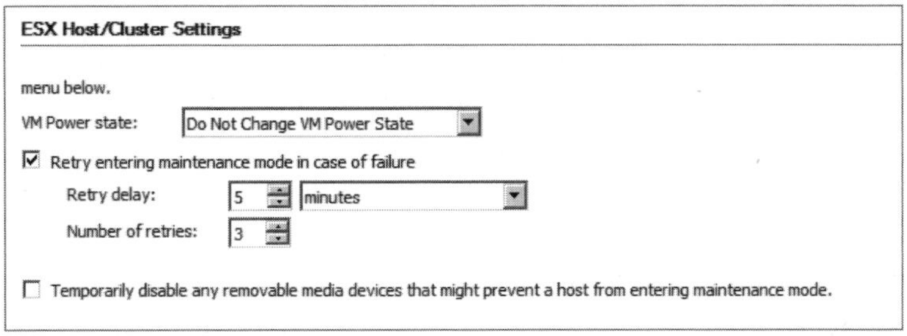

These options can be used to control how virtual machines behave when a host is placed
in maintenance mode. The VM Power State drop-down menu allows the configuration to
set virtual machines to power off, suspend, or be migrated. There are also retry settings, in
the event that the ESXi host does not successfully enter maintenance mode, and the ability
to temporarily disable removable media devices. Each of these options can be configured to
work as desired for the specific environment.

The next section of the ESXi Host/Cluster settings is the Cluster Settings. Exercise 9.27
covers the steps to configure these settings.

EXERCISE 9.27

Configuring vSphere Update Manager Cluster Settings

1. Connect to a vCenter Server using a vSphere Client with the vSphere Update
   Manager plug-in installed.

2. Click the Home icon in the navigation bar of the vSphere Client.

3. Click the Update Manager icon located in the Solutions And Applications section.

4. Click the Configuration tab.

(continued)

5. Click the blue ESX Host/Cluster Settings link in the Settings panel on the left.

Cluster Settings

Certain features might need to be temporarily disabled for cluster updates to succeed. These features will be automatically re-enabled when remediation is complete.

Update Manager does not remediate hosts on which the features are enabled.

Temporarily disable:

☑ Distributed Power Management (DPM)

☐ High Availability Admission Control

☐ Fault Tolerance (FT)

ⓘ To ensure that FT can be re-enabled, you should remediate all hosts in a cluster with the same updates at the same time. See the documentation for more details.

☐ Enable parallel remediation for hosts in cluster

☐ Migrate powered off and suspended virtual machines to other hosts in the cluster, if a host must enter maintenance mode

6. If DPM is configured on the cluster, ensure that the Distributed Power Management (DPM) option is selected. This will prevent DPM from interrupting vSphere Update Manager operations.

7. If your environment is very large, you may be able to speed the time to remediation by selecting the Enable Parallel Remediation For Hosts In Cluster option. This will allow Update Manager to update ESXi hosts simultaneously, as compared to sequentially when this option is not used.

8. Review the other settings listed here and determine whether they should be used in your environment.

The final setting in the ESX Host/Cluster settings is PXE Booted ESXi Host Settings. This setting can be used to allow vSphere Update Manager to update stateless ESXi hosts. This could be useful in cases where updates do not require a host reboot. This setting is disabled by default.

The last vSphere Update Manger setting is for vApps. There is one configurable option, known as Enable Smart Reboot After Remediation. This setting is shown in Figure 9.4.

This setting is enabled by default and will attempt to fulfill the startup order listed in the vApp, if any virtual machine in the vApp is remediated and requires a reboot. This is a useful setting, since rebooting a single virtual machine in the vApp could lead to failure of a tiered application.

Now that I have configured most of the vSphere Update Manager settings, I will move on to what are arguably the most important settings: the download options.

FIGURE 9.4   Update Manager vApp setting

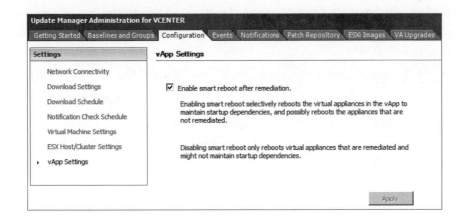

Configuring Patch Download Options

vSphere Update Manager can be configured to obtain files from three different download sources:

Direct Connection to Internet   This method can be used if vSphere Update Manager is installed on a server that has either direct or proxied Internet access.

Use a Shared Repository   This method can be used when vSphere Update Manager is installed on a server that does not have Internet access. It requires installing and configuring the Update Manager Download Service (UMDS) on an additional server that has Internet access.

Import Patches   This method can be used to import a ZIP file with the required patches.

> It is important to remember that either Internet downloads or a shared repository can be used, but they cannot be used simultaneously. It is strictly an either/or option.

Exercise 9.28 will cover the steps to configure the download settings for vSphere Update Manager.

EXERCISE 9.28

Configuring vSphere Update Manager Download Settings

1. Connect to a vCenter Server using a vSphere Client with the vSphere Update Manager plug-in installed.

2. Click the Home icon in the navigation bar of the vSphere Client.

3. Click the Update Manager icon located in the Solutions And Applications section.

4. Click the Configuration tab.

5. Click the blue Download Settings link in the Settings panel on the left. The default Download Settings are shown here.

Download Sources

⊙ Direct connection to Internet - download new patches and VA upgrades either at intervals specified in **Download**   Add Download Source...
Schedule or immediately by clicking the **Download Now** button below

Enabled	Update Type	Component	Download Source	Description	Connectivity Status
☑	VMware	ESX	https://hostupdate.vmware.com/softwareV..	Download vSphere ESX..	Connected
☑	VMware	ESX	https://www.vmware.com/PatchManageme..	Download ESX 3x patc...	Connected
☑	Custom	ESX	https://hostupdate.vmware.com/softwareV..	Download vSphere ESX..	Connected
☑	VMware	VAs	http://vapp-updates.vmware.com/vai-catal..	Download virtual applia...	Connected

○ Use a shared repository   What's this?

[Validate URL]   [Download Now] [Apply]

Note: you can also Import Patches manually from a local .zip file

Proxy Settings

☐ Use proxy   ☐ Proxy requires authentication

Proxy: [   ]   Username: [   ]

Port: [0   ]   Password: [   ]

[Test Connection] [Apply]

6. The first option in Download Sources is used when Update Manager is installed on a server with a connection to the Internet. Review the Enabled, Update Type, Component, Download Source, Description, and Connectivity Status columns.

7. If you recall from setup in Exercise 9.23, the option was chosen to not download the files. Download the files by clicking the Download Now button.

8. A dialog box will appear informing you that a download task has been started. Verify in the Recent Tasks pane that a Download Patch Definitions task has started.

9. While the patches download, note the second available option in the Download Sources section titled Use A Shared Repository. This option would be used with the UMDS mentioned earlier.

10. Look just below the Use A Shared Repository option, and you will see the third option, which is a blue Import Patches link.

11. Look in the Proxy Settings section in the lower part of the screen. These options can be configured as necessary when using the Direct Connection To Internet option in Download Settings.

12. There is also a Test Connection button included to test the proxy settings. If you use a proxy server, enter values for the Proxy Settings and click Test Connection to verify Internet connectivity.

13. When the Download Patch Definitions completes, browse to the directory that contains these files. If you accepted the default, the path will be C:\Program-Data\VMware\VMware Update Manager\Data\.

14. Review the directory structure and files contained here.

    Now that the download sources and proxy settings have been covered, I will cover the download schedule, which determines when vSphere Update Manager will actually download files.

15. Click the blue Download Schedule link in the Settings panel on the left.

16. Review the information here and notice that the scheduled downloads can also be disabled using the Enabled Scheduled Download option.

17. Take note of the date and time listed for the Next Run.

18. Click the blue Edit Download Schedule link to modify the schedule.

19. The Schedule Update Download Wizard will appear, as shown here.

(continued)

20. Change the Start Time and Interval setting to suit the needs of your environment. Click Next to continue.

21. If you want to be notified via email when new patches are downloaded, then enter an email address here. Click Next.

22. Review the information presented on the Summary screen and click Finish to modify the schedule.

23. Verify that the new schedule shows in the Download Schedule section of the Configuration tab.

Now that the download schedule has been covered, I will cover the Notification Check Schedule option. The notification check schedule is used to check for information about patch recalls, new fixes, and alerts.

24. Click the blue Notification Check Schedule link in the Settings panel on the left.

25. Review the information here and notice that the scheduled downloads can also be disabled using the Enabled Scheduled Download option.

26. The schedule can also be modified using the Schedule Update Wizard that was used previously in this exercise.

Now that the vSphere Update Manager download options have been covered, the next section will cover creating, editing, and deleting an Update Manager baseline.

Creating, Editing, and Deleting an Update Manager Baseline

vSphere Update Manager is used to scan hosts, virtual machines, and virtual appliances against a baseline or baseline group to determine their compliance level. A baseline is a collection of one or more patches, extensions, or upgrades, and a baseline group is a collection of baselines.

Baselines can be either dynamic or fixed. Dynamic baselines will update automatically as new patches are released, where fixed baselines are static and will not automatically include any newly released updates. Fixed baselines would typically be used when the virtual infrastructure administrator wants more control over what patches are installed.

The first type of baseline is the patch baseline. There are two patch baselines used for scanning hosts included with Update Manager by default. These baselines can be viewed on the Update Manager Baselines And Groups tab with the Hosts view. These two host baselines are as follows:

Critical Host Patches   These are used to check ESX/ESXi hosts for compliance with all critical patches.

Non-Critical Host   These are used to check ESX/ESXi hosts for compliance with all optional patches.

The second type of baseline is the extension baseline, which is used to deploy VMware or third-party software. An example of this might be vendor-specific CIM providers or a multipathing plug-in.

The third type of baseline is the upgrade baseline. There are three upgrade baselines used for scanning virtual machines and virtual appliances included with Update Manager by default. These baselines can be viewed on the Update Manager Baselines And Groups tab with the VMs/VAs view. The three upgrade baselines are as follows:

VMware Tools Upgrade to Match Host   Used to check virtual machines for compliance with the latest version of VMware Tools available on the ESX/ESXi 4 or newer host.

VM Hardware Upgrade to Match Host   Used to check the virtual hardware of a virtual machine for compliance with the most current version supported on the ESXi 5 host.

VA Upgrade to Latest   Used to check virtual appliance compliance with the latest available version of the virtual appliance.

Upgrade baselines can also be used in vSphere Update Manager to upgrade ESXi 4 hosts and to migrate ESX 4 hosts.

vSphere Update Manager cannot be used to upgrade an ESX 4 host that was upgraded from ESX 3.*x*. A fresh install will instead be required.

vSphere 5 surely has patches available for it. At the time this book was written, there were three patches already available for ESXi 5. Exercise 9.29 covers the steps to create a dynamic patch baseline for patching an ESXi 5 host to the latest release. This exercise will require a single ESXi 5 host that is not at the latest patch level.

EXERCISE 9.29

Creating a Dynamic Patch Baseline for ESXi 5

1. Connect to a vCenter Server using a vSphere Client with the vSphere Update Manager plug-in installed.

2. Click the Home icon in the navigation bar of the vSphere Client.

3. Click the Update Manager icon located in the Solutions And Applications section.

4. Click the Baselines And Groups tab. Note that the default view is the Hosts view.

5. On the Hosts view screen, click the blue Create link. The New Baseline Wizard will launch.

6. Give the baseline a descriptive name and provide a description for it in the Baseline Name And Description section. Ensure that the Host Patch option is selected in the Baseline Type section. The final settings should appear similar to what is shown here.

(continued)

EXERCISE 9.29 *(continued)*

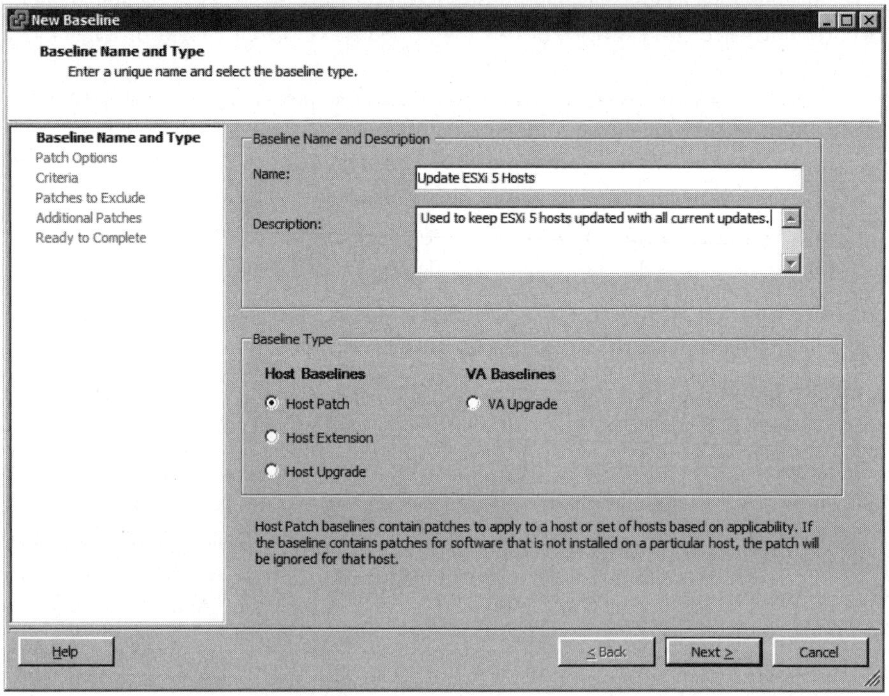

7. Click Next to continue.
8. Ensure that the Dynamic option is chosen for the baseline type and click Next to continue.
9. On the Dynamic Baseline Criteria screen, choose the Any option for the Patch Vendor. Select embeddedEsx 5.0.0 for Product. Accept the defaults for Severity and Category and do not specify any date ranges. The final settings should appear similar to what is shown here.

10. Note at the bottom of the screen that the number of patches that meet the selected criteria are listed. Click Next to continue.

11. On the Patches To Exclude screen, note the available patches are listed. The Patch Name, Release, Type, Severity, Category, Impact, and Vendor columns can each be used to discover more information about the available patches.

12. Accept the defaults and click Next to continue.

13. On the Additional Patches screen, review the additional patches that are available in the repository. Click Next to continue.

14. Review the information presented on the Ready To Complete screen. Expand Patches Matching Criteria Currently In The Repository and verify that the information listed is correct.

15. Click Finish and then verify that the new baseline is listed in the Hosts view of the baselines with the correct value in the Content column.

You have now created a dynamic baseline that can be used to update your ESXi 5 hosts to the latest version. I also included the Cisco Nexus 1000V in this baseline, and it's very likely that most test labs do not include this dvSwitch. If your lab does, then good for you! Exercise 9.30 covers how to edit the baseline just created to remove the Cisco Nexus 1000V patch.

EXERCISE 9.30

Editing a Dynamic Patch Baseline for ESXi 5

1. Connect to a vCenter Server using a vSphere Client with the vSphere Update Manager plug-in installed.

2. Click the Home icon in the navigation bar of the vSphere Client.

3. Click the Update Manager icon located in the Solutions And Applications section.

4. Click the Baselines And Groups tab. Note that the default view is the Hosts view.

5. On the Hosts view screen, locate the baseline created in the previous exercise. Right-click the baseline and choose the Edit Baseline option from the context menu that appears.

6. The Edit Baseline Wizard will appear. Note that on the Baseline Name And Type screen, you cannot edit the Baseline Type. Click Next to continue.

7. Leave the baseline as Dynamic and click Next to continue.

8. In the Dynamic Baseline Criteria settings, ensure that embeddedEsx 5.0.0 is selected for Product. Click Next to continue.

9. On the Patches To Exclude screen, select the Cisco Nexus 1000V patch by clicking it. Using the arrow buttons in the middle of the screen, move this patch to the Patches To Exclude section at the bottom of the screen.

10. Once the patch is moved, a red X will show beside it in the leftmost column in the top portion of the screen.

11. Click Next to continue.

12. On the Additional Patches screen, click Next.

13. Review the information presented on the Ready To Complete screen. Expand Patches Matching Criteria Currently In The Repository and Patches Matching Criteria To Exclude and verify that the information listed is correct.

(continued)

EXERCISE 9.30 *(continued)*

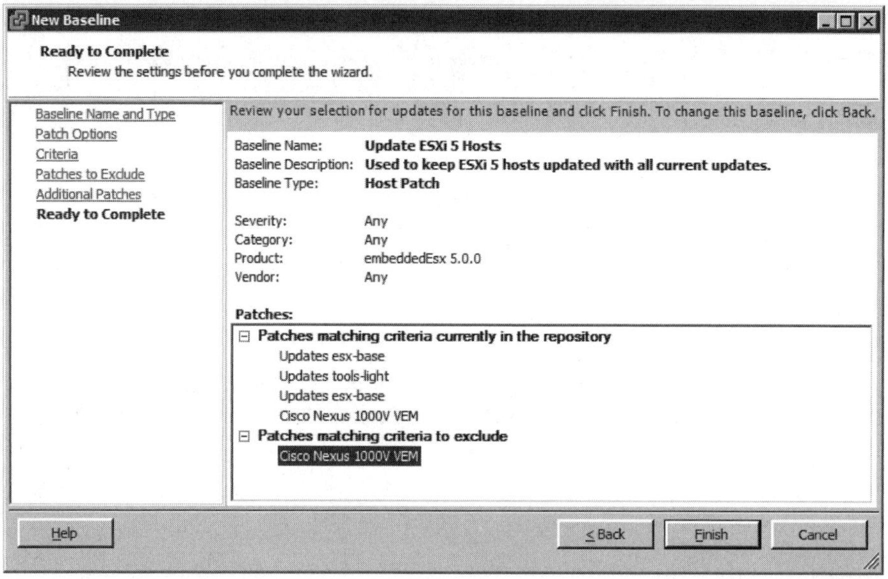

14. Click Finish and verify that the baseline is listed with the updated value in the Content column.

You have now created and edited a dynamic baseline. In the event that a baseline ever needs to be deleted, simply select the baseline to highlight it and then click the blue Delete link at the top of the screen. You will be prompted to confirm the deletion, as shown in Figure 9.5.

FIGURE 9.5 Deleting a baseline

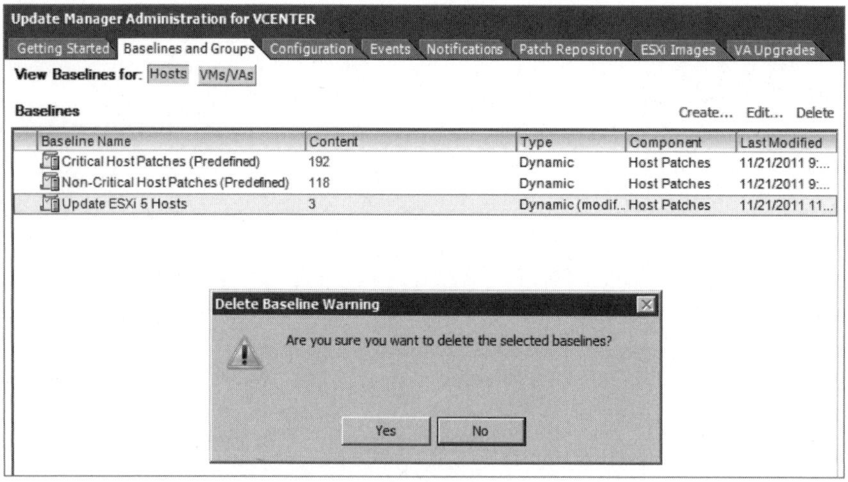

In the next section, I will cover attaching a vSphere Update Manager baseline to an ESXi host.

Attaching an Update Manager Baseline to an ESXi Host or Cluster

Attaching a baseline to an object allows you to view compliance information and remediate the object. Attaching baselines is performed from the Update Manager Client Compliance view. It is considered a best practice to attach baselines to a container object, such as a cluster, because this will help ensure consistency of all ESXi hosts in the cluster. In Exercise 9.31, this best practice will not be used. Instead, the steps to attach a baseline to a single ESXi host will be covered.

EXERCISE 9.31

Attaching a Baseline to an ESXi Host

1. Connect to a vCenter Server using a vSphere Client with the vSphere Update Manager plug-in installed.

2. Click the Home icon in the navigation bar of the vSphere Client.

3. Click the Hosts And Clusters icon.

4. Select an ESXi host in the left pane and then select the Update Manager tab in the right pane.

5. Click the blue Attach link in the upper right. The Attach Baseline Or Group windows will appear.

6. Select the baseline created in Exercise 9.28. The final configuration should appear similar to what's shown here.

(continued)

EXERCISE 9.31 *(continued)*

Attach Baseline or Group

Select the Baseline or Baseline Group that you want to attach to esxi1.test.local.

Individual Baselines by Type   Create Baseline...

Name	Type
☐ **Patch Baselines**	
☐ Critical Host Patches (Predefined)	Host Patch
☐ Non-Critical Host Patches (Predefined)	Host Patch
☑ Update ESXi 5 Hosts	Host Patch
Extension Baselines	
Upgrade Baselines	

Baseline Groups   Create Baseline Group...

Name	Type

| Help | | Attach | Cancel |

7. Click the Attach button.

8. Verify that the Update Manager tab has been updated.

Now that the baseline has been attached to an ESXi host, the next operation is to scan and remediate the ESXi host. The steps required to do this will be covered next.

Scanning and Remediating ESXi Hosts and Virtual Machine Hardware/Tools Using Update Manager

Scanning is how vSphere Update Manager discovers the compliance of hosts, virtual machines, or virtual appliances in the inventory. In the previous exercise, I covered how to attach a baseline to an ESXi host. The next step in patching this ESXi host is to scan it to check for compliance to the baseline you created. Scanning can be performed manually, or it can be scheduled using the Scheduled Tasks feature in vCenter Server.

ESXi host updates are all-inclusive, which means that the most recent update will contain all previous patches.

Exercise 9.32 covers the steps to perform a manual scan of an ESXi host.

EXERCISE 9.32

Manually Scanning an ESXi Host for Compliance

1. Connect to a vCenter Server using a vSphere Client with the vSphere Update Manager plug-in installed.

2. Click the Home icon in the navigation bar of the vSphere Client.

3. Click the Hosts And Clusters icon.

4. Select an ESXi host in the left pane and choose the Scan For Updates option from the context menu that appears.

5. A Confirm Scan dialog will appear, as shown here.

6. Ensure that the Patches And Extensions option is selected, and click the Scan button.

7. A Scan Entity task will begin. When this task completes, click the Update Manager tab in the right pane. The result should appear similar to what is shown here.

8. Review the information presented here in the Update Manager Compliance view.

The ESXi host should now be reported as noncompliant. The next and final step in the patching process of the ESXi host is to remediate it. Like scanning, remediating can also be performed manually or scheduled using the Scheduled Tasks feature in vCenter Server. Exercise 9.33 covers the steps to perform a manual remediation of an ESXi host.

EXERCISE 9.33

Manually Remediating a Noncompliant ESXi Host

1. Connect to a vCenter Server using a vSphere Client with the vSphere Update Manager plug-in installed.

2. Click the Home icon in the navigation bar of the vSphere Client.

3. Click the Hosts And Clusters icon.

4. Select an ESXi host in the left pane and right-click it. Choose the Remediate option from the context menu that appears.

5. The Remediate Wizard will begin.

6. On the Remediation Selection screen, ensure that the proper baseline is selected and that the proper ESXi host is listed at the bottom of the screen.

7. Click Next to continue.

8. Review the list of patches that will be applied and click Next.

9. Provide the task with a descriptive name and schedule. Ensure that the Remediate The Selected Hosts option is set for Immediately. Click Next to continue.

10. Review the Host Remediation Options settings. You may recall this same set of options from when the Update Manager configuration was originally performed.

11. Configure the Host options as appropriate for your specific test environment and click Next to continue.

12. Review the Cluster Remediation Options settings. You may recall this same set of options from when the Update Manager configuration was originally performed.

13. Configure the Cluster options as appropriate for your specific test environment and click Next to continue.

14. Review the information presented on the Ready To Complete screen and click Finish to begin the remediation of the ESXi host.

15. A Remediate Entity task will begin, and it can be followed by many others depending on how your test environment is set up.

    You should see Install, Check, Enter Maintenance Mode, Initiate Host Reboot, and Exit Maintenance Mode tasks as vSphere Update Manager remediates the host.

16. When the Remediate Entity task completes, verify that the ESXi host is reporting Compliant in the Compliance view.

 WARNING   As with any patching operation, always test the patches in a test environment before applying them in production.

I have now covered patching an ESXi host with vSphere Update Manager. I will next cover how to use vSphere Update Manger to update the VMware Tools and virtual machine hardware for a VM running on this ESXi host. To accomplish the VMware Tools and virtual hardware update as a single Update Manager operation, I will first create a baseline group. Exercise 9.34 covers the steps to create the baseline group and attach it to a virtual machine. This exercise will require a virtual machine with virtual hardware version prior to 8 and an older version of the VMware Tools installed.

EXERCISE 9.34

Creating a Group Baseline and Attaching It to a Virtual Machine

1. Connect to a vCenter Server using a vSphere Client with the vSphere Update Manager plug-in installed.

2. Click the Home icon in the navigation bar of the vSphere Client.

3. Click the Update Manager icon in the Solutions And Applications section.

4. Click the Baselines And Groups tab. Note that the default view is the Hosts view.

(continued)

5. Switch to the VMs/VAs view by using the view toggle buttons at the top of the tab.

6. In the VMs/VAs view, locate the Baseline Groups section on the right. Click the blue Create link. The New Baseline Wizard will launch.

7. In the Baseline Group Type section, select Virtual Machines And Virtual Appliances Baseline Group. Give the baseline group a descriptive name and then click Next.

8. In the VA Upgrades section, ensure that the None option is selected. In the VM Hardware Upgrades section, ensure that the VM Hardware Upgrade To Match Host (Predefined) option is selected. In the VMware Tools Upgrades section, ensure that the VMware Tools Upgrade To Match Host (Predefined) option is selected. The final configuration should look like this.

9. Click Next. Review the information on the Ready To Complete screen and then click Finish to create the baseline group.

10. Verify that the new baseline group is listed in the right pane. Expand it and ensure that both baselines are included.

You have now created the baseline group. The next step is to attach this baseline group to a virtual machine.

11. Click the Home icon in the navigation bar of the vSphere Client.

12. Select the VMs And Templates icon.

13. Locate the virtual machine that will be upgraded in the left pane and select it.

14. Select the Update Manager tab from the right pane.

15. Click the blue Attach link in the upper portion of the screen.

16. An Attach Baseline Or Group window will appear. Select the baseline group created earlier in this exercise. The baseline group will be located in the lower portion of the window. The final configuration will look similar to this.

17. Click the Attach button.

18. Verify that the Update Manager tab has been updated and that the virtual machine is reported as noncompliant.

The baseline group containing the predefined baselines for both the VMware Tools and the virtual machine hardware has now been attached to a virtual machine. The next step is to scan the virtual machine for compliance and to remediate it. Exercise 9.35 covers these steps.

EXERCISE 9.35

Manually Scanning and Remediating a Virtual Machine

1. Connect to a vCenter Server using a vSphere Client with the vSphere Update Manager plug-in installed.

2. Click the Home icon in the navigation bar of the vSphere Client.

3. Select the VMs And Templates icon.

4. Locate the virtual machine that will be upgraded in the left pane and select it.

5. Select the Update Manager tab in the right pane.

6. Select the virtual machine in the left pane and right-click it. Choose the Scan For Updates option from the context menu that appears.

7. A Confirm Scan dialog will appear. Deselect the Virtual Appliance Upgrades option and select the VM Hardware Upgrades and VMware Tools Upgrades options.

8. Click the Scan button to continue.

9. A Scan Entity task will begin. Verify the expected results are displayed on the Update Manager tab.

10. Right-click the virtual machine and choose the Remediate option from the context menu that appears.

11. The Remediate Wizard will launch.

12. Ensure that the baseline group is selected and that both of the included baselines are selected. Highlight the virtual machine in the bottom pane. The final configuration should appear similar to this.

13. Click Next.

14. Provide a detailed task name and description for this operation and choose the Immediately option for the scheduling. Click Next to continue.

15. Ensure that the Take Snapshot option is enabled. You may recall these settings from when vSphere Update Manager was initially configured. Provide a detailed name and description for the snapshot and choose whether to include the virtual machine's memory as part of the snapshot. Click Next to continue.

16. Review the information on the Ready To Complete screen and click Finish to begin the remediation.

17. A Remediate Entity task will begin, followed by a series of tasks that will be determined by which options were selected in the previous steps.

18. Watch the Recent Tasks list for entries; open the virtual machine's console, and watch the progress there as well.

19. When the Remediate Entity task completes, verify that the Compliance view reports the virtual machine as compliant.

20. Use the virtual machine's Summary tab to verify that the virtual machine hardware version and the VMware Tools have both been updated.

Remediation of the VMware Tools and the virtual machine hardware will initiate multiple virtual machine reboots.

I have now covered updating the VMware Tools and virtual machine hardware using vSphere Update Manager. In the next section, I will discuss staging ESXi updates.

Staging ESXi Host Updates

Earlier in this chapter, I showed how to use vSphere Update Manager to remediate an ESXi host. There is an additional option that can be used as part of the remediation process. Staging is the process of copying the patch files to the ESXi host, prior to the remediation task being run. This allows the files to be downloaded to the ESXi host before the remediation is performed and can save significant time in the remediation process. Exercise 9.36 covers the process to stage ESXi host updates.

EXERCISE 9.36

Staging ESXI Host Updates

1. Connect to a vCenter Server using a vSphere Client with the vSphere Update Manager plug-in installed.

2. Click the Home icon in the navigation bar of the vSphere Client.

3. Click the Hosts And Clusters icon.

4. Select an ESXi host in the left pane and right-click it. Choose the Stage Patches option from the context menu that appears.

5. The Stage Wizard will begin.

6. On the Baseline Selection screen, ensure that the proper baseline is selected and that the proper ESXi host is listed at the bottom of the screen.

7. Click Next to continue.

8. Deselect any undesired patches and click Next.

9. Review the information presented on the Ready To Complete screen and click Finish to stage the patches to the ESXi host.

10. A Stage Patches To Entity task will begin. When the Stage Patches To Entity task completes, the patches have been successfully staged to the ESXi host.

 ESX/ESXi 4 and newer hosts are supported for staging patches and extensions. PXE-booted ESXi 5 hosts are also supported, but Update Manager will not apply an update to a PXE-booted ESXi 5 host if an update requires a host reboot.

Staging ESXi patches concludes this chapter on maintaining service levels for ESXi and virtual machines.

Summary

The first part of this chapter focused on migrating virtual machines. This chapter began with discussing the procedure to migrate a powered-off or suspended virtual machine. Identifying ESXi host and virtual machine requirements for vMotion and Storage vMotion was covered, along with identifying Enhanced vMotion Compatibility CPU requirements. Snapshot requirements for vMotion and Storage vMotion were identified. Configuring the virtual machine swap file location was also covered. Migrating virtual machines using vMotion and Storage vMotion was covered, along with how to utilize Storage vMotion to change virtual disk types and the virtual machine working location and to rename virtual machines.

The second part of this chapter focused on backing up and restoring virtual machines. Snapshot requirements were identified. Creating, deleting, and consolidating virtual machine snapshots were all covered. VMware Data Recovery was installed, and a backup job was created with it. A test and live full/file-level restore with VMware Data Recovery was also covered. This section concluded with a discussion on determining an appropriate backup solution for a given vSphere implementation.

The final part of this chapter focused on patching and updating ESXi and virtual machines. This section began with identifying patching requirements for ESXi hosts, virtual machine hardware, and the VMware Tools. Creating, editing, and removing a host profile from an ESXi host were all covered, along with how to attach/apply a host profile to an ESXi host. I also performed compliance scanning and remediation of an ESXi host using host profiles. vSphere Update Manager was installed and configured, and the patch download options were also configured. I created, edited, and deleted an Update Manager baseline and attached an Update Manager baseline to an ESXi host or cluster. Scanning and remediating ESXi hosts, virtual machine hardware, and the VMware Tools using Update Manager were all also covered. This chapter concluded with staging ESXi host updates.

Exam Essentials

Know how to migrate virtual machines. Know how to migrate a powered-off or suspended virtual machine. Be able to identify ESXi host and virtual machine requirements for vMotion and Storage vMotion. Be able to identify Enhanced vMotion Compatibility CPU requirements and snapshot requirements for vMotion and /Storage vMotion. Know how to configure the virtual machine swap file location and understand the implications of doing so. Be able to migrate virtual machines using vMotion and Storage vMotion. Know how to utilize Storage vMotion to change virtual disk types, rename virtual machines, and change the working directory of a virtual machine.

Know how to back up and restore virtual machines. Be able to identify snapshot requirements and know how to create, delete, and consolidate virtual machine snapshots. Know how to install and configure VMware Data Recovery and create a backup job with it. Be able to perform a test and live full/file-level restore with VMware Data Recovery. Understand how to determine an appropriate backup solution for a given vSphere implementation.

Know how to patch and update ESXi and VMs. Be able to identify patching requirements for ESXi hosts, virtual machine hardware, and the VMware Tools. Know how to create, edit, and remove a host profile from an ESXi host. Know how to attach and apply a host profile to an ESXi host or cluster. Understand how to perform compliance scanning and remediation of an ESXi host using host profiles. Be able to install and configure vSphere Update Manager. Know how to configure patch download options and create, edit, and delete an Update Manager baseline. Know how to attach an Update Manager baseline to an ESXi host or cluster. Be able to scan and remediate ESXi hosts, virtual machine hardware, and the VMware Tools using Update Manager. Know how to stage ESXi host updates.

Review Questions

1. You have a virtual machine stored on a datastore on an ESXi host's local disks. The host that this VM is running on needs maintenance, and your vCenter Server is licensed for vSphere Standard. Which of the following methods can be used to migrate this virtual machine with no downtime?

    A. Cold migration

    B. vMotion

    C. Storage vMotion

    D. None of these

2. Which of the following are supported for use with snapshots?

    A. A powered-on virtual machine that is protected with VMware FT

    B. A powered-on virtual machine that has an independent disk

    C. A powered-on virtual machine with an RDM in physical compatibility mode

    D. A powered-on virtual machine with an RDM in virtual compatibility mode

3. Which of the following components are part of VMware Data Recovery? (Choose all that apply.)

    A. Client plug-in

    B. Backup appliance

    C. File Level Restore client

    D. vSphere Management Assistant

4. A virtual infrastructure administrator plans to manually update the virtual machine hardware and the VMware Tools in a maintenance window for a virtual machine with a Windows Server 2008 R2. How many times will the guest OS need to be restarted in this process?

    A. Three: one for the virtual machine hardware update and two for the VMware Tools update

    B. Three: two for the virtual machine hardware update and one for the VMware Tools

    C. Two: one for the virtual hardware and one for the VMware Tools

    D. Two: two for the virtual hardware

5. Which of the following are available vMotion priority options? (Choose two.)

    A. Reserve CPU For Optimal vMotion Performance

    B. Limit CPU For Optimal vMotion Performance

    C. Perform With Available CPU Resources

    D. Perform With Optimal vMotion Performance

6. A cluster has the virtual machine swap file option configured to store the swap file in the datastore specified by the host. The ESXi hosts in the cluster are configured to place the swap file on a datastore named NFS-SWAP. A newly created virtual machine located in this cluster has its virtual machine swap file option configured to always store with the virtual machine. The newly created virtual machine is located on NFS-VOL1. Where will this virtual machine's swap file be located when the virtual machine is powered on?

   A. The NFS-SWAP datastore

   B. The NFS-VOL1 datastore

   C. Both NFS-SWAP and NFS-VOL1

   D. None of these

7. Which of the following are download sources that can be used with vSphere Update Manager? (Choose all that apply.)

   A. Direct Connection To Internet

   B. Use A Shared Repository

   C. Proxy Settings

   D. Import Patches

8. You want to update the VMware Tools and virtual machine hardware in one scheduled task. Which of the following will allow this?

   A. Create one scheduled task in vCenter and provide it the two update steps.

   B. Create a baseline to update the virtual machine hardware version, and the VMware Tools will be automatically updated.

   C. Create a baseline group that contains both of the predefined update baselines. Schedule the remediation using the baseline group.

   D. This is not possible.

9. You edited an Update Manager dynamic baseline specific for ESXi 5 hosts to exclude a patch, and after these edits, the baseline is reporting a much higher value in the Content column than was previously reported. What is the most likely reason for this?

   A. In the Fixed Baseline Criteria settings, the Product value was set to Any.

   B. In the Fixed Baseline Criteria settings, the Product value was set to embeddedEsx 5.0.0.

   C. In the Dynamic Baseline Criteria settings, the Product value was set to Any.

   D. In the Dynamic Baseline Criteria settings, the Product value was set to embeddedEsx 5.0.0.

10. You have a vSphere 5 environment with 250 virtual machines. Which of the following backup solutions can you use?

   A. VMware Consolidated Backup

   B. VMware Data Recovery

C. VMware snapshots

D. None of these

11. You need to move a virtual machine with an active snapshot to a different datastore. You intend to use Storage vMotion to accomplish this task, and all of hosts are ESXi 5. Which of the following statements is accurate in regards to this plan?

A. This plan will work.

B. This plan will work, but proceed with caution.

C. This plan will work but is unsupported.

D. This plan will not work.

12. Which of the following are required to apply a host profile to an ESXi host? (Choose all that apply.)

A. Enterprise Licensing

B. Enterprise Plus Licensing

C. ESX/ESXi host in maintenance mode

D. vSphere Update Manager

13. A virtual infrastructure administrator has taken a single snapshot of a virtual machine. The snapshot requestor has asked that the virtual machine be reverted, and the snapshot requestor no longer needs the virtual machine to be in snapshot mode. Which set of actions should the virtual infrastructure administrator now take?

A. Revert to the current snapshot. Delete the snapshot using the Delete All button in Snapshot Manager.

B. Revert to the current snapshot.

C. Delete the snapshot using the Delete button in Snapshot Manager.

D. None of these.

14. Which of the following guest operating systems are supported for use with the VMware Data Recovery FLR client? (Choose all that apply.)

A. Ubuntu 8.04

B. Windows XP

C. Solaris 10

D. Windows 2008 R2

15. What is the proper sequence in which vSphere Update Manager processes updates?

A. Scan object, create baseline, attach baseline, remediate object

B. Create baseline, scan object, attach baseline, remediate object

C. Create baseline, attach baseline, scan object, remediate object

D. Remediate object, scan object, create baseline, attach baseline

16. You have two virtual machines that need to be moved to a new datacenter. Which of the following migrations will allow you to do this? (Choose all that apply.)

   A. Migrating a powered-off VM

   B. Migrating a suspended VM

   C. Migrating with vMotion

   D. Migrating with Storage vMotion

17. Which of the following statements are true about EVC? (Choose two.)

   A. Mixing Intel and AMD processors in the same cluster is allowed.

   B. Mixing Intel and AMD processors in the same datacenter is allowed.

   C. Mixing Intel and AMD processors in the same cluster is not allowed.

   D. Mixing Intel and AMD processors in the same datacenter is not allowed.

18. You plan to install vSphere Update Manager on a dedicated server and use a remote SQL Server database. Which of the following are required on the server that vSphere Update Manager will be installed on? (Choose two.)

   A. 32-bit operating system

   B. 64-bit operating system

   C. 32-bit DSN

   D. 64-bit DSN

19. You have a vSphere environment that utilizes only NFS datastores, and your storage vendor does not support the VAAI NAS extensions that enable reserve space. When performing a Storage vMotion, which of the following options are available? (Choose all that apply.)

   A. Change Datastore Location

   B. Change Virtual Disk Format

   C. Change Storage Profile

   D. Disable Storage DRS

20. Which of the following can be used to create backup jobs with VMware Data Recovery?

   A. The vSphere Web Client

   B. The vSphere Client

   C. The vSphere Client with the VMware Data Recovery client plug-in

   D. vSphere Management Assistant

Chapter

10

Perform Basic Troubleshooting

VCP5 EXAM OBJECTIVES COVERED IN THIS CHAPTER:

✓ **Perform Basic Troubleshooting for ESXi Hosts**

- Troubleshoot common installation issues
- Monitor ESXi system health
- Identify general ESXi host troubleshooting guidelines
- Export diagnostic information

✓ **Perform Basic vSphere Network Troubleshooting**

- Verify network configuration
- Verify a given virtual machine is configured with the correct network resources
- Troubleshoot virtual switch and port group configuration issues
- Troubleshoot physical network adapter configuration issues
- Identify the root cause of a network issue based on troubleshooting information

✓ **Perform Basic vSphere Storage Troubleshooting**

- Verify storage configuration
- Troubleshoot storage contention issues
- Troubleshoot storage over-commitment issues
- Troubleshoot iSCSI software initiator configuration issues
- Troubleshoot Storage Reports and Storage Maps
- Identify the root cause of a storage issue based on troubleshooting information

✓ **Perform Basic Troubleshooting for HA/DRS Clusters and vMotion/Storage vMotion**

- Identify HA/DRS and vMotion requirements

- Verify vMotion/Storage vMotion configuration

- Verify HA network configuration

- Verify HA/DRS cluster configuration

- Troubleshoot HA capacity issues

- Troubleshoot HA redundancy issues

- Troubleshoot DRS load imbalance issues

- Interpret the DRS Resource Distribution Graph and Target/Current Host Load Deviation

- Troubleshoot vMotion/Storage vMotion migration issues

- Interpret vMotion Resource Maps

- Identify the root cause of a DRS/HA cluster or migration issue based on troubleshooting information

This chapter will cover the objectives of section 6 of the VCP5 exam blueprint. This chapter will focus on performing basic troubleshooting in a vSphere environment.

This chapter will first cover performing basic troubleshooting for ESXi hosts and troubleshooting common ESXi installation issues. Monitoring ESXi system health will be covered, along with identifying general ESXi host troubleshooting guidelines. The first section will conclude with detailing the procedure to export diagnostic information.

The second section of this chapter will cover performing basic vSphere network troubleshooting. Verifying network configuration and that a given virtual machine is configured with the correct network resources will be covered. Troubleshooting virtual switch and port group configuration issues and physical network adapter configuration issues will also be covered. This section will conclude with identifying the root cause of a network issue based on troubleshooting information.

The third section of this chapter will cover performing basic vSphere storage troubleshooting. Verifying storage configuration will be covered. Troubleshooting storage contention issues and storage overcommitment issues will also be covered. Troubleshooting iSCSI software initiator configuration issues will be covered, along with troubleshooting storage reports and storage maps. This section will conclude with identifying the root cause of a storage issue based on troubleshooting information.

The final section of this chapter will cover performing basic troubleshooting for clusters, vMotion, and Storage vMotion.

Perform Basic Troubleshooting for ESXi Hosts

The ability to troubleshoot a vSphere environment is an important skill set that any virtual infrastructure administrator should have. Knowing how to troubleshoot a vSphere environment will also be important for the VCP exam. This chapter will begin with troubleshooting common ESXi and vCenter Server installation issues.

Troubleshooting Common Installation Issues

Most of the common installation issues encountered with vCenter Server and ESXi will relate to not meeting the system requirements. The hardware-specific system requirements are often enforced at the software level of the installers and cannot be bypassed. Other software-specific system requirements can also prevent the installation of vCenter Server or its components.

There are also environmental factors that can impact installation, such as networking, storage, and more. The first step in ensuring a successful install is to meet all of the hardware, software, and environmental system requirements for both ESXi and vCenter Server.

Installation issues can also be encountered related to product interoperability. You should determine prior to installation if the version of vCenter Server you plan to use is compatible with the versions of ESX/ESXi you plan to use. In addition to vCenter Server and ESXi compatibility, there are compatibility requirements for the operating system that will house the vCenter Server and requirements for specific versions of the database that will be used.

You can find the VMware product interoperability matrixes at http://partnerweb.vmware.com/comp_guide2/sim/interop_matrix.php.

ESXi hosts and all of the components contained therein should be verified for compatibility in the VMware HCL. Hardware vendors will often have their own unique set of requirements to support certain versions of ESX/ESXi, so make sure you verify your hardware (and firmware levels) with your server vendor. Also check with your vendor's documentation for any recommended BIOS settings or known issues with the version of ESXi you plan to use. Finally, ensure that any storage systems in use are listed on the HCL and are running the required firmware levels.

You can find the VMware Hardware Compatibility List (HCL) at www.vmware.com/go/hcl.

Troubleshooting installation issues should begin with ensuring that system requirements are met, that product interoperability is verified, and that all components are listed on the HCL. It is also good practice to read the release notes for the version of vCenter Server or ESXi that is being used, since these documents often contain known issues and workarounds. Always verify downloads using the provided checksums, since corrupt media will often produce interesting or unusual results. Using these practices can save significant amounts of both time and effort spent troubleshooting a problem that very likely won't be solved.

Now that I have covered troubleshooting common installation issues, I will cover monitoring ESXi system health.

Monitoring ESXi System Health

The vSphere Client can be used to monitor system health when connected to either an ESXi host or a vCenter Server. One of the simplest ways to monitor system health is to have the vSphere Client open and connected to an ESXi host or a vCenter Server. As health conditions occur, the ESXi host icons will have alerts and warnings placed on them. This is often a quick and easy way for operations staff to monitor ESXi hosts. When more detail is needed, the vSphere Client can be used to obtain this information as well. Remember that the approach used to discover the hardware status information is different when the vSphere Client is connected directly to an ESXi host in comparison to when the vSphere Client is connected to a vCenter Server managing the host.

When connected directly to an ESXi host, select the ESXi host in the left pane and then select the Configuration tab in the right pane. Then select the blue Health Status link in the Hardware panel on the left. The health of the ESXi host's hardware will be shown in the right pane. Figure 10.1 shows an ESXi host in an alert state, because it has a missing power supply.

In the ESXi Health Status view, the Sensor, Status, and Reading columns are used to provide information about the sensors and their current status. The blue Refresh link located in the upper right of the right pane can be used to refresh this information.

 The blue Reset link can also be used to reset sensor data. This can be useful when cumulative data needs to be cleared and new data needs to start being collected.

When using the vSphere Client connected to a vCenter Server, the hardware health information is obtained in a different location. Select the ESXi host in the left pane and then select the Hardware Status tab. Figure 10.2 shows a vCenter Server managed ESXi host in a healthy state.

FIGURE 10.1 ESXi Health Status view

Sensor	Status	Reading
Reset Sensors Refresh		
Cisco Systems Inc R210-2121605W	Alert	
Processors	Normal	
Memory	Normal	
Power	Alert	
System Board 0 POWER_USAGE --- Normal	Normal	184 Watts
Power Supply 2 PSU2_PIN --- Normal	Normal	0 Watts
Power Supply 2 PSU2_IOUT --- Normal	Normal	0 Amps
Power Supply 1 PSU1_PIN --- Normal	Normal	184 Watts
Power Supply 1 PSU1_POUT --- Normal	Normal	168 Watts
Power Supply 1 PSU1_IOUT --- Normal	Normal	14 Amps
Processor 1 VR_CPU1_IOUT --- Normal	Normal	8.55 Amps
Power Supply 1: Running/Full Power-Enabled	Normal	650 Watts
Power Supply 2: Off Line-Disabled	Normal	650 Watts
[Device] Power Supply 15	Unknown	
Power Supply 0 PSU_REDUNDANCY- Redundancy lost	Warning	
Power Supply 2 PSU2_STATUS: Power Supply AC lost - Assert	Alert	
Power Supply 1 PSU1_STATUS: Power Supply AC lost - Deassert	Normal	
Temperature	Normal	
Fan	Alert	
Voltage	Normal	
Other	Alert	
Software Components	Normal	
Storage	Normal	
Platform Alert	Normal	
Chip Set	Normal	

In the vCenter Server Hardware Status view, the Sensor, Status, and Details columns are used to provide information about the sensors and their current status. Note the drop-down menu that can be used to change the View options. This allows the viewing of all sensor data, alerts, and warnings or system event log. Also note the system summary located at the top of the tab, which includes detailed information about the host system. The blue Update link located in the upper right of the right pane can be used to refresh the information in this view, and the last update time is included at the very top left of this tab. This information can also be exported using the blue Export link at the top of the tab.

FIGURE 10.2 ESXi Hardware Status view in vCenter Server

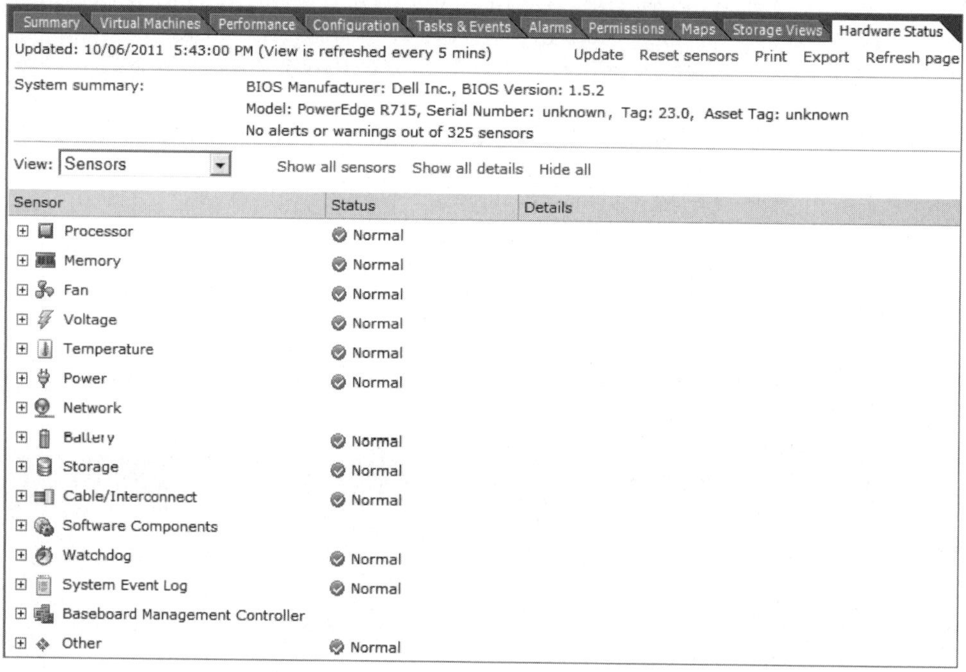

Summary	Virtual Machines	Performance	Configuration	Tasks & Events	Alarms	Permissions	Maps	Storage Views	Hardware Status

Updated: 10/06/2011 5:43:00 PM (View is refreshed every 5 mins)   Update   Reset sensors   Print   Export   Refresh page

System summary: BIOS Manufacturer: Dell Inc., BIOS Version: 1.5.2
                         Model: PowerEdge R715, Serial Number: unknown , Tag: 23.0, Asset Tag: unknown
                         No alerts or warnings out of 325 sensors

View: Sensors ▼   Show all sensors   Show all details   Hide all

Sensor	Status	Details
⊞ 🖳 Processor	🟢 Normal	
⊞ ▓ Memory	🟢 Normal	
⊞ 🌀 Fan	🟢 Normal	
⊞ ⚡ Voltage	🟢 Normal	
⊞ 🌡 Temperature	🟢 Normal	
⊞ 🔌 Power	🟢 Normal	
⊞ 🌐 Network		
⊞ 🔋 Battery	🟢 Normal	
⊞ 💾 Storage	🟢 Normal	
⊞ 🔗 Cable/Interconnect	🟢 Normal	
⊞ 🗂 Software Components		
⊞ 🕐 Watchdog	🟢 Normal	
⊞ 📋 System Event Log	🟢 Normal	
⊞ 🗄 Baseboard Management Controller		
⊞ ◆ Other	🟢 Normal	

The blue Reset Sensors link can also be used to reset the sensor data. This can be useful when cumulative data needs to be cleared and new data needs to start being collected.

There are also various vendor-provided and third-party solutions that can be used to monitor ESXi system health. If these tools already exist in your environment, it often makes sense to leverage them when monitoring the health of your ESXi systems.

Now that I have covered monitoring ESXi system health, I will identify general ESXi host troubleshooting guidelines.

Identifying General ESXi Host Troubleshooting Guidelines

The health status information provided in the vSphere Client can generally be used to start troubleshooting ESXi issues, and the vSphere Client is often where most issues will first be identified. If the issue cannot be resolved using this information, then the next location to look in is the actual ESXi log files. Some of these log files can be viewed in the vSphere

Client by using the System Logs view. The System Logs view can be accessed from the Administration options on the vSphere Client home page.

The ESXi log files can also be viewed in the DCUI under the View System Logs option, as shown in Figure 10.3.

FIGURE 10.3   DCUI view system logs

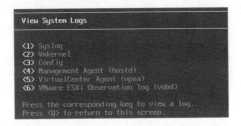

The different logs can be selected by choosing the appropriate number. All of the logs can also be accessed from /var/run/log when using the ESXi Shell.

 The VirtualCenter Agent (vpxa) log option will appear in the DCUI only if the host is being managed by a vCenter Server.

Ideally, most environments will also be configured to use a syslog server for remote logging, so this could be an additional option to use for troubleshooting ESXi hosts.

Knowing where to find the logs is great, but the order in which to troubleshoot ESXi hosts is equally important. The general troubleshooting flow for an ESXi host, as defined by VMware, is as follows:

1. Check the VMware Tools status in the virtual machine.
2. Check the ESXi host CPU usage.
3. Check the virtual machine CPU usage.
4. Check for ESXi host swapping.
5. Check storage usage.
6. Check ESXi for dropped receive packets.
7. Check ESXi for dropped transmit packets.

Now that I have covered general ESXi host troubleshooting guidelines, I will next cover exporting diagnostic information.

Exporting Diagnostic Information

System log files can be exported from both vCenter Server and ESXi hosts. If connected to a vCenter Server, then the diagnostic information for the ESXi hosts it manages can also be exported at the same time. If the vSphere Client is connected directly to an ESXi host, then only that host's diagnostic information can be exported. Exercise 10.1 covers the steps to export the diagnostic information from vCenter Server.

EXERCISE 10.1

Exporting System Logs from vCenter Server

1. Connect to a vCenter Server with the vSphere Client.

2. Select the Host and Clusters view.

3. Select the vCenter Server root inventory object in the left pane.

4. Select File ➢ Export ➢ Export System Logs.

5. The Export System Logs window will appear. Select the highest-level inventory object available, which should the vCenter Server root object. The results should look like this.

6. Click Next to continue.

7. Ensure that all of the system logs are selected by clicking the blue Select All link. Select the Gather Performance Data option and accept the default values for both Duration and Interval.

8. Click Next to continue.

9. Use the Browse button to select a location for the exported system logs to be downloaded to. Click Next.

10. Review the information presented on the Ready To Complete screen and click Finish to begin the export(s).

11. A Generate System Logs Bundles task will begin, and a Downloading System Logs Bundles window will appear to show the progress.

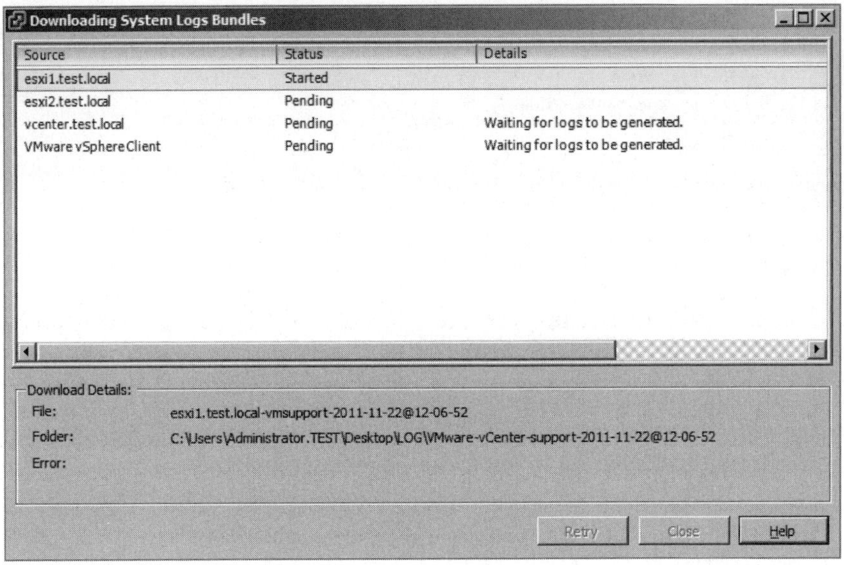

12. When all files have been successfully downloaded, click the Close button and verify that the log bundle is in the location you specified.

   Another useful option to generate this same log bundle is to use the vc-support.wsf script. One advantage this option provides is the ability to collect the log bundle when VMware VirtualCenter Server service is not running. The remainder of this exercise will cover the steps to use this option.

13. Obtain local console access to the Windows system that vCenter Server is installed on.

14. Launch the vc-support.wsf script by using Start ➢ All Programs ➢ VMware ➢ Generate vCenter Server Log Bundle.

15. A Generate vCenter Server Log Bundle command window will appear, as shown here.

(continued)

EXERCISE 10.1 *(continued)*

16. Take note of the lines in this command window that show the location the log bundle is being saved to.

17. When the command completes, verify the log bundle has been created. Compare its contents to the bundle created in the first part of this exercise.

If the vSphere Client is not available, then diagnostic information can also be obtained for ESXi hosts from the ESXi Shell by using the following command:

/usr/sbin/vm-support

Figure 10.4 shows the output of this command.

FIGURE 10.4 vm-support command output

```
~ # /usr/sbin/vm-support
17:40:12: Creating /var/tmp/esx-esxi1.test.local-2011-11-22--17.40.tgz
17:41:35: Done.
Please attach this file when submitting an incident report.
To file a support incident, go to http://www.vmware.com/support/sr/sr_login.jsp
To see the files collected, run: tar -tzf '/var/tmp/esx-esxi1.test.local-2011-11-22--17.40.tgz'
~ # _
```

Now that I have covered exporting diagnostic information from ESXi hosts and vCenter Server, I will move on to the next section in this chapter, which covers performing basic network troubleshooting.

Perform Basic vSphere Network Troubleshooting

Troubleshooting vSphere network connectivity is often one of the first things a virtual infrastructure administrator will perform, after the initial install of ESXi is complete. Networking and storage can be two of the more complex issues to troubleshoot in a virtual infrastructure, and this section will cover network troubleshooting.

Verifying Network Configuration

It is not unusual for a virtual infrastructure administrator to perform an ESXi install with one or more network cables plugged in to the host. There is often consistency between similar hosts in how the vmnics will be assigned, but sometimes this will not work as planned. One of the easiest ways to verify network connectivity is to use the DCUI. The Configure Management Network feature will allow you to view which vmnic is being used by the management network connection. Figure 10.5 shows the Configure Management Network feature.

FIGURE 10.5 Configure Management Network feature

```
Network Adapters

Select the adapters for this host's default management network
connection. Use two or more adapters for fault-tolerance and
load-balancing.


     Device Name  Hardware Label (MAC Address)   Status
 [X] vmnic0       N/A (00:0c:29:4b:8f:76)        Connected
 [ ] vmnic1       N/A (00:0c:29:4b:8f:80)        Connected (...)
 [ ] vmnic2       N/A (00:0c:29:4b:8f:8a)        Connected (...)
 [ ] vmnic3       N/A (00:0c:29:4b:8f:94)        Connected (...)




<D> View Details  <Space> Toggle Selected       <Enter> OK  <Esc> Cancel
```

The Configure Management Network feature shows the device name, the MAC address, and the status. Using the Configure Management Network feature is an effective way to verify that the correct NIC is actually reported as connected.

To verify additional networking configurations, the ESXi Shell can be used. The following command can be used to list the physical network adapters' properties and status:

```
esxcli network nic list
```

Figure 10.6 shows the output of this command from the ESXi Shell.

FIGURE 10.6 Listing NICs from the ESXi Shell

```
~ # esxcli network nic list
Name      PCI Device      Driver  Link  Speed  Duplex  MAC Address         MTU   Description
--------  --------------  ------  ----  -----  ------  ------------------  ----  ----------------------
vmnic10   0000:00b:00.0   bnx2    Down     0   Half    00:10:18:a3:83:b8   1500  Broadcom Corporation
vmnic11   0000:00b:00.1   bnx2    Down     0   Half    00:10:18:a3:83:ba   1500  Broadcom Corporation
vmnic12   0000:00c:00.0   bnx2    Down     0   Half    00:10:18:a3:83:bc   1500  Broadcom Corporation
vmnic13   0000:00c:00.1   bnx2    Up    1000   Full    00:10:18:a3:83:be   1500  Broadcom Corporation
vmnic14   0000:012:00.0   igb     Up     100   Full    e8:b7:48:7b:c1:b8   1500  Intel Corporation 82\$
vmnic15   0000:012:00.1   igb     Up     100   Full    e8:b7:48:7b:c1:b9   1500  Intel Corporation 82\$
~ #
```

If you are ever unsure which network cable is attached to a particular physical network adapter, you can detach the network cable and use this command to verify the Link status for the physical adapter.

In addition to listing the vmnics in the ESXi host, it is also useful to view the vSwitch or dvSwitch configuration for the ESXi host. The following commands can be used to list the vSwitch and dvSwitch information for an ESXi host:

```
esxcli network vswitch standard list
esxcli network vswitch dvs vmware list
```

Figure 10.7 shows the output of the vSwitch command from the ESXi Shell. Note that the format shown in this output has been modified to better fit the pages in this book.

FIGURE 10.7 Listing vSwitches from the ESXi Shell

```
vSwitch0                              vSwitch1                              vSwitch2
  Name: vSwitch0                        Name: vSwitch1                        Name: vSwitch2
  Class: etherswitch                    Class: etherswitch                    Class: etherswitch
  Num Ports: 128                        Num Ports: 128                        Num Ports: 128
  Used Ports: 4                         Used Ports: 3                         Used Ports: 14
  Configured Ports: 128                 Configured Ports: 128                 Configured Ports: 128
  MTU: 1500                             MTU: 1500                             MTU: 1500
  CDP Status: listen                    CDP Status: listen                    CDP Status: listen
  Beacon Enabled: false                 Beacon Enabled: false                 Beacon Enabled: false
  Beacon Interval: 1                    Beacon Interval: 1                    Beacon Interval: 1
  Beacon Threshold: 3                   Beacon Threshold: 3                   Beacon Threshold: 3
  Beacon Required By:                   Beacon Required By:                   Beacon Required By:
  Uplinks: vmnic14                      Uplinks: vmnic13                      Uplinks: vmnic15
  Portgroups: Management Network        Portgroups: iSCSI                     Portgroups: VM Network
```

The output of these three commands can typically be used to sort out any network configuration issues, and always remember that ping and vmkping are both available in the ESXi Shell. While the ESXi Shell offers much functionality, in many cases it is easier to use the vSphere Client.

If basic management network connectivity is available, the vSphere Client can be used to verify network configurations for the ESXi host. Network configuration was discussed in great detail in Chapter 4, but here is a brief review. Virtual machines will use virtual machine connection types, and all host-based connections will use VMkernel connection types. These host-based connections can include the management network, vMotion, FT logging, iSCSI, and NFS networking. These two connection type rules will always be the same regardless of whether a vSwitch, dvSwitch, or both is being used. Verifying these configurations can be easily performed using the information available in the vSphere Client, and the vSphere Client will also report any unavailable network links.

> Remember that the CDP (Cisco Discovery Protocol) and LLDP (Link Layer Discovery Protocol) information provided to the vSphere Client can be very useful in verifying network configurations.

Now that I have covered verifying network configurations, I will move on to verifying that a given VM is configured with the correct network resources.

Verifying a Given Virtual Machine Is Configured with the Correct Network Resources

When virtual machine connectivity issues arise, verifying the virtual machine network configuration might be necessary. This usually involves verifying the following:

- Verify the virtual machine has a network adapter, that it is connected, and that the virtual machine is using the correct network label in the virtual machine properties.
- Verify the virtual machine's network adapter type and check to see whether the guest OS is using the VMware Tools, if required.
- Verify that other virtual machines using the same virtual machine connection type are working properly.
- Verify the networking configuration inside the guest OS is correct, including testing the TCP/IP stack.
- Verify that the virtual switch has not lost connectivity to the physical network.
- Verify that the virtual switch has enough ports available.
- Verify that the port group is configured to use the required VLAN(s).

I have now covered verifying virtual machine network resources and will move on to troubleshooting virtual switch and port group configuration issues.

Troubleshooting Virtual Switch and Port Group Configuration Issues

Troubleshooting virtual switch and port group configuration issues will depend on the connection type. In the previous section, troubleshooting virtual machine connections was covered, so in this section VMkernel port group connection types will be covered. Some of these troubleshooting steps will be the same. The steps include the following:

- Verify that the virtual switch has not lost connectivity to the physical network.
- Verify that the virtual switch has enough ports available.
- Verify that VMkernel networking is configured correctly and that the IP address and subnet mask information are both correct.
- Verify that the port group is configured to use the correct VLAN(s), if applicable.
- For VMkernel port groups, verify that the correct use case is selected: vMotion, FT, management traffic, or no selection for network storage.
- If jumbo frames are used, verify that they are configured properly on the vSwitch and are enabled from end to end.

- Verify that the remote addresses can be reached with the vmkping command in the ESXi Shell.

- Verify that traffic shaping is configured properly, if applicable.

- Verify that NIC teaming is configured as required for the environment.

- Ensure that the ESXi firewall is configured correctly.

The vmkping command was mentioned in the preceding list, and Exercise 10.2 will cover the steps for using the vmkping command from the ESXi Shell. Before beginning this exercise, use the vSphere Client to locate the IP address of a storage system or another VMkernel interface on a different ESXi host. This IP address will be used in this exercise.

EXERCISE 10.2

Using the vmkping Command from ESXi Shell

1. Connect to the local console of an ESXi host.

2. Press the F2 key to log in to the DCUI. Log in using the root account.

3. Scroll down and select the Troubleshooting Options entry in the left pane. Press the Enter key.

4. In the left pane, Disable ESXi Shell is selected by default. If the right pane reports ESXi Shell Is Disabled, press the Enter key.

5. Once the right pane reports ESXi Shell Is Enabled, press the Alt+F1 combination to enter the ESXi Shell.

6. Log in to the ESXi Shell using the root account.

7. Type the following command and press Enter:

    vmkping

8. The output will appear similar to this.

```
~ # vmkping
vmkping [args] [host]
  args:
    -6                 use IPv6 - ICMPv6 Echo request
    -4                 use IPv4 (default)
    -I                 outgoing interface - for IPv6 scope
    -D                 vmkernel TCP stack debug mode
    -c <count>         set packet count
    -d                 set DF bit on IPv4 packets
    -i <interval>      set interval
    -s <size>          set send size
    -X                 XML output format for esxcli framework.
    -v                 verbose

  NOTE: In vmkernel TCP debug mode, vmkping traverses
        VSI and pings various configured addresses.
~ #
```

9. Review the different vmkping arguments before continuing.

10. Enter the following command and press Enter, replacing <IP Address> with the IP address obtained prior to the start of this exercise:

```
vmkping <IP Address>
```

11. The ping should return results, indicating a success.

12. Review these results and then type the following command and press Enter:

    ```
    exit
    ```

13. Press the Alt+F2 combination to enter the DCUI.

14. Press the F2 key again to log in to the DCUI.

15. Log in using the root account and disable ESXi Shell access.

Now that I have covered troubleshooting virtual switch and port group configuration issues, I will move on to troubleshooting physical network adapter configuration issues.

Troubleshooting Physical Network Adapter Configuration Issues

Physical network adapter configuration issues can be addressed from the vSphere Client or the ESXi Shell. As mentioned earlier, the vSphere Client is often easier to use. The "ESXi Shell Complications" real-world scenario can help explain why.

🌐 Real World Scenario

ESXi Shell Complications

A virtual infrastructure administrator wants to troubleshoot what she believes to be a physical network adapter configuration issue for an ESXi host that is a member of a cluster with HA and DRS enabled. This cluster is used for production systems and is monitored 24 hours a day.

The virtual infrastructure administrator uses many of the VMware best practices in her environment and leaves the ESXi Shell disabled by default for all of her ESXi hosts. Based on past experience, she knows to use the vSphere Client to troubleshoot this current physical network adapter issue.

Previously when troubleshooting a similar issue, she used an IP KVM to obtain console access to the ESXi host. She enabled the ESXi Shell and then logged in to the ESXi Shell. Within minutes, the operations team was calling her to report that a configuration issue was being reported on one of her ESXi hosts; they had noticed the alert in the vSphere Client. After taking several minutes to explain to the operator that everything was OK and to ignore the error, she resumed her work. She ran the appropriate esxcli commands and identified the problem. Her phone then rang again with an emergency "production down" situation for

---

a physical Windows server. She quickly exited esxcli and sped off to help with the production issue. The next day, a member of the security team contacted the virtual infrastructure administrator to inquire about why the ESXi Shell had been enabled on a production system for more than 24 hours. She quickly realized that she forgot to disable the ESXi Shell before speeding off to help with the emergency situation.

When troubleshooting physical network adapter configuration issues, using the vSphere Client provides the same information and doesn't require as many steps or risks. The virtual infrastructure administrator learned this from her experience.

Although the esxcli command can be used to troubleshoot physical network adapter configuration issues, Exercise 10.3 covers the steps required to troubleshoot physical network adapter configuration issues using the vSphere Client. A vSwitch and a dvSwitch will both be required for this exercise.

EXERCISE 10.3

Troubleshooting Physical Network Adapter Configuration Issues Using the vSphere Client

1. Connect to a vCenter Server with the vSphere Client.

2. Select the Hosts and Clusters view and then select an ESXi host in the left pane.

3. Select the Configuration tab in the right pane and click the blue Network Adapters link in the Hardware panel.

4. Note that the information presented in the right pane, as shown here, is very similar to the output of the esxcli network nic list command in the ESXi Shell.

Device	Speed	Configured	Switch	MAC Address	Observed IP ranges
Broadcom Corporation Broadcom NetXtreme II BCM5709 1000Base-T					
vmnic13	1000 Full	Negotiate	vSwitch1	00:10:18:a3:83:be	None
vmnic12	Down	Negotiate	None	00:10:18:a3:83:bc	None
vmnic11	Down	Negotiate	None	00:10:18:a3:83:ba	None
vmnic10	Down	Negotiate	None	00:10:18:a3:83:b8	None
Intel Corporation 82576 Gigabit Network Connection					
vmnic15	100 Full	Negotiate	vSwitch2	e8:b7:48:7b:c1:b9	None
vmnic14	100 Full	Negotiate	vSwitch0	e8:b7:48:7b:c1:b8	None

The adapters are listed by vendor, and device names, speed, configured speed, switch use, MAC address, and observed IP ranges are all available for troubleshooting purposes.

5. Click the blue Networking link in the Hardware panel.

6. Choose any vSwitch listed in the right pane and click the blue Properties link for it.

7. When the vSwitch Properties window opens, click the Network Adapters tab.

Much of the same information available in the Network information is also available here, but the location, driver, and iSCSI port binding information are additional pieces of information provided by this tab.

8. Close the vSwitch properties window.

9. Switch to the vSphere Distributed Switch view using the toggle buttons at the top of the tab.

10. Pick a dvSwitch and click the blue Manage Physical Adapters link.

11. When the Manage Physical Adapters window opens, hover the mouse over one of the listed vmnics. It will turn into a blue link. Click it.

The physical adapter details will be listed in the right pane.

(continued)

EXERCISE 10.3 *(continued)*

```
┌─ Manage Physical Adapters ──────────────────────────────────────────── ✕
│                                   ┌─ Physical Adapter Details ──────────────┐
│  ┌────────────────────────────┐   │ General                                 │
│  │ ⊟ dvSwitch-DVUplinks-463   │   │   Vendor/Model:      Intel Corporation  │
│  │   <Click to Add NIC>       │   │                      82545EM Gigabit    │
│  │   ⊟ 🖧 dvUplink1           │   │                      Ethernet Controller │
│  │     vmnic3      Remove     │   │                      (Copper)           │
│  │                            │   │   Location:          PCI 02:03.0        │
│  │                            │   │   Driver:            e1000              │
│  │                            │   │ Status                                  │
│  │                            │   │   Link Status:       Connected          │
│  │                            │   │   Configured Speed, Duplex: Auto negotiate ▼ │
│  │                            │   │   Actual Speed, Duplex: 1000 Mb, Full Duplex │
│  │                            │   │   Observed IP Networks: None            │
│  │                            │   │   DirectPath I/O:    Not supported  ⓘ   │
│  │                            │   │   Network I/O Control: Allowed          │
│  │                            │   │   iSCSI Port Binding: Disabled          │
│  │                            │   │ Cisco Discovery Protocol                │
│  │                            │   │   Device ID:         --                 │
│  │                            │   │   Port ID:           --                 │
│  └────────────────────────────┘   └─────────────────────────────────────────┘
│   Help                                              OK          Cancel
└──────────────────────────────────────────────────────────────────────────────┘
```

12. Click the Cancel button to close the Manage Physical Adapters window.

When certain configurations are in use, such as Route Based On IP Hash Load Balancing, it will often be necessary to involve the staff responsible for managing the upstream physical network devices. Troubleshooting the virtual switch alone might not be sufficient in these cases.

Now that I have covered troubleshooting physical network adapter configuration issues, I will move on to identifying the root cause of a network issue based on troubleshooting information.

Identifying the Root Cause of a Network Issue Based on Troubleshooting Information

The troubleshooting techniques used to identify the root cause of a network issue were covered thoroughly in this chapter. Determining the root cause of an issue can sometimes be simple. It can also be a long process that involves going through a vast number of log files, searching the VMware knowledge base, posting a discussion in the VMTN communities, or even opening a support request with VMware. For the VCP5 exam, use the troubleshooting content in this section as your guide for troubleshooting network issues.

Perform Basic vSphere Storage Troubleshooting

Troubleshooting vSphere storage can be far more involved than troubleshooting vSphere network issues. The variety of storage options and vendors presents many unique combinations, and storage systems even have their own category in the VMware HCL. This section will cover performing basic vSphere storage troubleshooting.

Verifying Storage Configuration

Verifying the correct configuration of storage systems is an important step for the vSphere environment. Misconfigured storage can create significant problems, and it is best to not discover these problems after virtual machines are running in the environment. Storage configuration verification is a multistep process, which involves a minimum of the following:

- Verify the host's storage adapters are listed on the HCL and used only as described in the HCL.
- Verify that the storage systems used are listed on the HCL and are at the required firmware versions.
- Verify that no configuration maximums have been exceeded.
- Verify that no ESXi patches are required for the configuration.
- Verify that SAN zoning and/or LUN masking are configured correctly.
- Verify that the storage network (Fibre Channel or Ethernet) is connected and configured properly.
- Verify that iSCSI or NFS systems are reachable via `vmkping` from all required ESXi hosts.
- Verify that iSCSI targets have been configured.
- Verify that iSCSI or NFS permissions are set up properly.
- Verify that authentication works properly to iSCSI systems.
- Verify that the chosen iSCSI adapter is configured properly.
- Verify that jumbo frames are set up properly.
- Verify the speed and duplex settings of network storage adapters.
- Verify that datastores are accessible and/or mounted by all required ESXi hosts.
- Verify that a supported path selection policy is being used.

- Verify VMFS versions, volume sizes, and block sizes.
- Verify that disks used for RDM are accessible.

Many of these verifications can take place in the vSphere Client, but some will have taken place in the design phase. If the storage or storage network is not under the direct responsibility of the virtual infrastructure administrator, then other staff members will often need to be involved in the verification of storage configurations in vSphere. Chapter 5 discussed how to create and verify storage configurations in detail, but the key thing to remember with verifying storage configuration is this: ensure that everything is configured in a supported configuration. For example, using a supported SAN with an unsupported path selection policy would be an undesirable storage configuration.

Always remember to read storage vendors' support statements for vSphere implementations to ensure that you use a fully supported storage configuration.

Now that verifying storage configuration has been covered, I will move on to troubleshooting storage contention issues.

Troubleshooting Storage Contention Issues

With all these virtual machines accessing the same shared storage, there will inevitably be periods of contention as the virtual machines fight for resources on the storage systems. These issues can be further compounded if the SAN or NAS being used by the virtual infrastructure is also shared with other physical systems in the environment.

🌐 **Real World Scenario**

Contention with Storage Not Dedicated to the vSphere Environment

A virtual infrastructure administrator wants to troubleshoot what he believes to be a storage contention issue for several of the virtual machines he is responsible for. He has collected performance data, and it appears that latency from the storage system is fairly high. Interestingly enough, he is not seeing a large number of I/O commands from the virtual machines.

The storage system is shared among other physical servers as well, in this smaller environment. The virtual infrastructure administrator decides to use the tools included with the storage system to monitor it. He quickly finds that a physical file server is the culprit. He tracks it down to a backup job that was started by an operator, since this server missed its normally scheduled backup window the previous day. The backup job is cancelled, and the performance of the virtual machines returns to normal.

> The virtual infrastructure administrator learned that when sharing storage systems with other physical servers, or even other virtual environments, sometimes it will become necessary to troubleshoot the issue from the storage side. vSphere includes many great utilities and metrics that can be used to troubleshoot problems, but these utilities cannot be used outside of their specific realm.

As the real-world scenario showed, storage issues sometimes need to be tracked on the storage side. This can be performed with tools provided by the storage vendor or with various third-party tools. vSphere includes two ways to monitor the storage performance of the storage systems. These two ways are as follows:

esxtop or resxtop   esxtop is used in the ESXi Shell to monitor storage performance, and resxtop (remote esxtop) is used in the same way from a remote environment like the vMA or vCLI. The advantage of using resxtop is that it works with the ESXi Shell and SSH both disabled.

vSphere Client   The performance charts in the vSphere Client can be used to monitor storage performance.

In esxtop or resxtop, there are different screens that can be used to obtain information about the storage adapters or virtual machines. The metrics on these screens include the following:

ADAPTR	HBA name, which will be shown as vmhba#.
CMDS/s	Total number of I/O operations per second.
READS/s	Number of read I/O commands issued per second.
WRITES/s	Number of write I/O commands issued per second.
MBREAD/s	Megabytes read per second.
MBWRTN/s	Megabytes written per second.
DAVG/cmd	Average amount of time in milliseconds a device takes to service a single I/O request. The device includes the vmhba, the storage device, and any devices between.
KAVG/cmd	Average amount of time in milliseconds the VMkernel spends servicing I/O requests.
GAVG/cmd	Total latency as seen from the virtual machine. This metric is the sum of DAVG and KAVG.
LAT/rd	Average latency in milliseconds for a read I/O operation. This is a virtual machine–specific metric.
LAT/wr	Average latency in milliseconds for a write I/O operation. This is a virtual machine–specific metric.

Exercise 10.4 covers the steps to view storage contention with esxtop. Note that if you wanted to use resxtop instead, the process is nearly identical.

EXERCISE 10.4

Viewing Storage Contention with esxtop

1. Connect to the local console of an ESXi host.

2. Press the F2 key to log in to the DCUI. Log in using the root account.

3. Scroll down and select the Troubleshooting Options entry in the left pane. Press the Enter key.

4. In the left pane, Disable ESXi Shell is selected by default. If the right pane reports ESXi Shell Is Disabled, press the Enter key.

5. Once the right pane reports ESXi Shell Is Enabled, press the Alt+F1 combination to enter the ESXi Shell.

6. Log in to the ESXi Shell using the root account.

7. Type the following command and press Enter on the keyboard:

   esxtop

8. When esxtop starts, press the d key. This will switch to the disk adapter screen, as shown here.

ADAPTR	PATH	NPTH	CMDS/s	READS/s	WRITES/s	MBREAD/s	MBWRTN/s	DAVG/cmd	KAVG/cmd	GAVG/cmd	QAVG/cmd
vmhba0	-	0	0.00	0.00	0.00	0.00	0.00	0.00	0.00	0.00	0.00
vmhba1	-	0	0.00	0.00	0.00	0.00	0.00	0.00	0.00	0.00	0.00
vmhba32	-	3	0.00	0.00	0.00	0.00	0.00	0.00	0.00	0.00	0.00
vmhba33	-	1	0.00	0.00	0.00	0.00	0.00	0.00	0.00	0.00	0.00
vmhba34	-	0	0.00	0.00	0.00	0.00	0.00	0.00	0.00	0.00	0.00
vmhba35	-	0	0.00	0.00	0.00	0.00	0.00	0.00	0.00	0.00	0.00
vmhba36	-	0	0.00	0.00	0.00	0.00	0.00	0.00	0.00	0.00	0.00
vmhba37	-	5	10.84	1.61	9.24	0.05	0.09	0.67	0.01	0.68	0.00
vmhba38	-	0	0.00	0.00	0.00	0.00	0.00	0.00	0.00	0.00	0.00
vmhba39	-	1	0.00	0.00	0.00	0.00	0.00	0.00	0.00	0.00	0.00
vmhba4	-	3	0.00	0.00	0.00	0.00	0.00	0.00	0.00	0.00	0.00

4:30:46pm up 29 days 1:26, 322 worlds, 5 VMs, 8 vCPUs; CPU load average: 0.01, 0.02, 0.02

   Review the information presented on the disk adapter screen. Note the values listed for CMDS/s, DAVG/cmd, and KAVG/cmd. Note that to find out which adapter is associated with the vmhba# listed, you can use the vSphere Client. Select the ESXi host's Configuration tab and use the Storage Adapters link in the Hardware panel.

9. Press the v key to view the virtual machine screen.

```
4:37:08pm up 29 days 1:31, 319 worlds, 5 VMs, 8 vCPUs; CPU load average: 0.01, 0.02, 0.03

     GID VMNAME        VDEVNAME NVDISK  CMDS/s  READS/s WRITES/s MBREAD/s MBWRTN/s LAT/rd LAT/wr
    1728 ESXi1              -        2    0.00     0.00     0.00     0.00     0.00   0.00   0.00
  104258 CentOS-NFS         -        1    2.41     0.00     2.41     0.00     0.01   0.00   0.63
  391016 WinDC              -        2    0.40     0.00     0.40     0.00     0.00   0.00   0.66
  922298 vCenter            -        2    2.01     0.00     2.01     0.00     0.12   0.00   2.45
 1116818 ESXi2              -        2    0.00     0.00     0.00     0.00     0.00   0.00   0.00
```

Review the information presented on the virtual machine screen. Again, note the CMDS/s, but this time note the LAT/rd and LAT/wr metrics as well. The virtual machine metrics are useful when a storage adapter is reporting latency and you want to find out whether a specific virtual machine is impacted or possibly even responsible.

10. Type the q key to exit esxtop.

11. Exit the ESXi Shell and then disable it in the DCUI.

The previous exercise focused on viewing storage contention, but in most environments storage contention will be sporadic and unpredictable. If you have a dedicated test environment, you can use tools like Iometer to create a storage contention situation. Another option would be to start multiple virtual machines that are stored on common storage simultaneously. If you have the means to re-create contention in a test environment, then you can repeat the previous exercise and create the contention condition. Be sure to start monitoring with esxtop or resxtop before the contention in order to establish a proper baseline.

 You can download Iometer from www.iometer.org/.

Viewing the metrics without context does not provide any value, so the following values are considered the threshold values for the metrics:

DAVG/cmd	A value greater than 20 usually indicates a problem.
KAVG/cmd	A value greater than 1 or 2 is considered high.

These are considered threshold values, but all environments and their workloads are different. What constitutes high latency in one environment may not in another. It is important to establish baselines of storage latencies in order to know when something truly unusual is happening.

Where `esxtop` and `resxtop` provide real-time data, historical storage contention data can be viewed with the vSphere Client. Exercise 10.5 covers the steps to view storage contention data with the vSphere Client.

EXERCISE 10.5

Viewing Storage Contention Data

1. Connect to a vCenter Server with the vSphere Client.

2. Open the Hosts and Clusters view and select an ESXi host in the left pane.

3. Click the Performance tab in the right pane.

4. The Overview view will load by default. In the upper portion of this view, there are two drop-down menus that can be used to customize the view. Make sure that the Home view is selected and that Time Range is specified as 1 Day.

5. Scroll down and locate the Disk (ms) chart. It will appear similar to this.

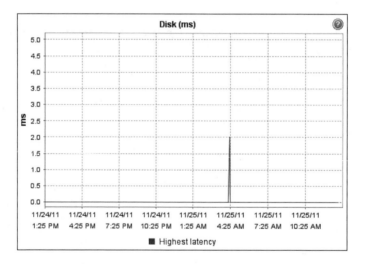

6. Note the peak value reported.

7. Repeat steps 4–7, choosing the 1 Week and 1 Month options. Note the peak values reported in each sampling period.

 The Advanced View in performance charts can be used to obtain even more granular information about these latencies.

Now that I have covered storage contention issues, I will move on to troubleshooting storage overcommitment issues.

Troubleshooting Storage Overcommitment Issues

With the capability of vSphere to thinly provision virtual disks, one of the very real possibilities is an out-of-space condition when using overcommitment with datastores. To help avoid this problem, the vCenter Server alarm Datastore Usage On Disk can be configured to alert operational staff or the virtual infrastructure administrator of this condition. Without this preemptive action, the first notice that the virtual infrastructure administrator will receive is likely crashing thinly provisioned virtual machines.

If your storage system has firmware that supports *T10-based Storage APIs* – Array Integration (Thin Provisioning), then you can leverage advanced warnings and errors when thresholds are realized for thinly provisioned datastores. This was a hidden feature of vSphere 4 and is officially considered a new feature in vSphere 5. A mechanism has been added to allow virtual machines to be paused when the datastore is exhausted, which will prevent the virtual machines from crashing or worse. When the virtual machine is paused, it can be migrated to another datastore, or space can be added or reclaimed on the current datastore. With the T10-based Storage APIs – Array Integration (Thin Provisioning) support, the first notice that the virtual infrastructure administrator will receive is likely that of warning events in vCenter Server.

With either scenario, freeing up space is likely the solution to the out-of-space condition. Once free space is sufficient on the datastore, then normal operations can resume.

Now that I have covered storage overcommitment issues, I will discuss troubleshooting iSCSI software initiator configuration issues.

Troubleshooting iSCSI Software Initiator Configuration Issues

Troubleshooting the iSCSI software initiator involves verifying the configuration of the iSCSI software adapter. The first step is to make sure that the iSCSI software adapter is listed in the ESXi host's storage adapters. The iSCSI initiator should also be enabled. If the iSCSI initiator is available and enabled, then further investigation will be required.

The Network Configuration tab can be used to verify that a VMkernel is bound to the iSCSI initiator. Figure 10.8 shows an example configuration.

If the port binding is verified, then the virtual switch configuration should also be verified. These steps were discussed earlier in this chapter. Also ensure that an iSCSI target is listed on either the Dynamic Discovery or Static Discovery tab in the iSCSI initiator properties. Verify that these targets can be reached by using the vmkping command from the ESXi Shell. Ensure that CHAP is configured correctly, and verify that the CHAP settings are correct if they are inherited. Also ensure that any advanced settings used are well understood and only used if required.

FIGURE 10.8 VMkernel port binding details

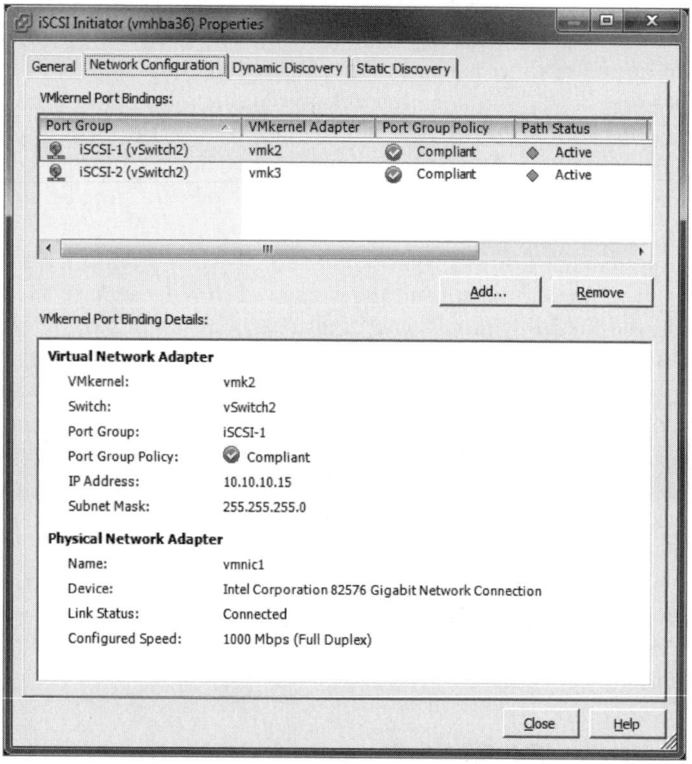

Now that I have covered troubleshooting iSCSI software initiator configuration issues, I will move on troubleshooting storage reports and storage maps.

Troubleshooting Storage Reports and Storage Maps

Storage reports are used to show relationships between an object and its associations with storage. Figure 10.9 shows a Storage Report view for a virtual machine with the available columns option expanded.

Storage maps show the relationship between a selected object and its associated virtual and physical storage entities. Figure 10.10 shows a storage map for a single virtual machine.

FIGURE 10.9   Storage report for VM

Summary	Virtual Machines	Performance	Configuration	Tasks & Events	Alarms	Permissions	Maps	Storage Views

View: Reports   Maps   Las

Show all Virtual Machines ▾   VM or Multipathin

VM	Multipathing Status	Space Used	Snapshot Space	Disks
VM1	✓ VM	794.39 KB	44.00 B	1
	Cluster			
	Resource Pool			
	✓ Multipathing Status			
	✓ Space Used			
	✓ Snapshot Space			
	Virtual Disk Space			
	Swap Space			
	Other VM Space			
	Shared Space			
	Provisioned Space			
	Uncommitted Space			
	✓ Disks			
	Datastores			

FIGURE 10.10   Storage map for VM

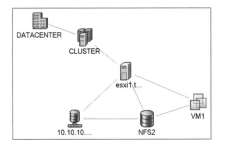

The VMware vCenter Storage Monitoring Service plug-in is used to populate the Storage Views tab. This plug-in is installed and enabled by default, but if this tab is missing or there are problems with the data, ensure that the plug-in is listed in the Plug-in Manager and shows a status of Enabled.

If storage views are missing or unavailable, the blue Update button can be used to refresh the view. Objects on the storage maps can be hidden by right-clicking the object on the map and choosing the Hide Node(s) option from the context menu that appears. If any objects appear to be missing, right-click anywhere on the map and verify that the Show Hidden Nodes option is not available.

Now that troubleshooting storage reports and storage maps has been covered, identifying the root cause of a storage issue based on troubleshooting information will be covered.

Identifying the Root Cause of a Storage Issue Based on Troubleshooting Information

The troubleshooting techniques used to identify the root cause of an issue with storage were covered thoroughly in this chapter. Like with network issues, determining the root cause of a storage issue can sometimes be simple. It can also be a long process that involves going through vast amounts of log files, searching the VMware knowledge base, posting a discussion in the VMTN communities, or even opening a support request with VMware or the storage vendor. For the VCP5 exam, use the troubleshooting content presented in this section as your guide for troubleshooting storage issues.

Perform Basic Troubleshooting for HA/DRS Clusters and vMotion/Storage vMotion

Performing basic troubleshooting for clusters with HA and DRS enabled is a key skill for any virtual infrastructure administrator. DRS and HA allow for a highly available infrastructure, along with vMotion and Storage vMotion. Keeping these functionalities working at all times is very important. The final section of this chapter will cover basic troubleshooting for clusters, vMotion, and Storage vMotion.

Identifying HA/DRS and vMotion Requirements

To ensure a properly working and supported environment, certain requirements must be met to use advanced vSphere features such as vSphere HA, DRS, and vMotion. vSphere HA has the following requirements:

- All ESX/ESXi hosts must be licensed to use vSphere HA.
- ESX 3.5 hosts need patch ESX350-201012401-SG.
- ESXi 3.5 hosts need patch ESXe350-201012401-I-BG.
- There must be at least two hosts in the cluster.
- Static IP addresses are recommended for all hosts in the cluster.
- A minimum of one common management network between the hosts in the cluster is required.
- All hosts must have access to the same VM networks and shared storage.
- All virtual machines in the cluster must be located on shared storage.
- The VMware Tools are required in virtual machines, if VM Monitoring will be used.

- Host certificate checking should be enabled.

  A DRS cluster has the following requirements:
- All hosts in the DRS cluster must be licensed to use DRS.
- All hosts must have access to the same shared storage.
- All virtual machines in the cluster must be located on shared storage.
- Processor compatibilities should be maximized to most effectively use EVC.

vMotion and Storage vMotion requirements were discussed in detail in Chapter 9, so as a quick review, the vMotion requirements are as follows:

- ESXi hosts must be licensed to use vMotion.
- ESXi hosts must have access to the same shared storage.
- ESXi hosts must have VMkernel networking established for the vMotion traffic.
- Virtual machines that use raw disks for clustering cannot be migrated.
- Virtual machines that use a virtual device backed by a device that is not accessible on the destination host cannot be migrated.
- Virtual machines that use a virtual device backed by a device on the client computer cannot be migrated.
- Virtual machines that use USB pass-through devices can be migrated, only if the devices are enabled for vMotion.

The Storage vMotion requirements include the following:

- ESXi hosts must be licensed to use Storage vMotion.
- Virtual machine disks must be in persistent mode or be RDMs for Storage vMotion.
- If ESX/ESXi 3.5 hosts are used, then they must also be licensed and configured for vMotion.

Now that the HA, DRS, vMotion, and Storage vMotion requirements have been covered, verifying the vMotion and Storage vMotion configurations will be covered.

Verifying vMotion/Storage vMotion Configuration

Verifying the vMotion and Storage vMotion configuration involves the following:

- Verify vSwitch/dvSwitch configuration on all ESX/ESXi source and target hosts.
- If vSwitches are used, ensure that consistent network labels are used across all hosts in the cluster.
- If dvSwitches are used, ensure that all hosts in the cluster are also all members of all dvSwitches used by virtual machines.
- Verify that a Gigabit Ethernet (GigE) network connection exists between all hosts that will use vMotion/Storage vMotion.

- A single Gigabit Ethernet interface should be dedicated to vMotion use.
- Verify that the vMotion traffic is on an isolated network.
- Verify that virtual machines have access to the same subnets on all ESXi hosts in the DRS cluster.
- Verify that jumbo frames are configured from end to end properly, if applicable.

 Virtual machines attached to an internal vSwitch cannot be migrated with vMotion, even if the destination host has an internal vSwitch with the same network label.

The final step in verifying the vMotion and Storage vMotion configuration is to test each by performing both a vMotion and Storage vMotion operation. Now that I have covered verifying the vMotion and Storage vMotion configurations, I will cover how to verify the vSphere HA network configuration.

Verifying HA Network Configuration

Ensuring that the vSphere HA networking is configured properly is essential to the proper operation of vSphere HA. The following list of items can be used to verify the HA network configuration for ESXi hosts in the HA-enabled cluster:

- Verify that all hosts in the cluster have static IP addresses used for their management network(s).
- Verify that the management network redundancy is present by using NIC Teaming or creating a second management network.
- Verify that the network isolation address can be pinged from the ESXi Shell. The network isolation address is the default gateway, unless it has been manually modified.
- Verify that the upstream physical network switches support PortFast or an equivalent setting.
- Verify that consistent port group names and network labels are used on all virtual switches.
- Verify that the entire configuration is fully documented.

 Be aware of the vSphere HA design changes in vSphere 5, when verifying your networking configuration. In prior versions, failing the management network(s) was an easy way to test vSphere HA. In vSphere 5, datastore heartbeating is introduced to determine if the host is isolated or partitioned.

Now that verifying HA network configuration has been covered, the next section will cover verifying the HA/DRS cluster configuration.

Verifying HA/DRS Cluster Configuration

The first step in verifying a cluster configuration is to ensure that all of the system requirements have been met. This includes verifying DNS resolution and network connectivity, as discussed in the previous section. Once these prerequisites have been covered, the Summary tab for the cluster can provide a significant amount of information about both HA and DRS.

The General panel on the Summary tab for the cluster shows the current status of vSphere DRS, vSphere HA, and the EVC mode. The number of hosts in the cluster and other relevant information are also included. Figure 10.11 shows the General panel.

FIGURE 10.11 Cluster Summary tab's General panel

General	
vSphere DRS:	On
vSphere HA:	On
VMware EVC Mode:	Disabled
Total CPU Resources:	10 GHz
Total Memory:	16.00 GB
Total Storage:	485.44 GB
Number of Hosts:	2
Total Processors:	4
Number of Datastore Clusters:	0
Total Datastores:	6
Virtual Machines and Templates:	3
Total Migrations using vMotion:	14

When the cluster has HA enabled, there will be a vSphere HA panel in the Summary tab for the cluster. This panel contains many details about the HA configuration. Figure 10.12 shows the vSphere HA panel.

FIGURE 10.12 vSphere HA panel

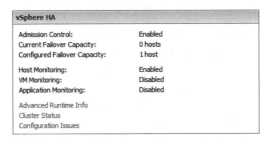

vSphere HA	
Admission Control:	Enabled
Current Failover Capacity:	0 hosts
Configured Failover Capacity:	1 host
Host Monitoring:	Enabled
VM Monitoring:	Disabled
Application Monitoring:	Disabled
Advanced Runtime Info	
Cluster Status	
Configuration Issues	

In Figure 10.12, the Host Failures The Cluster Tolerates admission control policy was used in the vSphere HA settings. Selecting this admission control policy added a blue

Advanced Runtime Info link in the vSphere HA panel. Clicking this link will open a window that will allow you to view the slot size information for the cluster. Figure 10.13 shows the vSphere HA Advanced Runtime Info window.

FIGURE 10.13   vSphere HA Advanced Runtime Info

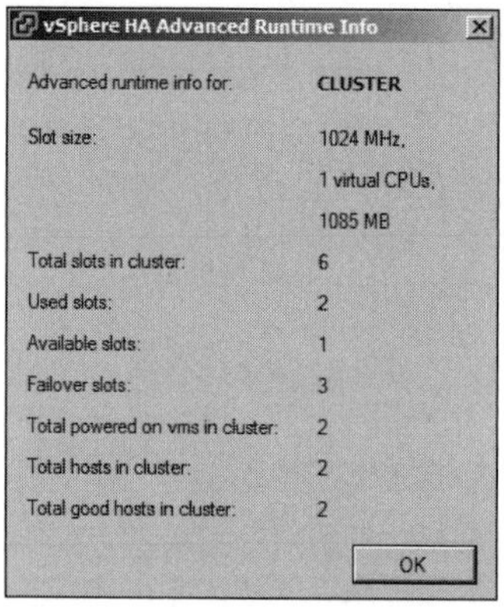

On the vSphere HA panel, there is also a blue Cluster Status link that can be used to view the number of hosts, master host, number of VMs protected, and heartbeat datastores being used. Figure 10.14 shows the vSphere HA Cluster Status window with the VMs tab selected.

FIGURE 10.14   Cluster status

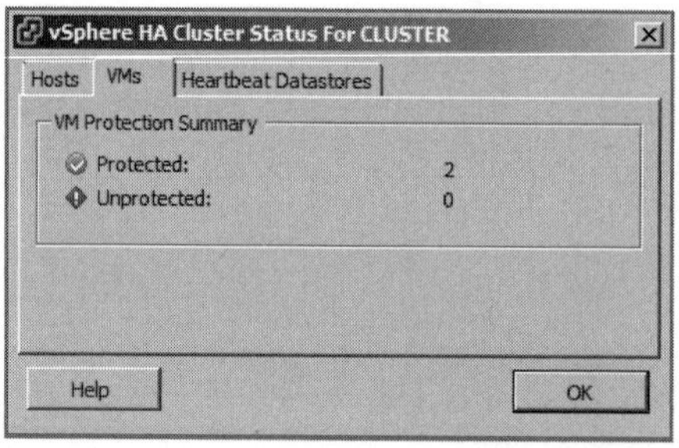

Also available on the vSphere HA panel is a blue Configuration Issues link that can be used to view any cluster configuration issues. Figure 10.15 shows the Cluster Configuration Issues window.

When the cluster has DRS enabled, there will also be a vSphere DRS panel in the Summary tab for the cluster. This panel contains many details about the vSphere configuration. Figure 10.16 shows the vSphere DRS panel.

FIGURE 10.15 Cluster Configuration Issues window

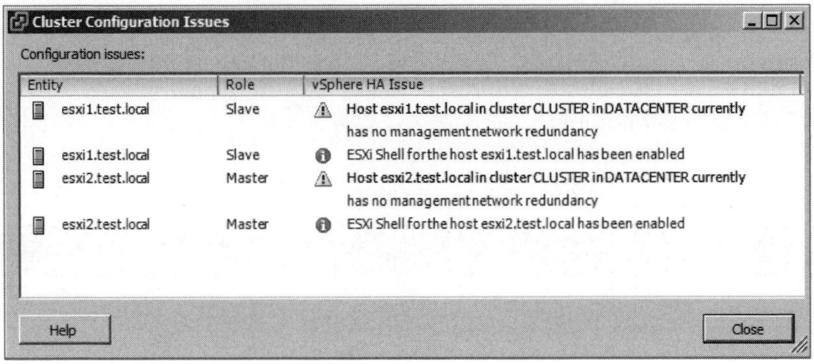

FIGURE 10.16 vSphere DRS panel

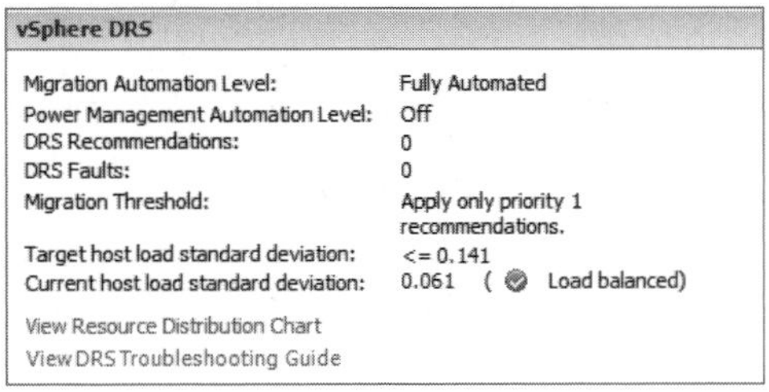

As discussed in Chapter 8, the blue View Resource Distribution Chart link can be used to view details about how DRS has allocated resources from the different hosts in the cluster.

Now that the verifying the vSphere HA and vSphere DRS configurations has been covered, troubleshooting HA capacity issues will be covered.

Troubleshooting HA Capacity Issues

Sometimes it will be necessary to troubleshoot capacity issues in an HA-enabled cluster. HA capacity issues will most often be related to the chosen admission control policy. An important thing to remember is that HA will only consider healthy hosts in its calculations. Hosts placed in maintenance mode or failed hosts will make a direct impact on the amount of resources available for virtual machines. These calculations need to be taken into consideration before the cluster is populated with virtual machines. The admission control policies were covered in detail in Chapter 8, but a brief review will be provided here.

When using the Host Failures The Cluster Tolerates admission control policy, a user-specified number of hosts can fail, and vSphere HA will reserve resources to fail over the virtual machines running from this number of failed hosts. The calculation used for this is based on a slot size, and the slot size is compared to the capacity of the hosts in the cluster to determine how many total slots are available. vSphere HA will then attempt to reserve enough resources to be able to satisfy the number of needed slots. If sufficient resources are no longer available, then the cluster will report that it has insufficient failover resources. Figure 10.17 shows this condition.

FIGURE 10.17 HA insufficient resources

CLUSTER											
Summary	Virtual Machines	Hosts	DRS	Resource Allocation	Performance	Tasks & Events	Alarms	Permissions	Maps	Profile Compliance

Configuration Issues
Insufficient resources to satisfy vSphere HA failover level on cluster CLUSTER in DATACENTER

If this condition exists, further virtual machines can be prevented from powering on. To correct this condition, the unavailable ESXi hosts need to be returned to the cluster or virtual machine CPU, and memory reservations may need to be checked to ensure they are not too high.

If the CPU and/or memory reservations cannot be changed, consider using the Percentage Of Cluster Resources Reserved As Failover Spare Capacity admission control policy.

When the Percentage Of Cluster Resources Reserved As Failover Spare Capacity admission control policy is used, the percentages may need to be adjusted to lower values to accommodate capacity needs.

Remember that resources are finite in a vSphere environment. Setting the percentages too low in the Percentage Of Cluster Resources Reserved As Failover Spare Capacity admission control policy can prevent HA from protecting all of your virtual machines in a failover event.

Now that troubleshooting HA capacity issues has been covered, troubleshooting HA redundancy issues will be covered.

Troubleshooting HA Redundancy Issues

To troubleshoot vSphere HA redundancy issues, it is important to understand how vSphere HA works. vSphere HA was covered in detail in Chapter 8, but here is a brief review. When host monitoring is enabled in the vSphere HA options, ESXi hosts in the cluster will exchange network heartbeats via the HA agents over their management networks. For network heartbeating, the master host monitors the status of the slave hosts. If the master host stops receiving network heartbeats from a slave host, it must determine whether the host is failed, isolated, or partitioned. To determine which type of event has occurred, the master host will try to exchange heartbeats with a datastore. This is known as *datastore heart-beating* and allows the master host to better determine the true state of the slave host(s).

As discussed earlier in this chapter, redundant management network connections are preferred when using HA. As a best practice, datastore connections should always be fully redundant, regardless of whether vSphere HA is used. When only one part of a redundant connection is lost, vSphere HA should continue to work as planned. Troubleshooting vSphere HA redundancy is really more about troubleshooting network redundancy and storage connection redundancy. vSphere HA will report lost network redundancy, as was previously shown in Figure 10.15. These warnings will stop being reported when the redundancy is restored.

Now that troubleshooting vSphere HA redundancy issues has been covered, troubleshooting DRS load imbalance issues will be covered.

Troubleshooting DRS Load Imbalance Issues

DRS attempts to balance loads based on the resource requirements of the virtual machines running in the cluster. Imbalanced load issues can sometimes occur, usually because of certain constraints. These include the following:

- ESXi hosts in maintenance mode
- VM-Host affinity/anti-affinity rules
- VM-VM affinity rules

Exercise 10.6 covers the steps to manually create and correct an imbalanced load. This exercise will utilize a two-node DRS cluster and two virtual machines configured with identical CPU and memory settings. If your lab has more virtual machines, simply power off the additional VMs. If your lab has more than two hosts, use maintenance mode to temporarily remove the extra capacity from the cluster.

EXERCISE 10.6

Creating and Correcting a DRS Load Imbalance

1. Connect to a vCenter Server with the vSphere Client.

2. Open the Hosts and Clusters view and select the cluster in the left pane.

3. Right-click the cluster and choose the Edit Settings option from the context menu that appears.

4. Select the vSphere DRS item in the left pane and then select the Fully Automated level.

5. Move the slider for the Migration Threshold option to the Conservative setting. The final configuration should appear exactly as shown here.

(continued)

EXERCISE 10.6 *(continued)*

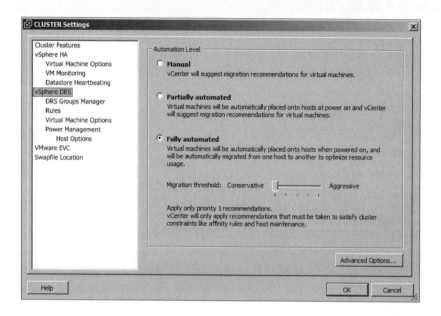

6. Click OK to save these changes. A Reconfigure Cluster task will begin. Wait for this task to complete.

   At this point, DRS has been effectively disabled, and it will not perform any automated actions.

7. Ensure that the cluster is selected in the left pane and click the Summary tab in the right pane.

8. Review the Target Host Load Standard Deviation value in the vSphere DRS panel. It should report a value of N/A.

   If the Target Host Load Standard Deviation value in the vSphere DRS panel does not immediately report N/A, wait for several minutes and the information will eventually refresh.

9. Migrate all virtual machines to one ESXi host in the cluster.

   Both virtual machines have now been moved to one ESXi host, and you will now create an affinity rule to keep them there together.

10. Right-click the cluster and choose the Edit Settings option from the context menu that appears.

11. Select the Rules option under vSphere DRS in the left pane.

12. Create a new rule by clicking the Add button in the lower left.

13. When the Rule window appears, give the rule a descriptive and unique name and choose the Keep Virtual Machines Together option for Type.

14. Click the Add button in the lower portion of the screen.

15. Add the two virtual machines by clicking the All button.

16. Click OK to add the virtual machines.

17. Verify the rule is accurate and click OK on the Rule window to save this rule.

The virtual machines have been placed on one ESXi host now, and an affinity rule has been created to keep them there. In the remaining steps, I will cover how to change the automation level and migration threshold to generate the cluster load imbalance.

18. Select the vSphere DRS item in the left pane and verify that the Fully Automated automation level is selected.

19. Move the slider for the Migration Threshold option to the Aggressive setting.

20. Click OK to save these changes. A Reconfigure Cluster task will begin. Wait for this task to complete.

21. Click the Summary tab in the right pane.

22. Review the Target Host Load Standard Deviation value in the vSphere DRS panel. It should now report a value. Review the Current Host Load Standard Deviation value, and note the area to the left of this value. A warning icon should appear and state Load Imbalanced.

You have now created an imbalanced load. In the next steps, you will remove the affinity rule.

(continued)

23. Right-click the cluster and choose the Edit Settings option from the context menu that appears.

24. Select the Rules option under vSphere DRS in the left pane.

25. Select the rule created earlier in this exercise and click the Remove button located in the lower-left corner of the screen.

26. Confirm the rule removal by clicking the Yes button.

27. Click OK in the cluster settings window to save the changes. A Reconfigure Cluster task will begin. Wait for this task to complete.

28. Wait patiently for DRS to migrate one of the virtual machines. The full DRS invocation cycle of 300 seconds may have to first pass.

29. Eventually, one of the two virtual machines will be migrated with vMotion to the other ESXi host, creating a one-to-one host-VM relationship.

30. Review the cluster Summary tab for the Current Host Load Standard Deviation value, and note the area to the left of this value. The load should now be reported as Balanced.

If you are fortunate enough to have a test lab with many resources, this exercise may not work as expected beyond step 28. If the Current Host Load Standard Deviation reports Load Balanced at the conclusion of step 28, then DRS will not migrate one of the virtual machines. If this happens, then you will need to simply read through the exercise and understand the remaining steps.

Now that I have covered troubleshooting DRS load imbalance issues, I will cover interpreting the DRS resource distribution charts and host load standard deviations.

Interpreting the DRS Resource Distribution Graph and Target/Current Host Load Deviation

The host standard load deviations represent the load imbalance metric of the hosts in the cluster. A priority level for migration recommendations is computed using this information, and the recommendation's priority level is compared to the migration threshold configured in the vSphere DRS settings. If the priority level is less than or equal to the threshold setting, the recommendation is applied or displayed. The automation of this action depends entirely on the automation level chosen in vSphere DRS.

The DRS host load standard deviations can also be viewed on the Cluster Summary tab in the vSphere DRS panel. There is an entry for Target Host Load Standard Deviation and for Current Host Load Standard Deviation, as shown in Figure 10.18.

FIGURE 10.18   Host Load Standard Deviation entries

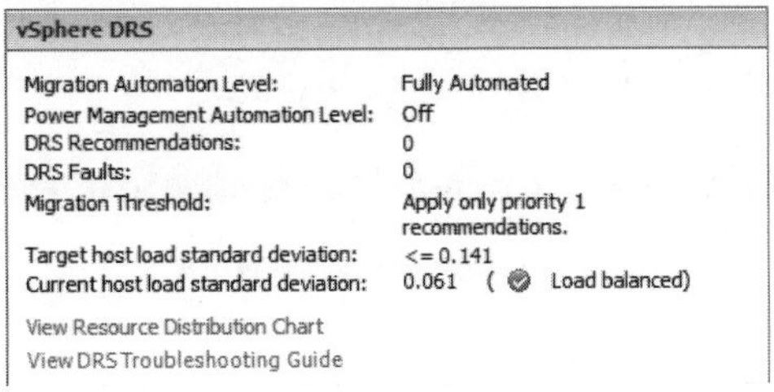

vSphere DRS	
Migration Automation Level:	Fully Automated
Power Management Automation Level:	Off
DRS Recommendations:	0
DRS Faults:	0
Migration Threshold:	Apply only priority 1 recommendations.
Target host load standard deviation:	<= 0.141
Current host load standard deviation:	0.061 (⊘ Load balanced)
View Resource Distribution Chart	
View DRS Troubleshooting Guide	

> **NOTE**   If the DRS migration threshold is set to Conservative, the Target Host Load Standard Deviation entry will report a value of N/A, since no attempt to load balance is made when this setting is selected.

If a cluster is balanced, the Current Host Load Standard Deviation entry will report Load Balanced, as previously shown in Figure 10.18. If the cluster is imbalanced, the Current Host Load Standard Deviation entry will report load Imbalanced, as shown in Figure 10.19.

FIGURE 10.19   Imbalanced load entry

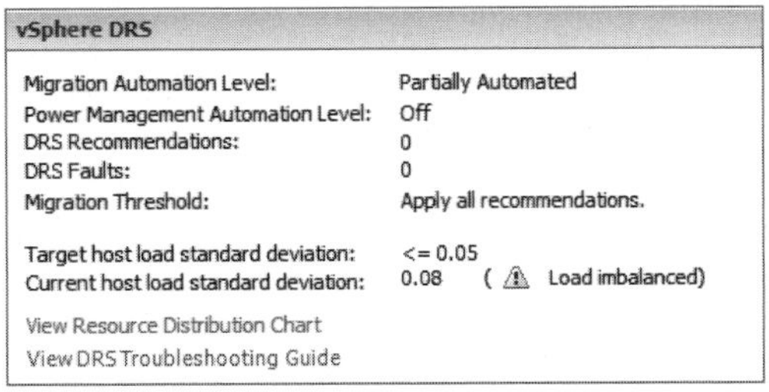

vSphere DRS	
Migration Automation Level:	Partially Automated
Power Management Automation Level:	Off
DRS Recommendations:	0
DRS Faults:	0
Migration Threshold:	Apply all recommendations.
Target host load standard deviation:	<= 0.05
Current host load standard deviation:	0.08 (⚠ Load imbalanced)
View Resource Distribution Chart	
View DRS Troubleshooting Guide	

The DRS Resource Distribution Graph can be accessed from the Cluster Summary tab in the vSphere DRS panel. There is a blue link titled View Resource Distribution Chart that is used to open the Resource Distribution Chart. Figure 10.20 shows the DRS Resource Distribution window.

The default view in the DRS Resource Distribution window is for CPU resources. Using the gray % and MHz buttons at the top of the window will allow the view to be toggled between utilization views. Each ESXi host in the cluster will be listed in the left column, and each of the colored boxes represents either a single virtual machine or a group of what are essentially idle virtual machines. Green boxes are good to see here. The legend at the bottom of the window shows that green indicates 100 percent of the entitled resources are being delivered for the VM. Any other color means the VM is not receiving all of its entitled resources. By hovering the cursor over any of these colored boxes, you can obtain the name of the virtual machine and information about its current resource usage.

FIGURE 10.20   DRS Resource Distribution window

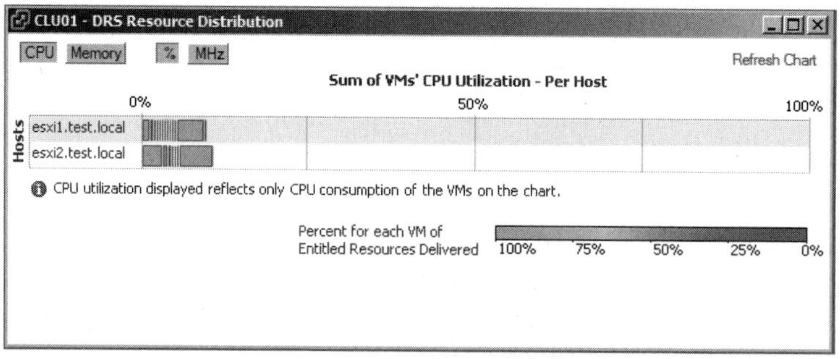

The memory settings for the cluster are also available in the DRS Resource Distribution window, and this view can be selected by clicking the gray memory button at the top of the window. Figure 10.21 shows the memory view.

FIGURE 10.21   DRS memory utilization view

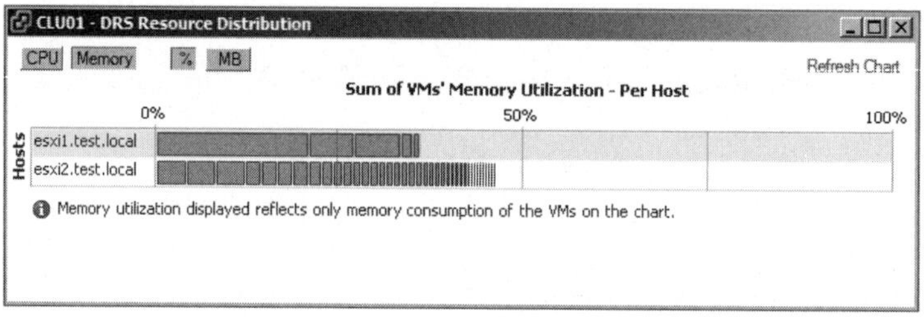

Using the gray % and MB buttons at the top of the window will allow the view to be toggled between utilization views. Each ESXi host in the cluster will be listed in the left column, and each of the gray boxes represents a single virtual machine. Just like with the CPU resources, hovering the cursor over any of these gray boxes will allow you to obtain the name of the virtual machine and information about its current resource usage.

Interpreting the DRS resource distribution charts and host load standard deviations has now been covered, and in the next section I will troubleshoot vMotion and Storage vMotion migration issues.

Troubleshooting vMotion/Storage vMotion Migration Issues

The first step in troubleshooting vMotion and Storage vMotion migrations is to ensure that all system requirements have been met. If vMotion and/or Storage vMotion are not working, then the following steps can be taken to troubleshoot:

- Ensure that all hosts are licensed for vMotion and/or Storage vMotion.
- Verify EVC and/or the processor compatibility of the hosts in the cluster.
- Ensure that vMotion networking exists on all hosts in the cluster.
- If vSwitches are used, ensure that consistent network labels are used across all hosts in the cluster.
- If dvSwitches are used, ensure that all hosts in the cluster are also all members of all dvSwitches used by virtual machines
- Use `vmkping` to verify network connectivity of the vMotion VMkernel interface for all hosts in the cluster.
- Verify that no firewalls are between hosts in the cluster.
- Verify virtual switch settings, including VLAN and MTU.
- Verify that time is synchronized across all hosts in the cluster.
- Verify that virtual machines aren't attached to devices on the local ESXi hosts.
- Ensure that the virtual machine is not in the middle of a VMware Tools installation.
- Verify that virtual machines are not connected to an internal-only virtual switch.
- Verify required disk space is available in datastores when using Storage vMotion.
- Verify that all hosts in the cluster have access to the same shared storage.

Now that the troubleshooting steps for vMotion and Storage vMotion migrations have been covered, the next section will cover interpreting vMotion resource maps.

Interpret vMotion Resource Maps

vMotion resource maps are a quick and convenient way to visually see the relationships between a virtual machine, the ESXi hosts in the cluster, and both the datastores and networks that the virtual machine and the hosts use. Figure 10.22 shows the vMotion resource map for a virtual machine using datastore NFS1 and a virtual machine port group named Intranet.

vMotion resource maps are a useful tool for troubleshooting vMotion issues. In Figure 10.22, there are green circles around the ESXi hosts. These green circles represent that each host has access to the same datastores and networks. The storage and networking requirements for vMotion both pass in Figure 10.22.

FIGURE 10.22 vMotion resource map

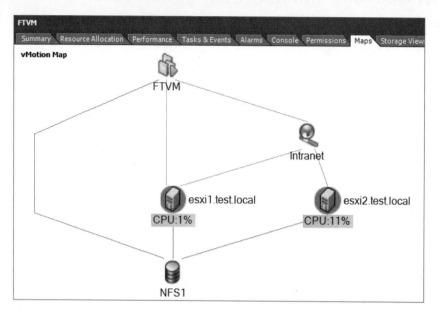

Figure 10.23 shows a vMotion resource map for a virtual machine that is stored on local storage on one of the ESXi hosts.

FIGURE 10.23 vMotion resource map

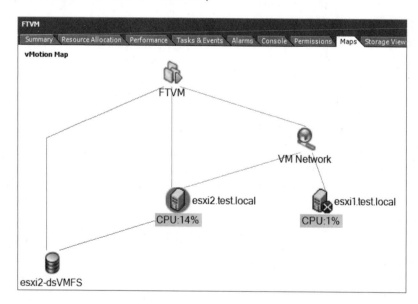

Notice in this image that the ESXi host that does not have access to the datastore has a red *X* on it and there is no line connecting the ESXi host and the datastore. The networking requirements pass, as is shown by the green line drawn between the ESXi host and the VM Network connection. This vMotion resource map shows that because of the local storage, using vMotion with this virtual machine will not be possible.

As good as the resource maps are as a troubleshooting tool, keep in mind that these maps can show networking and storage compatibilities only between the hosts in the cluster. In both of the previous images, the virtual machine used was connected to a host DVD-ROM that would prevent it from being migrated with vMotion. The virtual switch used in both of these examples was also an internal-only vSwitch, which would also prevent migration with vMotion. Be aware of these caveats when working with vMotion resource maps.

Now that vMotion resource maps have been covered, I will wrap up this chapter with identifying the root cause of a DRS/HA cluster or migration issue based on troubleshooting information.

Identifying the Root Cause of a DRS/HA Cluster or Migration Issue Based on Troubleshooting Information

The troubleshooting techniques used to identify the root cause of an issue with a cluster or virtual machine migration were covered thoroughly in this chapter. Determining the root cause of these issues can sometimes be simple. It can also be a long process that involves going through a vast number of log files, searching the VMware knowledge base, posting a discussion in the VMTN communities, or even opening a support request with VMware. For the VCP5 exam, use the troubleshooting content presented in this section as your guide for troubleshooting cluster and/or migration issues.

Summary

The first part of this chapter focused on performing basic troubleshooting for ESXi hosts. Troubleshooting common ESXi installation issues was covered. Monitoring the ESXi system health was also covered. General ESXi host troubleshooting guidelines were identified. Exporting diagnostic information completed the first section.

The second part of this chapter focused on performing basic vSphere network troubleshooting. Verifying network configuration was covered, along with verifying a given virtual machine configuration for the correct network resources. Troubleshooting virtual switch and port group configuration issues was covered, along with troubleshooting physical network adapter configuration issues. This section concluded with identifying the root cause of a network issue based on troubleshooting information.

The third part of this chapter focused on performing basic vSphere storage troubleshooting. Verifying a storage configuration was covered. Troubleshooting storage contention issues was also covered, along with troubleshooting storage overcommitment issues and iSCSI software initiator configuration issues. Storage reports and storage maps troubleshooting were covered. This section concluded with identifying the root cause of a storage issue based on troubleshooting information.

The final section of this chapter focused on performing basic troubleshooting for HA/DRS clusters and vMotion/Storage vMotion. The HA, DRS, and vMotion requirements were reviewed. Verifying a vMotion/Storage vMotion configuration was covered, along with verifying the HA network configuration. HA/DRS cluster configuration verification was discussed. Troubleshooting HA capacity and redundancy issues was covered, along with troubleshooting DRS load imbalance issues. I discussed troubleshooting vMotion/Storage vMotion migration issues. Interpreting the DRS Resource Distribution Graph and Target/Current Host Load Deviation was covered, along with interpreting vMotion resource maps. The chapter concluded with identifying the root cause of a DRS/HA cluster or migration issue based on troubleshooting information.

Exam Essentials

Know how to perform basic troubleshooting for ESXi.   Be able to troubleshoot common installation issues. Know how to monitor ESXi system health. Be able to identify general ESXi host troubleshooting guidelines. Understand how to export diagnostic information.

Know how to perform basic network troubleshooting.   Know how to verify a network configuration. Know how to verify whether a given virtual machine is configured with the correct network resources. Be able to troubleshoot virtual switch and port group configuration issues. Understand how to troubleshoot physical network adapter configuration issues. Be able to identify the root cause of a network issue based on troubleshooting information.

Know how to perform basic storage troubleshooting.   Know how to verify a storage configuration. Understand how to troubleshoot storage contention issues. Understand how to troubleshoot storage overcommitment issues. Be able to troubleshoot iSCSI software initiator configuration issues. Know how to troubleshoot storage reports and storage maps. Be able to identify the root cause of a storage issue based on troubleshooting information.

Know how to perform basic HA/DRS cluster, vMotion, and Storage vMotion troubleshooting.   Be able to identify HA/DRS and vMotion requirements. Know how to verify vMotion and Storage vMotion configuration. Be able to verify the HA network configuration and HA/DRS cluster configuration. Understand how to troubleshoot HA capacity issues, HA redundancy issues, and DRS load imbalance issues. Be able to troubleshoot vMotion and Storage vMotion migration issues. Understand how to interpret the DRS Resource Distribution Graph and Target/Current Host Load Deviation. Be able to interpret vMotion resource maps. Understand how to identify the root cause of a DRS/HA cluster or migration issue based on troubleshooting information.

Review Questions

1. You need to put a host in maintenance mode to replace a failed NIC card. When you attempt to put the host in maintenance mode, it gets stuck at 2 percent. Which of the following are likely reasons why the maintenance mode task will not complete? (Choose two.)

   A. A virtual machine does not have the VMware Tools installed.

   B. A virtual machine has a snapshot.

   C. A virtual machine is attached to an internal-only network.

   D. A virtual machine is attached to an ISO on a local datastore.

2. Your vSphere environment has hundreds of virtual machines and utilizes multiple vSwitches for all virtual machine connections. You created a new virtual machine, but it cannot get network connectivity. If you power off another virtual machine, this virtual machine works as expected. What is the most likely reason for this?

   A. The virtual machine has the same MAC address as another virtual machine.

   B. The VMware Tools are not installed in the guest OS.

   C. The virtual machine is using the wrong virtual machine hardware version.

   D. The vSwitch has run out of ports.

3. Where can all of the ESXi logs be accessed from? (Choose all that apply.)

   A. The vSphere Client

   B. The vSphere Web Client

   C. /var/run/log from the ESXi Shell

   D. /var/vmware/log from the ESXi Shell

4. If the Host Failures The Cluster Tolerates admission control policy is selected, which of the following links will appear in the vSphere HA panel on the cluster's Summary tab?

   A. Advanced Runtime Info

   B. Advanced Cluster Info

   C. Advanced Failure Info

   D. Advanced HA Info

5. You are troubleshooting what you believe to be a storage contention issue. Historically, the DAVG/cmd value returns an average of 7. Today the DAVG/cmd command returns a value of 30. What statement best summarizes the situation?

   A. There is no storage contention.

   B. There is minimal storage contention but not enough to worry about.

   C. There is storage contention.

   D. None of these.

6. You have a single virtual machine that fails when using vMotion. Other virtual machines work as expected with vMotion. Which of the following troubleshooting steps should be taken? (Choose all that apply.)

   A. Verify that no firewalls are between hosts in the cluster.

   B. Verify virtual switch settings, including VLAN and MTU.

   C. Verify that the virtual machine is not attached to any devices on the local ESXi host.

   D. Verify that the virtual machine is not in the middle of a VMware Tools installation.

7. Which of the following links can be used in the vSphere HA panel on the cluster's Summary tab to troubleshoot HA redundancy?

   A. Advanced Runtime Info

   B. Cluster Status

   C. Configuration Issues

   D. Resource Distribution Chart

8. Which of the following system requirements do HA, DRS, and vMotion all share? (Choose all that apply.)

   A. All hosts must be licensed to use the feature.

   B. All hosts must have access to the same shared storage.

   C. The VMware Tools are required in virtual machines.

   D. The VMware Tools must be the most recent version.

9. You need to export the diagnostic information for your vCenter Server and all of the ESXi hosts it manages. What is the simplest way to accomplish this task?

   A. Start ➤ Programs ➤ VMware ➤ Generate vCenter Server Log Bundle

   B. vSphere Client connected to vCenter Server

   C. vSphere Client connected to each ESXi host

   D. None of these

10. Which of the following is specifically used to measure virtual machine I/O latency? (Choose two.)

   A. KAVG/cmd

   B. DAVG/cmd

   C. LAT/rd

   D. LAT/wr

11. Which of the following could cause a DRS cluster to become imbalanced? (Choose all that apply.)

   A. VMs with individual memory reservations

   B. ESXi hosts in maintenance mode

   C. VM-Host affinity/anti-affinity rules

   D. VM-VM affinity rules

12. Which of the following can be viewed on a vMotion resource map? (Choose all that apply.)

   A. Virtual machine–connected devices

   B. vSwitches

   C. Datastores

   D. ESX/ESXi hosts

13. You are connected directly to an ESXi host with the vSphere Client. How do you obtain the health information for this system?

   A. Select the host and use the Hardware Status tab.

   B. Select the host and use the Configuration tab.

   C. Select the host and use the Health Status tab.

   D. Select the host and use the System Info tab.

14. Your NFS storage system firmware version does not support T10-based Storage APIs – Array Integration (Thin Provisioning). What will happen if an NFS volume fills to capacity on this storage system?

   A. Virtual machines will shut down gracefully.

   B. Virtual machines will be powered off.

   C. Virtual machines will be paused.

   D. Virtual machines will crash.

15. Which of the following is defined as the average amount of time in milliseconds a device takes to service a single I/O request?

   A. DAVG/cmd

   B. KAVG/cmd

   C. GAVG/cmd

   D. QAVG/cmd

16. You have just installed ESXi on a server and are having trouble getting management network connectivity established. When troubleshooting this issue, the network administrator has asked for the MAC address of the network adapter you are trying to use. Which of the following can be used to obtain the MAC address? (Choose all that apply.)

   A. From the ESXi Shell, run the command`esxcli network nic list`.

   B. The DCUI Configure Management Network feature.

   C. vSphere Client.

   D. vSphere Web Client.

17. You are trying to install ESXi on a white-box server built from parts you bought. During the installation, the installer fails to find a hard disk. What is the most likely cause of this problem?

   A. The server's BIOS is not configured properly.

   B. The installation media is corrupt.

   C. This server and storage controller are not on the HCL and are therefore not supported.

   D. The storage controller needs a driver.

18. Which of the following are valid steps in verifying a storage configuration? (Choose all that apply.)

   A. Verify the host's storage adapters are listed on the HCL and used only as described in the HCL.

   B. Verify that storage systems used are listed on the HCL and are at the required firmware versions.

   C. Verify that no configuration maximums have been exceeded.

   D. Verify that no ESXi patches are required for the configuration.

19. Your vSphere environment uses NFS for the storage. The connectivity to the NFS server was set up with a standard vSwitch using the Route Based On IP Hash load balancing. There have recently been issues with connectivity to the NFS server. There have been no changes to the vSphere networking, and your troubleshooting has found no problems. What is the next step in troubleshooting this issue?

   A. Reboot each ESXi host one at a time.

   B. Restart the NFS storage system.

   C. Involve the networking staff to verify that the physical switch is working properly.

   D. Open a support request with VMware.

20. When viewing the VMware DRS panel on the cluster's Summary tab, the value of N/A is reported for Target Host Load Standard Deviation. Why is this?

   A. Automation Level is set to Partially Automated.

   B. Automation Level is set to Fully Automated.

   C. Migration Threshold is set to Aggressive.

   D. Migration Threshold is set to Conservative.

Monitor a vSphere Implementation and Manage vCenter Server Alarms

---

VCP5 EXAM OBJECTIVES COVERED IN THIS CHAPTER:

✓ **Monitor ESXi, vCenter Server, and Virtual Machines**

- Describe how Tasks and Events are viewed in vCenter Server
- Create/Edit/Delete a Scheduled Task
- Configure SNMP for vCenter Server
- Configure Active Directory and SMTP settings for vCenter Server
- Configure vCenter Server timeout settings
- Configure vCenter Server logging options
- Create a log bundle
- Start/Stop/Verify vCenter Server service status
- Start/Stop/Verify ESXi host agent status
- Monitor/Administer vCenter Server connections
- Configure/View/Print/Export resource maps
- Explain common memory metrics
- Explain common CPU metrics
- Explain common network metrics
- Explain common storage metrics
- Compare and contrast Overview and Advanced Charts
- Create an Advanced Chart
- Identify critical performance metrics

- Determine host performance using resxtop and guest Perfmon
- Given performance data, identify the affected vSphere resource

✓ **Create and Administer vCenter Server Alarms**

- List vCenter default utilization alarms
- List vCenter default connectivity alarms
- List possible actions for utilization and connectivity alarms
- Create a vCenter utilization alarm
- Create a vCenter connectivity alarm
- Configure alarm triggers
- Configure alarm actions
- For a given alarm, identify the affected resource in a vSphere implementation

This chapter will cover the objectives of section 7 of the VCP5 exam blueprint. This chapter will focus on monitoring a vSphere implementation and managing vCenter Server alarms. This chapter will first cover monitoring ESXi hosts, vCenter Server, and virtual machines. How tasks and events are viewed in vCenter Server will be described, and critical performance metrics will be identified. Common memory, CPU, network, and storage metrics will be explained. I will compare and contrast the overview and advanced charts and show how to create an advanced chart. How to configure SNMP, Active Directory, and SMTP settings for vCenter Server will be covered, along with configuring vCenter Server logging options. I will show how to create a log bundle. I will cover how to create, edit, and delete a scheduled task in vCenter Server. I will also cover how to configure, view, print, and export resource maps. Starting, stopping, and verifying the vCenter Server services will be covered, along with starting, stopping, and verifying the status of the ESXi host agent. vCenter Server timeout settings will be configured. I will cover how to monitor and administer vCenter Server connections. Determining host performance using `resxtop` and Windows guest Perfmon will be covered. The first section will conclude with identifying the affected vSphere resource when given performance data.

The second section of this chapter will cover creating and administering vCenter Server alarms. The vCenter Server default utilization and connectivity alarms will be listed. The possible actions for utilization and connectivity alarms will also be listed. I will cover how to create both a vCenter Server utilization alarm and a connectivity alarm. I will also cover how to configure alarm triggers and alarm actions. This chapter will conclude with identifying the affected resource in a vSphere implementation for a given alarm.

Monitor ESXi, vCenter Server, and Virtual Machines

The ongoing monitoring of virtual machines, ESXi hosts, and vCenter Server is critical to the success of any virtual infrastructure. Monitoring allows virtual infrastructure administrators to be proactive in the virtual infrastructure and to better know what is happening on a day-to-day basis. This chapter will cover how to monitor virtual machines, ESXi hosts, and vCenter Server. I will first describe how tasks and events are viewed in vCenter Server.

Describing How Tasks and Events Are Viewed in vCenter Server

When using the vSphere Client to connect to a vCenter Server, the Recent Tasks pane is by default visible at the bottom of the screen. This pane will show any active tasks, in addition to any tasks that were started and completed within approximately the last 10 minutes. This brief view is good for obtaining real-time task information, but it is often necessary to go back further than this brief time period.

When using the vSphere Client connected directly to an ESXi host, the Recent Tasks pane is the only task history that is available. Events can be viewed in the vSphere Client connected directly to an ESXi host by selecting an object in the left pane and then using the Events tab. Figure 11.1 shows the Events tab for an ESXi host.

FIGURE 11.1   Events tab

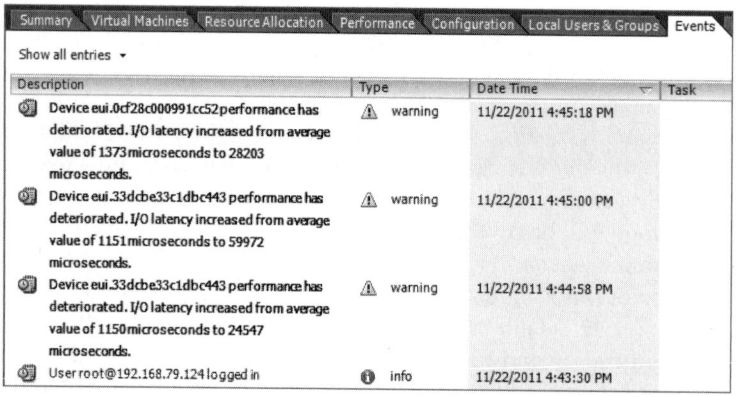

When the vSphere Client is connected to a vCenter Server, the Tasks & Events tab can be used to view both events and tasks. vCenter Server includes the ability to view historical task information and the ability to create and schedule tasks. The reporting of these tasks and any other tasks in vCenter Server can be found in the Tasks & Events tab, alongside the events. vCenter Server uses two different views to separate the tasks from the events, as shown in Figure 11.2.

FIGURE 11.2   Events view in vCenter Server

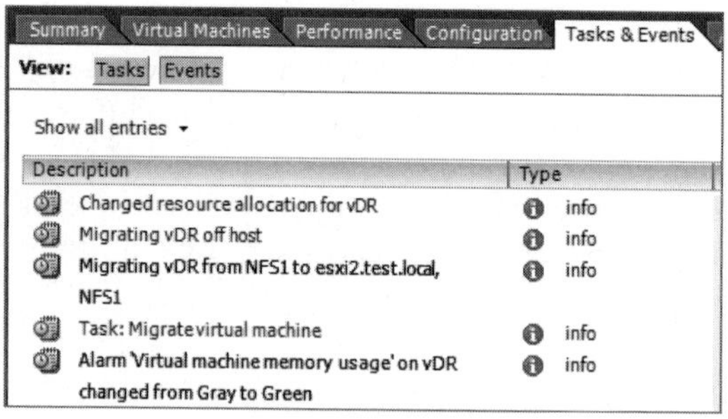

When viewing tasks and events, it is important to remember that the entries in the list will include all tasks and events for any child objects of the chosen object. For example, selecting a cluster will give you the events for every host and virtual machine in the cluster. Because of this, it is usually easier to begin with the lowest-level inventory object possible. Events can also be sorted by clicking the column header for the column you want to sort the data on. If you still need to be able to narrow the entries in this list, you can use the filtering options available in each view. Figure 11.3 shows a filtered view with the root vCenter Server inventory object chosen in the left pane.

FIGURE 11.3 Filtered Events view in vCenter Server

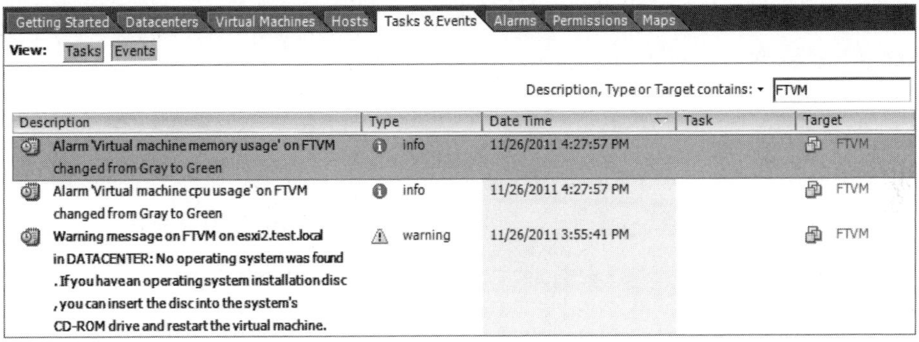

Additional information can be obtained for each event or task listed by clicking the entry in the list. The additional details will be displayed in the details pane below the event or task entries, as shown in Figure 11.4.

FIGURE 11.4 Event details

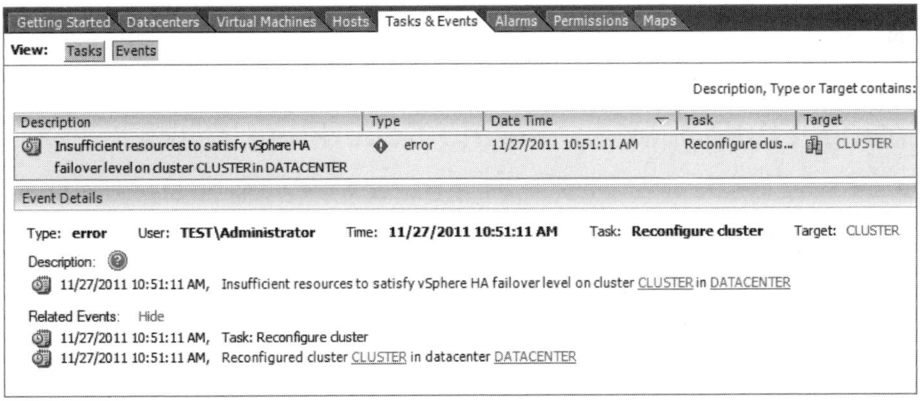

There is an additional way to view tasks and events in the vSphere Client when connected to a vCenter Server. This view can be accessed by clicking the Home icon in the navigation bar and choosing the Events icon listed under the Management section or by using the menus and choosing View ➤ Management ➤ Events. This view will provide one large pane to view tasks and events in and can be useful when you need to make the Name column very wide to view more information.

The number of entries displayed in the tasks and events lists in the vSphere Client can be adjusted. Use the Edit ➢ Client Settings menu option and then select the Lists tab from the Client Settings window. Change the Page Size value to any number between 10 and 1000.

In addition to historical tasks and events, there is one other task view that needs to be covered. vCenter Server scheduled tasks have their own view, and this view can be accessed by clicking the Home icon in the navigation bar and choosing the Scheduled Tasks icon listed under the Management section or by using the menus and choosing View ➢ Management ➢ Scheduled Tasks. Figure 11.5 shows the Scheduled Tasks view.

FIGURE 11.5   Scheduled Tasks view

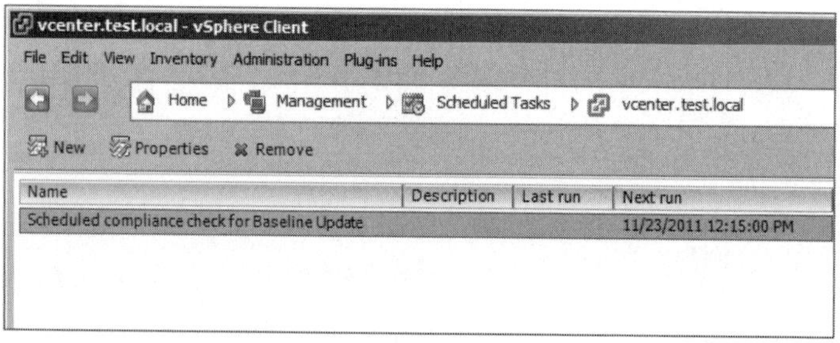

vcenter.test.local - vSphere Client
File Edit View Inventory Administration Plug-ins Help
Home ▷ Management ▷ Scheduled Tasks ▷ vcenter.test.local
New   Properties   ✖ Remove

Name	Description	Last run	Next run
Scheduled compliance check for Baseline Update			11/23/2011 12:15:00 PM

This section has focused on the vSphere Client, but it should be noted that the vSphere Web Client does have some ability to view tasks and events through the Task Console feature. The vCenter Server root object is shown, with all of its child objects, and there is no filtering availability. Scheduled tasks cannot be viewed or configured from the vSphere Web Client.

Now that viewing events and tasks in vCenter Server and ESXi hosts has been covered, vCenter Server scheduled tasks will be covered.

Creating, Editing, and Deleting Scheduled Tasks

A feature missing in ESXi hosts not managed by vCenter Server is the ability to create scheduled tasks. vCenter Server provides the ability to create tasks that can be used to perform a variety of administrative and operational tasks in the vSphere environment. The tasks available for scheduling will ultimately depend on the vSphere features and plug-ins in use, but the following list includes many of the options:

- Change the power state of a VM
- Clone a virtual machine
- Deploy a virtual machine
- Migrate a virtual machine
- Create a virtual machine
- Create a snapshot of a virtual machine
- Add a host

- Change cluster power settings
- Change resource pool or VM resource settings
- Check compliance of a profile
- Scan for Updates
- Remediate

🌐 Real World Scenario

Scheduling Virtual Machine Shutdowns

A virtual infrastructure administrator for an SMB is the sole responsible person for the entire vSphere environment. He has been asked to power off a two-tiered application that runs in two virtual machines. Normally this would not be a problem, but the requested shutdown date corresponds to a time that the virtual infrastructure administrator will be on a flight. The shutdown time cannot be changed, and the application owner insists that the servers be powered off.

Rather than changing his flight plans, the virtual infrastructure administrator decides to use a scheduled task in vCenter Server to accomplish this. He creates two separate tasks to shut down the virtual machines. He schedules them according to the proper shutdown sequence for the application and configures each task to send him an email notification when it completes.

Later in the week, as the virtual infrastructure administrator is waiting for a cab at the airport, he checks his email. There are two emails, each reporting that the virtual machine was shut down successfully. The scheduled tasks in vCenter Server allowed him to accomplish his work when he couldn't physically be there to do it.

Exercise 11.1 covers the steps to create, edit, and delete a scheduled task in vCenter Server.

EXERCISE 11.1

Creating, Editing, and Deleting a Scheduled Task in vCenter Server Using the vSphere Client

1. Connect to a vCenter Server with the vSphere Client.

2. Click the Home icon in the navigation bar and choose the Scheduled Tasks icon listed under the Management section.

3. Click the New Task button located just beneath the navigation bar, or right-click anywhere in the whitespace of the Scheduled Tasks list and choose New Scheduled Task from the context menu that appears.

4. The Schedule Task dialog box will appear. Use the drop-down menu to select the Change The VM Power State option.

(continued)

EXERCISE 11.1 *(continued)*

5. Click OK to continue.

6. The Change A Virtual Machine's Power State Wizard will launch.

7. Expand the hierarchy of inventory objects and select a virtual machine that has the VMware Tools installed and that can also be shut down at any time.

8. Click Next to continue.

9. Choose the Shut Down option from the Power Operation selections and click Next.

10. Give the scheduled task a descriptive task name and task description. Use the drop-down menu to set Frequency to Once and set Start Time for Later. Pick a date and time two weeks in the future.

11. Click Next to continue.

12. If your environment has SMTP configured, select the Send Email option and enter your email address. Otherwise, proceed to the next step and know that this is an available option with scheduled tasks.

Note that configuring vCenter Server to use an SMTP server will be covered later in this chapter.

13. Click Next.

14. Review the information presented on the Summary screen and click Finish to create this scheduled task.

15. A Create Scheduled Task task will begin. When this task completes, verify that the scheduled task is listed in the Scheduled Tasks view.

The scheduled task has now been completed. For the purposes of this exercise, assume that the task requestor has changed his mind and wants the virtual machine to be shut down at a different time. In the next part of this exercise, you will edit the scheduled task to accommodate this request.

16. Select the scheduled task created earlier in this exercise and click the Properties button located just beneath the navigation bar. Alternately, you can right-click the scheduled task and choose the Properties option from the context menu that appears.

17. The Change A Virtual Machine's Power State Wizard will launch with the scheduled task's information prepopulated.

18. Click Next to begin and move through the wizard until you get to the Schedule Task section.

19. Change the time of the scheduled task and move through the wizard until you reach the Summary screen.

20. Click Finish to save the changes made to the time.

21. A Reconfigure Scheduled Task task will begin. When this task completes, verify that the new start time is listed in the Scheduled Tasks view. This value will be reported in the Next Run column.

The scheduled task has now been modified. For the purposes of this exercise, now assume that the task requestor has cancelled the maintenance window entirely and he no longer wants the virtual machine to be shut down. In the final part of this exercise, I will cover the steps to remove this scheduled task.

22. Select the scheduled task that has been used in this exercise and choose the Remove button located just beneath the navigation bar. Alternately, you can right-click the scheduled task and choose the Remove option from the context menu that appears.

(continued)

EXERCISE 11.1 *(continued)*

> **vcenter.test.local - vSphere Client**
>
> File   Edit   View   Inventory   Administration   Plug-ins   Help
>
> ⬅️   ➡️   🏠 Home ▷ 🖥️ Management ▷ 🗓️ Scheduled Tasks ▷ 🗄️ vcenter.test.local
>
> 🗓️ New   📝 Properties   ✖ Remove
>
> | Name | Description | Last run |
> | --- | --- | --- |
> | Scheduled compliance check for Baseline Update | | |
> | Shut Down FTVM | Shut Down FTVM for Mainten... | |
>
> Run
> **Remove**
> Properties...
> ──────────────
> Copy to Clipboard   Ctrl+C

23. Click the Yes button when prompted to confirm.

24. Verify that the scheduled task is no longer listed in the Scheduled Tasks view.

25. Click the Home icon in the navigation bar and choose the Events icon listed under the Management section.

26. Verify that the scheduled task operations from this exercise are listed.

> **vcenter.test.local - vSphere Client**
>
> File   Edit   View   Inventory   Administration   Plug-ins   Help
>
> ⬅️   ➡️   🏠 Home ▷ 🖥️ Management ▷ 🗓️ Events ▷ 🗄️ vcenter.test.local
>
> 💾 Export Events
>
> Description, Type or Target co
>
> | Description | Type | Date Time | Task |
> | --- | --- | --- | --- |
> | Removed task Shut Down FTVM on FTVM in datacenter DATACENTER | ⓘ info | 11/28/2011 11:29:29 AM | Remove schedul... |
> | Task: Remove scheduled task | ⓘ info | 11/28/2011 11:29:29 AM | Remove schedul... |

If the Run option is chosen from the context menu of a scheduled task, it will run immediately, and you will not be prompted.

I have covered creating, editing, and deleting a scheduled task, and in the next section I will cover how to configure SNMP for vCenter Server.

Configuring SNMP for vCenter Server

vCenter Server includes an SNMP agent that can be configured to send SNMP traps to up to four receivers. This agent serves as a trap emitter only. Traps will be sent when vCenter Server is started and when alarms are triggered in vCenter Server. These traps would typically be sent to other management programs, or receivers, and these applications would need to be installed and configured properly as a prerequisite to configuring SNMP in vCenter Server. If existing monitoring tools are in place that can leverage the vCenter Server SNMP data, then this can be a great feature for enhancing the monitoring of vCenter Server. Configuring the SNMP settings requires the use of the vSphere Client connected to a vCenter Server. Exercise 11.2 covers the steps to configure SNMP for vCenter Server.

EXERCISE 11.2

Configuring SNMP for vCenter Server

1. Connect to a vCenter Server with the vSphere Client.

2. Click the Home icon in the navigation bar and choose vCenter Server Settings listed under the Administration section.

3. The vCenter Server Settings window will appear. Select SNMP in the left pane.

4. Enter the receiver URL and port information and the community string for the primary receiver.

Note that to use the additional receivers, you must select the Enable Receiver # box first.

5. Click OK to save these settings changes.

6. If your test environment has a working SNMP implementation, check it to verify that vCenter Server is sending events.

Now that configuring SNMP for vCenter Server has been covered, I will cover configuring Active Directory and SMTP settings for vCenter Server.

Configuring Active Directory and SMTP Settings for vCenter Server

vCenter Server's interactions with Active Directory can be configured using the vCenter Server settings. The vCenter Server settings are easily accessible from the Administration menu in the vSphere Client. Figure 11.6 shows the default settings for the Active Directory settings.

FIGURE 11.6   vCenter Active Directory settings

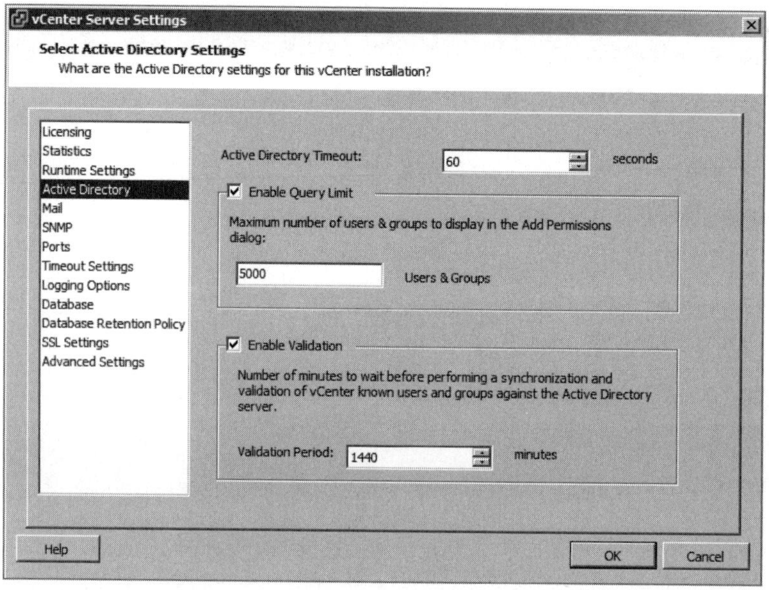

Active Directory Timeout is the number of seconds specified for the Active Directory connection timeout. If there are ever issues with all users and groups not being listed in large domains, increasing the timeout interval can resolve this issue.

The Enable Query Limit option is used to limit the number of domain users and groups that will be displayed in the Add Permissions dialog box when assigning permissions. The value can be adjusted in the Users & Groups field. Setting this value to a low number can be useful in troubleshooting situations with Active Directory. Note that setting this value to 0 will produce the same effect as deselecting the Enable Query Limit option. Either of these settings will place no limit on the maximum number of domain users and groups that will be displayed when assigning permissions in vCenter Server.

The Enable Validation option is used by vCenter Server to periodically validate its list of known domain users and groups against the current list in Active Directory and update its permissions accordingly. The Validation Period can be customized as desired, but validation will also occur at vCenter Server host startup.

vCenter Server can be configured to use an existing SMTP server to send email in response to alarm actions. Figure 11.7 shows the vCenter Server settings for SMTP.

The SMTP Server field can include the FQDN or IP address of the SMTP server, and the Sender Account must be configured with a full email address. Figure 11.7 shows a proper Sender Account configuration.

Configuring Active Directory and SMTP settings for vCenter Server have been covered, so next I will configure vCenter Server timeout settings.

FIGURE 11.7   vCenter SMTP settings

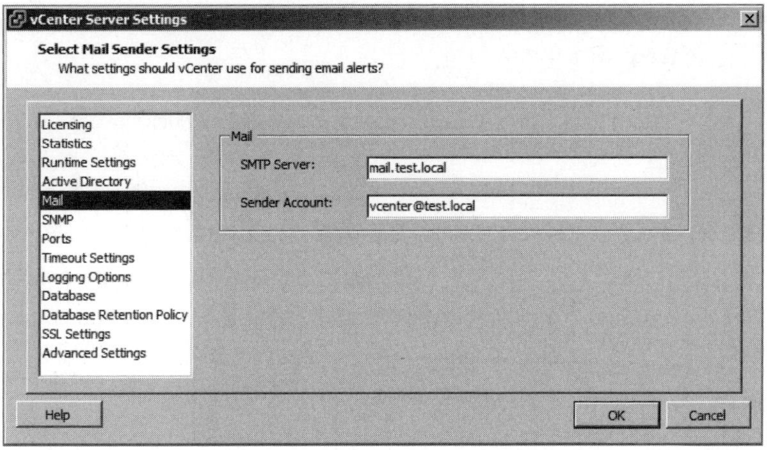

Configuring vCenter Server Timeout Settings

The vCenter Server timeout settings for vCenter Server operations can also be configured in the vCenter Server settings. These settings specify the interval of time after which the vSphere Client will time out. The vCenter Server settings are easily accessible from the Administration menu in the vSphere Client, and Figure 11.8 shows the vCenter Server timeout settings.

FIGURE 11.8   vCenter timeout settings

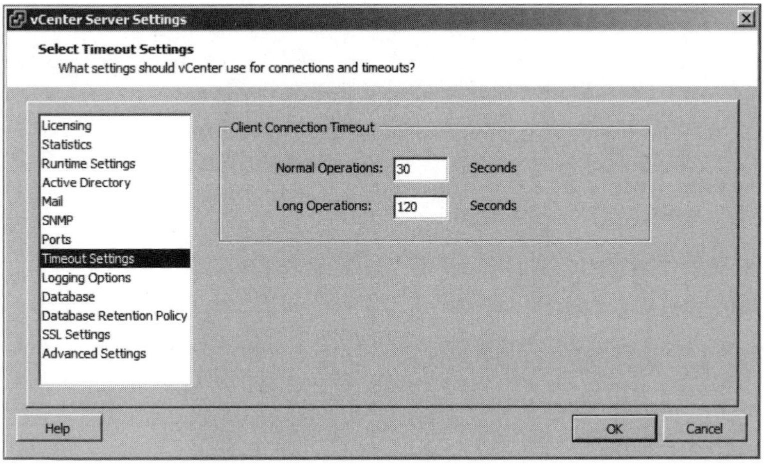

Increasing these values can sometimes be necessary for slow network links. The default value for long operations is 2 minutes, and the default value for normal operations is 30 seconds.

 Never set the Normal Operations timeout or the Long Operations timeout to a value of 0.

Now that configuring the vCenter Server timeout settings has been covered, I will cover configuring the vCenter Server logging options.

Configuring vCenter Server Logging Options

vCenter Server logging detail can also be configured in the vCenter Server settings. There is one drop-down menu that is used to configure the logging level for vCenter Server, as shown in Figure 11.9.

FIGURE 11.9 vCenter logging options

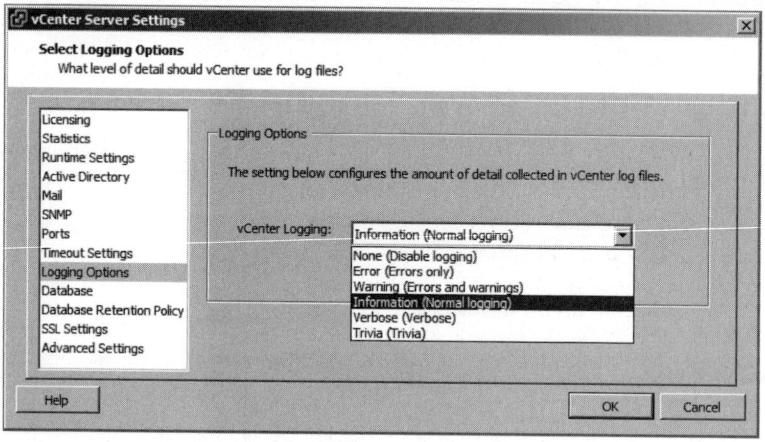

The vCenter Server logging detail is by default configured at Information (Normal Logging). The available logging levels are as follows:

None (Disable Logging)   Used to turn off logging

Error (Errors Only)   Used to display only error log entries

Warning (Errors and Warnings)   Used to display only error and warning log entries

Information (Normal Logging)   Used to display information, error, and warning log entries

Verbose (Verbose)   Used to display information, error, warning, and verbose log entries

Trivia (Trivia)   Used to display information, error, warning, verbose, and trivia log entries

Changes made to the Logging Options section in the vCenter Server settings take effect as soon as you click OK. vCenter Server system services do not need to be restarted for this change to take effect.

The default logging level of Information would typically be used, unless there was a specific requirement to change the level of logging. Logging levels might be increased when working with VMware Support, for example.

Configuring vCenter Server logging options has now been covered; in the next section I will review how to create a log bundle in vCenter Server.

Creating a Log Bundle

Creating a log bundle for vCenter Server was covered in Chapter 10 in Exercise 10.1. As a review, Figure 11.10 shows the Export System Logs Wizard that was used in Exercise 10.1 to create the vCenter Server log bundle.

FIGURE 11.10   Creating a vCenter log bundle

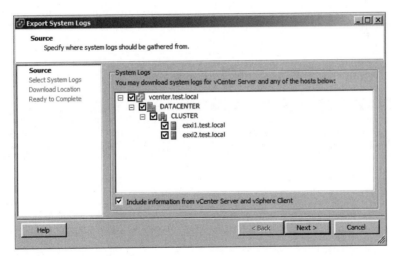

The log bundle can also be created regardless of the status of the vCenter Server services by selecting Start ➤ Programs ➤ VMware ➤ Generate vCenter Server Log Bundle.

Now that creating a log bundle has been reviewed, I will move on to working with the vCenter Server services.

Starting, Stopping, and Verifying vCenter Server Service Status

The vCenter Server service runs as a Windows service on the server it is installed on. The service is actually named VMware VirtualCenter Server, and it is configured to start automatically with the system by default. Exercise 11.3 will cover the steps to verify whether the VMware VirtualCenter Server service is running and stop and start the service.

EXERCISE 11.3

Verifying, Stopping, and Starting the VMware VirtualCenter Server Services Using the Windows Services Management Console

1. Connect to a console session on the Windows server that vCenter Server is installed on.

2. Open the vSphere Client and connect to vCenter Server.

3. Verify that no tasks are actively running. If there are, wait for them to complete. Leave the vSphere Client open.

4. In Windows, access the Run window or a command prompt. Type the following command in the Run window or command prompt:

   `services.msc`

5. The Services MMC snap-in will launch, as shown here.

6. Check the Status column beside the VMware VirtualCenter Server service. If it reports Started, then vCenter Server is running.

You have now confirmed that the VMware VirtualCenter Server service is running. This was actually a fairly safe bet, since you had just connected to it using the vSphere Client! In the next part of this exercise, you will manually stop the VMware VirtualCenter Server service.

7. In the Services MMC snap-in, select the VMware VirtualCenter Server service and then right-click it. Choose Stop from the context menu that appears.

8. A Stop Other Services dialog box will appear, similar to the one shown here.

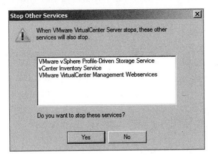

9. Note which services are going to be stopped, because they will need to be restarted. Click Yes to proceed.

10. Wait for the services to be stopped. Verify the Status column reports no value before continuing.

The VMware VirtualCenter Server services have now been stopped. In the next steps, you will see how this impacts vSphere Client connections and then restart the required services.

11. Return to the vSphere Client. You should see the error message shown here.

(continued)

EXERCISE 11.3 (continued)

12. In the Services MMC snap-in, select the VMware VirtualCenter Server service and right-click it. Choose Start from the context menu that appears.

13. Repeat this process for the VMware VirtualCenter Management Webservices service, the vCenter Inventory Service service, and the VMware vSphere Profile-Driven Storage Service service.

    Note that your list of services can vary. Refer to the specific services that were stopped in your environment in step 9 of this exercise. Depending on the number of services and their dependencies, it can sometimes be faster and easier to simply reboot Windows.

14. Return to the vSphere Client. Log in again, if prompted to do so.

The vCenter Service Status feature can also be used inside the vSphere Client connected to a vCenter Server to view vCenter Server service status information. Click the Home icon in the navigation bar and then select vCenter Service Status from the Administration options. Figure 11.11 shows the vCenter Service Status screen.

FIGURE 11.11 vCenter Service Status screen

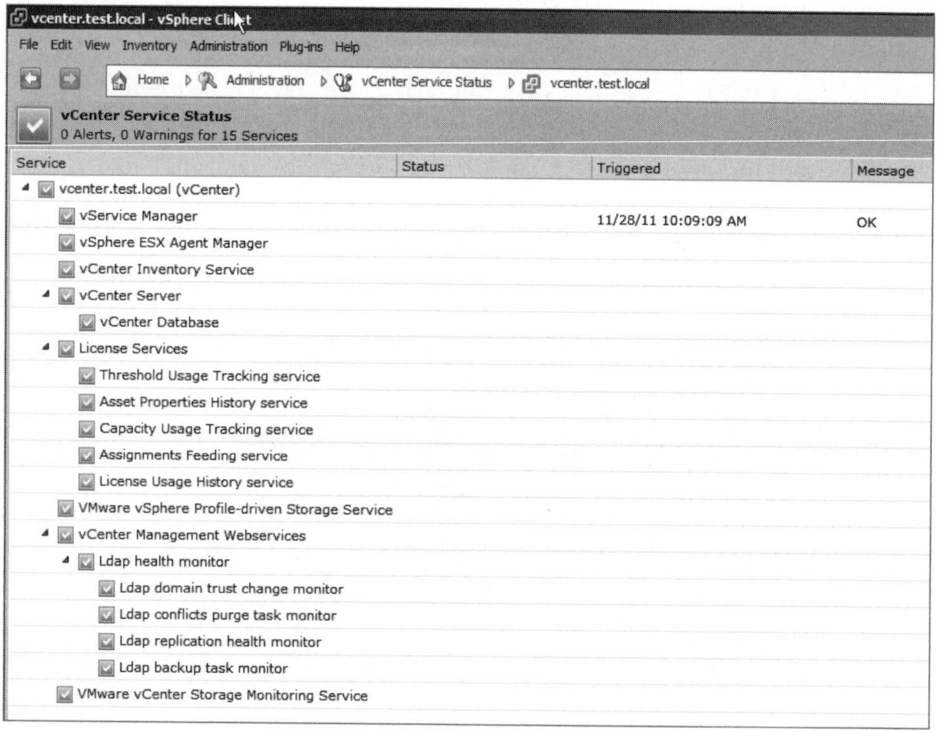

Now that verifying, stopping, and starting the vCenter Server Service has been covered, I will cover verifying, stopping, and starting the ESXi host agent status.

Starting, Stopping, and Verifying ESXi Host Agent Status

The ESXi *host agent* communicates to the vSphere Client, vCenter Server, and other vSphere interfaces through the vSphere API. The ESXi host agent runs as the hostd service in ESXi. It is installed as part of the default ESXi installation, and its architecture is shown in Figure 11.12.

FIGURE 11.12   ESXi host agent

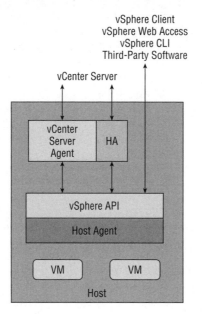

The steps to verify, stop, and start the ESXi host agent will be covered in Exercise 11.4. Make sure that no active tasks are running in vCenter Server before stopping the hostd service on an ESXi host.

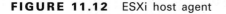

EXERCISE 11.4

Verifying, Stopping, and Starting the ESXi Host Agent

1. Connect to the console of an ESXi host.

2. Press the F2 key to log in to the DCUI.

3. Log in with the root account.

(continued)

4. Select the View System Logs option in the left pane.

5. Press the 4 key to view the Management Agent (hostd) log.

6. Press the G key to go to the end of the hostd log. The results should appear similar to what is shown here.

```
2011-11-29T14:33:07.165Z [33C81B90 verbose 'SoapAdapter'] Responded to service state request
2011-11-29T14:33:11.334Z [33FA5B90 verbose 'Cimsvc'] Ticket issued for CIMOM version 1.0, user root
2011-11-29T14:33:25.297Z [33C81B90 verbose 'Default'] Power policy is unset
2011-11-29T14:33:25.299Z [33A40B90 verbose 'Default'] Power policy is unset
2011-11-29T14:33:33.956Z [33D44B90 verbose 'SoapAdapter'] Responded to service state request
2011-11-29T14:33:37.167Z [33CC2B90 verbose 'SoapAdapter'] Responded to service state request
2011-11-29T14:33:55.294Z [33C81B90 verbose 'Default'] Power policy is unset
2011-11-29T14:33:55.296Z [FFBEAA90 verbose 'Default'] Power policy is unset
2011-11-29T14:34:03.958Z [3406EB90 verbose 'SoapAdapter'] Responded to service state request
2011-11-29T14:34:07.168Z [34019B90 verbose 'SoapAdapter'] Responded to service state request
2011-11-29T14:34:25.292Z [3406EB90 verbose 'Default'] Power policy is unset
2011-11-29T14:34:25.294Z [3406EB90 verbose 'Default'] Power policy is unset
<Q> Quit </> RegExp Search <H> Help
```

Pressing the G key will jump to the end of the file. Pressing it again will be similar to using the Tail command and will allow you to view the hostd log as it updates. If you are seeing current events here, then hostd is running. Remember that the times will be in UTC, so you will need to convert accordingly.

7. Press the Q key to exit the hostd log viewer.

You have now verified that the hostd log has entries. In the next part of this exercise, I will cover how to use the ESXi Shell to obtain the status for the hostd service.

8. While still in the DCUI, enable the ESXi Shell.

9. Press the Alt+F1 key combination on your keyboard and log in to the ESXi Shell using the root account.

10. Type the following command:

./etc/init.d/hostd status

The output should look like this.

```
~ # ./etc/init.d/hostd status
hostd is running.
~ # _
```

You have now verified that the hostd service is running. In the remainder of this exercise, the steps to stop and start the hostd service will be covered.

12. To stop the hostd service, type the following command:

./etc/init.d/hostd stop

13. To start the hostd service, type the following command:

`./etc/init.d/hostd start`

14. To restart the hostd service, type the following command:

`./etc/init.d/hostd restart`

15. To restart all management services, including hostd, ntpd, sfcbd, slpd, wsman, and vobd, use the following command:

`./sbin/services.sh restart`

Note that the management agents can also be restarted from the DCUI Troubleshooting Options menu item.

 For the procedure to handle hostd, if it ever becomes stuck, check the VMware KB article at http://kb.vmware.com/kb/1005566.

Now that I have covered verifying, stopping, and starting the ESXi host agent, I will cover how to monitor and administer vCenter Server connections.

Monitoring and Administering vCenter Server Connections

When using the vSphere Client connected to a vCenter Server, it is possible to view the current sessions of all users logged in to the system. To view the sessions, click the Home icon in the navigation bar of the vSphere Client and then choose Sessions from the Administration options. Figure 11.13 shows the session information for vCenter Server.

FIGURE 11.13   vCenter Server sessions

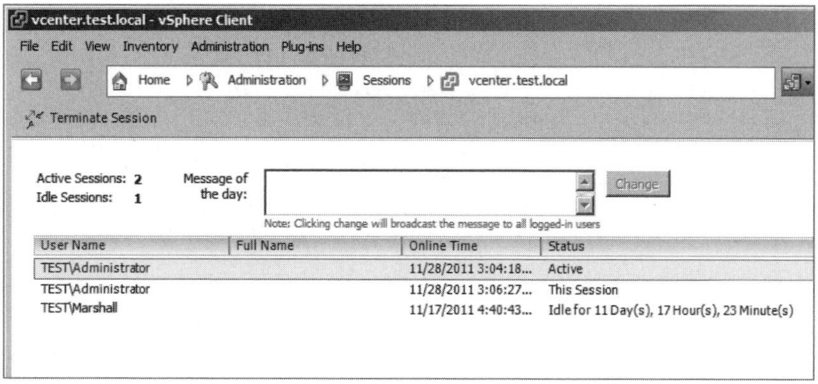

The Sessions pane shows the total count of active and idle sessions and lists the username, the user's full name, the online time, and the current status. Any idle or active session can be terminated by using the Terminate Session button located just beneath the navigation bar or by right-clicking the session and choosing Terminate from the context menu that appears. You will be prompted to confirm the session termination, as shown in Figure 11.14.

FIGURE 11.14   Session management

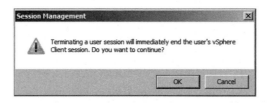

A message of the day can be sent to currently active session users of the vSphere Client. This message will also be sent to any newly logged in users of the vSphere Client. This is useful when you need to notify users of events such as upcoming maintenance windows. To configure the message of the day, simply enter the desired text in the Message Of The Day text box and click the Change button. Figure 11.15 shows the message of the day configuration and the dialog box that results from clicking the Change button.

FIGURE 11.15   Message Of The Day text box

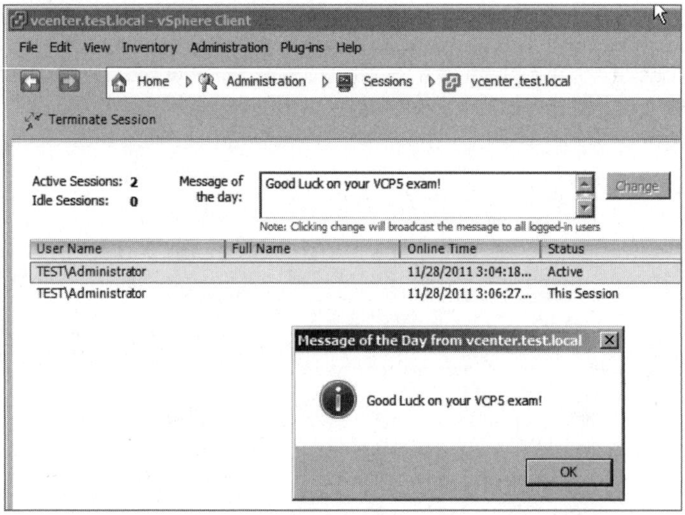

Now that vCenter Server connections have been covered, I will move on to configuring, viewing, printing, and exporting resource maps.

Configuring, Viewing, Printing, and Exporting Resource Maps

vCenter Server resource maps are used to display a visual representation of the relationships between virtual and physical resources. The following resource map views are available in vCenter Server:

- Virtual Machine Resources
- Host Resources
- Datastore Resources
- Custom
- vMotion

Chapter 10 covered vMotion resource maps, and one notable difference between the vMotion resource map and the other maps is that the vMotion resource map cannot be customized. Also note that the vMotion resource map is available only in the Hosts and Clusters or VMs and Templates view when the virtual machine is selected in the left pane and the Maps tab is selected in the right pane.

Configuring resource maps begins with checking the maximum number of objects the map will display. For very large vSphere environments, this can help control the usability of the resource maps. To set the maximum number of objects, use the vSphere Client menu and select the Edit ➢ Client Settings option. Select the Maps tab and change the value of Maximum Requested Topology Entities to the desired number. Figure 11.16 shows the default value of Maximum Requested Topology Entities for maps.

FIGURE 11.16   Max number of map objects

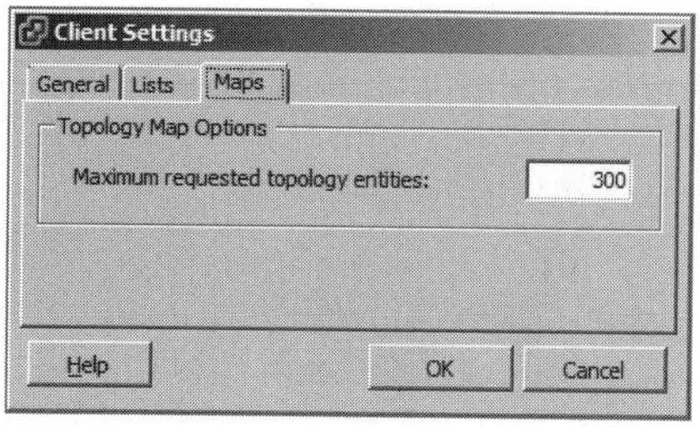

Once the maximum requested topology entities value has been configured, the resource maps are ready to be used. Exercise 11.5 covers the steps to configure, view, print, and export a resource map.

EXERCISE 11.5

Configuring, Viewing, Printing, and Exporting a Resource Map

1. Connect to a vCenter Server with the vSphere Client.

2. Click the Home icon in the navigation bar and choose Maps under the Management section.

3. The Virtual Machine Resources view will load by default, as shown here.

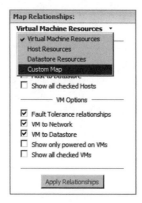

4. Using the Map Relationships panel, click the down arrow located to the right of Virtual Machine Resources to reveal the view options.

5. Select Custom Map from the menu that appears.

Note that even though there are check marks placed in several of the options in the Map Relationships panel, there are no objects placed on the map yet. This is because no object has been selected in the left pane.

6. Expand the inventory in the left pane to show all objects.

7. Select a single virtual machine in the left pane and note how the map updates immediately.

8. Click and drag any object in the map to reposition the map.

9. Right-click the virtual machine shown in the map. You should see the same context menu as shown here.

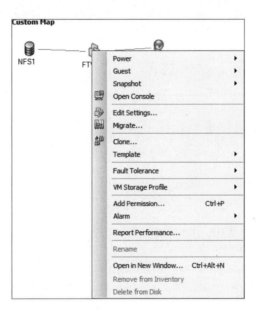

10. Press the Esc key to remove the context menu, and in the Map Relationships panel, deselect the VM To Network option.

11. Click the Apply Relationships button to apply this change.

12. Review the relationship.

13. In the Map Relationships panel, select the VM To Network option and deselect the VM To Datastore option.

14. Click the Apply Relationships button to apply this change.

15. Review the relationship.

16. Use the zoom controls in the Overview panel to zoom in and out on the map. Click the icon in the lower-right corner of the Overview panel to return to the default zoom level.

(continued)

EXERCISE 11.5 (continued)

17. Deselect the virtual machine in the left pane and choose a single ESXi host instead.

18. Select the listed Host Options in the Map Relationships panel.

19. Click the Apply Relationships button and review the results. The results should look similar to this.

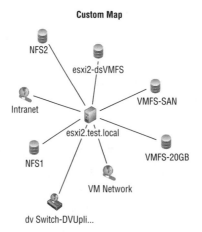

20. Print the map by using the File menu in the vSphere Client and choosing the Print Maps ➤ Print option.

21. Export the map by using the File menu in the vSphere Client and choosing the Export ➤ Export Maps option. You will be prompted to enter the location, name, and file type.

22. Click the Save As Type drop-down menu and review the different options available.

Now that configuring, viewing, printing, and exporting resource maps have been covered, I will explain the common metrics used in vSphere.

Explaining Common Memory Metrics

Memory metrics are used to track memory usage for different objects in the vSphere environment. The two most common tools used to monitor memory usage will be the vSphere Client and resxtop/esxtop. Table 11.1 details the common memory metrics used for ESXi hosts as they appear in resxtop and the vSphere Client.

TABLE 11.1 Common memory metrics for ESXi hosts

resxtop	Performance chart	Description
PMEM: total	Total Capacity	The total amount of memory installed in the ESXi host
PMEM: vmk	Memory: Used by VMkernel	The amount of memory being used by the VMkernel
PSHARE shared	Memory: Shared	The amount of physical memory that is being shared by virtual machines
SWAP curr	Memory: Swap used	The current swap file usage
ZIP zipped	Memory: Compressed	The total compressed physical memory
MEMCTL curr	Memory: Balloon	The total amount of physical memory reclaimed by ballooning

Virtual machines have their own unique set of metrics as well; Table 11.2 details these metrics.

TABLE 11.2 Common memory metrics for virtual machines

resxtop	Performance chart	Description
MEMSZ	N/A	The amount of physical memory allocated to the virtual machine
%ACTV	Memory: Usage	The percentage of guest physical memory being referenced by the guest
OVHD	Memory: Memory Overhead	The current amount of space used by the virtual machine overhead
SHRD	Memory: Shared	The amount of physical pages that are shared in memory
MEMCTLSZ	Memory: Balloon	The amount of physical memory reclaimed by way of ballooning
SWCUR	Memory: Swapped	The amount of memory being swapped out to disk on the ESXi host

(continued)

TABLE.11.2 Common memory metrics for virtual machines *(continued)*

resxtop	Performance chart	Description
SWR/s	Memory: Swap In Rate	The rate at which memory is being swapped in from disk on the ESXi host
SWW/s	Memory: Swap Out Rate	The rate at which memory is being swapped out to disk on the ESXi host
CACHEUSD	Memory: Compressed	The size of the used compression memory cache
ZIP/s	Memory: Zipped Memory	The compressed memory per second
UNZIP/s	Memory: Zipped Memory	The uncompressed memory per second

Now that the common memory metrics have been explained, the common CPU metrics will be explained.

Explaining Common CPU Metrics

CPU metrics are used to track CPU usage for different objects in the vSphere environment. The two most common tools used to monitor CPU usage will be the vSphere Client and resxtop/esxtop. Table 11.3 details the common CPU metrics used for ESXi hosts as they appear in resxtop and the vSphere Client.

TABLE 11.3 Common CPU metrics for ESXi Hosts

resxtop	Performance chart	Description
PCPU USED (%)	CPU: Usage	The percentage of CPU usage per PCPU and the percentage of CPU usage averaged over all PCPUs
PCPU UTIL (%)	CPU: Idle	The percentage of real time that the PCPU was not idle

Virtual machines have their own unique set of metrics as well; Table 11.4 details these metrics.

TABLE 11.4 Common CPU metrics for virtual machines

resxtop	Performance chart	Description
%USED	CPU: Used	The percentage of physical CPU core cycles used by the virtual machine
%RDY	CPU: Ready	The percentage of time the VM was not provided CPU resources but was ready to run
%SWPWT	CPU: Swap wait	The percentage of time spent waiting for the VMkernel to swap memory

The %SWPWT metric included in the CPU metrics will often also be used when monitoring memory.

Now that the common CPU metrics have been explained, the common network metrics will be explained.

Explaining Common Network Metrics

Network metrics are used to track network usage for different objects in the vSphere environment. The two most common tools used to monitor network usage will be the vSphere Client and resxtop/esxtop. Figure 11.17 shows the common network metrics used for both ESXi hosts and virtual machines as they appear in resxtop.

FIGURE 11.17 resxtop networking metrics

```
7:55:09pm up  1:00, 302 worlds, 1 VMs, 1 vCPUs: CPU load average: 0.03, 0.04, 0.04

    PORT-ID      USED-BY  TEAM-PNIC DNAME     PKTTX/s   MbTX/s   PKTRX/s   MbRX/s %DRPTX %DRPRX
    16777217  Management        n/a vSwitch0     0.00     0.00      0.00     0.00   0.00   0.00
    16777218      vmnic0          - vSwitch0     0.79     0.00      0.98     0.00   0.00   0.00
    16777219        vmk0    vmnic0 vSwitch0     0.79     0.00      1.18     0.00   0.00   0.00
    33554433  Management        n/a vSwitch1     0.00     0.00      0.00     0.00   0.00   0.00
    33554434      vmnic1          - vSwitch1     0.00     0.00      1.77     0.00   0.00   0.00
    50331649  Management        n/a vSwitch2     0.00     0.00      0.00     0.00   0.00   0.00
    50331650      vmnic5          - vSwitch2     0.20     0.00      0.20     0.00   0.00   0.00
    50331651        vmk1    vmnic5 vSwitch2     0.20     0.00      0.39     0.00   0.00   0.00
    67108865  Management        n/a vSwitch3     0.00     0.00      0.00     0.00   0.00   0.00
    67108866      vmnic2          - vSwitch3     0.00     0.00      1.77     0.00   0.00   0.00
    67108867        vmk2    vmnic2 vSwitch3     0.00     0.00      0.00     0.00   0.00   0.00
    83886081  Management        n/a vSwitch4     0.00     0.00      0.00     0.00   0.00   0.00
    83886082      vmnic3          - vSwitch4     0.00     0.00      1.77     0.00   0.00   0.00
    83886083    4138:VM1    vmnic3 vSwitch4     0.00     0.00      0.00     0.00   0.00   0.00
```

Table 11.5 details the common network metrics used for both ESXi hosts and virtual machines.

TABLE 11.5 Common network metrics

esxtop	Performance chart	Description
PKTTX/s	Network: Packets transmitted	The number of packets transmitted per second
PKTRX/s	Network: Packets received	The number of packets received per second
MbTX/s	Network: Data transmit rate	The number of megabits transmitted per second
MbRX/s	Network: Data receive rate	The number of megabits received per second
%DRPTX	Network: Transmit packets dropped	The percentage of transmit packets that were dropped
%DRPRX	Network: Receive packets dropped	The percentage of receive packets that were dropped

Now that the common network metrics have been explained, the common storage metrics will be explained.

Explaining Common Storage Metrics

Storage metrics are used to track storage contention, latencies, patterns, and more. The common storage metrics were discussed and used in Exercise 10.4 in Chapter 10, but they are also included here as a review. Table 11.6 lists the common storage metrics used in resxtop/esxtop and the vSphere Client.

TABLE 11.6 Common storage metrics

resxtop	Performance chart	Description
CMDS/s	Disk: Commands issued	The total number of I/O operations per second.
READS/s	Disk: Read requests	The number of read I/O commands issued per second.
WRITES/s	Disk: Write requests	The number of write I/O commands issued per second.

resxtop	Performance chart	Description
MBREAD/s	Disk: Read rate	The megabytes read per second.
MBWRTN/s	Disk: Write rate	The megabytes written per second.
DAVG/cmd	Disk: Physical device command latency	The average amount of time in milliseconds a device takes to service a single I/O request. The device includes the vmhba, the storage device, and any devices between.
KAVG/cmd	Disk: Kernel command latency	The average amount of time in milliseconds the VMkernel spends servicing I/O requests.
GAVG/cmd	Disk: Command latency	The total latency as seen from the virtual machine. This metric is the sum of DAVG and KAVG.
ABRTS/s	Disk: Commands terminated	The number of commands aborted per second.
RESETS/s	Disk: Bus resets	The number of commands reset per second.
LAT/rd	Datastore: Read latency	The average latency in milliseconds for a read I/O operation; this is a VM-specific metric.
LAT/wr	Datastore: Write latency	The average latency in milliseconds for a write I/O operation; this is a VM-specific metric.

Now that I have explained the common storage metrics, I will compare and contrast overview and advanced charts.

Comparing and Contrasting Overview and Advanced Charts

There are two different types of charts used in the vSphere Client when connected to vCenter Server. These charts are available in two different views on the Performance tab. Overview charts show the metrics that VMware considers the most useful for both monitoring performance and diagnosing problems. Overview charts consist of a predefined view that can be selected from a drop-down menu. The different views available depend on the object selected. Table 11.7 shows the object and associated views combinations.

TABLE 11.7   Object and views in overview charts

Object	Views available
Datacenter	Clusters, Storage
Datastore	Storage
Cluster	Home, Resource Pools & Virtual Machines, Hosts
Host	Home, Virtual Machines
Resource Pool	Home, Resource Pools & Virtual Machines
Virtual Machine	Home, Storage, Fault Tolerance

 All of these views cannot always be available. For example, if no virtual machines are protected with VMware FT, the Fault Tolerance view will be unavailable in the overview charts.

A key component of the overview charts is the thumbnail charts that are presented. These thumbnail charts are available for any child objects of the selected inventory object. Figure 11.18 shows the thumbnail charts available when an ESXi host object is selected.

FIGURE 11.18   VM thumbnail charts

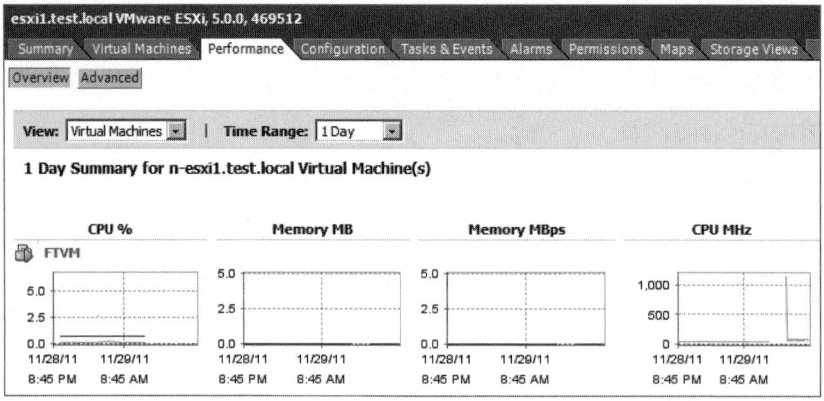

Another unique aspect of overview charts is that they are predefined, so no customization is possible, other than the time range that can be specified. Also note that the Datacenter object allows a Storage view that can show space utilization for the datastores in the datacenter. Figure 11.19 shows an overview chart with the datacenter object's Storage view.

FIGURE 11.19   Storage View in an overview chart

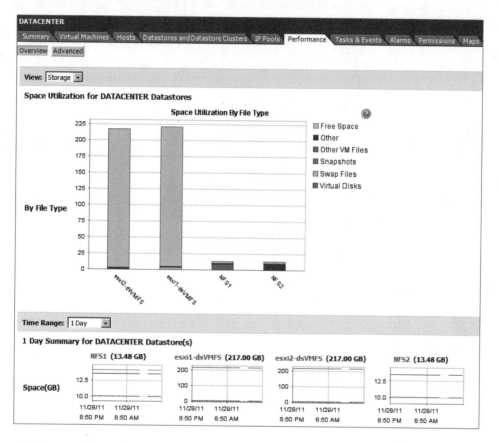

Where overview charts are predefined, advanced charts are extremely customizable and can allow very granular metrics to be obtained for datacenters, clusters, hosts, resource pools, and virtual machines. Advanced charts also offer the following:

- Additional details can be obtained in a chart by hovering the mouse over specific data points.

- Chart data can be exported.

- Chart data can be saved as an image.

- Separate windows can be opened to view performance data.

Figure 11.20 shows the additional detail available when hovering the mouse over a specific data point. The icons used to print, refresh, save/export, and open a new chart window are also seen in the upper-right corner.

FIGURE 11.20   Data point detail in advanced chart

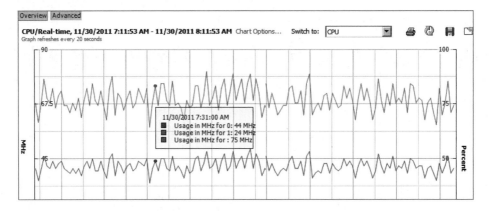

Advanced charts will be covered in much more detail in the next section, where the steps to create an advanced chart will be given.

Creating an Advanced Chart

Creating an advanced performance chart can be very useful when you need to obtain more granular or very specific information. The advanced charts allow you to do the following:

- Use multiple user-selected counters
- Define date/time ranges using the Custom chart option
- Select the chart type
- Select objects to use in the chart
- Save chart settings for future use

Figure 11.21 shows the Customize Performance Chart window, where an advanced chart is created.

To create an advanced chart that can be used again, you can also save a customized chart. Exercise 11.6 covers the steps to create an advanced performance chart.

FIGURE 11.21   Creating an advanced chart

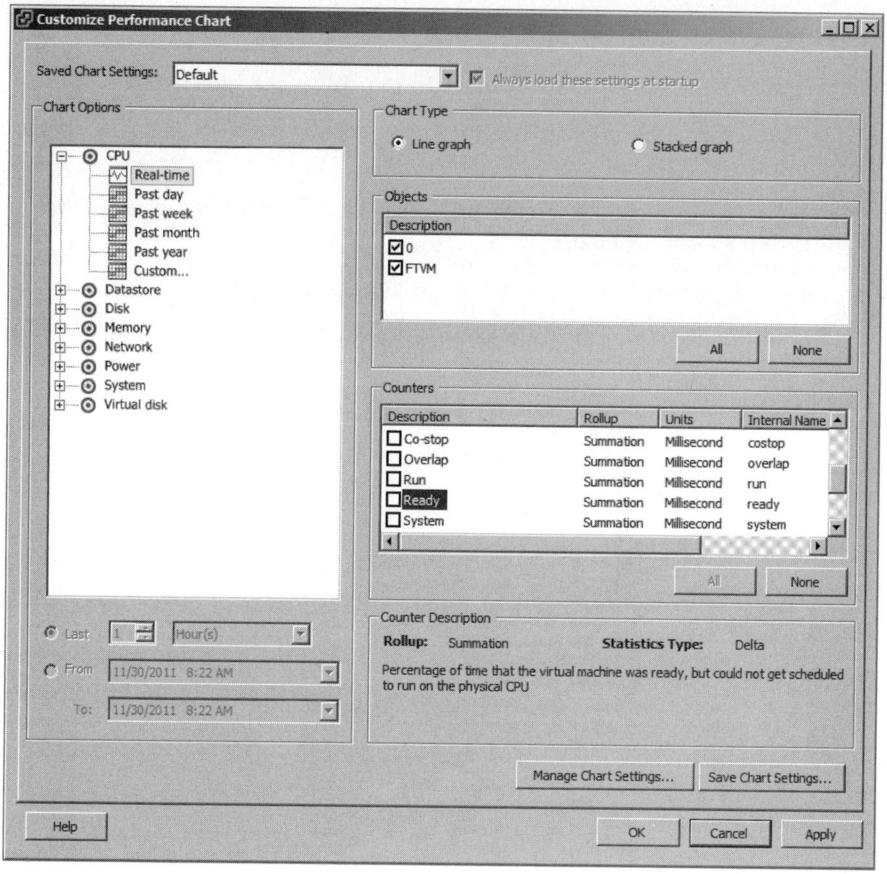

EXERCISE 11.6

Creating an Advanced Performance Chart

1. Connect to a vCenter Server with the vSphere Client.

2. Select the Hosts and Clusters view and select a virtual machine in the left pane.

(continued)

3. Click the Performance tab in the right pane.

4. Click the gray Advanced button to switch to the Advanced chart view.

5. Click the blue Chart Options link located in the center of the screen toward the top of the tab.

6. The Customize Performance Chart window will open. This is the window that was shown previously in Figure 11.21.

7. Expand the CPU object in the left pane and choose the Custom option.

8. At the bottom of the Chart Options, change the Last value to 3 Hours.

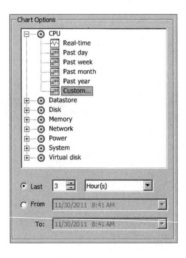

9. Accept the default Chart Type setting of Line Graph.

10. In the Objects panel, ensure that the virtual machine is selected.

11. Click to select the Usage counter and review the Counter Description information presented at the bottom of the window.

12. Select the Usage box.

13. Click the Ready counter and review the Counter Description information presented at the bottom of the window.

14. Select the Ready box.

15. The Counters panel should look exactly like what is shown here.

16. Click the Save Chart Settings button located toward the bottom of the screen.

17. When prompted, enter a name for the chart and then click OK.

18. Note that the value at the top of the screen for Saved Chart Settings updates to reflect the name just given to this chart.

19. Click the Apply button to save the changes.

20. Click OK and review the chart.

21. Click the Popup Chart icon located at the far right of the screen. Review the chart, and note that while in this view the Chart Options link is grayed out.

22. Close the pop-up chart.

23. Click the Refresh Chart icon to refresh the chart.

24. Click the Save Chart icon. When prompted, save the chart as either an image or an Excel spreadsheet.

Now that creating an advanced chart has been covered, critical performance metrics will be identified.

Identifying Critical Performance Metrics

While there are many common metrics used in vSphere, certain metrics are considered to be critical in monitoring the environment. These metrics also have thresholds associated with them, and several of the critical storage metrics were discussed in Chapter 10. The actual threshold values for many of these critical metrics will also be covered later in this chapter. Table 11.8 lists the critical performance metrics.

TABLE 11.8   Critical performance metrics

Esxtop	Performance chart	Description
SWAP curr	Memory: Swap used	The current swap file usage.
ZIP zipped	Memory: Compressed	The total compressed physical memory.
MEMCT curr	Memory: Balloon	The total amount of physical memory reclaimed by ballooning.
PCPU USED (%)	CPU: Usage	The percentage of CPU usage per PCPU and the percentage of CPU usage averaged over all PCPUs.
%RDY	CPU: Ready	The percentage of time the VM was not provided CPU resources but was ready to run.
%SWPWT	CPU: Swap wait	The percentage of time spent waiting for the VMkernel to swap memory.
%DRPTX	Network: Transmit packets dropped	The percentage of transmit packets that were dropped.
%DRPRX	Network: Receive packets dropped	The percentage of receive packets that were dropped.
CMDS/s	Disk: Commands issued	The total number of I/O operations per second.
DAVG/cmd	Disk: Physical device command latency	The average amount of time in milliseconds a device takes to service a single I/O request. The device includes the vmhba, the storage device, and any devices between.
KAVG/cmd	Disk: Kernel command latency	The average amount of time in milliseconds the VMkernel spends servicing I/O requests.
GAVG/cmd	Disk: Command latency	The total latency as seen from the virtual machine. This metric is the sum of DAVG and KAVG.
ABRTS/s	Disk: Commands terminated	The number of commands aborted per second.
RESETS/s	Disk: Bus resets	The number of commands reset per second.

These metrics are deemed critical because they can be used to discover resource exhaustion, contention, or error conditions. Now that the critical performance metrics have been identified, determining host performance using `resxtop` and guest Perfmon will be covered.

Determining Host Performance Using resxtop and Guest Perfmon

This chapter has covered using `esxtop`, `resxtop`, and the vSphere Client performance charts to monitor ESXi hosts. One additional option for monitoring the performance of an ESXi host is to use the Windows Perfmon utility to view exported `esxtop` or `resxtop` data.

Exercise 11.7 covers the steps to use Perfmon to view exported `resxtop` data. This exercise will require the use of the vMA or vCLI, and this exercise will assume that the vMA is used. This exercise will also use Perfmon on Windows 2008 R2 and make use of the free WinSCP utility. WinSCP can be downloaded from `http://winscp.net/`.

EXERCISE 11.7

Using resxtop Data and Perfmon to Monitor ESXi Host Performance

1. Connect to the console or SSH to the vMA.

2. Log in with the vi-admin account.

3. Type the following command:

   `resxtop --server <vCENTER FQDN> --vihost <ESXi HOST FQDN> --username <DOMAIN>\\<USERNAME> -b -d 2 -n 60 > resxtop-export.csv`

   Add the FQDN of your vCenter Server and one of your ESXi hosts in the previous command.

   Use a domain user account that has Administrator permissions on the vCenter Server to log in.

   Note that there are two backslashes (\\) between the domain and username. This command will create a file containing the resxtop data in it. The -b switch is used to indicate batch mode for resxtop. The -d switch is the delay between statistics snapshots, and the -n switch is used to specify the number of iterations. In the previous example, two minutes worth of data will be collected.

4. Wait for the previous command to complete.

5. When the command completes, enter the following command:

   `ls -l`

   (continued)

6. Verify that the export file exists and appears to be a valid size.

   The resxtop data has now been collected. The next step is to copy the data off the vMA and onto the Windows system that Perfmon will be used on.

7. On a Windows guest, open WinSCP and connect to the vMA using the vi-admin credentials. In the right pane, locate the resxtop data file.

8. Select a destination directory in the left pane and copy the resxtop export file from the vMA.

   The captured data file has now been copied to a Windows guest. In the remaining steps of this exercise, the steps to view this data with Perfmon will be covered.

9. In Windows, use the Run window or a command prompt and type the following command:

   Perfmon

10. When Performance Monitor opens, select Performance Monitor in the left pane.

11. Press the Ctrl+L key combination on your keyboard. The Performance Monitor Properties window will appear.

12. Click the Source tab and select the Log Files option for the Data Source. Click the Add button and locate the `resxtop` data file that was copied earlier in this exercise.

The completed configuration should look like this.

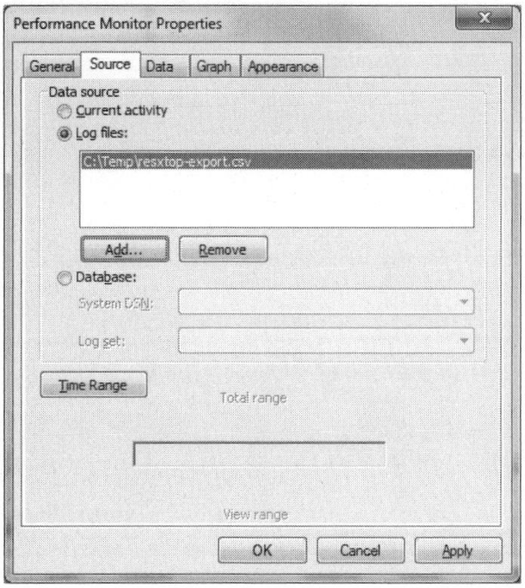

13. Click the Time Range button and verify that the time range is accurate.

14. Click the Data tab in the Performance Monitor Properties window.

15. If any Windows-specific counters are listed, remove them using the Remove button.

16. Click the Add button. The Add Counters window will appear.

17. Expand the Memory object in the left pane. Select the Free Mbytes counter and use the Add>> button at the bottom of the counter list to add this counter.

18. Expand the Physical CPU object in the left pane. Select the % Processor Time counter and use the Add>> button at the bottom of the counter list to add this counter.

The final configuration should appear similar to what is shown here.

(continued)

EXERCISE 11.7 *(continued)*

19. Click OK to close the Add Counters window.

20. Review the Counters listed in the Performance Monitor Properties window and click OK.

21. Use the Change Graph Type button in the toolbar to change to the graph type to Report.

22. Review the information listed in the Report chart. It should appear similar to what is shown here.

> This exercise captured an enormous amount of information from resxtop. When using this approach to monitor your ESXi hosts, it would likely make much more sense to configure resxtop to capture the data only for metrics you deem important.

Determining host performance using resxtop and Perfmon has now been covered. Identifying the affected vSphere resource, given performance data, will be the next topic.

Given Performance Data, Identifying the Affected vSphere Resource

As seen in the previous sections, certain metrics will immediately identify affected resources in the vSphere environment. Table 11.9 shows some common metrics and their threshold values that would indicate a likely problem.

TABLE 11.9   Common metrics and affected vSphere resource

resxtop	Performance chart	Threshold
%RDY	CPU: Ready	10
%SWPWT	CPU: Swap wait	5
MEMCTLSZ	Memory: Balloon	1
SWCUR	Memory: Swapped	1
SWR/s	Memory: Swap In Rate	1
SWW/s	Memory: Swap Out Rate	1
CACHEUSD	Memory: Compressed	0
ZIP/s	Memory: Zipped Memory	0
UNZIP/s	Memory: Zipped Memory	0
%DRPTX	Network: Transmit packets dropped	1

(continued)

TABLE 11.9 Common metrics and affected vSphere resource *(continued)*

resxtop	Performance chart	Threshold
%DRPRX	Network: Receive packets dropped	1
DAVG/cmd	Disk: Physical device command latency	25
KAVG/cmd	Disk: Kernel command latency	2
GAVG/cmd	Disk: Command latency	25
ABRTS/s	Disk: Commands terminated	1
RESETS/s	Disk: Bus resets	1

There is an excellent and constantly updated resource that details the thresholds for these and many other metrics available at www.yellow-bricks.com/esxtop/.

Now that identifying the affected vSphere resource when given the performance data has been covered, the first part of this chapter is complete. In the next part of this chapter, I will cover how to create and administer vCenter Server alarms.

Create and Administer vCenter Server Alarms

As a VMware Certified Professional, you will be expected to know how to create and administer vCenter Server alarms. vCenter Server alarms are user-configurable and allow the specification of the conditions required to trigger the alarm. vCenter Server alarms are shown in the vSphere Client when connected to a vCenter Server, and they can be configured to perform a variety of actions. These alarms can be quite useful for the virtual infrastructure administrator and allow the administrator to be more proactive in the administration of the vSphere environment. In this section, I will cover how to detail, create, and administer vCenter Server alarms.

Listing vCenter Default Utilization Alarms

Utilization alarms are used to notify the vSphere administrator of a capacity issue. The default utilization alarms in vCenter Server are as follows:

- Virtual machine CPU usage
- Virtual machine memory usage
- Datastore usage on disk
- License capacity monitoring
- Host service console swap rates
- Datastore cluster is out of space
- Thin-provisioned LUN capacity exceeded
- Host memory usage
- Host CPU usage

Now that the default utilization alarms have been listed, the default connectivity alarms will be listed.

Listing vCenter Default Connectivity Alarms

Connectivity alarms are used to notify the vSphere administrator of a connectivity issue. The default connectivity alarms in vCenter Server are as follows:

- Pre-4.1 host connected to SIOC-enabled datastore
- Cannot find vSphere HA master agent
- Network uplink redundancy degraded
- Network uplink redundancy lost
- Cannot connect to storage
- Host connection failure

Now that the default connectivity alarms have been listed, listing possible action for utilization and connectivity alarms will be covered.

Listing Possible Actions for Utilization and Connectivity Alarms

vCenter Server alarms have configurable actions. Each alarm has an Actions tab that can be used to specify the action to take if the alarm is triggered. These available actions vary, depending on the alarm type monitor configured. There are eight alarm-type monitor options, which are shown in Figure 11.22.

FIGURE 11.22 Alarm-type monitor options

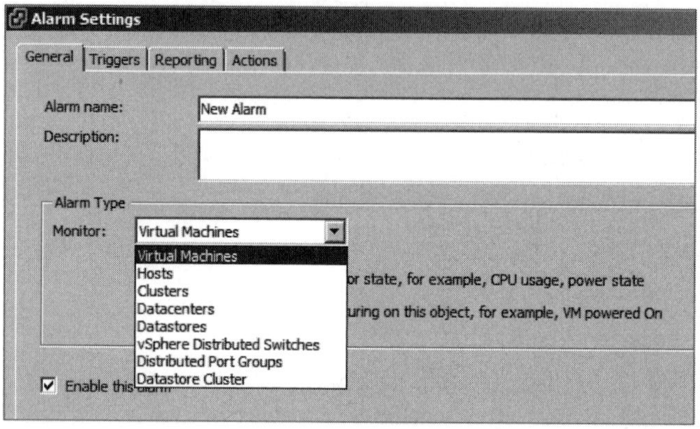

All eight of these alarm-type monitors have the following actions in common:

- Send a notification email
- Send a notification trap
- Run a command

The Host alarm-type monitor includes the following additional specific actions:

- Enter maintenance mode
- Exit maintenance mode
- Enter standby
- Exit standby
- Reboot host
- Shutdown host

The Virtual Machine alarm-type monitor includes the following additional specific actions:

- Power on VM
- Power off VM
- Suspend VM
- Reset VM
- Migrate VM
- Reboot guest on VM
- Shutdown guest on VM

Now that I have covered the default utilization and connectivity alarms and their possible actions, I will cover the steps required to create a vCenter Server utilization alarm.

Creating a vCenter Utilization Alarm

Creating a vCenter Server utilization alarm is a fairly simple process that can be used to provide impressive levels of detail and automation. Exercise 11.8 coves the steps to create a vCenter Server utilization alarm for a virtual machine.

EXERCISE 11.8

Monitoring Virtual Machine CPU and Memory Usage with a vCenter Server Utilization Alarm

1. Connect to vCenter Server using the vSphere Client.

2. Select the Host and Clusters view and select a virtual machine in the left pane.

3. Click the Alarms tab in the right pane.

4. Note that the default view is Triggered Alarms. Use the gray view toggle buttons at the top to switch to the Definitions view.

5. Review the definitions listed, and take note of the Defined In column. This column allows you to see which inventory object the alarm is defined on.

Name		Defined In	Description
	Timed out starting Secondary VM	vcenter.tes...	Default alarm to monitor time-outs ...
	No compatible host for Secondary VM	vcenter.tes...	Default alarm to monitor if no comp...
	Virtual Machine Fault Tolerance vLockStep interval Status Changed	vcenter.tes...	Default Alarm to monitor changes in...
	Virtual machine error	vcenter.tes...	Default alarm to monitor virtual mac...
	Migration error	vcenter.tes...	Default alarm to monitor if a virtual...
	Virtual machine Fault Tolerance state changed	vcenter.tes...	Default alarm to monitor changes in ...
	vSphere HA virtual machine failover failed	vcenter.tes...	Default alarm to alert when vSphere...
	vSphere HA virtual machine monitoring action	vcenter.tes...	Default alarm to alert when vSphere...
	vSphere HA virtual machine monitoring error	vcenter.tes...	Default alarm to alert when vSphere...
	Virtual machine cpu usage	vcenter.tes...	Default alarm to monitor virtual mac...
	Virtual machine memory usage	vcenter.tes...	Default alarm to monitor virtual mac...

FTVM — Summary | Resource Allocation | Performance | Tasks & Events | Alarms | Console | Permissions | Maps | Storage Views

View: Triggered Alarms | Definitions

6. Right-click in the whitespace of the Definitions view and choose New Alarm from the context menu that appears.

7. The Alarm Settings window will appear.

8. Give the alarm a unique and descriptive name and a description.

(continued)

9. Ensure that the drop-down menu for the Monitor option is set to Virtual Machine and that the Monitor For Specific Conditions Or State option is selected. Also ensure that the Enable This Alarm option is selected. The final configuration should look similar to this.

10. Click the Triggers tab.

11. Click the Add button located at the bottom of the window.

12. An entry will appear on the list of triggers. Click this entry under the Trigger Type column heading to access a drop-down menu.

13. Select the VM CPU Usage (%) option.

14. Ensure the Condition column value reports Is Above.

15. Click the entry below the Warning column and enter the value **50**.

16. Click the entry below the Alert column and enter the value **60**.

17. Click the Add button located at the bottom of the window.

18. An entry will appear at the bottom of the list of triggers. Click this entry under the Trigger Type column heading to access a drop-down menu.

19. Select the VM Memory Usage (%) option.

20. Ensure the Condition column value reports Is Above.

21. Click the entry below the Warning column and enter the value **50**.

22. Click the entry below the Alert column and enter the value **60**.

23. Ensure that the Trigger If All Of The Conditions Are Satisfied option is selected. The final configuration should look like this.

24. Click the Actions tab.

25. Click the Add button at the bottom of the window.

26. An entry will appear on the list of actions. Click this entry under the Action column heading to access a drop-down menu.

27. Select the Send A Notification Email option.

28. Click the entry below the Configuration column header and enter a valid email address to send the notification to.

29. Ensure that all other columns have the Once value selected.

The final configuration should look like this.

(continued)

EXERCISE 11.8 *(continued)*

Alarm Settings   ☒

General | Triggers | Reporting | **Actions** |

Specify the actions to take when a type of alarm changes.
Select whether the action should be repeated.
Specify how often actions should be repeated.

Action	Configuration	✓→⚠	⚠→◆	◆→⚠	⚠→✓
Send a notification email	admin@test.local	Once	Once	Once	Once

                                                                        Add   Remove

Frequency
Repeat actions every:

5 ⇕ minutes

Actions will repeat until the alarm type changes.

                                                        OK   Cancel   Help

30. Click OK to save this alarm.

31. Review the list of alarms and verify that the new alarm is listed. Note its value in the Defined In column.

Creating the alarm at the virtual machine inventory object level makes it specific to the virtual machine. Keep in mind the most appropriate inventory object level for alarms when they are created.

The previous exercise created a utilization alarm that monitored both CPU and memory for its trigger. CPU or memory utilization alone would not be capable of triggering this alarm. In your test environments, you could experiment with some of the other alarm actions like Run A Command or Reboot Guest On VM on the alarm. These actions can make utilization alarms a very powerful tool for managing your vSphere environment.

🌐 **Real World Scenario**

Monitoring and Taking Action on Snapshots

A virtual infrastructure administrator has been asked to put a virtual machine in snapshot mode; the virtual machine is running a large database used for testing. She is reluctant to perform this task, because she knows that the snapshot will grow very large. She decides to use a vCenter Server alarm to monitor this snapshot.

She creates an alarm at the virtual machine object level so that it will apply only to this specific VM. She configures the alarm using the VM Snapshot Size (GB) trigger type. She configures the warning value for 100 and the alert value for 150. She adds an action of Send A Notification Email and configures it to send her an email on the normal-to-warning transition and the warning-to-alert transition.

She places the virtual machine in snapshot mode. The next day, she receives an email stating that the snapshot has reached the warning threshold. She contacts the owner of the test server and reports what she is seeing. The application owner verifies that the testing has failed and requests that the virtual machine be reverted and the snapshot deleted.

Using vCenter Server alarms allowed the virtual infrastructure administrator to keep track of the virtual machine's snapshot size without having to manually check it periodically.

I have now covered creating a vCenter Server utilization alarm. In the next section, I will cover how to create a vCenter Server connectivity alarm.

Creating a vCenter Connectivity Alarm

Similar to creating a utilization alarm, creating a vCenter Server connectivity alarm is also a fairly simple process that can be used to provide impressive levels of detail and automation. Exercise 11.9 covers the steps to create a vCenter Server connectivity alarm for a virtual machine.

EXERCISE 11.9

Monitoring Datastore Connectivity with a vCenter Server Connectivity Alarm

1. Connect to vCenter Server using the vSphere Client.

2. Select the Host and Clusters view and select the root vCenter Server object in the left pane.

3. Click the Alarms tab in the right pane.

4. Note that the default view is Triggered Alarms. Use the gray view toggle buttons at the top to switch to the Definitions view.

5. Select the File menu in the vSphere Client and choose New ➢ Alarm from the context menu that appears.

6. The Alarm Settings window will appear.

7. Give the alarm a unique and descriptive name and a description.

(continued)

8. Ensure that the drop-down menu for the Monitor option is set to Datastore and that the Monitor For Specific Conditions Or State option is selected. Also ensure that the Enable This Alarm option is selected. The final configuration should look like this.

9. Click the Triggers tab.

10. Click the Add button located at the bottom of the window.

11. An entry will appear on the list of triggers. Click this entry under the Trigger Type column heading to access a drop-down menu.

12. Select the Datastore State To All Hosts option.

13. Ensure the Condition column value reports Is Equal To.

14. Click the entry below the Warning column and choose the value None from the drop-down menu.

    None is chosen in this case since a datastore disconnected from all hosts would be an alert condition only.

15. Click the entry below the Alert column and choose the value Disconnected from the drop-down menu.

16. Ensure that the Trigger If Any Of The Conditions Are Satisfied option is selected. The final configuration should look like this.

17. Click the Actions tab.

18. Click the Add button at the bottom of the window.

19. An entry will appear on the list of actions. Click this entry under the Action column heading to access a drop-down menu.

20. Select the Send A Notification Email option.

21. Click the entry below the Configuration column header and enter a valid email address to send the notification to.

22. Ensure that only the Warning To Alert column has the Once value selected.

The final configuration should look like this.

(continued)

EXERCISE 11.9 *(continued)*

23. Click OK to save this alarm.

24. Review the list of alarms and verify that the new alarm is listed. Note its value in the Defined In column.

The previous exercise created a connectivity alarm that monitored datastore connectivity to all hosts. In your test environments, you could experiment with some of the other connectivity alarms and the alarm actions to get a better understanding of the events that vCenter Server alarms can monitor and respond to.

You have now created a vCenter Server connectivity alarm. In the next section, I will review configuring vCenter Server alarm triggers.

Configuring Alarm Triggers

vCenter Server alarms consist of three parts:

- Type
- Trigger
- Action

Triggers were specifically covered in the previous two exercises, and it is important to remember that multiple trigger types can be defined in a single alarm. The trigger types can each act individually or as a group. Keep in mind that when using the Trigger If All Of The Conditions Are Satisfied option, the more trigger types that are added, the more complex the alarm becomes. Figure 11.23 shows a virtual machine–type alarm with multiple triggers defined.

FIGURE 11.23   Multiple triggers in alarm

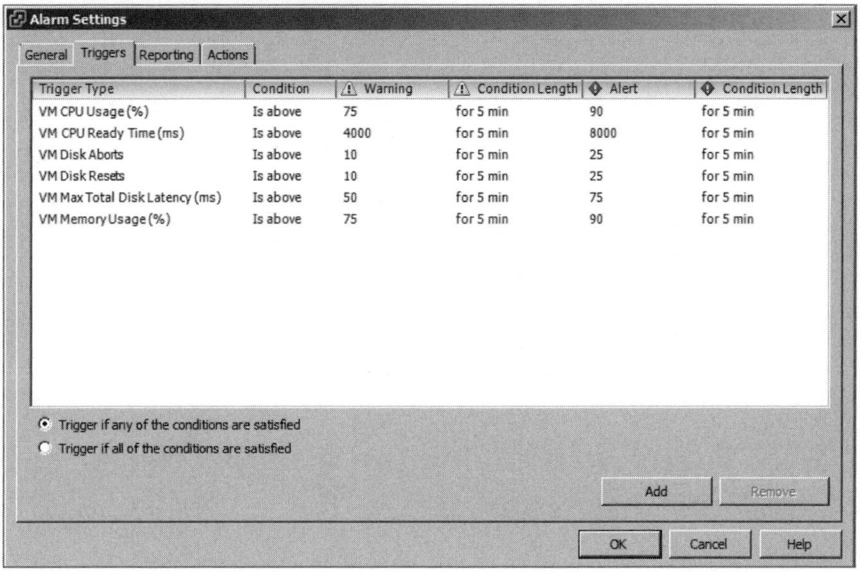

Trigger Type	Condition	⚠ Warning	⚠ Condition Length	◆ Alert	◆ Condition Length
VM CPU Usage (%)	Is above	75	for 5 min	90	for 5 min
VM CPU Ready Time (ms)	Is above	4000	for 5 min	8000	for 5 min
VM Disk Aborts	Is above	10	for 5 min	25	for 5 min
VM Disk Resets	Is above	10	for 5 min	25	for 5 min
VM Max Total Disk Latency (ms)	Is above	50	for 5 min	75	for 5 min
VM Memory Usage (%)	Is above	75	for 5 min	90	for 5 min

Alarm Settings — General | Triggers | Reporting | Actions

⦿ Trigger if any of the conditions are satisfied
○ Trigger if all of the conditions are satisfied

Add   Remove

OK   Cancel   Help

> The VM Total Size On Disk and VM Snapshot Size triggers cannot be used in combination with any other triggers.

Now that configuring alarm triggers has been reviewed, I will review configuring alarm actions.

Configuring Alarm Actions

The key thing to remember with vCenter Server alarm actions is that multiple actions can be defined on each alarm. These actions can correlate to any of the four condition changes, which are represented in the four columns on the Actions tab. Figure 11.24 shows a virtual machine type alarm with multiple actions defined.

Configuring alarm actions has now been reviewed. In the next section, I will identify the affected resource in a given vSphere implementation for a given alarm.

FIGURE 11.24   Multiple actions in alarm

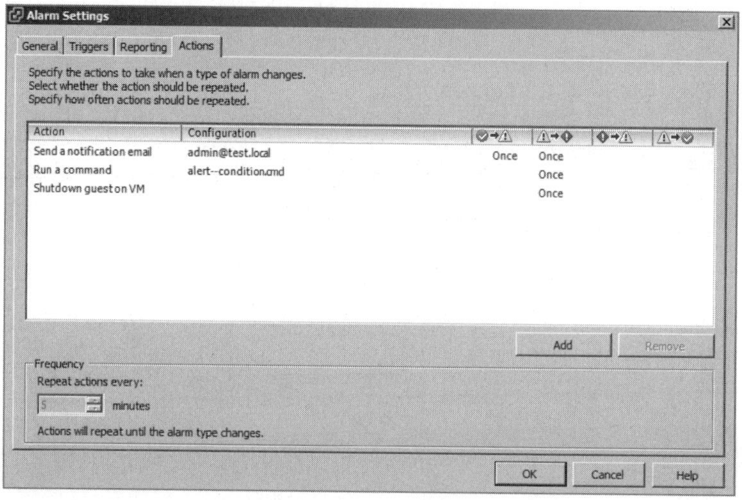

For a Given Alarm, Identifying the Affected Resource in a vSphere Implementation

For most vCenter Server alarms, the Name column will provide sufficient detail to identify the affected resource. Figure 11.25 shows vCenter Server–triggered alarms in the alert state.

FIGURE 11.25   vCenter Server alarms for power

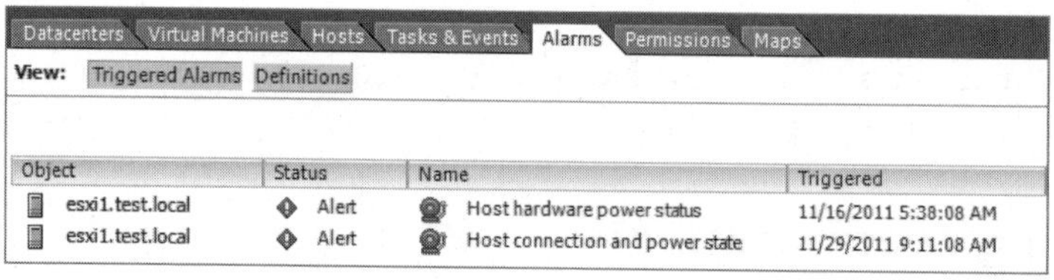

The first entry is for an ESXi host that was running on a single power supply. The second entry is for this same host when the power feed was interrupted to the host. Both of these alerts provide adequate detail in the Name column to identify the affected resource.

Figure 11.26 shows another vCenter Server alarm scenario.

FIGURE 11.26   vCenter Server alarms for vSphere HA

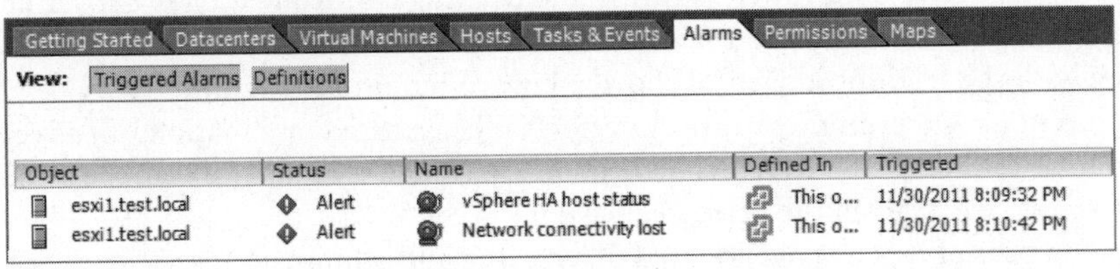

Object	Status	Name	Defined In	Triggered
esxi1.test.local	◆ Alert	vSphere HA host status	This o...	11/30/2011 8:09:32 PM
esxi1.test.local	◆ Alert	Network connectivity lost	This o...	11/30/2011 8:10:42 PM

For this set of alerts, the management network was disconnected for the ESXi host. The first alert about vSphere HA host status is not quite immediately obvious, but network connectivity should almost always be first suspected in HA alerts. The second alert is obvious as to the affected resource.

Figure 11.27 shows one final set of vCenter Server alarms.

FIGURE 11.27   vCenter Server custom alarms

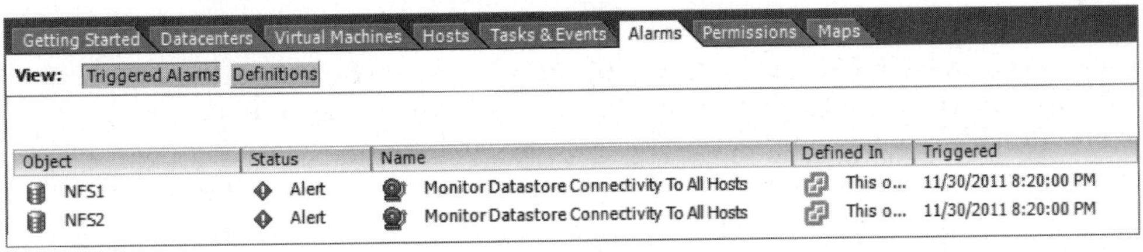

Object	Status	Name	Defined In	Triggered
NFS1	◆ Alert	Monitor Datastore Connectivity To All Hosts	This o...	11/30/2011 8:20:00 PM
NFS2	◆ Alert	Monitor Datastore Connectivity To All Hosts	This o...	11/30/2011 8:20:00 PM

In this alarm, an NFS server used as a datastore on multiple ESXi hosts was disconnected from the network. Again, the information provided in the Name column is sufficient to identify the affected resource.

This last alarm is not a default vCenter Server alarm but rather the alarm that was created in Exercise 11.9 of this chapter.

I have now covered identifying the affected resource in a vSphere implementation for a given alarm. This concludes this chapter and my coverage of the VCP5 exam objectives.

Summary

The first part of this chapter focused on monitoring ESXi hosts, vCenter Server, and virtual machines. This chapter began by describing how tasks and events are viewed in vCenter Server. Critical performance metrics were identified. Common memory, CPU, network, and storage metrics were covered. I compared and contrasted overview and advanced charts, as well as covered the process to create an advanced chart. vCenter Server settings were configured for SNMP, Active Directory, SMTP, logging, and timeouts. I covered creating a log bundle. I also covered creating, editing, and deleting a scheduled task. I cover how to configure, view, print, and export resource maps. The vCenter Server services were covered, along with the ESXi host agent. I showed how to monitor and administer vCenter Server connections. Determining the host performance using a combination of `resxtop` and Windows Perfmon was covered. This section concluded with identifying the affected vSphere resource when given the performance data.

The second part of this chapter focused on creating and administering vCenter Server alarms. The vCenter Server default utilization and connectivity alarms were covered, along with their possible actions. I created a vCenter Server utilization and connectivity alarm and configured alarm triggers and alarm actions. This chapter concluded with identifying the affected resource in a vSphere implementation when given an alarm.

Exam Essentials

Know how to monitor ESXi, vCenter Server, and VMs.   Be able to describe how tasks and events are viewed in vCenter Server. Be able to identify critical performance metrics. Be able to explain common memory, CPU, network, and storage metrics. Know the difference between an overview and an advanced chart and how to create an advanced chart. Know how to configure SNMP, Active Directory, SMTP, logging, and timeout settings for vCenter Server. Understand how to create a log bundle. Be able to create, edit, and delete a scheduled task. Know how to configure, view, print, and export resource maps. Understand how to start, stop, and verify vCenter Server services and how to start, stop, and verify the ESXi host agents. Be able to monitor and administer vCenter Server connections. Understand how to use `resxtop` and Windows Perfmon to determine host performance. Be able to identify the affected vSphere resource when given performance data.

Know how to create and administer vCenter Server alarms.   Be able to list vCenter Server default utilization and connectivity alarms. Be able to list the possible actions for utilization and connectivity alarms. Know how to create a vCenter utilization alarm and connectivity alarm. Understand how to configure alarm triggers and alarm actions. Be able to identify the affected resource in a vSphere implementation for a given alarm.

Review Questions

1. Which of the following can be used to restart the ESXi host agent? (Choose all that apply.)

   A. DCUI

   B. ESXi Shell

   C. vSphere Client

   D. All of these

2. You need to restart the vCenter Server services as part of a routine maintenance window. You have multiple virtual infrastructure administrators connected to vCenter Server at any given time. What is the best way to immediately notify these users of the maintenance?

   A. Select all users in the Sessions pane and right-click. Use the Send Message option on the context menu.

   B. Use Message Of The Day in the Sessions pane.

   C. Use the Notify Users option in the Sessions pane.

   D. Use the System Messages option in the Sessions pane.

3. When viewing the Tasks & Events tab, you notice that there are a limited number of entries and the information available does not go back far enough. What setting could be used to adjust the number of entries?

   A. This is not possible.

   B. Edit menu ➢ Client Settings ➢ Lists tab.

   C. Filtering.

   D. vCenter Server Settings ➢ Administration ➢ Statistics.

4. Which of the following is defined as the percentage of time a VM was not provided CPU resources but was ready to run?

   A. %SYS

   B. %WAIT

   C. %USED

   D. %RDY

5. You need to collect resxtop data for two minutes. This data will be used in Perfmon on a Windows guest. Which of the following commands should be used?

   A.
   ```
   resxtop --server <vCENTER FQDN>
   --vihost <ESXi HOST FQDN>
   --username <DOMAIN>\\<USERNAME>
   -b -d 3 -n 120 > resxtop-export.csv
   ```

   B.
   ```
   resxtop --server <vCENTER FQDN>
   --vihost <ESXi HOST FQDN>
   --username <DOMAIN>\\<USERNAME>
   -b -d 120 -n 1 > resxtop-export.csv
   ```

C. `resxtop --server <vCENTER FQDN>`
    `--vihost <ESXi HOST FQDN>`
    `--username <DOMAIN>\\<USERNAME>`
    `-b -d 2 -n 60 > resxtop-export.csv`

D. `resxtop --server <vCENTER FQDN>`
    `--vihost <ESXi HOST FQDN>`

    `--username <DOMAIN>\\<USERNAME>`
    `-b -d 1 -n 120 > resxtop-export.csv`

6. You created a vCenter Server alarm at the root vCenter Server level to monitor a single virtual machine for the snapshot space used. You are now getting warnings from multiple VMs. What is the best way to solve this problem?

A. Re-create the rule at the virtual machine object level.

B. Exclude the virtual machines you don't want to see from the rule.

C. Move the rule to the host level.

D. None of these.

7. How many SNMP receivers can be configured in vCenter Server?

A. 1

B. 2

C. 3

D. 4

8. You collect metrics for your vSphere environment. You see %DRPRX has a value of 1. Which of the following is most likely the problem?

A. CPU.

B. Network.

C. Disk.

D. There is no problem.

9. Which of the following is defined as the average amount of time in milliseconds a device takes to service a single I/O request?

A. DAVG/cmd

B. GAVG/cmd

C. KAVG/cmd

D. None of these

10. When adding permissions to objects in vCenter Server, you notice that many domain accounts are not available. Your Active Directory domain is small and contains only 250 users. What setting could you change to best attempt to correct this?

A. Adjust the Active Directory settings and disable the Enable Query Limit.

B. Adjust the Active Directory settings and disable the Enable Validation option.

C. Increase the Active Directory Timeout value.

D. None of these.

11. You notice an alarm on your vCenter Server that states vSphere HA Host Status. What is the most likely cause of this alarm?

    A. Host hardware power supply failure

    B. Host hardware NIC failure

    C. Host hardware memory failure

    D. Host hardware Fibre Channel HBA failure

12. When monitoring your vSphere environment, you notice that the VMware FT view is not available in the overview charts. What is the most likely reason for this?

    A. There is no VMware FT view.

    B. The advanced charts have the VMware FT views.

    C. This view is contained in the cluster view.

    D. No VMs are protected with FT.

13. Which of the following can be scheduled using the scheduled tasks feature in vCenter Server? (Choose all that apply.)

    A. Cloning a VM

    B. Migrating a VM

    C. Adding a host

    D. Deleting a VM

14. You created a vCenter Server alarm with multiple trigger types and an action to send email. One of the triggers should have fired by now, but you have not received any emails. You are receiving emails from other alarms. Which of the following is most likely the reason why?

    A. The Trigger If All Of The Conditions Are Satisfied option was used.

    B. The Trigger If Any Of The Conditions Are Satisfied option was used.

    C. SMTP is not configured in the vCenter Server settings.

    D. Alarms cannot have multiple trigger types.

15. Which of the following are required to configure SMTP in the vCenter Server settings? (Choose two.)

    A. IP address of SMTP server

    B. Port number of SMTP server

    C. SMTP server authentication information

    D. Sender account

16. Which of the following make up an alarm? (Choose all that apply.)

    A. Type

    B. Trigger

    C. Action

    D. Condition

17. Which of the following actions do all of the alarm-type monitors have in common? (Choose all that apply.)

    A. Send a notification email

    B. Send a notification trap

    C. Run a command

    D. Enter maintenance mode

18. You need to view all events for a recent HA problem. What is the lowest-level inventory object that would be considered the best starting point?

    A. Virtual machine

    B. ESXi host

    C. Cluster

    D. vCenter Server root object

19. Which of the following metrics are used to monitor current SWAP file usage? (Choose two.)

    A. Memory: Swap Used

    B. SWAP curr

    C. SZTGT

    D. CACHEUSD

20. Which vCenter Server logging level will include information, error, warning, and verbose log entries?

    A. Warning

    B. Information

    C. Verbose

    D. Trivia

Appendix

A

Answers to Review Questions

Chapter 2: Plan, Install, Configure, and Upgrade vCenter Server and VMware ESXi

1. C, D. The version of VMware Tools that is included with vSphere 5 is supported on both vSphere 4.*x* and vSphere 5 virtual machines.

2. A. The bundled Microsoft SQL Server 2008 R2 Express edition database can be used with up to 5 VMware ESX hosts and 50 virtual machines in the inventory.

3. D. During the install, you can leave this password blank. Obviously, this is not a recommended practice.

4. C. ESX/ESXi 3.5 hosts will require the use of the legacy license server, which may be downloaded as a separate component from the VMware website.

5. A, B. vCenter Server 5 requires two vCPUs or one dual-core vCPU to be a supported configuration.

6. C. You can upgrade a dvSwitch to version 5.0.0 only if all of the ESXi hosts are also running ESXi 5.

7. A, B, C. ESXi 5 can create, edit, and run virtual machine hardware versions 8 and 7. ESXi 5 can edit and run virtual machine hardware version 4.

8. A. vCenter Server is always upgraded first. The vSphere Client would be next, because the latest version would be required to manage the vCenter Server 5 instance.

9. B, C. ESXi 5 hosts can PXE boot and receive an IP address from a DHCP server. Then the Auto Deploy server will stream the ESXi image into the host's memory.

10. B. ESXi 5 requires a minimum of two processor cores.

11. C. The vSphere Client can be used to apply license keys to ESXi hosts.

12. B. Mem.MemZipEnable is used to enable/disable the memory compression cache. By default the setting is 1, or enabled.

13. A, D. DNS and routing can be configured using either vSphere Client or the DCUI.

14. C. The vSphere Web Client is a web application that can be used on Linux, and it is particularly well-suited for virtual machine administrators.

15. A, B, C, D. These are the four available vCenter Server Support Tools that can be installed from the VMware vCenter Installer.

16. B, D. VMware vCenter Server Standard is used in the vSphere 5 Standard, Enterprise, and Enterprise Plus kits.

17. A. The vCenter Server Appliance requires a minimum of 7GB of disk space and a maximum of 80GB.

18. A, C. A virtual machine must be powered off to upgrade the virtual hardware, and a virtual machine that is already using the latest version of the virtual hardware would be ineligible for an upgrade to the latest version.

19. B. An existing ESX/ESXi host must have a static IP address if it is going to be updated by Update Manager.

20. D. Update Manager, interactive, and scripted upgrades are the supported upgrade methods when upgrading ESX/ESXi 4.*x* versions to ESXi 5.

Chapter 3: Secure vCenter Server and ESXi and Identify vSphere Architecture and Solutions

1. B. There are three default system roles: Administrator, Read-Only, and No Access.

2. C. A privilege defines individual user rights.

3. C. A role is a collection of privileges.

4. B. A permission is created by pairing a role with a user or group and associating it with an object in the vCenter Server inventory.

5. A, D. Any permission defined on a child object will override permissions propagated from parent objects, and virtual machines do inherit multiple permissions.

6. B. The ESXi firewall is enabled by default and also blocks all traffic by default, except for default management services traffic.

7. A. Start Automatically If Any Ports Are Open, And Stop When All Ports Are Closed is the VMware-recommended setting.

8. C. All operations performed against an ESXi host in lockdown mode must originate from the vCenter Server that is managing the ESXi host. The exceptions are the ESXi Shell, SSH, or the Direct Console User Interface (DCUI), if these services are enabled on the ESXi host in lockdown mode.

9. B, C. MAC Address Changes and Forge Transmits are set to Accept by default, and Promiscuous Mode is set to Reject by default.

10. B. The list of local ESXi users and groups is accessible from the vSphere Client connected directly to the ESXi host. vCenter Server has no ability to view these local ESXi accounts.

11. C. Active Directory security groups are the preferred method for managing permissions in vCenter Server.

12. D. The default system roles of No Access, Read-Only, and Administrator cannot be edited or removed. The Administrator and Read-Only roles can be cloned; however, the No Access role cannot be cloned.

13. D. There must be a group in Active Directory with the name ESX Admins, and the Active Directory user accounts that should have access to the ESXi host(s) will be placed in this group.

14. A, B, C, D. Permission changes via host profiles require vSphere 4.0 or newer hosts to be configured to use Active Directory. The Enterprise Plus edition of vSphere is required from a licensing perspective, and the use of vCenter Server is also required.

15. A, C. The Virtual Machine.State.Create Snapshots privilege and the Datastore.Allocate privilege are both required to take a snapshot of a virtual machine.

16. B, D. Storage I/O Control and Storage DRS are both included only in the Enterprise Plus Edition of vSphere 5.

17. A, B, C, D. All four of these features are available only in Enterprise or higher editions of vSphere 5.

18. A, C, D. The vSphere architecture is composed of three distinct layers: the virtualization layer, the management layer, and the interface layer.

19. A. You are running a private cloud, if vSphere is running in your datacenter, is running on your hardware, and is providing services to your internal customers.

20. A. The Enterprise Plus edition of vSphere would be required in this case, because the customer could use the Auto Deploy feature to achieve the diskless and stateless ESXi hosts.

Chapter 4: Plan and Configure vSphere Networking

1. C. CDP information can be obtained for peer devices connected to the network adapters on vNetwork standard switches by clicking the information icon beside the vSwitch.

2. A, D. The two connection types available when creating a vSwitch are virtual machine and VMkernel. Connection types are also known as port groups.

3. A, B, C, D. All of these are common policies in both the vSwitch and the dvSwitch.

4. B, C. Virtual Switch Tagging (VST) and Virtual Guest Tagging (VGT) each require the use of trunked VLANs.

5. A, B, C, D. Any vSphere environment can make use of a vSwitch.

6. B. The Route Based On Physical NIC Load policy is available only in the dvSwitch.

7. A. Adding and removing NICs from a vSwitch with a virtual machine port group is a non-disruptive action, as long as there remains at least one active NIC.

8. D. The dvSwitch version 5.0.0 provides Network I/O Control, NetFlow, and port mirroring.

9. A, C. Add Now and Add Later are the two options presented in the wizard.

10. B. VLAN trunking allows a range of trunked VLANs to be entered, which requires only a single dvPort group in the dvSwitch.

11. A. The virtual machine will need a virtual machine port group to connect to this network, since only the ESXi host can use the VMkernel port group. The best practice would be to remove this virtual machine port group, once it is no longer in use, to limit potential access to this isolated network.

12. A, D. Route Based On IP Hash requires etherchannel, and standby adapters/uplinks should not be configured when using the Route Based On IP Hash load-balancing policy.

13. C, D. To utilize TSO in a virtual machine, either the VMXNET 2 or VMXNET 3 network adapter is required. The VMware Tools are also required to load the drivers in the guest OS, but the VMware Tools alone will not allow the VM to use TSO.

14. A, C, D. The VMkernel can be used for host-based connections such as vMotion, iSCSI, and Management traffic.

15. D. Use of the dvSwitch requires both vCenter Server and Enterprise Plus licensing.

16. B. A Distributed Virtual Uplink (dvUplink) is used to provide a level of abstraction between the physical network adapters (vmnics) on the ESXi host and the dvSwitch.

17. A. The dvSwitch provides bidirectional virtual machine traffic shaping capability.

18. A, B, C. Using jumbo frames in a virtual machine requires the VMXNET 2 or VMXNET 3 adapter, guest OS configuration changes, and ensuring that all devices on the network segment support jumbo frames.

19. C. With static binding a dvPort is immediately assigned and reserved when the virtual machine is connected to the dvPort.

20. B, C, D. In a dvSwitch, virtual network adapters are used to provide VMkernel connections such as ESXi management traffic, vMotion, FT, iSCSI, and NFS.

Chapter 5: Plan and Configure vSphere Storage

1. B. The Software iSCSI Adapter is not enabled by default.

2. A. eui.5577bd49251ddb52 is an example of a SCSI INQUIRY device identifier.

3. A, B, C. All of these answers are supported configurations, because four NICs are required. However, the single quad-port NIC introduces a single point of failure.

4. B. A VMDK can be no larger than 2TB minus 512 bytes on a VMFS-5 datastore.

5. A, C, D. The three path selection policies included by default in ESXi are Fixed, Most Recently Used, and Round Robin.

6. B. With Mutual CHAP, the target (storage system) authenticates the iSCSI adapter (initiator), and the iSCSI adapter also authenticates the target. This is also known as bidirectional.

7. C. Since the independent hardware iSCSI adapter handles the workload for both the iSCSI processing and the iSCSI traffic, it would place the least amount of additional load on the ESXi host resources.

8. A, B. VSA clusters can exist in two-node and three-node configurations only.

9. B, C. vCenter Server cannot run on a virtual machine hosted by an ESXi host that is part of a VSA cluster. It would have to be run on a different ESXi host or in a physical server.

10. B, C. VMFS datastores can be extended or expanded to increase their size.

11. A, B, C, D. All four are correct and represent the four vCenter Server storage filters.

12. A. VMFS-3 datastores will retain their original block size after an upgrade to VMFS-5.

13. A, B, C, D. All of these statements are true of the VSA.

14. A, B, D. The NFS server's name, the IP address or NFS UUID, the path to the NFS share, and the NFS datastore name to be used in vSphere are all required when adding an NFS datastore.

15. A, C. Blade servers often do not have the slots available for multiple cards, and FCoE can be a good use case here. Network consolidation is another use case for FCoE.

16. C. Once an NFS datastore is unmounted, the Add Storage Wizard can be used to mount it again.

17. C. The independent hardware iSCSI adapter performs the iSCSI processing and the iSCSI networking traffic on one card. These adapters are also known as iSCSI HBAs.

18. B. VMware FT requires Thick Provision Eagerly Zeroed VMDKs. This means a 50GB VMDK will consume 50GB of space both at the VMDK level and at the storage array level.

19. D. The VSA cluster uses NFS, so an iSCSI adapter is not used at all to access the VSA storage resources.

20. D. The Rescan For Datastores option from the context menu that appears on the cluster object would scan all hosts in one operation. This would be the fastest option.

Chapter 6: Create and Deploy Virtual Machines and vApps

1. C. The VMware Converter can be used to change the virtual hardware configuration for virtual machines, including the virtual machine hardware version.

2. B, C. New virtual machines can be configured and deployed with either the vSphere Client or the vSphere Web Client.

3. A. An RDM in Physical Compatibility Mode allows the guest OS to access the raw device directly and is used for SAN-aware applications running in a virtual machine.

4. A, B, C, D. All of these are device drivers included with the VMware Tools.

5. D. The VMware vCenter Converter plug-in is not available in vSphere 5. The VMware vCenter Converter Standalone is the replacement product, and it is a free download.

6. B. Cloning a vApp is accomplished with the vSphere Client.

7. D. The Virtual SCSI bus sharing type allows virtual disks to be shared by virtual machines located on the same ESXi host.

8. B. Both IPv4 DHCP Servers and IPv6 DHCP servers can be specified.

9. D. The VMXNET 3 is a paravirtualized NIC that is used for high performance.

10. A, B, C. Objects that can be added to an existing vApp include virtual machines, resource pools, and other vApps.

11. B, C. The VMware Tools are not required for any virtual machine, but they do offer advanced functionality and management for virtual machines. An automatic VMware Tools upgrade is not interactive and can reboot the guest OS without prompting.

12. B, C. Each virtual machine in the same group is started in the order specified, before the next group in the list begins. Shutdown is performed in reverse order of the start order.

13. C. All changes made to an independent nonpersistent disk are lost at VM power-off or reset.

14. B. Hyper-V virtual machines can be imported with the VMware Converter, but they must be powered off.

15. C, D. DRS requires either the Enterprise or Enterprise Plus edition of vSphere.

16. A, D. Virtual machine hardware version 8 supports a maximum of 32 vCPUs and 1TB of RAM.

17. A, B, C. Virtual disk files can be stored with the virtual machine, or a different datastore or datastore cluster can be specified for them.

18. A, B, C, D. All of these methods can be used to convert a thin disk to a thick disk.

19. A, B. `VmwareToolboxCmd.exe` can be used to disable periodic time synchronization in Windows, and `vmware-toolbox-cmd` can be used on Linux, Solaris, and FreeBSD.

20. A, B. The vSphere Client or the vSphere Web Client can be used to obtain virtual machine console access.

Chapter 7: Manage and Administer Virtual Machines and vApps

1. A, B, C, D. All of these options are listed in the context menu when right-clicking a template using the vSphere Client.

2. A. ESXi 5 hosts can have up to 2TB of RAM.

3. B. Creating the VM and cloning it would be the least amount of work. Cloning can be used to avoid repetition of tasks.

4. A. Advanced parameters are added using the Configuration Parameters button in the Advanced/General section of the Options tab in the virtual machine properties. These options can be configured only when the virtual machine is powered off.

5. A. The Disable Acceleration option is used to slow down a virtual machine if there is a problem running or installing software in the virtual machine.

6. A, D. The two types of storage capabilities are system-defined and user-defined.

7. B. vApps are built on an industry-standard format known as the Open Virtualization Format (OVF).

8. B. The option to force the virtual machine to enter the BIOS/EFI setup is one of the few that may be configured while the virtual machine is powered on.

9. A. Templates cannot be powered on, and they must first be converted to virtual machines to be powered on. After converting a template to a VM, the VM can be updated as required, powered off, and then converted to a template again.

10. A, B. Virtual machines that are noncompliant with their VM storage profile can be cold migrated or moved to new datastores via Storage vMotion to make them compliant again.

11. A, B, C, D. Virtual machine security consists of securing the virtual machine, the ESXi host(s) it runs on, the storage and Ethernet networks it uses, the vCenter Server used to manage it, the backup server used to protect it, and likely more. Each environment will be different, but securing virtual machines encompasses a lot of different parts of the infrastructure.

12. A, B, C. Shares, limits, and reservations can all be specified on the Resources tab of the Virtual Machine Properties editor.

13. C. When a virtual machine is converted to a template, its configuration file will have the `.vmtx` extension.

14. B. Windows Server 2008 R2 supports extending OS volumes, and vSphere supports hot extending disks. Neither of these procedures requires downtime to accomplish.

15. B, C. Setting a power-on delay will provide additional time to access the BIOS setup; even better is the Force BIOS Setup option, which will ensure that the virtual machine boots into the BIOS setup.

16. A, D. Virtual machine swap files (VSWP) and virtual disk files (VMDK) can be moved to locations outside of the virtual machine working location.

17. D. The `.vmsd` file is a database that stores information and metadata about snapshots for a virtual machine.

18. A, B. vCenter Server and the vSphere Client are both required to create and use clones and templates.

19. A, C. Windows as the guest OS is always a requirement for Wake on LAN, and both the vmxnet and vmxnet 3 virtual adapters are supported.

20. A, D. Virtual appliances and vApps can both be deployed by using the Deploy OVF Template function in the vSphere Client.

Chapter 8: Establish Service Levels with Cluster, Fault Tolerance, and Resource Pools

1. A, B, C. All of these are correct, except the EVC mode setting. EVC mode is not a requirement to use VMware FT.

2. B, C. Storage DRS requires ESXi 5 hosts and all NFS or all VMFS datastores.

3. B. ESXi hosts must be in maintenance mode before they can be removed from a cluster.

4. B, C. It is recommended to have a dedicated 1GbE NIC for fault tolerance logging and to isolate the traffic to secure it.

5. C. The VMware Tools are required for a proper shutdown of the guest OS, so the virtual machine without the VMware Tools would be powered off.

6. A. A VM-Host affinity rule can be created to require VMs in the specified VM group to run on ESXi hosts in the specified host group.

7. C. FT has an overhead of 5 to 20 percent that must be accounted for.

8. B, D. Enabling DRS on a cluster will create a second layer of scheduling architecture to go along with the local scheduler on each ESXi host. This second scheduler is called the global scheduler.

9. B. Selecting the expandable reservation allows a child resource pool to request resources from its parent or ancestors. If there is only a single resource pool or resource pools that are siblings, then the request would go to the root resource pool.

10. B, D. Raising the EVC mode for cluster involves moving from a lower feature set to a greater feature set. Virtual machines can continue to run during this operation.

11. D. If resource pools do not exist in the destination, the Migrate Virtual Machine Wizard will not offer you the option to select a resource pool.

12. B. In the partially automated automation level, vCenter Server will inform of suggested virtual machine migrations and place the virtual machines on ESXi hosts at VM startup.

13. C. When choosing the specify failover hosts admission control policy, no virtual machines can be powered on when they are on the specified failover hosts, unless an HA event has occurred.

14. A, B, D. Resource pools allow shares, reservations, and limits to be configured, and the resource pool name can be changed.

15. A, C, D. The slave host could be failed, isolated, or partitioned.

16. A, B. The vSphere Client is required to enable FT. The power state of the VM is irrelevant, since the VM's virtual disk files are eager zeroed thick provisioned.

17. D. The Fault Tolerance Test Failover option is both noninvasive and fully supported.

18. D. The migration threshold is configured beneath the automation level settings of the DRS cluster. Moving the slider to the far right will set the migration threshold to Aggressive.

19. A, B, C, D. VMware FT can be used in all of these cases, as long as the virtual machine meets the FT requirements.

20. B. VM monitoring works by monitoring VMware Tools heartbeats and I/O activity from the VMware Tools process running in the guest OS and can reset failed and/or unresponsive virtual machines.

Chapter 9: Maintain Service Levels

1. D. Cold migration would require powering off the virtual machine. vMotion cannot be used to change datastores, and Storage vMotion is not a feature with vSphere 5 Standard edition licensing.

2. D. Of the choices presented, only snapshots with RDMs in virtual compatibility mode are supported.

3. A, B, C. The VMware Data Recovery solution consists of the vSphere client plug-in, the backup appliance(s), and the optional File Level Restore client.

4. B. The VMware Tools should be installed first and will require a reboot. The second restart will be when the virtual machine hardware is upgraded, since this requires the virtual machine to be powered off. After the VM is powered up, Windows will find new devices and then require a third and final reboot.

5. A, C. There are two options for the vMotion priority level: Reserve CPU For Optimal vMotion Performance and Perform With Available CPU Resources.

6. B. The swap file location specified on a virtual machine will override swap file settings defined at either the ESXi host or cluster level.

7. A, B, D. vSphere Update Manager can be configured with a direct connection to the Internet to use a shared repository or to import patches.

8. C. Creating a baseline group allows the VMware Tools and virtual machine hardware to be updated in a single vSphere Update Manager remediation operation that can be scheduled.

9. C. When a baseline is edited, the Product value defaults to Any. When this baseline was edited, this value was likely changed from embeddedEsx 5.0.0 to Any.

10. B. Each vCenter Server instance supports up to ten VMware Data Recovery backup appliances, and each appliance is supported for use with up to 100 virtual machines. VMware Data Recovery could be used for this environment. VCB is not supported in vSphere 5, and snapshots are not a backup solution.

11. A. Storage vMotion can be used to migrate a virtual machine that has snapshots, as long as the VM is located on an ESXi 5 host.

12. B, C. Enterprise Plus licensing is required to use host profiles, and ESX/ESXi hosts must be placed in maintenance mode to have a host profile applied.

13. A. Reverting the virtual machine to the current snapshot will restore it to its previous state. The snapshot will still exist, so deleting it in Snapshot Manager using either the Delete or Delete All button will remove the snapshot.

14. A, B, D. Each of these guest operating systems is supported for use with the FLR client. No version of Solaris is supported.

15. C. The proper sequence is create baseline, attach baseline, scan object, and remediate object.

16. A, B. Migrating a powered-off or suspended VM to a new datacenter is supported. vMotion and Storage vMotion cannot be used to migrate VMs to different datacenters.

17. B, C. The requirement for EVC is that all hosts in the cluster must have the same brand of processors.

18. B, C. vSphere Update Manager requires a 64-bit operating system and a 32-bit DSN.

19. A, C, D. NFS servers that do not support the VAAI NAS extensions that enable reserve space will not allow the disk format to be changed, and the option to change virtual disk formats will be grayed out.

20. C. The VMware Data Recovery client plug-in is used with the vSphere Client to connect to a vCenter Server and create backup jobs.

Chapter 10: Perform Basic Troubleshooting

1. C, D. Virtual machines attached to an internal-only virtual switch cannot be migrated with vMotion, and neither can virtual machines that are using an ISO on local storage.

2. D. vSwitches have 120 ports available by default. It is likely that the ports have been exhausted for the vSwitch.

3. A, C. All of the ESXi logs are accessible from `/var/run/log` in the ESXi Shell or from the vSphere Client's Export System Logs option.

4. A. If the Host Failures The Cluster Tolerates admission control policy is used, there will be a blue Advanced Runtime Info link available. This link is available only when this admission control policy is selected.

5. C. A DAVG/cmd value greater than 20 usually indicates a problem, and the value currently reported is nearly 4 times higher than normal. It is a safe conclusion that there is storage contention in this situation.

6. C, D. A single virtual machine is affected, so checking host-specific or network settings is simply not necessary in this case.

7. C. The Configuration Issues link can be used to view HA status, including warning and error conditions.

8. A, B. All hosts must be licensed and have access to the same shared storage. The VMware Tools are never required for these features.

9. B. If connected to a vCenter Server, then the diagnostic information for the ESXi hosts it manages can also be exported at the same time.

10. C, D. The LAT/rd and LAT/wr metrics are virtual machine specific and used to measure I/O latency.

11. B, C, D. Each of these can lead to a DRS cluster imbalance.

12. B, C, D. Virtual switches, datastores, hosts, and virtual machines can all be viewed in vMotion resource maps, but there is no ability to show connected devices for virtual machines.

13. B. When connected directly to an ESXi host with the vSphere Client, use the Configuration tab to view the Hardware Health Status information.

14. D. Without the T10-based Storage APIs – Array Integration (Thin Provisioning) support, virtual machines will crash if an out-of-space condition occurs.

15. A. DAVG/cmd is the average amount of time in milliseconds a device takes to service a single I/O request.

16. A, B. From the local console, the ESXi Shell or the Configure Management Network feature will show the device name, the MAC address, and the status. The vSphere Client and vSphere Web Client cannot be used if there is no management network connectivity.

17. C. When building a white-box server, as many parts as possible should be verified to be on the VMware HCL.

18. A, B, C, D. Each of these are valid steps in verifying a storage configuration.

19. C. When certain configurations are in use, like Route Based On IP Hash Load Balancing, it will often be necessary to involve the staff responsible for managing the upstream physical network devices.

20. D. When Migration Threshold is set to Conservative, no attempt to load balance will be made by DRS. This will result in the target host load standard deviation being reported as N/A.

Chapter 11: Monitor a vSphere Implementation and Manage vCenter Server Alarms

1. A, B. The ESXi Shell can be used to restart the host agent service. The DCUI Troubleshooting Options menu item can also be used to restart all management agents, including hostd.

2. B. The message of the day can be used to send a message to all users with active sessions. The message of the day will also be sent to any newly logged in users of the vSphere Client.

3. B. The number of entries displayed in the tasks and events lists in the vSphere Client can be adjusted using the Edit ➢ Client Settings ➢ Lists tab.

4. D. %RDY or CPU Ready is used to measure the percentage of time a VM was ready to run but was not provided with CPU resources.

5. C. The -d switch is the delay between statistics snapshots, and the -n switch is used to specify the number of iterations. Option C will perform 60 iterations at 2 second intervals, capturing 2 minutes of data.

6. A. Alarms are inherited down the chain of inventory objects, so the only way to solve this problem is to re-create the alarm at the VM object level.

7. D. vCenter Server can be configured to send SNMP traps to up to four receivers.

8. B. %DRPRX indicates that network receive packets are being dropped. This is a likely indicator of a problem.

9. A. The DAVG/cmd metric is the average amount of time in milliseconds a device takes to service a single I/O request. The device includes the vmhba, the storage device, and any devices between.

10. C. Increasing the Active Directory Timeout value will allow more time for the users and groups from Active Directory to populate.

11. B. vSphere HA alarms could likely be the result of a management network communication failure.

12. D. If no virtual machines are protected with VMware FT, the Fault Tolerance view will be unavailable in the Overview charts.

13. A, B, C. Cloning a virtual machine, migrating a virtual machine, and adding a host are all tasks that can be scheduled in vCenter Server. There is no scheduled task to delete virtual machines.

14. A. If the Trigger If All Of The Conditions Are Satisfied option is used, then each trigger type must have the condition met before the trigger will fire. Remember that the more trigger types that are added, the more complex the alarm becomes.

15. A, D. The SMTP settings must include the FQDN or IP address of the SMTP server and the sender account.

16. A, B, C. A vCenter Server alarm consists of three parts: type, trigger, and action.

17. A, B, C. All of the alarm-type monitors have the actions of send a notification email, send a notification trap, and run a command.

18. C. All event entries for a selected object include the child objects. When troubleshooting an HA problem, the Cluster object would include events for all hosts (and virtual machines) in the cluster.

19. A, B. To monitor current swap file usage, SWAP curr is used in resxtop and esxtop, and Memory: Swap Used is used in performance charts of the vSphere Client.

20. C. Verbose logging includes information, error, warning, and verbose log entries.

About the Additional Study Tools

IN THIS APPENDIX:

✓ Additional study tools

✓ System requirements

✓ Using the study tools

✓ Troubleshooting

Additional Study Tools

The following sections are arranged by category and summarize the software and other goodies you'll find on the companion website. If you need help installing the items, refer to the installation instructions in the "Using the Study Tools" section of this appendix.

> **NOTE** You can find the additional study tools at www.sybex.com/go/vcp5. You'll also find instructions on how to download the files to your hard drive.

Sybex Test Engine

The files contain the Sybex test engine, which includes two bonus practice exams, as well as the assessment test and the chapter review questions, which are also included in the book.

Electronic Flashcards

These handy electronic flashcards are just what they sound like. One side contains a question, and the other side shows the answer.

PDF of Glossary of Terms

We have included an electronic version of the glossary in .pdf format. You can view the electronic version of the glossary with Adobe Reader.

Adobe Reader

We've also included a copy of Adobe Reader so you can view PDF files that accompany the book's content. For more information on Adobe Reader or to check for a newer version, visit Adobe's website at www.adobe.com/products/reader/.

System Requirements

Make sure your computer meets the minimum system requirements shown in the following list. If your computer doesn't meet these requirements, you may have problems using the software and files. For the latest and greatest information, please refer to the ReadMe file located in the download.

- A PC running Microsoft Windows 98, Windows 2000, Windows NT4 (with SP4 or newer), Windows Me, Windows XP, Windows Vista, or Windows 7

- An Internet connection

Using the Study Tools

To install the items, follow these steps:

1. Download the .zip file to your hard drive, and unzip it to your desired location. You can find instructions on where to download this file at www.sybex.com/go/vcp5.

2. Click the Start.EXE file to open the study tools file.

3. Read the license agreement, and then click the Accept button if you want to use the study tools.

   The main interface appears and allows you to access the content with just a few clicks.

Troubleshooting

Wiley has attempted to provide programs that work on most computers with the minimum system requirements. If a program does not work properly, the two likeliest problems are that you don't have enough memory (RAM) for the programs you want to use or you have other programs running that are affecting the installation or running of a program. If you get an error message such as "Not enough memory" or "Setup cannot continue," try one or more of the following suggestions and then try using the software again:

Turn off any antivirus software running on your computer.   Installation programs sometimes mimic virus activity and may make your computer incorrectly believe that it's being infected by a virus.

Close all running programs.   The more programs you have running, the less memory is available to other programs. Installation programs typically update files and programs, so if you keep other programs running, installation may not work properly.

Have your local computer store add more RAM to your computer.   This is, admittedly, a drastic and somewhat expensive step. However, adding more memory can really help the speed of your computer and allow more programs to run at the same time.

Customer Care

If you have trouble with the book's companion study tools, please call the Wiley Product Technical Support phone number at (800) 762-2974, or email them at `http://sybex .custhelp.com/`.

Index

Note to the Reader: Throughout this index **boldfaced** page numbers indicate primary discussions of a topic. *Italicized* page numbers indicate illustrations.

A

actions, alarm
  configuring, 689, 690, **693–696**, *694*, *696*
  listing, **685–687**, *686*
Actions tab, 689, 690, 693, 694
Active Adapters/Uplinks option, 201
Active Directory
  ESXi hosts, **121–123**, *122–123*
  permissions, 100
  vCenter Server settings, **651–653**, *652–653*
Active Directory Application Mode (ADAM), 55–56
Active Directory Timeout setting, 652
adapters, virtual
  configuring, **186–187**, *186–187*
  creating, **182–185**, *183–185*
  migrating, **187–191**, *188–190*
Add Adapter Wizard
  Fault Tolerance logging traffic, *470*, 471
  vmnics, 152–153, *152–153*
Add Counters window, 681–682, *682*
Add Hardware window
  disk controllers, 326, *327*
  TSOs, 207, *208*
  virtual disks, 330–331, *330–331*
  virtual NIC adapters, 338
  VMware Data Recovery backup appliance, 533, *533*
Add Host To vSphere Distributed Switch Wizard, 170–171, *171–172*
Add Host Wizard, 108, *108*, 429–430, *429*
Add Hosts And Physical Adapters screen, 167

Add Network Wizard
  Fault Tolerance logging traffic, 469–471, *470*, *472*
  port groups, 160, *160*
  VMkernel ports, 155–158, *155–158*
  vNetwork standard switches, 149–150, *150*
Add New License Key dialog box, 53, 73
Add New Role window, 119, *119*
Add Physical Adapter window, 181, *181*
Add Storage Adapter window, 236, *236*
Add Storage Capability window, 410
Add Storage Wizard
  NFS, 270, *271*
  VMFS, 249, *249*
Add Virtual Adapter Wizard, 183–185, *183–185*, 190
Additional Patches screen, 573, *575*
Administrator system role, 97
admission control, **435–441**, *437–438*, *440*
advanced charts
  creating, **674–677**, *675–677*
  features, **673–674**, *674*
advanced feature enablement in VMFS, 247
Advanced IP Allocation window, 361–362, *362*
Advanced Options screen, 327
advanced parameters for virtual machines, **402–403**, *402*
Advanced Settings window
  memory compression cache, 71–72, *71*
  storage filters, 229–230, *229*
affinity rules
  VM-Host, **448–453**, *449–450*, *452*
  VM-VM, 448, **454–456**, *454–455*
Alarm Settings window, 687–688, *688–689*, 691–692, *692*, 695, *695*

alarms, 462, *462*, **684–685**

actions

configuring, 689, *690*, **693–696**, *694,*
696

listing, **685–687**, *686*

connectivity

actions, **685–687**, *686*

creating, **691–694**, *692–694*

default, **685**

exam essentials, **698**

High Availability, 462

resources affected, **696–697**, *696–697*

review questions, **699–701**

summary, **697–698**

triggers, **694–695**, *695*

utilization, **685**, **687–690**, *687–690*

Alarms tab, 462

Allow Override Of Port Policies option, 178

Always Store With The Virtual Machine
option, 392, 507

anti-affinity rules, 448, **454–456**

appliance maintenance mode, **290–291**, *290*

Apply Profile window, 128, *128*, 556, 558

array thin provisioning

use case, **246**

vs. virtual disk thin provisioning, **245–
246**

Assign License dialog box

DRS/HA clusters, 430

ESXI hosts, 73, *74*

vCenter Server, 53, *54*

Assign Permissions window

inventory objects, 114–116, *115–116*

vCenter Server, 99, *99*

Assign User-Defined Storage Capability
window, 409–410, *410*

Associations tab, 361

ATS enhancement, 248

Attach Baseline or Group dialog

baselines, 577, *578*

host upgrades, 85, *85*

virtual machines, 583, *583*

Attach Profile window, 126,
556–557, 556

attaching

baselines

to ESXi hosts, **577–578**, *578*

to virtual machines, **581–583**, *582–
583*

ESXi host profiles, **556–557**, *556–557*

attributes for resource pools, **485–486**, *486*

Audio device driver, 321

Auto Deploy feature

architecture, **22**, *23*

ESXi hosts, **60–61**

installing, **48–49**, *49*

Automatic Tools Upgrade option, 318

automation levels, **443–446**, *444, 446*

availability. *See* High Availability (HA)

average bandwidth, 202

B

back-end IP addresses, 286

Backup Job - Backup Wizard, 541–543,
541–543

backups

backup appliance

configuring, **536–538**, *537–538*

connections, **538–540**, *538–540*

installing, **531–532**, *531–532*

virtual disks, **533–534**, *533*

exam essentials, **588**

jobs, **541–543**, *541–543*

options, **550–552**

restore tests

file-level, **544–546**, *545–546*

virtual machines, **547–550**, *547–550*

review questions, **589–592**

snapshots. *See* snapshots

summary, **587–588**

VMFS, 247

bandwidth policies, 202

Baseline Selection screen, **586–587**, *586*

baselines

dynamic patches, 571

ESXi host updates, 85, *85*, **586–587**, *586*

group, **581–583**, *582–583*
vSphere Update Manager
    attaching to ESXi hosts, **577–578**, *578*
    creating, **570–573**, *572–573*
    editing, **574–576**, *575–576*
Baselines And Groups tab
    ESXi dynamic patches, 571, *572*
    ESXi host upgrades, 85
    virtual machines, 582
Beacon Probing option, 200
bidirectional CHAP, 242
Bind With VMkernel Network Adapter
    window, 234–235, *234–235*, 240, *240*
binding
    dvPort groups, **178**
    iSCSI ports, **239–241**, *240–241*
    VMkernel network adapters, 234–235,
      234–235
    VMkernel ports, 617–618, *618*
blocking policies, **196–197**, *197*
boot options, **397–399**, *398*
burst size, 202
bus sharing, 325
BusLogic parallel controllers, 325

C

capabilities
    storage, **247–248**, 409–410, *410*
    virtual machine hardware, **301–303**
    vNetwork Distributed Switches, **163–165**,
      163
    vNetwork standard switches, **145–148**,
      146–148
capacity of HA clusters, **625–626**, *626*
CDP (Cisco Discovery Protocol), 16, 148,
    149, 604
certificate authorities, 84
Certificate Warning screen, 46
Challenge Handshake Authentication
    Protocol (CHAP), **242–245**, *243–244*
Change A Virtual Machine's Power State
    Wizard, 648–649, *648*

Change Access Rule window, 117, *117*
Change EVC Mode window, 458
Change SCSI Controller Type window, 328,
    328
channels in storage, 225
CHAP (Challenge Handshake
    Authentication Protocol), **242–245**,
    243–244
CHAP Credentials window, 239, 243–245,
    243–244
CHAP (Target Authenticates Host) settings,
    244
Chart Options window, 676, *676*
charts
    advanced
      creating, **674–677**, *675–677*
      features, **673–674**, *674*
      overview, **671–673**, *672–673*
Check Prerequisites screen, 253
Cisco Discovery Protocol (CDP), 16, 148,
    149, 604
Cisco Nexus 1000V switch, 164
claim rules, 265
CLI (command-line interface), **8**
Client Settings window, 663, *663*
clients
    NTP
      disabling, **101–103**, *102*
      IP address settings, **103–104**, *104*
    vSphere Client. *See* vSphere Client
    vSphere Web Client. *See* vSphere Web
      Client
Clone vApp Wizard, 493, *493*
Clone Virtual Machine Wizard, 376, 379
clones
    cold, 341
    linked, 468
    modes, 340
    roles, **120**, *120*
    vApps, **364–365**, 493, *493*
    virtual machines
      options, **375–376**
      process, **376–379**, *377–379*
      provisioning, 387

cloud computing, **134–135**

Cluster Configuration Issues window, 625, *625*

Cluster Settings window
    swap files, 508
    VM-VM affinity rules, 455

Cluster Summary tab, 631

clusters, 55
    affinity rules
        VM-Host, **448–453**, *449–450*, *452*
        VM-VM, 448, **454–456**, *454–455*
    baseline attachments, *577*
    capacity, **625–626**, *626*
    configuration verification, **623–625**,
        623–625
    creating, **425–428**, *425–428*
    datastore, 21, *21*
    deleting, 428, *428*
    ESXi hosts, 132, *132*
        adding and removing, **428–431**, *429*
        monitoring, **433–435**, *434*
        upgrades, 87
    EVC, **456–458**, *457*
    exam essentials, **494**
    failover methodology, **423–424**
    host load standard deviation, 630–631
    load imbalance, **627–630**, *628–629*
    monitoring, **458–462**, *459–462*
    resource pools, **132**, *132*
    resource requirements, **423–424**, 620–
        621
    review questions, **495–498**
    root cause identification, **635**
    storage DRS, **462–466**, *464–465*
    summary, **493–494**
    virtual machines
        adding and removing, **431–433**,
            431–432
        admission control, **435–441**, *437–438*,
            440
        automation levels, **443–446**, *444*, *446*
        configuring, **439–441**
        datastore locations, 335

        disks for, 332
        entitlement, **424–425**, *424*
        migration thresholds, **447–448**
        monitoring, **441–443**, *442–443*
        placing in, **313**
        swap file location, 508
    VMFS, 247
    VSA
        configurations, **275–276**, *275*
        requirements, 278
        VSA Manager, **283–289**, *284–289*
    vSphere Update Manager settings, **565–**
        566, *565–567*

CNAs (Converged Network Adapters), 231

cold cloning, 341

cold migration, 433, 502

command-line interface (CLI), **8**

community PVLAN ports, 165

compatibility and Compatibility window
    EVC, **456–458**, *457*
    virtual disks, 329–330
    virtual hardware, 82
    virtual machine clones, 376
    virtual machine templates, 382, 384

Compliance Details tab, 555, *555*

compliance scanning
    ESXi hosts, **557–559**, *558*, **578–579**, *579*
    virtual machines, **584**, *584*

compression cache, **70–73**, *71*

Configuration Details tab, 125, 555, *555*

configuration files location, **391–392**, *392*

configuration maximums, **5–6**, **387–389**

Configuration Maximums document,
    388–389

Configuration Parameters window, 394–
    395, *394*, **402–403**, *402*

Configuration tab
    CHAP, 243
    extents, 260
    Fault Tolerance traffic logging, 469–470
    iSCSI, 233, 236–237
    jumbo frames, 209
    network adapters, 608, *608*

NFS, 270, 272
port groups, 159–160, 162
rescanning storage, 225–226
storage adapters, 222
swap file location, 509
uplink adapters, 180, *180*
virtual adapters, 186, 188
virtual machines, 192
VMFS datastores, 250, 255, 262
vmnics, 152, 154
vNetwork standard switches, 151
vSphere Update Manager, *563–565, 563–564, 568–570*
Configure Management Network screen, 67–68, 603, *603*
Configure Management Network Confirmation screen, 67, *68*
Configure Reset At Disconnect option, 178
Confirm Consolidate window, 528
Confirm Datastore Unmount window, 252
Confirm Maintenance Mode window, 430
Confirm Removal screen, 118, *118*
Confirm Scan dialog
    ESXi hosts
        compliance, 578, *579*
        upgrades, 86, *86*
    virtual machines, 584, *584*
Connect-VIServer command, *527*
connections
    backup appliances, **538–540**, *538–540*
    vCenter Server, **661–662**, *661–662*
    vNetwork standard switches, 146, 150
connectivity, VSA, 279
connectivity alarms
    actions, **685–687**, *686*
    creating, **691–694**, *692–694*
    default, **685**
consistency of snapshots, **519–520**
console
    DCUI. *See* Direct Console User Interface (DCUI)
    virtual machine, **313–316**, *314–315*
Console window, 315–316

consolidating snapshots, **525–528**, *526–528*
contention, storage, **612–617**, *614–616*
converged adapters
    Converged Network Adapters, 231
    and vNetwork standard switches, 162
Conversion Wizard, 346–348, *346–348*
    physical servers to virtual machines, 342–344, *342, 344*
    V2V conversions, 350–353, *350–353*
Convert Template to Virtual Machine Wizard, 384
Converter Security Warning screen, 350–351
converting
    P2V, **340–345**, *341–345*
    thin disks to thick, **332–334**, *333*
    V2V, 350–353, *350–353*
counters
    advanced charts, 676–677, *677*
    Perfmon, 681–682, *682*
CPUs
    alarms, **687–690**, *687–690*
    EVC requirements, **506**
    metrics, **668–669**
    multi-core, **14**, *15*
    virtual machines, **336–337**
    VSA requirements, 277
Create Distributed Port Group Wizard, 173–174, *174*
Create New Virtual Machine Wizard, 303–307, *304–305, 307*
    clusters, 431, *431*
    resource pools, 482
Create New VM Storage Profile Wizard, 411, *411*
Create Profile From Wizard, 125, 554
Create Resource Pool window, 481–482, *481–482*, 489
Create vSphere Distributed Switch Wizard, 166–168, *167–168*
credentials
    Active Directory, 121–123, *122–123*
    CHAP, 243–245, *243–244*
critical host patches baselines, 570

critical performance metrics, **677–679**

cross-platform web application, 42

current host load deviation, **630–632**, *630–631*

Custom DNS Suffixes window, 67

Custom VM Monitoring Settings window, 442, *442*

customer needs, vSphere editions based on, **135–136**

Customization Specification Manager window, 382

Customize Hardware screen, 309, *310*

Customize Performance Chart window, 674–676, *675*

Customize Using The Customization Wizard option, 377

D

Data Migration Tool, 77

data source names (DSNs), 34

Database Browser
  files in, 390, *391*
  swap file location, 509–511, *510–511*
  virtual disks, 333, *333*

Database Size calculator, 39

database size for vCenter Server, **39–41**, *40*

Datastore Properties window, 257, *258*, 260–261, 267–268

datastores
  clusters, 21, *21*
  heartbeating, 9, **433–434**, 627
  IP addresses, 285
  NFS. *See* Network File System (NFS) datastores
  virtual machines workload factors, **335–336**
  VMFS. *See* Virtual Machine File System (VMFS) datastores

DAVG/cmd metric, 615

DCUI (Direct Console User Interface)

ESXi hosts
  DNS and routing configuration, **65–69**, *65–68*
  lockdown mode, **108–109**, *108–109*
  system logs, 599, *599*

Dead Space Reclamation, 17

deduplication, 336

default alarms, **685**

default swap file location, 392, 507

default system roles, 97

deleting
  clusters, 428, *428*
  dynamic patch baselines, 576, *576*
  scheduled tasks, 647
  snapshots, **523–525**, *524*
  VMFS datastores, **254**
  vNetwork standard switches, 165
  vSwitches, 151, *151*

delta disks, **518–519**

departmental use case, 273

dependent hardware iSCSI adapters
  configuring and editing, **233–235**, *234–235*
  requirements, **231–232**
  use case, **232–233**

Deploy OVF Template Wizard, 31, *31*, 386, 531, *531*

Deploy Template Wizard, 382

deploying
  ESXi hosts, **60–61**
  vCenter Server Appliance, **30–34**, *31–33*
  virtual appliances and vApps, **384–385**
  virtual machines
    methodology selection, **386–387**
    from templates, **381–383**, *382–383*
    vSphere Client, **308–312**, *308–312*

Destination Maintenance Windows, 23

Destination Selection screen, 547–549, *548*

Destination System screen
  P2V conversions, 343, *343*
  V2V conversions, 351

Destination Virtual Machine screen
    P2V conversions, 344
    V2V conversions, 351
    VMware Converter, 348, *348*
Details window
    VM-Host affinity rules, 453
    VM-VM affinity rules, 455
device drivers, **319–320**
DHCP
    IP allocation policy, 363
    IP pools, 361
    VMware Data Recovery backup
        appliance, 537
DHCP tab, 361
diagnostic information, exporting, **599–602,**
    600–602
differencing disks, 519
Direct Console User Interface (DCUI)
    ESXi hosts
        DNS and routing configuration,
            65–69, *65–68*
        lockdown mode, **108–109,** *108–109*
        system logs, 599, *599*
directory services, **121–123,** *122–123*
Directory Services Configuration window,
    122, *122*
Disable Fault Tolerance dialog box, 477
Disabled virtual machine option, 439
disabling
    Fault Tolerance, **477–478,** *477*
    NTP client, **101–103,** *102*
    software iSCSI initiators, **237–238,** *238*
    VMFS path datastores, **268–269,** *269*
    vSphere Client plug-Ins, **50–51**
disk based cloning, 340
disk controllers, **324–328,** *326–328*
Disk File settings, 323
Disk Management screen, 405, *405*
disk mirroring use case, 273
disk operations factor for virtual disks, 332
Disk Provisioning settings, 323
disk shares, **334–335,** *335*

disks. *See* virtual disks
Distributed Resource Scheduler (DRS), 34
    automation levels, **443–446,** *444, 446*
    clusters. *See* clusters
    migration thresholds, **447–448**
    resource distribution graphs, **630–632,**
        630–631
    storage, **20–21,** *21,* **462–466,** *464–465*
    virtual machine entitlement, **424–425,**
        424
    VM-Host affinity rules, **449–451,** *449–*
        450
Distributed Switches. *See* vNetwork
    Distributed Switches (vDS)
Distributed Virtual Uplink groups, **179–182,**
    180–182
DNS
    ESXi hosts, **64–69,** *64–68*
    IP pools, 361
    VMware Data Recovery backup
        appliance, 537, *537*
    VSA, 279
DNS and Routing dialog box, 64, *64*
DNS Configuration window, 66–67, *67*
DNS tab, 361
Do not use CHAP security level, 242–243
Do not use CHAP unless required by target
    security level, 242
domain names, 122
download options for patching, **567–570,**
    568–569
Downloading System Logs Bundles window,
    601, *601*
drivers, **319–320**
DRS. *See* Distributed Resource Scheduler
    (DRS)
DRS Group window, **449–451,** *449–450*
DRS Resource Distribution window, 460–
    461, *461,* 632, *632*
DSNs (data source names), 34
dvPort groups
    blocking policies, **196–197,** *197*

vNetwork Distributed Switches, **173–179**, *174, 176–177*

dvPortGroup Settings window, 197, *197*, 199, *199*

dvSwitches. *See* vNetwork Distributed Switches (vDS)

dvUplink groups, **179–182**, *180–182*

Dynamic Baseline Criteria screen, 572–573, *573*

dynamic binding, 178

Dynamic Discovery tab, 234

dynamic disk mirroring use case, 273

dynamic growth in VMFS, 247

dynamic patch baselines
    creating, **571–573**, *572–573*
    editing, **574–576**, *575–576*

E

E1000 NICs, 337

Edit Profile window, 125–126, *126*, 555

Edit Role window, 120, *120*

Edit Settings window, 486, *486*

Edit vApp Settings window
    IP pools, 361–362, *362*
    settings, 357–359, *357–358*

Edit Virtual Adapter window, 186, *187*

Edit VM window
    boot options, 398
    disk shares, 334, *335*
    hot extending virtual disks, 404

editing
    dynamic patch baselines, **574–576**, *575–576*
    ESXi host profiles, **555**, *555*
    iSCSI, **233–235**, *234–235*
    port groups, **159–160**, *159*
    roles, **120**, *120*
    software iSCSI initiator settings, **238–239**
    vApp settings, **357–359**, *357–359*

editions
    ESXi, 57
    vCenter Server, **29–30**

vSphere, 130–131, 135–136

egress traffic with vNetwork Distributed Switches, 164

Enable Query Limit option, 652

Enable Validation option, 652

Enable VM Storage Profiles window, 410–411, *411*

enabling
    Fault Tolerance, **475–477**, *475–476*
    storage profiles, 410–411, *411*
    vSphere Client plug-Ins, **50–51**

encapsulation, 247

End-User Patent Agreement screen
    Auto Deploy, 49
    Syslog Collector, 47
    vCenter Server, 35
    VSA Manager, 281
    vSphere Client, 42, 44
    vSphere Update Manager, 560

Enhanced vMotion Compatibility (EVC)
    configuring, **456–458**, *457*
    CPU requirements, **506**
    status, 460

ephemeral binding, 178

Error (Errors Only) logging option, 654

EST (External Switch Tagging), 213

ESX retirement, **3**

esxcli command-line interface, 8
    enhanced logging, 11
    esxcli network nic list command, 603
    esxcli network vswitch list command, 604
    esxcli refresh command, 6
    firewalls, 101
    network adapters, 608
    patching, 553
    for upgrades, 76

ESXi
    architectures, **130**
    dynamic patch baselines
        creating, **571–573**, *572–573*
        editing, **574–576**, *575–576*
    editions, **57**
    exam essentials, **89–90**

hosts. *See* ESXi hosts
hyperthreading, **69–70**, *70*
interactive installation, **58–59**, *59*
review questions, **91–94**
summary, **89**
ESXi hosts
agent status, **659–660**, *659*
alarm-type monitor, 686
architectures, **132–134**
baseline attachment, **577–578**, *578*
clusters, **132**, *132*
adding and removing, **428–431**, *429*
monitoring, **433–435**, *434*
upgrades, 87
deployment, **60–61**
directory services, **121–123**, *122–123*
DNS and routing configuration, **64–69**, *64–68*
firewalls, **6**
configuring and administering, **100–104**, *102*, *104*
services, **105–107**, *106–107*
group lists, **112–113**, *113*
licensing, **73–74**, *74*
lockdown mode, **108–110**, *108–110*
maximums, **387–389**
memory compression cache, **70–73**, *71*
metrics
CPU, **668**
memory, **667**
NTP configuration, **61–63**, *62–63*
patching requirements, **553–554**
Perfmon utility, **679–683**, *680–682*
profiles, 60
attaching, **556–557**, *556–557*
compliance scanning and remediating, **557–559**, *558*
creating, 554
editing, **555**, *555*
permissions, **124–128**, *124–128*
remediating, **580–581**, *580*
rescanning storage, **225–227**, *226–227*
scanning, **578–579**, *579*

troubleshooting
exporting diagnostic information, **599–602**, *600–602*
guidelines, **598–599**, *599*
installation issues, **595–596**
system health, **596–598**, *597–598*
UEFI support, 8
update staging, **586–587**, *586*
upgrades
process, **83–89**, *84–88*
requirements, **75–76**
virtual machines, 313
vMotion and Storage vMotion requirements, **505**
vNetwork Distributed Switches, **169–173**, *170–172*
VSA hosts, 278
VSA resources, **277–278**
vSphere Update Manager settings, **565**, *565*
esxtop command, **613–616**, *614–615*, 666
Evaluation Mode
ESXi host license keys, **73–74**, *74*
vCenter Server licensing, **53–55**, *53–54*
vNetwork Distributed Switches, 166
EVC (Enhanced vMotion Compatibility)
configuring, **456–458**, *457*
CPU requirements, **506**
status, 460
events, **644–646**, *644–646*
Events tab, 644, *644*
Expandable Reservation parameter, **481–484**, *481–483*
expanding VMFS datastores, **257–262**, *258–259*, *261*
Export OVF Template window, 365, *366*
Export System Logs window, 600, *600*, 655, *655*
exporting
diagnostic information, **599–602**, *600–602*
OVF templates, **385–386**
system logs, **600–602**, *600–602*
vApps, **365–366**, *366*

Extend Volume Wizard, 405, *405*

extending

virtual disks, **403–406**, *405*

VMFS datastores, **257–262**, *258–259,
261*

extent volumes in VMFS, 248

External Switch Tagging (EST), 213

F

failover

methodology, **423–434**

policies, 196, **198–201**, *198–199*

Fault Tolerance (FT), *55*, **466**

configuration testing, **478–479**, *479*

disabling, **477–478**, *477*

enabling, **475–477**, *475–476*

exam essentials, **494**

improvements, **13**

requirements, **467–468**

review questions, **495–498**

summary, **493–494**

traffic logging, **469–475**, *470–474*

use cases, **466–467**

virtual disks, 332

FC (Fibre Channel) SANs, 230

FCoE (Fibre Channel over Ethernet) adapters

support, 7

use cases, **231**

feature IP addresses in VSA, 285

features, vSphere editions, **130–131**

Fibre Channel (FC) SANs, 230

Fibre Channel over Ethernet (FCoE) adapters

support, 7

use cases, **231**

File Level Restores (FLR)

client installation, **534–535**

VMware Data Recovery, **544–546**,
545–546

files

virtual machines use, **389–391**, *391*

VMFS, 248

filters in storage, **227–230**, *229*

Firewall Properties window, 102–103, *102,
104*

Firewall Settings window, 103

firewalls

configuring and administering, **100–104**,
102, 104

new features, **6**

services, **105–107**, *106–107*

Fixed IP allocation policy, 363

flat disks, 246

Flexible NICs, 337

flow control for iSCSI adapters, 233

FLR (File Level Restores) client

client installation, **534–535**

VMware Data Recovery, **544–546**,
545–546

Folder Of Files (OVF) option, 365

Forged Transmits policy, 111–112

frames, jumbo, **209–212**, *209–212*

FT. *See* Fault Tolerance (FT)

FT Test Failover functionality, 478

Fully automated automation level, 444–445

G

General settings

cluster configuration, 623, *623*

EVC, 460

iSCSI initiator, 237–239, *239*

jumbo frames, 209–210, *210*

Generate vCenter Server Log Bundle
window, 601

Get-View command, 527

Getting Started Wizard, 539–540, *539–540*

global entities, permissions for, 99

global schedulers, 424, *424*

groups

baselines, **581–583**, *582–583*

dvPort

blocking policies, **196–197**, *197*

vNetwork Distributed Switches, **173–
179**, *174, 176–177*

dvUplink, **179–182**, *180–182*

lists, **112–113**, *113*
permissions, **114–118**, *115–118*
port
 verifying configuration, **605–607**, *606*
 vNetwork standard switches, 146, *147*, 150, **158–162**
growing extents, **257–260**, *258–259*
Guest Customization screen
 clones, 377–378, *377–378*
 templates, 382, *383*
guest OS on virtual machine, **303–307**, *304–305, 307*

H

HA. *See* High Availability (HA)
hard disks for VSA, 277
hardware
 patching requirements, **553–554**
 virtual machines
  capabilities, **301–303**
  settings, **349–353**, *350–353*
  upgrading, **82–83**
 VMware Converter settings, **349–353**, *350–353*
 VSA requirements, 277
Hardware Compatibility List (HCL), 75
hardware FCoE, 7, 231
hardware iSCSI adapters
 configuring and editing, **233–235**, *234–235*
 requirements, **231–232**
 use case, **232–233**
HCL (Hardware Compatibility List), 75
heartbeating
 datastore, **433–434**, 627
 network, 626
 vCenter Server improvements, **11–13**, *12*
hierarchy of resource pools, **480–481**, *480*
High Availability (HA), 34
 admission control, **435–441**, *437–438, 440*

clusters. *See* clusters
failover methodology and resources, **423–434**
improvements, **8–9**
network configuration, **622**
redundancy issues, **626–627**
use case, 273
vCenter Server, **55–56**
Host Failures the Cluster Tolerates policy, 435, *625*
host load deviation, **630–632**, *630–631*
Host Rescan Filter, 228–230
Host Summary screen, 430
hostd restart command, 661
hostd start command, 661
hostd status command, 660
hostd stop command, 660
hosts. *See* ESXi hosts
Hosts And Clusters tab, 558
hot extending virtual disks, **403–406**, *405*
hybrid clouds, **135**
Hyper-V VMs, **346–349**, *346–348*
hyperthreading, **69–70**, *70*

I

Image Builder feature, **21**, *22*, 60
Import ESXi Image Wizard, 84–85, *84–85*
importing
 OVF templates, **385–386**
 patches, 567
 virtual machines, **345–349**, *346–348*
in-place upgrades, **88–89**, 248
Increase Datastore Capacity Wizard, 258–260, *259, 261*
independent hardware iSCSI adapter requirements, **231–232**
independent nonpersistent mode, 324
independent persistent mode, 324
Inflating window, 333
Information (Normal Logging) logging option, 654

ingress traffic with vNetwork Distributed
  Switches, 164
inherited permissions, **98–100**, *99*
initiators, iSCSI
  configuration, **617–618**, *618*
  enabling and disabling, **236–238**,
    236–238
  port binding, **239–241**, *240–241*
  requirements, **231–232**
  settings, **238–239**
  use case, **232–233**
Install/Upgrade Tools dialog box, 318
installing
  ESXi, **58–59**, *59*
  ESXi hosts, **595–596**
  File Level Restores client, **534–535**
  vCenter Server into virtual machines,
    34–39, *36–38*
  VMware Converter Standalone, **341**, *341*
  VMware Data Recovery
    backup appliance, **531–532**, *531–532*
    client plug-in, **529–530**, *530*
  VMware Tools, **316–318**, *317*
  vSphere Client, **41–43**, **46–50**, *48*, *50*
  vSphere Update Manager, **560–562**,
    560–562
  vSphere Web Client, **42–46**, *44–45*
Intel SMT enhancements, **5**
interactive ESXi installation, **58–59**, *59*
interface layer, 130, **132–133**
Internet Small Computer System Interface
  (iSCSI)
  CHAP, **242–245**, *243–244*
  configuring and editing, **233–235**,
    234–235
  GUI support, **13**, *14*
  initiators
    configuration, **617–618**, *618*
    enabling and disabling, **236–238**,
      236–238
    port binding, **239–241**, *240–241*
    requirements, **231–232**
    settings, **238–239**
    use case, **232–233**

Inventory object permissions, 100, **114–118**,
  115–118
Inventory screen, 71
Inventory Service, **37–38**
Iometer tool, 615
IP addresses
  NTP client, **103–104**, *104*
  VSA, 278, **284–286**, *286*
IP Configuration window, 66, *66*
IP pools, **359–363**, *360–362*
iSCSI. *See* Internet Small Computer System
  Interface (iSCSI)
iSCSI Alias property, 239
iSCSI HBA, 232
iSCSI Initiator Properties window, 233,
  236–237, *237*
  CHAP, **243–244**
  port binding, **239–241**, *241*
ISO use case, 273
isolated PVLAN ports, 165

J

Java Virtual Machine (JVM) memory, 39
jumbo frames support, **209–212**, *209–212*

K

KAVG/cmd metric, 615

L

labels, network, 161, *161*
LAHF (Load Register AH From Flags)
  instruction sets, **5**
large file numbers, 248
large physical RDMs, 248
large single extent volumes, 248
Legacy device identifiers, 224
levels, logging, **654–655**
License Information screen, 281

licensing
    clusters, 430
    ESXi hosts, **73–74**, *74*
    new features, **24–25**
    vCenter Server, **51–55**, *53–54*
    VSA, 278, 281
    vSphere Client, 42
    vSphere Web Client, 43–44
limits
    resource pools, **488–492**, *489–492*
    virtual machines, **406–408**, *406*, *408*
Link Layer Discovery Protocol (LLDP)
    enabling, 16
    vNetwork Distributed Switches, 165
Link Status Only option, 200
linked clones, 468
Linked Mode, 37, *38*
LLDP (Link Layer Discovery Protocol)
    enabling, 16
    vNetwork Distributed Switches, 165
load balancing
    policies, 196, **198–201**, *198–199*
    troubleshooting, **627–630**,
        628–629
load-based NIC teaming, 164
load distribution use case, 273
Load Register AH From Flags (LAHF)
        instruction sets, **5**
local schedulers, 424, *424*
Local Users & Groups tab, 113
Locate Network File System window, 270
lockdown mode, **108–110**, *108–110*
logs and logging
    bundles, **655**, *655*
    system
        exporting, **600–602**, *600–602*
        viewing, 599, *599*
    traffic, **469–475**, *470–474*
    vCenter Server
        enhancements, **11**
        options, **654–655**, *654*
LSI device driver, 321
LSI Logic Parallel controllers, 325
LSI Logic SAS controllers, 325

LUNs
    description, 222
    masking, **230–231**
    in storage names, 225

M

MAC Address Changes policy, 111–112
Mac OS X Server support, **11**
Machine Details window, 342
maintenance mode
    appliance, **290–291**, *290*
    ESXi host upgrades, 87
    VMFS datastores, **264**
    VSA clusters, **288–289**, *288–289*
Manage Physical Adapters window, 180–
        182, *181*, 609–610, *610*
Manage Storage Capabilities window, 409,
        409
Manage Virtual Adapters window, 183–191,
        186
Manage vSphere Licenses Wizard, 54–55, *54*
managed entities, permissions for, 99
management IP addresses in VSA, 285
management layer, 130, **133**
Manual automation level, 444
Map Relationships panel, 665–666
maps
    resource
        vCenter Server, **663–666**, *663–666*
        vMotion, **633–635**, *634*
    storage, **618–619**, *619*
masking, LUN, **230–231**
master hosts, **433–434**
Maximum Requested Topology Entries
        setting, 663, *663*
maximum transmission units (MTUs),
        209–212
Mem.MemZipEnable setting, 71–72
memory
    compression cache, **70–73**, *71*
    DRS utilization, 461, *461*, 632, *632*
    Java Virtual Machine, 39

metrics, **666–668**
resource pool reservations, **489–492**, *489–492*
usage alarms, **687–690**, *687–690*
virtual machines, 305
VSA requirements, 277
Memory Control device driver, 320
Memory screen, 305
Message Of The Day text box, 662, *662*
metrics
advanced charts, **674–677**, *675–677*
CPU, **668–669**
critical performance, **677–679**
memory, **666–668**
network, **669–670**, *669*
overview charts, **671–673**, *672–673*
Perfmon, **679–683**, *680–682*
resources affected, **683–684**
storage, **670–671**
Metro vMotion, **19**
Microsoft Cluster Services (MSCS), 55, 329
Migrate Virtual Adapter window, 188, *189*
Migrate Virtual Machine Networking Wizard, 192–194, *193*
Migrate Virtual Machine Wizard, 432, *432*
powered-off virtual machines, 502–504, *503*
Storage vMotion, 513–516, *514, 516*
migration
threshold settings, **447–448**
troubleshooting, 633, 635
virtual adapters, **187–191**, *188–190*
virtual machines, 501
EVC CPU requirements, **506**
exam essentials, **588**
powered-off, **501–503**, *503*
review questions, **589–592**
snapshot requirements, **507**
Storage vMotion, **505–507**, **513–518**, *514–517*
summary, **587–588**
suspended, **503–504**, *504*
swap file locations, **507–511**, *508–511*

vMotion, **505–507**, **511–513**, *512*
vNetwork distributed switches, **191–195**, *192–194*
monitoring, **643**
clusters, **458–462**, *459–462*
ESXi system health, **596–598**, *597–598*
exam essentials, **698**
metrics. *See* metrics
Perfmon, **679–683**, *680–682*
review questions, **699–701**
summary, **697–698**
tasks and events, **644–650**, *644–646, 648, 650*
virtual machines, **441–443**, *442–443*
Mount Datastore Wizard, 253
mounting
NFS datastores, **272–273**, *272*
VMFS datastores, 253
Mouse device driver, 321
MPP (multipathing plug-in), 265
MSCS (Microsoft Cluster Services), 55, 329
MTUs (maximum transmission units), 209–212
multi-core virtual CPUs, **14**, *15*
multipathing plug-in (MPP), 265
Must Not Run On Hosts In Group option, 453
Must Run On Hosts In Group option, 453
mutual CHAP, 242

N

names
device identifiers, **223–225**
domains, 122
VMFS datastores, **248–251**, *249–250*
NAS (networked-attached storage) devices, 221
connecting to, **270–271**, *271*
provisioning, 245
Native Multipathing plug-in (NMP), 265

NetFlow feature
 visibility, **15**
 vNetwork Distributed Switches, 165–166
network adapter configuration, **607–610**, *608–610*
Network Adapters tab
 Fault Tolerance traffic logging, 470–471
 vmnics, 152, 154
Network Configuration tab, 240
Network Connectivity screen, 171
Network File System (NFS) datastores
 mounting and unmounting, 272–273, *272*
 NAS devices, **270–271**, *271*
 properties, **272**, *272*
 shares, **269–270**
 support improvements, **18**
 use case, **273–274**
 volumes, 221
Network I/O Control (NIOC) feature
 improvements, **17**
 vNetwork Distributed Switches, 165
Network Load Balancing, 112
Network tab for iSCSI, 234
Network Time Protocol (NTP)
 client
  disabling, **101–103**, *102*
  IP address settings, **103–104**, *104*
 ESXi hosts, **61–63**, *62–63*
networked-attached storage (NAS) devices, 221
 connecting to, **270–271**, *271*
 provisioning, 245
networks, **145**
 exam essentials, **214**
 heartbeating, 626
 metrics, **669–670**, *669*
 policies. *See* policies
 review questions, **215–218**
 summary, **213–214**
 troubleshooting, **602**
  physical network adapter configuration, **607–610**, *608–610*
  root cause identification, **610–611**

verifying configuration, **603–604**, *603–604*
 virtual machine configuration, **605**
 virtual switch and port group configuration, **605–607**, *606*
 VMkernel port configuration, **155–158**, *155–158*
 vNetwork Distributed Switches. *See* vNetwork Distributed Switches (vDS)
vNetwork standard switches
 capabilities, **145–148**, *146–148*
 creating and deleting, **148–151**, *149–151*
 port groups, **158–162**, *159–161*
 use case, **162–163**
 vmnics on, **151–154**, *152–153*
VSA
 requirements, 277–278
 storage, **279–280**, *279*
vSphere Update Manager settings, 563–**564**, *563*
New Baseline Wizard, 571–576, *572–573, 576, 582, 582*
New Cluster Wizard, 425–427, *425–427, 457, 457*
New Datastore Cluster Wizard, 464–465
New IP Pool Properties window, 360, *360*
New vApp Wizard, *356*
NFS. *See* Network File System (NFS) datastores
NIC teaming
 settings, 148, *148*
 vNetwork Distributed Switches, 164
NIC Teaming tab, 148, *148*
NIC with FCoE Support, 231
NIOC (Network I/O Control) feature
 improvements, **17**
 vNetwork Distributed Switches, 165
NMP (Native Multipathing plug-in), 265
No Access system role, 97
non-critical host patch baselines, 571
None (Disable Logging) logging option, 654
not-shared storage, 324

Notification window, 310
NTP (Network Time Protocol)
    client
        disabling, **101–103**, *102*
        IP address settings, **103–104**, *104*
    ESXi hosts, **61–63**, *62–63*
NTP Daemon (ntpd) Options screen, *62*, *63*,
    107, *107*

O

on-demand fault tolerance, 467
on-demand provisioning, 387
one-way CHAP, 242
online in-place upgrades, 248
Open Virtualization Format (OVF)
    templates, 30
    deploying virtual appliances and vApps
        from, **384–385**
    importing and exporting,
        385–386
Options screen
    IP pools, 361
    NTP, 62–63, *63*
    P2V conversions, 344, *344*
    swap file location, 510
    V2V conversions, 352
    vApp settings, 357–358, *357*
    virtual machines
        importing, 348
        settings, 393
        troubleshooting options, **399**, *399*
OS on virtual machine, **303–307**, *304–305*,
    307
Out-of-Space Conditions, 17–18
overcommitment
    memory, 70
    storage, **617**
overview charts, **671–673**, *672–673*
OVF (Open Virtualization Format)
    templates, 30
    deploying virtual appliances and vApps
        from, **384–385**

importing and exporting, **385–386**
OVF/virtual appliances provisioning, 387

P

P2V (physical to virtual machine)
    conversions, **340–345**, *341–345*
Paravirtual SCSI device driver, 320
Partially automated automation level, 444
passwords as VSA requirements, 278
Patches To Exclude screen, **573–574**, *575*
patching, **552–553**. *See also* updates and
    Update Manager
    download options, **567–570**, *568–569*
    exam essentials, **588**
    requirements, **553–554**
    review questions, **589–592**
    summary, **587–588**
Path-based device identifiers, 224
Path Selection Plug-in (PSP), 266
paths to VMFS datastores
    disabling, **268–269**, *269*
    preferred, **266–268**, *267*
    selection policies, **264–266**, *265*
peak bandwidth traffic shaping policies, 202
Percentage of Cluster Resources Reserved
    as Failover Spare Capacity policy, 435–
    436, *625*
Perfmon utility, **679–683**, *680–682*
performance
    monitoring, **679–683**, *680–682*
    snapshots, 519
    virtual disks, 332
Performance Monitor Properties window,
    681–682, *681*
periodic time synchronization, 320
permissions
    ESXi host profiles, **124–128**, *124–128*
    inventory objects, **114–118**, *115–118*
    vCenter Server, 99, *99*
physical compatibility mode, 329
physical network adapter configuration,
    607–610, *608–610*

physical RDMs, 248
physical to virtual machine (P2V)
　conversions, **340–345**, *341–345*
ping command, 604
pinning virtual machines to hosts, 445
plug-ins, 46
　MPP, 265
　PSP, 266
　vCenter Server, 133
　VMware Data Recovery client, 529–530,
　　530
　vSphere Client, **46–51**, *48*, *50*, *52*
　vSphere Update Manager, 561–562, *562*
Pluggable Storage Architecture (PSA), 265,
　265
policies, **196**
　common, **196**
　dvPort group blocking, **196–197**, *197*
　IP allocation, 362–363
　jumbo frame support, **209–212**,
　　209–212
　load balancing and failover, **198–201**,
　　198–199
　security, **110–112**, *111*, 196
　traffic shaping, **202–207**, *203–206*
　TSO for virtual machines, **207–208**, *208*
　virtual machine storage
　　assigning, **408–413**, *409–412*
　　verifying, **413–414**, *413*
　VLANs
　　configuration determination, **212–213**
　　settings, **201–202**, *201–202*
　VMFS datastore path selection, **264–266**,
　　265
political use case for VMFS and NFS
　datastores, 273
port binding
　dvPort groups, 178
　iSCSI, **239–241**, *240–241*
　VMkernel, 617–618, *618*
Port Group Override Settings window, 177,
　177
Port Group Properties window, 473

port groups
　Fault Tolerance traffic logging, 473
　policy overrides, 177, *177*
　troubleshooting configuration, **605–607**,
　　606
　vNetwork standard switches, 146, *147*,
　　150, **158–162**
Port Settings window, 206, *206*
ports and Ports tab
　Fault Tolerance traffic logging, 471–472
　jumbo frames, 209–210
　mirroring, **15–16**, 165
　port groups, 159–160, 162
　TCP and UDP, **100–101**
　traffic shaping, 206, *206*
　vmnics, 152
　vNetwork standard switches, 146, *147*
power settings, **395–397**, *396–397*
powered-off virtual machines
　Fault Tolerance
　　disabling, **477–478**, *477*
　　enabling, **475–477**, *475–476*
　migrating, **501–503**, *503*
Preboot Execution Environment (PXE), 60
preferred paths for VMFS datastores, **266–
　268**, *267*
Preview window for vNetwork standard
　switches, 150, *150*
priority of virtual machines, 438–439
private clouds, **135**
Private VLANs (PVLANs)
　dvPort groups, 175
　vNetwork Distributed Switches, 165
privileges for vCenter Server, **96–100**,
　97–99, **129–130**
profile-driven storage, 21, 408–409
profiles, 60
　ESXi hosts
　　attaching, **556–557**, *556–557*
　　compliance scanning and remediating,
　　　557–559, *558*
　　creating, 554
　　editing, 555, *555*

permissions, **124–128**, *124–128*
virtual machine storage, **408–413**,
    409–412
Promiscuous Mode policies, 110
promiscuous PVLAN ports, 165
Propagate to Child Objects option, 99, *99*
Provision Virtual Machine Wizard, 308
provisioning
    array thin vs. virtual disk thin, **245–246**
    virtual machines, 324, 387
Proxy tab, 361
PSA (Pluggable Storage Architecture), 265,
    265
PSP (Path Selection Plug-in), 266
public clouds, **135**
PVLANs (Private VLANs)
    dvPort groups, 175
    vNetwork Distributed Switches, 165
PXE (Preboot Execution Environment), 60

Q

quality of service (QoS), 165
quiescing, 519–520

R

RAID
    virtual machines, 336
    VSA requirements, 277
raw device mapping (RDM), 246, 329
RDM devices
    adding to virtual machines, **330–332**,
        330–331
    VMFS, 247–248
RDM Filter, **228**
Read-Only system role, 97
Ready To Complete The Profile screen, 554
Record/Replay device driver, 320
recoverability in VMFS, 247
recovery. *See* VMware Data Recovery
redundancy issues in HA, **626–627**

Register vCenter Server window, 45, *45*
remediation and Remediate Wizard
    ESXi hosts
        noncompliant, 580–581, *580*
        profiles, **557–559**, *558*
        upgrades, 86–87, *87*
    virtual machines, 584–585, *585*
Remediation Selection screen
    ESXi host upgrades, 87, *87*
    ESXi hosts, 580, *580*
Remove Cluster dialog box, 428, *428*
Remove Resource Pool prompt, 485, *485*
Rename window, 251
renaming VMFS datastores, **248–251**,
    249–250
replication use case, 273
reports and Reports tab
    storage, **618–619**, *619*
    virtual machine restores,
        548, *548*
    VMware Data Recovery, 543
Rescan window, 225, 226, 241
Rescan For Datastores Warning window,
    226–227, *227*
rescanning storage, **225–227**, *226–227*
reservations
    adjusting, **406–408**, *406, 408*
    evaluating, **488–492**, *489–492*
    expandable, **481–484**, *481–483*
Resource Allocation tab, 462
resource distribution graphs, **630–632**,
    630–631
resource maps
    vCenter Server, **663–666**, *663–666*
    vMotion, **633–635**, *634*
resource pools
    adding and removing, 313, **487–488**
    attributes, **485–486**, *486*
    clusters, **132**, *132*
    creating and removing, **484–485**, *484*
    exam essentials, **494**
    expandable reservations, **481–484**,
        481–483
    hierarchy, **480–481**, *480*

requirements, **488**

review questions, **495–498**

shares, reservations, and limits, **488–492**

summary, **493–494**

resources

adjusting, **406–408**, *406, 408*

alarms, **696–697**, *696–697*

HA implementation, **423–434**

metrics, **683–684**

VSA clusters, **283–289**, *284–289*

Restore Rehearsal From Last Backup option, **549–550**, *549–550*

restore tests

file-level, **544–546**, *545–546*

virtual machines, **547–550**, *547–550*

resuming vApps, **363–364**, *363–364*

resxtop command, **613–616**

exported data, **679–683**, *680–682*

memory metrics, 666

networking metrics, 669, *669*

reverting to snapshots, 522–523

roles in vCenter Server

creating, cloning, and editing, **118–121**, *119–120*

identifying, **96–98**, *97–98*

permissions, **98–100**, *99–100*

root cause identification

clusters, **635**

migration, **635**

networks, **610–611**

storage, **620**

Route Based On IP Hash option, 199

Route Based On Physical NIC Load option, 199

Route based On Source MAC Hash option, 199

Route Based On (The) Originating Virtual Port (ID) option, 199

routing ESXi hosts, **64–69**, *64–68*

Rule window

DRS load imbalance, 629

VM-Host affinity rules, 451–453, *452*

VM-VM affinity rules, 454, *454*

Runtime Name device identifiers, 224

RX traffic, 164

S

SAHF (Store AH Register into Flags) instruction sets, 5

Same Host and Transports Filter, 228

SANs (storage area networks), 221, 230

SATP (Storage Array Type Plug-in), 266

scanning

ESXi host profiles, **557–559**, *558*

ESXi hosts, **578–579**, *579*

storage, **225–227**, *226–227*

virtual machines, **584**, *584*

Schedule Task dialog box, 647

Schedule Update Download Wizard, 569–570, *569*

scheduled tasks, **646–650**, *648, 650*

Scheduled Tasks view, 646, *646*

schedulers, global and local, 424, *424*

SCSI bus sharing, 325

SCSI device driver, 321

SCSI INQUIRY device identifiers, 223

SDRS maintenance mode, 265, *265*

security, **96**

CHAP, **242**

cloud computing, **134–135**

ESXi firewalls

configuring and administering, **100–104**, *102, 104*

new features, **6**

services, **105–107**, *106–107*

ESXi hosts

architectures, **130, 132–134**

directory services, **121–123**, *122–123*

lockdown mode, **108–110**, *108–110*

permissions, **124–128**, *124–128*

exam essentials, **137**

group lists, **112–113**, *113*

policies, **196**

common, **196**

dvPort group blocking, **196–197**, *197*

load balancing and failover, **198–201**, *198–199*

network, **110–112**, *111*

review questions, **138–141**

summary, **136–137**

vCenter Server

architectures, **130**, **132–134**

privileges, **98–100**, *99–100*, **129–130**

roles, **96–98**, *97–98*, **118–121**, *119–120*

virtual machines, **400–401**

vSphere editions and features, **130–131**, **135–136**

Security Alert window, 430

Security Warning window, 84

Select A Datastore Or Datastore Cluster window, 516–517, *517*

Select a Disk screen

disk controllers, 326

virtual disks, 330, *330*

Select Disk/LUN screen, 249

Select Disks screen, 405, *405*

Select Hosts and Clusters screen, 465

Select VMs To Migrate screen, 193–194

sensitivity in virtual machine monitoring, 441

server-managed ESXi host maximums, **387–389**

service levels. *See* clusters

services

ESXi firewalls, **105–107**, *106–107*

vCenter Server status, **656–658**, *656–658*

Services MMC snap-in, 656–658, *656*

Services Properties window, 105–107, *106*

Session Management window, 662, *662*

sessions in vCenter Server, **661–662**, *661–662*

Set-ExecutionPolicy command, 526

Settings screen in NTP, 63

shared repositories for patches, 567

shared storage. *See* storage

shares

disk, **334–335**, *335*

NFS datastores, **269–270**

resource pools, **488–492**, *489–492*

virtual machines, **406–408**, *406, 408*

sharing SCSI buses, 325

Should Not Run On Hosts In Group option, 453

Should Run On Hosts In Group option, 453

shrinking disks, 349

Simple Network Management Protocol (SNMP)

configuring, **650–651**, *651*

support, 8

simplified administration, VMFS for, 247

simultaneous multithreading (SMT) enhancements, 5

Single File (OVA) option, 365

size

burst traffic, 202

memory compression cache, **72–73**

vCenter Server databases, **39–41**, *40*

VMFS blocks, 247–248

slave hosts, **433–434**

small and medium-size business (SMB) customers, 274

small file support in VMFS, 248

SMT (simultaneous multithreading) enhancements, 5

SMTP settings, **651–653**, *652–653*

Snapshot Manager, 521–527, *522, 524*

snapshots, 34

consolidating, **525–528**, *526–528*

creating, **521–523**, *521–522*

deleting, **523–525**, *524*

migrating, 507

requirements, **518–521**

SNMP (Simple Network Management Protocol)

configuring, **650–651**, *651*

support, 8

soft licenses, 52
software FCoE, 7, 231
software iSCSI adapters
    CHAP, **243–245**, *243–244*
    requirements, **231–232**
software iSCSI initiators
    enabling and disabling, **236–238**, *236–238*
    port binding, **239–241**, *240–241*
    requirements, **231–232**
    settings, **238–239**
    use case, **232–233**
software requirements in VSA, 278
solid-state drive (SSD) devices
    support, **7**
    virtual machines, 336
Source Machine screen, 350, *351*
SPAN (Switch Port Analyzer), 15, 165
Specify Failover Hosts window, 436–437, *437*
SSD (solid-state drive) devices
    support, **7**
    virtual machines, 336
Stage Wizard, 586–587, *586*
staging ESXi host updates, **586–587**, *586*
standard switches. *See* vNetwork standard switches (vSS)
Standby Adapters/Uplinks option, 201
Start And Stop Manually policy, 105–106
Start And Stop With Host policy, 105
Start Automatically If Any Ports Are Open, And Stop When All Ports Are Closed policy, 105–107
Start Order tab, 358, *358*
startup policies for services, **105–107**, *106–107*
static binding, 178
status
    cluster, 460, *460*
    ESXi host agent, **659–660**, *659*

vCenter Server services, **656–658**, *656–658*
Stop Other Services dialog box, 657, *657*
storage, **221**
    adapter and device identification, **222–223**
    array thin provisioning
        use case, **246**
        vs. virtual disk thin provisioning, **245–246**
    exam essentials, **292–293**
    FCoE use case, **231**
    iSCSI. *See* Internet Small Computer System Interface (iSCSI)
    metrics, **670–671**
    naming conventions, **223–225**
    NFS. *See* Network File System (NFS) datastores
    profile-driven, 21
    review questions, **294–297**
    scanning and rescanning, **225–227**, *226–227*
    summary, **291–292**
    troubleshooting. *See* troubleshooting
    vCenter Server filters, **227–230**, *229*
    virtual disks, 332
    virtual machines
        policies, assigning, **408–413**, *409–412*
        policies, verifying, **413–414**, *413*
        reports, **618–619**, *619*
        resources, **323–324**, *323–324*
        workload factors, **335–336**
    VMFS. *See* Virtual Machine File System (VMFS) datastores
    VSA. *See* vSphere Storage Appliance (VSA) and VSA Manager
    zoning and LUN masking practices, **230–231**
storage accelerator, **18**
Storage Adapter properties window, 234
Storage Adapters screen, 222, *222*

storage area networks (SANs), 221, 230
Storage Array Type Plug-in (SATP), 266
storage DRS feature
    configuring, **462–466**, *464–465*
    overview, **20–21**, *21*
Storage vMotion
    configuration verification, **621–622**
    improvements, **17**
    migrating virtual machines, *502*
        process, **513–514**, *514*
        techniques, **514–518**, *515–518*
        troubleshooting, **633**
    requirements
        ESXi host, **505**
        identifying, **620–621**
        snapshots, **507**
        virtual machine, **506**
    VMFS and NFS datastore use case, *273*
Store AH Register into Flags (SAHF)
    instruction sets, **5**
Store In The Host's Swapfile Datastore
    option, *392*, *507*
strong licenses, *52*
sub-blocks in VMFS, *248*
Summary screen
    cluster configuration, *623*, *623*
    DRS load imbalance, **629–630**
    dvPort groups, *174*, *174*, *176*
    ESXi host profiles, **556–557**
    EVC, *459*, *459*
    Fault Tolerance traffic logging, *471*, *474*
    host profiles, *126*, *127*
    P2V conversions, *344*
    resource pools, *490*
    scheduled tasks, *649*
    snapshots, *525*
    storage DRS feature, *466*
    swap file location, *509*
    V2V conversions, *353*
    virtual machines, *585*
    VMware Data Recovery, *532*
    vNetwork standard switches, *150*
    vSphere Update Manager, *570*

suspended virtual machines, migrating,
    503–504, *504*
suspending vApps, **363–364**, *363–364*
SVGA device driver, *321*
swap files, **391–392**, **507–511**, *508–511*
Switch Port Analyzer (SPAN), *15*, *165*
switches
    vNetwork Distributed Switches. *See*
        vNetwork Distributed Switches (vDS)
    vNetwork standard switches. *See*
        vNetwork standard switches (vSS)
synchronization of virtual machines, **320–
    322**, *322*
syslog server, *46*
System Customization screen, *68*
system-defined storage, *408*
system health, ESXi hosts, **596–598**, *597–
    598*
system logs, **599–602**, *599–602*

T

target host load deviation, **630–632**, *630–
    631*
targets, storage, *222*, *225*
tasks
    creating, editing, and deleting, **646–650**,
        648, *650*
    viewing, **644–646**, *644–646*
Tasks & Events tab
    EVC, *462*
    event view, **644–645**, *644–645*
TCP port access, **100–101**
TCP segmentation offload (TSO) support,
    207–208, *208*
templates
    deploying virtual appliances and vApps
        from, **384–385**
    importing and exporting, **385–386**
    provisioning, *387*
    virtual machines
        creating, **379–381**, *380–381*

deploying from, **381–383**, *382–383*
options, 375–376
updating, **383–384**
VMFS and NFS datastores, 273
Test Management Network window, 68, *68*
tests
Fault Tolerance configuration, **478–479**, *479*
VMware Data Recovery restores
file-level, **544–546**, *545–546*
virtual machines, **547–550**, *547–550*
TFTP servers, 60
Thick Provision Eager Zeroed disks, 329
Thick Provision Lazy Zeroed disks, 329
thick provisioned disks
converting thin to, **332–334**, *333*
description, 246, 339
thin provisioned disks
array vs. virtual disk, **245–246**
converting to thick, **332–334**, *333*
use case, 246
VMFS, 247
third-party clustering solutions, 55
three-node VSA clusters, **275–276**, *276*
thresholds, migration, **447–448**
thumbnail charts, 672, *672*
tiered vApps, **354**
time synchronization, **320–322**, *322*
timeout settings, **653–654**, *653*
traffic logging, **469–475**, *470–474*
traffic shaping policies, 196, **202–207**, *203–206*
Transient IP allocation policy, 362–363
triggers, alarms
configuring, **694–695**, *695*
creating, 688–689, *689*, 692–693, *693*
Triggers tab, 688–689, *689*, 692–693, *693*
Trivia logging option, *655*
troubleshooting, **595**
clusters
capacity, **625–626**, *626*
configuration, **623–625**, *623–625*
requirements, **620–621**

root cause identification, *635*
DRS load imbalance, **627–630**, *628–629*
ESXi hosts
exporting diagnostic information, **599–602**, *600–602*
guidelines, **598–599**, *599*
installation issues, **595–596**
system health, **596–598**, *597–598*
exam essentials, **636**
High Availability
configuration, **622**
redundancy issues, **626–627**
host load deviation, **630–632**, *630–631*
migration, **633**, *635*
networks, **602**
physical network adapter configuration, **607–610**, *608–610*
root cause identification, **610–611**
verifying configuration, **603–604**, *603–604*
virtual machine configuration, **605**
virtual switch and port group configuration, **605–607**, *606*
review questions, 637–640
storage, **611**
configuration, **611–612**
contention, **612–617**, *614–616*
iSCSI software initiators, 618, *618*
overcommitment, **617**
root cause identification, **620**
storage reports and storage maps, **618–619**, *619*
Storage vMotion configuration, **621–622**
summary, 635–636
virtual machine options, 399, *399*
vMotion
configuration, **621–622**
requirements, **620–621**
resource maps, **633–635**, *634*
TSO (TCP segmentation offload) support, **207–208**, *208*

Turn On Fault Tolerance dialog box, 475–476, *475*, 491
two-node VSA clusters, 275, *275*
TX traffic, 164

U

Ubuntu operating system, **535**
UDP port access, **100–101**
UEFI (Unified Extensible Firmware Interface) boot support, 8
UMDS (Update Manager Download Service), 567
unidirectional CHAP, 242
unified 1MB file block size in VMFS, 247–248
Unified Extensible Firmware Interface (UEFI) boot support, 8
Unmount Datastore Wizard, 253, *253*
unmounting
    NFS datastores, **272–273**, *272*
    VMFS datastores, **252–254**, *252–253*
Unused Adapters/Uplinks option, 201
Update Manager Download Service (UMDS), 567
updates and Update Manager
    ESXi hosts upgrades, **83–89**, *84–88*
    improvements, **24**
    virtual machine templates, **383–384**
    VMware Tools, 81
    vSphere Update Manager. *See* vSphere Update Manager
Upgrade to VMFS-5 dialog box, 80, *81*
Upgrade vSphere Distributed Switch To Newer Version Wizard, 79–80, *79–80*
upgrades
    ESXi hosts
        process, **83–89**, *84–88*
        requirements, **75–76**
    in-place, **88–89**, 248
    virtual machine hardware, **82–83**
    VMFS, **80–81**, *81*, 248, **262–264**, *263*
    VMware Tools, **81–82**, **317–319**, *318–319*

vNetwork distributed switches, **78–80**, *79–80*
vSphere implementations, **76–78**
uplink adapters
    dvUplink groups, **179–182**, *180–182*
    types, 200–201
use cases
    array thin provisioning, **246**
    Fault Tolerance, **466–467**
    FCoE, **231**
    iSCSI, **232–233**
    VMFS and NFS datastores, **273–274**
    vNetwork Distributed Switches, **195–196**
    vNetwork standard switches, **162–163**
    VSA, **274**
    vSphere Client and Web Client, **56–57**
Use CHAP security level, 242
Use CHAP unless prohibited by target security level, 242
Use Explicit Failover Order option, 200
Use This Port Group For Fault Tolerance Logging option, 158
Use This Port Group For Management Traffic option, 158
Use This Port Group For vMotion option, 158
used storage, 324
user-defined storage, 408
user permissions, **114–118**, *115–118*
UTC time, 58, 61
utilization alarms
    actions, **685–687**, *686*
    creating, **687–690**, *687–690*
    default, **685**

V

V2V (virtual machines to virtual machines) conversions, 340, **349–353**, *350–353*
VA Upgrade to Latest upgrade baseline, 571
VAAI Thin Provisioning improvements, **17–18**

vApps, 114, **301**, **354**
  adding objects to, **356–357**, *356*
  cloning, **364–365**, **493**, *493*
  creating, **355–356**, *355–356*
  deploying, **384–385**
  exam essentials, **367**, **414–415**
  exporting, **365–366**, *366*
  IP pools, **359–363**, *360–362*
  review questions, **368–371**, **416–419**
  settings, **357–359**, *357–359*
  summary, **366–367**, **414**
  suspending and resuming, **363–364**,
    363–364
  tiered, 354
  vSphere Update Manager settings, 566,
    567
vc-support command, 602
vc-support.wsf script, 601
VCB (VMware Consolidated Backup), **4**
vCenter Server, **29**
  Active Directory settings, **651–653**,
    652–653
  alarms. *See* alarms
  architectures, 130, **132–134**
  availability requirements, **55–56**
  connections, **661–662**, *661–662*
  database size, **39–41**, *40*
  editions, **29–30**
  ESXi host system health, **597–598**,
    598
  exam essentials, **89–90**
  exporting system logs, **600–602**, *600–602*
  heartbeat improvements, **11–13**, *12*
  installing into virtual machines, **34–39**,
    36–38
  inventory object permissions, **114–118**,
    115–118
  licensing, **51–55**, *53–54*
  log bundles, **655**, *655*
  logging enhancements, **11**
  logging options, **654–655**, *654*
  plug-ins, 133
  privileges, **98–100**, *99–100*, **129–130**
  resource maps, **663–666**, *663–666*
  review questions, **91–94**
  roles, **96–98**, *97–98*, **118–121**, *119–120*
  scheduled tasks, **647–650**, *648*, *650*
  service status, **656–658**, *656–658*
  SMTP settings, **651–653**, *652–653*
  SNMP settings, **650–651**, *651*
  storage filters, **227–230**, *229*
  summary, **89**
  tasks and events, **644–646**, *644–646*
  timeout settings, **653–654**, *653*
  upgrading, 77
  VMware Data Recovery backup appliance
    connections, **538–540**, *538–540*
  vSphere Client and Web Client use case,
    56–57
  vSphere Client installation, **41–43**
  vSphere Client plug-ins, **46–51**, *48*,
    50, *52*
  vSphere Web Client installation, **42–46**,
    44–45
vCenter Server Appliance (vCSA)
  deploying, **30–34**, *31–33*
  description, **19**
vCenter Server Installer screen, 36, *36*
vCenter Server Settings window
  Active Directory settings, **652–653**,
    652–653
  logging, **654–655**, *654*
  SNMP settings, **651**, *651*
  statistics, 40, *40*
  storage filters, **229–230**, *229*
  timeouts, **653–654**, *653*
vCenter Storage Monitoring Service plug-in,
  619
VCS (Veritas Cluster Services), 55
vCSA (vCenter Server Appliance)
  deploying, **30–34**, *31–33*
  description, **19**
VDI (VMware View), 18
Verbose logging option, 655
verifying
  cluster configuration, **623–625**, *623–625*
  HA network configuration, **622**

network configuration, 603–604, *603–604*

storage configuration, 611–612

virtual machines

   configuration, 605

   storage policies, 413–414, *413*

virtual switch and port group

   configuration, 605–607, *606*

vMotion configuration, 621–622

VGT (Virtual Guest Tagging), 213

virtual adapters

   configuring, 186–187, *186–187*

   creating, 182–185, *183–185*

   migrating, 187–191, *188–190*

virtual application deployment, 384–387. *See also* vApps

virtual compatibility mode, 330

virtual CPU resources, 336–337

Virtual Device Node settings, 323

virtual disks

   converting thin disks to thick, 332–334, *333*

   disk controllers, 324–328, *326–328*

   hot extending, 403–406, *405*

   location, 391–392, *392*

   thin provisioning, 245–246

   types, 329–332, *330–331*

   VMware Data Recovery backup appliance, 533–534, *533*

Virtual Guest Tagging (VGT), 213

virtual hardware

   boot options, 398

   compatibility, 82

   hot extensions, 404

virtual machine console, 313–316, *314–315*

Virtual Machine File System (VMFS)

   datastores, 227

   capabilities, 247–248

   creating and renaming, 248–251, *249–250*

   deleting, 254

   extending and expanding, 257–262, *258–259, 261*

   maintenance mode, 264

   paths

      disabling, 268–269, *269*

      preferred, 266–268, *267*

      selection policies, 264–266, *265*

   properties, 255–257, *255–256*

   unmounting, 252–254, *252–253*

   upgrading, 80–81, *81*, 248, 262–264, *263*

   use case, 273–274

   VMFS-5, 18–19

Virtual Machine Interface (VMI) paravirtualization, 4

Virtual Machine Networking screen, 171

Virtual Machine Options screen, 438, *438*, 440, *440*

Virtual Machine Properties window, 10, *10*

   disk controllers, 326–328, *326*

   memory reservation, 489

   power settings, 396–397, *397*

   profiles, 412, *412*

   resources, 406–408, *406, 408*

   settings, 393

   snapshots, 522–524

   Storage vMotion, 515

   swap file location, 510

   troubleshooting options, 399

   TSOs, 207–208

   virtual disks, 330–333

   virtual NIC adapters, 338

   VMware Data Recovery, 532, 550

Virtual Machine Restore Wizard, 547, *547*, 549

virtual machine swap (.vswp) files, 391

Virtual Machine Swapfile Location window, 509, *509*

virtual machines (VMs), 30, **301**

   advanced parameters, 402–403, *402*

   alarm-type monitor, 686

   backups. *See* backups

   boot options, 397–399, *398*

   clones

      options, 375–376

      process, 376–379, *377–379*

provisioning, 387
clusters
    adding and removing, **431–433,**
        431–432
    admission control, **435–441,** *437–438,*
        440
    automation levels, **443–446,** *444, 446*
    configuring, **439–441**
    datastore locations, 335
    disks for, 332
    entitlement, **424–425,** *424*
    migration thresholds, **447–448**
    monitoring, **441–443,** *442–443*
    placing in, **313**
    swap file location, 508
configuration file and virtual disk
        location, **391–392,** *392*
configuring, **308–312,** *308–312,* **393–**
        395, *394*
console, **313–316,** *314–315*
converting physical servers to, **340–345,**
        341–345
CPU and memory usage alarms, **687–**
        690, *687–690*
deploying
    methodology selection, **386–387**
    from templates, **381–383,** *382–383*
    vSphere Client, **308–312,** *308–312*
disk controllers, **324–328,** *326–328*
disk shares, **334–335,** *335*
enhancements, **9**
exam essentials, 367, **414–415**
files used, **389–391,** *391*
group baselines attached to, **581–583,**
        582–583
guest OS on, **303–307,** *304–305, 307*
hardware
    capabilities, **301–303**
    settings, **349–353,** *350–353*
    upgrading, **82–83**
importing, **345–349,** *346–348*
maximums, **387–389**
metrics

CPU, **669**
    memory, **667–668**
migrating. *See* migration
patching requirements, **553–554**
power settings, **395–397,** *396–397*
remediating, **584–585,** *585*
resource pools, **487–488**
resources, 313, *313,* **406–408,** *406, 408*
review questions, **368–371, 416–419**
scanning, **584,** *584*
security, **400–401**
snapshots
    consolidating, **525–528,** *526–528*
    creating, **521–523,** *521–522*
    deleting, **523–525,** *524*
    requirements, **518–521**
storage
    policies, assigning, **408–413,** *409–412*
    policies, verifying, **413–414,** *413*
    reports, **618–619,** *619*
    resources, **323–324,** *323–324*
    workload factors, **335–336**
summary, **366–367,** 414
swap file locations, **507–511,** *508–511*
TCP segmentation offload support, **207–**
        208, *208*
templates
    creating, **379–381,** *380–381*
    deploying from, **381–383,** *382–383*
    options, **375–376**
    updating, **383–384**
time synchronization, **320–322,** *322*
troubleshooting options, **399,** *399*
vCenter Server installation into, **34–39,**
        36–38
verifying configuration, **605**
virtual CPU and memory resources,
        336–337
virtual disks
    converting thin disks to thick, **332–**
        334, *333*
    types, **329–332,** *330–331*
virtual NIC adapters, **337–339,** *339*

vMotion and Storage vMotion
   requirements, **506**
VMware Data Recovery restores, **547–**
   550, *547–550*
VMware Tools. *See* VMware Tools
vNetwork standard switches, 146, *146*
VSA, 278
vSphere Update Manager settings, **564–**
   565, *564–565*
virtual machines to virtual machines (V2V)
   conversions, 340, **349–353**, *350–353*
virtual memory resources, **336–337**
virtual NIC adapters, **337–339**, *339*
Virtual Printing device driver, 320
Virtual Switch Tagging (VST), 213
virtual switches
   troubleshooting, **605–607**, *606*
   vNetwork Distributed Switches. *See*
      vNetwork Distributed Switches (vDS)
   vNetwork standard switches. *See*
      vNetwork standard switches (vSS)
VirtualCenter Agent (vpxa) log option,
   599
virtualization layer, 130, **132**
VLAN Trunking option, 175
Vlance NICs, 337
VLANs
   configuration determination, **212–213**
   dvPort groups, 175
   policy, 196
   settings, **201–202**, *201–202*
   vNetwork Distributed Switches, 165
   vNetwork standard switches, 146
   VSA hosts, 278, 285
vLockstep technology, 466
VM Hardware Upgrade to Match Host
   upgrade baseline, 571
VM-Host affinity rules, **448–453**, *449–450*,
   452
VM Network Properties window, 201, *201*,
   204–205, *204–205*
VM Network Settings window, 202, *202*
VM Storage Profiles, 21, 412–413

VM-VM affinity rules, 448, **454–456**,
   454–455
vMA (vSphere Management Assistant), 108
VMCI device driver, 321
VMCI sockets, 5
VMDK files, 389
VMFS. *See* Virtual Machine File System
   (VMFS) datastores
VMFS Filter, 228
VMFS Properties window, 256, *256*
vmhba storage adapters, 225
VMI (Virtual Machine Interface)
   paravirtualization, **4**
VMkernel
   network service ports, **155–158**,
      155–158
   port binding, 617–618, *618*
   vNetwork standard switches, 146
vmkfstools command, 334
vmkping command, 604, **606–607**, *606*
vmnics
   firewalls, 100
   iSCSI, 234
   on vNetwork standard switches, **151–154**,
      152–153
vMotion
   configuration verification, **621–622**
   improvements, **19**
   migrating virtual machines, 502,
      511–513, *512*, 633
   requirements
      ESXi hosts, **505**
      identifying, **620–621**
      snapshots, **507**
      virtual machine, **506**
   resource maps, **633–635**, *634*
   swap file location, *508*
.vmtx file extension, 380
VMW_PSP_FIXED PSPs, 266
VMW_PSP_MRU PSPs, 266
VMW_PSP_RR PSPs, 266
VMware Auto Deploy feature, **49–50**, *50*
VMware Consolidated Backup (VCB), **4**

VMware Converter
  hardware settings, **349–353**, *350–353*
  importing virtual machines, **345–349**,
    346–348
  physical machine conversions, **340–345**,
    341–345
VMware Converter Standalone window,
  348, 353
VMware CPU Identification Utility, 75
VMware Data Recovery, **528–529**
  backups. *See* backups
  client plug-in, **529–530**, *530*
  improvements, **23–24**
  restore tests
    file-level, **544–546**, *545–546*
    virtual machines, **547–550**, *547–550*
VMware Data Recovery Restore Client
  window, 544–546, *545–546*
VMware Distributed Resource Scheduler, 34
VMware ESXi. *See* ESXi; ESXi hosts
VMware Fault Tolerance. *See* Fault
  Tolerance (FT)
VMware GUI Toolbox, **4**
VMware Paravirtual controllers, 325
VMware Remote Console Plug-in
  application, 315
VMware Syslog Collector, **47–49**, *48*
VMware Tools
  device drivers, **319–320**
  installing, **316–317**, *317*
  support for, **9–10**, *10*
  upgrading, **81–82**, **317–319**, *318–319*
VMware Tools Upgrade to Match Host
  upgrade baseline, 571
VMware vCenter Database Sizing Calculator
  for Microsoft SQL Server, 40
VMware vCenter Database Sizing Calculator
  for Oracle, 40
VMware vCenter Server. *See* vCenter Server
VMware View (VDI), 18
VMwareRestoreClient.exe program, 544
VmwareToolbox.cmd command, 322
VMX files, 389

VMXNET network adapters, 337
VMXNET 2 network adapters, 207–208,
  211, 337
VMXNET 3 network adapters, 207–208,
  211, 338
VMXNET NIC driver, 321
vNetwork Distributed Switches (vDS)
  capabilities, **163–165**, *163*
  creating and deleting, **165–168**, *167–169*
  dvPort groups, **173–179**, *174*, *176–177*
  ESXi hosts, **169–173**, *170–172*
  improvements, **14–17**, *16*
  listing, 604, *604*
  policies, 196, **205–207**, *205–206*
  upgrading, 78–80, *79–80*
  uplink adapters, **179–182**, *180–182*
  use case, **195–196**
  virtual adapters
    configuring, **186–187**, *186–187*
    creating, **182–185**, *183–185*
    migrating, **187–191**, *188–190*
  virtual machine migration, **191–195**,
    192–194
vNetwork standard switches (vSS)
  capabilities, **145–148**, *146–148*
  creating and deleting, **148–151**, *149–151*
  jumbo frames, **209–210**, *209–210*
  port groups, **158–162**, *159–161*
  traffic shaping policies, **203–204**, *203–
    204*
  use case, **162–163**
  vmnics on, **151–154**, *152–153*
volume based cloning, 340
Volume Shadow Copy Service Support
  device driver, 321
vRAM, 24, 30, 43, 52
VSA. *See* vSphere Storage Appliance (VSA)
  and VSA Manager
vSMP, 468
vSphere Authentication Proxy, 121
vSphere CLI commands, 108
vSphere Client
  cluster creation, **425–428**, *425–428*

disk controllers, **326–328**, *326–328*
ESXi hosts, DNS and routing
    configuration, **64–65**, *64*
installing, **41–43**
lockdown mode, **109–110**, *110*
migrating virtual machines, **502–503**,
    503
network adapter configuration, **608–610**,
    608–610
plug-ins, **46–51**, *48, 50, 52*
RDMs for virtual machines, **330–332**,
    330–331
scheduled tasks, **647–650**, *648, 650*
use case, **56–57**
vApps
    cloning, **364–365**
    exporting, **365–366**, *366*
    suspending and resuming, **363–364**
VMware Tools, **317–319**, *318–319*
vSphere Client Windows Guest
    Customization window, 377–378,
    377–378
vSphere distributed switches. *See* vNetwork
    Distributed Switches (vDS)
vSphere DRS panel, 460, 625, *625*
vSphere Essentials Kits, 30
vSphere HA Advanced Runtime Info
    window, 624, *624*
vSphere HA Cluster Status window, 460,
    460
vSphere Hardening Guide, 400–401
vSphere High Availability, 34
vSphere Management Assistant (vMA), 108
vSphere Storage Appliance (VSA) and VSA
    Manager, 274
    appliance maintenance mode, **290–291**,
    290
    architecture, **275–277**, *275–276*
    clusters
        configurations, **275–276**, *275*
        requirements, 278
        storage resources, **283–289**, *284–289*
    ESXi host resources, **277–278**

overview, **19–20**, *20*
storage networks, **279–280**, *279*
use case, **274**
VSA Manager
    clusters, **283–289**, *284–289*
    deploying and configuring, **280–282**,
        280–282
vSphere Update Manager, 559
    baselines
        attaching to ESXi hosts, **577–578**, *578*
        creating, **570–573**, *572–573*
        editing, **574–576**, *575–576*
    cluster settings, **565–566**, *565–567*
    download settings, **568–570**, *568–569*
    ESXi host update staging, **586–587**, *586*
    exam essentials, **588**
    group baselines, **581–583**, *582–583*
    installing, **560–562**, *560–562*
    network settings, **563–564**, *563*
    patching requirements, **553–554**
    remediating
        ESXi hosts, **580–581**, *580*
        virtual machines, **584–585**, *585*
    review questions, **589–592**
    scanning
        ESXi hosts, **578–579**, *579*
        virtual machines, **584**, *584*
    summary, **587–588**
    virtual machine settings, **564–565**,
        564–565
vSphere Web Client
    disk shares, **334–335**, *335*
    installing, **42–46**, *44–45*
    use case, **56–57**
    vApps, **355–356**, *355–356*
    virtual disk hot extensions, **403–406**, *405*
    virtual machines
        boot options, **398–399**, *398*
        configuration and deployment,
            308–312, *308–312*
        console, **313–316**, *314–315*
        migrating, **503–504**, *504*, **512–513**,
            512

virtual NIC adapters, **338–339**, *339*
vSphere Web Client Administration application, 44
VST (Virtual Switch Tagging), 213
vSwitch Properties window
    Fault Tolerance traffic logging, 470, 472–474
    jumbo frames, 209–210, *209*
    network adapters, 609, *609*
    port groups, 159–162
    traffic shaping policies, 203–204, *203*
    vmnics, 152–154
vSwitches. *See* vNetwork Distributed Switches (vDS); vNetwork standard switches (vSS)
.vswp (virtual machine swap) files, 391

Warning window for ESXi host upgrades, 84
Windows 2000 guest OS customization support, 4
Windows services management console, **656–658**
WinSCP utility, 679–680
working location, 391
workload factors
    resource pool shares, reservations, and limits, **488–492**, *489–492*
    virtual machine resources, **406–408**, *406, 408*
    virtual machine storage, **335–336**
    VMFS and NFS datastores use case, 273
Wyse Multimedia Support device driver, 321

W

Wake on LAN feature, 395–396, *396*
warning condition for EVC, 458, *459*
Warning (Errors and Warnings) logging option, 654

Z

zoning, 230

Free Online Study Tools

Register on Sybex.com to gain access to a complete set of study tools to help you prepare for your VCP5 Exam

Comprehensive Study Tool Package Includes:

- **Assessment Test** to help you focus your study to specific objectives

- **Chapter Review Questions** for each chapter of the book

- **Two Full-Length Practice** Exams to test your knowledge of the material

- **Electronic Flashcards** to reinforce your learning and give you that last-minute test prep before the exam

- **Searchable Glossary** gives you instant access to the key terms you'll need to know for the exam

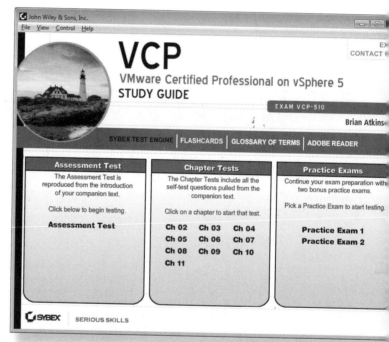

Go to www.sybex.com/go/vcp5 to register and gain access to this comprehensive study tool package.